ISBN 978-0-266-01856-8
PIBN 10960754

1 MONTH OF
FREE
READING

at

www.ForgottenBooks.com

By purchasing this book you are
eligible for one month membership to
ForgottenBooks.com, giving you
unlimited access to our entire
collection of over 1,000,000 titles via
our web site and mobile apps.

To claim your free month visit:
www.forgottenbooks.com/free960754

English
Français
Deutsche
Italiano
Español
Português

www.forgottenbooks.com

Mythology Photography **Fiction**
Fishing Christianity **Art** Cooking
Essays Buddhism Freemasonry
Medicine **Biology** Music **Ancient
Egypt** Evolution Carpentry Physics
Dance Geology **Mathematics** Fitness
Shakespeare **Folklore** Yoga Marketing
Confidence Immortality Biographies
Poetry **Psychology** Witchcraft
Electronics Chemistry History **Law**
Accounting **Philosophy** Anthropology
Alchemy Drama Quantum Mechanics
Atheism Sexual Health **Ancient History**
Entrepreneurship Languages Sport
Paleontology Needlework Islam
Metaphysics Investment Archaeology
Parenting Statistics Criminology
Motivational

REPORTS

OF

CIVIL AND CRIMINAL CASES

DECIDED BY

COURT OF APPEALS

OF KENTUCKY

———

VOLUME XXVII
T. R. McBEATH. Reporter

VOLUME 135 KENTUCKY REPORTS
Containing Cases Decided From October 20, 1909, to December 17, 1909

———

FRANKFORT. KY.
FRANKFORT PRINTING CO., PRINTERS AND BINDERS
1910

JUDICIAL OFFICERS OF THE STATE

COURT OF APPEALS OF KENTUCKY

(As constituted during the period covered by this volume, 1909.)

Hon. T. J. NUNN, Chief Justice

ASSOCIATE JUSTICES

Hon. J. P. HOBSON
Hon. W. E. SETTLE
Hon. HENRY S. BARKER
Hon. JOHN M. LASSING
Hon. JOHN D. CARROLL
Hon. ED. C. O'REAR
Hon. WM. ROGERS CLAY, Commissioner.

(As constituted now—1910.)

Hon. HENRY S. BARKER, Chief Justice

ASSOCIATE JUSTICES

Hon. J. P. HOBSON
Hon. JOHN M. LASSING
Hon. JOHN D. CARROLL
Hon. ED. C. O'REAR
Hon. W. E. SETTLE
Hon. T. J. NUNN
Hon. WM. ROGERS CLAY, Commissioner.

OFFICERS OF COURT

JAMES BREATHITT, Attorney General.
JOHN F. LOCKETT, First Assistant Attorney General.
THEODORE B. BLAKEY, Second Assistant Attorney General.
TOM B. McGREGOR, Third Assistant Attorney General.
T. R. McBEATH, Reporter.
NAPIER ADAMS, Clerk.

JUDGES OF CIRCUIT COURTS

(Who Presided During the Period Covered by This Volume.)

1st District—R. J. BUGG.............................Bardwell
2nd District—W. M. REED............................Paducah
3rd District—THOS. P. COOK........................Murray
4th District—J. F. GORDON.....................Madisonville
5th District—J. W. HENSON..........................Dixon
6th District—T. F. BIRKHEAD....................Owensboro
7th District—W. P. SANDIDGE....................Russellville
8th District—JOHN M. GALLOWAY...........Bowling Green
9th District—WEED S. CHELF.................Elizabethtown
10th District—SAMUEL E. JONES....................Glasgow
11th District—I. H. THURMAN.....................Springfield
12th District—R. F. PEAK........................Shelbyville
18th District—W. C. BELL........................Harrodsburg
14th District—R. L. STOUT........................Versailles
15th District—J. W. CAMMACK.....................Owenton
16th District—W. McD. SHAW.....................Covington
17th District—A. S. BERRY..........................Newport
18th District—L. P. FRYER........................Falmouth
19th District—Jas. P. HARBESON...............Flemingsburg
20th District—S. G. KINNER.....................Catlettsburg
21st District—ALLIE W. YOUNG..................Mt. Sterling
22nd District—WATTS PARKER....................Lexington
23rd District—ROBERT RIDDELL.......................Irvine
24th District—A. J. KIRK...............................Inez
25th District—J. M. BENTON......................Winchester
26th District—M. J. ROSS...........................Pineville
27th District—H. C. FAULKNER...................Barbourville
28th District—M. L. JARVIS..........................Albany
29th District—H. C. BAKER....'.....................Columbia
30th District—Jefferson Circuit Court—Louisville—
    JOSEPH PRYOR—Criminal Branch.
    SHACKELFORD MILLER—Chancery Branch, First Division.
    SAMUEL B. KIRBY—Chancery Branch, Second Division.
    HOMER BATSON—Common Pleas Branch, First Division.
    THOS. R. GORDON—Common Pleas Branch, Second Division
    MATT O'DOHERTY—Common Pleas Branch, Third Division.
31st District—D. W. GARDNER..................Salyersville
32nd District—J. B. HANNAH.....................Sandy Hook
33rd District—L. D. LEWIS...........................Hyden

COMMONWEALTH ATTORNEYS

(During the Period Covered by This Volume—1909.)

1st District—W. H. HESTER .... Mayfield

2nd District—JOHN G. LOVETT ....Benton

3rd District—DENNY P. SMITH .... Cadiz

4th District—JOHN L. GRAYOT ....Smithland

5th District—S. V. DIXON ....Henderson

6th District—BEN D. RINGO........................Hartford

7:n District—R. Y. THOMAS.....................Central City

8th District—NAT T. HOWARD .... Morgantown

9th District—J. R. LAYMAN .... Elizabethtown

10th District—DAVID J. WOOD...................Munfordville

11th District—R. L. DURHAM .... Greensburg

12th District—CHAS. H. SANDFORD .... New Castle

13th District—CHARLES A. HARDIN...............Harrodsburg

14th District—ROBT. B. FRANKLIN .... Frankfort

15th District—FRANK C. GREEN ....Owenton

16th District—MAURACE L. GALVIN...............Covington

17th District—W. A. BURKAMP .... Newport

18th District—JAS. C. DEDMAN.................. ......Cynthiana

19th District—M. J. HENNESSEY .... Augusta

20th District—J. B. WILHOIT......................Grayson

21st District—ALEX CONNOR ....Owingsville

22nd District—JOHN R. ALLEN ....Lexington

23rd District—JAMES P. ADAMS.....................Beattyville

24th District—JOHN F. BUTLER ....Pikeville

25th District—B. A. CRUTCHER ....Nicholasville

26th District—J. B. SNYDER .... Williamsburg

27th District—WILLIAM LEWIS........................Hyden

28th District—B. J. BETHURUM..................Williamsburg

29th District—A. A. HUDDLESTON .... Burksville

30th District—JOSEPH M. HUFFAKER .... Louisville

31st District—A. B. STEPHENS..................Prestonsburg

32nd District—J. M. WAUGH .... Grayson

33rd District—IRA FIELDS .... Whitesburg

TABLE OF CASES

DECISIONS

OF THE

COURT OF APPEALS OF KENTUCKY

SEPTEMBER TERM, 1909.

CASE 1,—INDICTMENT AGAINST FRED MARCUM FOR MUR-
DER—Oct. 29, 1909.

Commonwealth v. Marcum.

Appeal from Lawrence Circuit Court.

J. B. HANNAH, Circuit Judge.

After a mistrial the Commonwealth certified certain questions to the Court of Appeals.

1. Searches and Seizures—Misdemeanors—Arrest Without War-
    rant—Statutes.—Ky. St. Sec. 806, makes it an offense, pun-
    ishable by a fine and imprisonment in the county jail, for any
    person while riding on a train in the hearing or presence of
    other passengers, and to their annoyance, to use obscene or
    profane language, or behave in a boisterous or riotous man-
    ner, and makes it the duty of the conductor either to put such
    person off the train, or to give notice of violation of the sec-
    tion to some peace officer at the first stopping place where
    such officer may be, who may arrest the offender without a
    warrant. Held, that such act was valid, and not objectiona-
    ble in so far as it authorized such arrest, as violating Const.
    Sec. 10, providing that the people shall be secure from un-
    reasonable searches and seizures.

2. Carriers — Passengers—Ejection—Disorderly   Conduct.—Ky.
    St. Sec. 806, providing for the ejection of passengers on rail-
    road trains guilty of disorderly conduct or obtaining or at-
    tempting to obtain money or property from any person by
    any game or device, etc., is reasonable and valid.

3. Homicide—Arrest—Misdemeanors—Use of Force.—An officer having a right to arrest for a misdemeanor may use such force, if resisted. as is necessary or reasonably appears to the officer necessary in the exercise of a sound judgment to overcome the resistance and make the arrest. but he may not, while the resistance is not forcible, wantonly shoot or injure the person sought to be apprehended.

4. Homicide—Defenses — Resistance—Force—Instructions.—An instruction that it was a public offense for a passenger to behave boisterously in the presence of other passengers, and that it was the conductor's duty either to eject the offending person or give notice to a peace officer at the first stopping place, and that it was the peace officer's duty to arrest the offender and carry him to the most convenient magistrate of the county, and in making the arrest the officer could use such force as was necessary, even to taking the life of the offender, but that he should not use unnecessary violence, nor shoot the offender unless the arrest could not otherwise be made—was objectionable, as eliminating the necessity that the resistance must be forcible, and the idea that the officer might act on appearances in the exercise of reasonable judgment.

5. Homicide—Execution of Duty—Resistance to Arrest—Instruction.—In a prosecution for homicide, an instruction as to the right of defendant, a city marshal, to shoot one whom a train conductor had requested to have arrested for disorderly conduct in case of resistance to the arrest, held proper.

BYRD & DAVIS, CALLOWAY HOWARD and HOPKINS & HOPKINS for appellant.

JAS. BREATHITT, Attorney General, and TOM B. McGREGOR, Assistant Attorney General, for Commonwealth.

OPINION OF THE COURT BY JUDGE BARKER.

The appellee, Fred Marcum, was jointly indicted with Frank Blevins and James Sizemore by the grand jury of Lawrence county, Ky., charged with the offense of willful murder, committed by shooting John Whittaker with a pistol and inflicting wounds upon him of which he then and there died. The defendants all pleaded not guilty to the indictment, and, when the case was called for trial, the appellee, Fred Marcum demanded a severance from his code-fendants, which was granted him. Thereupon the commonwealth elected to try him first, and a trial was then and there had, with the result that the jury were unable to agree upon a verdict, and were dis-charged by the court from further consideration of the case.

Afterwards the commonwealth's attorney, as by law authorized, certified the record to this court for the purpose of having adjudicated the propriety of giving instructions Nos. 5 and 6 to the jury, and of the court's refusal to give to the jury instruction No. 1 asked for the commonwealth. The court gave the usual instructions in murder cases, and in addi-tion gave Nos. 5 and 6, which are as follows:

"(5) The court further instructs the jury that it is a public offense for any person while riding on a passenger train, to, in the hearing or presence of the passengers, and to their annoyance, use or utter ob-scene or profane language, or behave in a boisterous or riotous manner, and it is the duty of the conductor in charge of a train upon which any such offense is committed either to put the person so offending off the train, or to give notice of such offense to some peace officer at the first stopping place where any such peace officer may be, and it is the duty of such peace officer when so notified by such conductor to arrest such offender, and carry him to the most convenient magistrate of the county in which such arrest is made; and in making such arrest such peace officer has the right to use such force as is necessary therefor, even to the taking of the life of the offender, but not the right to use unnecessary violence, nor to shoot the offender, unless such offender resist such arrest, and such arrest cannot be otherwise made.

"(6) A city marshal is a peace officer of the county in which the city is located of which he is marshal, and if the jury should believe from the evidence that Frank Blevins was the conductor in charge of the train upon which the deceased Whittaker was riding at the time that he was killed, and further believe from the evidence that said Blevins as such conductor, in Lawrence county, Ky., while such conductor in charge of said train and on said run, and before said killing was done, complained to and notified the defendant, Marcum, as marshal of the city of Louisa, Lawrence county, Ky., that the deceased Whittaker had on his (Blevins') train, on said run, committed a public offense as defined in said instruction No. 5, and that as such marshal in the discharge of his official duties in good faith attempted to arrest the deceased, and while so engaged the deceased, with the intent to prevent and with force resisted such arrest and assaulted the defendant, and there appeared to defendant Marcum, exercising a reasonable judgment on the time and under the circumstances, no other safe way to save his life or to protect himself from great bodily harm or to make such arrest than to shoot and kill the deceased, then in such event the jury will acquit the defendant upon the grounds of self-defense or apparent necessity."

The commonwealth tendered to the court, and asked that it be given to the jury, instruction No. 1, which was refused. It is as follows: "It was the duty of the defendant in attempting to arrest the deceased to inform him of his intention to arrest him, and of the offense charged against him, and if the jury believe from the evidence beyond a reasonable doubt that the defendant failed to perform said duties, or either of them, and they further believe from the evidence beyond a reasonable doubt that the deceased did not know the defendant's purpose and the offense charged against him, then the deceased had the right under the law to use such force as was necessary or reasonably appeared to him to be necessary to protect him from danger or death, or great bodily harm then about to be inflicted on him by the defendant.''

The facts out of which grew the killing for which the appellant was indicted are as follows: The Chesapeake & Ohio Railroad Company on Sunday, January 11, 1909, ran an excursion train through Lawrence county, Ky., to Cattlettsburg. The deceased, John Whittaker, and his two brothers, Caleb and Frank, with several friends and acquaintances, went on this excursion. When the party reached Catlettsburg, John Whittaker and his friends proceeded to have a good time by getting drunk and visiting houses of prostitution. At one of these, John Whittaker got into an altercation with one of the women in the house, and drew his pistol, flourishing it about in a reckless manner. One of his companions, Sam Robinson, in order to keep him out of trouble, took the pistol from the drunken man, and placed it in his own pocket. The train returned at night, and John Whittaker and his party had with them a suit case containing six quarts of whisky and gin, of which they partook freely, and were in a hilarious and boisterous mood. The conductor, Frank Blevins, warned John Whittaker several times to keep quiet, and not to make a disturbance, and finally said to him: ''You have got to cut that out (meaning his boisterous behavior), for I have got a man on this train who will take you off." He referred to the appellee, Fred Marcum, who was marshal of Louisa. When the train reached Lawrence county, Marcum, at the instance and request of the conductor, Blevins, went into the car where Whittaker and his party were for the purpose of arresting those who were boisterous and unruly. They first arrested Sam Robinson, who, as before stated, had taken John Whittaker's pistol from him in Catlettsburg. In making this arrest they mistook Robinson for Whittaker; they both wearing white hats, and looking something alike. Robinson submitted quietly to the arrest, and went with the officer and conductor to another car, where he explained to them that they were mistaken in the man, and told them that he had taken a pistol from Whittaker to keep him out of trouble. Thereupon the officer released Robinson, and with the conductor went back into the car for the purpose of finding and arresting John Whittaker. Whittaker and his brothers, who had seen the arrest of Sam Robinson, undertook to avoid the arrest of John Whittaker by the following ruse: John left the seat he was occupying, went in the forward part of the car, and on the opposite side of the aisle from where he had been sitting or standing, and took a seat by a little boy; and, in order to conceal him, one of his brothers sat on the arm of the seat, and leaned over John so as to screen him from ordinary observation. This necessitated somewhat of a search by the officer and the conductor, with the result that the conductor, Blevins, finally discovered John, and said to the officer, "Here he is. This is your man," or words to that effect. Thereupon the marshal, Marcum, put his hand upon the shoulder or neck of Whittaker, and said to him: "You must go with me. You are under arrest." Thereupon Whittaker replied: "I haven't done anything, and I will not go." The marshal then said, "Oh, yes; you will," and then gave him a pull or jerk with his hand. Thereupon John Whittaker immediately assaulted the officer, knocking him down, or very nearly knocking him down, and his brothers, and perhaps others at once assaulted the marshal and conductor, Blevins, and a general and free fight resulted, creating the greatest confusion and consternation among the passengers, many of whom left or tried to leave the car. The marshal was badly beaten about the face, the blood running freely from a wound on his head down in his eyes. In the midst of the melee he drew his pistol and shot John Whittaker in the left breast, and he sank into his seat, and there died within a few minutes.

We have not recited all of the mass of testimony that was adduced upon the trial. The evidence for the commonwealth and that for the defendant differs as to the degree of noise or boisterous conduct of Whittaker and his friends, but the evidence for the commonwealth sufficiently shows the facts to be substantially as stated in this opinion. We feel that it is sufficient for the purposes of this case merely to give a general outline of the evidence so that the principles of law certified to us may be properly understood. The arrest of John Whittaker by the constable was under the authority of section 806, Ky. St., which is as follows: "If any person whilst riding on a passenger or other train, shall, in the hearing or presence of other pasengers, and to their annoyance, use or utter obscene or profane language, or behave in a boisterous or riotous manner, or obtain or attempt to obtain, money or property from any passenger by any game, or device, he shall be fined for each offense not less than twenty-five nor more than one hundred dollars, or imprisoned in the county jail not less than ten nor more than fifty days, or both so fined and imprisoned; and it shall be the duty of the conductor in charge of any train upon which there is a person who has violated the provisions of this section either to put such person off the train, or to give notice of such violation to some peace officer at the first stopping place where any such officer may be." The commonwealth challenges the constitutionality of the foregoing statute as being inimical to section 10 of the Constitution, which provides: "The people shall be secure in their persons, houses, papers and possessions, from unreasonable search and seizure. * * *" And in support of this view cite the case of Jamison v. Gaernett, etc., 10 Bush, 221. In that case it was insisted that the charter of the city of Louisville authorized policemen to arrest, with or without a warrant, persons guilty of offenses against the laws or ordinances of the city. The court in denying that the charter authorized policemen to make arrests contrary to the general law of the state said, after quoting the charter: "We do not regard this enactment as necessarily conflicting with the general law which denies and limits the power of the arresting officer; but, if we did so construe it, we should hesitate to decide that it was not an infringement of the constitutional guaranty of security to the people 'in their persons, houses, papers, and possessions, against unreasonable seizure and searches.'" And then the opinion goes on to hold that policemen of the city of Louisville must make arrests in accordance with the general law bearing upon the subject. The opinion in this case is not conclusive of the question of the constitutionality of the statute we have under consideration. ⟨It may well be doubted whether policemen could constitutionally be authorized to make arrests for violations of municipal ordinances not committed in their presence without a warrant; and there would be ample room for the argument that the granting of such power would be unreasonable within the meaning of section 10 of the Constitution. But that is not the case we have here.⟩ The statute we are construing was enacted for the protection of the traveling public—men, women, and children—from unlawful conduct on the part of fellow passengers. If a conductor could not be empowered to forcibly eject a pasenger violating the foregoing statute, or to have the offender arrested as soon as a peace officer could be obtained, then we are not able to see how a railroad corporation could protect its passengers from the unlawful deeds of boisterous or disorderly or drunken persons on the train. Railroad corporations are engaged in the business of carrying passengers for long distances. Their trains ordinarily run through many counties as well as through different states. The passengers are necessarily more or less crowded together in close proximity, and their safety is in a measure at the mercy of each other. If the law-abiding cannot be protected from insult or violence by the lawless, it necessarily follows that traveling by railroad will become essentially a hazardous undertaking, independently of the ordinary dangers of accident or misfortune. The law is a growing science, and the Legislature is constantly engaged in advancing its protecting sanctions so as to safeguard the lives and the liberty of the citizen against outrage and violence. Wherever there is a special need for a new statute to protect the citizen in his rights, then it is the duty of the Legislature to enact such a statute. It was in obedience to this duty that the statute under consideration was enacted for the protection of the traveling public in their right to be transported in railroad cars free from the danger of insult, outrage, or violence by lawless men.

So much of the statute under consideration as authorized the conductor under the circumstances described in the statute to eject a passenger from his train was recognized and upheld as lawful by this court in the case of Chesapeake & Ohio Ry. Co. v. Crank, 128 Ky. 329, 108 S. W. 276; 32 Ky. Law Rep. 1202, 16 L. R. A. (N. S.) 197.

But the statute not only authorizes the conductor to eject a passenger who offends against its provisions, but authorizes him to obtain the assistance of a peace officer as soon as he can get into the presence of such an officer and empowers the peace officer upon the demand of the conductor to arrest the offender without a wararnt. This must necessarily be so if the statute is to have any efficient force or effect. The train could not be held at a station until the conductor could go and swear out the warrant for the arrest of the offender. To require this would nullify the statute. Laws are not made for the benefit of criminals, but for the protection of the innocent, and, if the statute was so framed as to require the issuance of the warrant as a prerequisite to the arrest of the violator of the statute, it would enable the guilty always to escape, and thus take from the innocent all hope of protection. The statute is not only constitutional, but it is an exceedingly wise and beneficent law. It puts into the hands of the railroad corporation the power to protect its innocent passengers by authorizing the conductor to eject offenders from his train or to cause them to be arrested by the first peace officer whose services he can secure.

The question as to whether a search or seizure of the person of the citizen is reasonable under the Constitution is a relative one. It might not be reasonable to seize or search the person of a citizen for a misdemeanor where he was at large in the city or country, and where the circumstances would generally be such that a warrant could be secured in advance of the arrest. But it would not be reasonable to require the officers to wait for a warrant if the offense was a felony, because here the gravity of the offense and the importance to the public of the prompt seizure of the criminal overrides the unreasonableness of the search or seizure without a warrant. And so, in the case at bar the circumstances which require the arrest of an offender against the statute are such as to make it reasonable that a peace officer should be authorized upon the request of the conductor of a train to arrest a violator without a warrant and without the offense for which the arrest was to be made being done in the presence of the officer. The law, being a practical science, regards the necessities of the case, the danger to the public, and the opportunity for the escape of the offender, and arranges the remedy so as to protect the innocent, trespassing upon the liberty of the citizen as little as possible in order to secure the protection of the public. No law, therefore, can be considered unreasonable which is necessary to protect the public from violence or outrage at the hands of the lawless. And, if such a law seems to give an undue amount of absolute authority into the hands of the officers having in charge its administration, it must be remembered that this is the price that the people pay for protection; for, after all, government is but the sum total of the natural liberty of the citizen surrendered up in return for law and order and peace and safety.

We will now consider instructions 5 and 6, given by the court, and which are objected to by the commonwealth. In the case of Stevens v. Commonwealth, 124, Ky. 32, 98 S. W. 284, 30 Ky. Law Rep, 290, we had occasion to examine the question as to the force which a peace officer is authorized to use in making an arrest where the party is charged with a misdemeanor and in the opinion in that case the decisions by our court are reviewed, as well as the text-books bearing upon the subject, and from the principles there enunciated we have never departed. In the opinion it is clearly stated that an officer having a right to arrest for a misdemeanor, if he be forcibly resisted, may use such force as is necessary, or reasonably appears to the officer necessary in the exercise of a sound judgment, to overcome such force and to make the arrest. But he has not the right, where the resistance is not forcible, to wantonly shoot or injure the person charged with a crime. In the case cited an instruction was formulated which, with slight changes to meet the necessities of the varying facts, would have well served for the instruction in this case. Instruction No. 5, given by the court, is objectionable, in that it does not present the idea that the resistance of the offender to the proposed arrest must be a forcible resistance. Nor does it present the idea that the officer may act upon what appears to him to be necessary in the exercise of a reasonable judgment. Therefore No. 5 should be modified so as to make it read, commencing with the last semicolon, as follows: "* * * And in making such arrest, such peace officer has the right to use such force as is reasonably necessary therefor, if the arrest be forcibly resisted, even to the taking of the life of the offender but he has not the right to use unnecessary force or violence, nor to shoot or otherwise injure the offender unless such offender forcibly re-sists the arrest and the arrest can not be otherwise made, or it appears to the officer, in the exercise of a reasonable judgment, that it can not be otherwise made.''

Instruction No. 6 is not subject to criticism, and upon another trial may be given as on the first.

/The commonwealth was entitled to have the jury instructed, in accordance with the provisions of section 39 of the Criminal Code of Practice, that it was the duty of the officer, before making the arrest, to inform the offender that he was about to be arrested and the offense for which he was to be arrested, un-less the decedent knew these facts, in which latter case it was not necessary to inform him of that which he already knew.] The court should, in addition, have told the jury plainly that it was the duty of the peace officer to arrest the offender upon the verbal request or demand of the conductor, and that in making the arrest the peace officer was not required to examine into the guilt or innocence of the offender whom the conductor asked to have arrested, and it was the duty of the decedent to submit to a lawful arrest at the hands of the peace officer, whether or not he had done anything which justified the arrest. In order to make the statute effective, it was necessary to authorize the officer to make the arrest upon the verbal request of the conductor. It does not contemplate that the offense should have been committed in the presence of the officer, and therefore the officer was authorized to act under the direction of the conductor. It may be that this construction will occasionally work a hardship upon the citizen, but, as said before, this hardship is necessary in the individual instance in order to effectuate a statute which is intended to subserve a great and general good. And the citizen who is oppressed unlawfully by its operation has his remedy against the railroad corporation for malicious prosecution.

It is therefore now ordered that this opinion be certified to the trial court, as by law required.

CASE 2.—SUIT BY JOSEPH D. ARNETT AGAINST T. P. CARD-
WELL, JR., POLICE JUDGE, TO HAVE AN ORDI-
NANCE ADJUDGED INVALID AND TO ENJOIN
THE COLLECTION OF A REPLEVIN BOND.—Oct.
20, 1909.

'Arnett v. Cardwell, Police Judge

Appeal from Breathitt Circuit Court.

J. P. Adams, Circuit Judge.

From an order denying relief, plaintiff appeals.— Reversed.

1. Courts—Conflicting Jurisdiction.—Civ. Code Prac., Sec. 284, provides that no injunction shall be granted to stay the proceeding on a judgment of a justice of the peace or of a county court, if the value of the matter in dispute does not exceed $25. Section 285 provides that an injunction to stay proceedings on a judgment must be brought in the court where the judgment was rendered. A judgment was recovered against plaintiff in the police court, which he sought to enjoin, on the ground that the ordinance under which the judgment was recovered was invalid. Held, that, in a suit, the main purpose of which was to have an ordinance declared invalid, and the injunction prayed for was only incidental to the main relief asked, sections 284 and 285 have no application, and that the circuit court had jurisdiction.

2. Municipal Corporations—Ordinances—Void for Uncertainty.
—While a town ordinance which prescribes a penalty for its
violation may leave a margin for the discretion of the court
so that the fine or imprisonment imposed may be graded in
proportion to the aggravation of the circumstances, it is void
for uncertainty, where it only prescribes for a minimum, and
not for a maximum penalty.

G. W. FLEENOR, attorney for appellant.

We rest our rights in this action and our claims for jurisdiction,
not alone on the common sense view of the situation, but upon
the authority in the cases of Boyd v. Board of Councilmen, 25
Ky. Law Rep. 1311; 77 S. W. 669; Moody v. City of Middles-
borough, 28 Ky. Law Rep. 60.

W. S. HOGG for appellees.

The judgment of the circuit court herein should be affirmed for
the following reasons:

First. The petition is not sworn to, and no affidavit filed setting forth grounds for injunction. The amended petition is verified but does not state facts authorizing an injunction, and the
prayer does not seek one.

Second. The plaintiff has never executed an injunction bond
in the circuit court, and therefore no valid injunction can be
granted herein. Civil Code, Sec. 278.

Third. Section 284, Civil Code, provides no injunction shall be
granted to stay proceedings upon a judgment of a justice of the
peace if the amount in controversy is less than $25. In this case
the plaintiff seeks to enjoin the collection of six judgments of
$16 each.

Fourth. The injunction must be sued out in the court which
rendered the judgment sought to be enjoined, and in this case
the circuit court had no jurisdiction to grant an injunction to
stay the collection of a judgment of the police court. Civil
Code, sec. 285; Davis v. Davis, 10 Bush, 274; Jacobson v. Wir-
nest, 1917 Law Rep. 662; Shackelford v. Patterson, 23 Ky. Law
Rep. 316.

Fifth. The circuit court can not take jurisdiction in this case,
the plaintiff seeks no real relief except to be relieved from paying these fines, and there is no threatened injury to plaintiff
from this ordinance; he does not state that he is threatened and
prevented thereby from continuing the sale of any malt drink
prohibited in said ordinance.

OPINION OF THE COURT BY WM. ROGERS CLAY, COMMISSIONER—Reversing.

The board of trustees of the town of Jackson, Ky., enacted the following ordinance: "Be it ordained by the board of trustees of the town of Jackson, Ky., as follows: That it shall be unlawful for any person to sell within the corporate limits of the town of Jackson, Ky., any drink known as Malt Meade or Beerine, and any person violating this ordinance shall, upon conviction, be fined not less than ten ($10.00) dollars for each offense, and each sale shall constitute a separate offense. This ordinance shall take effect from and after its publication. (Signed) R. T. Davis, Chairman. M. S. Crain, Clerk." Thereafter six warrants were issued against Joseph Arnett, charging him with violation of the above ordinance. He was tried before appellee, T. P. Cardwell, Jr., police judge of Jackson, and fined $10 and costs for each offense, the costs amounting to $6. Thereafter appellee replevied the fines and costs, amounting to $98, all of which were put in a single replevin bond. Appellant instituted this action against appellee, T. P. Cardwell, Jr., police judge of Jackson, Ky., and the town of Jackson, to have the aforesaid ordinance adjudged invalid, and to enjoin the collection of the replevin bond. The lower court denied the relief prayed for; hence this appeal.

Appellee took the position below that appellant's application for injunction should have been made in the police court, as that court rendered the judgment. He also contended that even the police court had no jurisdiction, as the amount in controversy did not exceed $25. See secs. 284 and 285 of the Civil Code of Practice. The circuit court agreed with appellee. Our conclusion, however, is that sections 284 and 285 have no application to a case like this. Here the main purpose of the suit is to have declared invalid the ordinance in question. The injunction prayed for is incidental only to the relief asked. This distinction was made by this court in the case of Boyd et al. v. Board of Council of the City of Frankfort, 117 Ky. 199, 77 S. W. 669, 25 Ky. Law Rep. 1311, Moody v. City of Williamsburg, etc., 121 Ky. 92, 88 S. W. 1075, 28 Ky. Law Rep. 60, and Combs v. Sewell, etc., 59 S. W. 526, 22 Ky. Law Rep. 1026.

The next question is: Is the ordinance void? It will be observed that the ordinance provides a minimum penalty, but not a maximum penalty. In ordinances and by-laws the penalty must be certain. The old English rule was that the precise amount should be fixed. This rule was followed in New Jersey. State v. Zeigler, 32 N. J. Law, 262. North Carolina holds to the same doctrine. State v. Worth, 95 N. C. 615. For a while Alabama had the same rule. · Mobile v. Yuille, 3 Ala. 137, 36 Am. Dec. 441. The latter case was afterwards overruled. Huntsville v. Phelps, 27 Ala. 55. According to the decided weight of authority, it is proper for penal ordinances to leave a margin for the discretion of the court, so that the fine or imprisonment imposed may be graded in some proportion to the aggravation of the circumstances. Thus the ordinance may provide that the fine shall not be less than a named sum, nor greater than a specified amount; or that the imprisonment shall not be less than a specified time, nor greater than a time named; or that the fine shall not exceed a named sum, or the imprisonment extend beyond a specified time. McQuillen on Municipal Ordinances, sec. 175. The ordinance in question does not conform to the general rule. While it prescribes a minimum fine, it does not fix a maximum

mum, thus leaving to the court the power to impose any fine in excess of $10. The ordinance is therefore void for uncertainty. It follows that appellant is entitled to the relief prayed for.

We deem it unnecessary to pass upon the other questions raised.

Judgment reversed, and cause remanded for proceedings consistent with this opinion.

CASE 3.—ACTION BY H. M. RUNYONS AND ANOTHER AGAINST T. H. BURCHETT, IN WHICH HE FILED A COUNTERCLAIM.—Oct. 20, 1909.

Runyons v. Burchett

Appeal from Floyd Circuit Court.

D. W. Gardner, Circuit Judge.

Judgment for defendant, plaintiff appeals.—Affirmed.

1. Pleading—Sufficiency—Aider by Verdict.—In an action against a seller of standing timber for a deficiency in the timber which had been paid for, an answer alleging for a counterclaim that the buyer unlawfully cut and removed from the land timber which did not belong to him, that 800 or more trees which belonged to the seller were removed, and that each tree was worth $1.50, was sufficient after verdict and judgment for the seller to state a cause of action on a counterclaim.

2. Appeal and Error—Record—Instructions—Bill of Exceptions.—Instructions can not be considered by the appellate court where they are not made a part of the record by bill of exceptions or by order of court.

3. Logs and Logging—Sale of Standing Timber—Counterclaim—Evidence.—In an action against a seller of standing timber for a deficiency in timber, which had been paid for, evidence

held to justify a verdict for the seller on his counterclaim based on the buyer taking trees not included in the contract of sale.

WALTER S. HARKNESS and JAMES GOBLE for appellants.

MAY & MAY for appellees.

OPINION OF THE COURT BY JUDGE HOBSON—Affirming.

On August 18, 1902, a written contract was entered into between T. H. Burchett of the first part, and A. L. James of the second part, which among other things contained the following provisions:

"Party of the first part does this day bargain and sell to party of the second part all the white oak and chestnut belonging to him. Party of the second part do bind himself to mark said timber from twenty inches clear the bark at an ordinary stump, with all trees that will make a clean log 30 feet long. Second party agrees to pay first party $1.00 per tree. Party of the second part binds himself to begin to brand said timber 24th day of August. Second party agrees to brand as speedy as possible until trees are branded. When done branding second party is to pay for said timber."

After the writing was entered into, Burchett and James went upon the land with their helpers and measured and marked with a cross-mark with a hatchet the trees which were accepted under the contract. After this had been done James sold the trees to S. W. Patten for $1.25 apiece; and, to save the cost of making two deeds, he and Burchett executed a deed to Patten, the granting clause of which is as follows:

"That for and in consideration of one dollar per tree, in hand paid to the said Thomas H. Burchett;

and the further consideration of twenty-five cents per tree in hand paid to the said A. L. James, for thirty-three hundred and eighty-six white and chestnut oak trees, branded with an 'X' cut with a hatchet on the said trees, now standing on the land of the said Thomas Burchett, on Buffalo creek, Floyd county, Kentucky, and on the Clerk branch and Wolf branch of said Buffalo creek, including all the land owned by the said Burchett on the waters of Buffalo creek. The said trees to be twenty inches in diameter inside of bark, reasonable stump high, and thirty feet and upward in length, the said trees now being marked with the 'X' in the bark, by the party of the second part.''

Patten sold the trees to the American Car & Foundry Company for $1.75 apiece, that company agreeing to take all trees 20 inches in diameter clear of bark and 24 feet long. It then went into the woods and began cutting the timber. It cut off the land 2,534 trees which came up to the contract; also 490 trees which were branded but were not 20 inches in diameter at the stump clear of bark. Thereupon this suit was filed by Patten and H. M. Runyons, who was a partner with him in the deal, against Burchett to recover for the deficiency in the timber which had been paid for upon the basis that there were 3,386 trees filling the contract. Burchett filed an answer in which he denied that there was a deficiency, and alleged that the plaintiffs and those claiming under them had cut and taken 800 of his trees not included in the contract, which were of value of $1,200, and this he pleaded as a counterclaim. The allegations of the reply were controverted, and a trial was had before a jury which resulted in a verdict and judgment in favor of Burchett for $400. The plaintiffs appeal.

It is insisted that the allegations of the plaintiffs' answer are not sufficient to state a cause of action on the counterclaim. The allegation of the original answer is as follows: "Defendant says * * * that plaintiffs unlawfully cut and removed from this defendant's land 800 or more trees which belonged to this defendant, and that said trees were worth $800, and he is entitled to recover the value thereof on his counterclaim herein."

But he thereafter filed an amended answer which was in these words:

"The defendant, Thomas H. Burchett, amends his original answer and counterclaim herein by leave of the court, and for amendment says that the allegation that the value of the 800 trees taken by the plaintiffs that were not branded and did not belong to them, instead of being stated at $800 should have been stated at $1,200, or $1.50 per tree."

The reply filed by the plaintiffs to the amended answer is as follows:

"The plaintiffs for reply to amended answer of defendant filed herein September 9, 1908, say it is untrue, and they deny that defendant's answer should have stated that the 800 trees which were taken by the plaintiffs which were not branded and did not belong to them, instead of being stated at $800, should have been stated at $1,200, or $1.50 per tree. They deny that they took any trees which did not belong to them which were worth $1,200, or any other amount, or were worth $1.50 per tree."

It is manifest that the amended answer and the reply made up an issue as to whether the plaintiffs had cut 800 trees or any other number from the land which were not branded, and did not belong to them, and, if there was any doubt of this, the pleading is certainly good after verdict and judgment. Hill v. Ragland, 114 Ky. 209, 70 S. W. 634, 24 Ky. Law Rep. 1053.

It is also insisted that the court misinstructed the jury, but this matter is not so presented by the record that we can consider it. The instructions given by the court are not embodied in the bill of exceptions, or made part of the record in any way. The bill of exceptions contains these words:

"Here copy instructions Nos. 2, 3, 4"—also as to cther instructions these words: "Here copy said instructions."

It has been often held that, although the instructions may be copied elsewhere in the record by the clerk, they can not be considered by this court where they are not made part of the record by bill of exceptions or by order of court. Forest v. Crenshaw, 81 Ky. 51, 4 R. 596-613, Johnson v. Postal Telegraph Co., 50 S. W. 1, 20 Ky. Law Rep. 1821; Housman v. Long, 66 S. W. 821, 23 Ky. Law Rep. 1994. We have examined, however, the instructions copied in the record, and find no substantial error in them. The question whether the plaintiffs had cut trees which they had not bought, and whether there was a deficiency in the trees bought below 3,386, the number specified in the deed, and if a deficiency, how much, were so submitted to the jury that under the evidence before them they could not have been misled.

Lastly, it is earnestly insisted that the verdict of the jury is palpably against the evidence. In this we can not concur. There was evidence warranting the jury in concluding that the plaintiffs had cut from 400 to 800 trees that were not branded or included in the contract. It was admitted that the plaintiffs had cut and taken away 2,534 trees which filled the contract. It was also admitted that they had cut and taken away 490 trees which were branded, but which were not 20 inches in diameter at the stump clear of the bark. There was also evidence warranting the jury in concluding that there were yet standing on the land and not cut 400 branded trees; thus showing that there were 3,424 trees branded if these figures are correct, while the deed only called for 3,386 trees.

The proof for the plaintiffs was to the effect that the 490 trees which were less than 20 inches in diameter were taken by them under an agreement with Burchett that they were to be counted two for one. But he denies this, and under all the circumstances we can not say that the jury were not warranted in accepting his version of the transaction. We are satisfied from the evidence that there were a number of trees which were branded which were not twenty inches in diameter at the stump clear of bark; but inasmuch as the jury were warranted in finding that the plaintiffs had cut and carried away three or four hundred more trees than they had bought, we can not say that the verdict in favor of the defendant for $400 is palpably against the evidence.

Judgment affirmed.

CASE 4.—ACTION BY FRED E. STEVENS AND OTHERS
AGAINST CITY OF LOUISVILLE TO RESTRAIN IT
FROM PROSECUTING PLAINTIFFS FOR SELLING
PISTOLS AT RETAIL WITHOUT A LICENSE.—Oct
20, 1909.

Stevens, &c. v. City of Louisville

Appeal from Jefferson Circuit Court (Chancery
Branch, First Division).

Shackelford Miller, Judge.

Plaintiffs' petition dismissed and they appeal.—
Affirmed.

Pawnbrokers—Licenses—Sale of Pistols.—The license ordinance
of a city in one section provided for a pawnbroker's license,
and in another section for a license to sell pistols at retail.
Held, that the taking out of a pawnbroker's license did not
authorize the pawnbroker to sell pistols at retail without taking out a license for the sale of pistols.

CHATTERSON & BLITZ for appellant.

POINTS AND AUTHORITIES.

1. The right in a municipality to levy or collect taxes is a special
delegated authority, and must be strictly complied with. Kentucky Statutes, Section 2980; Schuster v. City of Louisville, 28
Ky. Law Rep. 528; City of Louisville v. Button, 26 Ky. Law Rep.
606.

2. Where the main business pays a tax by way of license, it is
to be presumed that the licensee shall have all of the privileges
ordinarily included in, or incident to, that business. New Galt
House Co. v. City of Louisville, 111 S. W. 351.

3. Both the statute of the State and the ordinance of the city
defines what the business of a pawn broker is, and provides for
a licensing of that business; and the appellants in this case have
paid that license tax in both instances, and to compel them to pay
a second license tax upon an incidental business is to require a

Stevens, &c. v. City of Louisville.

double license or tax which is abhorrent to the Constitution of this State. New Galt House Co. v. City of Louisville, Ibid; City of Newport v. Fitzer, 115 Ky. Dec. 742.

4. Where an ordinance is valid upon its face, and the alleged invalidity consists in matters to be established by extrinsic evidence, a court of equity will always interfere to determine the rights of the parties by injunction pending that determination. Brown v. Trustees of Catlettsburg, 11 Bush 437; Ludlow & Cin. Coal Co. v. City of Ludlow, 19 Ky. Law Rep. 1381; Shinkle v. City of Covington, 83 Ky. 420; Ewing v. City of St. Louis, 5 Wallace 413.

5. Also to prevent a multiplicity of actions (whether criminal or civil) or irreparable injury.

6. The license ordinance in this case is a revenue ordinance.

7. The city of Louisville has never received authority of law to impose upon any business or occupation a regulation ordinance, and the purposes of all ordinances must be specified in the ordinance. Schuster v. City of Louisville, 28 Ky. Law Rep. 528; City of Louisville v. Button, 26 Ky. Law Rep. 606.

8. The petition in this case alleges all of the facts necessary under these decisions to establish equitable jurisdiction, and these facts are admitted to be true by the demurrer. Norman v. Ky. Board of Managers, 93 Ky.; page 537.

CLAYTON B. BLAKEY and ELMER C. UNDERWOOD for City of Louisville.

POINTS AND AUTHORITIES.

1. The law presumes that the Police Court of the City of Louisville would have correctly decided the law and the fact had appellants been actually present before it for trial.

2. Kentucky Statutes, Section 2922, provides an ample remedy at law in cases like the one at bar. Where the fine inflicted by the Police Court is more than $20.00 the defendant may appeal to the Jefferson Circuit Court; where the fine imposed is $20.00 or less the defendant is entitled to a writ of prohibition to test the validity of the ordinance involved.

3. No warrants or summonses have ever been issued, but have only been threatened. As Kentucky Statutes, Sec. 2922, affords a complete remedy at law a Court of Equity will not interfere by injunction to restrain criminal proceedings. Smiser v. City of Cynthiana, 97 S. W. 35; In re Sawyer, 124 U. S. 209; Rogers v. Cincinnati, 5 McLean (U. S.) 337; Am. & Eng. Enc. of Law, 2d. Ed., vol. 16, p. 337; Shinkle v. City of Covington, 83 Ky. 420; Ludlow & Cincinnati Coal Co. v. City of Ludlow, 102 Ky. 354;

High on Injunctions, 3d Ed., sec. 1244; Louisville & Nashville
Railroad Co. v. Barrall, 25 Ky. Law Rep. 1395.

4. A pawn broker's license does not confer the right to sell
any class of personal property that the pawn broker may choose
to take in pledge. If this were not so, a pawn broker could sell
cigarettes, intoxicating liquor, playing cards, and bowie knives
as well as pistols. The ordinance requiring a license to sell pistols is a police measure and the fact that a pawn broker has paid
a pawn broker's license does not justify him in evading such police measure. Commonwealth v. Fowler, 17 Ky. Law Rep. 1209;
Am. & Eng. Enc. of Law, Vol. 21, page 807; Bowser v. Thompson,
20 Ky. Law Rep. 21, 103 Ky. 331; Commonwealth v. Fowler, 96 Ky.
166.

OPINION OF THE COURT BY JUDGE HOBSON—Affirming.

The license ordinance of the city of Louisville
among other things contains the following:

"Section 1. That hereafter the following licenses
shall be paid into the sinking fund of the city of
Louisville for the purposes of the sinking fund, for
doing the business, following the callings, occupations
and professions, or using or holding, or exhibiting the
articles hereinafter named in the city of Louisville
in addition to the ad valorem taxes heretofore levied
or hereafter to be levied on any species of property
in the city of Louisville."

"Sec. 66. Every person, firm, or corporation whose
business is to take or receive by way of pledge, pawn
or exchange any goods, wares or merchandise, or any
personal property whatever, as security for the payment of money lent thereon, other than banks or trust
companies, shall be deemed a pawn broker and shall
pay a license of three hundred and fifty dollars per
year."

"Sec. 72. Every person, firm or corporation who
sells pistols at retail shall pay a license of one hundred dollars per year."

"Sec. 106. Any person, firm or corporation violating any of the provisions of this ordinance, where a different fine has not been provided, shall be fined not less than five dollars nor more than one hundred dollars for each offense. Each day the violation is continued shall constitute a separate offense."

Appellants are pawnbrokers in the city of Louisville, and took out license as such; but they did not take out license to sell pistols at retail. The city was threatening to institute prosecutions against them, and they thereupon brought this suit the purpose of which was to obtain an injunction or prohibition restraining the city from prosecuting them for selling pistols at retail without license. The circuit court dismissed their petition, and they appeal.

The only question we deem it necessary to consider on the appeal is the validity of section 72, as to pawnbrokers. It is insisted for appellants that as they have taken out license as pawnbrokers to require them to take out a license to sell pistols at retail will be to tax them twice on their business, and the case cf Newport v. Fitzer (Ky.) 115 S. W. 742, is relied on. In that case there was a city ordinance which required the payment of $20 for a license for peddling when carried on with a wagon, and $10 if carried on on foot. There was also another ordinance requiring the payment of $3 by the owner of a vehicle for the right to use it upon the streets. It was held that, as the $20 was paid for the privilege of peddling with a wagon, this necessarily carried with it the right to use the wagon on the streets, as there could be no peddling with a wagon unless the wagon was run on the streets, and that, therefore, it must be presumed that the $3 tax was levied on vehicles not otherwise licensed. That is not this case. The business of a pawnbroker may be carried on without selling pistols at retail. Sections 66 and 72 are to be read together. The license under section 66 authorizes the pawn·broker to carry on the business, and to deal in all those things for which no special license is required. But, if a pawnbroker wishes to deal in those things which can only be sold at retail under a special li·cense, then, in order to sell at retail these things, he must take out the license required for that business. To hold otherwise would be to say that a pawnbroker who had taken out a license as such might carry on under this license the business of retailing other goods of any kind for the sale of which a special li·cense is required by the ordinance of the city. Such a construction of the ordinance would defeat the manifest purpose of the council in requiring a special license for the retailing of certain things, and it would enable a pawnbroker under one license to carry on any kind of retail business he pleased without the payment of a special license tax. To illustrate: If he may sell pistols without paying the special tax, he may upon the same principle sell playing cards, whisky, cigars, tobacco, soft drinks, and all other things for which a special license may be required.

Judgment affirmed.

CASE 5.—ACTION BY B. F. WILLIAMSON AND OTHERS
AGAINST W. H. MAYNARD AND OTHERS.—Oct.
20, 1909.

Williamson, &c. v. Maynard, &c.

Appeal from Pike Circuit Court.

A. J. KIRK, Circuit Judge.

Judgment for defendants, plaintiffs appeal.—Appeal dismissed.

1. Wills—Probate—Appeal—Time of Taking Proceedings.—Ky.
   St. 1909, Sec. 4850, limits the time to appeal from a judgment
   of the circuit court probating a will to one year. Held that,
   if an appellant from such a judgment was unavoidably delayed in preparing his transcript, he should, within the year,
   apply to the appellate court for an extension of the time to
   file the transcript, as prescribed under Civ. Code Prac. Secs.
   738, 740, 758, and that, on failure to do so, the appeal may
   be dismissed if not taken within the prescribed time.
2. Wills—Probate—Appeal—Dismissal—Time of Taking Proceedings.—That the limitation of one year prescribed by Ky. St.
   1909, Sec. 4850, for taking an appeal from a judgment of the
   circuit court probating a will, has expired, may be raised by
   motion upon a proper plea made at or before the time the
   case is submitted on the merits.

S. M. CECIL, W. H. FLANNERY, J. F. BUTLER, JAMES M.
ROBERSON attorneys for appellants.

HAGER & STEWART and W. S. HARKINS of counsel.

PROPOSITION.

1. The will was not signed by the testator nor acknowledged by
him to be his will.
2. The subscribing witnesses contradict each other and the will
is not therefore proven as the law requires.
3. Undue influence was used by W. H. Maynard to have C. W.
Williamson make the will.

Williamson, &c. v. Maynard, &c.

4. The testator's physical condition and mind were such that he could not make a valid will.

5. The will is unnatural; C. W. Williamson is made to forget his father and mother and attempt to put the title to the land in strangers to whom he owed no duty, except his wife should have had a reasonable provision if he was in condition to make the will. Wherefore the appellants ask a reversal of the judgment appealed from.

N. J. AUXIER, YORK & JOHNSON and F. W. STOWERS for appellees.

QUESTIONS OF LAW AND AUTHORITIES CITED.

1. One year limitation for appeal from judgment of circuit court in will case. Kentucky Statutes, Section 4850.

2. Appeal granted by clerk of this court by application made to him and filing copy of judgment. Carroll's Code, Section 734.

3. Will may be probated on testimony of one of the subscribing witnesses. Cornelison v. Browning, 10 B. Mon. 425; Hall, &c. v. Sims, &c., 2 J. J. Mar. 511; Overall v. Overall, Lit. Sel. Cases, 503.

OPINION OF THE COURT BY JUDGE O'REAR—Dismissing appeal.

This is an appeal from the judgment of the Pike Circuit Court, finding the paper in contest to be the last will of C. W. Williamson. The final judgment became effective in October of 1907. This appeal was prosecuted January 25, 1909. Appellees have interposed and rely upon the plea of limitation of one year in such cases.

In avoidance of the plea appellants assert that parts of the record were lost, and that because of that fact and other unavoidable casualty they were not able to have the transcript of the record filed in this court within one year from the time the final judgment was entered.

Section 4850, Ky. St. limits to one year the period within which appeals may be prosecuted to this court from judgments of the circuit court probating wills. If some casualty delayed the appellants in having the transcript prepared within that time, they should during that year, and while this court still had jurisdiction of the matter, have applied to this court for an extension of the time within which to have filed the transcript. Sections 738, 740, 758, Civ. Code Prac.; Hernstein v. Depue, 65 S. W. 805, 23 Ky. Law Rep. 1498; Bush v. Lisle, 86 Ky. 504, 6 S. W. 330, 9 Ky. Law Rep. 667.

It was held by this court in the case of Duff v. Duff, 103 Ky. 348, 45 S. W. 102, 20 Ky. Law Rep. 52, that the statutory bar of one year in will cases may be available to the appellee by motion based upon proper plea, and made at or before the case is submitted on the merits. Such was the practice in this case, and the court has no option but to sustain the plea and motion.

Appeal dismissed.

CASE 6.—AMBROSE FERGUSON WAS INDICTED FOR OB-
TAINING MONEY BY FALSE PRETENSES.——October 20, 1909.

Commonwealth v. Ferguson

Appeal from Morgan Circuit Court.

J. B. HANNAH, Circuit Judge.

Demurrer to indictment sustained and Commonwealth appeals.—Reversed.

1   False Pretenses—Indictment.—Under Ky. St. 1909, Sec. 1208,
    making criminal the obtaining of money, property or other
    thing by false pretense, it is not necessary that the indict-
    ment charge that the person to whom the false pretense was
    made sustained any loss, and an indictment charging defend-
    ant with obtaining money by falsely representing that he was
    of age, and thereby inducing the prosecuting witnesses to pur-
    chase land of him, was not defective, though impliedly ad-
    mitting that the witnesses afterwards obtained a good title
    to the land.

2. False Pretenses—Infants—Representation as to Age.—Under
    Ky. St. 1909, Sec. 1208, making criminal the obtaining of
    money, property or other thing by false pretenses, a state-
    ment by a minor that he is of age is a false statement, if
    made to induce another to enter into a contract that he would
    not have otherwise entered into, and the one to whom the
    statement is made is induced to, and does, part with his
    money or property on the faith of it.

JAS. BREATHITT, Attorney General, TOM B. McGREGOR, Assistant Attorney General, and JOHN W. WAUGH for Commonwealth.

S. M. NICKELL and A. N. CISCO for appellee.

(No briefs—record out).

OPINION OF THE COURT BY JUDGE CARROLL—Reversing.

The only question in this case is whether or not
the lower court ruled correctly in sustaining a demurrer to the following indictment:

"The grand jury of Morgan county, in the name
and by the authority of the Commonwealth of Kentucky, accuse Ambrose Ferguson of the crime of obtaining money by false pretense, committed as follows:

The said defendant, Ambrose Ferguson, on the 23d
day of March, 1908, in the county and circuit aforesaid, did unlawfully, willfully and feloniously, and by
falsely representing and pretending to K. S. Lykins
and S. M. Freese that he, the said Ferguson, was 21
years of age on the 26th day of March, 1904, and able
to contract for himself, and did thereby induce and
procure the said Lykins to purchase and take conveyance from him (Ferguson) of a certain tract of land
in Morgan county, Ky., and to pay him therefor the
sum of $2,400, when in truth and in fact he was under
21 years of age at that time, and he well knew same,
and said statements and representations when so
made by him were false and fraudulent, and known
to him to be false at the time, and were made by him
with the intention of defrauding the said Lykins and
Freese, and that they did not get said land under the
said conveyance, but were induced and did pay to the
said Ferguson the sum of $2,400 believing and, by
reason of said statements, not knowing the same to be
false, against the peace and dignity of the Commonwealth of Kentucky."

We are not accurately advised as to the grounds
upon which the demurrer was sustained. It may
have been because the indictment failed to charge
that Lykins and Freese suffered any loss by reason of

the fraudulent representations made to them by Ferguson, or upon the ground that a false statement made by an infant as to his age does not come within the statute. But, whatever the reason that influenced the lower court, his ruling was erroneous, as in our opinion the indictment was sufficient.

It will be observed that the indictment charges that Lykins and Freese did not get the land under the conveyance made to them by Ferguson at the time they paid the $2,400, but impliedly admits that they afterwards obtained a good title to the land, and so we will assume that they did not suffer any loss. It is not necessary that an indictment for false pretense shall charge that the person to whom the false pretense was made sustained any loss. Section 1208 of the Kentucky Statutes, describing the crime of obtaining money or property by false pretenses, reads as follows:

"If any person by any false pretense, statement or token, with intention to commit a fraud, obtain from another money, property or other thing which may be the subject of larceny, or if he obtain by any false pretense, statement or token, with like intention, the signature of another to a writing, the false making whereof would be forgery, he shall be confined in the penitentiary not less than one nor more than five years."

Under this statute it is the obtention by fraudulent pretenses of money or property that may be the subject of larceny that constitutes the offense. When the owner is induced to, and does, part with his property by reason of the false and fraudulent statement or pretense, the offense in this particular is completed.

It is wholly immaterial whether he actually or ultimately suffers a loss or not. If he should regain his property, or the person obtaining it or another should fully compensate him, it would not lessen the offense, or prevent the Commonwealth from prosecuting and convicting the offender.

Although this precise question has not, so far as our investigation goes, been heretofore passed upon by this court, it has often been considered by courts of last resort in other jurisdictions, and the rulings are entirely uniform. Thus, in People v. Genung, 11 Wend. (N. Y.) 18, 25 Am. Dec. 594, Genung by false pretenses procured Conly to sign a note. In passing upon an objection to the indictment similar to the one made in this case the court said:

"It was suggested upon the argument that the indictment was bad in not charging loss or prejudice to have been sustained by Conly. * * * The offense is complete when the signature is obtained by false pretenses with the intent to cheat or defraud another. It is not essential to the offense that actual loss or injury should be sustained."

In Commonwealth v. Coe, 115 Mass. 481, in considering a prosecution for obtaining money and property under false pretenses under a statute substantially like ours, the court said:

"The offense consists in obtaining property of another by false pretenses. The intent to defraud is the intent, by the use of false means, to induce another to part with his possession and confide it to the defendant, when he would not otherwise have done so. Neither the promise to repay, nor the intention to do so, will deprive the false and fraudulent act in obtaining it of its criminality. The offense is complete when the money or property has been obtained by such means, and would not be purged by subsequent restoration or repayment."

In People v. Bryant, 119 Cal. 595, 51 Pac. 960, in disposing of a similar question, the court said:

"If a person is induced to part with his property by reason of fraudulent pretenses and misrepresentations, he is thereby defrauded of the property so parted with, even though he may eventually make himself whole in some manner not then contemplated. It is not necessary to show that the property has been absolutely lost to him in order to sustain the charge. He is defrauded of his property when he is induced to part with it by reason of the false and fraudulent pretenses and representations, and the offense is complete when by means of such false pretenses the fraud thereby intended is consummated by obtaining possession of the property sought, * * * notwithstanding the defrauded party may recover the value of the property in a civil action against him."

And so in the case of People v. Cook, 41 Hun (N. Y.) 67, the court said:

"In the case at bar the representations, alleged to have been made with intent to cheat and defraud the party who was thereby induced to part with his money, were that the note presented was made by a particular person, when in fact it was not, but was made by another having the same name. The obtaining money by such means was clearly within the statute, and the indictment contains all the elements of crime required by its provisions, although there is no allegation that the maker of the note was less responsible than the person represented as the maker. * * * The purpose of the statute is to protect against imposition, and not to permit guilt to depend upon the uncertainty of the determination of the question whether any pecuniary injury necessarily resulted in some view which might be taken of the situation."

Likewise, in Lowe v. State, 111 Ga. 650, 36 S. E. 856, it is said:

"The crime, then, was certainly complete when the accused failed to pay for the goods after the prosecutor had become aware of his misrepresentations, and demanded payment of him. * * * The fact that he afterwards settled with the accused for the value of the goods is not pretended as a settlement of the crime that had been committed, even if the parties had authority to settle such a crime; but it must be construed simply as a settlement of a civil liability, one, who for the purpose of deceiving another and obtaining credit, makes a false and fraudulent representation to the effect that he has purchased and has become the owner of valuable property, and who in this manner defrauds the person to whom the representation is made of money or other thing of value, is guilty of being a cheat and swindler; and a settlement between such wrongdoer and the person defrauded, made after the commission of the offense, and the arrest of the former upon a warrant charging him therewith, constitutes no bar to his conviction thereof upon an indictment subsequently returned. As well might it be said that one guilty of larceny could escape prosecution by returning the stolen goods after being arrested for the offense."

In Commonwealth v. Schwartz, 92 Ky. 510, 18 S. W. 775, 13 Ky. Law Rep. 929, 36 Am. St. Rep. 609, it was ruled that if a person obtains a loan of money from another by false pretense of an existing fact,

although he intends to repay it, he will be guilty of
the crime denounced by the statute.

It is equally clear that a statement made by a person that he is over 21 years of age, when in fact, as
he well knows, he is not, is a false statement within
the meaning of the statute, if it be made for the
fraudulent purpose of inducing a person to enter into
a contract or engagement that he would not have
entered into if he had known that the person was an
infant, and the person to whom the statement is made
is induced to, and does, part with his money or property on the faith of it. An infant's contract is voida-
able at his election. Generally speaking, he may or
may not perform it. Persons who deal with an infant may or may not suffer loss, depending upon the
election of the infant to perform the contract or
avoid it. But whether loss is sustained or not is not
important, nor is it material that the infant may be
estopped from relying on his infancy to defeat the
contract. It is the fact that a false statement was
made to obtain the property, and that on the credit
of it the property was obtained, that constitutes the
gist of the offense. Whenever a person is induced to
part with his money or property by fraudulent and
false statements of existing or past facts, no matter
in what the fraudulent settlement consists, the statute has been violated. The purpose of the law is to
suppress cheating and fraud. It is a broad statute,
and embraces all persons who "by any false pretense
statement or token, with the intention to commit a
fraud, obtain from another money, property, or other
thing which may be the subject of larceny." Lefler
v. State, 153 Ind. 82, 54 N. E. 439, 45 L. R. A. 424,
74 Am. St. Rep. 300; Barton v. People, 135 Ill. 405,

25 N. E. 776, 10 L. R. A. 302, 25 Am. St. Rep. 392; 2 Bishop's New Criminal Law, Sec. 414.

There is no exception in favor of infants. The infant of mature years is placed on the same footing as the adult. If an infant by falsely and fraudulently representing that he is the son of A., when in fact he is not, and this is unknown to C., who on the faith of his statement advances him money which he would not· have done had he known the truth, he· is guilty of the offense denounced. And so an infant who appears and represents himself to be of age, or makes any other false and fraudulent statement upon the faith and credit of which he obtains money or property, is equally guilty. In each case he has been enabled to procure the money or property by reason of the false statement. People v. Kendall, 25 Wend. (N. Y.) 399, 37 Am. Dec. 240. It is not important in what the false statement consists, so that it relates to some material past or existing fact, and is calculated to, and does, deceive. Bishop's New Criminal Law, Secs. 433-436; 2 Wharton's Criminal Law, Sec. 1186; Commonwealth v. Grady, 13 Bush, 285, 26 Am. Rep. 192; Commonwealth v. Haughey, 3 Metc. 223; Commonwealth v. Beckett, 119 Ky. 817, 84 S. W. 758, 27 Ky. Law Rep. 265, 68 L. R. A. 638, 115 Am. St. Rep. 285.

Wherefore the judgment is reversed, for proceedings consistent with this opinion.

CASE 7.—ACTION BY JOHN V. LeMOYNE AGAINST ENOS A.
ROUNDTREE TO RECOVER LAND.—October 21, 1909.

Le Moyne v. Roundtree

Appeal from Whitley Circuit Court.

WM. H. HOLT, Special Judge.

Judgment for defendant, plaintiff appeals.—Reversed.

Adverse Possession—Possession of Trespasser—Evidence.—Evidence that one owning land gave it to his son-in-law with other conterminous land which he did not own, and the son-in-law entered on the latter land which was rough, uninclosed, mountain land and inclosed a few acres, and occasionally cut timber and tan bark on the part uninclosed, but did not claim to any well-defined boundary, is insufficient on which to base adverse possession of such land other than the inclosed portion, since a trespasser can not obtain necessary title unless he claims to a well-defined boundary.

GILLIS & GILLIS and CHAS. H. RHODES for appellant.

A reversal of the judgment is asked on the following grounds:
1. Because of error in instructing the jury.
2. Refusal to give a peremptory instruction to find for appellant.
3. The admission of incompetent testimony.
4. The verdict is flagrantly against the evidence.
5. Because of refusal to give instruction asked by appellant.
6. Because of improper argument by counsel for appellee.
7. Because of error in ordering by-standers to serve on jury.

AUTHORITIES CITED.

116 S. W. 755, Steele v. Bryant; 110 Ky. 787, Mann v. Cavanaugh; 20 Ky. Law Rep., 383, Ohio & Big Sandy R. R. Co. v. Wooten; 22 Ky. Law Rep., 416, Barr v. Potter; 9 Ben Mon., 82 Floyd v. L. & N. R. R. Co.; 25 Ky. Law Rep. 2148, Inter State Ins. Co. v. Bailey, 93 S. W. 578; 3 A. K. Marshall, 313, Trotter v. Cas-

sady; 105 S. W. 106, Jones v. McCauley's Heirs; 22 Ky. Law Rep. 1919, Helton v. Straube; 31 Ky. Law Rep. 1099, Fuller v. Kesee; 30 Ky. Law Rep. 592, Kountz v. Hatfield; 23 Ky. Law Rep. 1234, Strange v. Commonwealth; 27 Ky. Law Rep. 250, L. & N. R. R. Co. v. Carter.

R. S. ROSE and TYE & SILER attorneys for appellee.

AUTHORITIES CITED.

Stone, Auditor v. Sanders, 106 Ky. 904; Eichman's Committee v. South Covington C. St. Ry. Co., 31 R. 880; Miller v. South Covington St. Ry Co., 25 R. 207; Kentucky R. R. Co. v. Warren & Co., 10 Bush 711; Anderson v. Winfree, 85 Ky. 597; American & English Encyclopedia of Law, page 462; Meaux v. Meaux, 81 Ky. 475; L. & N. R. R. Co. v. Lawson, 11 S. W. 511; Murphey v. May, 9 Bush 33; also 79 Ky. 205; Commonwealth v. Gibson, et al., 85 Ky. 666; Fox v. Hinton, 4 Bibb 559; Whitley County Land Co. v. Lawson, 94 Ky. 613; Ware v. Bryant's Adm'r., 14 R. 852; Northup's Trustee v. Summer's Trustee, et al., 116 S. W. 698; Cates v. Loftus' Heirs, 4 T. B. Monroe 439; Young v. Withers, 8 Dana 167; Griffith v. Dicken, 2 B. Monroe 24; Overton v. Perry, Jr., 111 S. W. 369; Scott v. Mineral Develpoment Co., 130 Fed. 497; Burt v. Brabb, 109 S. W. 348; Robinson v. Huffman, 113 S. W. 458; Metlock v. Suter, 80 Ky. 101; Creech v. Abner, 106 Ky. 239; Thompson v. Thompson, 93 Ky. 435; Gilbert v. Kelly, 22 R. 353.

OPINION OF THE COURT BY JUDGE BARKER—Reversing.

This action involves the title to 148 1-2 acres of land in Whitley county, Ky. It was begun by the appellant, John V. Le Moyne, filing a petition in the Whitley circuit court describing the land in question by metes and bounds, alleging himself to be the owner and entitled to the immediate possession thereof, and that he had been ousted from his lawful possession by the appellee (defendant) Enos A. Roundtree. The appellee filed an answer putting in issue appellant's title and right to possession of the land described in the petition, and by a second paragraph pleaded title in himself by prescription. The affirmative allegations of the answer were denied and the issues thus completed. A trial by jury resulted in a verdict in favor of the defendant (appellee), and of the judgment based upon this verdict the appellant complains.

The first question involved on this appeal is the correctness of the trial court's ruling in refusing to grant the appellant's (plaintiff's) motion for a peremptory instruction to the jury to find for him at the close of the evidence. The appellee made no sort of claim to the land except by prescription, and the appellant established a complete and perfect paper title, which was in no wise denied or impeached by any evidence for appellee. The question, then, recurs: Was there sufficient evidence of adverse possession for the statutory period by appellee to warrant the court in submitting his claim to the jury? Except as to a small part (some 10 or 12 acres) of the land sued for which appellee testified to having fenced in and held and used, he showed no possession which would ripen into a title by the expiration of the statutory period. In 1890 he says that his father-in-law, Tom Meadors, put him in possession of a house on the Creekmore survey which the latter owned, and told him he could have it and the surrounding land, consisting of certain fields. He understood his father-in-law to make him a present of the land. The Creekmore survey was conterminous to the land in question, the public road, however, running between the two tracts. The possession which Meadors gave to his son-in-law is thus described by appellee himself: After having stated that his father-in-law gave him the land in controversy which he did not own, and a part of his own land, he was asked this question: "What did Tom Meadors say about this land in question? A. He just waved his hand up that way, and said I could have all that land. Q. Did he give you this land? A. Yes, sir; that is what I understood him. Q. What did you do, if anything, toward taking possession of the land or improving it? A. In the spring of 1890 I fenced up ten to twelve acres of it, and cleared a half or three-quarters of an acre." The witness does afterwards say that he claimed all of the land to a well-defined boundary, but showed on cross-examination that he knew nothing of the lines, and more especially showed that he did not know whether the lines of the tract were marked or not. It was conceded that Tom Meadors, the father-in-law of appellee, neither had any sort of title to the land in controversy nor claimed to have. He did own, however, several boundaries of land lying contiguous to it, among which was the Creekmore survey. It is also conceded that the house of which Tom Meadors gave appellee the possession was not on any part of the land involved in this litigation, but was on the Creekmore tract which was separated from the land in dispute by a public road. Appellee having no title or shadow of legal claim to the land in dispute, he could only obtain a possessory title by actual occupancy with claim of ownership for the full term of 15 years. The property was rough, uninclosed mountain land; and, while appellee shows that he occasionally cut timber and tan bark, and committed other occasional acts of trespass, he had no sort of actual occupancy except of the ten or twelve acres he says he inclosed.

In Interstate Inv. Co. v. Bailey, 93 S. W. 578, 29 Ky. Law Rep. 468, we said: "Actual possession to oust the owner must be an actual occupancy, as by residence upon, or cultivation, or inclosure of the premises claimed. It is the pedis possessio of the law, a foothold upon the land, a possession in fact, an actual physical entry. Such a possessor by his acts and claim sets the statute of limitation to running, because he has not only effectually ousted any other claimant, thereby giving to him a cause of action, but its notorious character is so calculated to direct attention of any other claimant as to raise the presumption that he does know of it, and imposes on him the duty to recover his own in timely season, or thereafter be heard no more to assert his right to it." In Ohio & Big Sandy R. R. Co. v. Wooten, 46 S. W. 681, 20 Ky. Law Rep. 383, it was said: "It seems to us that the well-settled rule of law in this state is that actual occupancy of the tract or parcel of land is necessary to enable a plaintiff without title to recover against a trespasser, and also that actual occupancy for the statutory period is necessary to vest title in the occupant, in the absence of paper title; that mere claim of ownership, with frequent cutting and removing of timber from the tract of land, does not constitute actual occupancy or possession within the meaning of the law." In Barr, etc., v. Potter, 57 S. W. 479, 22 Ky. Law Rep. 418, the following language is used: "The court also erred in refusing to instruct the jury that a mere claim of ownership, with occasional cutting of timber on the land in controversy or removing it therefrom, by those under whom defendant claims, and the building of a cabin thereon without actual residence upon the land, or without inclosing it, or cultivating it, was not such adverse possession as could be added to the time defendant had actually resided upon the land so as to defeat the plaintiff's right of recovery." In

Fuller v. Keesee, etc., 104 S. W. 700, 31 Ky. Law Rep. 1099, this court, speaking through Judge Hobson, said: "To say he held in adverse possession all the land in this great boundary by simply laying claim to run with the top of the cliffs would be to ignore the reasons for the rule protecting the bona fide occupants of land, who hold it in adverse possession. He had, as the record shown, no shadow of title, and he gained possession only of so much of the land in controversy as he cleared or inclosed." And in Kountze v. Hatfield, 99 S. W. 265, 30 Ky. Law Rep. 592, we said: "It may be conceded that their adverse holding extended to the full limit of the land cultivated or inclosed by fence. But outside of that their holding does not go. * * * * Appellant traces his title to the land in controversy back to the commonwealth, while appellees rest their claim entirely on adverse possession." To the same effect are Floyd v. Louisville & Nashville R. R. Co., 80 S. W. 204, 25 Ky. Law Rep. 2149; Helton v. Strubbe, 62 S. W. 12, 22 Ky. Law Rep. 1919; Mann v. Cavanaugh, 110 Ky., 787, 62 S. W. 854, 23 Ky. Law Rep. 238.

The cases cited by appellee do not militate against the principle here enunciated. We have never held that a mere trespasser could obtain a possessory title unless he claimed to a well-marked or well-defined boundary. His possession must be such as gives the world, and especially those in interest, notice of the extent of his claim; and then, if the owner stands by and allows the trespasser to occupy and claim his property for the full term of fifteen years, he loses it, and the trespasser, under the statute, obtains title to the extent of his possession. The appellee had no such possession as is necessary to the acquisition of title by prescription, and what he did upon appellant's land, according to his own testimony, did not give notice of his adverse holding, except to the few acres he inclosed. A wrong-doer cannot acquire title to another's land by occupancy without giving notice for fifteen years of what he is doing and claiming.

Upon the conclusion of the evidence, the court should have sustained appellant's motion for a peremptory instruction to the jury to find for him for the whole tract sued for except 10 or 12 acres which appellee says he fenced up, and submitted to the jury only the question as to whether or not the appellee did use and occupy this inclosure continuously and adversely under a claim of ownership for 15 years.

Judgment reversed for further procedure consistent with this opinion.

CASE 8.—ACTION BY W. H. SALMON AGAINST GEORGE SNADON.—Oct. 21, 1909.

Snadon v. Salmon

Appeal from Todd Circuit Court.

W. P. SANDIDGE, Circuit Judge.

Judgment for plaintiff, defendant appeals.—Reversed.

1. Covenants—Covenant of Warranty—Breach—Actions.—A grantee who has been evicted, or who has suffered such a loss as entitles him to sue on a covenant of general warranty, may sue a remote grantor who conveyed the land with warranty, and he is not confined to an action against his immediate grantor, but a grantee seeking to recover on a warranty in a deed made by a remote grantor, with knowledge of the fact that the conveyance was not intended to pass the title, but was only a mortgage, takes the place of the immediate grantee of the grantor whom he sues, and can occupy no better position than such grantee.

2. Covenants—Covenant of Warranty—Breach—Actions.—An agreement between a grantor in a deed with covenant of warranty, and the grantee therein, by which the latter relieves the former of liability on the covenant, does not operate as an estoppel on a subsequent or remote grantee or prevent him from suing on the warranty.

3. Covenants—Covenant of Warranty—Breach—Actions.—A purchaser purchased with notice of the character of the conveyance his vendor took. At the time of the conveyance to the vendor his grantor was not invested with title or possession, but both remained in the original owner. The vendor knew when he took the conveyance that the grantor only had a mortgage. Held, that the purchaser could not sue on the covenant of warranty in the deed by the grantor to the vendor, for he took the position of the vendor who could not recover on the covenant in the deed to him.

4. Covenants—Covenant of Warranty.—A covenant of warranty presupposes that the title to the property is conveyed, and,

---

Snadon v. Salmon.

---

where the title was not intended to pass, the grantee, if evicted, has not suffered any loss because he had no title.

S. WALTON FORGY for appellant.

POINTS AND AUTHORITIES CITED.

1. The judgment of the lower court is inequitable and oppressive to appellant, causing him to bear the cost of appellee's wrongdoing.

2. The judgment of the lower court is contrary to the judgment of this court in the case of Jennings v. Salmon, 30 Ky. Law Rep. 168, which case should control the court in this action.

3. Salmon was not an innocent purchaser and could take only what Fort could give. Jones on Mortgages, Secs. 255, 339, 841, 841a and 842; Jennings v. Salmon, 30 Ky. Law Rep. 168; Gill v. Fugate, 117 Ky. 256; Washburn on Real Property, Sec. 985; Interstate Investment Co. v. Bailey, 29 Ky. Law Rep. 468.

4. The purchaser or mortgagee of land must inquire into the claims and rights of the party in possession. Possession alone is notice. Interstate Investment Co. v. Bailey, 29 Ky. Law Rep. 468; Graves v. Leathers, 17 B. Monroe 665; Jones on Mortgages, Secs. 339 and 255.

5. The testimony of witnesses, Mimms and Jennings, records show that Salmon had actual notice of Jenning's title.

6. If the instrument from Snadon to Fort and from Fort to Salmon be treated as deeds, then they are void. Ky. Statutes, Sec. 210.

7. The instruments being void no action can be maintained upon the warranty by Salmon or anyone else. Ky. Statutes, Secs. 210 and 216; Graves v. Leathers, 17 B. Monroe. 665; Crowley v. Vaughn 11 Bush, 517; Altemus v. Nickell, 115 Ky. 506; Caldwell v. Spriggs' Heirs, 7 Dana 38.

8. Snadon may rely upon this statute. Crowley v. Vaughn, 11 Bush 517; Altemus v. Nickell, 115 Ky. 506; Caldwell v. Spriggs' Heirs, 7 Dana 38; Ky. Statutes, Sec. 211.

9. The implied agreement to return the amount paid by Salmon only applies to Fort and does not extend to Snadon.

10. If this could be extended to Snadon it is barred by limitations. Graves v. Leathers, 17 B. Monroe, 665.

SELDEN Y. TRIMBLE for appellee.

POINTS MADE BY APPELLANT'S BRIEF.

1. Appellee's alleged knowledge of the defect of title. Jones v. Jones, 87 Ky. 82; Pryse v. McGuire, 81 Ky. 608; 11 Cyc., page 1066; Interstate Investment Co. v. Bailey, 29 Ky. Law Rep. 468.

2. Res Adjudicata. Meade v. Ratliff, 118 S. W. 271; Scholl v. Hopper, 119 S. W. 771.

3. Champerty.—(a) Appellant's line of Cases.—Cardwell v. Sprigg's Heirs, 7 Dana 36; Graves v. Leathers, 17 B. Mon. 665; Crowley v. Vaughn, 11 Bush 517; Altemus v. Nickels, 115 Ky. 506, 24 R. 2401. (b) Appellee's line of Cases.—1 Morehead & Brown Statutes, pp. 285-6; 1 Revised Statutes, Chapter 12, pp. 226, &c.; Kentucky Statutes, Secs. 209 to 216; Hobson v. Hendrick, 7 K. L. R. 362; Marman v. Brewster, 7 Bush 355; Luen v. Wilson, 85 Ky. 503; Ft. Jefferson, &c. v. Dupoyster, 108 Ky. 792, 21 R. 515; Meade v. Ratliff, 118 S. W. 271; Madison Stock Yards v. Frasee, 30 Ky. Law Rep. 254; Smith v. Cornett, 30 Ky. Law Rep. 302.

OPINION OF THE COURT BY JUDGE CARROLL—Reversing.

In 1899 Albert Jennings conveyed with covenant of general warranty to George Snadon a small parcel of land. Afterwards Snadon conveyed with covenant of warranty the land to Fort, and in 1902 Fort conveyed with covenant of warranty to W. H. Salmon. After Salmon obtained title to the land, he brought suit against Jennings, who was in possession, to recover it, and succeeded in the lower court. From the judgment Jennings prosecuted an appeal to this court, and in an opinion that may be found in 98 S. W. 1026, 30 Ky. Law Rep. 168, it was held that the deed executed by Jennings to Snadon was in fact a mortgage to secure a debt due by Jennings to Snadon. In the course of the opinion the court further said: "Fort got from Snadon no better title than Snadon had. The facts that Snadon told Fort put him on notice as to the condition of the title if he did not know them before. The only title that Fort got he got from Snadon, and Snadon had nothing but a mortgage. Salmon lived in 250 yards of Jennings, and, aside from the proof showing that he had notice

vol. 135—4

of the infirmity of the title, the fact that Jennings was living on the land, giving it in for assessment in his own name and paying the taxes, was sufficient to put him on inquiry. On the whole case we are satisfied that the deed to Snadon should be treated as a mortgage, and we are also satisfied that the $73 paid by Jennings to Fort covered everything that was due upon the land.''

Upon a return of the case the petition of Salmon was in accordance with the opinion of this court dismissed, and a judgment entered adjudging Jennings his costs. Thereupon Salmon brought this suit against Snadon upon the covenant contained in his deed to Fort, basing his action upon the ground that, as he purchased from Fort, he was entitled to the benefit of the convenant contained in the deed made by Snadon to Fort. The lower court rendered a judgment in favor of Salmon, and Snadon appeals.

There is no doubt that a vendee who has been evicted, or who has suffered such a loss as would entitle him to maintain an action upon a covenant of general warranty, may bring his action to recover damages for the breach against a remote vendor who conveyed the land with covenant of warranty. He is not confined to an action against his immediate vendor. Thomas v. Bland, 91 Ky. 1, 14 S. W. 955, 12 Ky. Law Rep. 640, 11 L. R. A. 240; Hunt v. Orwig, 17 B. Mon. 74, 66 Am. Dec. 144; Cummins v. Kennedy, 3 Litt. 118, 14 Am. Dec. 45.

But, when a vendee seeks to recover on a warranty contained in a deed made by a remote vendor, with full knowledge of the fact that the conveyance was not intended to pass the title, he takes the place of the immediate vendee of the vendor whom he sues, and can occupy no better position than did such vendee.

If, as between A. and B., A. was not liable on his covenant, neither can he be made liable by any person to whom B. may convey, with notice of the fact that the conveyance of A. was a mortgage, and not a deed. Subsequent conveyances would not increase his responsibilities or obligations to vendees with such notice beyond what they were when he conveyed. Of the correctness of this proposition we think there can be no doubt. If a vendor could be held liable upon a covenant by a remote vendee, who purchased with notice of the fact that his conveyance was not intended to pass title, when he could not be held by his immediate vendee, it would follow that his liability would attach. not by virtue of his act or deed, but because of the act or deed of some other person with whom he had no privity of contract whatever. But, if one conveys a title with covenant of warranty, and at the same time or afterwards enters into some agreement or arrangement with his vendee by which as between them he is relieved of liability on his covenant or that would estop his vendee from looking to the warranty for indemnity, this would not operate as an estoppel on a subsequent or remote vendee, or prevent him from maintaining an action on the warranty. It is only when the remote vendee is chargeable with notice of the facts that work an estoppel on the person whose place he takes that he will not be permitted to assert any claim that such person could not make.

Assuming, then, that Salmon, who purchased with notice of the character of conveyance Fort took and who consequently occupies no better position than Fort did, is remitted to the rights and remedies of Fort, the question naturally arises, could Fort, if he had been evicted, have maintained an action against

Snadon upon the covenant contained in his deed?
Snadon only had a mortgage on the land. At the
time of the conveyance to Fort he was not invested
with either the title or possession; both being in Jennings. Fort got from Snadon no better title than
Snadon had, and Fort knew when he took the conveyance from Snadon that he only had a mortgage.
If Snadon had been evicted, he could not recover on
the covenant contained in the deed made by Jennings,
and so it follows that Ford could not recover on the
covenant contained in the deed made to him by Snadon, as neither Jennings nor Snadon conveyed the
title. A covenant of warranty presupposes that the
title to the property is conveyed. If, in fact, the title
does not and is not intended to be conveyed, of course,
the vendee, if evicted, has not suffered any loss because he had no title to lose. As said in Tiedeman on
Real Property, section 624: "But, in order that a
covenant may run with the land to assignees, the
grantee must by the conveyance acquire the actual
or constructive seisin. If at the time of the conveyance the grantor had neither title nor seisin, nothing
passes by the deed, and the covenant remains in the
grantee, and cannot be enforced by an assignee."
This is not a case of a purchaser buying land with
chance of defects in the title. Here the title cannot and was not intended to be conveyed. It may be
conceded to be settled law that the mere fact that the
vendee has notice of defects in the title at the time
of his purchase will not estop him from recovering
on a covenant contained in the deed he accepted.
Jones v. Jones, 87 Ky. 82, 7 S. W. 886, 9 Ky. Law
Rep. 942; 11 Cyc. 1066. But this principle has
no application to the facts of this case. To
permit Salmon to recover against Snadon on account

of the warranty contained in the deed to Fort would be to permit Salmon, who must be treated as having notice of the character of the conveyances, to occupy a better position than Fort did, and to disregard the rights of Snadon as between himself and Fort.

The judgment is reversed, with directions to dismiss the petition.

CASE 9.—ACTION BY THE PADUCAH COOPERAGE CO. AGAINST THE PADUCAH VENEER & LUMBER CO.—Oct. 22, 1909.

Paducah Cooperage Co. v. Paducah Veneer Co.

Appeal from McCracken Circuit Court.

W. M. REED, Circuit Judge.

Judgment for defendant, plaintiff appeals—Reversed.

1. Quieting Title—Actions—Admissibility of Evidence.—In an action between parties owning the north half and south half of a lot to quiet title to a strip of land claimed by both near the middle of the lot, evidence that plaintiff's president saw and knew of the erection by defendant seven years before, of a boiler room, on a part of the strip in controversy, and made no objection thereto, was material as bearing on the question of defendant's possession of the ground and the understanding of the parties as to the true location of the line separating the lot of plaintiff from that of defendant.

2. Witnesses—Competency—Effect of Decree of Party in Interest.—Civ. Code Prac. Sec. 606, providing that no person shall testify concerning statements of a person deceased at the time testimony is offered, does not prevent an agent from testifying for his principal as to transactions had by him as such agent through the agent of another, although the agent of the other person be dead at the time of the giving of such testimony, where it appears that the agent has no personal interest in the business of his principal.

Paducah Cooperage Co. v. Paducah Veneer Co.

3. Quieting Title—Instructions.—Evidence, in an action to quiet
    title, held insufficient to warrant submission to the jury of
    defendant's claim of possession of the land in contro-
    versy.
4. Adverse Possession—Nature and Requisites—Actual Posses-
    sion—Inclosure.—Where plaintiff has title to one-half of a lot,
    and defendant has title to the other half, and there is a dispute
    as to the location of the line separating the two parts, a
    claim by one of them for more than 15 years that the strip
    in controversy is its property will not give title to the strip,
    in the absence of inclosure or actual occupancy thereof ad-
    versely to all others.
5   Trial—Taking Case from Jury—Directing Verdict.—Where, in
    an action to quiet title, the issue is as to the true location of
    a line separating the land of plaintiff from that of defendant,
    and there is some evidence to support the location of the line
    contended for by defendant, the case should go to the jury,
    although the weight of the evidence seemed to show the true
    location of the line was the one claimed by plaintiff.
6. Quieting Title—Answer—Description of Land.—Under Civ.
    Code Prac. Sec. 125, subsec. 2, providing that in an action for
    the recovery of land the answer must so describe the land
    that it may be identified, an answer is sufficient which claims
    the whole of the ground in controversy, the petition having
    given a particular description of the land, and the answer in
    effect adopting such description; and it would be only in the
    event that defendant claimed only a part of the ground in dis-
    pute that it would be necessary for the answer to describe
    such part so that it may be identified.

J. D. MOCQUOT for appellant.

1. The motion for a judgment non obstante veredicto should
have been sustained by the court.

2. Testimony of an interested party as to admissions or transactions with the deceased agent of a corporation was inadmissible.

3. Instruction "B" offered by appellant clearly embodies the law
and should have been given instead of No. 1 given by the court.

AUTHORITIES CITED.
Section 25, Civil Code; Brent v. Long, 99 Ky. 245; Bailey v. Mc-
Connell, 12 Ky. Law Rep. 473; Holmes v. Herringer, 12 Ky. Law
Rep. 22; Mann v. Cavanaugh, 110 Ky. 776; Hughes v. Owen, 29
Ky. Law Rep. 140; Warden v. Addington, 115 S. W. 241.

WHEELER, HUGHES & BERRY for appellee.

POINTS AND AUTHORITIES.

1. In ejectment not necessary that answer should contain a description of the land in controversy if the defendant claim all thereof. Brent v. Long et al., 99th Ky. 245; Bailey v. McConnell, 12th Ky. Law Rep. 473; Sub-sec. 2 of Sec. 125, Civil Code of Practice; Jones v. Griffin, 25th Ky. Law Rep. 117.

2. Evidence of agent of corporation that the agent of another corporation was claiming certain land, which evidence is given in court after the death of the agent of the second corporation, not incompetent. Cobb's Adm'r v. Wolfe, 96 Ky. 418; F. & C. Co. v. Gaff, 17 Ky. Law Rep. 214; Brooks v. Spain, 22 Reporter 1178; Lyon's Executor v. Bank, 25 Ky. Law Rep. 1668.

3. Actual enclosure by a fence not necessary to support possession. Brisco v. McGee, 8th Ky., 1st A. K. Marshall 139 (side page 190); Cameron v. Beatty, 6th Ky. Law Rep. 589; Ky. L. & I. Co. v. Sloane. 25 Ky. Law Rep. 1515; Waite v. Gover, 11 Ky. Law Rep. 750; Ky. L. & I. Co. v. Crabtree, 113 Ky. 922; Sommers v. Green. 4th J. J. M. 137; Holmes v. Herringer, 12th Reporter 22.

OPINION OF THE COURT BY JUDGE SETTLE—Reversing.

This action brought by appellant against appellee raises a controversy as to the ownership of a strip of ground in the city of Paducah. The strip of ground is of triangular shape, and begins at a point on Meyers street, extends a distance of 30 poles, and has a width of, perhaps, 30 feet at the end of the 30 poles. The trial in the circuit court resulted in a verdict and judgment in favor of appellee. In the motion and grounds for a new trial filed by appellant in that court, it was contended that numerous errors were committed by the court to its prejudice, and it now insists that these alleged errors entitle it on this appeal to a reversal of the judgment.

One of the appellant's contentions is that the trial court erred in permitting Sowell, appellee's manager, to testify that Kilgore, at the time appellant's president, saw and knew of appellee's erecting seven years ago the boiler room of its mill on a part of the ground

in controversy, and yet made no objection thereto, it
being claimed that this testimony should have been
excluded because Kilgore was dead at the time of its
admission. The testimony was material because of
its bearing on the question of appellee's possession of
the ground in controversy, and also on the matter of
the understanding of the parties as to the true location of the line separating the lot of appellant from
that of appellee, for the failure under the circumstances, of appellant's president to object to the erection
of appellee's boiler house upon the ground in controversy, allowed the presumption that it was not included within the lines of appellant's deed, and amounted
in some sort to a recognition on his part of appellee's
right thereto. The admission of the testimony in
question was not error. Section 606, Civ. Code Prac.,
does not prevent an agent from testifying for his
principal as to transactions had by him as such agent
with the agent of another, although the agent of the
other person be dead at the time of the giving of such
testimony. It does not appear that appellee's manager, Sowell, had any personal interest in the appellee
corporation. He therefore, incurs no financial loss
nor gains any material benefit by the result of the
litigation. An examination of the following authorities will show that this court has frequently recognized the competency of such evidence: Cobb's Adm'r
v. Wolfe, 96 Ky. 418, 29 S. W. 303, 16 Ky. Law Rep.
591; F. & C. Co. v. Goff, 30 S. W. 626, 17 Ky. Law
Rep. 214; Brooks v. Spain, 60 S. W. 184, 22 Ky. Law
Rep. 1178; Lyon's Ex'r v. Bank, 78 S. W. 454, 25
Ky. Law Rep. 1668.

Appellant also contends that the trial court erred
in instructing the jury. But one instruction was
given. It is as follows, viz.:

"Gentlemen of the Jury: It is undisputed in this case that the plaintiff, Paducah Cooperage Company is the owner of the north half of lot No. 24 in the city of Paducah, Ky., and that the defendant, Paducah Veneer & Lumber Company. is the owner of the scuth half thereof. and that the plaintiff and defendant have paper titles and deeds to their respective halves of said lot from the same common grantor, and that the defendant has the oldest deed, and the court now instructs you that if you shall believe from the evidence in this case that the strip of land in controversy in this suit is embraced by, or included in, plaintiff's deed, then the law is for the plaintiff, and you will find for it said strip of ground in controversy, unless you shall believe from the evidence that said strip of land is also embraced by, or included in, defendant's deed; or that defendant, and those under whom it claims, was at any time, before the bringing of this suit, for a period of as much as 15 years, in the actual, continuous, adverse and peaceable possession of said south half of said lot No. 24 by having buildings or inclosures thereon, and claiming to a marked boundary or dividing line between plaintiff's and defendant's part of said lot, which marked or division boundary included the land in controversy in this suit then and in either of these events, and if you shall so believe, the law is for defendant, and you will so find."

We have reached the conclusion that the instruction contains one error. It should not have submitted to the jury the question of appellee's claim of possession, as there was no evidence upon which to base it. It is true that appellee's answer, after denying appellant's title and alleging title in itself to the ground in controversy, pleaded the statute of lim-

itations based on its alleged actual, adverse possession of the ground to a well-defined marked boundary
for more than 15 years before the institution of appellant's action, but the evidence did not prove such
possession or any other, except to a small part thereof occupied by its boiler shed for a period of 7 years.
According to the evidence, appellee about 7 years
ago rebuilt its mill, following a fire, at which time its
boiler house was so constructed as to extend upon
and occupy from 11 to 13 feet of the ground in controversy; its first actual adverse possession of the
ground in dispute then began and has since continued,
but back of that time no actual or adverse possession
on its part of the ground was shown. Therefore its
plea of the statute was unavailing. We do not overlook the fact that appellee as far back as 1884 caused
Postlethwaite to survey its entire lot; that the latter
then attempted to so establish a line between appellees' lot and that of appellant as to apparently include the land in controversy in the lot of appellee,
and that stakes were driven in the ground, and perhaps a cottonwood tree marked on the bank of the
Tennessee river to indicate the line attempted to be
established; but it does not appear from the evidence
by what, if any, title papers this work was done, or
that appellant's vendor and then owner of its lot adjoining appellee's was present or had any notice
thereof. Postlethwaite is dead, and no plat or other
evidence of the survey in question was left by him;
the stakes placed by him have long since been removed and the cottonwood destroyed, and the evidence as to where stakes and cottonwood stood was
quite indefinite. There was some evidence tending
to prove that appellee, since the surveying of Postlethwaite was done, has made claim to the ground

out to the line staked by Postlethwaite, but it failed
to prove any actual possession by it of the ground
in controversy, except what has been occupied during
the last seven years by the boiler house of the mill.

It is true appellee has for more than 15 years had
the actual and adverse possession of that part of lot
24 conveyed by its deed, but, unless the ground in
controversy is in fact covered by the deed, such possession as it had did not extend to or include it. If
it is not embraced by the boundary of appellee's deed,
the latter by merely claiming it to the line staked by
the surveyor, could have acquired no right to it as
against the title of another without an inclosure or
actual occupancy thereof adversely to all others for
as much as 15 years.

It is admitted that appellant and appellee derived
title from a common source; that by the plat recorded
by the vendor, as well as the deeds to them, the
ground owned by appellant is one half of lot 24, and
that owned by appellee the other half of lot 24; that
each deed purports to convey the same quantity of
ground, and that appellee's deed is the elder of the
two. Eliminating the question of possession from the
case, it is manifest that the only issue that should
have been submitted to the jury was as to the true
location of the line separating the lots of appellant
and appellee. As appellee's deed antedates that of
appellant, it goes without saying that, if the ground
in controversy is a part of the lot conveyed by its
deed, the jury should have found for it; but on the
other hand, if it is included in the boundary contained
in the deed to appellant, the verdict should have
been for the latter. Looking to the evidence on this
issue, we find that that of appellant, consisting in the
main of the surveys shown by the three plats found

in the record, and the testimony of the surveyors by
whom they were made, strongly conduces to prove
that the ground in question is a part of its lot and
embraced by its deed. It further appears from the
evidence that, by including the ground in controversy,
appellant's lot will contain the precise quantity its
deed purports to convey; but if it is added to appellee's lot, it will be found to exceed by perhaps as
much as its size the quantity the deed of appellee purports to convey. On the other hand, appellee's claim
to the ground in controversy finds some support in
the evidence as to the Postlethwaite survey and the
fixing of the line by him, evidence as to the building
of the boiler house upon the ground in controversy
with the knowledge and apparent acquiescence of appellant's president, Kilgore, and other evidence as
to appellee's possession of the part occupied by the
boiler house after that time; the evidence as to appellant's acquiescence in the erection of the boiler
house being competent as tending to show that both
parties understood the true line between their lots
to be located as claimed by appellee. While it is apparently true that the weight of the evidence conduced to prove that the true location of the line separating the lot of appellant from that of appellee is
as claimed by the former, as there was some evidence
to support appellee's location of the line, the case
should have gone to the jury; therefore, the peremptory instruction asked by appellant, which would
have required the jury to find for it, was properly
overruled.

In lieu of instruction No. 1, the court upon a retrial
should give the following: "The jury are instructed
that it is admitted plaintiff and defendant derived title, each to its own lot, from a common source, and

that defendant's deed antedates that of plaintiff. And if the jury believe from the evidence that the deed of the plaintiff embraces the strip of ground in controversy, and it is not embraced in the deed of the defendant, they should find for the plaintiff. But on the other hand, if the jury shall believe from the evidence that the strip of ground in controversy is embraced in the deeds of both plaintiff and defendant, or in the deed of defendant alone, they should find for the defendant.''

As previously intimated, an instruction on the ques tion of adverse possession will not be necessary or proper, unless appellee should introduce proof showing actual occupancy, or an inclosure of the ground in controversy for the statutory period. Indeed, in the state of case here presented, if the ground in controversy is not embraced in appellee's deed, but is included in that of appellant, the only possession that would defeat appellant's title is such as appellee could have acquired by an inclosure of the ground, or actually occupying it for the statutory period no proof of which was made on the trial in the circuit court. Except as to the small part of it covered by appellee's boiler house for seven years it has had no other possession of the ground in controversy that appellant has not had and exercised, and neither has claimed title to or possession of it, except upon the ground that it was embraced by its deed, and therefore the possession of each has been and is limited to the true location of the line of division between the lots.

The case is, we think, governed by the rule announced in that of Holmes v. Heringer, 13 S. W. 359, 913, 12 Ky. Law Rep. 22, in the opinion of which it is said: ''For as both parties claim under the same

patent, no question of superiority arises in the case.
Nor has either acquired any legal advantage by adverse possession of the land in contest, for both parties having the undisputed title to and possession of
two adjoining tracts, respectively owned by them,
must be regarded as claiming and holding up to the
division line, wherever that may be, until one or the
other, by actual inclosure, takes possession beyond.
It is true appellee did have the disputed land under
fence when the action was commenced by appellant,
but as there is no evidence whatever showing it had
been inclosed 15 years, he acquired no right thereby."

It is further contended by appellant that its motion
for a judgment non obstante should have been sustained by the trial court. We decline to accept appellant's view of that matter. The motion was bottomed
upon the idea that, as the answer failed to give a particular description of the strip of ground in controversy, judgment by reason of that fact should have
gone in appellant's favor. Waiving the question of
whether the objection to the answer should have been
presented by a demurrer or motion to make more specific, we do not think the pleading defective, for,
as amended, it claimed for appellee title to, and alleges his possession of, the whole of the ground in
controversy. The petition of appellant gave a particular description of the part in controversy. The
answer in effect adopts this description and claims
the whole of it as described. This was a sufficient
compliance with the provisions of section 125, subsec.
2, Civ. Code Prac. If in the answer appellee had
claimed only a part of the ground in dispute, then it
would have been necessary for the answer to state
what part of it was claimed, and "so describe such
part that it may be identified." But as already stated,

it claimed the whole of it as described in the petition.

The views we have expressed make it unnecessary to consider the refused instructions. On account of the error in the one instruction given, the judgment is reversed, and cause remanded for a new trial consistent with the opinion.

CASE 10.—ACTION BY KEEL ROBERTS AGAINST W. J. THOMAS.—Oct. 22, 1909.

Roberts v. Thomas

Appeal from Henry Circuit Court.

CHAS. C. MARSHALL, Circuit Judge.

Judgment for defendant, plaintiff appeals.—Affirmed.

1. False Imprisonment—Distinguished from Malicious Prosecution.—False imprisonment lies where the imprisonment is without legal authority, and, where it is valid or apparently so, the remedy is by malicious prosecution.
2. Malicious Prosecution—Elements Of.—To render a person liable for malicious prosecution, he must have acted maliciously and without probable cause.

PEAK & HOLLAND and EDWARDS, OGDEN & PEAK for appellant.

POINTS AND AUTHORITIES.

The only point we make in this case is that the action is for false imprisonment, and in actions of that character it is not necessary to allege in the petition want of probable cause or malice. Malice is not an ingredient of an action of this character. Southern Railway in Kentucky v. Sherley, 28 L. R. 861; 21 Ky. 865; Reynolds, By, &c. v. Price, 22 L. R., page 5.

WILLIS & TODD for appellee.

W. P. THORNE and MOODY & BARBOUR of counsel.

AUTHORITIES CITED ON PETITION.

Words and Phrases, Vol. 3, page 2660; A. & E. Ency. (second edition), page 739; Gordon v. West, Vol. 13, L. R. A. (new series 1908), page 549; A. & E. Ency. Vol. 7, page 664; Reynolds, By, &c. v. Price, 22 Ky. Law Rep. page 5; Mitchell v. Ripy, &c., 82 Ky. page 516; A. & E. Ency. (second edition), Vol. 19, page 650.

AUTHORITIES CITED ON AMENDED PETITION.

Brashears v. Frazier, 110 S. W. page 826; Hegan Mantel Co. v. Alford, 114 S. W., page 219.

OPINION OF THE COURT BY JUDGE HOBSON—Affirming.

Keel Roberts filed his petition in the Henry circuit court, in which he sought to recover damages in the sum of $10,000 against W. J. Thomas. Thomas filed a demurrer to the petition which the court sustained. Roberts thereupon filed an amended petition. The court sustained the demurrer to the petition as amended. The plaintiff declining to plead further, the petition was dismissed, and he appeals.

The facts stated in the petition are these: Thomas subscribed and swore to an affidavit before the judge of the Shelby quarterly court in which Roberts was charged with the crime of unlawfully confederating and banding together with one John W. Thomas, Jr., and going forth armed for the purpose of intimidating and alarming another person or persons. By this affidavit Thomas caused the judge of the quarterly court to issue a warrant of arrest against Roberts for the crime. Roberts was arrested under the warrant of arrest in Henry county on March 3, 1909, and was confined in the Shelby county jail until March 7, when he executed a bond before the judge of the quarterly court, and was released on bond, Thereafter he was tried before the judge of the quarterly court and was acquitted, and the charge against him was dismissed. It was alleged in the petition that all of this was done unlawfully, wrongfully, willfully, , forcibly, and against the plaintiff's will and consent. In the amended petition it was charged that all this was done wrongfully and without probable cause. The affidavit filed by Thomas with the judge and the warrant of arrest issued by the judge which was in proper form were made part of the petition.

There is a well-marked distinction between an action for false imprisonment and an action for malicious prosecution. An action for false imprisonment may be maintained where the imprisonment is without legal authority. But, where there is a valid or apparently valid power to arrest, the remedy is by an action for malicious prosecution. The want of lawful authority is an essential element in an action for false imprisonment. Malice and want of probable cause are the essentials in an action for malicious prosecution. The petition shows that the plaintiff was not arrested without lawful authority. He was arrested under a warrant of arrest legally issued by the proper officer. The person who procured the warrant to be issued and thus caused the arrest is liable to an action for malicious prosecution if he acted with malice and without probable cause. But he is not liable for procuring the warrant to be issued and executed unless he acted with malice and without probable cause. 19 Cyc. 321, 7 Am. & Eng. Encyc. of Law, 664; Gordon v. West, 129 Ga. 532, 59 S. E. 232, 13 L. R. A. (N. S.) 549, and cases cited. In the case of Southern Railway Co. v. Shirley, 121 Ky. 865, 90 S. W. 597, 28 Ky. Law Rep. 860 this distinction is pointed out. In that case Shirley was arrested without a warrant of arrest and without legal authority. His arrest was unlawful. In this case the plaintiff was arrested under a legal wararnt and he was legally held in custody. In the case of Reynolds v. Price, 56 S. W., 502, 22 Ky. Law Rep. 5, the arrest was also without legal authority. It is not averred in the petition that Thomas acted with malice and without probable cause in swearing out the warrant. Malice is essential to the cause of action for malicious prosecution, and, this not being averred, the circuit court properly sustained the demurrer to the petition.

Judgment affirmed.

CASE 11.—ACTION BY ERNEST EVANS' ADMINISTRATOR AGAINST THE CUMBERLAND TELEPHONE & TELEGRAPH COMPANY.—Oct. 26, 1909.

Evans' Adm'r. v. Cumb. Tel'p. & Tel'g Co

Appeal from Oldham Circuit Court.

CHARLES C. MARSHALL, Circuit Judge.

Dismissed on demurrer and plaintiff appeals—Affirmed.

1. Death—Negligence of Telephone Company—Failure to Transmit Message.—The negligent failure of a telephone company to connect a message dispatched to call a doctor for a person who had sustained an accidental gunshot wound with the doctor's telephone, thereby depriving such person of medical attention, is too remote to constitute it a proximate cause of the death; it not appearing that, but for the negligence, the death would not have resulted.

2. Action—Ground of Action—Conjecture.—A thing not susceptible of being proved can not be made the basis for a recovery in an action at law, as it would base the recovery on conjecture alone.

LLOYD W. GATES, EDWARDS, OGDEN & PEAK and S. E. DEHAVEN for appellant.

Evans' Admr. v. Cumb. Telp. & Telg. Co.

POINTS AND AUTHORITIES.

1. A telephone company is liable for the natural and proximate damage caused by its delay in giving telephone connection, where it is shown that such damage would not have occurred if it had performed its duty. 2 Greenleaf, Evidence 210; Smith v. W. U. Telegraph Co., 83 Ky. 116.

2. Where a person suffering from a gun shot wound in the leg, dies as the result of a telephone company's negligence in refusing to give a telephone connection with a doctor's residence, whereby the injured party could have obtained the said physician's services, and his life thereby saved, the company is liable in damages for the death caused by its negligence.

3. The lower court erred in sustaining demurrer to plaintiff's petition on the ground that the damages were too remote and speculative. The case of Lebanon, &c., Tel. Co. v. Lanham Lumber Co., 115 S. W. 824, relied upon by defendant, does not sustain its contention.

4. An allegation that the life of a person suffering from a gun shot wound in the calf of the leg would have been saved with proper medical attention is not so speculative and conjectural as to authorize a court to release a telephone company from liability for its gross negligence in failing to deliver a message.

5. Proximate cause is a question for the jury to determine from the facts. L. & N. R. R. Co. v. Kiefer, 113 S. W. 435.

6. Appellee should be held liable for Evans' death, because of its wanton, willful and reckless negligence. Metallic, &c., Co. v. Pittsburg, 109 Mass. 277; Little Rock Tract. Co. v. McCaskill, 75 Ark., 86 S. W. 997; Mott v. Hudson River Ry. Co., 1 Rob. (N. Y.), 585; Kiernan v. Metropolitan Constr. Co., 170 Mass. 378.

FAIRLEIGH, STRAUS & FAIRLEIGH for appellee.

A. The action of the trial court in sustaining the general demurrer to the petition was right.

B. The trial court erred in ruling that it had jurisdiction to hear and determine this action. Lebanon, Louisville & Lexington Telephone Co., &c. v. Lanham Lumber Co., 115 S. W. 824; Civil Code, Sec. 73; Sections 35 and 36; Newman's Pleading and Practice (DuRelle's Edition).

OPINION OF THE COURT BY JUDGE O'REAR—Affirming.

Ernest Evans sustained an accidental gunshot
wound in the leg, producing considerable hemorrhage.
A messenger, who was dispatched to call a doctor
applied at a pay station of the appellee, and asked
that he be furnished telephone connection with the
doctor's residence, offering to pay the required toll.
It is alleged that owing to the negligence of the operator there was a failure to make the connection with
the doctor's telephone, in consequence of which he did
not get the message, and Evans was thereby deprived
of his services. It is further alleged that, if the connection had been made, the doctor would or could
have got to the patient in time to have stanched the
flow of blood and have saved his life; but, as the doctor did not get there, the patient for the lack of medical attention bled to death. This is a suit at law by
the administrator of Ernest Evans against the telephone company to recover $25,000 damages for the
alleged negligent destruction of the intestate's life.
A demurrer was sustained to the petition. An amended petition was allowed. In the amendment it was
averred that the doctor mentioned was the nearest
doctor available, or who could have been secured by
the decedent at that time. Evans was about four miles
from the doctor's residence. A general demurrer
was sustained to the petition as amended, and, plaintiff electing to stand by the cause of action as stated,
his petition was dismissed. He appeals.

We think the alleged negligence too remote in law
from the fact of the decedent's death to constitute it
a proximate cause of the death. Nothing appears
that, but for the alleged negligence, the death would
not have resulted. The injury to the young man was
inflicted before the negligent act sued upon, and, of
course, has no casual connection with it. If the send-

ing of the message itself, and it alone, could have prevented the death, a different state of case would be
presented.   But the office of the message was to set
in motion an entirely new and independent agency,
the result of which is purely speculative.   It does not
necessarily follow that the doctor would or could
have got to the young man before he died. Nor does it
necessarily result that, if the doctor had got there,
he could have saved the life of the youth.   It is true,
both propositions are alleged in the petition. But
neither is susceptible of proof.   A thing not susceptible of being proved cannot be made the basis for a
recovery in a lawsuit.   That would be to base the
recovery upon conjecture alone, which is never allowed.

The lower court followed the opinion in Lebanon,
Louisville & Lexington Telephone Company v. Lanham Lumber Company (Ky.) 115 S. W. 824, 131
Ky. ——. The principal announced in that case is adhered to.

Judgment affirmed.

CASE 12.—ACTION BY IDA BARNHILL AND OTHERS
AGAINST HENRY SHARON AND OTHERS.—Oct.
26, 1909.

Barnhill, &c. v. Sharon, &c.

Appeal from Scott Circuit Court.

R. L. Stout, Circuit Judge.

Judgment for defendants, plaintiffs appeal.—Reversed.

Wills—Beneficiaries—Substitution—"Sister."—Ky. St. 2064 provides that where a devise is made to several as a class, and one or more shall die before, and another or others shall survive testator, the share or shares of those dying shall go to his or their descendants, or, if none, to the surviving devisees. Section 4841 (section 3964) provides that if a devisee dies before testator, or is dead at the making of the will, leaving issue who survive testator, such issue shall take as the devisee would have done. Testator devised the remainder, after a life estate in land, to his brothers and sisters. He had one sister who died without issue, before he did, and a half-sister who died before the will was made leaving issue who survived him. Held, that the will must be construed to mean "sisters" as a class, which being the case, the devise was controlled by section 4841, and the descendants of the half-sister took the share she would have had she survived testator.

J. C. B. SEBREE for appellants.

FORD & FORD for appellees.

OPINION OF THE COURT BY WM. ROGERS CLAY, COMMISSIONER—Reversing.

Appellants, Ida Barnhill and others, who are the children and grandchildren of Mary Elizabeth Williamson, instituted this action against Henry Sharon

and others, to recover a one-fifth interest in a tract
of land consisting of 47 acres and situated in Scott
county, Ky.   The court sustained a demurrer to the
petition, and it was dismissed.   Ida Barnhill and others appeal.

The petition is as follows: "The plaintiffs state:
That one Thos. Sharon, on the ―――― day of 190―
departed this life testate, a resident and citizen of
Scott county, Ky., having first made and published
his last will in writing, a certified copy of which is filed
herewith marked "W." and which was duly probated and admitted to record in the clerk's
office of said county.   At the time of his death he was
the owner of a tract of land in said county of about
47 acres bounded and described as follows: Adjoining
the land of Henry Sharon on the west, Hugh Sharon
and Annie Morris on the south, Jas. N. Sharon on the
east, and Patsy Williamson on the north.   That by
the said will said testator devised said land to Mary
Sharon, his wife, for life, remainder to his brothers
and sisters.   That on the ―――― day of   January,
1909, his wife, the said Mary Sharon, the said life tenant, departed this life.   That the four defendants who
survive are the only brothers he ever had.   That said
testator had one sister, who died before the testator
died, without issue or parents, and a half-sister,
whose name was Mary Elizabeth Williamson, who
died before the said will was made and left surviving her the three children, a daughter, Ida Barnhill,
the plaintiff, and the plaintiff Arthur Barnhill is her
husband, Rosa Ann Barnhill, who married the plaintiff Jno. E. Barnhill and died, leaving as her only
children the plaintiffs Ethel, Mary, and Ward Barnhill and another daughter, Artymacy Barnhill, now
dead, who married plaintiff, Joe Sutton, and

of that marriage she left the following children: The plaintiffs Claud, Cambridge, Mary, Sindy, Arthur, and Pearl Sutton, all infants except Claud and Cambridge and have no guardian, curator or committee, and they sue by their father and next friend, the plaintiff Joe Sutton. Plaintiffs say that they as the only children and grandchildren of the said Mary Elizabeth Williamson, are entitled to one-fifth of said land, and the defendants are entitled to the other four-fifths in equal shares. Wherefore plaintiffs pray that commissioners be appointed to make partition of said land among the plaintiffs and defendants. That one-fifth of said land be allotted to plaintiffs. The plaintiff John E. Barnhill is the guardian of his children, Esther, Mary, and Ward.''

The will of Thomas Sharon, referred to in the petition, is as follows:

''May 17, 1897.

''I, Thomas J. Sharon, of the county of Scott and state of Kentucky, do this day make and publish this my last will and testament:

''(1) I give and bequeath to my wife, Mary A. Sharon, all my estate, both real and personal, to have and to hold the same during her lifetime.

''(2) And the real estate to go to my brothers and sisters, at the death of my wife.

''(3) I do hereby appoint and make my wife, Mary A. Sharon, my sole executrix without giving any bond.

''(4) I further order my executrix to pay my just and honest debts, and funeral expenses.

''In testimony whereof I have this day set my hand in the presence of

''THOMAS J. SHARON.

''Witnesses: JOHN MORRIS,
''JOHN F. COX,
''W. O. BARNHILL.''

In the case of Fuller v. Martin, 96 Ky. 500, 29 S. W. 315, 16 Ky. Law Rep. 576, the will of George W. Robinson was before this court for interpretation. After directing the sale of his personal property and the application of the proceeds to the payment of his debts, the will is as follows: "Second. After the payment of my debts and funeral expenses as above provided for, I give and bequeath to my brothers and sisters all my real and personal property to be divided equally between them. * * *" The testator then appoints certain friends as executors of his will. In its opinion is first set forth section 1, art. 2, c. 50, of the General Statutes of 1883 and section 18, c. 113, of the General Statutes of 1888, which are the same as sections 2064 and 4841 of the Kentucky Statutes and are as follows:

"Sec. 2064. When a devise is made to several as a class or as tenants in common, or as joint tenants, and one or more of the devisees shall die before the testator, and another or others shall survive the testator, the share or shares of such as so die shall go to his or their descendants, if any; if none, to the surviving devisees, unless a different disposition is made by the devisor. A devise to children embraces grandchildren when there are no children, and no other construction will give effect to the devise."

"Sec. 4841. If a devisee or legatee dies before the testator, or is dead at the making of the will, leaving issue who survive the testator such issue shall take the estate devised or bequeathed, as the devisee or legatee would have done if he had survived the testator, unlss a different disposition thereof is made or required by the will."

"The court then uses the following language: "These statutes, however, cannot aid us until we first

determine who are the devisees or legatees meant to
be described by the words in question. The words of
first statute, 'when a devise is made to several as a
class,' require the ascertainment of the class before
we can say that the descendants of a member of the
class shall be substituted as a devisee and so with
the words, 'if a devisee or legatee dies before the
testator, or is dead at the making of the will,' etc.,
the question must first be determined who is the devisee or legatee under the will before we can substitute the issue. The statute in effect leaves the question where we found it. It is conceded that, if the testator meant to include his dead brothers and sisters
by the words 'brothers and sisters,' then these children take what their parents would have taken. It
seems to us that, as the words used cannot be applied as a description of living objects, the testator
must have meant to describe all his brothers. He
could not properly describe his living brother as
'brothers,' and, if effect be given the language used,
we must suppose that the testator, knowing that the
issue of the dead brothers and sisters took by substitution, meant to include all his brothers and sisters
as a class, the dead as well as the living. By this construction all those who are the natural objects of the
testator's love partake of his bounty, and not a part
only.'' In support of the construction adopted in the
above case, this court relied upon the case of Hun-
tress v. Place, 137 Mass. 409, and upon Jarman on
Wills (6th Ed.) vol. 2, p. 713.

From an examination of the will and facts of the
above case, it will be seen that the question involved
in the case at bar is substantially the same. In the
will under consideration the testator uses the words
''brothers and sisters.'' In order to give the word

"sister" any meaning at all, it must be made to include more than one sister. It is contended by appellees that the petition does not allege that the sister who died before the testator, and the half-sister, whose descendants have instituted this action, are the only sisters that the testator ever had. We are inclined to the opinion that this fact is immaterial. There is nothing in the will to show that the testator intended to limit his estate to his full-sisters. We must construe the will to mean "sisters" as a class. That being the case, the devise is controlled by section 4841 of the Kentucky Statutes. Under that section it is immaterial that Mary Elizabeth Williamson was dead at the time of making the will, if as a matter of fact she was included in the class "sisters." As it appears from the petition that the full-sister died without issue or parents, her share passed under section 2664 to the surviving devisees under the will.

Judgment reversed and cause remanded, with directions to overrule the demurrer to the petition.

CASE 13.—ACTION BY ANTHONY A. LANG'S ADMINISTRA-
TRIX AGAINST THE CHESAPEAKE & OHIO RAIL-
WAY CO.—Oct. 26, 1909.

Ch. & Ohio Ry. Co. v. Lang's Adm'x

Appeal from Mason Circuit Court.

JAMES P. HARBESON, Circuit Judge.

Judgment for plaintiff, defendant appeals.—Reversed.

1. Master and Servant—Injury to Servant—Negligence After Discovered Peril.—Direction to find a verdict for defendant in
an action against a railroad company for the killing by a
train of its section hand while riding by permission a velocipede on its track was properly refused; the evidence for
plaintiff being that no warning of the approach of the train
was given, that deceased was ignorant of its approach, and
that it might have been checked, if not stopped, after he
was seen by the engineer, in time to avoid the accident.

2. Evidence—Opinions—Qualification of Witnesses.—Witnesses,
while not knowing the engine or cars of a train, having run
other trains, are competent to testify as to the distance
within which such a train could be stopped.

3. Master and Servant—Injury to Section Hand on Track—Liability of Company.—The place on a railroad track where a section hand riding a velocipede by permission was struck by
a train being outside the town, and where the presence of
persons was not to be expected, the company was liable only
in case there was negligence after his peril was discovered;
it having been incumbent on him to keep a lookout for, and
get out of the way of, trains.

4. Trial—Instructions—Conformity to Evidence.—There being no
evidence that the peril of a section hand on the track was discovered by any one except the engineer of the train which
struck him, instructions as to "agents and servants" of the

company in control and management of the train having discovered him, and not used proper care to prevent the injury, should use the word "engineer" in place of the words "agents and servants."

5. Master and Servant—Injury to Sectionman on Track—Care Required of Engineer.—The engineer of a train, on discovering the peril of a section hand on the track, was not bound to use the utmost diligence to prevent his injury, but only such care as might be reasonably expected of a person of ordinary prudence under the circumstances.

6. Master and Servant—Injury to Section Hand on Track—Duty of Engineer—Instructions.—In place of the words "promptly used all the means in his power" in the instruction, in an action against a railroad company for the killing of its section hand by its train, that if the train was being run by the engineer in an ordinarily careful and prudent manner, and, after discovering decedent's peril, he "promptly used all the means in his power" to prevent the accident, defendant was not liable, there should have been inserted the words "used ordinary care in the exercise of all reasonable means at his command consistent with the safety of the train."

7. Master and Servant—Injury to Section Hand—Liability Notwithstanding Servant's Negligence.—Though a section hand was guilty of negligence in going on the track with his velocipede knowing that a train was coming, the company was liable for his death from being struck by the train, if, after it discovered his peril, it did not exercise ordinary care to avoid injuring him.

8. Master and Servant—Injury to Servant—Assumption of Risk. —Where a section hand riding a velocipede on the track. knowing of the approach of the train, jumped off,and was safe from the train, and then trying to get his velocipede off the track when it was too late for those in charge of the train to do anything to avoid injuring him, was struck and killed by it, he assumed the risk, and the company was not liable, unless he had reason to believe the velocipede endangered the train, and he used such care as may be reasonably expected of a person of ordinary prudence situated as he was.

9. Pleading—Disjunctive Allegations—Injury to Servant—Negligence After Knowledge of Peril.—The allegation in the petition for death of a section hand struck by a train that the persons in charge of the train saw or could have seen by ordinary care his danger is only one that they could have seen, and does not involve one that they saw his peril.

WORTHINGTON, COCHRAN & BROWNING for appellant.

Ch. & Ohio Ry. Co. v. Lang's Admx.

POINTS AND AUTHORITIES.

1. The demurrer to the petition of plaintiff should have been sustained. Reusch v. Licking Rolling Mill Co., 118 Ky. 369; 80 S. W. 1168; Heindrick v. Louisville Elevator Co., 92 S. W. 608; King v. Creekmore, 77 S. W. 689; Simons v. Gregory, 85 S. W. 751; Jacobs' Adm'r v. C. & O. Ry. Co., 72 S. W. 308; Louisville, H. & St. L. Ry. Co. v. Jolly's Adm'x., 90 S. W. 977; Dilas' Adm'r. v. C. & O. Ry. Co., 71 S. W. 492; Eastern Ky. Ry. Co. v. Powell, 33 S. W. 629; Davis' Adm'r v. C. & O. Ry. Co., 116 Ky., 144; 75 S. W. 275; Gregory v. L. & N. R. R. Co., 79 S. W. 238; Gains & Co. v. Johnson, 105 S. W. 381.

2. The trial court should have peremptorily instructed the jury to find for defendant.

(a) Because no negligence upon the part of the defendant was shown which can be said to have been the proximate cause of the accident. Jacobs' Adm'r. v. C. & O. Ry. Co., supra; Louisville, H. & St. L. Ry. Co. v. Jolly's Adm'r. Supra; Mobile & Ohio Ry. Co. v. Dowdy's Adm'x., 91 S. W. 709; Dilas' Adm'r. v. C. & O. Ry. Co. supra; Eastern Ky. Ry. Co. v. Powell, supra; 3 Elliott on Railroads, Sec. 1298; Illinois Central R. R. Co. v. Murphy's Adm'r., 97 S. W. 729; L. & N. R. R. Co. v. Redmon's Adm'r., 91 S. W. 722; C. & O. Ry. Co. v. Nipp's Adm'r., 100 S. W. 246; L. & N. R. R. Co. v. Lowe's Adm'r., 118 Ky. 260; Illinois Central R. R. Co. v. Tyson's Adm'x., 108 S. W. 863; Nashville, &c., Ry. Co. v. Bean's Ex'or., 110 S. W. 328; Cummings v. Illinois Central R. R. Co., 110 S. W. 809; Gregory v. L. & N. R. R. Co., supra; Edwards' Adm'r. v. C. & O. Ry. Co., 108 S. W. 303; Illinois Central R. R. Co. v. Willis' Adm'r., 97 S. W. 21; L. & N. R. R. Co. v. Taafe's Adm'r., 50 S. W. 850; Helm v. L. & N. R. R. Co., 33 S. W. 396; Gresham's Adm'r. v. L. & N. R. R. Co., 24 S. W. 869; L. & N. R. R. Co. v. Penrod, 56 S. W. 1.

(b) Because of the contributory negligence of plaintiff intestate. Dilas' Adm'r v. C. & O. Ry. Co., supra; Jacobs' Adm'r v. C. & O. Ry. Co., supra; Louisville, H. & St. L. Ry. Co. v. Jolly's Adm'x., supra; Long's Adm'r v. Illinois Central R. R. Co., 68 S. W. 1094; 113 Ky. 806; Illinois Central R. R. Co. v. McIntosh, 80 S. W. 496; 118 Ky. 145; Goodlet v. L. & N. R. R. Co., 122 U. S. 1391; Nelling v. Chicago, &c., Ry. Co. (Iowa), 67 N. W. 404; Wright v. Southern Ry. Co., 80 Fed. 260.

3. The trial court erred in giving certain instructions and in refusing others. Hovius v. C., N. O. & T. P. Ry. Co., 107 S. W. 214; Flint v. Illinois Central R. R. Co., 88 S. W. 1055; Wilmurth's Adm'r. v. Illinois Central R. R. Co., 76 S. W. 193; L. & N. R. R. Co. v. Brown, 107 S. W. 321; C. & O. Ry. Co. v. Crank, 108 S. W. 276; L. & N. R. R. Co. v. King's Adm'r., 115 S. W. 196; L. & N. R. R. Co. v. Harrod, 115 Ky., 377; 75 S. W. 233.

TH   D. SLATTERY for   ellee.

Ch. & Ohio Ry. Co. v. Lang's Admx.

AUTHORITIES.

1. On the proposition that demurrer to petition was properly overruled, and the action of the court thereon will not now avail appellant. 2 Chitty on Pleadings, 650; Childs v. Drake, 2 Met. 149; L. C. & L. R. R. Co. v. Cases' Adm'r., 9 Bush 732; L. & N. R. R. Co. v. Mitchell, 87 Ky. 334; Fagg's Adm'r. v. L. & N. R. R. Co., 111 Ky. 30; L. & N. R. R. Co. v. Wolfe, 80 Ky. 82; Connell v. C. & O. Ry. Co., 22 Ky. Law Rep. 501; Lowe v. Miller, 104 S. W. 257; Duncan v. Brown, 15 Ben. Mon. 197; Western Assurance Co. v. Ray, &c., 105 Ky. 523; Bently v. Bustard, 16 B. Monroe, 690; Daniel v. Holland, 4 J. J. Mar. 18; Drake's Adm'r. v. Semonin, 82 Ky. 291; Hill v. Ragland, &c., 114 Ky. 209; C. & O. Ry. Co. v. Thieman, 96 Ky. 507; Drakesboro Coal, Coke & Mining Co. v. Jeonegan, 99 S. W. 235; Harmon v. Thompson, 27 Ky. Law Rep. 181; L. & N. R. R. Co. v. Daulton, 113 S. W. 842.

2. On the proposition that the court did not err in refusing to instruct the jury peremptorily to find for defendant. Wilmurth's Adm'r. v. Ill Central R. Co., 76 S. W. 193; Newport News, &c. v. Deuser, 97 Ky. 94; I. C. R. R. Co. v. Hocker, 55 S. W. 438; L. & N. R. R. Co. v. Tinkham's Adm'r., 44 S. W. 439; Wren v. L. St. L. & T. Ry. Co., 14 Ky. Law Rep. 324.

3. On the proposition that defendant owed plaintiff's intestate a lookout duty. Thompson on Negligence, Vol. 4, Sec. 4478; 2 Thompson on Negligence, Sec. 1839; Thompson on Negligence, Vol. 2, Sec. 1735; Hammill v. L. & N. R. R. Co., 93 Ky. 343; L. & R. R. Co. v. Lowe, 118 Ky. 260; Shelby's Adm'r. v. Cin., New Orleans & T. P. R. R. Co., 85 Ky. 229; L. & N. R. R. Co. v. Creighton, 106 Ky. 42; L. & N. R. R. Co. v. Seibert's Adm'r., 21 Ky. Law Rep. 1603; Cin., N. O. & T. P. Ry. Co. v. Hill, 89 S. W. 523; Cason's Adm'r. v. C. C. & C. E. R. & T. & B. Co., 93 S. W. 19; Perkins v. C. & O. Ry. Co., 94 S. W. 636; Davis v. Louisville H. & St. L. Ry. Co., 97 S. W. 1122.

The following cases cited by appellant distinguish from the case at bar: Eastern Ky. Ry. Co. v. Powell, 33 S. W. 629; Dilas' Adm'r. v. Chesapeake & Ohio Ry. Co., 71 S. W. 492; Louisville & Henderson & St. Louis Ry. Co. v. Jolly's Adm'r., 90 S. W. 977; Jacobs' Adm'r. v. C. & O. Ry. Co., 72 S. W. 308.

4. The question of contributory negligence was properly left to the jury. L. & N. R. R. Co. v. Lowe, 118 Ky. 260; Young v. I. C. R. R. Co., 24 Ky. Law Rep. 789.

5 Appellant was not prejudiced by the instructions given in this case. Southern Ry. Co. in Kentucky v. Otis' Adm'r., 25 Ky. Law Rep. 1686; Young v. I. C. R. R. Co., 24 Ky. Law Rep. 789; Childs v. Jones, 7 Dana, 540; Lynch v. Sanders, 9 Dana, 59; L. & N. R. R. Co. v. Connelly, 9 Ky. Law Rep. 993; Sims v. Reed, 12 B. Monroe 51; Sears' Adm'r. v. L. & N. R. R. Co., 22 Ky. Law Rep.

OPINION OF THE COURT BY JUDGE HOBSON—Revers.
ing.

Anthony A. Lang was a section hand in the service of the Chesapeake & Ohio Railway Company. It
was a part of his duty to act as track walker between
South Ripley and Dover, a distance of about six miles.
One of his duties was the lighting of the signal and
switch lights between these points, and to save time
he was allowed to use a velocipede. On December 19,
1905, he had been to South Ripley and was returning
to Dover, where he lived. Just before the road
reaches Dover it passes over a trestle. While Lang
was going over this trestle, a rapidly moving passenger train came up behind him, knocking him off the
track and killing him. This suit was brought by his
personal representative to recover for his death, on
the ground that those in charge of the engine and train
perceived his danger and, after perceiving it, could
by proper care have avoided killing him. There was
a verdict and judgment in the plaintiff's favor for the
amount sued for, $2,000, and the railroad company
appeals.

One witness, who lived about 100 feet from the railroad track and about 800 feet east of the trestle, tes-
tied that he was sitting in his room, and saw Lang go
by on the velocipede. He seemed to be going along
very leisurely. The witness then got up and went into his kitchen, and just as he got into the kitchen he
heard the whiz of the passenger train. He was un-
easy about Lang, for he had seen him pass, so he
stepped to the window to see if he had gotten across
the bridge, and, as he reached the window, he saw
him at the end of the bridge, and the witness could
only see him half way across the bridge. The train
was only about 100 feet behind decedent when the

witness last saw him. The train did not whistle or give
any signal until after it had gotten beyond the bridge.
Another witness testified that she lived just west of
the bridge. She was tired and went to the window.
She saw Lang going by, and watched him until he
got about across the bridge. While she was standing there the train came along. She looked until it
got close to him. She turned her eyes, and the train
struck him. The window at which she was standing
faced the bridge. She also testified that there was no
whistle or ringing of the bell until after Lang was
struck. Lang did not look back, so far as she saw.
The train was an extra, consisting of an engine and
three baggage cars, running at the rate of 45 or 50
miles an hour. There was proof on behalf of the
plaintiff that it could have been stopped in 400 or
500 feet.

The conductor of the train testified that he was in
the rear car, and that the engineer whistled and put
on the emergency brakes on the curve before reaching
the straight track approaching the trestle. The track
was straight for about 800 feet east of the point
where Lang was struck. The engineer testified that
he was two or three rail lengths west of the distance
signal when he first saw Lang. A rail length is 33
feet. The distance signal was 780 feet from the point
where Lang was struck; so, according to his testimony, Lang was about 700 feet from him when he
saw him. He said he saw Lang when he came around
the curve into the straight track. The fireman was
busy shoveling coal, and did not see him at all at that
time. The engineer testified that he at once set his
emergency brakes and blew the alarm whistle; that
Lang was at about the end of the viaduct, and got off

the velocipede, and was trying to pull it from the track, when he was struck and killed. The fireman testified that, after the alarm was given, he looked out and saw Lang trying to pull the velocipede from the track when he was struck. On the other hand, the section hands who were working on the track a little below the trestle testified that no warning of the approach of the train was given until after Lang had been struck; and two persons walking east along the track, who passed Lang a short distance from the trestle, gave similar testimony.

It is insisted for the defendant that the court should have instructed the jury peremptorily to find for it; but we cannot concur in this conclusion. If a signal of the approach of the train had been given, Lang might have protected himself by jumping from the velocipede. The evidence for the plaintiff was that no warning of the approach of the train was given, and that Lang was struck when he was proceeding along in ignorance of the approach of a train behind him. In addition to this, there was evidence tending to show that the train might have been checked, if not stopped, in time to avert the catastrophe. While the witnesses who testified for the plaintiff did not know this engine or these cars, they had run other trains and were competent to testify as to the distance within which such a train could be stopped. The evidence shows that Lang was seen by the engineer when he came around the curve into the straight track, and, if he had whistled then, Lang could, at least, have jumped from the velocipede. It is true the testimony for the company is to the effect that the engineer did blow the whistle then, but the great weight of the evidence is to the effect that no whistle was blown until after Lang had been struck and the train was some feet west of the point at which the accident occurred.

The court gave the jury these instructions:

"(1) The court instructs the jury that if they believe from the evidence that the decedent, Anthony Lang, was on the 19th day of December, 1905, while riding on a velocipede on the track of defendant's railroad, killed by being run into by an engine of defendant as described in the proof, and if they further believe that at the time of such injury and killing he was upon the track in the usual course of his employment by said railroad company, and that the agents and servants of said railroad company in control and management of the train after discovering the peril of decedent, Lang, failed to use the utmost diligence to prevent his injury, then they will find for the plaintiff.

"(2) If the jury believe from the evidence that at the time of the killing of decedent, Lang, the train was being run by the agents and servants of the defendant railroad in an ordinarily careful and prudent manner, and that after the discovery of the decedent, Lang's, peril they promptly used all the means in their power to prevent the injury, then they will find for the defendant.

"(3) If the jury believe from the evidence that the decedent was himself guilty of such negligence that as without his negligence the injury would not have happened, notwithstanding the defendant may have been guilty of negligence, still the law is for the defendant and the jury will so find.

"(4) If the jury finds for the plaintiff, they should assess the damages at such sum as will fairly compensate the estate of the decedent for the destruction of his power to earn money, not to exceed, however, the sum of $2,000, the amount claimed in the petition.

"(5) The jury are instructed that the rate of speed of defendant's train prior to the time its engineer saw the peril of Lang was not negligence. Defendant had the right to run its train at the speed that it was running."

The court did not err in telling the jury that the defendant was only responsible in case there was negligence after the peril of Lang was discovered. The point at which he was struck was one where the presence of persons on the track was not to be expected. It was outside of the town limits, and there was no reason why the presence of persons at this point should be anticipated. It is true Lang was not a trespasser. He had a right to be on the road with a velocipede; but it was incumbent on him to keep a lookout for trains and get out of their way. Those in charge of the train had no reason to anticipate his presence on the trestle, and were not required to keep a lookout for him. But they were required to exercise proper care to avoid injuring him after his peril was discovered. There was no evidence that his peril was discovered by any one but the engineer, and in instructions 1 and 2, in lieu of the words "agents and servants," the court should have used the word "engineer." The engineer was not required to use the utmost diligence to prevent his injury after he discovered his peril. He was required to exercise such care as might be reasonably expected of a person of ordinary prudence under the circumstances. The court, therefore, erred in telling the jury that the company was liable if the engineer failed to use the utmost diligence to prevent the injury.

In the second instruction, in lieu of the words "promptly used all the means in their power," the court should have inserted these words, "used ordinary care in the exercise of all reasonable means at his command consistent with the safety of the train." Hovius v. Cincinnati, etc., Ry. Co., 107 S. W. 214, 32 Ky. Law Rep. 786; Flint v. Illinois Central R. R. Co., 88 S. W. 1055, 28 Ky. Law Rep. 1.

The defendant introduced proof on the trial to the effect that Lang, before leaving the last station, received warning from the station master that this passenger train was coming, and it is insisted for the railroad company that, if he received this warning, he was guilty of negligence in going upon the track with his velocipede in front of the passenger train. But, although he was guilty of negligence in thus going upon the track, the defendant would still be liable if, after it discovered his peril, it did not exercise ordinary care to avoid injuring him; and, as the plaintiff cannot recover in any view of the case except for negligence after his peril was discovered, no instruction should be given based upon this evidence. There was proof for the defendant to the effect that Lang, after he knew of the approach of the train and after he had jumped from his tricycle and was safe from the train, lost his life in an effort to get his tricycle off the track. When he did this, it was too late for those in charge of the train to do anything more than they had already done to avoid injuring him; and, if with knowledge of the approaching train and when he was safe from it he thus put himself in danger in an effort to save the tricycle when it did not endanger the train, he cannot recover. The proof for the plaintiff does not sustain this view of the transaction, but it is supported by the proof for the

defendant. A person may lawfully imperil his life
to protect the lives of the persons on a train. In lieu
of the third instruction, the court will tell the jury
that if they believe from the evidence that Lang
jumped from the tricycle, and when he was at a point
of safety, with knowledge of the approach of the
train, he undertook to take the tricycle off the track
end thus lost his life, he took the risk and the defendant is not liable, unless he had reason to believe the
tricycle endangered the train, and he used such care
as may be reasonably expected of a person of ordinary prudence situated as he was. Nelling v. Chicago, etc., Ry. Co., 98 Iowa, 554, 67 N. W. 404; Wright
v. Southern Railway Co. (C. C.) 80 Fed. 260; Illinois
Central v. Jackson, 65 S. W. 342, 23 Ky. Law Rep.
1405; Louisville & Nashville R. R. Co. v. Molloy's
Adm'x, 122 Ky. 219, 91 S. W. 685, 28 Ky. Law Rep.
1113; Barber v. Cincinnati, etc., R. R. Co., 21 S. W.
340, 14 Ky. Law Rep. 869; Becker v. Louisville &
Nashville R. R. Co., 110 Ky. 474, 61 S. W. 997, 22 Ky.
Law Rep. 1893, 53 L. R. A. 267, 96 Am. St. Rep. 459.

We see no other prejudicial error in the record.
The petition is defective, in that it does not aver that
those in charge of the train saw the peril of the deceased, and, after perceiving it, were negligent as
therein alleged. The allegation that they saw or
could have seen by ordinary care is only an allegation
that they could have seen. On the return of the case
the plaintiff may amend her petition.

Judgment reversed and cause remanded, with directions for a new trial consistent with this opinion.

Nunn, C. J., dissenting.

CASE 14.—MANDAMUS BY J. C. BRODIE AGAINST WILLIAM F. HOOK TO COMPEL HIM TO PLACE HIS NAME ON THE OFFICIAL BALLOT AS A CANDIDATE FOR THE OFFICE OF CIRCUIT COURT CLERK.— Oct. 28, 1909.

Brodie v. Hook.

Appeal from Breckinridge Circuit Court.

WEED S. CHELF, Circiut Judge.

Writ denied and plaintiff appeals—Affirmed.

1. Elections—Nominations—Time for Filing Certificate.—Ky. St. Sec. 1456, requiring certificates and petitions of nomination to be filed with the clerk of the county not more than 60 and not less than 15 days before election, is mandatory, and the clerk has no right to place the name of a candidate upon the ballot, the certificate for which has been filed within 15 days of the date of election.

2. Mandamus—Sufficiency of petition.—A petition for mandamus to the county clerk to compel him to place petitioner's name on the official ballot alleged that petitioner's name was omitted by mistake from the original certificate of nomination, and that another certificate was prepared in which petitioner's name was inserted; that the clerk refused to place petitioner's name on the ballot; that the clerk discovered the omission of petitioner's name from the first certificate, and took it from the box where he kept such certificates, and put it in a different box where it was not likely to be found; that he did this to conceal the omission from petitioner. Held not sufficient to justify mandamus, the time having elapsed within which under Ky. St. Sec. 1456 (Russell's St. Sec. 4015), certificates should be filed before the amended certificate was filed, as the petition does not allege that the act of the clerk concealed from him the omission of his name from the original certificate, or that petitioner was prevented from seeing the certificate by reason of the change, or that he ever called

on the clerk to produce it, and was refused, or that the removal of the certificate from one box to the other was in any way hurtful to him.

W. H. HOLT, A. R. KINCHELOE and JOHN P. HASWELL for appellant.

AUTHORITIES.

26 Ky. Law Rep. 487, Mason v. Bryley; 113 Ky. Rep. 785, Denny v. Bosworth; 83 S. W. 154, Bennett, v. Richards per Justice Nunn; Combs case, 27 Ky. Law Rep. 753-756; 120 Ky. Rep. 378; Mc-Creary on Elections (Third Edition) (Sections 190-194).

ADDENDA.

This case, in its facts, reaches beyond the Hallon case. No question of fraud or mistake was raised in it.

The Legislature did not mean or intend to make the statute as to the time of filing the certificate mandatory as against fraud or mistake. It did not intend to shield a fraud or bar relief in case of an honest mistake. Suppose a case of fraud without the county court clerk being implicated—suppose by fraud the names proper to a certificate were erased and the clerk therefore refused to put the name of the candidate, fairly and honestly nominated, upon the ballot—would not a court of equity compel it?

It is fair to presume that the appellant has been at much labor and expense in prosecuting his canvass, and is it right to keep him off the ballot, although fairly nominated?

The legislative object in fixing a limit of time to file certificates was to give the clerk time to have the ballots printed; and this does not prevent the courts from affording relief in a case of mistake or omission; and especially when the ballots have not yet been printed.

The facts admitted by the appellee fully support the appellant's contention. No objection was entered of record to the appellant's motion for a mandatory injunction, and common fairness would dictate that it ought not to be objected to by anyone. There was no neglect on his part; as soon as he discovered the mistake and oversight an amendment was filed.

MERCER & MERCER and MURRAY & MURRAY for appellee.

We submit that the court will affirm the judgment of the lower court, and we presume that much will be said as to the office of the chancellor, and that it is his province to correct mistakes and right wrongs arising from fraud, but the chancellor is absolutely controlled by any constitutional mandatory law that the law making power may enact.

Brodie v. Hook.

The appellant must suffer the consequences of the error of his legal representatives, who were the chairman and secretary of the nominating convention, who failed to notify appellee within the time limit of appellant's nomination as required by law.

AUTHORITIES CITED.

Ky. Statutes, Sec. 1456; Hallon v. Center, 102 Ky. 109; Parrish v. Powers, 32 Ky. Law Rep. 125; Commonwealth v. Combs, 120 Ky. 368; Cyc. Vol. 15, page 338.

OPINION OF THE COURT BY CHIEF JUSTICE NUNN— Affirming.

In the month of August, 1909, the Republicans of Breckinridge county held a convention to nominate candidates for the various offices of the county to be voted for at the election to be held November 2, 1909. The chairman and secretary prepared and signed a certificate showing the persons nominated for the respective offices, in due form, and same was filed with the county court clerk of that county within the time prescribed by the statutes, but it failed to be stated in the certificate who was nominated, if any one, for the office of circuit court clerk. Matters stood thus until October 19, 1909, at which time the same chairman and secretary prepared another certificate reciting the nominees of the August convention, in which they inserted the name of appellant as the nominee for the office of circuit court clerk but the county court clerk refused to regard it and place appellant's name upon the ballots. Appellant then instituted this action for a mandamus requiring him to place his name upon them. The facts above stated were alleged in the petition, and also that his name was left out of the first certificate by oversight of the chairman and secretary. He also averred that the county court clerk discovered the omission of his name from the first

certificate and charged that he then took the certificate from the box where he kept all such certificates,
and put it in a different box where it was not likely to
be found, and that this was done to conceal the same
from appellant. While we must concede this allegation as true, the case having gone off on demurrer, it
is justice to the clerk to say that he denied it.

We have a case before us in which it is conceded
that the certificate declaring appellant's nomination
was filed within 15 days next before the election to be
held November 2, 1909, with a bare pretense that his
failure to file it 15 days before the election was caused
by the clerk changing the first certificate, which did
not contain his name, from its place of deposit to another box in his office. He did not allege that he made
any effort to see the certificate or request anyone to
examine it for him, or that anyone was prevented
from examining the certificate by reason of any act
of the clerk, or that the clerk at any time failed to
produce the certificate when called upon for it; nor
is there any allegation in the petition that the removal of the certificate from its original place of deposit to another was in any way hurtful to appellant.
It is provided by section 1456, Ky. St. that: "Certificates and petitions of nomination herein directed to
be filed with the clerk of the county shall be filed not
more than sixty and not less than fifteen days before
election." If this language is mandatory, the clerk
had no right to place appellant's name upon the ballots to be voted at the election to be held November
2, 1909; but, if the statute is merely directory, he had
the right to put it on. In 15 Cyc. 338, it is said:
"Statutory provisions in regard to the time of filing
certificates of nomination are mandatory, and a certificate offered after the time limited is properly re-

jected''—and in support of the rule are cited cases from California, Kansas, New York, and Ohio, but cite none holding the contrary.

In the case of Griffin v. Dingley, 114 Cal. 481, 46 Pac. 457, the court held the statute of that state in regard to filing certificates of nominations to be mandatory. The statutes of that state declare that the certificate should be filed not less than 30 days before the day of the election. The court in that case said: "To hold that it (the certificate) could be filed 28 days before the day of election would be in manifest disregard of the provisions of the statute." In that case the candidate offered his certificate of nomination 28 days before the election, when the statute said "it shall be filed not less than thirty days before the election." In the case of Hollon v. Center, etc., 102 Ky. 119, 43 S. W. 174, 19 Ky. Law Rep. 1134, this court construed our statute above quoted. In that case Center and others, who were candidates for the county offices in Wolfe county, sued Hollon, the county court clerk, to mandamus him to place their names upon the ballots. The lower court granted the writ and Hollon appealed. All the candidates filed with the clerk certificates of their nomination, except James R. Ross and John Creech. All the certificates were filed within the period prescribed by the statute, except G. W. Sally's and J. F. Sample's, which were not offered until the 19th day of October, less than 15 days before the election, exactly what was done in the case at bar with reference to appellant's certificate. The certificates of the other candidates filed were defective, in that they did not state the place of residence of the candidates nor of the chairman and secretary of the convention; nor did the chairman and secretary acknowledge the same before an officer authorized to administer an oath. The court in that case decided that these defects in the certificates could be supplied by other evidence or by the clerk, if he had personal knowledge of the facts omitted in the certificates, that the statute, in respect to the defects named, was merely directory, and not mandatory; but with reference to the certificates of Sally and Sample, which were filed October 19th, less than 15 days before the election, the court determined that the statute was mandatory, and that the certificates were inoperative because the statute required· that such certificates be filed not less than 15 days before the day of the election, and reversed the case as to these appellees and also as to the two parties who failed to file any certificates. Bouvier's Law Dictionary defines the word "mandatory" as follows: "In the construction of statutes, this word is applied to such as require to be obeyed, under penalty of having proceedings under them declared void. Directory statutes must be obeyed, but, if not, do not invalidate the act."

In view of these authorities, and it seems that there are none to the contrary, we are of the opinion that appellee was correct in refusing to print appellant's name on the ballots to be voted at the election to be held November 2, 1909. We are of the opinion that the General Assembly enacted this mandatory provision requiring the certificates and petitions of nomination to be filed not less than fifteen days before the election, so as to give the clerk that much time to prepare and have the ballots printed and distributed among the polling places in the county before the day of the election, and without being annoyed by litigation by some one attempting to get some name on or off the ballotts, and without being importuned by

candidates and their friends for that purpose. The
statute makes it obligatory upon all persons who desire to be candidates at an election to see to it that
their certificates of nomination, or the necessary papers entitling them to have their names placed on the
ballots to be voted, are filed not less than fifteen days
before the election. If they neglect to do this, they
must suffer the loss. Of course, the rule would be
otherwise if the clerk fraudulently or otherwise
wrongfully prevented the filing of the certificate or
petition within the time required by the statute. It
is true that appellant alleged that the clerk changed
the first certificate from one box to another for the
purpose of concealing it from him, but it is not alleged that it was concealed from him, or that he was
prevented from seeing it by reason of the change, or
that he ever called on the clerk to produce it and was
refused, or that he had anyone else to do so with a
like result, or that he ever looked into the box where
such certificates were usually kept and failed to find
it; nor does he allege that the removal of the certi-
cate from one box to another was in any way hurtful
to him

For these reasons, the judgment of the lower court
must be affirmed.

BARKER and O'REAR, JJ., dissent.

CASE 15.—ACTION BY THE EXECUTOR OF ROBERT BOYD,
SR., AND OTHERS AGAINST NATHAN BUCHANAN
AND OTHERS TO RECOVER LAND.—Oct. 28, 1909.

Buchanan v. Boyd's Ex'r, &c.

Appeal from Whitley Circuit Court.

M. J. Moss, Circuit Judge.

Judgment for plaintiffs, defendants appeal.—Affirmed.

1. Descent and Distribution—Conveyances by Heirs—Debts of
   Intestate—Bona Fide Purchaser for Valuable Consideration.—
   Under Ky. St. 1909, Sec. 2087, providing that any estate
   aliened by the heir or devisee before suit was brought shall not
   be liable to the creditors of decedent in the hands of a bona
   fide purchaser for a valuable consideration unless action is
   instituted within six months, a "bona fide purchaser for a
   valuable consideration" is one who in good faith buys the
   land and pays therefor.

2. Descent and Distribution—Conveyance by Heirs—Debts of Intestate—Bona Fide Purchaser.—Under said section, that the
   purchaser was judge of the circuit court and had notice of the
   pendency of an action against the ancestor to recover a
   money judgment did not prevent his being a bona fide purchaser; the suit not seeking to subject the land.

3. Descent and Distribution—Debts of Intestate—Action Against
   Purchaser—Limitations.—Under said section, one purchasing
   land in good faith from the widow and heirs of the deceased
   owner and paying therefor acquired title, unless an action
   to subject the land to debts was filed within six months after
   it descended.

4. Appeal and Error—Right to Allege Error—Inviting Error.—
   Where, in an action to recover land, an amended reply and
   rejoinder, though unnecessary, were filed without objection,
   and the parties elected to set forth their respective titles, and
   it appeared from the pleadings that defendants had no title,
   they could not on appeal complain, where the court decided
   the issue presented in such pleadings without objection on
   their part.

5. Appeal and Error—Harmless Error—Though an amended reply was improperly filed to prevent the case going to the jury, the case will not be reversed and remanded for a jury trial on an issue playing no part in the action.

See original appeal, 115 S. W. 222; 120 S. W. 295; 131 Kentucky Reports, Case 48, page —.

TYE & SILER for appellants.

QUESTIONS DISCUSSED AND AUTHORITIES CITED.

1. In an action of ejectment issue is joined by filing an answer denying the allegation of ownership in plaintiff. Civil Code, subsection 2, section 125; Simms v. Simms, 88 Ky. 642; Howton v. Roberts, 20 R. 1331; Anderson v. Proctor Coal Co., 25 R. 131; Williams v. Watson, 19 R. 1798.

2. It is surplusage to plead evidence of title in an action of ejectment.

3. In an action of ejectment it is not incumbent on defendant to respond to a pleading, setting forth mere evidence of title in plaintiff and nothing more. Tinsley v. Ross, 15 R. 44; Combs v. Combs, 19 R. 439; Grigsby v. Hart, 13 R. 920; Fuqua v. Bogard, 22 R. 1910.

4. A general demurrer searches the entire record and thus brings all previous pleadings before the court, and judgment on such demurrer should be against the party who committed the first error. Wile v. Sweeney, 2 Duvall, 161; Martin v. McDonald, 14 B. M. 544.

5. It is not negligence in a party in failing to find a deed of record, but not indexed, and such record is not notice. Elliott v. Harris, &c., 81 Ky. 470; Gill v. Fugate, 117 Ky. 266.

6. A stranger to a deed can not be estopped by it. Hume v. Breck, 4 Littell, 286.

7. Before a matter can operate as an estoppel in pais, it must be shown that the party pleading it has been prejudiced in some right of his by the act complained of; that he would have done something which he could have done but for the act, or that he was induced to do something that he would not have done but for it. Western Bank v. Coldewey's Ex'tx., 26 R. 1250; Wright v. Williams, 25 R. 1379.

8. The law protects the party in possession against all but the rightful owner. Plaintiff must recover land upon the strength of his own title and not upon the want of title in the defendant. Green v. Wilson, 8 R. 601; Ratliff v. Elam, 14 R. 772; Long v. L. & N., 89 Ky. 544.

9. In action of ejectment defendant, under general issue, may prove that he was in adverse possession of land in controversy at the time it was conveyed to plaintiff and thus defeat the action. Kentucky Statutes, Sec. 212; Shaw v. Revel, 21 R. 348.

10. A defendant in ejectment is always at liberty to show that the legal title or present right of possession is vested in a third person, and thus prevent a recovery. Warrelle on Ejectment, Sec. 246.

H. C. CLAY for appellee.

ROBT. BOYD, Jr., Ex'or.

AUTHORITIES.

Motion to dismiss appeal, Code Secs. 506, 734, 767; Hopkins v. Hopkin's Adm'r., 91 Ky. 310; Magee v. Frazier's Ex'or, 21 R. 254; 51 S. W. 174. Creditors of a decedent have no lien on real estate unless suit to settle the estate is filed within six months from his death. Ky. Stat. Sec. 2087; Parks v. Smoot's Adm'r., 105 Ky. 63; 20 R. 1043; 48 S. W. 146.

OPINION OF THE COURT BY WM. ROGERS CLAY COMMISSIONER—Affirming.

R. Boyd, Sr., instituted this action against appellants, Nathan Buchanan and others, to recover two tracts of land lying in Whitley county, Ky. Appellants filed an answer pleading that they were in possession of the first tract named in the petition, but were not in possession of the second tract. They denied plaintiff's title to the first tract and pleaded title in themselves. Thereafter R. Boyd, Sr., filed a reply denying the affirmative allegations of the answer. Subsequently, and without objection on behalf of the appellants, plaintiff amended his reply and set forth the sources of his title. He pleaded: That the tracts of land described in the petition were conveyed to him on August 14, 1889, by Juda Leforce and Lee Leforce. That Juda Leforce was then the widow of D. H. Leforce, who had theretofore died intestate in Whitley county, Ky. That Lee Leforce, the other

grantor in the deed, was the only child and heir of D.
H. Leforce.   That at the death of the latter he was
seised in fee simple of the tracts in controversy.   That
by reason of D. H. Leforce's intestacy the
legal title thereto descended on his death to
Lee Leforce, subject to the dower rights of
Juda Leforce.   That · plaintiff purchased said
lands from Juda Leforce and Lee Leforce in
good faith and for a valuable consideration then paid
l·y him to them.   That on the date of said deed to-
wit, August 14, 1889, each of the grantors therein
duly acknowledged and delivered the same to the
plaintiff, and he thereby became the owner of the fee-
simple title to each of said tracts of land.   Said deed
was duly lodged for record and recorded on the 20th
day of August, 1889, in the clerk's office of the Whitley county court.   A copy of the deed is filed with the
amended reply.   In said reply it is further alleged:
That on the 13th day of September, 1893, the appellants, in an action which was then pending in the
Whitley circuit court wherein they were plaintiffs,
and others, including the heirs of D. H. Leforce, were
defendants, an amended petition was filed by the
plaintiffs, by which for the first time the plaintiffs in
that action sought to subject to the payment of the
claim which they were asserting against the estate of
D. 'H. Leforce the land in controversy; that nearly
four years theretofore, for a valuable consideration
paid by the plaintiff, Juda Leforce and Lee Leforce
had conveyed the lands in question to him by deed of
general warranty; that, in the action wherein appellants were plaintiffs and said Juda Leforce and others were defendants, an order was made by the Whitley circuit court at its January term, 1894, directing

that the land in question be sold to satisfy the claim of appellants against the estate of D. H. Leforce; that in obedience to that order the first named of the tracts described in the petition was sold by the master commissioner on March 5, 1894; that J. S. G. Farris became the purchaser thereof for the benefit of appellants; that thereafter a deed was made to the appellants. It is further charged that the last conveyance is the only semblance of title which the appellants have to the tract first named, and that they purchased the same subject to notice of plaintiff's prior purchase of said land in good faith from the widow and heirs of D. H. Leforce.

Thereafter appellants, Nathan Buchanan and others, filed a rejoinder to plaintiff's reply, wherein they pleaded: That in 1881 they instituted an action against D. H. Leforce to recover judgment for many hundred dollars; that said action remained on the docket of the Whitley circuit court until the death of D. H. Leforce, which occurred on the 3d day of May, 1887; that after the death of D. H. Leforce, and within six mouths thereof, said action against D. H. Leforce was revived against Lee Leforce, his only child and heir at law, and the administrator of said D. H. Leforce; that said action was thereafter transferred to the equity side of the court's docket, and an amended petition filed, by which it was sought to settle the estate of D. H. Leforce and to sell his land for the purpose of paying their debt; that the plaintiff in this action failed to cause his deed to be recorded in the clerk's office of the Whitley county court, or failed to have it indexed in the index of records of deeds in said clerk's office; and that appellants had no knowledge of the existence of said deed, and said deed was not in fact recorded in the clerk's office of the Whitley county court as required by law. It is further pleaded: That by the action to settle the estate appellants had a lien upon the land in controversy to secure the payment of their debts, which lien was prior and superior to the rights of plaintiff; that said lien was enforced by a sale of said land, and they became the purchasers thereof; that said sale was confirmed by order of the Whitley circuit court and a deed of conveyance made by the commissioner of said court.

It is further charged: That plaintiff was judge of the Whitley circuit court in which such action was pending from January, 1886, until January, 1893, and had notice of the pendency of said action; that plaintiff took title to said land subject to the rights and liens of appellants and all other creditors of D. H. Leforce. Plaintiff filed a demurrer to the foregoing rejoinder, which was sustained by the court. Appellants then declined to amend their rejoinder or otherwise plead further. Judgment was then entered in favor of plaintiff. From that judgment this appeal is prosecuted. Robert Boyd, Sr., died after the rendition of the foregoing judgment, and the case has been revived against his heirs.

It will be observed that the rejoinder admits that the amended petition, by which the appellants sought to subject D. H. Leforce's land to the payment of his debts, was not filed within six months after the death of said Leforce. Moreover, the rejoinder does not deny that appellants had notice of the fact that R. Boyd, Sr., had actually purchased the land in question from the widow and heir at law of D. H. Leforce. The question, then, arises: Did appellants acquire a good title to the property in question by their purchase under such circumstances?

Section 2087, Ky. St., is as follows: "When the heir or devisee shall alien, before suit brought, the estate descended or devised, he shall be liable for the value thereof, with legal interest from the time of alienation, to the creditors of the decedent or testator; but the estate so alienated shall not be liable to the creditors in the hands of a bona fide purchaser for valuable consideration, unless action is instituted within six months after the estate is devised or descended to subject the same." It will be observed that the foregoing section provides that any estate aliened by the heir or devisee shall not be liable to the creditors in the hands of a bona fide purchaser for valuable consideration, unless action is instituted within six months after the estate is devised or descended to subject the same. While it appears from the rejoinder that the original action of appellants against D. H. Leforce was revived within six months, it further appears that the amended petition seeking to subject the land was not filed within the required time. Under that section a "bona fide purchaser for a valuable consideration" is one who in good faith buys the land and pays therefor. The fact that R. Boyd, Sr., was a purchaser for a valuable consideration, was not denied by the rejoinder, and the fact that he was judge of the circuit court and had notice of the pendency of the original case of appellants against D. H. Leforce did not make him any the less a bona fide purchaser for a valuable consideration. In that suit it was not sought to subject the land. Having bought the land in good faith, and having paid for it, he was entitled to it, unless an action to subject the land was filed within six months after it descended to D. H. Leforce's widow and heirs. Parks v. Smoot, 105 Ky. 63, 48 S. W. 146, 20 Ky. Law Rep. 1043. No such action having been filed, he acquired title under the deed made to him by Juda Leforce and Lee Leforce.

But it is insisted: That the petition, answer, and reply made an issue as to the ownership of the land; that the subsequent pleadings, consisting of the amended reply and rejoinder, in which R. Boyd, Sr., and appellants set forth their respective titles, were mere surplusage, and the court erred in determining the controversy by those pleadings instead of trying the case upon the issues which had been completed by the petition, answer, and reply. In support of this position, it is insisted that appellants might, under the general issue, have shown adverse possession for the statutory period. As appellants' however, claimed title only from the time of the execution of the deed to them in the year 1894, and as this action was instituted in the year 1904, it is manifest that adverse possession can play no part in this case. Moreover, even though the filing of the amended reply and rejoinder was unnecessary, yet where each of these pleadings was filed without objection, and the parties elected to set forth their respective titles, and it is apparent from the pleadings that appellants have no title, they cannot now complain because the court decided the issue which was presented in such pleadings without objection upon their part.

But it is argued that the amended reply was filed for the purpose of preventing the case from going to the jury. That may be true; but it is perfectly manifest that, with the question of adverse possession eliminated, the only other question in the case was one of law. Under these circumstances, substantial justice does not require that this case be reversed and remanded for a trial by jury upon an issue which it is apparent from the record plays no part in the case. Judgment affirmed.

CASE 16.—ACTIONS BY G. W. UPTON'S COMMITTEE AGAINST S. H. BUSH AND OTHERS AND AGAINST W. R. GADDIE AND OTHERS.—Oct. 28, 1909.

Upton's Committee v. Bush, &c.
Same v. Gaddie, &c.

Appeal from Hardin Circuit Court.

WEED S. CHELF, Circuit Judge.

Judgment for defendants, plaintiff appeals.—Reversed.

1. Insane Persons—Guardianship—Statutes—Construction.—Ky. St. Sec. 2156, authorizing proceedings to inquire into the state of persons alleged to be of unsound mind or imbecile, or incompetent to manage their estates, and to a committee, applies to persons who are incompetent by reasons of mental unsoundness or imbecility, and not to incompetency by mere physical infirmity, because of sickness, infancy, or age.

2. Insane Persons—Unsoundness of Mind—Adjudication of Insanity—Setting Aside—Jurisdiction.—Where a court has found a person to be of unsound mind, an application to vacate such decree must be made to the same court, and is not within the jurisdiction of a court of another county.

3. Insane Persons — Inquisition — Committee—Appointment—Grounds—Verdict.—A verdict in a lunacy inquisition finding that defendant is incompetent to manage his estate, but not finding that he is a person of unsound mind, or stating in what the incompetency consists, was insufficient to warrant the appointment of a committee.

4. Insane Persons—Inquisition—Subsequent Inquest.—Where a person has been found incompetent, but one subsequent inquiry is permitted in which the issue to be tried is whether the original condition has ceased to exist, whether the first

inquest was obtained by fraud, or whether the inquest was false when judgment was entered.

5.   Insane Persons—Actions—"Next Friend."—The office of next friend is to represent a person under disability in the litigation, being authorized to appear only when there is no legal and statutory representative discharging that duty.

6.   Insane Persons—Action—Next Friend.—Though the Attorney. General or the attorney for the commonwealth might have maintained a suit to recover property belonging to an incompetent who had no committee, such suit was also maintainable by the incompetent by his next friend, where the representative of the commonwealth did not act.

7.   Insane Persons—Action by Next Friend—Qualification.—Where a next friend suing for an incompetent having no committee failed to file the affidavit of qualification, he should be allowed to supply the defect on timely objection being made, in the absence of which his failure to do so is waived.

8.   Insane Persons—Actions—Next Friend.—Where an order appointing a committee of an incompetent was invalid for want of jurisdiction, and the committee, after having sued to recover property belonging to the incompetent, offered to prosecute the suit as next friend, and it appeared that defendants had imposed on the incompetent to obtain the property sought to be recovered improperly and for an inadequate consideration, the court should not have dismissed the suit by the committee, but should have permitted him to continue it as the incompetent's next friend.

JAMES MONTGOMERY for appellant.

QUESTIONS DISCUSSED.

1st. The responsibility of appellees to the estate of Geo. W. Upton.

2nd. The right of appellant to counterclaim.

3rd. The attack of appellees is a collateral attack.

4th. Presumption that Upton was present at the inquest.

5th. And being present no notice was necessary.

6th. That appellees must plead he was not present and that a demurrer will not reach any defect, if any, in the inquest.

7th. That the appellants were made parties by the appellees and sought relief of them, and they are estopped to claim that appellants cannot counterclaim.

8th. That the court erred in not permitting Upton to sue in person or by next friend.

9th. The record showing Upton was an imbecile, that it was the duty of the chancellor, in consideration of his estate, to appoint a guardian ad litem for him or allow him to sue by next friend.

10th. That the demurrer being special came too late, reply being filed April 22, 1902, and shortly thereafter an amendment tenaered.

That the case was prepared for a trial a long time, and, as limitation would not bar another action, Upton being conclusively shown an imbecile for years, and as the appellees by demurring and not pleading indicated they could not plead absence of Upton at the inquest, the court now ought to adjudge appellants $483.34. $333.84 and $25, with interest on them from time gotten, as shown by the answer and cross petition of appellees and the deposition of S. H. Bush.

BUSH & IRWIN for appellees.

QUESTIONS DISCUSSED AND AUTHORITIES CITED.

1. The inquest under which Rush was appointed committee was void, because the jury did not find any mental unsoundness. Menifee v. Ends, 97 Ky. 388; Hendricks v. Settle, 21 Rep. 1058; Taylor v. Moore, 23 Rep. 1572; Tipton v. Tipton's Com., 97 S. W. 413.

2. The inquest was also void because found by a jury of only six members. Ky. Stats. 2151-2158; Constitution of the State, Secs. 7 and 248.

3. The court properly refused to permit Rush to proceed with the suit in his name as next friend. Civil Code, Sec. 37; Upton v. Handley, 30 Ky. Law Rep. 170.

OPINION OF THE COURT BY JUDGE O'REAR—Reversing.

G. W. Upton was found by the verdict and judgment of the Larue Circuit Court to be a person of unsound mind, and incompetent thereby to manage his affairs. A committee was appointed to take charge of his estate, an inheritance. In 1895 by proceedings had in the circuit court of Larue as well as the county court of Hardin (he having removed to the latter county) instituted by himself he was found by the verdict of the juries to be of a sound mind. It is not

pretended that there was a substantial change in his
condition at any time. He was not a lunatic. His
imbecility was a weakness of understanding, by reason of which he could not properly comprehend the
value of property, or make contracts with respect to
it. His was the mind of a child in those respects.
Some things he could do. As a school boy he could
learn certain lessons. He was good at penmanship,
and could memorize certain rules of grammar, and
do sums in arithmetic, as a boy 10 years old could do.
But it seems that his mind never matured so that he
could appreciate the value of property, or how its
ownership affected his welfare. He knew how to
spend money, for in that, of course, he had plenty of
help. But the value of it to him was practically unknown or unappreciated by him. He would sell anything he had for any kind of a price, and make bar-
gains such as no mature mind would have made. Nor
was he an idiot. As to business matters he was simply weak-minded. Just as very young persons are,
or very old ones sometimes get to be. It is difficult
to classify his mental condition. It is enough to say
of it that he had not contractual capacity. Such is
the man as this record shows him to be and to have
been.

The statute of this state (section 2156, Ky. St.),
deals with the subject of a "person found to be of
unsound mind, or imbecile, or incompetent to manage his estate," and confers upon the circuit and
county courts the jurisdiction to inquire into such
state of the person, and, if found incompetent, to
commit his estate, and, if need be, the care of his person to a committee, or, if a lunatic or dangerous, the
care of his person to an asylum.

This section has been construed not to apply to
persons who are incompetent from mere physical
infirmity to manage their estates, as because of sickness or old age, or mere infancy; but it covers only
the instances where the person is incompetent by
reason of mental unsoundness or imbecility. Menifee v. Ends, 97 Ky. 388, 30 S. W. 881, 17 Ky. Law
Rep. 280; Taylor v. Moore, 112 Ky. 330, 65 S. W.
612, 23 Ky. Law Rep. 1572.

The central thought in the statute is the abnor-
mally deficient mind, the purpose being to protect
the property of such persons from becoming the
prey to the avaricious who would overreach them in
contracting.

Upton had some mind. He could communicate his
wants in intelligible language, and was, of course,
capable of thought and purpose. He wanted to get
his property into his control so that he could spend
it. He got two lawyers, Haynes and Irwin, to institute the proceedings mentioned to have his committee discharged. They proceeded under section
2160, Ky. St., which provides:

"Whenever it shall appear to a county or circuit
court, from an affidavit filed, that a person found of
unsound mind has been restored to his proper senses,
or that the inquest was false or fraudulent, the court
shall forthwith direct the facts to be inquired into
by a jury in open court and make all necessary orders or decrees in the premises."

The court which found the person to be of unsound
mind is the tribunal that should open up the judgment in the case; for the person is a ward of that
court, and his estate is in its custody till the judgment is vacated. Consequently the Hardin County
Court had not jurisdiction to inquire into the mat-

ter.   The proceedings in the Hardin County Court
may then be disregarded.   In the Larue Circuit
Court the following proceeding appears to have
been entered:

"Larue Circuit Court.   May term, 1895.   Commonwealth of Kentucky v. G. W. Upton, Jr.   This day
came parties by attorneys and announced ready for
trial: thereupon came the following jury, to wit:
(names the jury, T. J. Wilkins and eleven others)
who were duly sworn and impaneled to try the issue,
and after hearing the evidence and receiving the instructions of the court and hearing the arguments of
counsel, they were permitted to return to their
jury room to consider of their verdict, and after
some time returned into open court the following
verdict, to-wit; 'We, the jury, believe from the evidence that G. W. Upton has sufficient mind to manage
his estate.   T. J. Wilkins.' " Upon that verdict this
judgment was entered: "This cause having been submitted, and the court having ordered an inquest
herein to determine the competency of the defendant
to manage his estate and the jury impaneled having
returned a verdict that G. W. Upton was competent
to manage his estate, it is now adjudged and agreed
by the parties that Jacob Hubbard, committee for
G. W. Upton, settle his accounts as said committee
with the Larue Circuit Court, and he will after said
settlement turn over all notes, choses in action, and
money in his hands as said committee to defendant
Upton, and will surrender to the defendant the possession of said defendant's estate.   It is also adjudged that the costs of this action and of the inquest to be paid by the plaintiff and taxed as costs
herein, including a reasonable attorney's fee to Murray R. Hubbard, plaintiff's attorney."

Another suit involving some part of Upton's estate (which was prepared and tried with these suits) was recently before this court, where it was said (Rush, Committee v. Handley, 97 S. W. 726, 30 Ky. Law Rep. 170): ·

"It is further contended that at the time Nelson purchased from Upton he had been declared by a court competent to transact business for himself. The evidence upon this point is rather meager, but in substance is as follows:

"About the time of the death of G. W. Upton's father, the question of his sanity was tried in a court of competent jurisdiction, and the jury adjudged that he was of unsound mind, and a committee was appointed for him by the court. Soon after this some parties made an effort to have a jury declare him competent and finally succeeded in having a jury so adjudge (one of the appellees, D. S. Handley, being a witness on these trials). It further appears that these parties who had interested themselves in Upton as above set forth at once took charge of his affairs, and within 30 days thereafter he had wasted all the estate left to him by his father, about $2,500." Messrs. Haynes and Irwin had a contract with Upton for 30 per cent. of his estate for their fee in these (and possibly in other) matters; Haynes' part being assigned subsequently to appellee Bush, an attorney at law residing in the same town with Upton, and who knew him well. On November 1, 1895, Upton made a deed to appellees, Bush and Irwin (the latter having been one of his attorneys in the foregoing proceedings) for all his interest in the estate of the grantor's grandfather. The consideration was $200, most of which was debt created by Upton for a stock of merchandise to wholesale houses a short while before.   The evidence shows the property then conveyed was worth nearer $2,000.   Irwin and Bush conveyed by general warranty two parcels of the property to appellee Gaddie.

This suit was brought in equity by Albert Rush, as committee for G. W. Upton, against Gaddie to recover the real estate last mentioned.   Gaddie pleaded his purchase from Bush and Irwin, and denied that Rush was the committee of Upton.   Gaddie made his answer a cross-petition against his warrantors, Bush and Irwin.   They made their answer a cross-petition against the plaintiff.   They put in issue appellant's claim that Upton was of unsound mind, but asserted that he was of sound mind when they bought from him.   Although they had not the right to make their answer a cross-petition against the plaintiff, yet the parties joined an issue on whether Bush and Irwin had not under their deed from Upton collected considerable money due him of the personal estate derived from his ancestor.   It turned out that they had collected at least $334 on that score.   On the trial of these consolidated and cross-actions the circuit court dismissed appellant's petition.   He prosecuted appeals.   One has been disposed of as stated above. 97 S. W. 726, 30 Ky. Law Rep. 170.

In the record now before us something more appears concerning appellant's appointment as committee than was shown on the other appeal.   It now appears that in July, 1896, the Hardin County Court impaneled a jury to inquire into the state of mind of G. W. Upton.   Their verdict was:

"We, the jury, find from the evidence that Geo. W. Upton is a person who is incompetent to manage his estate; that he was born in Hardin county and resides in Hardin county, and is 23 years old; that he was not brought into this state for the purpose of becoming a charge on the commonwealth; that he owns no estate of any kind; that his father is dead, mother is living and resides in Hardin county.''

It is said in brief that the circuit court dismissed appellant's petition because the proceedings just mentioned had in the Hardin County Court were void; that, as the verdict did not show that Upton was of unsound mind, that court had not jurisdiction to appoint a committee for him, citing Menifee v. Ends, supra; Hendricks v. Settle, 53 S. W. 1051, 107 Ky. 344, 21 Ky. Law Rep. 1058; Taylor v. Moore, supra; and Tipton v. Tipton's Committee, 30 Ky. Law Rep. 80, 97 S. W. 413.

The authorities sustain appellee's contention as to the jurisdiction. Still we think the circuit court should not have dismissed the petition. It is true that Upton was not otherwise a party to this cause, so far as the record before us discloses, than by his committee, Rush. But the record is in a very imperfect condition. Much of it was left out of the transcript, and has been brought up later. Some of it is not here yet. Briefs on both sides allude to the fact that Rush offered to prosecute the suit as next friend, but was denied. It is said that he did not tender the affidavit required by section 37 of the Civil Code of Practice.

From earliest times imbeciles have been regarded as wards of the chancellor. In Nailor's Children v. Nailor, 4 Dana 339, some of the children of George Nailor filed a bill against him and his wife, charging that he was of unsound mind because of extreme age, and was under the influence of his wife, who had seduced him late in life to marry her in order that she might get control of his property for herself and her own children, and that she was squandering his estate. They prayed a restraining order against her selling the property and for other general relief. A demurrer was sustained to the bill. This court reversing the judgment said, inter alia:

"It is unquestionable that in England the chancellor exercised jurisdiction over the persons and estates of idiots and lunatics. The form of proceeding there was by petition to the chancellor, which might be filed by the Attorney General or by any creditor, friend or relative of the individual, praying for a commission of idiocy or lunacy. * * * Though the proceedings in this case are not technically formal when tested by the English practice, yet the bill contains substantially all the allegations which would be proper in a petition, and is verified by affidavit, as required by the common law. And though there are many specific prayers which are unwarranted by the forms of practice, and can not be granted, there is a general prayer, which will authorize the chancellor to afford that redress which is consistent with the rules of law, and the powers of the court, according to the circumstances of the case."

There was then a statute in this state respecting the holding of inquests substantially like the existing statute. The arm of the chancellor has not been shortened since then. Rush's suit brought before the court a state of facts with defendants in possession of an imbecile's property upon a disclosure that should have aroused the chancellor's concern and vigilance, and enlisted his ancient equitable jurisdiction. He should not have turned the parties and property loose upon the showing before him.

Going back a step, we will remark that the late proceedings in the Larue Circuit Court (of May,

1896), seem to us to have been unauthorized. The statute permits, after one has been found of incompetent mind, but one subsequent inquiry: Has the original condition ceased to exist; or was the first inquest obtained by fraud; or was the inquest false when judgment was entered? In this case it is not pretended now, nor then so far as this record shows, that the first inquest was obtained by fraud. The unsoundness of mind found by the first jury was one that does not abate short of death. It was of the kind like a deformity. It was not lunacy. It was more like idiocy. But whether or not it was curable, or susceptible of improvement, it is not shown in the proceedings, and is not asserted that those proceedings were based upon the fact that there had been such improvement. If the practice indulged is permissible, then one jury may, without finding any change in the mind of the person after the first inquest, conclude that the first jury decided the matter wrong, and proceed to find it the other way, either on the same or different evidence. The statute does not contemplate such unseemly course. On the contrary, it inferentially forbids it. It recognizes that a verdict and judgment regularly entered fixes the status of the party, except where the proceeding was tainted by fraud or was false. In the latter event the correct practice is by direct attack, and the question would be, was the first inquest false? In addition, it recognizes and provides for the contingency of a change in a person's mind when the change is to restore it to soundness. All the inquests after the first were irregular and unauthorized. As the first committee has been discharged, the trial court should have allowed the suit of Upton to be prosecuted by a friend; and, if the affidavit of qualification was not filed, if the objection was made in due season, it could have been supplied, or a prochein ami suffered who could have qualified. But there was not a motion before answer in this case to have Rush file the affidavit. Thereafter it is deemed waived. Staton v. Bryant, 5 Ky. Law Rep. 426; Henning v. Barringer, 10 S. W. 136, 10 Ky. Law Rep. 674.

Although Rush did not denominate himself next friend, yet his attitude in the case was the equivalent of that office, and he should have been so treated. As said in Nailor v. Nailor, supra, that, though .the statute imposes a duty upon certain attorneys of the commonwealth to put in motion the proceedings, this is but directory to them, and a means used by the Legislature to insure attention to the condition of that unfortunate class when they might otherwise be neglected by their relations, or friends, or have none. "But," it was said, "the statute containing no repealing clause, it is remedial and cumulative, and can not be fairly construed (as contended by counsel for appellees) as repealing any provision of the common law which recognizes the right of the other persons, such as friends or relations or even others, filing the petition."

The office of next friend in court is to represent the person under. disability in that litigation. He can come in only when there is not a legal and statutory representative discharging the duty. The Attorney General or the attorney for the commonwealth might have maintained this suit as well. There being no committee and the commonwealth's representative not acting, Rush may be deemed next friend for that purpose. We are of the same opinion upon this record as was reached in Handley's Case, supra, namely:

"The testimony introduced is overwhelming that he (Upton) was incompetent to transact business, and that appellees knew that fact."

The circuit court should have adjudged Upton a recovery of the 73 acres of land described in the amended petition, subject to a lien in behalf of Gaddie for a sum the equivalent of the vendable value added to the land by permanent and lasting improvements put on it by him, less reasonable rents; also, the recovery of the storehouse and lot in Upton village named in the petition, and rents, less taxes and repairs, if any.

As to appellees, Irwin and Bush, the judgment should have been for $334 and interest from the time it was collected. Upon the return of the case, and before judgment is entered, let Rush qualify as next friend by executing the bond required by the Code; or, if the Larue Circuit Court has appointed another committee in lieu of Jacob Hubbard, let him be joined as a party plaintiff, if he will, otherwise as a defendant.

Reversed and remanded for proceedings consistent herewith.

CASE 17.—ACTION BY JASPER STORY AGAINST R. B. LIT-
TLE AND OTHERS.—Oct. 20, 1909.

Story v. Little, &c.

Appeal from Fleming Circuit Court.

Jas. P. Harbeson, Circuit Judge.

Judgment for defendants, plaintiff appeals.—Affirmed.

1. Highways—Petition to Open Road—Sufficiency.—Ky. St. 1909,
Sec. 4288, provides that applications for opening roads shall
be allowed only for the convenience of traveling to the county
courthouse, to a public warehouse, an established town, etc.
Section 4289 provides that applications to have a new road
opened shall be to the county court signed by at least five
landowners of the county, etc. Held, that a petition which is
otherwise sufficient need not state that the proposed road
was required to enable the petitioners to travel to one of the
places named in section 4288.

2. Highways—Establishment—Insufficiency of Petition—Demurrer.—Were it necessary that the petition should state that
the proposed road was required to enable the petitioners to
travel to one of the places named in Section 4288, Ky. St.
1909, the defect in failing to so state should have been taken
advantage of by demurrer.

3. Highways—Opening—Sufficiency of Petition—Review.—The
failure of a petition for a new road to state that it was necessary to provide access to any of the places to reach which
a public road may be established under section 4288, Ky. St.
1909, is immaterial on appeal from a judgment establishing
the road, where the report of the commissioners shows its necessity in order to reach several of the places mentioned in
the statute, as the necessity for the road will be determined
from the entire record.

4. Highways—Opening—Commissioner's Report—Amendment—
Statutes.—While road commissioners could not amend their
reports under the "General Statutes" under the Kentucky
Statutes now in force, road commissioners may amend their
report.

5. Highways—Petition for Road—Death of Petitioner.—Where
one of six landowners, who had signed a petition for opening
a road, died, it was not error for the circuit court to refuse to
enter an order of revivor and to continue the case for that
purpose, where there still remained five landowners concurring in the application, whose names still remained to the
petition; Ky. St. 1909, Sec. 4289, only requiring the petition
to be signed by five landowners.

6. Highways—Road Commissioner's Report.—The report of road
commissioners was written in the office of the attorneys of
the petitioners. One of the attorneys, at the request of the
commissioners, calculated and arrived at the quantity of
land that would be taken from each landowner for the proposed road. It is not claimed nor shown that the calculations were in any respect incorrect. The correctness of the
report was testified to by the commissioners and approved
by two juries which had viewed the entire route of the new
road and lands over which it ran. Held, that in the absence
of allegations and proof of fraud or undue influence on the
part of the attorney as to the preparation of the report, the
fact that the commissioners received the assistance of the
attorney in the preparation of their report would not invalidate it.

7. Highways—Road Commissioner's Report.—Road commissioners took luncheon with two of the petitioners for a new road
during their work of viewing the route of the proposed
road. It does not appear that they were improperly influenced by the hospitality of the petitioners, nor was it shown that
they were talked to on the subject of the road. Held, that
it was not error to refuse to quash the report because of
this, in the absence of testimony tending to show any improper conduct or conversation upon the part of the petitioners.

8. Highways—Establishment—Commissioners' Report.—It is not
ground for dismissal of a petition for a public road that
neither the petition nor the commissioners' report gives the
width of the proposed road. The statute prescribing the
commissioners' duties does not require their report to state
the width, where the report which, with the petition, follows
the statute, fixes the beginning and end of the road and the
course and distances thereof, and where the order establishing the road fixes the width thereof at 30 feet, and makes
the line of the survey the center thereof.

9. Highways—Turnpikes and Toll Roads—Establishment—
Statutes.—The legislature, after having already passed a law

providing for the opening of all public roads (Ky. Stat. 1909. sec. 4289), later enacted the free turnpike statute (Ky. Stat. 1909, chap. 129, art. 6), which provided that all turnpikes thereafter constructed should be public roads. Sec. 4748b, subd. 5, provided that the fiscal court could acquire turnpike roads by gift, lease, or purchase, and provided for the construction of turnpikes when the public good demanded it, and subd. 6, declares all turnpikes so acquired or constructed to be public roads to be maintained by the fiscal court. Held, that the failure of the Legislature to provide a manner for opening turnpikes, as distinguished from other public roads. shows conclusively that it considered the earlier law, for the opening of public roads ample for the purpose, and proceeding to open either a public road or a turnpike may be had under the earlier statute.

10. Highways—Opening—Proceedings—Review—Court of Appeals—Scope.—Under the direct provisions of Ky. Stat. 1909, sec. 4303. relating to appeals in proceedings to open highways, the Court of Appeals have jurisdiction only of matters of law arising on the record.

11. Highways—Costs—Appeal—Refusal to Accept Damages.—Where a party refused to accept damages allowed him by the report of road commissioners, and failed to recover as much either in the county or circuit court, he was not entitled to the costs.

J. H. POWERS and R. J. BABBETT for appellant.

AUTHORITIES CITED.

Sec. 4288, Ky. Stat.; Portland & Greenwood Turnpike Co. v. Bobb, 88 Ky. 226; Chamberlain v. Hignite, 97 S. W. 396; Vogle v. Bridges, 15 Ky. Law Rep. 6; Gen. Stat., sec. 7, art. 1, chap. 94; Ky. Stat. 4292-4293; Am. & Eng. Ency. of Law, 2d ed., vol. 24, p. 230; Lewis on Eminent Domain, sec. 423; Ky. Stat., sec. 4295; Louisville, St. Louis & Texas R. R. v. Barrett, 91 Ky. 487; Lewis on Eminent Domain, sec. 511; Stanton's Revised Stat. of Ky., vol. 2, chap. 84, art. 1, sec. 18; Gen. Stat., chap. 94, art. 1, sec. 20; Session Acts of the Legislature for the year 1893, chap. 232, art. 1, sec. 22; Ky. Stat., 4287-4347 inclusive; Secs. 4712 to 4748b inclusive, Ky. Stat.; Cyc., vol. 15, p. 5678; Ligare v. Chicago, 32 Am. St. Rep. 171; United States v. Certain Tract of Land, 70 Fed. 940; Elliott on Roads, pp. 147-8; Postal Telegraph Cable Co. v. Mobile & Ohio R. R. Co., 21 Ky. Law Rep. 1188; Lances Appeal, 53 Am. Dec. 722; Imlay v. W. B. Traction Co., 68 Am. Dec. 392; Brown v. Gerald, 109 Am. St. Rep. 526; Kansas City v. Hyde,

Story v. Little, &c.

113 Am. St. Rep. 766; Cyc., vol. 15, p. 85 2; Foster v. Chicago, &c. R. R. Co., 31 S. W. 529; Barnes v. Chicago, &c. R. R. Co., 33 S. W. 601; Ky. Stat., 889; Ky. Stat., 4289; Civil Code, secs. 363 to 367 inclusive, sec. 102; Ky. Stat., 4303; Hedges v. Downs, 2 Mich. 160; Mattingly v. Mosley, 2 Met. 443; Howards v. Maxwell, 98 S. W. 1013.

JNO. P. McCARTNEY and B. F. GRANNIS for appellees.

AUTHORITIES CITED.

Ky. Stat., secs. 950, 4288, 4289, 4292, 4293, 4348, 4356, 4783; Civil Code, 102, 363, 565, 640, 727, 728; Gen. Stat., p. 1125; Chamberlain v. Hignite, 97 S. W. 396; Louisville N. R. Co. v. Gerard. 112 S. W. 915; Ford v Collins, 108 Ky. 553; Vogel v. Bridges, 15 Ky. Law Rep.; Hedges v. Downs, 2 Met. 160; Mattingly v. Mosley, 2 Met. 443; Howard v. Maxwell, 98 S. W. 1013; Louisville, St. Louis & Texas R. R. Co. v. Barrett, 91 Ky 487; Tingle v. Tingle, 12 Bush, 160.

OPINION OF THE COURT BY JUDGE SETTLE—Affirming.

Appellees, following the giving of the required statutory notice, filed in the Fleming county court a petition to obtain the opening of a public road through their own lands and those of appellant and others. Commissioners appointed by the court viewed the route of the proposed new road and duly assessed the damages that would result from its establishment to the persons over whose lands it would run, and thereafter made a report to the court showing performance of the duties required of them. Later an amended report was filed by them for the purpose of supplying certain omissions in the first report. The appellant, Jasper Story, being opposed to the opening of the road, filed numerous exceptions to the report of the commissioners. The issues of fact raised by the exceptions were tried in the county court by a jury resulting in a verdict sustaining the report, and the court thereupon entered judgment overruling the exceptions, confirming the report, and establishing the road. Appellant, being dissatisfied with the judgment, prosecuted an appeal to the Fleming circuit court, and, the trial in that court having likewise resulted in a verdict in favor of appellees, appellant by the present appeal seeks a reversal of the judgment of the circuit court.

We will endeavor to pass upon such of appellant's exceptions to the report of the proceedings as we regard material. His first objection is that the petition does not state the proposed new road is necessary for the convenience of the petitioners or others traveling to one of the several places mentioned in section 4888, Ky. St., Section 4289, Ky. St., provides: "Applications to have a new road opened or a former one changed or discontinued, or to have the privilege of erecting gates across any such road, shall be by petition to the county court signed by at least five land owners of the county, which petition shall set forth, in writing, a description of the road, and what part thereof is to be altered or vacated. If for a new road, the names of the owners and tenants of lands, if known, and if not known it shall be so stated, over which the road is to pass, the points at or near which it is to commence, its general course, and the place at or near which it is to terminate, and if to erect gates the place proposed for that structure." A reading of the petition will show that it contains the signatures of five landowners of Fleming county, and sets forth every fact required by the section, supra, to be therein stated. This we think was sufficient, but if we were of opinion that the petition should have stated that the proposed road was required to enable the petitioners to travel to one of the places named in section 4288, and that the omission to state that fact in the petition made it defective, we should hold that the defect was one that appellant should have taken advantage of by demurrer. The report of the commissioners shows that the road will be necessary to enable the petitioners and others to reach several of the places to which it is permissible under section 4288 to open a public road, and, in addition, the fact is abundantly established by the evidence appearing in the record. The question of whether the opening of a proposed road is or not necessary is to be determined by the court from the record as a whole.

Appellants complain that the county court improperly allowed the commissioners to amend their report, and, in support of this contention, his counsel cites the case of Mitchell v. Bond, 11 Bush, 614. That case was decided when the "General Statutes" were in force, the provisions of which, with respect to the road law, were in many respects unlike those of the present law on the same subject contained in the Kentucky Statutes. Ford v. Collins, 108 Ky. 553, 56 S. W. 993, 22 Ky. Law Rep. 251; L. & N. R. R. Co. v. Gerard (Ky.) 112 S. W. 915; 130 Ky. 18.

Under the present law the court has recognized the right of road commisiosners to amend their report and approved it as correct practice. Chamberlain v. Hignite, 97 S. W. 396, 30 Ky. Law Rep. 85.

We find no force in appellant's complaint that the circuit court after the death of Allen Boyse, one of the petitioners, failed to enter an order of revivor, and refused him (appellant) a continuance of the case for that purpose. The name of Boyse was one of six landowners appearing to the petition, and, as after his death there were still five landowners concurring in the application for the new road whose names remained to the petition, an order of revivor was unnecessary following the death of Boyse.

We do not think the county or circuit court erred in refusing to quash the commissioners' report on appellant's motion because it was written in the office of appellee's attorneys. It does not clearly appear from the evidence by whom the report was written, but does appear that one of appellee's attorneys at the request of the commissioners calculated and arrived at the quantity of land that would be taken from each landowner, for the proposed road. It is not, however, claimed nor did the evidence show, that the calculations of the attorney were in any respect incorrect, and if, as there was some evidence to prove, it be conceded that the report of the commissioners was typewritten in the office and presence of the attorney and by his stenographer in the presence of the commissioners, that fact should not be held to invalidate the report, as it is not denied it was written by their direction or in conformity to their views, even though they may have received the assistance of the attorney in its preparation. Neither fraud nor undue influence on the part of the attorney with reference to the preparation of the report was alleged or proved, and its correctness was testified to by the commissioners and approved by two juries, one on the trial in the county and the other in the circuit court, who were permitted to view the entire route of the new road and the lands over which it ran before returning their verdicts.

Another of appellant's complaints is that the county and circuit courts refused to quash the report because of the fact that the commissioners took luncheon with two of the petitioners during their work of viewing the route of the proposed road. This ruling

of the court was not error. It does not appear from
the evidence that the commissioners were improperly
influenced by the hospitality of the petitioners, nor
was it shown that they were talked to by the latter on
the subject of the road while partaking of their hospitality. The commissioners were some distance from
their own homes and not convenient to a hotel. Under
the circumstances, and in the absence of testimony
tending to show any improper conduct or conversation on the part of their hosts, we are unwilling to im-
pugn the intelligence or condemn the work of the commissioners by assuming that they were influenced by
the meal furnished them to make a report more favorable to the petitioners than was authorized by the
law and facts.

Appellant further contends that the petition should
have been dismissed because neither the petition nor
the report of the commissioners indicates the width of
the proposed road. The report of the commisisoners,
like the petition, follows the statute. The report
states the points of beginning and ending of the road
to be opened, as well as the courses and distances
thereof; and also the names of the owners over whose
lands it will run. It does not, it is true, give the
width of the road, nor does the statute defining the
duties of the commissioners seem to require that
their report shall indicate the width of the road. We
find, however, that the width of the road, 30 feet, is
fixed by the order establishing it, which also makes
the line of survey the center. This we think sufficient.
In the case of Tingle v. Tingle, 12 Bush, 160, the report of the viewers was excepted to because it failed
to give the metes and bounds of the road to be opened.
In overruling the exception the court said: "It was
also objected that the report was defective because

it did not give the metes and bounds of the proposed change. The courses and distances are given, and the width of the road is fixed by the order establishing the alteration; but neither that order nor the report indicates on which side of the single line run and reported as the route the road is located; and the question arises, Is the running of a single line on the proposed route a substantial compliance with the statute which requires the report to describe the route laid out and reported by metes and bounds and by general courses and distances? * * * We are not aware of any case in which a report of viewers has been held insufficient because the road was not bounded by two parallel lines on the opposite sides of the road, including it within those external lines, but upon a careful examination of the reported cases we are satisfied that it has heretofore been deemed a sufficient meeting and bounding of a proposed road to fix with certainty and distinctness the points of beginning, of termination, end the location of the road from one to the other of those points by a survey and fixing the width of the road, making the line of survey the center thereof.'' According to the testimony of the commisisoners, the land of the appellant taken for the road is 30 feet in width, and he was allowed by the report for the quantity appropriated at the rate of $40 per acre.

Appellant insists that though the petition in this case seeks the establishment of a public road it is the purpose of the appellees and the county court to convert it into a turnpike, which, it is claimed, cannot legally be done without a proceeding to condemn the right of way as and for a turnpike. We regard this contention unsound. The present road law was in force when the Legislature on March 18, 1896, passed the free turnpike statute. Article 6, c. 129, Ky. St.

By a vote under the latter law Fleming county made all turnpikes in the county free. Therefore all new pikes constructed are to be such roads as the statute declares them to be. Subsection 5, Sec. 4748b, provides that the fiscal court may acquire all turnpikes or gravel roads by gift, or lease, or purchase, and also provides for the construction of turnpikes or gravel roads when the public good demanded it. Subsection 6 declares: "All turnpikes and gravel roads thus acquired or constructed shall become public roads and shall be maintained by the fiscal court." We quite agree with counsel for appellees that the Legislature, having already enacted a statute providing the manner of opening all public roads, and later enacting that all turnpikes hereafter constructed shall be public roads and maintained by the fiscal court as such, declined to confuse the public mind and incumber the statute with any re-enactment of a provision for the manner of opening turnpikes as distinguished from other public roads, and the fact that such provision is omitted from the free turnpike statute is conclusive that the Legislature regarded the public road statute ample for the purpose. As the converting of the road in controversy into a turnpike cannot increase or lessen appellant's damages or put him to any additional cost, and will give him a far better road through his premises than a dirt road, we are unable to see any good reason for his opposition to the change.

Several of appellant's exceptions based upon alleged insufficiency of the evidence we deem it unnecessary to consider, further than to say that the two juries regarded it sufficient to sustain the report of the commissioners and upon it and their own inspection of the route of the proposed road based their verdicts.

We have to do only with questions of law arising on the record, for section 4303, Ky. St. provides: ''In all such cases the party aggrieved may prosecute an appeal within 60 days by executing bond as required in other cases to the circuit court of the county, and the appeal shall be tried de novo, and from the decision of the circuit court either party may prosecute an appeal in the Court of Appeals, and the latter court shall have jurisdiction only of the matters of law arising on the record of such cases.''

Finally, appellant complains that the circuit court gave appellees judgment against him for costs. This was not error. Appellant, having refused to accept the damages allowed him by the report of the commissioners, and having failed to recover as much either in the county or circuit court he was not entitled to his costs and the circuit court properly so adjudged. As on the whole case the necessity for the road and its convenience to the traveling public seem to have been sufficiently established, and it is fairly apparent that the proceedings show a substantial compliance with the requirements of the statutes as to the opening of public roads, no reason is perceived for disturbing the judgment.

Wherefore it is affirmed.

CASE 18.—ACTION BY T. H. PICKRELL AGAINST THE CITY
OF CARLISLE.—October 20, 1909.

Pickrell v. City of Carlisle

Appeal from Nicholas Circuit Court.

L. P. FRYER, Circuit Judge.

Judgment for defendant, plaintiff appeals.—Reversed.

1. Municipal Corporations—Streets—Obstructions.—Streets, including the pavements of a town, belong to the municipality for the use of the public traveling upon them for their whole length and width.
2. Municipal Corporations—Obstructions of Streets—Nuisances —Abatement.—Any permanent structure built upon any part of the public   streets which interferes   with their use by the public may be abated by the municipality, or be abated by the courts, at the instance of the town.
3. Municipal Corporations—Use of Streets—Rights of Abutting Owners..—The public will not be heard in equity to complain of an abutting owner's act in obstructing a street, which does not unreasonably interfere with the public's use of a street for travel.
4. Adverse Possession—Street—Right to Obstruct—Title by Prescription.—A lot owner may acquire by prescription an exclusive right to occupy a public street with his building or partial obstruction.
5. Adverse   Possession—Obstructions   of   Streets—Nuisance— Abatement.—Plaintiff erected in front of his house steps that extended upon the sidewalk. A former owner maintained an obstruction of the same character at the same place for more than 15 years prior to 1873. Others on the same block and in other blocks, where the sidewalks were narrow, were allowed to maintain other similar partial obstructions. Held, that the steps were not a purpresture and a public nuisance, which could be abated, the present owner having the right to maintain them, having an easement to continue the obstruction maintained by the former owner, or one no more an

Pickrell v. City of Carlisle.

obstruction, and the fact that others maintained like obstructions was evidence that it was not unreasonable, but a common custom.

6. Words and Phrases—"Common."—What is "common" is generally known to all.

7. Municipal Corporations—Ordinances—Prohibiting Obstruction of Streets.—A town may prohibit the erection of steps extending upon the sidewalks by a general ordinance of uniform application.

SWINFORD & SWINFORD for appellant.

AUTHORITIES CITED.

Dillon on Mun. Corp. Vol. 2, Sec. 734, 888; Commonwealth, etc., v. First Nat'l Bank of West Newton, 56th Atl. Rep., 437; Livingston v. Wolf, 136 Pa., 519; Bosworth v. City of Mt. Sterling, 12th K. L. R., 157; Wolf v. District of Columbia, 69th L. R. A., 84; City of Georgetown .v. Hambrick, 31st. K. L. R., 1276; City of Mt. Carmel v. McClintock, 155 Ill., 608; Dudley v. Trustees of Frankfort, 12th B. Monroe, 617; Newcome v. Crews, 17th K. L. R., 900; City of Bowling Green v. Gaines. 29th Rep. 1013; Dudley v. Trustees of Frankfort, 12 B. Monroe. 616; Dillon on Mun. Corp. Vol. 1, Sec. 734, 4th Ed.; Dillon on Mun. Corp., Vol. 2, Sec. 734, 888; Commonwealth, by, etc., v. First Nat'l Bank of West Newton, 56th Atl. Rep. 437 and 438; Teager v. City of Flemingsburg, 109 Ky., 746; Bouvier, Vol. 2, 14th Ed., 245; Hundley v. Harrison, 123 Ala., 292; Commonwealth, by etc., v. Borough of Beaver, 33rd. Atl. Rep., page 112; Elliott on Roads and Streets, page 291; Fox v. Halcomb, 32nd Mich, 494; Kerr on Injunctions (Star P. 201); Dickerson v. Mayor of City of LeRoy, vol. 72, page 588, appellate Dec. of Ill.; City of Logansport v. Uhl, etc., 99 Ind., 539; L. & N. R. R. Co. v. Smith, 25th. K. L. R., 459.

HOLMES & ROSS, attorneys for appellees.

AUTHORITIES.

4 Metc. 110; Thompson on Nuisance, 619; Covington v. Hall, &c., 30 Rep. 358; City of Louisville v. Snow's Adm'r, 21 K. L. R. 1268; City of Paducah v. Johnson. 29 Rep. 535; Trustees of Hazlegreen v. McNabby. 23 L. R., 812; Bogard &c. v. O'Brien et al., 14 Ky., 649; Sec. 3637, Ky. Stat.; McQuillin on Municipal Ordinances. Sec. 460; McQuillin on Municipal Ordinances, Sec. 444; Hundley v. Harrison, 123 Ala., 292; Pennsylvania Co. v. City of Chicago. 54 N. E., 825; Hibbard et al. v. City of Chicago, 50 N. E. 256; Elliott on Roads and Streets, page 478; Snyder v. City of Mt. Pulaski, 52 N. E., 63; People v. Harris, 67 N. E., 785; Barker

v. Mayor &c.. of Macon, 39 Ga., 735; Shaw v. Kennedy, 1 N. C.
Term Rep, 158; Harvey v. DeWoode, 18 Ark. 252; Hutton v.
Camden, 39 N. J. L., 122; Kansas City v. McLear, 31 Mo. App.,
433; VanWormer v. Albany, 15 Wend., 264; Lassing v. Americus,
86 Ga., 756; Denver v. Mullen, 7 Col. 345; Nazworthy v. Sullivan,
55 Ill. App., 48; Baumgartner v. Hasty, 100 Ind.. 575; Irvin v.
Wood &c., 51 N. Y., 224, 10 Am. Rep., 603; Wood on Nuisances,
Sec. 748; Wood on Nuisances, Sec. 749; Wood on Nuisances, Sec.
259; Joyce v. Woods, 78 Rep. 386; Varden v. Mount, 78 Ky. Rep.,
92; Teager v. City of Flemingsburg, Dubois v. Kington, City of
Covington v. Lee. 28 Rep. 492; City of Henderson v. Reed, etc.,
23 Rep., 463; Fugate v. City of Somerset, 16 Rep., 808; House
v. City of Covington, 26 Rep. 660; Thompson on Negligences, Sec.
6167, Vol. 5; Thompson on Negligences, Sec. 6170, Vol. 5; Thompson on Negligences, Sec. 6175, Vol. 5; City of Carlisle v. Secret,
25 Rep., 336; City of Louisville v. Brewer's Adm'r 24 L. Rep., 1671;
Dillon on Municipal Corporations, 1007; White v. City of New
berne, 59, S. E., 992; Curry v. Town of Mannington, 23 W. Va., 14;
City of Denver v. Utzler. 38 Colo., 300; Dudley v. City of Flemingsburg, 115 Ky., 5; Faulkner v. City of Aurora, 85 Ind., 130; Calla-
nan v. Gilman. 107 N. Y., 360; Gray v. Henry County, 19 Rep., 885;
Hurst v. Cassiday &c., 5 Rep. 771; Churchill v. Commonwealth,
13 B. Mon., 333; Wood on Nuisances, 357; Jones on Easements,
Sec. 855; Jones on Easements, Sec. 870; Palestine Bldg. Assoc.
v. Minor &c., 27 Rep. 783; Elliott on Roads and Streets, Sec.
659; Daekalb v. Luney, 61 N. E., 1036; Ashbrook v. Commonwealth, 1 Bush 13. A.; Yates v. Town of Warrenton, 84 Va,
337; City of Lexington v. Auger, Jr., &c., 4 Rep. 24; City of
Glascow v. Gillenwaters, 23 Rep., 1375; Commonwealth v. Find-
ley, 15 Rep., 650; Modern Law Municipal Corporations. Sec. 1311;
First National Bank v. Tyson, 133 Ala., 459; James Adm'r v. Trustees of Harrodsburg, 8 Rep., 899; State v. Goodwin, 145 N. C.,
461; Stein v. Chesapeake & Ohio Railway Co., 116 S. W., 737.

OPINION OF THE COURT BY JUDGE O'REAR—Reversing.

The town of Carlisle, county seat of Nicholas
county, was laid out in 1816. A plot of the town was
then recorded in the county clerk's office, showing
location and width of streets. The town is now a city
of the fifth class, with a population of less than
2,000. The part of the town occupied by business

houses is Main street. The courthouse square fronts
Main street on the south, and extends to Chestnut
street on the north.   On the west is Locust street
(originally named Main Cross street), and runs at
right angles to Main and Chestnut.   That block of
Locust street opposite the courthouse square is occupied by a bank, a clothing store, a lawyer's office,
and the postoffice building on the south end of the
block, while the north end is occupied by dwelling
houses except at the corner of Chestnut, which is occupied by the Christian church building.   Locust
street is 70 feet wide along this block, and is 60 feet
wide throughout the remainder of its length.   All of
Locust street north of the postoffice (except the Christian church) is fronted by residence property only.
Nor are there any business houses north or northeast
of the block named. Appellant owned a lot immediately
south of the Christian church, fronting on Locust
street.   He applied to the town council for, and was
granted, a permit to build a dwelling house on his
lot. The surface of the ground on which Carlisle is
situated is hilly.   Locust street and the block west
of the courthouse square have a sharp slope to the
south and west.   All the buildings on that block except the Christian church have a greater elevation
of the foundations on their south side above the surface of the street, owing to that fact.   All the buildings on that block fronting Locust street are built
on the line of the street, several of them being resi-
dences.   The most of them have steps and porches
extending a foot or so, to three or four feet, out on
the pavement. The pavement along that block is 12
feet wide, and constructed of cement. Appellant's lot
has a frontage on Locust street of 55 feet. When he

came to build his house, he excavated for his cellar
and foundation, placing his building so that it would
come up to the property line on the street. After his
foundation was built, and when he began to build his
steps, extending them out on the pavement for 3 1-2
feet, as was necessary to enable him to get into the
house if it was built on the property line as it was
begun, the town council ordered the steps removed,
and, the marshal threatening to tear them down, ap- ·
rellant filed this suit for injunction against the town
and its officers, restraining them from interfering
with the plaintiff's steps. Pending the suit the building was finished at a cost of about $8,000 or $9,000.
The circuit court adjudged that plaintiff was not entitled to the relief sought, dissolved the injunction,
and ordered the steps removed. From that judgment
this appeal is prosecuted.

· In addition to the foregoing, the proof discloses
the following facts: Many other buildings in the town
on Main street and other streets had steps extending
out on the pavements. On this lot where plaintiff
erected his house there formerly stood an old stone
building used as a store for many years. It had stood
there longer than the memory of the oldest inhabi-
tant. It was built on the property line also. There
was a stone step 18 inches wide, 6 or 8 inches high,
and 5 feet long in front of it and extending for its
full length and width on the pavement. Just south
of that step there was a cellar door in the pavement
next to the building. It was a double wooden door,
slanting from the pavement to the building, being
some 2 1-2 feet higher at the building than at the
pavement. On its south side it was much higher
above the surface of the pavement than at its north
side. The door extended out onto the pavement four·

feet, and its width when open was eight feet.   The steps now in question occupy part of the space formerly taken up by that cellar door, and partly by the old step above referred to.   The old cellar door was doubtless built when the stone house was.   At least it was there when witnesses 55 to 75 years old, and who had always lived in the town, first knew it.

Under these circumstances, were the plaintiff's steps a purpresture, and a public nuisance, which the town might abate or prevent, and which it ought to prohibit.   It is old and familiar law that the streets, including the pavements, of a town, belong to the municipality for the use of the public traveling upon them for their whole length and width; likewise, that any permanent structure built upon any part of the public streets so as to interfere with their use by the public for travel may be per se a nuisance, and may be abated by the municipality, or be abated by the courts at the instance of the town.   But it is not true that the municipality and the traveling public have the right to the exclusive use of the public streets. The owners of abutting lots have rights in the streets in addition to those enjoyed by the general public, and it may be in spite of their rights.   For example, the abutting owner has a particular easement in the street immediately fronting his lot, or leading to it, of ingress and egress, to a not unreasonable extent, although the exercise of his right might interfere with the public use.   If it were not so, then towns could not exist, for the title to the street would in effect, or could, absorb the value of the abutting lot as a city lot.   This right of ingress and egress must be exercised in a reasonable manner, so as to interfere not excessively with the public right of travel. It will vary according to the circumstances of the particular case. The location of the lot, the purposes for which it may be used, and is used, the natural grade of the street and lot, or artificial grade of the street as made by the city, all are pertinent factors entering into the question. So will the number of the population of the town, and the extent, present and probable of the necessity for the public's use of the street for traveling purposes. The dominant idea of the common law is ''reasonableness.'' Neither the city nor the abutting lot owner is allowed to act the dog in the manger—at least, will not be given the aid of a court of equity in so acting. It is therefore that a lot owner is confined to a reasonable use of his right of ingress, and egress, of ornamentation of his lot and the street in front of it (as by planting and main·taining shade trees, awnings, lamp posts, and the like), and the city and public will not be heard in equity to complain of the abutting owner's act which does not unreasonably interfere with the public's use of the street for travel.

The general rule is fairly summarized in the following paragraph from Dillon on Municipal Corporations (volume 2, Sec. 734) : ''The owners of lots bordering upon streets or ways have or may have in other respects a right to make a reasonable and proper use of the street or way. What may be deemed such a use depends, in absence of legislative or authorized municipal declaration, much upon the local situation and public usage—that is, the use which others similarly situated made of their land—this being evidence of reasonable use. Conformably to these principles, it was held that common and well-established usage in the city of Boston justified the owner of the land in erecting thereon warehouses on the line of the streets or ways with doors or windows opening onto the street or highway, and shutters projecting into the same when open, and with sidewalks in front, having on their surface iron gratings for admitting light to, and trapdoors for communicating with, the cellar or underground apartments of the warehouses and used for putting in or taking out goods. . So, for the same reasons, it is not an unreasonable use of the street in a populous place, where land is valuable, so to erect structures as that the grates and doors, when opened, swing over the line of the street. Whatever may be the rights of the public, certain it is that these acts do constitute a trespass upon the privy owner of the soil of the street.''

The Supreme Court of Pennsylvania had our question before it in the Commonwealth v. First National Bank of West Newton, 207 Pa. 255, 56 Atl. 437. West Newton was a town about the size of Carlisle. The controversy was as to the right of a property holder to construct steps on the sidewalk of Main street, a street 42 feet wide, practically where other projections of like character had existed to a former building. The steps extended two feet nine inches on a sidewalk seven feet wide. The court observed:

''In the absence of municipal regulation, lot owners may for purposes of necessity, ornament, or convenience partially obstruct a highway in a reasonable manner, so as not to prevent the use of the highway by the public; and the municipal authorities may by ordinance or otherwise regulate the manner of this public use and the ornamentation. What is a reasonable exercise of this discretion depends on the circumstances.''

The same court in Livingston v. Wolf, 136 Pa. 519, 20 Atl. 551, 20 Am. St. Rep. 936, said:

"The footways, no less than the carriageways, are under municipal control, and the authorities may determine the extent to which the walks and pavements may be obstructed by cellar doors, door steps, awnings, projecting windows, cornices, and the like. This power must be exercised by regulations that are general and uniform, that are reasonable and certain, and that are in conformity with the Constitution and laws."

In Georgetown v. Hambrick, 127 Ky. 43, 104 S. W. 997, 31 Ky. Law Rep. 1276, 13 L. R. A. (N. S.) 1113, this court declared that while a municipality has control of its streets and sidewalks, and may regulate the width of each, it must do so in a reasonable manner, and not arbitrarily; that the abutting lot owner has certain rights therein that must be respected, and can not be capriciously or unreasonably curtailed.

In Commonwealth v. Borough of Beaver, 171 Pa. 542, 33 Atl. 112, the Supreme Court of Pennsylvania said:

"The general proposition that the public have a right to travel on foot or in vehicles over every portion of the highway is modified largely by exceptions.

In Commonwealth (City of Allegheny) v. Zimmerman, 95 Pa. 292, 40 Am. Rep. 649, Mercur, J., in delivering the opinion of the court, says: 'So shade trees may stand between the sidewalk and the central part of the street without constituting a nuisance per se.' The mere partial obstruction of a street, when in fact such obstruction does not interfere with the public use, does not create a nuisance. * * * The right to partially obstruct a street does not appear to be limited to cases of necessity. It may extend to cases of convenience or ornament, provided it does not unnecessarily interfere with public travel."   .

Appellee relies on certain text-writers. Elliott on
Roads; Thompson on Negligence; and Wood on Nuisances. These authors lay down the principle more
broadly' than the adjudged cases, so far as we have
noticed or they have been cited to us. When courts
charged with the responsibility of declaring governing principles and applying them in actual cases between litigants have spoken, a less strict rule has been
observed. The cases recognize the fact, of which we
are all cognizant, that in nearly every town, and particularly the old towns of the states which were early
settled, the custom was to build houses fronting on
the streets and abutting on the property line so as to
make some part of the approach extend out on the
pavement. This is perhaps more frequently so as to
cellar doors and similar so-called obstructions. Most
of the states hold to the doctrine that limitation does
not run against the public, and that no length of time
could ripen into a right what was originally a common nuisance. Notwithstanding, the weight of authority, and what seems to us to be the right of the
matter, tends to support a milder doctrine than that
the public authorities must at all hazards require removed, and that the lot owner must under pain of having his property demolished or materially impaired,
remove those inoffensive obstructions which for gen-
erations and in a great number of instances have
been suffered to exist upon some portion of the
streets. All agree that the municipality may by general ordinance, or by a consistent course, regulate
such obstructions even to prohibiting them entirely.
But, unless it does so, where they are suffered in a
number of instances, and where they do not appear
to be an unreasonable use of the street, it is deemed,
not that they are there as a matter of right, but that

their presence is usual and customary, and does not materially or unreasonably interfere with the public use.   Dillon on Municipal Corporations (4th Ed.) Sec. 657.

Noticing some of the adjudged cases cited by ap·pellee, and which seems to be the most persuasive au·thority cited to sustain the judgment in this case, we find that the expressions most strongly supporting appellee's contention are dicta, or turn upon other facts not here present.   For example, People v. Har·ris, 203 Ill. 272, 67 N. E. 785, 96 Am. St. Rep. 304, was a mandamus, to compel certain municipal officers to remove an obstruction consisting of a bay window. An ordinance of the city permitted lot owners to ap·propriate three feet of the pavement. It is not shown what the width of the street was, nor whether the encroachments were not unreasonable or usual in that city.   The question turned on the power of the council to enact such general ordinance.   It was held to be beyond its power.   This excerpt will show the thought of the court:

"If bay windows may be authorized to be extended into the street eighteen inches when near the ground, then why not cities authorize property holders owning properties on each side of the street to cover the entire street, so long as they will place their projections and obstructions high enough that the tallest man in the community, or the highest wagon or the biggest load that may be conceived of, may pass readily? It seems to us the very suggestion carries with it its own answer, and that there is no safe field of speculation other than to keep within the limits placed by the books, by saying that the streets in the entirety are public properties, exclusively for public use, and that they, or any part of them, cannot be devoted exclusively to private purposes or private use.''

Yet the fact is that no city enforces the ironclad doctrine announced. Cornices, awnings, shade trees, hitch posts, cellar openings, coal holes, gratings to protect windows, door sills or single steps, shutters, show windows a few inches wide, all structures of a permanent nature, and tradesmen's exhibitions of wares in boxes, barrels, or otherwise, temporary, but so constant, as to be practically permanent matters, are universally suffered, and are not found either dangerous or annoying to pedestrians. The question always comes back to the point: Are they unreasonable and do they make the street unsafe for the public use? In Parker v. Mayor, 39 Ga. 725, 99 Am. Dec. 486, the city charter seems to have required the city authorities to keep the streets free from buildings, posts, steps, fences, or other obstructions or nuisances. The court said: ''To this end it is the duty of the city authorities to remove any nuisance from the streets or sidewalks, and anything that endangers the life of a person passing along the sidewalk is a nuisance which they are bound to abate.'' We are not prepared to criticise that statement. Irvine v. Wood, 51 N. Y. 224, 10 Am. Rep. 603, was a case where a coal hole was excavated in the pavement, but left with a defective covering. The landlord and tenant of the premises were sued. The case opens with this statement: ''The defendants did not allege in their answer that the coal hole was constructed by any license from the proper city authorities. * * * It may then be treated as a nuisance, being an unauthorized excavation in the street. * * * Even if this hole was excavated on the street by permission of competent authority, the person who originally excavated it was bound to do it in a careful manner, and to see that it was properly and carefully covered, so as not to be perilous to travelers upon the street.'' The case turned entirely upon the fact that the hole was negligently maintained without suitable covering. White v. City of New Berne, 146 N. C. 447, 59 S. E. 992, 13 L. R. A. (N. S.) 1166, 125 Am. St. Rep. 476, was an action against the city for personal injury inflicted on the plaintiff by his stumbling over steps projecting into the street. The case was made to turn upon that fact, coupled with the further fact that the city had failed to maintain a light at or near that point to show the obstruction. We apprehend it would have been equally liable had the plaintiff fallen over some unevenness in the street, which was structural and dangerous if not lighted. Callahan v. Gilman, 107 N. Y. 360, 14 N. E. 264, 1 Am. St. Rep. 831, was a case where the defendant had by use of drays and other accessories in his business practically appropriated a street, excluding the public. It was held that was an unreasable use, even though the magnitude and nature of the defendant's business seemed to require it. Other cases for personal injury to the plaintiff's falling over obstructions in streets, such as steps and the like, lay down the general doctrine that the streets are primarily for the public use, and that any permanent appropriation by lot owners is a purpresture, and a nuisance, where it endangers the public safety. Appellee expresses the fear that such would be its predicament should some one stumble upon these steps, and sustain injury. The question would be for the jury whether the presence of the steps was unsafe, and, in view of the lay of the ground, the width of the pavement at that point, and other steps similar in the same locality, made the street not reasonably safe for the travel of pedestrians. The jury might find it one way or the other. So might that body find any other situation alleged as constituting a common or private nuisance. We must decide the fact as it appears to us, assuming that any other body who may come to view the question will be governed by the law and the facts. In this state the doctrine obtains that a lot owner may obtain by operation of the statutes of limitation an exclusive right to occupy a public street with his building or partial obstructions. Bosworth v. City of Mt. Sterling, 13 S. W. 920, 12 Ky. Law Rep. 157.

The fact that more than 15 years prior to 1873 the owner of the lot had maintained an obstruction substantially at the same place, and not differing in character from that now sought to be removed, gave the present owner an easement to continue it, or another no more an obstruction. And the fact that others in the same block, and in other blocks where the pavements were not so wide, were suffered, and had been for a great many years, to maintain similar partial obstructions, is evidence that such steps were not unreasonable, but were a common custom in that town. What is common is generally known by all, and would seem not to be an unreasonable course. The town might have prohibited such steps by a general ordinance of uniform application. As it has not done so, unless it shows that the particular obstruction complained of is in fact a nuisance, and is an unreasonable use of the public way under the conditions shown to exist there, appellant ought not to be singled out for discipline merely to vindicate a previously unused power.

The judgment will be reversed, and the cause remanded, with directions to grant the injunction prayed for.

CASE 19.—ACTION BY C. C. BROWN AND OTHERS AGAINST
     W. S. DYCUS AND OTHERS TO REMOVE DEBTS
     DUE UNDER A PARTNERSHIP SETTLEMENT.—
     October 21, 1909.

Dycus, &c. v. Brown, &c.

Appeal from McCracken Circuit Court.

W. M. REED, Circuit Judge.

Judgment for plaintiffs, defendants appeal.—Reversed.

1. Pleading—Answer—Admissions—Failure   to   Deny.—Averments of a petition are confessed by failure to deny them.

2. Bankruptcy—Discharge—Claims Barred.—Creditors who had
    actual notice of the adjudication of their debtor in bankruptcy, and of the steps taken in the proceedings, were
    bound to present their claim, though not mentioned as creditors, and on failure so to do their claim is barred by the
    discharge.

3. Partnership—The Relation—Creation.—Defendants executed
    a contract with plaintiffs which stated that it was for the
    purpose of buying and selling tobacco on joint account during the season, and by which defendants agreed to buy tobacco to be paid for with money furnished by plaintiffs; and
    ship it for sale by plaintiffs, defendants to receive a certain
    amount as compensation for buying and delivering it, and
    the contract further provided that when the tobacco was
    sold and the expenses paid, including defendant's commission,
    the profits or loss should be divided equally. Held, that
    plaintiffs and defendants were partners in the transaction.

4. Bankruptcy—Unliquidated Claims—Evidence.—In an action
    against bankrupts, after their discharge, by persons engaged
    in a joint transaction with them for the purchase and sale
    of tobacco, to recover losses in the partnership transaction,
    in which defendants set up their discharge in bankruptcy, evidence held to show that plaintiff knew, when defendants filed
    their petition in bankruptcy, that the transaction would result in loss, leaving defendants indebted to them, though the
    amount was uncertain.

5. Bankruptcy—Discharge —"Unliquidated   Claim"— Debts between Partners.—Bankr. Act July 1, 1898, c. 541; 30 Stat. 544
(U. S. Comp. St. 1901, p. 3418), provides that if one or more, but
not all of the members of a firm are adjudged bankrupt, the
firm property shall not be administered in bankruptcy. unless on
consent of the non-bankrupt partners but that such partners
shall settle the partnership business as soon as possible, and
account for the interest of the bankrupt partners. By section
63 debts of the bankrupts may be proved and allowed against
their estate which are (1) a fixed liability as evidenced by
a judgment or an instrument in writing, owing at the filing
of the petition, whether then payable or not; (4) founded upon an open account or upon contract; (5) founded upon provable
debts reduced to judgments after the petition is filed and
before discharge. Section 63, subd. "b" permits unliquidated
claims against the bankrupt to be liquidated as the court
may direct, and may thereafter be proved. Plaintiffs were
partners with defendants in buying and selling tobacco, and
plaintiffs knew, when defendants filed a petition in bankruptcy that the venture would result in loss leaving defendants
indebted to plaintiffs though the exact amount was not
then known and could not be known until the rest of the
tobacco was sold. Held that plaintiffs had an "unliquidated
claim" against defendants within section 63, subd. "b" which
was provable when plaintiffs filed their petition, and was
barred by failure to present it, and the provisions of the bankrupt act, permitting nonbankrupt partners to, administer the
assets, did not relieve them from reporting to the court the
amount received in the settlement of the partnership affairs;
its purpose not being to defeat the rights of creditors of bankrupt partners.

6. Bankruptcy—Construction of Act—Provable Debts.—The provision of Bankr. Act July 1, 1898, c. 541, 30 Stat. 544 (U. S.
Compt. St. 1901, p. 3418), relating to provable debts, should
be construed to make all debts fairly within its meaning
provable debts, in order to effectuate the purpose of the act
in relieving insolvents, and any doubt whether a debt is provable, or whether it is an unliquidated demand which may be
made provable, should be resolved in favor of its provability.

MILLER & MILLER and E. H. JAMES for appellants.

POINTS AND AUTHORITIES.

1. It is not denied that appellees had "actual knowledge" of
the filing of the petition in bankruptcy and actually advised and
assisted in making the composition with creditors and they are

therefore, now precluded from asserting this claim which arose
long prior to those proceedings. Jones v. Walter 115 Ky., 556,
(74 S. W., 249); Gatliff v. Mackey, 104, S. W., 379.

Confirmation of a composition discharges bankrupt. Bankruptcy
Act, 1898, Sec. 14 c.

2.   The claim sued on was for money advanced long prior to the
filing of the petition in bankruptcy to purchase tobacco for a partnership composed of Appellees and Appellants under a written
contract and was a "fixed liability" under section 63 Bank Act,
1898.

Liability was fixed from the moment the money was advanced and the judgment appealed from really so considers it
because interest is charged on the advancements from the time
they were made long prior to the institution of the bankruptcy
proceedings.

3.   But if we assume for the sake of argument that the liability
was not actually fixed when the petition in bankruptcy was filed
or prior thereto, the filing of the petition in this case was such a
disenablement or repudiation of the contract as made it the right
and duty of appellees to take steps to liquidate and prove their
claim and they could have made it provable and are barred. In
Re Pettingill, 137 Fed. 143; In Re Hilton, 104 Fed., 981.

4.   Facts show the agreement alleged.

5.   Facts shown to exist constitute an estoppel and appellees
can not take advantage of their own wrong, and if appellee's
contention is correct, a fraud was perpetrated to which they were
a party and they are not entitled to relief therefrom.

J. D. MOCQUOT for appellees.

1.   S. H. Cassidy & Co., nor their trustee in bankruptcy had
any personal interest in the tobacco until the partnership was
wound up, and the surviving partners were entitle to wind it up
without the intervention of the bankrupt court.

2.   The claim of appellees was not a provable debt against
S. H. Cassidy & Co., on October 16 1903, and was not affected by
their discharge in bankruptcy. In re Pettingill & Co., 137 Fed.
Rep., 143; In re Imperial Brewing Co., 143, Fed Rep, 579; Rawin
v. Maguire, 15 Wall 549.

OPINION OF THE COURT   BY JUDGE CARROLL—Reversing.

In November, 1902 the appellants W. S. and J. B.
Dycus and S. H. Cassidy, now deceased composing
the firm of S. H. Cassidy & Co., entered into a contract

with the appellees Brown and Bloom "for the purpose of buying and selling tobacco on joint account
during the season of 1902-1903." By the terms of the
contract Cassidy & Co. agreed to buy tobacco in the
country to be paid for with money furnished by
Brown and Bloom and ship the same to the Western
District Warehouse Company at Paducah for sale
by Brown and Bloom. Cassidy & Co. were to receive
60 cents per hundred pounds as compensation for
buying and delivering the tobacco. And it further
stipulated: "When all the tobacco prized and delivered under this contract shall have been sold, and all
legitimate expenses of the business have been paid
(said expenses to include commission of sixty cents
per hundred pounds paid S. H. Cassidy & Company,
all fire and marine insurance on tobacco, interest on
all money used in the business, freight, drayage and
regular warehouse charges for selling said tobacco)
then all profits or losses arising from this business
shall be divided as follows—One-half to Brown and
Bloom and one-half to. Cassidy & Company." After
this contract was entered into, Cassidy & Co. bought
a large quantity of tobacco with money furnished by
Brown and Bloom, and shipped the tobacco to the
warehouse named in the contract. In October, 1903,
Cassidy & Co. composed of the members above mentioned, filed their petition in bankruptcy, and in Feb-
rūary, 1904, settled with their creditors on the basis
of 25 per cent. of their claims, which settlement was
approved by the bankrupt court, and thereupon the
firm was discharged and acquitted of its indebtedness.
Brown and Bloom were not mentioned in the bankruptcy proceedings as creditors of Cassidy & Co., nor
was any part of the tobacco in the possession of
Brown and Bloom scheduled among the assets of the

firm, although at that time a large quantity of the tobacco purchased by Cassidy & Co., and shipped to Brown and Bloom, was unsold and in the custody of the latter in Paducah. Some time in 1904 or 1905 Brown and Bloom sold all of the tobacco that had been purchased by Cassidy & Co., and it was then ascertained that a loss of about $11,000 had been sustained. In 1908 Brown and Bloom brought this action against W. S. and J. B. Dycus and M. A. Cassidy, the wife of S. H. Cassidy, to recover from them one-half the loss. Upon hearing the case the lower court rendered a judgment in favor of Brown and Bloom for the amount claimed, and it is of this judgment that the appellants complain.

There does not seem to be any serious dispute concerning the fact that the sale of the tobacco resulted in a loss, or the amount of it; but appellants insist that the discharge in bankruptcy released them from all liability to Brown and Bloom growing out of the tobacco transactions and that the judgment against Mrs. M. A. Cassidy was erroneous.

Taking up first the question as to the liability of Mrs. M. A. Cassidy, her connection with the transaction arose in this way: In December, 1907, her husband, S. H. Cassidy, conveyed to her all his real and personal estate, and in consideration thereof she agreed "to meet and comply with all his obligations so far as the property herein conveyed may enable her to do and comply with them." And it was averred in the petition of Brown and Bloom that "the value of the property so conveyed to and received by Mrs. Cassidy was more than sufficient to satisfy the claim of Brown and Bloom, and all other obligations of S. H. Cassidy, and that Mrs. Cassidy took said property in trust for the purpose of discharging the obligation due to Brown and Bloom, as well as all other indebtedness of S. H. Cassidy.'' These averments of the petition were confessed by the failure to deny them. We are therefore of the opinion that, unless there be some other reason for setting aside the judgment against Mrs. Cassidy, the objections to it in her behalf cannot avail her.

Cassidy & Co.—and for purposes of brevity we include Mrs. Cassidy—set up in their answer that prior to their adjudication in bankruptcy they agreed with Brown and Bloom that the latter would take all of the tobacco that had been purchased by Cassidy & Co. for the firm ''for better or worse,'' and pay all debts and expenses growing out of the purchase and sale of the tobacco; and, in consideration of this undertaking on the part of Brown and Bloom, Cassidy & Co. surrendered all interest they had in the tobacco and thereafter did not concern themselves about it, but treated the tobacco as the sole property of Brown and Bloom. They further averred that because of the agreement and transfer of the tobacco to Brown and Bloom it was not mentioned in the schedule filed by them in bankruptcy proceedings. All this was denied in a reply filed by Brown and Bloom. On the issue of fact thus presented the evidence is conflicting, but in the view we have of the case it does not seem important to further consider this phase of it.

As it is conceded that Brown and Bloom had actual notice of the adjudication in bankruptcy, and all the steps taken in the bankruptcy proceedings, they occupied towards the bankrupts the same attitude as if they had been mentioned in the petition in bankruptcy as creditors of Cassidy & Co. Jones v. Walter, 115 Ky. 556, 74 S. W. 249, 24 Ky. Law Rep. 2459.

It follows from this that if the claim of Brown and
Bloom was a "provable" one under the bankrupt act,
they should have presented it in the bankrupt court,
and, failing to do so, are barred by the discharge in
bankruptcy from recovering the amount of it in this
action.   If their claim against Cassidy & Co. was not
a "provable" one in bankruptcy, then neither the
failure to present it nor the discharge affects their
right to recover.   It will thus be seen that the question
narrows down to the single issue of whether or not
the claim of Brown and Bloom was a "provable"
claim aginst Cassidy & Co. at the time the latter filed
their petition in bankruptcy.   That Cassidy & Co.,
on the one side, and Brown and Bloom, on the other,
were partners in this tobacco venture is manifest from
the contract.   This being so it is the contention of
counsel for Brown and Bloom that they were not required to surrender the tobacco to the bankrupt court,
or present to the court any claim on account of probable or possible loss resulting to the partnership, and it
is further insisted that their claim was not a "provable debt."   Bankr. Act. July 1, 1898, c. 541, 30
Stat. 544 (U. S. Comp. St. 1901, p. 3418), provides
in part that: "In the event of one or more but not
all of the members of a partnership being adjudged
bankrupt, the partnership property shall not be administered in bankruptcy unless by consent of the
partner or partners not adjudged bankrupt; but such
partner or partners not adjudged bankrupt shall settle the partnership business as expediously as its nature will permit and account for the interest of the
partner or partners adjudged bankrupt."   And, also:
"Debts of the bankrupt may be proved and allowed
against his estate, which are (1) a fixed liability as
evidenced by a judgment or an instrument in writing

absolutely owing at the time of the filing of the petition against him, whether then payable or not, with any interest thereon which would have been recoverable at that date, or with rebate of interest upon such as were not then payable and did not bear interest; * * * (4) founded upon an open account or upon a contract express or implied; (5) founded upon provable debts reduced to judgments after the filing of the petition and before the consideration of the bankrupt's application for discharge * * * unliquidated claims against the bankrupt may pursuant to application to the court be liquidated in such manner as it shall direct and may thereafter be proved and allowed against his estate.''

In the assumption that Brown and Bloom did not have a provable debt against Cassidy & Co., in October, 1903, we cannot agree. Bloom was asked the following questions: "Q. Tell whether at the time of the filing of the petition in bankruptcy, or the composition that was made, it was known whether or not the partnership venture engaged in between you, Mr. Brown, and the defendants would result in a profit or a loss. A. I expected it to be a loss—in fact, I knew it. Q. Was it known at that time whether there would be a profit or a loss? A. Not exactly; the account was not closed up yet. It was open, and some tobacco had to be sold yet.'' From this it appears that Brown and Bloom knew at the time Cassidy & Co. filed their petition in bankruptcy that there would be a loss, and consequently an indebtedness due by Cassidy & Co. to them, although the amount of it was not then ascertained. The mere fact that the total amount of the loss was not then ascertained, or the fact that it could not be ascertained until all of the tobacco was sold, did not, in the fair meaning of the bankrupt act, leave it all an unprovable debt. Although the precise amount of the loss was not known when the petition in bankruptcy was filed, yet it was susceptible of ascertainment, and might properly be treated as an unliquidated claim, and as such it was the duty of Brown and Bloom to make application to the bankrupt court to have it liquidated, in order that it might when liquidated be proved and allowed against the bankrupt's estate. It only required a sale of the tobacco to fix the exact amount of the loss and consequent liability of Cassidy & Co., and if application had been made to the bankrupt court, it cannot be doubted that the court would have allowed a reasonable time to ascertain the loss, and have entered such orders as would protect the rights of Brown and Bloom in the meantime. The provisions of the bankrupt act in reference to provable debts should be so construed as to permit all debts that come fairly within the meaning of the law to be treated as provable to the end that the purpose of the act in permitting insolvents to be relieved of their debts may be carried out; and, where there is doubt as to whether a debt is provable or not, or as to whether it comes within the meaning of an unliquidated demand that may be made a provable debt, the doubt should be resolved in favor of the provability of the debt, or that it is an unliquidated demand in the meaning of the act, as the case may be.

That there is some confusion and apparent conflict in the cases as to what are and are not provable debts, and as to the proper meaning of the words, "unliquidated claims," must be conceded, but the weight of authority favors the view we have taken. Thus, in the case of In re Hilton (D. C.) 104 Fed. 981, the facts were that in November, 1895, Johnson made a

written contract with the firm of Hilton, Hughes &
Co., in which the bankrupt Hilton was a partner,
whereby Johnson was employed for five years at an
annual salary payable monthly. Johnson continued
in this employment until August, 1896, when the firm
made a general assignment for the benefit of their
creditors. Johnson was paid up to that time, and discharged from further service. In 1899 Hilton became
a voluntary bankrupt and in his schedule Johnson was
named as a creditor for an unliquidated demand arising from the breach of contract, but took no steps to
liquidate his claim for damages. The question afterwards came before the court, in the bankruptcy proceedings, as to whether or not Johnson's claim was a
provable debt.

In considering the case the court said: "It
only remained to liquidate the amount of the damages
arising out of the breach of contract to make it provable like any other debt. Section 63b expressly provides for the proof of such claims to be liquidated 'in
such manner as the court shall direct.' Having made
this provision, it is impossible to suppose that it was
the intent of the act to allow a creditor voluntarily
to withhold such claim from liquidation, and thereby
preserve it as a claim against any subsequently acquired property, and thus practically defeat the object of the bankrupt act as respects the debtor; to free
him from the load of former obligations. Section 17
provides that the discharge shall release the bankrupt
from all his 'provable debts.' A provable debt as here
used means in my judgment any claim that the creditor may make provable through the means provided
by section 63b. * * * I cannot doubt that the intent of these words 'claim provable in bankruptcy'
was to include every claim that under the provisions

of the bankrupt act might be made provable; and the definite provisions of section 63b for making unliquidated claims provable is, I think, precisely what is intended to be included in those words as distinguished from the previous word 'debt.' In my judgment, therefore, this claim as a claim that could be made provable in the manner provided by the act would be barred by the bankrupt's discharge." In the case of In re Stern et al., 116 Fed. 604, 54 C. C. A. 60, it appears that the Manhattan Ice Company entered into contracts with sundry customers to supply them with ice for a fixed period. Before the period expired, the ice company was adjudicated a bankrupt, and the question presented for decision was whether or not the persons with whom it had made contracts to furnish ice had "provable debts" against it for the damages growing out of its failure to fulfill its contract. The court held that they did. In the case of In re Silverman et al. (D. C.) 101 Fed. 219, the facts were that Rosenburg presented a claim against the bankrupt Silverman Bros. for unliquidated damages growing out of a breach of contract for his employment as manager of one of their departments. In considering the case the court, among other things, stated: "The claim being unliquidated, its allowance against the estate is provided for by subsection 'b' of section 63 of the bankrupt act, which provides that 'unliquidated claims against the bankrupt may pursuant to application of the court be liquidated in such manner as it shall direct and may thereafter be proved and allowed against his estate." The claimant was therefore premature in presenting his claim for allowance before the referee, without first making application to the court to direct the manner of liquidating it."

In the light of these authorities, and others that we have examined, we are of the opinion that Brown and Bloom had, within the meaning of the bankrupt act, an unliquidated claim against Cassidy & Co. that was a provable debt, and should have been presented in the bankruptcy proceedings; and, failing to do so, their right of recovery is barred by the discharge. In our opinion section 63b relating to unliquidated claims was intended to, and does, embrace a claim such as Brown and Bloom had at the time the petition in bankruptcy was filed. Their claim arose out of a contract. It was capable of definite ascertainment; and, although unliquidated in the sense that the exact amount they were entitled to recover was not ascertained, it was nevertheless a provable claim. Provable claims are not confined to the debts or liabilities mentioned in subsections 1, 2, 3, 4, and 5 of section 63, but include unliquidated claims arising out of contract that are capable of definite ascertainment, such as the claim we are considering. An unliquidated claim of this character may be barred by the discharge, as well as an ascertained claim due upon a note, judgment, or open account, if the creditor holding such claim fails to present it. A creditor having an unliquidated claim within the meaning of the bankrupt act can no more withhold it, and after the discharge maintain an action upon it, than he could if his claim was founded upon a judgment or a note.

In Dunbar v. Dunbar, 190 U. S. 340, 23 Sup. Ct. 757, 47 L. Ed. 1084, in considering the proper construction of the words "unliquidated claims" in the bankrupt act, the court, said: "In section 63b provision is made for unliquidated claims against the bankrupt, which may be liquidated upon application to the court in such maner as it shall direct, and may thereafter be proved and allowed against his estate. This paragraph 'b,' however, adds nothing to the class of debts that might be proved under paragraph 'a' of the same section. Its purpose is to permit an unliquidated claim, coming within the provisions of section 63a, to be liquidated as the court should direct. We do not think that by the use of the language in section 63a it was intended to permit proof of contingent debts or liabilities or demands, the valuation or estimation of which it was substantially impossible to prove." In Crawford v. Burke, 195 U. S. 176, 25 Sup. Ct. 9, 49 L. Ed. 147, the court upon the same subject said: "As to paragraph 'b,' two constructions are possible: It may relate to all unliquidated demands, or only to such as may arise upon such contracts, express or implied, as are covered by paragraph 'a.' Certainly paragraph 'b' does not embrace debts of an unliquidated character, and which in their nature are not susceptible of being liquidated." See also, Brown v. United Button Co. 149 Fed. 48, 79 C. C. A. 70, 8 L. R. A. (N. S.) 961; 9 Am. & Eng. Ann. Cas. 445.

Although the precise question presented in the case before us was not involved in the cases mentioned, the reasoning of the court supports the view we have taken.

Nor does the fact that the claim grew out of a partnership venture which must be settled add anything to the strength of the argument presented by Brown and Bloom that it was not necessary to assert their claim in the bankrupt court. It may be conceded that Brown and Bloom had the right to settle the partnership business, but it is also manifest that it was their duty to report the settlement made to the bankrupt court. If a profit had been realized on the

tobacco, the creditors of the bankrupts were entitled
·to their interest in it; and if a loss resulted, the partners sustaining the loss had the right to present their
claim against the bankrupt's estate.   It cannot be
successfully maintained that, because the bankrupt
act permits those members of a partnership who are
not adjudged bankrupt to administer the assets, it
was intended to release so much of such assets as
might belong to the bankrupt partner from the payment of his debts.   It seems evident that the purpose
of the act, in giving to the members of the partnership
not adjudged bankrupt the right to settle up the partnership affairs, was to protect their interest, and not
fo defeat the rights of the creditors of the bankrupt
partner.   And in our opinion when some members of
a partnership are adjudged bankrupt, and the other
partners take charge of the partnership assets, it is
their duty to report to the bankrupt court all steps
taken by them in the winding up of the partnership
business, and to report to the court the amounts received in settlement of the partnership affairs.
Brown and Bloom, however, did not pay any attention to the bankrupt proceedings, or make any report
of the partnership affairs.   Their failure to do this
lends support to the contention of Cassidy & Co. that
they were to take the tobacco and relieve Cassidy &
Co. from all liability on account thereof.   But, without further extending this opinion, we may conclude
by saying that, as Cassidy & Co. were discharged
from their indebtedness to Brown and Bloom, the
judgment against them was erroneous.

Wherefore the judgment is reversed, with directions to dismiss the petition.

Nunn, J., not sitting.

CASE 20.—ACTION BY B. C. HICKS AGAINST A. S. WINSTEAD
AND OTHERS.—October 26, 1909.

Winstead, &c. v. Hicks

Appeal from Henderson Circuit Court.

J. W. HENSON, Circuit Judge.

Judgment for plaintiff, defendants appeal.—Affirmed.

1. Sheriffs and Constables—Levy on and Sale of Exempt Property—Action on Bond—Petition—Sufficiency.—In an action
    on an indemnity bond given to the sheriff by an execution
    plaintiff, allegations of the petition that the two horses
    levied on and sold were plaintiff's only work beasts, and
    that by such levy and sale he was deprived of their use. etc.,
    that he did not have sufficient provisions, including bread
    stuff, and animal food, to sustain his family for more than
    one week, nor sufficient provender to sustain his live stock
    for more than one week, nor any other personal property,
    wages, money, or growing crops out of which the said provisions or provender could be provided, were sufficient to
    sustain a judgment for plaintiff, as against the objections
    that plaintiff did not state that the horses were his only work
    beasts at the time of the levy, or that he had not then other
    personal property not disclosed sufficient to have made up
    the deficit in his provision.

2. Pleading—Construction—Aider by Verdict or Judgment.—
    While, on demurrer and before judgment, pleadings are strictly construed against the pleader, after verdict or judgment
    they are liberally construed to sustain the judgment, and at
    that time mere formal defects will be held cured.

3. Exemptions—Time for Claim.—While a judgment debtor may
    waive his exemption. the statute does not require him to notify the sheriff before the execution sale or before the execution of the indemnity bond that he claims the proprty as
    exempt.

Winstead, &c. v. Hicks.

4. Sheriffs and Constables—Indemnity to Sheriff—Action—Notice of Exemption—Sufficiency of Evidence.—In an action by an execution defendant on an indemnity bond given the sheriff, evidence held to support a finding that plaintiff notified the sheriff that he claimed the property levied on to be exempt.

5. Trover and Conversion—Measure of Damages.—The general rule is that in trover the measure of damages is the value of the property, with interest (in the discretion of the jury) from the time of its conversion.

6. Detinue—Measure of Damages.—In detinue the measure of damages is, as a general rule, the value of the use of the property, plus its deterioration and the necessary expense of recovering it.

7. Sheriffs and Constables—Indemnity to Sheriff—Effect—Recovery of Exempt Property Siezed.—While the effect of the giving of an indemnity bond to an officer holding an execution is, if the surety is good, to restrict the right of action for damages for the conversion of the property under the execution to an action on the bond, the makers being substituted in liability for the sheriff, the execution of the bond does not prevent the debtor claiming as exempt the property levied on from maintaining an action against the sheriff or the purchaser to recover the property as in detinue.

8. Sheriffs and Constables—Levy on and Sale of Exempt Property—Action on Indemnity Bond—Measure of Damages.—In an action by the execution defendant on an indemnity bond given the sheriff, the measure of damages for levying on and selling exempt property is the same as in trover, viz., the value of the property, with interest (in the discretion of the jury) from the time of its conversion.

9 Exemptions—Levy on and Sale of Exempt Property—Action to Recover—Measure of Damages.—In an action by an execution debtor against the sheriff or the purchaser at execution sale of exempt property to recover the property, the measure of damages is the same as in detinue. viz., the value of the use of the property, plus its deterioration and the necessary expense of recovering it.

10. Set-Off and Counterclaim—Subject-Matter—Wrongful Levy and Sale—Action on Indemnity Bond.—In an action by an execution debtor on an indemnity bond given the sheriff for damages for the levy on and sale of exempt property, it was error to adjudge that the damages be set off by the amount of the original judgment.

YEAMAN & YEAMAN for appellants.

POINTS AND AUTHORITIES.

1. The pleadings do not support the judgment. The appellant, sued only for the value of provisions and provender not on hand.

2. An execution defendant must notify either the sheriff or the plaintiff of his claim of exemptions. He cannot stand by and see the property sold, and then claim his exemptions. Commonwealth, for &c., v. Burnett, 19 Ky. L. R., 1856:; 44 S.W. 967.

3. 'The measure of damages for the wrongful conversion of personal property, is its value at the time of the conversion, plus interest in the discretion of the jury. The plaintiff cannot recover the value of the property and also the value of its use. Sutherland on Dam. Vol. 1, p. 173-4; Vol. 3, p. 480-490; Newcomb-Buchanan Co., v. Baskett, 14 Bush, 680; Rogers v. Twyman, 22 Ky. L. R. 40; White, &c., Co. v. Connor, 111 Ky. 830.

4. The case of Manning v. Grinstead, 28 Ky. L. R. 787, 90 S. W. 553 was where the property itself was recovered, and compensation allowed for the detention.

R. G. HILL and VANCE & HEILBRUNNER for appellee.

We submit that if interest on the value of the horse is all that can be recovered, then not only is there nothing to deter an aggressive plaintiff and officer from making an illegal levy and sale, but the defendant suffers beyond the remedy given to him by law.

He must be made whole for the loss done to him and he is only made whole with a judgment for the value of his work beasts and in addition thereto a judgment for the value of their use.

OPINION OF THE COURT, BY JUDGE O'REAR—Affirming.

An execution issued upon a judgment in favor of Winstead against Hicks was levied upon two horses and a buggy, the property of the latter. A bond of indemnity was required by the sheriff before selling the property, which was executed by the appellants. Thereupon the property was sold. This suit is upon that bond by the execution defendant, who claims that he was a housekeeper of this commonwealth, with a family, that those were his only work beasts, and that he had not the provision for his family and the provender for his exempt live stock allowed by law, and consequently all the property was exempt from sale under the execution. He laid his damages at $525. The case was submitted to the judge without a jury, who, upon a separate finding of the law and facts, adjudged that the live stock was specifically exempt; that the buggy was exempt under the provision of the statute allowing other personal property in lieu of exempt provision and provender not on hand, fixing the value of the exempt articles at $300, and finding the damages to be $125. The latter sum was arrived at by deducting from the value of the use of the live stock sold the reasonable cost of keeping it for the time the defendant was deprived of it by its seizure and sale under the execution.

The appellants complain of the trial court's conclusion of law and fact, as follows:

First. That the petition was not sufficient to allow a recovery for the animals. It is claimed the plaintiff did not specifically state that they were his only work beasts at the time of the levy, or that he had not then other personal property not disclosed sufficient to have made up the deficit in his provision. The allegations of the petition are that "the said two horses seized, levied on, and sold were his only work beasts, and by the said illegal levy and sale he has been deprived of the use and services of said horses from the 7th of May, 1908, the date of said seizure, whereby he has been damaged as set out," etc. As to the exempt provisions and provender, the allegation is: "That he did not have sufficient provisions, including bread stuff and animal food, to sustain his family for more than one week; nor did he have sufficient provender suitable to live stock to sustain his live stock for more than one week;

nor did he have any other personal property,
wages, money, or growing crops out of which
the said provisions or provender could be provided.'' These allegations are sufficient, but, if not,
after verdict or judgment in plaintiff's behalf, are
sufficient to sustain the judgment. The rule is pleadings are liberally construed after verdict or judgment
to sustain the judgment, whereas on demurrer and before judgment they are strictly construed against the
pleader. Any formal defect in pleadings is deemed
cured by the verdict or judgment. Hill v. Ragland,
Sheriff, 114 Ky. 209, 70 S. W. 634, 24 Ky. Law Rep.
1053; Dunekake v. Beyer, 79 S. W. 209, 25 Ky. Law
Rep. 2002; Ashland, etc., R. Co. v. Lee, 82 S. W. 368,
26 Ky. Law Rep. 700; Harmon v. Thompson, 84 S.
W. 569, 27 Ky. Law Rep. 186.

Second. It is not now denied that Hicks was a
housekeeper, entitled to the exemptions claimed; nor
that the property was of less value than that found
by the court. But it was made a ground for the motion for a new trial in the lower court, and for a reversal here that the evidence did not justisfy the
finding of the court of the fact that the execution defendant notified the sheriff before the sale, or before
the execution of the bond of indemnity, that he
claimed the property as exempt. The statute does
not impose upon a debtor that duty. True, he may
expressly or by his conduct waive the exemption.
But, unless he does so, it is not perceived by what authority the court could impose upon him a condition
upon which his statutory exemption was made to depend different from or in addition to what the statute
had imposed. The courts have taken two views of
the question whether the debtor must claim his exemption to be entitled to it. The principal difference

arises out of the difference in the phraseology of the statutes. In some of the states the condition is ·expressly or impliedly imposed in the statute creating the exemption that the debtor must claim it before it will be allowed to him. In those states it is held he must claim the exemption at or before the time of sale. Freeman on Executions, Sec. 211. But in others the exemption is absolute, and the defendant need not expressly claim it in order to avail himself of his statutory right. Id. Sec. 212, and cases collected. Our statute belongs to the latter class. In the early history of the statutes of exemption from execution the decisions were not in harmony on the subject, but modernly the question seems to have become settled in conformity with the foregoing statement, which seems to us to be in accord with the spirit and reason of the legislation. In this state that rule was applied in Stirman v. Smith, 10 Ky. Law Rep. 665, 10 S. W. 131.

In McGee v. Anderson, 1 B. Mon. 187, 36 Am. Dec. 570, it was held that the execution defendant would be put to his election to claim one of three or more horses (where only two were exempt), one having been levied· on by the sheriff under execution. This case seems to be the same in principle in its main aspect as the case relied on by appellants, viz., Commonwealth for the benefit of Breef v. Burnett, 44, S. W. 966, 19 Ky. Law Rep. 1836. In that opinion, in discussing an instruction properly refused (but not copied in the opinion), the court observed: "Instruction No. 9 was properly refused for the reason it was the duty of appellant on or before the day of sale to make known to the officer or plaintiff in the execution that he (appellant) did not have on hand the provisions allowed by law to himself and family, and that

he claimed a sufficiency of the live stock suitable for
that purpose as exempt from levy and sale. These
facts being peculiarly within his own knowledge, and
could not have been known to the officer or the plaintiff in the execution, it was his duty to make that fact
known, if it was a fact, in time to assert any claim.''
The above quotation, as will be observed, was with
reference to property claimed as exempt in lieu of
specific exempt property not on hand. Just what instruction No. 9 was that was then rejected we do not
now know. The facts shown in the opinion were that
the execution defendant probably had other property
out of which he might have claimed his exemption
in lieu of that not on hand in specie. In such instance
the execution defendant ought not to put the plaintiff
and officer to the hazard of guessing at what the defendant had in his larder. Failing to apprise them,
or one of them, when he had opportunity to do so,
might justly be regarded as a waiver of his right to
claim such property. That opinion did not overrule
Stirman v. Smith, supra, and did not advert to the
prevailing rule deduced from the authorities elsewhere. Harmonizing it with McGee v. Anderson and
Stirman v. Smith, we must hold that it was intended
to apply only to those instances where the execution
defendant was put upon his election, and, failing to
elect, would be deemed to have waived his right. Appellee Hicks practiced this case by the opinion in
Commonwealth, etc., v. Burnett, supra. He attempted to show that he gave the sheriff notice of his claim
to the exemption. He testified that he lived some distance from the county seat; that he had a young lady,
who was operator of the long-distance telephone line
between his point and the county seat, to call up the
sheriff at the county seat, and notify him that he

(Hicks) claimed the property as exempt, and advised that he protect himself by a bond of indemnity. He further testified that he did not personally use the telephone because he was slightly hard of hearing; but that he stood by and heard the operator repeat the message over the telephone to the sheriff. The sheriff testified that he remembered having been called over the long-distance telephone on the subject of that execution, and that the talking from the other end of the line was a woman's voice; that he did not remember what was said, whether a lien was claimed by some one or whether the property was claimed as exempt. He at first testified that it was the latter, but on cross-examination retracted so far as to say that he had not sufficient recollection on that point to state, but was rather of the impression that it was concerning a lien. He said he had been called but once on the subject. While not conclusive, this evidence persuades the mind that the conversation related by the plaintiff was had. The sheriff corroborates the plaintiff as to the fact of the conversation, and the time and manner of it. There was no testimony to the contrary. There was a mortgage lien on the property, but it was not contended that the lienholder or any one other than Hicks called the sheriff to notify him of the fact. It is a reasonable inference that the plaintiff, even if he mentioned the mortgage, also mentioned his own claim of exemption. The circuit judge believed his testimony, and we find no ground for rejecting it.

Third. The general rule is that in an action of trover the measure of damages is the value of the property, with interest (in the discretion of the jury) from the time of its conversion (Sanders v. Vance, 7 T. B. Mon. 209, 18 Am. Dec. 167), while in actions of detinue the criterion is the value of the use of the property, plus its deterioration and necessary expense in recovering it. Exceptional circumstances under proper averments admit of a somewhat different criterion in the latter cases. Manning v. Grinstead, 90 S. W. 553 28 Ky. Law Rep. 789; Schulte v. L. & N. R. R., 108 S. W. 941, 33 Ky. Law Rep. 31.

Although this is an action on the bond of indemnity, it is properly classified as belonging to that of actions of trover at the common law. The effect of the execution of the bond is, if the surety is good, to restrict the right of action for damages for the conversion of the property under the execution to an action on the bond. The makers of the bond are substituted in liability for the sheriff. But the execution of the bond does not prevent the debtor claiming the property levied on as exempt from maintaining an action against the sheriff who has levied upon it or the purchaser to recover the property as in detinue. Bethel v. Van Meter, 9 Ky. Law Rep. 331; Hoskins v. J. M. Robinson Co., 101 Ky. 667, 42 S. W. 113, 19 Ky. Law Rep. 877.

In neither instance is the character of the action, whether on the bond or against the officer or the purchaser or the plaintiff in the execution, different from the common-law actions of trover and detinue. It follows that the measure of damages allowed in those cases from ancient times and consistently is the correct measure upon the bond. Sections 492, 493, Sedgwick on Damages; Freeman v. Luckett, 2 J. J. Marsh, 390; Daniel v. Holland, 4 J. J. Marsh, 18; Justice v. Mendell, 14 B. Mon. 12.

In allowing a recovery of $125 for the use of the horses, and in addition to their value, the trial court erred in this case. But the court went further, and adjudged that the damages of $125 be set off by the debt of $100, for which the plaintiff in the execution had judgment against the defendant (appellee). That, too, was error. Mulliken v. Winter, 2 Duv. 256, 87 Am. Dec. 495; Collett v. Jones, 7 B. Mon. 586.

The plaintiff (appellee) should have had judgment for the value of the exempt property and interest, but no more. The result of the judgment appealed from is not substantially different from what it would have been had the court pursued the correct course in estimating the damages.

The original judgment of appellant against the appellee is not affected by the judgment appealed from.

Affirmed.

CASE 21.—ACTION BY THE LOUISVILLE DRY GOODS COMPANY AGAINST J. W. LANMAN AND OTHERS.— October 26, 1909.

Louisville Dry Goods Co. v. Lanman

Appeal from Mercer Circiut Court.

W. C. BELL, Circuit Judge.

Judgment dismissed and plaintiff appeals.—Reversed.

1. Sales—Remedies of Seller—Fraud of Buyer.—If an insolvent, buying goods of plaintiffs, mortgaged the entire stock in or to be in his store, to secure a bank holding his notes and a surety thereon to the exclusion of his other creditors, plaintiffs could avoid the sales on the ground of the buyers' actual fraud in buying without intention or means of paying for the goods, and in intending that they should, the moment they came into his possession, pass to preferred creditors, and retain the goods by detinue or claim and delivery under the Code, or could sue for damages for the deceit and could pursue the additional remedy of sequestrating the debtor's property for payment of his debts under the act of 1856 relating to conveyances by insolvents in contemplation of in-

solvency, or could proceed against the debtor in involuntary bankruptcy proceedings in the United States ,court, if, when they learned of the deceit, that court had power under the limitation of time, to grant them relief.

2. Bankruptcy—Debts Discharged—Liability Growing Out of Fraud.—Under Bankr. Act July 1, 1898, c. 541, Sec. 17, subd. 4, 30 Stat. 550 (U. S. Comp. St. 1901, p. 3428), excluding debts created by fraud from the release of the discharge in bankruptcy, the debt of the insolvent, incurred by purchasing goods on credit with the intention of setting over the goods to certain other favored persons leaving nothing with which he could pay for them or out of which the sellers could make their debt would not be released by a discharge.

3. Bankruptcy—Remedy of Seller—Obtaining Personal Judgment Against a Buyer Adjudicated a Bankrupt.— The federal court being unable to discharge the buyer from the debt, plaintiffs could pursue him in the state courts and obtain a personal judgment against him, though he had been adjudged bankrupt, upon which, after the federal court had exercised its jurisdiction, the writ of fieri facias might issue; but, pending the proceedings in bankruptcy, the state court should stay its execution until the bankruptcy case is finally adjudicated.

4. Bankruptcy—Construction of Statutes.—Act of 1856 (Ky. St. Secs. 1910-1917), providing that a mortgage by a debtor in contemplation of insolvency and to prefer certain creditors shall operate as an assignment of all his property for the benefit of all creditors, except as provided, such transfers to be under the control of equity, etc., is not a bankrupt or insolvency statute.

5. Bankruptcy—Preferential Mortgages by Insolvent.—Ky. St. Sec. 1910, makes a mortgage by a debtor in contemplation of insolvency and with design to prefer creditors an assignment of all the debtor's property for benefit of all creditors, except as provided. Section 1911 (section 2105) gives equity control of perferential mortgages made by a debtor in contemplation of insolvency upon petition of an interested person within six months after the transfer is lodged for record or the property is delivered. Bankr. Act July 1, 1898, c. 541, Sec. 3a (2), 30 Stat. 546 (U. S. Comp. St. 1901, p. 3422), makes the transfer while insolvent of any portion of his property by a debtor to his creditor with intent to prefer the creditor an act of bankruptcy, and provides that a petition may be filed against an insolvent who has committed an act of bankruptcy within four months after commission of the act. Sec. 60b makes a preference given four months before

Louisville Dry Goods Co. v. Lanman.

filing a petition voidable by the trustee. Held, that the
federal statute does not invalidate either a perferential mortgage by an insolvent debtor or his voluntary deed of assignment, and if such mortgage is not attacked within the time
which will give the bankrupt court jurisdiction, or if the assignor is not proceeded against by his creditors or does not
file petition to be adjudged a bankrupt within the four months
allowed by the federal statute, the instruments may be enforced and the parties thereto granted appropriate relief by
the state court when invoked within six months, and, where
the state court has been invoked and has taken jurisdiction
and possession of the property, it may proceed to a final adjudication, though the federal court may also have taken
jurisdiction of the bankrupt and his affairs.

6. Bankruptcy—Jurisdiction of State Court.—The state court,
having taken jurisdiction, could adjudge a recovery against
the debtor in personam in favor of the creditor against whom
the preference was made, staying the execution until his application for discharge in bankruptcy has been acted upon
by the federal court.

C. E. RANKIN for appellant.

AUTHORITIES CITED.

Kentucky Statutes, 1910-1911, &c.; Ebersole &c. v. Adams 10th
Bush 83; Downer &c. v. Porter &c., 116 Ky., 422, 76 S. W. 135;
Heidrich v. Silva, 89 Ky., 422, 11 R. 645; Linthicum v. Fenley, 11th
Bush, 131; Eblen v. Brooks &c., 106 S. W.. 308; Collier on Bank-
ruptcy, 6th Edition, 1907, pages 292, 145, 539, 901, 951; Bankrupt
Law of 1867; Bankrupt Law of 1898; Bankrupt Law of 1898, sec.
11; In re Girdes, 4 Am. B. R. 346, 102 Federal 318; Matter of
Bay City Irrigation Co., 14 Am. B. R., 370, 135 Fed. 850; In re Eng-
lish, 11 Am. B. R. (C. C. A.) 127 Federal, 940; In re Price, 1 Am.
B. R., 602, 92 Federal, 987; Chattanooga Nat. Bank v. Rome Iron
Co., 4 Am. B. R., 441, 102 Fed. 516; Thompson v. Fairbanks, 13
Am. B. R., 437, 445, 196 U. S., 516.

OPINION OF THE COURT BY JUDGE O'REAR—Reversing.

J. W. Lanman was a merchant doing business at
Cornishville, in Mercer county. The petition alleges:
That the plaintiffs were wholesale merchants, and had
sold him bills of merchandise from April to June,

1908, amounting to $473.82, and from June 23, 1908, to July 28, 1908, of $50.46; that on April 28, 1908, the defendant Lanman, being then insolvent, and with the design to prefer some of his creditors to the exclusion of the others, executed a mortgage to the Union Bank of Cornishville, Ky., upon a storehouse and lot situated in Cornishville, "and the stock of merchandise now within or to be within said storeroom, consisting of dry goods, boots, shoes, notions, and whatever articles there may be therein, including furniture and fixtures," to secure the bank in the sums of $1,495.75 on a note due March 8, 1908, $1,323 on a note due June 4, 1908, and $148.42 overdraft then due the bank; that these debts were in existence prior to the execution of the mortgage, and were secured by a prior pledge of 30 shares of the stock of the bank as collateral; that one S. P. De Baun had since the filing of the suit been subrogated to the rights of the bank by an assignment of the mortgage to him by the bank; and that the mortgage was fraudulent, and executed with the design to prefer the bank and De Baun. It is also alleged that De Baun was bound as surety on the original notes to the bank, and that the mortgage covers all the property of the mortgagee. The mortgage was acknowledged on April 28, 1908, but was not recorded until July 28, 1908. This suit was begun by the filing of the petition and issual of summons on January 14, 1909. The summons was executed by personal service on Lanman, De Baun, and the Union Bank of Cornishville on January 16, 1909. On January 27, 1909, the day on which an appearance and answer were due, the defendants filed a joint answer which they term a "plea in bar," stating that on January 25, 1909, the defendant J. W. Lanman filed in the District Court of the United States for the Eastern

District of Kentucky his petition in bankruptcy, that said Lanman was thereupon on that day adjudged a bankrupt by said court, and that the affairs of the bankrupt had been referred by that court to its referee in bankruptcy. Upon that showing they prayed to be dismissed. A demurrer was filed to the answer by the plaintiffs. The circuit court overruled the demurrer. The plaintiffs declined to plead further, and their petition was dismissed. The plaintiffs have prosecuted this appeal from the judgment.

We have concluded that the judgment is erroneous, when considered upon either of several grounds. The allegations of the petition in this case are not denied. They are confessed as true. It follows that J. W. Lanman was insolvent when he gave the mortgage, and inferentially, when he bought the goods for which he is sued in this case; that he designed by the mortgage to prefer the bank and De Baun to the exclusion in whole of his other creditors. What were the rights of the plaintiffs when they filed this suit? Depending upon the whereabouts of the goods, they had a choice of four courses open to them: (1) To avoid the sales to Lanman, on the ground of his actual fraud in buying the goods without intention or means of paying for them, but intending that they should the moment they came into his possession pass to his preferred creditor, the bank, or his favored surety at the bank, De Baun. This was such fraud as in law, at the election of the sellers, would have avoided the sale, and they could have regained their goods by detinue, or, what is the same practice under our Code, an action of claim and delivery; but perhaps the goods had been disposed of to innocent purchasers before the plaintiffs learned of the fraud. At any rate, it was at the election of the plaintiffs whether they pursued that

remedy, or (2) to proceed in an action at law to recover the value of the goods from the fraudulent vendee—not upon the contracts of sale, but upon the deceit practiced upon them. And (3) the plaintiffs might
pursue the additional remedy afforded by the laws
of this state to sequestrate the debtor's property for
the payment of his debts under the act of 1856 (Ky.
St. Secs. 1910-1917), or (4) proceed against him in
involuntary bankruptcy proceedings in the United
States District Court. The last-named course would
depend, for its efficacy, upon whether, at the time the
plaintiff's learned of the deceit and of the debtor's
transfer of his property, the United States court had
the power, under the limitation of time prescribed by
the act of Congress, to grant them full relief. These
remedies are at the election of the creditors, the vendees. The plaintiffs elected to sue in the state court
to pursue the second and third of the remedies outlined above. The question is: Does National Bankruptcy Act July 1, 1898, c. 541, 30 Stat. 544 (U. S.
Comp. St. 1901, p. 3418), give the United States
courts exclusive jurisdiction of the affairs and property of a voluntary bankrupt under the circumstances recited above? It is remarked that the existing act
defines more clearly the demarcation of the jurisdictions of the federal and state courts, and shows more
disposition to not interfere with the local jurisdiction
of the latter than did Act March 2, 1867, c. 176, 14
Stat. 517. Certain it is that Congress did not intend
to aid fraud in any of the provisions of the act. In
truth, the fraudulent were placed beyond its intended
benefits, and held to the strictest accountability when
their acts came within the jurisdiction of the courts of
the United States.

No debtor can be discharged in bankruptcy of a liability which grows out of his fraud.   Section 17, Act
1898. It was held in Classen v. Schoeneman, 80 Ill.
304, and Ames v. Moir, 130 Ill. 582, 22 N. E. 535, that
if a debtor buys goods for cash on delivery, obtains
possession of them without payment and immediately
ships them beyond reach of the seller, and then
refuses to pay, his conduct is such as to make the
debt a fraudulent one within the meaning of the bankrupt law. It is equally fraudulent, in law and morals,
for one to buy goods with a positive intention not to
pay for them, for if such intention were known to the
vendor he certainly would not sell. "Its suppression
therefore is a legal fraud." Benjamin on Sales, 442,
and cases collected by that author. The cases hold
that such design may be inferred from the conduct
and circumstances of the vendee. It is admitted here
that he was insolvent, and intended to set over to certain favored persons the very goods he purchased
from the plaintiffs on credit, leaving nothing with
which he could pay for them, or out of which they
could make their debt. That is very black fraud. As
the United States District Court could not have discharged Lanman from the plaintiff's debts created by
his fraud, they were at liberty to pursue him in the
state courts, and obtain a personal judgment against
him, even though he had been adjudged bankrupt, upon which, after the federal court had exercised its jurisdiction, the writ of fieri facias might issue; but,
pending the proceedings in bankruptcy, the state
court should have stayed its execution until the United States courts had finally adjudicated the bankrupt's case.

But there is still another branch of this case, of more
importance than the one just discussed. That is the

right of the state court to proceed to a judgment in
rem as against the property embraced in the mortgage and as affecting the bank and De Baun. The
determination of that question involves the nature of
the mortgage as it affected the debtor's property
covered by it, and the rights of the plaintiffs created
by that instrument in relation to that property. The
statute of Kentucky (sec. 1910, Ky. Stat.), commonly
known as the "Act of 1856," concerning the conveyance by insolvents in contemplation of insolvency, is
not a bankrupt or insolvency statute. Ebersole v.
Adams, 10 Bush, 83; Downer v. Porter, 116 Ky. 423,
76 S. W. 135, 25 Ky. Law Rep. 571.

It does not declare that the transaction shall be
void. It operates independently of motives of fraud
by the parties. It is voidable only for a specific purpose, at the instance only of creditors of the debtor
making the mortgage or conveyance, and then only if
they take action to that end in a court of equity within
six months from the execution or recordation of the
instrument. The effect of such mortgage or conveyance, if so attacked, is made by the statute to operate
as voluntary assignment of all the debtor's property
for the benefit of all his creditors. It is precisely as if
he had executed voluntarily a deed of trust in behalf
of all his creditors, conveying the title to all his property (except exemptions) to a trustee upon the express trust that the latter would sell it and pay the
proceeds pro rata to his creditors. Linthicum v. Fenley, 11 Bush, 131.

It is true the act of Congress of 1898 makes both
a preference by an insolvent debtor of some one or
more creditors to the exclusion of others, the execution of a voluntary deed of assignment, acts of bankruptcy, but, unless they are proceeded on as such

within four months from the time when filed for record, they are not affected by the bankrupt statute.
Sections 3 and 60, Act Cong. 1898. But the federal
statute does not prohibit or invalidate either a preferential mortgage by an insolvent debtor, or his voluntary deed of assignment. If such mortgage is not attacked within the time which will give the bankrupt
court jurisdiction of the matter, or if the assignor is
not proceeded against by his creditors, or does not
file his petition to be adjudged a bankrupt within the
four months allowed by the federal statute, those instruments may be enforced, and the parties to them
granted all appropriate relief by the state courts. Or,
further, if the jurisdiction of the state court has been
invoked, and the latter has taken jurisdiction and
possession of the property, it may proceed to a final
adjudication of the rights of the parties, although the
United States District Court may also have taken
jurisdiction of the bankrupt and his affairs. Linthicum v. Fenley, supra; Louisville Trust Co. v. Com-
ingor, 184 U. S. 18, 22 Sup. Ct. 293, 46 L. Ed. 413.

It was held in Linthicum v. Fenley that the filing
of the petition in the state court gave that court possession of the res, and entitled it to proceed with the
case. However, there can scarcely be apprehended
any conflict of jurisdiction in this matter, for, while
the state court had jurisdiction of the subject-matter
and parties when the suit was begun down there, the
federal court did not have when the bankrupt filed
his petition in that court Janury 25, 1909, more than
four months after the mortgage had been recorded in
the proper office of registry. While then the debtor
may have been adjudged a bankrupt, and the United
States District Court had jurisdiction of his
estate, it would have had to administer it,

except as to conveyances and incumbrances executed or suffered within four months of the filing of the petition in that court, subject to existing liens and conveyances. Neither the act of Congress nor the statute of this state (the act of 1856) make a preferential conveyance by an insolvent debtor void, or deem it a fraud. Each statute gives to it, if the remedy is invoked within the prescribed times, the effect of a voluntary assignment by the debtor for the benefit of all his creditors. The state statute allows two months more of time in which the conveyance may be attacked.

While this transaction was such that the bankrupt court might have acquired jurisdiction of it, and have administered the estate embraced as if the mortgage did not exist, yet it did not within the time when it might, consequently the trust created by our statute survives unaffected by the provisions of the act of Congress. The state court can and should proceed to execute the trust, by requiring the property to be sold and the proceeds applied to the payment ratably of all the debts of Lanman then in existence. Property since acquired by him and before his application in bankruptcy will be subject alone to the bankrupt proceedings. And, in addition, the state court may adjudge a recovery by the plaintiff against the defendant Lanman in personam, staying the execution till his application for discharge in bankruptcy has been acted on by the United States District Court.

Wherefore the judgment is reversed, and cause remanded for proceedings consistent herewith.

CASE 22.—ACTION BY MARIA LAKES AGAINST T. C. BRON-
STON'S ADMINISTRATOR ON A PROMISSORY
NOTE.—October 27, 1909.

Bronston's Admr. v. Lakes

Appeal from Madison Circuit Court.

J. M. BENTON, Circuit Judge.

Judgment for plaintiff, defendant appeals.—Affirmed.

1. Bills and Notes—Actions—Pleading—Consideration—Necessity of Alleging.—Act 1812 (Laws 1811-12, p. 180, c. 375, substantially readopted in Rev. St. 1852, c. 22, Sec. 2, Gen.. St.
1873, c. 22, Sec. 2, and in Ky. St. 1894, Sec. 471, placing all
writings executed without seal for the payment of money,
etc., upon the same footing with sealed writings containing
like stipulations, abolished the common-law distinction between sealed and unsealed instruments, so that every written
promise imports a consideration, and hence it is not necessary to allege a consideration in an action on a promissory
note.

2. Bills and Notes—Actions—Proof—Consideration—Necessity.
—If, in an action a note, which imports a consideration, the
pleader unnecessarily alleges a consideration, it must be
proved.

3. Bills and Notes—Actions—Burden of Proof—Want of Consideration.—Where, in an action on a note, the consideration therefor is impeached by a verified answer, the burden of
proving want of consideration is on the one alleging it.

J. A. SULLIVAN and S. A. WALLACE for appellants.

CITATION OF AUTHORITIES.

Sec. 471, Ky. Stat.; Lord Mansfield in Pillans v. Van Mierop, 3 Bur-
rows, 1663; Rann v. Hughes, 7 Term R., 350, 4 Bro. P. V. 27; Bliss
on Code Pleadings, sec. 286; Phillips on Code Pleading; Letcher v.
Taylor, 2 Bibb, 585; Hart v. Coran, 3 Bibb, 26; Beauchamp & Yies-
ter v. Bosworth, 3 Bibb, 115; 26 Am. & Eng. Ency. of Law, 529; Pen-

dleton v. State Bank, 2 J. J. Met. 148; Johnson v. State Bank, 5 T.
B. Mon. 119; 26 Am. & Eng. Ency. of Law, 616; Covington v. Mc-
Nickle, 18 Ben Mon., 286; 2 Coke's Institutes, 200; Rosin v. Lid-
gerwood Mfg. Co., 89 N. Y., App. Div. 245; 26 Am. & Eng. Ency.
of Law, 610; Rodes v. Weldy, 46 O. St. 242, 15 A. St. Reps. 584;
Shaw v. Railroad Company, 101 U. S., 565.

SMITH & SMITH for appellee.

OPINION OF THE COURT BY JUDGE CARROLL—Affirming.

The appellee, Maria Lakes, instituted this action
against the administrator of Bronston, alleging that
Bronston "on the 5th day of May, 1892, executed and
delivered to her his promisory note, by which he
promised to pay her on the 2d day of August, 1892, the
sum of $1,000, with interest at the rate of 7 per cent.
per annum from date until paid, that no part of said
debt or interest had been paid, and that the same was
due and owing to her." She filed with and as a part
of her petition the note, reading: "On the 2d day of
August next I promise to pay Maria Lakes one thous-
and dollars with interest at the rate of seven per cent.
per annum from this date until paid, for value received. May 5, 1892. T. C. Bronston."

The only question presented by the record is whether or not a general demurrer filed by Bronston's administrator should have been sustained. In support
of the proposition that the demurrer should have been
sustained, counsel for appellant insist that the petition was fatally defective because it failed to aver the
consideration for the execution of the note. The argument of counsel is: "That at the common law, and
in the absence of a statute to the contrary, every contract, except contracts under seal, which by law dis-
penses with the necessity of a consideration, and ne-

gotiable instruments which under the law merchant
are presumed to have been given for a consideration,
requires a consideration to support it; and as a necessary corollary thereto, it is incumbent upon the
pleader, in declaring upon such a contract, to both
aver and prove a consideration for it." And that unless section 471, Ky. St. changes the rule, the lower
court was in error in overruling a demurrer to the petition. The statute referred to reads: "A seal or
scroll shall in no case be necessary to give effect to
a deed or other writing. All unsealed writings shall
stand upon the same footing with sealed writings,
having the same force and effect, and upon which the
same actions may be founded. But this section shall
not apply to, nor shall it alter, any law requiring the
state or county seal, or the seal of a court, corporation, or notary, to any writing." Counsel correctly
state the common-law rule; and, if it controlled the
practice in cases like this, the argument that the petition in failing to aver a consideration did not state
a cause of action would be well taken. At the common
law there was a marked difference in the effect given
to a sealed and an unsealed instrument of writing. In
the case of deeds and other writings of like import the
seal was as necessary as the signature to make it a
valid and enforceable instrument. Indeed at common
law contracts were classed as simple or sealed contracts. All contracts, whether verbal or reduced to
writing, but not under seal, were simple contracts,
and written contracts under seal were spoken of as
sealed contracts. A contract, although in writing, unless a seal was attached, was treated as a parol contract, and it was necessary in declaring on it to set out
the consideration, and also to prove it. Interesting
information concerning the origin, use, and necessity

for seals upon deeds and written contracts, and the difference between sealed and unsealed instruments, can be found in Blackstone's Commentaries, book 2, p. 305; Chitty's Pleadings, vol. 1, p. 299; Chitty on Contracts, vol 1, p. 5.

In this state, prior to the act of 1812 (Laws 1811-12, p, 180, c 375), the distinction between sealed and unsealed instruments of writing was recognized by our court, and it was held in a number of cases to be necessary, in declaring upon what might be termed a simple contract—that is a verbal contract or a contract in writing but not sealed—to aver the consideration for its execution. Thus in Letcher v. Taylor 2 Bibb 585 a common-law action of debt was brought upon an agreement in writing but without a seal. The declaration contained no averment of the consideration upon which the agreement was made. In ruling that the general demurrer interposed should have been sustained the court said: "The objection to the declaration for want of an averment of the consideration of the agreement is fatal. In a case founded upon a deed or a mercantile instrument as the law in such a case implies a consideration, none is necessary to be stated in the declaration; but in all other cases the consideration, not being implied, must be averred." To the same effect is Hart v. Coram, 3 Bibb, 26; Beauchamp v. Bosworth, 3 Bibb, 116; Jackson v. Berry, 3 Bibb, 85.

But in 1812 the Legislature enacted: "That all writings hereafter executed, without a seal or seals, stipulating for the payment of money or property, or for the performance of any act or acts, duty or duties, shall be placed upon the same footing with sealed writings, containing the like stipulations; receiving the same consideration in all courts of justice;

and to all intents and purposes having the same force
and effect and upon which the same species of actions
may be founded, as if sealed.'' This act was in substance readopted in 1852 as a part of the Revised
Statutes, and may be found in chapter 22, Sec. 2,
was again re-enacted in the adoption of the General
Statutes of 1873, chap. 22, sec. 2, and readopted in
sec. 471, as a part of the Kentucky Statutes, in 1894.
So that since 1812 there has been in effect no distinction between sealed and unsealed instruments 'of
writing. A writing without a seal stands on the
same footing as a writing with a seal. The purpose
and effect of the Act of 1812, as well as
the subsequent legislation upon the same subject, was to abolish in every particular, both as
to substance and procedure, the common law
distinction between sealed and unsealed instruments.
Since the enactment of this legislation, every writing
signed and delivered, whereby the obligor uncondi-
tionally promises to do a specified thing, imports a
sufficient consideration, and it is not necessary in declaring on it to aver that it was executed for a consideration, or to prove that there was any consideration for its execution, unless the consideration is denied. But, if in declaring on a writing that imports
a consideration, thereby dispensing with the averment that it was executed for a consideration, the
pleader unnecessarily sets out the consideration, he
must prove it. Steadman v. Guthrie, 4 Metc. 147; L.
& N. R. Co. v. Literary Society, 91 Ky. 395, 15 S. W.
1065, 13 Ky. Law Rep. 5.

And so the consideration of any writing with or
without a seal may be impeached or denied by a pleading verified by oath, as authorized by section 472 of

the Kentucky Statutes.   But when so denied, the ·burden of proving the want of consideration is placed on the person relying on this plea to defeat the action. Andrews v. Hayden, 88 Ky. 455, 10 Ky. Law Rep. 1049, 11 S. W. 428; Trustees v. Fleming, 10 Bush, 234; Brann v. Brann, 44 S. W. 424, 19 Ky. Law Rep. 1814; Keisewetter v. Kress, 68 S. W.. 633, 24 Ky. Law Rep. 405.

The court properly overruled the demurrer and the judgment is affirmed.

CASE 23.—ACTION BY THE BOARD OF COUNCILMEN OF THE CITY OF FRANKFORT AGAINST MRS. JOHN H. MORGAN TO RECOVER TAXES ON CERTAIN REAL ESTATE.—October 28, 1909.

Morgan v. City of Frankfort

Appeal from Franklin Circuit Court.

R. L. STOUT, Circuit Judge.

Judgment for plaintiff, defendants appeal.—Reversed.

1.   Taxation—Rate of Taxation—Constitutional Limitations.— As Const. Sec. 157, expressly permits the tax rate, exclusive of the school tax in a city of the third class to exceed 75 cents on $100, if necessary to pay the interest on and provide a sinking fund for an indebtedness contracted before the adoption of the Constitution, where it is neither alleged nor proved that the tax the collection of which is resisted, was not levied in part, or at least to the excess over 75 cents and the school tax, to pay the interest on, and provide a sinking fund for, an indebtedness contracted before the adoption of the Constitution, the presumption will not be indulged that the Constitution has been violated.

2.   Taxation—Taxes Barred by Limitation—Recovery.—Where, in an action for taxes, those for certain years were admittedly barred by limitation, it was an error to include them in the judgment.

1. By Section 157 Constitution the tax rate is fixed by the number of population and where it is less than 10,000 the rate is 75 cents on the $100. By population is meant an enumeration of the inhabitants, or persons who dwell permanently in such city. An enumeration that includes the convicts in the state penitentiary, the inmates of the school for feeble minded children and state officials and their families, is too large. Such persons should not be included. Am. & Eng. Ency., 2nd Ed. Vol. 16, page 328.

2. The court takes judicial notice of the Federal census as well as of census taken by authority of law. Am. & Eng. Ency.; Vol. 17, page 898; Zimmerman v. Brooks, 118 Ky.. 85; O'Bryan v. Owensboro, 113 Ky., 680.

3. Where the petition was filed Jan 9th, 1903, and no summons issued thereon till Dec. 6th, 1906, taxes assessed Jan. 10th, 1897, 1898, 1900, and 1901 are barred by limitation of five years from assessment. Butts v. Turner & Lacy, 5 Bush, 435; Trabue v. Sayre, 1 Bush, 129; R. R. v. Smith, 87 Ky.. 501; Louisville v. Maglemary, 107 Ky., 124; Blackburn v. Louisville, 21 R.

The lien for taxes in cities of the third class runs five years from date of assessment. Sec. 3375 Ky. Stat.

WM. CROMWELL for appellee.

AUTHORITIES CITED.

O'Bryan, Clerk v. City Owensboro, 24 Ky. L. R., 471; Ky. Statutes, Secs. 3364 and 3400.

OPINION OF THE COURT BY JUDGE SETTLE—Reversing.

This is the second appeal in this case. The action was brought to recover in behalf of the city of Frankfort taxes alleged to be owing it by appellants on certain real estate for the years 1897 to 1905, inclusive, the payment of which the latter are resisting. On the first appeal this court, among other things, decided that the creation, assessment, and levy of the tax by the city of Frankfort must be presumed to be legal and correct, and that the burden of proving its illegality, if any, is upon the appellees. Board of Councilmen v. Morgan, 33 Ky. Law Rep. 297, 110 S. W. 286.

Various objections are made by appellees to the right of the city to collect the tax sued for, the principal one being that the levy for each year, exclusive of so much thereof as is to be applied to school purposes, is in excess of the limit fixed by section 157, state Constitution. In other words, that the rate of taxation adopted by the city in the levy of the taxes for which judgment is sought is greater than can be levied by a city of less than 10,000 population, and that the population of Frankfort is less than 10,000. Section 157 of the Constitution is as follows: "The tax rate of cities, towns, counties, taxing districts, and other municipalities, for other than school purposes, shall not at any time exceed the following rates upon the value of taxable property therein, viz.: For all towns or cities having a population of 15,000 or more, one dollar and fifty cents on the hundred dollars; for all towns or cities having less than 15,000, and not less than 10,000, one dollar on the hundred dollars; for all towns or cities having less than 10,000, seventy-five cents on the one hundred dollars, and for counties and taxing districts fifty cents on the $100.00; unless it should be necessary to enable such city, town, county or taxing district to pay the interest on, and provide a sinking fund for the indebtedness contracted before the adoption of the Constitution. * * *" Frankfort, by act of the Legislature, has been declared a city of the third class; and, while it may be true that its population is less than 10,000, and its tax rate for the years it is attempting to collect taxes of appellants was, exclusive of the tax for school purposes, in excess of 75 cents on the $100, it nevertheless had the right to exceed that rate, if the tax imposed was necessary to enable it to pay the interest on, and to provide a sinking fund for, an indebtedness contracted by the municipality before the adoption of the present Constitution, for section 157 of that instrument expressly confers such right. It is not alleged in appellant's answer or either amendment thereto, nor does it appear from the evidence, that the tax, the collection of which is resisted, for any of the years claimed was not levied in part, or at least to the extent of the excess over 75 cents and the school tax, for the purpose of paying the interest on and providing a sinking fund to liquidate an indebtedness contracted by the appellee city before the adoption of the Constitution. In the absence of such an allegation and proof we will not indulge the presumption that the Constitution has been violated.

This conclusion makes it unnecessary for us to consider the grounds relied on by appellants to defeat the tax.

It appears, however, that the judgment of the circuit court improperly includes in the recovery the tax for the years 1897, 1898, 1899, 1900, and 1901. As the tax for each of these years was admittedly barred by the statute of limitations, it was error to include them in the judgment.

For this error alone the judgment is reversed, and cause remanded, that the court may enter a judgment to conform to this opinion.

CASE 24.—ACTION BY DUQUESNE DISTRIBUTING CO. AGAINST JOSEPH GREENBAUM AND ANOTHER FOR SLANDER.—October 29; 1909.

Duquesne Distributing Co. v. Greenbaum

Appeal from Jefferson Circuit Court (Common Pleas Branch, Second Division).

THOS. R. GORDON, Judge.

From a judgment of dismissal on demurrer to the petition the plaintiff appeals.—Affirmed.

1. Libel and Slander—Actions—Parties.—Slander can only be committed by an individual, and two or more persons cannot jointly utter the same words, but each speaks for himself, and is liable for his own language, and two or more persons cannot be jointly sued.

2. Partnership—Liability for Torts—Slander.—Though partners are not jointly liable, and cannot be sued as a firm for slanderous words spoken by one of them unless by the direction or authority or approval of the others, they are liable as a firm for slander committed by a servant, whom they have directed or authorized to speak the words for them, or where, with knowledge of what their servant has done, they ratify it.

3. Partnership—Nature of Partnership.—A partnership is like a corporation, a legal entity, except in a more limited sense and a firm, like a corporation, may have agents, and may be liable for their acts of commission and omission in all cases where a corporation would be liable.

4. Partnership — Corporations — Torts of Agent — Liability of Principal.—A partnership or corporation is not liable for slander by its servants unless the actionable words were spoken by its express consent, direction, or authority, or were ratified or approved by it.

5. Master and Servant—Wrongful Acts of Servant—Liability of Master.—The general rule that, when it is attempted to hold a master liable for the wrongful act of his servant, it is sufficient to describe the wrongful act, and charge that it was

Duquesne Distributing Co. v. Greenbaum.

done by the servant while acting within the scope of his employment, is particularly true in cases involving injury to person or property by a physical act or omission of tha servant that involved a wrongful act or breach of the duty of the master to the person injured, but it does not apply when it is attempted to hold a master in slander for words spoken by his servant.

6. Master and Servant—Slander by Servant.—To charge a master with liability for the slanderous utterance of a servant, it is not sufficient to aver and prove that the servant at the time was engaged in the service of the master or was acting within the scope of his employment, but it must be further averred and proved that the master authorized the servant to speak the actionable words, or afterwards ratified their speaking.   •

7. Partnership—Slander by Agent—Liability of Principal.—A firm engaged in selling liquor to liquor dealers is not liable for slanderous words uttered by a traveling salesman with respect to a concern not a competitor, where the firm neither authorized the salesman to speak the words nor ratified them.

A. T. BURGEVIN for appellant, (no brief).

CHATTERSON & BLITZ for appellee.

POINTS AND AUTHORITIES.

1. A joint action against two or more for slander cannot be maintained. Webb v. Cecil & Vaughn, 9 B. M. 198 Townsend on Slander & Libel, Sec. 118 and note.

2. To hold the principal liable for the slanderous utterances of his agents or servants, there must have been express authority or a subsequent ratification. Newell on Defamation, Slander & Libel, 373; 18 Am. & Eng. Ency. of Law, 1059; S. M. Burgess & Co., v. Patterson, 32 Ky. Law Rep., 624.

3. The language charged is not actionable per se, consequently special damages must be alleged. 25 Cyc. 455; 5 Enc. Pleading & Practice, 768; Windsich Company v. Bacon, 21 Ky. Law Rep. 928; Newell on Defamation, &c., page 868; Tharp v. Nolan, 119 Ky. 870; McNamara v. Shannon, 8 Bush 558.

4. The language charged to appellees is not defamatory and not actionable, as it does not affect appellants in their trade, calling or occupation. Winsett v. Hunt, 21 Ky. Law Rep. 922.

Opinion of the court by Judge Carroll—Affirming.

In this action for slander by appellants against the appellees a demurrer was sustained to the petition as amended, and the petition dismissed; so that the only question we are called upon to consider is whether or not the petition as amended stated a cause of action.

It averred, in substance: That the Duquesne Distributing Company is a corporation engaged in the manufacture and sale of an aperient water known by the trade-name as "Red-Raven," sometimes known as "Red Raven Splits," which product had been extensively advertised by the plaintiff at great expense, and had become well known throughout the United States and elsewhere, and the plaintiff had enjoyed a profitable business arising from the sale thereof throughout the state of Minnesota and elsewhere. That "Red Raven" was sold principally to persons engaged in the sale of liquor at wholesale and retail, and the good will and friendship of such persons was in consequence of great importance and value to the plaintiff in the conduct of its business; and it did enjoy the confidence and good will of its customers and make very large sales of its product to them and realized large profits from such sales. That the defendants, desiring and intending to injure the plaintiff in its business standing and favor with its patrons and customers so engaged in the liquor trade, on or about March 1, 1908, at the city of Duluth, in Minnesota, falsely and maliciously made the following statement of and concerning the business of plaintiff to ———, who was and is engaged in the business of selling liquor at said place, and was a customer of the plaintiff and a dealer in the product of plaintiff: "They (meaning the plaintiff) contributed the sum of $10,000 to the anti-saloon cause"—and made the following statement to ———: "The Duquesne Distributing Company (meaning thereby the plaintiff) have appropriated $10,000 to further the prohibition movement." That said words spoken of and concerning the plaintiff were spoken and published by persons who were salesmen or traveling agents of the defendant, and they spoke and published the said words and statements while acting within the scope of their authority as such salesmen and agents. That by means of the false and malicious statements of defendants the plaintiffs lost the good will and confidence of many of their customers, who were led to believe the truth of said statements, and the business standing of plaintiffs with their customers was thereby injuriously affected, and the plaintiffs lost the custom and trade of their said customers, and the custom and trade of many other persons engaged in the sale of liquor who would otherwise have dealt in the product of plaintiffs. That by reason of the circulation of the said false and malicious statements of defendants the business of the plaintiff has fallen off and decreased so that the plaintiff has sustained loss and damage to the amount of $10,000.

In considering the case before us, two principal questions are presented: First, can a partnership be sued for slander; and, second, is a partnership liable for slanderous statements made by its agents or employes?

All the authorities are agreed that slander, which is an oral utterance of defamatory matter, must necessarily be committed by an individual. Two or more persons cannot in the very nature of things jointly utter the same words. Each must and does speak for himself, and each is liable for his own language. A dozen persons might repeat identically the same slan-

derous words at one and the same time or at different
times, and each would be liable in an action against
the individual; but two or more of them could not be
jointly sued. In Webb v. Cecil & Vaughan, 9 B. Mon.
198, 48 Am. Dec. 423, Cecil and Vaughan were jointly
sued for slander by Webb. A demurrer was sustained
to the petition. In passing on the case the court said:
"That the matters alleged would be sufficient to sustain civil actions against the defendants we apprehend
there can be no doubt, but we are not satisfied they are
sufficient to sustain an action against them jointly.
The tort complained of is verbal slander, and nothing
more, for which it seems a joint action against two
cannot be maintained. For a libel signed and published by two a joint action may be supported, upon
the ground that it is an entire offense, and one joint
act done by them both. But such an action cannot be
maintained against two for slanderous words because
the words of one are not the words of the other. The
act of each constitutes an entire and distinct offense.
And a further reason may be suggested that the same
words spoken by one may occasion greater injury
than spoken by another, and that each should only be
responsible for the injury inflicted by his own independent act." To the same effect is Cooley on Torts,
p. 124; Newell on Slander and Libel, p. 382; Townsend
on Slander and Libel, Sec. 118.

But, although partners are not jointly liable and
cannot be sued as a partnership for defamatory words
spoken by any one of them, unless by the direction or
authority or with the approval of the others, they may
be held liable as a firm for slander committed by an
agent or servant whom they have directed or authorized to speak the words for them, or in their behalf or
interest, or in furtherance of their business. And

this rule may with propriety be so extended as to make them liable, if, with the knowledge of what their agent or servant has done in this particular, they approve or ratify it, although in the first instance it may not have been done with their knowledge or consent or by their authority. A partnership in so far as its liability for the slanderous utterances of an agent or servant is concerned stands on the same footing as a corporation. A partnership is a legal entity as well as a corporation, except in a more limited sense. The firm as well as the corporation may have agents, and be liable for their acts of commission and omission in all states of case that a corporation would be liable. But this liability, as we shall presently point out, is not so general where it is sought to recover for slanderous words spoken by the agent as it is in the case of an ordinary tort committed by the agent. That a corporation or partnership may be sued in libel for actionable words written and published by its agents is well settled, not only by the decisions of this court but by the authorities generally.

In Newell on Slander and Libel, p. 373, it is said: "If a partner in conducting the business of a firm causes a libel to be published, the firm will be liable as well as the individual partner. And so, if an agent or servant of the firm defames any one by the express direction of the firm, or in accordance with the general orders given him by the firm for the conduct of their business. To hold either of the members of a partnership, it is not necessary that the partner should publish the libel himself. It is sufficient if he authorized, incited, or encouraged any other person to do it; or, if having authority to forbid it, he permitted it, the act was his." Burgess & Co. v. Patterson, 106 S. W. 837, 32 Ky. Law Rep. 624; Pennsylvania Iron Works

Co. v. Voght Machine Co., 96 S. W. 551, 29 Ky. Law
Rep. 8, 861 L. R. A. (N. S.) 1023; John Rivers v. Ya-
zoo & Miss. Val. R. Co., 90 Miss. 196, 43 South. 471, 9
L. R. A. (N. S.) 931; Gilbert v. Crystal Fountain
Lodge, 80 Ga., 284, 4 S. E. 905, 12 Am. St. Rep. 255;
Singer Manufacturing Co. v. Taylor, 150 Ala. 574, 43
South, 210, 9 L. R. A. (N. S.) 929, 124 Am. St. Rep.
90; Sawyer v. Norfolk Southern R. Co., 142 N. C. 1,
54 S. E. 793, 115 Am. St. Rep. 716, 9 Am. & Eng. Ann.
Cas. 440; Washington Gaslight Co. v. Lansden, 172
U. S. 534, 19 Sup. Ct. 296, 43 L. Ed. 543.

It is true that these authorities relate to actions
for libel, but upon principle there can be no sound
reason why the corporation or partnership may not
also be sued for the slanderous utterances of its
agents or servants. Libel is no more a tort than slander; the only difference between them being that in
libel the words are written, while in slander they are
spoken. If the principal may be liable for what his
agent writes, we think he should likewise be liable
for what he speaks. In each case the wrong is the
same, and although there is a dirth of authority on
the subject of the liability of a partnership or corporation for the slanderous utterances of its agents or
servants, we hold that within the limitations hereinafter set out they may be sued for slander. Without
including in what we say the rules applicable when the
action is for libel, and confining our opinion to actions
for slander, as that is the question we are dealing
with, we think that a partnership or corporation cannot be held liable for the slanderous utterances of its
agents or servants unless the actionable words were
spoken by its express consent, direction, or authority
or are ratified or approved by it. Generally speaking,
when it is attempted to hold the master or principal

liable for the wrongful acts of his servant or agent, it is sufficient to describe in a general way the wrongful act, and charge that it was done by the servant while acting within the scope of his employment. This is particularly true in cases involving injury to persons or property, where some physical act is done or omitted to be done by the servant that involved a wrongful act or a breach of duty upon the part of the master to the person injured. But a different rule should be applied when it is attempted to hold the master or principal in slander for defamatory words spoken by his agent or servant. Slanderous words are easily spoken, are usually uttered under the influence of passion or excitement, and more frequently than otherwise are the voluntary thought and act of the speaker. Or, to put it in another way, the words spoken are not generally prompted by or put into the mouth of the speaker by any other person, and represent nothing more than his personal views or opinions about the person or thing spoken of. If principals or masters could be held liable for every defamatory utterance of their servants or agents while in their service, it would subject them to liability that they could not protect or guard against. No person can reasonably prevent another, not immediately in his presence, from giving expression to his voluntary opinions, however defamatory they may be. It would be entirely out of the question to hold the principal or master responsible for every reckless, thoughtless, or even deliberate speech made by his agent or servant concerning or relating to persons that the agent or servant may meet, or know, or come in contact with while in the service of his principal or master. As to other torts or wrongful acts committed by the servant or agent, and for which the master or principal may be liable, they can as a general rule guard against by exercising care in the employment of agents and servants and in the selection and use of the appliances or things they work with. But no sort of reasonable care that the master or principal could exercise in employment or control would enable him to prevent his servant or agent from the use in his absence of language that might be actionable. A speech by the agent or servant when absent from the principal or master is absolutely within his power alone to regulate or control. He may be prudent and discreet, or reckless or careless in his conversation. He may have his tongue under perfect control, or under no control whatever, may talk freely about persons and things, or talk little. And so we think that, when it is sought to charge the master or principal in any state of case with liability for defamatory utterances of the servant or agent, it is not sufficient to aver or prove that the servant or agent at the time was engaged in the service of the master or principal, or acting within the scope of his employment in the ordinary use of that word. But it must be further averred and shown that the principal or master directed or authorized the agent or servant to speak the actionable words, or afterwards approved or ratified their speaking. Tested by this rule, the petition was bad. The charge is that "the agents or servants were salesmen or traveling agents of the defendant partnership, and that they spoke and published the said words and statements while acting in the scope of their authority as such salesmen or agents." The agents who spoke the words charged were at the time acting as the agents of Greenbaum Bros., in the sense that they were then engaged in selling liquor for them, but it does not appear from the petition that it was

any part of their duty under directions from Greenbaum Bros., to in any way speak of or concerning the
Duquesne Distributing Company or its product or
that the agents spoke the words charged by the consent or approval or in the interest of or to promote
the business of their employer. No reason is assigned
why Greenbaum Bros. should desire to injure the
trade or business of the distributing company. The
two concerns were not competitors in any sense of the
word. The goods sold by one did not interfere with
the sale of goods by the other. Greenbaum Bros. were
not concerned in or prejudiced in any personal or
business way by the sale of "Red Raven Splits." The
facts of this case as presented in the petition confirm
us in the correctness of the view we have as to the
facts necessary to be alleged and proven to hold a
partnership, individual, or corporation liable for defamatory words spoken by an agent or servant. Here
a firm having its principal place of business in this
state, with salesmen selling its goods all over the
country, is sought to be made responsible in damages
because one or two of its agents in a distant state uttered a slanderous speech concerning a party with
whom it had no business or other relations and no
reason to desire to prejudice or injure. If, under this
state of facts, Greenbaum Bros. could be sued for the
utterances of their agents, they could likewise be sued
for any slanderous statements made by them concerning any person whom they might meet or come in contact with or see proper to discuss in the course of
their travels. To lay down a rule like this would be
ruinous to persons who are obliged in the conduct of
their business to employ agents and servants. But
when the principal or master directs or authorizes
the agent or servant to speak certain words, or if

with knowledge of their speaking he approves or
ratifies them, he assumes a direct responsibility for
the acts of his agent or servant, and subjects himself
to an action to the same extent as if he had spoken
them himself.

This view of the case renders it unnecessary to consider the questions raised by counsel as to whether
or not the petition sufficiently sets out the special damages sustained to authorize a recovery.

Wherefore the judgment of the lower court is affirmed.

CASE 25.—ACTION BY SARAH GEIS AGAINST THE SOUTH
        COVINGTON & CIN. STREET RY. CO.—October 27,
        1909.

South Cov. & Cin. St. Ry. Co. v. Geis

Appeal from Campbell Circuit Court.

J. W. YOUNGBLUT, Circuit Judge.

Judgment for plaintiff, defendant appeals.—Reversed.

1. Carriers — Passengers — Injuries — Actions—Evidence.—In a
    street car passenger's action for injuries sustained while
    alighting, by the alleged sudden starting of the car, evidence
    held not to support a verdict for plaintiff.

2. Damages——Instructions—Personal Injuries.—Where the pe-
    tition in a personal injury action alleged that plaintiff lost
    20 weeks from her work because of the injuries, and was
    permanently injured, so that the only elements of damage
    were the time lost and permanent inpairment of earning pow-
    er, the instructions as to the latter item of damages should
    have permitted recovery only for the "permanent" impair-
    ment of plaintiff's ability to earn money, so as to exclude re-
    covery under that item for time lost.

L. J. CRAWFORD for appellant.

ARTHUR C. HALL for appellee.

OPINION OF THE COURT BY WM. ROGERS CLAY, COM-
MISSIONER—Reversing.

Appellee, Sarah Geis, instituted this action against
appellant, the South Covington & Cincinnati Street
Railway Company, to recover damages for personal
injuries. The jury returned a verdict in her favor in
the sum of $500. From the judgment based thereon,
this appeal is prosecuted.

It is earnestly insisted by appellant that the verdict
is flagrantly against the evidence. In view of this contention, it will be necessary to set forth the evidence
in some detail.

The accident occurred on December 12, 1907. About
6 o'clock a. m. on that date appellee boarded one of
appellant's cars at Fifth avenue and Kenton street
in the city of Dayton, Ky., for the purpose of taking
passage thereon to the place of her employment
in Cincinnati, Ohio. It was her custom to take car No.
1 on the Belleview and Dayton line. On the occasion
in question she failed to catch that car, but boarded
car No. 7, which was the next car following No. 1, at
Fifth avenue and Benham street. The latter street is
the next street eastwardly from Kenton street, where
the cars of appellant stop to take on and let off passengers. When car 7, on which appellee was a passenger, arrived at Fifth avenue and Benham street,
car No. 1, which it had been appellee's custom to ride
on, was standing at that point waiting for passengers
to get off or take passage. Car No. 7 moved up in
the rear of car No. 1. Before No. 7 had stopped, and
while it was moving slowly, appellee said to the conductor, "Can I catch that car?" The conductor replied: "Yes; I guess so, lady. He will wait for you."

Thereupon appellee started to the rear of the car for the purpose of getting off. From this point on there is a sharp conflict in the testimony.

Appellee testified that the car came to a full stop; that after the car stopped she stood on the platform for several minutes. She then attempted to alight from the platform, by placing one foot on the ground and the other on the step, and holding with one hand to the upright bar of the car. While she was in this position the car was caused to be suddenly started, thereby throwing her violently to the ground and injuring her. She was confined to her bed for about 5 weeks, and to her home about 20 weeks. She was earning $9 per week as a tailoress, and lost 20 weeks from her work. She expended for necessary services of physicians, nurses, and medicine the sum of $125. Up to the time of the trial, which was on March 23, 1909, she was still suffering from her injuries, and at that time required the services of a physician. The physician who treated her was of opinion that her injuries were permanent.

The testimony for appellant is as follows: The conductor on car No. 7 states that appellee boarded the car at Fifth avenue and Kenton street. When they reached the end of the line, there was another car there waiting for its time. The conductor started in the car to shake out the register. Appellee said: "Can I catch that car ahead?" The conductor replied: "Yes; I guess so, lady. He will wait for you." Appellee started out of the car. The conductor stopped about the middle of the car, looked back, and as he looked appellee stepped down and off the car before it came to a stop. At the time appellee spoke to the conductor the car in front was not over 20 feet away. Car No. 7 was moving slowly at the time appellee got off, and did not move over 5 feet after appellee was injured. The ground at the place where appellee got off was rough and frozen. Martin Schroath, the motorman on car No. 7, testified that at the time appellee stepped off the car it was just coasting along; that he did nothing to cause the car to go suddenly forward. Herman J. Fischer, who was on the car just behind car No..7, but who was not then in the employ of the company,.testified that he saw appellee fall. The car was barely moving when she attempted to alight. It moved a foot or two after she got off. Appellee did not stand on the back end of the car at all, but got right off. Jerry Mahoney, conductor upon the car in front of car No. 7, testified that he saw appellee walk to the rear of car No. 7 and step off. At the time the car was simply coming to a standstill. The car went probably two feet after appellee alighted. Miss Rose Berkemeier, the only passenger on the car besides appellee, testified that she knew the latter. When appellee attempted to alight, the car was moving very slowly. Appellee never stood at all upon the rear platform, but walked right out and stepped off the car. As she moved out of the car she walked faster than an ordinary walk.

In the above testimony it will be seen that no one corroborates appellee, while there are five witnesses for appellant, one of whom was a disinterested stranger, one not then in the employ of the company, but a former employe, and three others who were employes of the company at the time they testified. Although there is a great disparity in the number of witnesses testifying for appellee and for appellant, we would not be disposed to disturb the finding of the jury, if there were any circumstances of the case which tended to support the evidence of appellee. Ac-

cording to her own story, she was anxious to catch
car No. 1, which was immediately in front of car No.
7.   With that end in view she started to the rear of
car No. 7 for the purpose of alighting.   Notwithstanding her anxiety and hurry to catch the preceding car,
she nevertheless states that she stood on the platform
for several minutes after the car came to a stop. Furthermore, not only she, but every other witness, testified that car No. 1 was but a short distance in advance of car No. 7.   It is, therefore, altogether un-
likely that car No. 7 was permitted to stop within a
few feet of car No. 1, and was then suddenly started
up towards that car which was standing still.   Thus
it will be seen that the circumstances surrounding the
accident tend to support the statements of appellant's
witnesses, rather than the statement of appellee, and,
therefore, to make improbable the testimony given by
the latter.

After a careful consideration of all the evidence and
of all the circumstances, we are inclined to think that
the finding of the jury is flagrantly against the evidence, and that the ends of justice require that this
case be remanded for a new trial.

As the case must be reversed for the reason given,
we deem it proper to say that the instruction on the
measure of damages should be corrected so as to read
"and such permanent impairment, if any, of her ability to earn money," instead of, "and such impair-
m·nt, if any, of her ability to earn money," thereby
excluding from the latter item any damages that
might be allowed for loss of time.   The petition
charged that appellee had lost 20 weeks from her
work, and that she was permanently injured.   Therefore the only elements of damage, if any, were the

time lost and the permanent impairment of her power to earn money.

Judgment reversed, and cause remanded for a new trial consistent with this opinion.

CASE 26.—MOTION BY DAISY D. SEBASTIAN AGAINST W. C. ROSE TO SHOW CAUSE WHY HE SHOULD NOT BE PUNISHED FOR CONTEMPT FOR FAILING TO PAY ALIMONY ADJUDGED TO HER IN A DIVORCE ACTION.—November 12, 1909.

Sebastian v. Rose

Appeal from Owsley Circuit Court.

L. D. Lewis, Circuit Judge.

From a judgment denying the motion plaintiff appeals.—Reversed.

1. Divorce—Jurisdiction.—Divorce proceedings are exclusively within the jurisdiction of the chancery courts.

2. Divorce—Decree for Alimony—Enforcement—Summary Proceedings—Contempt.—While under the direct provisions of Ky. St. 1909, Sec. 1663, a judgment in chancery for money or other specified thing may be enforced by any appropriate writ allowable on a judgment at law, under subsection 2, providing that nothing herein shall prevent the carrying of a judgment into execution according to the ancient chancery practice, circuit courts have all the powers of the English chancery court, and may as an incident thereto summarily enforce their decrees by attachment and imprisonment, and hence payment of the balance of an alimony decree could be enforced by motion for a rule to show cause against punishment for contempt for nonpayment.

3. Divorce—Decree for Alimony—Modification.—Ky. St. Sec. 2123, permitting the court on final judgment to make orders for the care and maintenance of minor children, and at any time afterward, upon petition of either parent, to revise or alter the same, contemplates further control by chancery

courts over divorce decrees awarding alimony, so that the court granting the divorce may modify the decree by enlarging, lessening, or suspending the allowance of alimony.

4. Divorce—Absolute Divorce—Appeal.—A decree of absolute divorce is final, and cannot be reviewed on appeal by the trial court; only divorces from bed and board being subject to retrial under the direct provisions oι Civ. Code Prac. Sec. 427.

5. Divorce——Decree—.Construction—"Filed Away."—A recital in a divorce decree, that a part of the judgment for alimony was paid by defendant, and, that the case was "filed away,"' was, in effect, keeping control of the case to be redocketed upon notice; the parties not 'having been dismissed.

6. Divorce—Decree—On Agreement.—While a defendant in a divorce action may refuse to defend under an agreement with plaintiff, the decree of divorce cannot be subject of agreement, but it is the court's action upon the allegations and proof.

7   Divorce—New Trial—Award of Alimony.—While a new trial cannot be granted after entry of a decree of absolute divorce, and the judgment is final unless annulled upon petition of both parties under Civ. Code Prac. Sec. 426, a new trial may be granted upon the question of allowing or refusing alimony.

8. Divorce—Appeal — Decisions   Reviewable — Alimony.— Judgments allowing or refusing alimony are reviewable on appeal.

9. Attorney   and   Client—Authority—Compromise—Receiving Less Amount Than Judgment.—An attorney in a divorce action is without authority to compromise by accepting a less amount of alimony than awarded by the decree in satisfaction thereof, without express authority of his client; such compromise being voidable at the client's option.

10. Attorney and Client—Authority——Ratification by Client.— Where an attorney compromised a suit without authority .by accepting a less amount of alimony than was awarded his client by the judgment, the client, upon learning of the act, must either ratify or disaffirm it, and, on disaffirming, must occupy the same position as before the compromise, and cannot at the same time deny the attorney's authority and claim the benefits of the compromise.

11. Divorce—Appeal—Alimony—Scope of Review.—On appeal 'from an order denying a motion for rule to show cause why defendant should not be compelled to pay the balance of alimony awarded plaintiff in a divorce action, the question whether plaintiff is entitled to alimony is not open, the only question being the amount thereof; defendant claiming

Sebastian v. Rose.

that judgment for the amount awarded thereby was fraudulently or inadvertently entered.

12. Divorce—Alimony—Considerations in Awarding.—The dependent condition of defendant's abandoned wife, the needs of his infant child, defendant's wealth when the action begun as well as when the award was made, and his earning capacity and reasonable future expectancy and probable ability to pay alimony, should all be considered in determining the amount of alimony.

WM. H. HOLT for appellant.

POINTS AND AUTHORITIES.

1. Judgment for alimony may be enforced by Rule and Attachment. 18 Ky. Law Rep. 941, Evans v. Stewart, &c.; 99 Ky. Rep. 31, Tyler v. Tyler

2. The acts or statements of a person are not competent evidence against another in the absence of evidence showing that the one making them had authority from the other party to act for him as to the particular matter to which they relate.

3. The judgment is not sustained by competent evidence.

4. An attorney cannot in the absence of express authority release his client's claim or any part of it by way of compromise or otherwise. 3 Met. 438, Smith's Heirs v. Dixon, &c.; 21 Ky. Law Rep. 421, Cox v. Adelsdorf.

HAZELRIGG & HAZELRIGG for appellee.

We submit that this judgment should stand there being no error of law in the record and the evidence certainly being strong enough to come within the rule which, on mere questions of fact, is always followed by this court. We ask that the judgment of the lower court be affirmed.

OPINION OF THE COURT BY JUDGE O'REAR—Reversing.

Appellant and appellee were married June 13, 1901. Appellee was then a young man about 25 years old. His wife was a year or two younger Appellee's father was a man of wealth, and had considerable business interests. Appellee was a partner in some of his enterprises, was industrious, a good

business man of sound judgment, and successful; but
he had contracted the habit of inebriacy. Upon his
marriage he took his bride to his father's dwelling
to reside. A month later he abandoned her, leaving
her without means of support. She was compelled
to return to her father's home, where she resided
till his death in 1907. March, 1902, after the separa-
tion, she gave birth to a son, who is still living so far
as the record shows. In 1902 she brought this suit
against her husband for divorce and alimony, asking
also that she be given the permanent custody of the
child, and that she be restored to her maiden name.
Her father was a lawyer, a man of high social and
professional standing, but possessed of moderate
means. He had other children also. In appellant's
suit for divorce she joined as defendants the parents
and brothers of appellee, charging that her husband
had conveyed and transferred his property to them
in fraud of her rights, and to defeat her action for
alimony. Appellee did not file an answer in the case.
Appellant introduced evidence in support of her
claim. It showed her right to a divorce under the
statute on the ground of abandonment. As to the
alleged transfer of property the evidence was very
meager. A judgment was entered in the case on
May 14, 1903, granting to appellant an absolute divorce from appellee, restoring her to her maiden
name, and adjudging her the custody and control of
the child. She was also adjudged $1,500 as alimony,
and $50 as counsel fee in the case. The judgment con-
cludes: "Thereupon came G. B. Rose and paid $500
on the judgment to the plaintiff and $50 to John C.
Eversole and this case is filed away."

G. B. Rose was the father of appellee. John C.
Eversole was an attorney in the case for appellant.

Appellant's action against G. B. Rose and his wife
and sons concerning appellee's property was dismissed.   On December 11, 1907, appellant filed a
motion (of which due notice was given to appellee)
for a rule against appellee to show cause why he
should not be punished for contempt of court for his
failure to pay the balance of the judgment above
named.   Appellee responded that he ought not to
pay any part of the balance, because the judgment
was entered by the fraud or mistake of appellant's
counsel (her father having been one of her attorneys
in the suit for divorce and alimony); that the judgment was in fact a compromise of the suit; that appellee had a valid defense to the action, involving
matter that would have been humiliating or disgrace-
ful to her if disclosed, and that, upon her father's
being advised of the fact, he assented to the compromise, and induced appellant to likewise agree to it;
that the agreement was that appellee was to pay
appellant $500 only as alimony, and the $50 counsel
fee, but that as a salve to her feelings the judgment
was to recite that she was adjudged $1,500 as ali-
mony, all of which was to be indorsed satisfied upon
the payment of $500 and the $50 attorney fee; that
counsel relied upon appellant's father, James M. Sebastian, one of her counsel, to have the proper orders
entered, but that he failed to do so through fraud or
oversight.   Appellant replied, denying the authority
of her father to make the compromise of $500, and
denied that he did so.   She denied that appellee had
any defense to her action of divorce, and denied that
it involved her moral conduct.   Upon this issue the
motion was tried.   The evidence is that James M.
Sebastian acted as attorney for appellant in the divorce case; that while Mr. John C. Eversole was also

counsel Mr. Sebastion was the senior and managing attorney; that he did agree to take $500 in full settlement of his daughter's alimony, and upon his reporting that she had consented to it the $500 was paid, and the judgment entered. The evidence also shows that appellant did not authorize the settlement and knew nothing of it until it was disclosed in the response filed upon this motion. There was no evidence introduced nor offered impugning appellant's conduct or character. Thereupon the circuit court adjudged that the motion be denied, and that the collection of the balance of the judgment be perpetually enjoined. It is from that judgment that this appeal is prosecuted.

Divorce proceedings in this state come within the exclusive cognizance of courts of chancery jurisdiction. Judgments in chancery may be enforced by any appropriate writ allowed for the enforcement of judgments at law. Section 1663, Ky. St. But it is provided by subsection 2, section 1663, that "nothing in this article shall prevent either party from proceeding to carry an order or judgment of court into execution according to ancient practice of courts of chancery." The circuit courts of this state have all power anciently vested in the English Courts of Chancery. Rebhan v. Fuhrman, 21 Ky. Law Rep., 17, 50 S. W. 976. Those courts had, and circuit courts of Kentucky now have, the power, as an incident of their chancery jurisdiction, to enforce obedience to their orders and decrees by summary mode, attachment, and imprisonment. Said this court in Ballard v. Caperton, 2 Metc., 412: "This power belongs of necessity to the court, that its judgments and orders may be carried into execution and not remain powerless, and that its dignity and right to respect may be preserved by prompt punishment of contumacy.'' The practice of proceeding by rule in such cases is seemingly sustained by Evans v. Stewart, 38 S. W., 697, 18 Ky. Law Rep., 941, and Tyler v. Tyler, 99 Ky. 31, 34 S. W. 898, 17 Ky. Law Rep. 1341. Furthermore, the statute contemplates further control by courts of chancery over their decrees in cases where alimony has been adjudged (section 2123, Ky. St.) for, as observed in Logan v. Logan, 2 B. Mon., 150: ''If hereafter the circuit judge shall be satisfied that this allowance is either inadequate or superfluous, he will, of course, modify it by enlargement, curtailment, or suspension altogether, according to circumstances, retaining, as he must, the control of the case for that purpose, and for the benevolent purpose also of keeping open the door of ultimate reconciliation.'' The original decree in this case ''filing the case away'' was, in effect, keeping control of the case, to be redocketed upon notice, as the parties were not dismissed. The decree of divorce is final. It may not be reviewed on appeal, or a new trial granted by the trial court. Divorces *a mensa et thoro* may be retried in the circuit court (section 427, Civ. Code Prac.; McCracken v. McCracken, 109 Ky. 766, 60 S. W. 720, 22 Ky. Law Rep., 1448), but in no other. Hence, we are precluded, as was the circuit court, from re-examining the grounds of the judgment for divorce in this case, in so far as that judgment granted the divorce, even if there was an issue upon that point. But there is not. Th abandonment of appellant by her husband appears have been a cruel act, wholly unexplained, and wi out mitigation. The solemn and sacred vows o

altar, the highest form of contract, the most important social relation, were forgotten by the bridegroom
ere the honeymoon had waned; and it seems even the
pride of paternity was not enough to move to com-
passion a nature insensible to the demands of con-
jugal obligation.

Grounds for divorce may not be confessed. They
must be proved. Section 422, Civil Code Prac. They
cannot legally be the subject of agreement. Not the
consent of dissatisfied parties, but the judgment of
the courts alone, may dissolve the marital relation.
True, a defendant to an action for divorce may decline to defend, even though he has a defense. The
act may be the result of agreement. Nevertheless,
when the decree is entered, it is the court's judgment
upon the record as made, and establishes a new
status, not subject to retrial in court. The decree of
divorce in this case must therefore abide, unless the
parties by their joint personal petition to the court
granting the divorce procure its annulment as allowed by section 426, Civil Code Prac. But judgments allowing or refusing alimony are subject to
review on appeal; or to new trial upon proper
grounds therefor being shown.

This proceeding to enforce the payment of the
judgment for alimony was, as we have seen, one authorized by the practice in chancery. Relief will be
granted according to the rules of equity. We are
satisfied from the evidence that Mr. Sebastian, representing appellant as her attorney, did agree with
the father and the attorney for appellee that the payment of $500 and the attorney's fee of $50 would be
in satisfaction of the judgment for alimony, and that
the judgment fixing the amount was predicated upon

that agreement, rather than upon the proof in the record. We are also satisfied that appellant did not authorize the compromise and did not know of it. Her counsel had not the legal authority to enter into a compromise for her without her express authority. Smith v. Dixon, 3 Metc., 438; Cox. v. Adelsdorf, 51 S. W., 616, 21 Ky. Law Rep., 421.

The compromise was therefore voidable by her. When appraised of it, she must elect to either ratify or disaffirm it. If she ratify it, that ends it. If she disaffirms it, then she must consent to stand where she was before it was made. She will not in equity be allowed to say in one breath that she will claim the fruits of the agreement, and in the next breath to deny the condition upon which the agreement was made. The case then stands thus: A divorce has been granted to appellant upon allegation and proof of abandonment. Her claim for alimony asserted in the petition is undisposed of. She has been paid $500 on her claim for alimony, and $50 on her counsel fee. That she is legally entitled to alimony in this case is not now an open question. The only question is: How much should be awarded her? Even upon the showing she made in the partial preparation of the case, it seems to us that $1,500 was wholly inadequate. Just what property appellee then had is not satisfactorily shown. But it is shown that he had youth, health, strength, and business ability, no mean assets in these times. Many a man begins life with the charge of a family with no more, yet achieves success. The dependent condition of the wife, the helplessness and just needs of their child, both imposing legal and moral obligations upon the husband and father not discharged by divorce, nor diminished

by his abandonment, or want of affection, are elements which enter into the court's consideration in
fixing the amount of alimony. Not only what appellee
had when the action was begun, but what he has now,
and his reasonable expectancy (Muir v. Muir, 92 S.
W. 314, 28 Ky. Law Rep. 1355, 4 L. R. A. (N. S.) 909)
and his earning capacity (Canine v. Canine, 16 S. W.
367, 13 Ky. Law Rep. 124) may also be considered,
and should be, in ascertaining the just amount necessary to maintain appellant and her child comfortably,
and to educate the child fittingly, and the probability
of appellee to pay it. This is exacted of appellee not
as a penalty alone for his fault (though that may also
be considered), but is in discharge of his contractual,
and more particularly of his social, obligation imposed on him by law as an incident of manhood and
the head of a family.

Let the judgment be reversed and cause remanded
for further proceedings not inconsistent with this
opinion.

CASE 27.—INDICTMENT AGAINST W. P. YANCEY FOR
CRIMINAL LIBEL.—November 5, 1909.

Yancey v. Commonwealth

Appeal from Carroll Circuit Court.

SAMUEL M. WILSON, Special Judge.

Defendant convicted and· appeals.—Reversed.

1. Constitutional Law—Right of Peaceable Assembly—Right to
Petition Legislature—Circulation of Petition.—Under Const.
Sec. 1, subsec. 6, which provides that citizens of the state
shall have the right to assemble in a peaceable manner for
their common good, and to apply to the government for the
redress of grievances, or other proper purpose by petition, address, or remonstrance, any citizen or number of citizens
may petition the Legislature of the state for any necessary
and proper purpose,· which includes the right to lawfully
circulate a petition and procure others to sign it.

2. Libel and Slander—Circulation of Petition—Privileged Communication.—Defendant, in a prosecution for criminal libel,
was a judge of the county court. He caused to be sent to C.,
who was the foreman of a former grand jury, a letter asking
that C. sign an inclosed petition or an affidavit, to be used
in impeachment proceedings before the Legislature, to the
effect that G., who was the state attorney, for the judicial district in which all three parties lived, was an unfit and incompetent officer, he being frequently and almost constantly
drunk, etc. Held, that if defendant in good faith believed G.
to be such an unfit and incompetent officer as the letter and
petition appear to make him, the defendant had the right to
inquire of C. as to his knowledge of G.'s unfitness and
incompetency, and to ask his assistance in procuring the impeachment of G. by the Legislature.

3. Libel and Slander—Circulation of Petition—Impeachment Proceedings—Privileged Communication.—Ky. St. 1909, Sec. 2172
provides that a person desirous of procuring the impeachment
of any officer shall, by petition in writing to the House of Representatives signed by himself and verified by his own affida-

vit, and the affidavits of such others as he may deem necessary, set forth the facts upon which he prays an impeachment. Defendant, in a prosecution for criminal libel, was a
judge of the county court. He caused to be sent to C., who
was foreman of a former grand jury, an affidavit and petition addressed to the House of Representatives, charging G.,
the state attorney for the district in which all three parties
lived, with acts reprehensible in one of his official position.
Held, that if G.'s conduct was so bad as to make him a fit
subject for impeachment, in rendering such assistance as
would tend to bring it about, defendant and C. should be presumed to be discharging a social or public duty, and defendant's communication was within the scope of his duty as an
officer and good citizen; it not being alleged in the indictment that it was made without reasonable grounds.

4. Libel and Slander—Circulation of Petition—Privileged Communications.—The right conferred by Ky. St. 1909, Sec. 2172,
to file the affidavits of other persons in proceedings for the
impeachment of an officer necessarily carries with it the right
to make reasonable and proper inquiry to obtain them.

5. Libel and Slander—Impeachment Proceedings—Judicial Proceeding—Privileged Communications.—An impeachment proceeding is a judicial proceeding and whatever writings in the
way of petitions, affidavits, or pleas as may properly be used
in an impeachment proceeding are, as to statements of fact
contained therein, as much privileged as other writings or
pleadings prepared for use or filed in the course of ordinary
litigation.

GEO. B. WINSLOW, attorney for appellant.

JOHN J. HOWE, W. O. JACKSON, W. E. MOODY and M. H.
BONNIE, of counsel.

POINTS AND AUTHORITIES.

PART I. THE DEMURRER TO THE INDICTMENT.

(a) The failure to allege that the matter was written "of
and concerning" F. C. Greene, is fatal.   Criminal Code, sec. 132;
Newman's P. & P. (New Ed.) sec. 230; 2 Roberson's Crim. Law,
sec. 595, p. 807, citing Tracey v. Commonwealth, 87 Ky. 578; 13
A. & E. Ency. Plead. & Prac., page 99.

(b) The failure to allege that Greene had been, or was then,
holding or expecting to hold some office was fatal. 2 Roberson's
Crim. Law, sec. 595, p. 809; Commonwealth v. Stacy, 8 Phila.
(Pa.) 617; 13 A. & E. Ency. Plead & Prac., p. 99 and notes; New-

Yancey v. Commonwealth.

man's Plead & Prac. sec. 230; 13 A. & E. Ency. Plead & Prac.,
p. 55; Townsend on Slander & Libel, sec. 388, p. 586.

(c) The legal effect of an innuendo. 13 A. & E. Ency., P.
& P., p. 51, 52-54, 98, 99, 102; Townsend on Slan. & Lib., sec.
335-6, p. 579-80; 2 Roberson Crim. Law, sec. 595, p. 809; 2 Chit.
Crim. Law, 310.

(d) The indictment is bad for duplicity. Tracey v. Commonwealth, 87 Ky. 584; Townsend on Slan. & Libel, sec. 117, 347;
Nicholas v. Commonwealth, 78 Ky. 584; Ellis v. Commonwealth,
78 Ky. 133; Clymer v. Commonwealth, 23 K. L. R., 1042.

(e) The statements were absolutely, privileged. Ky. Cons.,
sec. 1, subsec. 6; Ky. Statutes, sec. 2172.

PART II.

(f) A peremptory instruction should have been given to find
for the defendant.

(g) If the matter was not absolutely privileged, it was a case
of qualified privilege.

(h) The law as to privilege communication. Bishop on Non-
Contract Law, secs. 295, 302, 303; 18 A. & E. Ency. Law; 1023,
1029, 1030, 1041; 2 Roberson Crim. Law, sec. 592; 13 A. & E.
Ency., P. & P., page 112, note 7; Nix v. Caldwell, 81 Ky. 291;
Nicholson v. Rust, 21 Ky. Law Rep. 645; Coles v. Wilson, 18
B. M. 212.

JAMES BREATHITT, Attorney General, T. B. McGREGOR,
Assistant; J. A. DONALDSON, M. S. DOWNS, CHAS. STRO-
THER, ARTHUR COX, F. C. GREEN, Commonwealth Attorney
of Counsel.

This is the first time that a jury of good citizens, the
peers of any jury that might be selected in this or any other
district in the State of Kentucky, has been called to pass on
these troubles, and after a full, fair and impartial hearing, not
influenced by any feeling or partiality or prejudice whatever,
guided only by the stubborn facts as presented by the sworn
statement of witnesses, examined before them and by the
law, the instructions given them by a just, fair, intelligent,
learned and upright Judge from another section of the State,
influenced by no other motive than to fairly expound the law and
instruct the jury as to the law that should control them in their
deliberations and in reaching a fair and just conclusion, this
jury, under all the facts as thus presented, and the law, as thus
fairly and correctly given, after duly considering the whole case,
rendered the verdict they did.

It was a just, fair and reasonable verdict, and the judgment ren. dered thereon should not be disturbed, but should be affirmed, with damages.

AUTHORITIES.

Section 132, Criminal Code; Section 118, Criminal Code; Section 122, Criminal Code; Section 124, Criminal Code; Commonwealth v. Magowan, 1 Met., 368; Clark v. Commonwealth, 16 B. Monroe, 206; Tracy v. Commonwealth, 87 Ky. 582.

OPINION OF THE COURT BY JUDGE SETTLE—Reversing.

At the January term, 1908 of the Carroll circuit court the grand jury found and returned against the appellant, W. P. Yancey, the following indictment: "The grand jury of Carroll county, in the name and by the authority of the commonwealth of Kentucky, accuse W. P. Yancey of the offense of criminal libel committed as follows, to-wit: The said W. P. Yancey in the county and circuit court aforesaid did, on the 17th day of January, 1908, within 12 months next before the finding of this indictment, unlawfully, willfully, maliciously, and knowingly write and publish a certain written statement, to-wit, a letter, which letter imputed to one F. C. Greene, then commonwealth attorney of the Fifteenth judicial district of Kentucky, dishonesty, misconduct in office, corruption in the discharge of his official duties, and incompetency in the performance of same, and did sign same and mail and deliver same to the following persons in Carroll county, Ky.: B. W. Ransdell, John Davis, A. S. Lee, A. G. Kendall, Arthur Carico, C. M. Bond, C. C. Coghill, J. C. Duvall, R. E. Crutcher, Harry Grobmeyer, Joe Hayes, Forrest Adcock, and divers others whose names are to this grand jury now unknown, all residents of Carroll county, Ky., said written letters being in words as follows: 'W. P. Yan-

cey, Judge of Owen County Court. Owenton, Kentucky, January 17, 1908. Mr. C. C. Coghill, Carrollton, Ky.—My Dear Sir: We should like very much
to have you sign a petition or affidavit would be better, something like the one I inclose. I only send this
thinking it might answer the purpose, if not, all right.
A petition has been circulated in this county pe-
titioning the Legislature to remove Greene from office. We would like very much to have an affidavit
signed by you as foreman of the May term of the
grand jury to the effect that Greene is wholly incompetent and corrupt in his office. If this meets your
approval you can write me by Wednesday of next
week as we want to go to Frankfort Thursday with
affidavits. Yours truly in confidence, W. P. Yancey.'
The inclosure in said letter and part of said letter is
in words and figures as follows: 'We, the undersigned
citizens of Carroll county, Ky., state that we were
members of the grand jury at the ———— term of the
Carroll circuit court, for the year 1907, and that during that said term of the court, the commonwealth attorney for the Fifteenth judicial district of Kentucky,
one F. C. Greene, was constantly and habitually
d·unk, so much so that he was incapacitated from attending to the duties of his said office in a proper and
becoming manner; that at the close of the term of our
said service as grand jurors, when several indictments had been prepared, the said F. C. Greene could
not be found, and that we found that he was trying
to make his escape from the city of Carrollton, and
that it was necessary for us to have·the said Greene
arrested by the sheriff of Carroll county and returned
to the jury room, in order that he might sign the said
indictments. The affiants state that the said F. C.
Greene has persistently and continuously shown his

incompetency and unfitness for the office of commonwealth attorney, in that he is frequently and almost constantly drunk, and they respectfully ask and petition the Legislature of Kentucky to impeach the said Greene and remove him from his said office.' Now 'he grand jury says that said Yancey wrote said letter and caused said inclosure to accompany same, and vouched for the truth of same, well knowing at the time he so published same that it was and is false, libelous, infamous, and malicious, and same was and is false and libelous, and same was so done by the said Yancey with the malicious purpose and criminal intent to injure said F. C. Greene in his profession and in the discharge of his official duties and against the peace and dignity of the commonwealth of Kentucky. F. C. Greene, Commonwealth Attorney, Fifteenth Dist. of Kentucky.'' The trial of appellant resulted in his conviction of the alleged criminal libel, his punishment being fixed by verdict of the jury at a fine of $500. Appellant entered motion in arrest of judgment, and also filed a motion and grounds for a new trial, but both motions were overruled by the circuit court, and these rulings gave cause for this appeal.

Appellant's first complaint is that the trial court erred in overruling his demurrer to the indictment. This complaint is mainly based upon the ground that both the letter and the inclosed petition set forth in the indictment were privileged communications, and therefore their publication did not constitute an indictable offense. Subsection 6, section 1, Bill of Rights, Const., provides that citizens of the state shall have "the right of assembling together in a peaceable manner for their common good, and of applying to those invested with the power of government for the redress of grievances, or other proper

purpose by petition, address or remonstrance.'' Manifestly, the foregoing declaration of the Bill of Rights
confers upon any citizen, or number of citizens, the
right to petition the Legislature of the state for any
necessary and proper purpose, and if one may lawfully sign his name to a petition to be presented to
the Legislature for a proper purpose, he may likewise lawfully circulate the petition and procure others to sign it.   The letter and inclosed petition set
forth in the indictment show that appellant was
seeking either a petition or affidavit from Coghill to
be used in an impeachment proceeding, to be instituted in the Legislature against Greene, and nothing
contained in the indictment negatives this idea.   If,
as these writings show appellant in good faith believed Greene, the commonwealth's attorney of the
judicial district in which he and Coghill reside, to
be such an unfit and incompetent officer as the letter
and petition appear to make him, then appellant had
the right to inquire of Coghill as to his knowledge
of the alleged unfitness and incompetency of Greene,
and to ask his assistance in procuring the impeachment of Greene by the Legislature.

Section 2172. Ky. Stat., provides: ''A person desirous of procuring the impeachment of any officer
shall, by petition in writing to the House of Representatives signed by himself and verified by his own
affidavit, and the affidavits of such others as he may
deem necessary, set forth the facts upon which he
prays an impeachment.''   It will be observed that
the paper Coghill was asked by appellant to sign
was an affidavit and petition addressed to the House
of Representatives.   As appellant was judge of the
Owen county court, and Coghill had been a member

of the grand jury during the Carroll circuit court at which Greene was charged with certain acts reprehensible in one of his official position, and both appellant and Coghill were citizens of the district of which Greene was commonwealth's attorney, the communication complained of was between persons having a common interest, and mainly in the nature of an inquiry of Coghill as to his knowledge of what Greene had done at the Carroll court. If Greene's conduct was so bad as to make him a fit subject of impeachment, it is no less than the truth to say that, in rendering such assistance as would tend to bring about his impeachment, appellant and Coghill should be presumed to have acted in the discharge of a social or public duty and from the standpoint of good citizenship. The communication was within the scope of appellant's duty as an officer and good citizen, and it is not alleged in the indictment that it was made without reasonable grounds. Not only were the letter and inclosure from appellant to Coghill in the nature of an inquiry and request for the latter's assistance, but it was also a confidential communication, for the letter closes with the words, ''Yours truly in confidence.'' The inclosure contains no statement of fact made by appellant; it is merely a part of the inquiry, and in addition a statement of the facts the writer supposed to be in Coghill's possession, and which, if true, he was expected to swear to, in which event it would be used by appellant, in connection with the contemplated impeachment proceedings, as a petition or one of the affidavits allowed by the statute in support of the petition praying Greene's impeachment. The right conferred by the statute to file the affidavits of other persons in such a proceeding necessarily carries with it the right to make reasonable and proper inquiry to obtain them.

An impeachment proceeding is a judicial proceeding; the Legislature being the trial court. This being true, whatever writings in the way of petitions, af· fidavits, or pleas as may properly be used in an impeachment proceeding are, as to the statements of fact contained therein as much privileged as other writings or pleadings prepared for use or filed in the course of ordinary litigation in the courts of the country. An excellent statement of the law on this subject, as we understand it, may be found in Roberson's Criminal Law, sec. 592: "There are certain communications which are privileged, and are not deemed libelous, because of the occasion upon which they are made, though the party making them may in fact be in error, and not able to prove them to be true. A communication is regarded as privileged if made in good faith, upon any subject-matter upon which the party communicating has an interest, or in reference to which he has a duty public or private and either legal, social, or moral, if the defamatory matter is honestly believed to be true by the person publishing it, and made to a person or body of men having a corresponding interest or duty. Thus proceedings in courts of justice, legislative proceedings, and petition and memorials to the Legislature are privileged." The rule here announced was approved by this court in Ranson v. West, 125 Ky. 457, 101 S. W. 885, 31 Ky. Law Rep. 82; Sebree v. Thompson, 126 Ky., 223; 103 S. W., 374, 31 Ky. Law Rep. 642, 11 L. R. A., (N. S.) 723. Also Cooley on Torts, sec. 251; Townsend on Slander and Libel, sec. 221; 18 Am. & Eng. Ency, of Law, 1023.

Being of opinion that the writings alleged in the
indictment to be libelous belong to the class of communications regarded by the law as absolutely privileged, we conclude that the learned special judge
erred in overruling the demurrer to the indictment.
This view of the matter makes it unnecessary for us
to consider the numerous additional contentions
urged by appellant for a reversal.

Judgment reversed, and cause remanded for proceedings consistent with this opinion.

CASE 28.—ACTION   BY   THE   CITY   OF   HARRODSBURG
    AGAINST THE EAST TENNESSEE TELEPHONE
    COMPANY.—November 3, 1909.

East Tennessee Telp. Co. v. City of Harrodsburg

Appeal from Mercer Circuit Court.

W. C. BELL, Circuit Judge.

Judgment for plaintiff, defendant appeals.—Reversed.

Telegraphs and Telephones—Regulation—Charges — "Business
    Service."—The words "business service," in a telephone com-
    pany's franchise fixing the maximum rate for such service,
    mean the ordinary service between business men and other
    citizens within the radius specified, and do not include ser-
    vice rendered to a telegraph company under a joint traffic
    arrangement which does not increase the cost of the service
    rendered by the latter company.

E. H. GAITHER for appellant.

C. E. RANKIN and R. W. KEENON for appellee.

OPINION OF THE COURT BY WM. ROGERS CLAY, COM-
MISSIONER—Reversing.

Appellant, East Tennessee Telephone Company, is the owner of a franchise for the maintenance and operation of a system of telephone service in Harrodsburg and Mercer county, Kentucky. Section 6 of the franchise is, in part, as follows: "The maximum rate during the term of this franchise shall be as follows: * * * For business service within a radius of one and one-half miles from the exchange, one party line, per month, $2.75; the same service, two party line, per month, $2.00. * * * In the event the foregoing provisions of this section, or any of them, shall be violated by the owner or operator of said system of said telephone, or any manager or agent, or servant of said owner or operator, or its assigns, by charging, demanding, collecting, or receiving any sum in excess of the rates herein provided for, said owner or operator shall forfeit to the city of Harrodsburg the sum of ten dollars in liquidated damages for each day said terms are violated, said damages to be for the benefit of the citizens of Harrodsburg, unless said owner or operator shall refund such amount of overcharge when demanded after giving proper evidence of each overcharge." This is an action by the city of Harrodsburg to enforce the penalty above referred to against appellant for an alleged overcharge in its telephone rates. It is charged in the petition that J. D. Parrish is a citizen and resident of Harrodsburg, Kentucky, engaged in transmitting to other points, and receiving from other points and transmitting to said citizens, telegraphic messages; that he is also engaged in the business of receiving for transportation by express freight from the citizens of said town and that community, and the business of delivering to said citizens freight transported to them from other cities, under an arrangement which he has with the telegraph and express companies which he represents; that he is required to furnish the office room and furniture, and to send out to persons residing a distance from his office the telegraphic messages of persons desiring them sent over the telegraph lines, and for all of his services in said business; that he has in his possession a store in said city, within 250 yards of defendant's Harrodsburg exchange; that, desiring a telephone service as contemplated in, and required by, the franchise referred to, he requested the defendant to furnish it to him; that, in compliance with his request it installed in his building a telephone instrument, and connected him with the Harrodsburg exchange; that he is now, and has at all times been, ready, willing, and able to pay to said defendant the sum of $2.75 for services per month; that said amount has been tendered appellant, but that it refused, and still refuses, to accept the same; that notwithstanding said franchise, the appellant has adopted a different method of charging him for said telephone service; that it demands and charges him 2 cents for each and every call, and 15 per cent. of all sums which he collects for transmitting telegraph messages from Harrodsburg, Ky., to other distant points; that during the month of March, 1909, it demanded, charged, collected, and received from him, for each and every day between February 28, 1909, and April 1, 1909, a period of 31 days, in excess of $2.75 per month for the services furnished him, which charges were paid by him under protest; that complaint of the overcharge was made, and proof thereof offered to appellant, but that it failed and refused to refund any sum on account thereof. It is then charged that, by reason of the violation of its franchise agreement and the overcharge exacted of J. D. Parrish, appellant had become indebted to plaintiff in the sum of $10 per day for 31 days amounting to $310. Appellant thereafter filed its answer. The first paragraph contained a general denial of certain allegations of the petition. By the second paragraph the defense is made that John D. Parrish is the agent of the Western Union Telegraph Company, a corporation duly and legally organized and engaged in the business of transmitting and receiving telegraph messages throughout the country; that said Parrish is also the agent of the Southern Express Company, a common carrier of goods and stock, and that said Parrish has no business other than as agent for the said corporations; that under the traffic arrangement with the Western Union Telegraph Company, duly executed in writing, between that company and appellant for the purpose of mutual benefit and profit, appellant made and entered into a contract whereby it agreed to transmit for the Western Union Telegraph Company to each of defendant's subscribers any messages received over the wires of the Western Union Telegraph Company. The charge for this service is 2 cents for each message. It is further stipulated that, for each message delivered over appellant's lines to the Western Union Telegraph Company for transmission over its lines, appellant is to receive 15 per cent. of the net cost of said message to said sender; that said contract embraces all of the exchanges of the appellant, and that it is a valid, binding, and equitable contract, and that the Western Union Telegraph Company and the appellant are mutually bound thereunder and are each attempting to perform and live up to said contract; that the said J. D. Parrish is attempting to nullify the contract and avoid the provisions thereof by demanding of the appellant a telephone ostensibly for his personal business, but with the fraudulent purpose of using the same to receive and transmit messages for and from the Western Union Telegraph Company, and to thereby nullify the said contract with said company. It is further averred in the second paragraph that it had offered to install for Parrish's use, individually and as agent of the Southern Express Company, a telephone at the business rate of $2.75 per month, and a second phone for the Western Union Telegraph Company under the said agreement and traffic arrangement with said company; that Parrish has refused to accept said phones under such conditions; that said contract with the Western Union Telegraph Company is in full force and effect in all the exchanges under appellant's control, and that the same was in existence at the time said telephone was installed in the office of the Western Union Telegraph Company at Harrodsburg. By amended answer it is further averred that the contract between appellant and the Western Union Telegraph Company was in existence, and that the appellant and the Western Union Telegraph Company were each operating under said contract before the passage of the franchise granted to appellant by the city of Harrodsburg in 1908; that it offered to said Parrish, agent of the Western Union Telegraph Company, a telephone for all purposes other than business of the latter company at the rates fixed by said ordinance, but that he refused to accept the same. A demurrer was sustained to the second paragraph of appellant's answer and to the amendment thereof. Evidence was then heard, and the case submitted to the jury. The court peremptorily instructed the jury to return a verdict in favor of appellee, city of Harrodsburg, for the sum of $310, and the telephone company appeals.

While several grounds for reversal are urged, we deem it necessary to consider only one; that is, the propriety of the court's action in sustaining the demurrer to the second pragraph of the original answer and the amendment thereof. It appears from these pleadings that appellant and the Western Union Telegraph Company are both public service corporations, engaged in the business of receiving and transmitting messages. They have made a joint traffic arrangement by which the cost of the messages transmitted by them is to be prorated upon a certain basis. This arrangement applies to all exchanges under the control of appellant, and to every place where the Western Union Telegraph Company has an office. According to the franchise the maximum rate is as follows: "For business service within a radius of one and one-half miles from the exchange, one party line, per month, $2.75; the same service, two party line, per month, $2.00." The question, then, arises: "What is meant by the words "business service" as used in the franchise? In our opinion the council meant the ordinary business service between the business men and other citizens within the radius specified in the ordinance granting the franchise. We do not believe the council intended that the words "business service" should include service of the kind rendered by appellant to the Western Union Telegraph Company. In our opinion the council did not intend to affect in any way the joint traffic arrangement between two such public service corporations as appellant and Western Union Telegraph

Company. If the service rendered by the Western Union Telegraph Company to the citizens of Harrodsburg and vicinity was rendered more costly by reason of the charge exacted by appellant, a different question would be presented. So far as it appears in the answer, the Western Union Telegraph Company alone pays the cost of such service, and pays it under and by virtue of a contract which it has with appellant. There is no increased cost that the citizen is required to pay. The increased cost required of Parrish is not exacted from him as a citizen of Harrodsburg, but only as the agent and representative of the Western Union Telegraph Company. He cannot therefore obtain for his personal use a telephone from appellant, and then as the agent of the Western Union Telegraph Company use the telephone for the purpose of nullifying the contract between appellant and the Western Union Telegraph Company. If the franchise ordinance were intended to apply to a commercial arrangement between two public service corporations, engaged in the same line of business, it is manifest that the telephone company would be placed at a great disadvantage. Its proportion of the profits of the business done would depend, not upon its contract with the telegraph company, but upon the maximum rate fixed for ordinary business service. As said above, we are of opinion that the council did not intend that the maximum rate fixed in the franchise ordinance should control the joint traffic arrangement between two such corporations. We, therefore, conclude that the trial court erred in sustaining appellee's demurrer to the second paragraph of appellant's answer and the amendment thereof.

Judgment reversed, and cause remanded, for proceedings consistent with this opinion.

Vol. 135.]   SEPTEMBER   TERM, 1909.   223

Cov. & Cin. Railroad Transfer & Bridge Co. v. Mulvey's Admr.

CASE 29.—ACTION BY JOHN MULVEY'S ADMINISTRATOR
AGAINST THE COVINGTON & CINCINNATI RAIL-
ROAD TRANSFER & BRIDGE COMPANY.—Novem-
ber 4, 1909.

Cov. & Cin. Railroad Transfer & Bridge Co. v. Mulvey's Admr.

Appeal from Campbell Circuit Court.

C. W. YUNGBLUT, Circuit Judge.

Judgment for plaintiff, defendant appeals.—Reversed.

Railroads—Injury to Person Near Track—Coal Falling from
Car—Negligence.—The probability that a boy, who with a
few other boys plays on the private premises of a railroad
company, adjoining its right of way, will be in a position
to be struck by a lump of coal falling from a passing car
is not so great as to impose on the company the duty of loading its cars with reference to his presence, or of inspecting its cars to see that he is not injured by falling coal; and
there is no liability for injury so occurring in the absence of
wantonness and recklessness.

GALVIN & GALVIN for appellant.

There is a long line of cases in this state holding that the testimony must be clear and unequivocal, connecting the negligence with the injury, and that if the injury could have resulted
from any one of two or more causes, for one of which the defendant would be liable, and for the other of which defendant would
not be liable, there can be no recovery.

AUTHORITIES CITED.

Willis Swartwood's guardian v. L. & N., 3 S. W., 305; L. & N
v. Reynolds, 24 Ky. L. R., 1402; Gleason v. Virginia Midland R.
R. Co., 140 U. S., 435; Thomas v. C. N. O. & T. P. Ry., 32 Ky.
L R., 67; C. & O. v. Raymond Davis, 22 Ky. L. R., 748; L. & N.
v. Wade, 18 Ky. L. R., 549; Wintuska's adm'r v. L. & N., 14 Ky.
L. R., 579; Johnson's adm'r v. E. T. V. & G R. R., 17 Ky. L. R.,

67; L. & N. R. R. Co. v. Wathen, 22 Ky. L. R. 82; Hughes v. Cincinnati, etc., R. R. Co., 91 Ky., 526; Louisville Gas Co. v. Kaufman, Straus & Co., 105 Ky., 156 & 157; Witten v. Bell & Coggeshall Co., 27 Ky. L. R., 805; Hurt v. L. & N., 25 Ky. L. R., 755; L. & N. v. McGary, 104 Ky., 509.

ARTHUR C. HALL and J. A. SHACKELFORD for appellee.

QUESTIONS DISCUSSED AND AUTHORITIES CITED.

1. The lot in question was an attractive place as a play-ground for children.

2. The appellant acquiescing in their use of it owed them a duty not to negligently injure them while they were upon said premises.

3. The court did not err in submitting the case to the jury and refusing to give a peremptory instruction to find for Appellant. Bronsom's Adm'r v. Labrot, 81 Ky., 638; Reliance T. & D. Wks. v. Mitchell, 24 Ky. L. R., 1287; C. & O. Ry. Co. v. Davis, 22 Ky. L. R. 748; L. & N. R. R. v. Eaden, 93 S. W., 7; Willis v. Mays. & D. S. R. R., 27 Ky L. R., 495; Gulf C. & S. F. R. R. v. Wood, 63, S. W., 164; Un. Pac. R. R. v. McDonald, 152 U. S., 280; Sioux Cy. & P. R. R. v. Stout, 84 U. S., 745; Young, &c., v. Trapp, &c., 26 Ky. L. R., 752; Harper v. Kopp, 24 Ky. L. R., 2343; Fletcher v. B. & O. R. R., 168 U. S., 135; and Thompson on Negligence, Secs. 1031, 1033, 1034-5 and White's Sup. to Thompson on Negligence, Sec. 1032.

4. The case at bar comes clearly within the rule of Res Ipsa Loquitur. Thompson on Negligence, Vo. 1, Sec. 15 and 4537; L. & N. v. Davis, 115 Ky., 270; L. & N. v. Reynolds, 24 Ky. L. R. 1403; Gulf C. & S. F. v. Wood, 63 S. W. 164; C. & O. v. Bercew, 23, Ky. L. R. 1509; Howser v. Cumb. & Penna. R. R., 27 L. R. A., 154; Barnowski v. Helson, 15 L. R. A., 33; Ford v. L. S. & M. S., 12 L. R. A. 455.

5. Every presumption of negligence on the part of appellant is authorized by the evidence in the case, and that negligence was the direct cause of the death of Decedent. L. & N. v. Mulfinger, 26 Ky. L. R., 3; I. C. R. R. v. Cane, 28 Ky. L. R., 1018.

OPINION OF THE COURT BY WM. ROGERS CLAY, COMMISSIONER—Reversing.

John Mulvey, as administrator of John Mulvey, Jr., deceased, instituted this action against the Louisville & Nashville Railroad Company, the Chesapeake &

Ohio Railway Company, and appellant, the Covington & Cincinnati Railroad, Transfer & Bridge Company, to recover damages for the death of his decedent. Upon the conclusion of the testimony the court gave a peremptory instruction in favor of the Louisville & Nashville Railroad Company and the Chesapeake & Ohio Railway Company. Judgment was entered in their favor, and from that judgment there is no appeal. The case as to appellant was submitted to the jury, which returned a verdict in favor of appellee for the sum of $2.500. From that judgment this appeal is prosecuted. The failure of the trial court to award it a peremptory instruction is the only ground for reversal urged by appellant.

The facts are as follows: Appellant is the owner of a' bridge which spans the Ohio River at Covington, Ky. It also owns and maintains railroad tracks running from Seventeenth street, in Covington, through said city and over said bridge to points in Cincinnati, Ohio. It has locomotives which it uses for the purpose of transportating trains over the bridge and roads owned by it. At Fifth and Johnson streets in Covington, Ky., there is a vacant and uninclosed lot, which has a frontage of about 50 feet on the south side of Fifth street, and a depth of about 100 feet. This lot is bounded on the west by a stone wall or approach to said bridge, and on the east by an alley. The top of the wall is about 10 feet above its base or the level of the lot. There are two tracks on this wall; the east track being used by trains going north, and the west track by those going south. This lot in question is owned by appellant. In the summer time it has been used as a playground by children. At times they would gather up the coal on the tracks and from cars, and make a fire on the lot. On December 11, 1907, about 7:30 o'clock p. m., and after dark, the decedent, John Mulvey, who was then about 12 years of age, in company with several other boys the same age, was playing on the lot referred to. Early in the day they had built a fire on the lot within a distance of 4 or 5 feet from the bridge wall. On the occasion of the accident they were sitting around the fire when they heard a train approaching from the south. The train consisted of about 20 cars, four of which were loaded with coal. As the engine approached, the boys all ran back 30 or 40 feet to escape the cinders and ashes from the engine. Shortly after the engine passed, young Mulvey ran back to the fire and took a seat thereby. In a short time one of his companions called the attention of the other boys to the fact that Mulvey was lying on the ground. About that time one of the boys saw a dark object rolling along the ground about three or four feet from young Mulvey's head. The witness who testified to this fact made a statement inconsistent with it, but on the trial of the case insisted that he had seen something rolling along the ground at the time Mulvey was injured. When their attention was called to young Mulvey, the boys rushed to his assistance. It was found that he had a wound in the top of his head. This wound contained particles of dirt. Mulvey's companions carried him to his home. It was found by the physician summoned to attend him, and by the coroner at the inquest, that young Mulvey's neck was broken. The lump of coal which it is claimed fell from the car, and which was seen rolling when young Mulvey was injured, was picked up by one of the boys, and later turned over to the coroner as evidence. There is also evidence to the effect that there was no other coal on the lot at the time of the injury. Some of the witnesses also testified that the coal in the coal cars was heaped up in the center of the cars. Appellant proved title to the lot, and also showed that the cars containing the coal were loaded at least 250 miles from the point where the accident occurred.

In discussing this case we may admit that there is some evidence tending to show that young Mulvey was killed by being struck on the head by a lump of coal which fell from one of the cars as the train passed by. The doctrine of the Turntable Cases, of course, has no application to this case. This is not a case where a dangerous agency that was alluring and attractive to children was left in such a position that they could and would use it. Nor is it a case where the premises were rendered unsafe by a spring gun or any trap that would injure a person if he came in contact with it. Appellee, however, insists that, as children had been playing upon the lot in question for a long time with the knowledge and acquiescence of appellant, it was the duty of the latter to anticipate their presence, and so load its cars as not to injure any one of them. This court has gone to the extent of holding that where a railroad track runs through a populous community, along or across streets, where from the nature of things persons may be reasonably expected at any time, it is the duty of those in charge of the train to have it under reasonable control, to keep a lookout for persons using the track, and to give timely warning of the approach of the train. Illinois Central R. R. Co. v. Murphy's Admr., 123 Ky. 787, 97 S. W. 729; 30 Ky. Law Rep. 93, 11 L. R. A. (N. S.) 352. The reason for this rule is that the long and continued use of the track at the

point in question by large numbers of persons is sufficient to indicate a reasonable certainty that persons
will be found there. This rule has never been extended to cases where there was no customary use of
the track at the point of the injury. The presence of
persons on the track because of its customary use by
the public being reasonably certain, there is a strong
probability of some one's being injured unless proper
precautions are taken to prevent accidents. The
necessity for precaution is due to the fact that the
very movement of a train is dangerous, and likely to
injure those caught unawares. But the probability
that a boy, who, with a few other boys, plays upon the
private premises of a railroad company, adjoining its
right of way will be in position to be struck by a
lump of coal falling from a passing car is not so great
as to impose upon the company the duty of loading
its cars with reference to his presence, or of inspecting its cars to see that he is not injured by falling
coal. Under such circumstances there is no liability,
unless the injury is wanton or reckless. There is no
evidence in this case to show either one of these
prerequisites to a recovery. The death of the decedent was simply the result of an unfortunate accident, which could not have been reasonably anticipated by appellant. We, therefore, conclude that the
court erred in failing to give a peremptory instruction in favor of appellant.

Judgment reversed and cause remanded for proceedings consistent with this opinion.

CASE 30.—ACTION BY SOUTH CONWAY AGAINST THE
LOUISVILLE & NASHVILLE RAILROAD COMPANY.
November 9, 1909.

Conway v. Louisville & Nashville R. R. Co.

Appeal from Franklin Circuit Court.

R. L. STOUT, Circuit Judge.

Judgment for defendant, plaintiff appeals.—Affirmed.

1. Railroads—Operation—Accidents at Crossings—Precautions
as to Persons Near Crossing.—Those in charge of a railroad
engine are not bound to take notice of the conduct or fright
of a horse on a parallel highway, or to stop or slacken the
speed of the train to avoid a possible collision, unless the horse
is so close to the railway that the engine operatives can, by
the exercise of ordinary care, discover that the horse is
frightened, and the attitude of the horse or the immediate
conditions are such as to lead a person of reasonable prudence to believe that there is danger of a collision.

2. Railroads—Operation—Accidents at Crossings—Signals from
Trains.—Under the statute requiring all trains to give the
statutory signals of their approach to a grade crossing, the
failure to give such signal is actionable negligence, for which
one injured in consequence thereof may recover.

3. Railroads—Operation—Accidents at Crossings—Contributory
Negligence.—While travelers on a public highway crossing
a railroad may rely for protection on the statutory signals
required to be given by trains, failure to give the signals does
not relieve the travelers from the duty of exercising ordinary care for their own safety.

4. Negligence—Contributory Negligence—Questions for Jury.—
The question of contributory negligence is generally for the
jury.

5. Negligence—What Constitutes.—To constitute actionable
negligence, there must be negligence and injury resulting as
a proximate cause of it.

6. Railroads—Operation—Accidents at Crossings—Evidence.—
Evidence held insufficient to show that the failure of defen-

dant railroad to give the statutory signals at a crossing caused plaintiff's horse to run away and injure him through a collision with the train.

IRA JULIAN for appellant.

1. If there was any evidence tending to show, or from which the jury could have reasonably inferred the alleged negligence, and that the injury was caused thereby, the case should have been submitted to the jury. Dodge v. Bank Ky., 9 Ky., 610; Bishop v. McNary, 41 Ky., 132; Martin v. Ry. Co., 29 Ky. L. R., 148.

2. The questions as to the proximate cause of the injury was a question of fact for the jury. Gen. Pass. Ry. v. Chatterson, 17 Ky. L. R., 5; Ashland Coal Ry. v. Wallace, 19 Ky. L. R., 849; L. & N. v. Mitchell, 87 Ky., 327; Connell v. C. & O. Ry. Co., 22 Rep., 501.

3. It is the duty of those in charge of trains to give some timely warning of its approach to a public crossing for the protection of those who may be riding or driving on the highway, that they may secure themselves against injury by reason of the frightening of horses. Encyc. of Law, Vol. 8, page 422; Rupard v. C. & O. Ry. Co., 88 Ky., 280; Hudson v. L. & N. R. R., 77 Ky., 303; C. & O. Ry. v. Ogls, 24 Ky. L. R., 2160.

And this Common Law duty is emphasized in our Statute. Section 786 Ky. Statutes; N. C. R. R. v. Higgins, 29 Ky. L. R., 89; L. & N. v. Ueltschi, 29 Ky. L. R., 1136.

4. Failure to give the crossing signal was the proximate cause of the injury to this boy. Ill. Cent. R. R. Co. v. Mizell, 18 Ky. L. R., 738; L. & N. R. R. v. Armstrong, 32 Ky. L. R., 252.

5. Negligence of train men in failing to keep a lookout, at public crossing, and check train to avoid injury, was gross negligence. See diagram used on the trial; A. M. and Eng. Encyc. of Law, Vol. 8, p. 393; and evidence of South Conway and his father, J. P. Conway; L. & N. R. R. Co. v. Getz's Adm'r, 79 Ky., 442.

6. If the evidence of South Conway was true (and there is no evidence to the contrary) then the train men could not avoid seeing the boy and horse, when they overtook or passed them on the roadway, and they ran a race with them, for seventy-three yards, to the crossing where the collision occured and this was gross negligence which authorized an instruction for punitive damages instead of a peremptory instruction for defendant. Ill. Cen. R. R. v. Stewart, 23 Ky. L. R., 637; L. & N. v. Simpson, 23 Ky. L. R., 1044; C. & O. v. Dodge, 23 Ky. L. R., 1959.

McQUOWN & BECKHAM for appellee.

BENJAMIN D. WARFIELD of counsel.

POINTS AND AUTHORITIES.

1. There is no denial of the allegation in the answer that the whistle was sounded and bell rung for the crossing; and that the horse ran into a car while the train was passing over the crossing. Newmans Pl. & Pr., Sections 207, 407; Preston v. Roberts, 12 Bush, 581.

2. The horse was alarmed by the noise of the train, and for this, and its consequences, the railroad company is not liable. L. & N. R. R. Co. v. Sights, 121 Ky. p. 210; Clinebell v. C., B. & Q. R. Co., 110 N. W., 347.

3. The horse, in its alarm, at the noise of the train, ran away and threw appellant. This and not the alleged failure to sound the signal, was the proximate cause of the injury. Hendricks v. F. E. & M. B. R. Co., 93 N. W., 141; Clinebell v. C., B. & Q. R. Co., 110 N. W., 347.

4. It is only where the traveler has listened for the crossing signal, and, not hearing it, has placed himself in a dangerous position, and thereby received the injury, that the omission to sound the signal has been held to be the proximate cause of the injury. Such cases are I. C. R. Co. v. Mizell, 18 Rep., 738; Rupard v. C. & O. R. Co., 88 Ky. 280; C. & N., Ry. v. Ogles, 24 Rep., 2160.

The rule of these cases does not apply where the traveler, in a position to see and hear, neither listens for the signal nor looks for the train, but recklessly places himself in a position of danger. He is not misled by the omission.

5. Neither does the rule of the Mizell and other like cases apply where a horse, ridden on a parallel road, is alarmed by the ordinary noise of the train, and, running away, injures the rider. In such case the railroad company is not liable because the horse was frightened by the noise, and the omission to sound the signal is not the cause of the fright or injury. Lynch v. N. P. R. Co., 54 Wis., 348; Pratt v. C. R. I. & P. R. Co., 107 Iowa. 287; Clinebell v. C., B. & Q. R. Co., 110 N. W. 347; Walters vs. R. Co., 104 Wis., 251.

6. The horse was daily ridden across the track, and along a parallel road, with only an overcheck rein, which was not sufficient to control it. It was well known that a great many trains passed daily. This was such contributory negligence as will bar a recovery. Givens v. L. & N. R. Co., 24 Rep., 1796; L. & N. R. Co. v. Webb, 99 Ky. 332; Graney v. Railway, 157 Mo., 666; Spilane v. Mo. Pac. Ry., 135 Mo. 414.

7. The company owed the Appellant, riding on a parallel road, no lookout duty. The duty of the trainmen was to watch the track and not animals straying or ridden in the highways or fields. L.

& N. R. Co. v. Smith, 107 Ky., p. 182; C. N. O. & T. P. Co. v. Bagby, 16 R. 533.

8. It is not the duty of an engineer to check or stop a train, even if he could do so, merely because a horse is running upon a parallel road. This duty does not arise until the horse is either upon, or so close to, the track as to clearly indicate a purpose to go upon it. C. N. O. & T. P. Ry. Co. v. Bagby, 16 R. 533; N. N. & M. V. R. Co. v. Howard, 14 R. 476; L. & N. R. Co. v. Murphy, 6 R., 664.

9. It was impossible to stop the train and avoid the accident when the horse turned from the parallel road and ran towards the crossing. L. & N. R. Co. v. O'Nan, 33 R., 462.

10. The proof does not connect the injury as a rational and proximate result of the alleged negligence, and hence there was no question for the jury. The peremptory instruction was, therefore, proper. C. N. O. & T. P. R. Co. v. Zachary's Adm'r, 32 R. C80; Hummer vs. L. & N. R. Co., 32 R., 1315.

OPINION OF THE COURT BY JUDGE CARROLL—Affirming.

The appellant, South Conway, a boy about 11 years old, brought this action against the appellee railroad company to recover damages for injuries received in a collision between a horse he was riding and one of its trains which was going east. Upon the conclusion of the evidence for the plaintiff the jury, under the direction of the court, returned a verdict in favor of the defendant company, so that the only question before us is whether or not there was sufficient evidence introduced on behalf of the plaintiff to take the case to the jury.

The negligence complained of in the petition as amended consisted in the failure of the train with which Conway's horse collided to give at the usual point, which was some distance west of the place the accident occurred, the statutory signals of its approach to a grade crossing, and the failure of the engineer in charge of the train to exercise ordinary care to prevent injury after the peril of Conway was discovered. The substantial facts shown by the evidence introduced for the plaintiff are these: South Conway, an intelligent boy, lived with his father in a house situated on the north side of the railroad track a few yards from the point where a public road that runs east and west crosses the railroad at grade. On the south side of the railroad there is a road that intersects the county road a short distance south of the crossing, and runs west from the county road parallel with the railroad and a few feet distant from it for some 200 yards, and then goes down an embankment into a creek. On the day of the accident young Conway, desiring to water one of his father's horses, rode it across the railroad, and thence on the road parallel with the railroad to the creek. When he had watered the horse, and was on his way back home, riding along the road that runs by the side of the railroad, and at a point about 75 yards west of the crossing, a freight train, going at a high rate of speed in the same direction that Conway was riding, came up behind him and frightened the horse, causing him to run off. The horse ran towards the crossing, and reached it about the time that the engine did, and was struck by some part of the train; the collision throwing Conway off and breaking his arm. Conway had frequently ridden this horse to water along the same road, and had often met trains about the same place, but the horse had never before become frightened by them.

The law in respect to the duty of trainmen when they come upon a frightened horse being driven or ridden on a parallel road is well stated in L. & N. R. R. Co. v. Smith, 107 Ky. 178, 53 S. W. 269. In that case the horse that Smith was driving on a road parallell with the railroad became frightened at the whistling of an engine, and ran away, injuring the driver. The lower court instructed the jury that they should find for Smith if they believed the employes on the train knew, or by the exercise of ordinary care could have known, that the whistling would cause the horse to run off. In holding this instruction erroneous the court said: "The instructions, so far as they permit a recovery for the whistling, by which the horses were frightened, if the employes saw that if they continued to blow it would cause the horses to be frightened, are proper, and the law; but there is no rule of law that requires employes in charge of an engine to discover the condition of a team or persons on a highway running parallel with the railroad. * * * While it is not their duty to discover such things, yet if the employes do see the apparent danger, it then becomes the duty of such employes to use care to avert the injury. As to persons not on the railroad the obligation to observe care begins when the danger is discovered. The rule that requires a lookout duty in cities and towns and at public or private crossings does not extend to persons on a highway parallel to the railroad." In C., N. O. & T. P. Ry. Co. v. Bagby (Ky.) 29 S. W. 320, in considering a case very much like the one before us, the court said: "It would therefore seem to follow that an engineer cannot be reasonably expected or required to look out for, or see, animals at all distances on each side of a railroad track, nor give the danger signals and stop the train to prevent injury to those straying, unless such animal is actually on the track, or else so near or in such attitude as would induce a person of ordinary care and prudence to believe there was danger of a collision. In this case the engineer did not discover appellee's horse until the train was too near to the private crossing to be checked in time to prevent the collision. * * * Conceding the horse might have been seen by the engineer at any point between appellee's gate and the crossing, still he was not required to stop the train unless he had reasonable grounds to believe the horse would be permitted by its owner to go upon the track in front of the train. It seems to us the engineer was not in this case guilty of actionable negligence, for it does not appear that he saw the horse, or had reasonable grounds to believe it would go upon the track in front of the train until it was about to jump on it." In L. & N. R. Co. v. Bowen (Ky.) 39 S. W. 31, the court, in considering a like question, said: "It would therefore seem to follow that an engineer cannot be reasonably expected or required to look out for, or to see, animals at all distances on each side of the railway track, nor to give the danger signal and stop the train to prevent injury to those straying, unless such animal be actually on the track, or else so near or in such attitude as would induce a person of ordinary care and prudence to believe that there was danger of a collision." To the same effect, Kean v. Chenault, 41 S. W. 24; C. & O. Ry. Co. v. Pace (Ky.) 106 S. W. 1176; L. & N. R. Co. v. McCandless, 123 Ky. 121, 93 S. W. 1041.

The rule to be deduced from these cases is that the persons in charge of an engine are not under any duty to take notice of the conduct or fright of a horse on a parallel highway, or to stop or slacken the speed of the train to avoid a possible collision, unless it is so close to the railroad that the persons in charge of the engine could by the exercise of ordinary care discover that the horse is frightened, and the attitude of the

horse or the immediate conditions are such as would
lead a person of reasonable prudence to believe there
was danger of a collision. The mere fact that the ingi-
neer saw Conway riding along the parallel road did
not require him to check his train, or sound any signal or warning, or take any precaution to avert an injury at the crossing, unless he knew, or by the exercise of ordinary care could have known, that the horse
was frightened and running away, and the circumstances were such as to induce a person of reasonable
prudence to believe that he would attempt to cross the
track in front of the train or come in contact with it
at the crossing. But we do not find in the record any
evidence or circumstance that would justify us in saying that the engineer was negligent in failing to take
any action to avoid a collision with Conway. If we
should assume—and it would be a mere assumption—
that the engineer saw, or in the exercise of reasonable care should have seen, the fright of the horse,
there is a total failure to show any fact or circum
stance from which it could be reasonably inferred that
by the exercise of ordinary care, or any degree of
care, the engine could have been stopped or the speed
of the train slackened so as to have avoided the collision after the fright of the horse was, or should have
been discovered. It is therefore manifest that, so
far as this charge of negligence is concerned, it was
not supported by sufficient evidence to warrant a submission of the case to the jury.

The next question is: "Was the injury due to the
failure to give the crossing signals? It is by statute
made the duty of all trains to give the statutory signals of their approach to a grade crossing, and the
failure to give these signals is actionable negligence
for which a recovery may be had by any person injur-

ed by a breach of duty in this respect. It is also true that travelers upon a public highway that crosses a railroad have the right to rely upon these signals for protection, although the failure to give the signals does not relieve the traveler from the duty of exercising ordinary care for his own safety; for, if by the exercise of ordinary care a traveler could see or hear an approaching train, he will be guilty of such contributory negligence as would defeat a recovery if he goes upon the crossing and receives an injury, although the signals were not given. Generally, the question of contributory negligence is for the jury, but a state of facts might be presented that would authorize the court to take the case from the jury. To illustrate: If it were shown that by exercising ordinary care a traveler could discover the approach of a train, and he testified that he did not take any precautions to learn whether a train was coming or not, and failed to offer any evidence upon this point, he could not recover, although the statutory signals were not given, unless it appeared that after his peril was discovered the persons in charge of the train could, by the exercise of ordinary care, have avoided injuring him. Southern Ry. Co. v. Winchester (Ky.) 105 S. W. 167; C., N. O. & T. P. Ry. Co. v. Champ (Ky.) 104 S. W. 988, 31 R. 1054. This rule, however, would not be applied if the traveler was killed, and there was no evidence introduced to show that he failed to exercise ordinary care for his own safety. As we said in L. & N. R. Co. v. Clark, 105 Ky. 571, 49 S. W. 323, 20 R. 1375, where this point was under consideration: "In this case plaintiffs intestate is not here to testify, and there is an absence of evidence as to the care exercised by him in attempting to cross defendant's track, but it cannot be presumed that deceased recklessly or carelessly imperiled his own life, or entered upon the track knowing of the train's approach. If the presumption of negligence arises from the mere fact that deceased was killed on the track at a place where he had a right to be, it must necessarily defeat recovery in all such cases, unless it appear that those in charge of the train, after discovering the dangerous condition of the parties injured, could, by the exercise of ordinary care, have avoided inflicting the injury." L. C. & L. R. Co. v. Goetz, 79 Ky. 447, 3 R. 221, 42 Am. Rep. 227; L. & N. R. R. Co. v. Taylor (Ky.) 104 S. W. 776, 31 R. 1142.

There is also a plain elementary principle of negligence law that to constitute actionable negligence there must be a concurrence of two things: First, negligence; and, second, injury resulting as a proximate cause of it. It matters not how negligent a person may be, his negligence, unless the injuries complained of were the proximate result of it, will not authorize a recovery in damages. C., N. O. & T. P. Ry. Co. v. Zackary (Ky.) 106 S. W. 842; Hummer v. L. & N. R. Co. (Ky.) 108 S. W. 885, 32 R. 1315. Applying to the facts of this case the rules of law that the traveler must exercise ordinary care for his own safety, and that there must·be some causal connection between the negligent act and the injury complained of before there can be a recovery, let us see what care Conway exercised, and if there is any evidence conducing to show that the injuries received by him were the proximate result of the failure on the part of the persons in charge of the train to give the crossing signals. Conway had frequently ridden the horse along this road when trains were passing, but never before had he become frightened. He does not pre-

tend to say that if the signal had been given he would
not have ridden the horse as he was riding him, or
that he would have remained at the creek, or that he
would have ridden his horse away from the railroad,
or that he would have taken any precautions whatever
for his safety. The evidence leaves no room to doubt
that Conway did not suspect that his horse would be
come frightened at the train, and consequently he did
not feel it incumbent or necessary to take any care to
look out for trains. For some unexplained reason the
passing train, although operated in the usual way and
making only the customary noises, frightened the
horse, but this would as surely have happened if the
crossing signals had been given. It was not the failure to give the crossing signals that caused the horse
to run off, or that resulted in the injury to Conway.
Both of these things were due to the fact that the
horse became frightened at the passing train. To hold
that the failure to give the crossing signals was the
proximate cause of the accident, we would be obliged
to infer, without any evidence whatever to support the
inference, that if the signals had been given, Conway
would have remained at the creek, or have avoided
the road he was accustomed to go over, or have taken
other precautions to prevent his horse from becoming
frightened. These inferences, in addition to having no
foundation in fact would be contradicted by the reasonable inferences that may be drawn from the evidence of Conway tending to show that, if he had
known that the train was coming, he would have ridden his horse along the road as he had done many
times before. If there was any evidence even tending
to show that Conway would have remained at the
creek, or not have ridden his horse along the parallel
road, or that he would have taken any precautions for

his safety, if the train had sounded the crossing signals, a very different question would be presented. The mere circumstance that the collision occurred at the crossing did not in any wise strengthen Conway's case. If the collision had occurred 35 feet from the crossing, or if the horse in his fright had run into a tree or fence or over an embankment, the case for Conway would be the same, because if the negligence of the company in failing to whistle caused the horse to become frightened and run away, it was not important or material how or in what manner Conway was injured by the horse. So that, looking at the question from any standpoint, it was necessary to connect the fright of the horse with the failure to whistle, and it is on this vital point that the case of Conway fails.

Counsel for appellant relies in his brief on a number of cases to sustain his contention that the failure to give the crossing signals was negligence and the proximate cause of the injury to his client; but, in our opinion the cases cited do not sustain the position taken. In Rupard v. C. & O. Ry. Co., 88 Ky. 280, 11 S. W. 70, 10 R. 1023, 7 L. R. A. 316, Mrs. Rupard was injured while riding horseback on the public road at a point where the railroad crosses the public road on an overhead trestle. The negligence complained of consisted in the failure of the persons in charge of the train to give any signals of its approach to this crossing; it being shown that if the signals had been given Mrs. Rupard "could and would, have kept at a safe distance from the crossing until the train passed it, whereby the injury would have been avoided." The court said: "Injury may occur to the traveler at the crossing in two ways, namely: By a collision with him, or by scaring the horse that he is riding or driving, whereby he is injured. It is the duty of the railroad company in approaching a crossing, if danger to the traveler in either of the ways above mentioned may be reasonably apprehend- ed, to give timely notice of its approach, in order that the traveler may not only be warned not to come in collision with the train, but secure himself from in- jury by his frightened horse.'' In this case, however, the court held that a peremptory instruction in favor of the railroad company was proper, because of the contributory negligence of Mrs. Rupard. In Chesa- peake & Nashville Ry. Co. v. Ogles (Ky.) 73 S. W. 751, 24 R. 2160, Lulu Ogles was injured by her horse be- coming frightened at the passing of a train on a tres- tle that crossed the public road upon which she was traveling. The evidence shows: ''That when appellee and her husband had arrived at within about 60 yards of the crossing, they stopped their horse, which was a young and inexperienced animal, and listened for a signal, or any noise that would indicate the ap- proach of a train. But, hearing none, they sent their brother-in-law, who was riding with them, for- ward to the crossing to see if he could discover any evidence of the approach of a train. He informed them that the way was clear. They then proceeded on their way, and while passing under the crossing appellant's train of cars came suddenly from the south, running rapidly over the crossing, making a loud noise, which so frightened their horse that he began to tremble, jump, and make efforts to escape.'' In Illinois Central R. Co. v. Mizell, 100 Ky. 235, 38 S. W. 5, 18 R. 788, Mrs. Mizell, in approaching a rail- road at a point where it was crossed at grade by the public road, on which she was riding, listened for the signal of the approach of a train, but, not hearing any, proceeded towards the crossing, when her horse became frightened at a train that suddenly came in view, causing her to sustain injuries for which she sought to recover damages. Putting the decision of the case upon the ground that the failure to give the signals induced Mrs. Mizell to approach the track, the court said: "The principal ground relied upon by the appellant is that the alleged negligence in failure to blow the whistle was not the proximate cause of the injury; but if, by reason of that failure, the appellee went upon the track and her horse was there frightened by the approaching train, the jury, if they believed appellee's witnesses, had evidence from which they were entitled to find that the negligence was the proximate cause of the injury, and that the damage followed as a continuous and natural sequence from the negligent act, and was a result which might have been foreseen and expected as the result of the conduct complained of, for it was to be expected that passengers on horseback might be traveling along the highway." These cases merely support the rule we have stated that, when the injury is traceable directly to the negligent act, there may be a recovery, but they do not hold that there can be a recovery when there is no proven or presumptive connection between the negligence and the injury.

In our opinion the evidence for Conway was not sufficient to take the case to the jury. Wherefore the judgment is affirmed.

Hobson and Nunn, JJ., dissent.

DISSENTING OPINION BY JUDGE HOBSON.

Section 786, Ky. St. (Russell's St. Sec. 5335), requires railroad companies to provide each locomotive engine passing upon its road with a bell of ordinary size and a steam whistle, and requires that the bell shall be rung, or the whistle sounded outside of in-corporated cities and towns at a distance of at least 50 rods from the place where the roads cross upon the same level any highway, and that the bell shall be rung or whistle sounded continuously or alternately until the engine has reached the highway crossing. Sec. 466 Ky. St. (Russell's St. Sec. 3), also provides that the person injured by the violation of any statute may recover from the offender such damages as he may sustain by reason of its violation, although a penalty is therein imposed. Accordingly it has been steadily held by this court that where the proper signals are not given of the approach of a train to a public crossing as required by the statute, and by reason thereof a traveler on the highway is hurt, he may recover damages. South Conway, a boy 11 years of age, took his father's horse to water, and while riding back from the creek along the county highway approaching the crossing, and on his way to the crossing was hurt in this way: The road ran, as it approached the crossing, for a few yards parallel with the railroad. A freight train, running rapidly, came up behind the horse, giving no signal of its approach to the crossing, and caused the horse to run away, thus injuring the child very seriously. The county road at this point ran along a fill just outside of the railroad ties. No signals of the approach of the train being given, the child was caught in a trap with the creek on one side of him and the rapidly approaching railroad train coming up behind his horse on the other side, where the ties of the railroad ran out nearly to the line of the county road. That the horse should become frightened when a rapidly running train suddenly dashed upon it from behind without warning was to be expected. The danger to the traveler at this narrow point was just as great for all practical purposes as far as the management of the horse went as it would have been if he was at the crossing. The purpose of requiring signals to be given of the approach of the train 50 rods from the crossing is that the traveler may know of the approach of the train, and have an opportunity to take steps for his own protection. When there was a failure of the train in question to give any notice of its approach to the crossing, the child was caught in a trap, and the first he knew of the approach of the train was from the fright of his horse. It is entirely immaterial whether he was at the crossing or 73 yards from it. He was on the county highway. He was riding to the crossing, and as a traveler on the highway, was entitled to notice of the approach of the train, as required by the statute. The fact that the county road for a short distance ran parallel with the railroad in no way lessened his rights. On the contrary, the danger of the situation required a greater degree of care on the part of those operating the train. The opinion seems to be based upon the idea that the child does not testify what he would have done if the proper signals of the approach of the train had been given. If he had undertaken to testify on this subject, the court would manifestly have excluded the evidence. He can tell what he did, but what he would have done under other conditions he cannot testify to; for he cannot be allowed after he is hurt to tell what was in his mind or what he would have done if something had happened that did not happen. He can testify to all that he did, and what he would have done if the signals had been given that were not given must be determined by the jury under the evidence and all the circumstances. The opinion intimates broadly

that, if the child had said that he would have waited at
the creek if signals had been given of the approach of
the train, then a peremptory instruction should not
have been given. It also intimates broadly that, if he
had testified that he would have protected himself in
some other way the peremptory instruction should
not have been given. What he may now say he would
have done if the signals had been given might be entirely different from what he would, in fact, have done.
in the emergency in which he was placed. The question he may testify to is what he could have done.
He was entitled by law to the signals of the approach
of the train. When they were not given, he was deprived of an opportunity to secure himself. If he
'could by ordinary diligence have protected himself
from danger if the signals had been given, then it
should be presumed that he would have exercised ordinary care for a child of his age under the circumstances. It is manifest from the proof that, if the
child had known that the train was coming a
minute before his horse took fright, he could have
turned him around and ridden back down to the
creek, even if it be conceded that he had left the creek
before the train had reached the whistling board.
When signals are not given of the approach of the
train, and the traveler on the highway is injured because he is not aware of the approach of the train,
and is thus caught at a disadvantage, it must
be a question for the jury whether or not his
injury is primarily due to the failure of those
in charge of the train to give the signals
of its approach. In Ill. Cent. R. R. Co. v.
Mizell, 100 Ky. 235, 38 S. W. 5, 18 Ky. Law Rep. 738,
no signals of the approach of a train to a crossing
were given, and the plaintiff's horse ran off with her,

throwing her and injuring her seriously. Sustaining a recovery, this court said: "The principal ground relied on by appellant is that the alleged negligence in failure to blow the whistle was not the proximate cause of the injury; but, if by reason of that failure the appellee went upon the track and her horse was there frightened by the approaching train, the jury, if they believe appellees' witnesses, had evidence from which they were entitled to find that the negligence was the proximate cause of the injury, and that the damage followed as a continuous and natural sequence from the negligent act, and was a result which might have been foreseen and expected as the result of the conduct complained of, for it was to be expected that passengers on horse back might be traveling along the highway."

The same rule is laid down in Rupard v. C. & O. R. R. Co., 88 Ky. 280, 11 S. W. 70, 10 Ky. Law Rep. 1023, 7 L. R. A. 316, although in that case a peremptory instruction was given because Mrs. Rupard was negligent in not looking out for the train. But in this case the child was only 11 years old. He was not upon the crossing, but simply approaching it, and if it is conceded, as in the Rupard Case, that an action may be maintained for the negligence of the railroad company unless there was contributory negligence on the part of the plaintiff, then manifestly the case should have gone to the jury under a long line of opinions by this court. See L. & N. R. R. Co. v. Clark, 105 Ky. 571, 49 S. W. 323, 20 Ky. Law Rep. 1375; L.&N.R. R. Co. v. Ueltschi, 97 S. W. 14, 29 Ky. Law Rep. 1136; C. & O. R. R. Co. v. Vaughn, 97 S. W. 774, 30 Ky. Law Rep. 215; L. & N. R. R. Co. v. Lucas, 99 S. W. 959, 30 Ky. Law Rep. 359; C., N. O. & T. P. Ry. Co. v. Champ,

104 S. W. 988, 31 Ky. Law Rep. 1054; L. & N. R. R.
Co. v. Taylor, 104 S. W. 776, 31 Ky. Law Rep. 1142.

This case is practically on all fours with C. & N.
R. R. Co. v. Ogles, 73 S. W. 751, 24 Ky. Law Rep. 2160,
except that there were in that case facts showing that
the plaintiff was not guilty of contributory negligence. But, as the child here was only 11 years old,
he could only be required to use such care as might
be reasonably expected from a child of his age; and,
if the railroad company was negligent, it cannot
shield itself from the consequences of its own negligence because the child did not take those precautions
that might reasonably be expected of an adult. In so
far as the opinion is predicated in any degree upon
contributory negligence on the part of the child, it
is in conflict with the opinions of this court above
cited; and, in so far as it is based on the ground that
the child does not testify what he would have done if
the signals had been given, it disregards the settled
rules of evidence. In L. & N. R. R. Co. v. McNary's
Adm'r, 128 Ky. 408, 108 S. W. 898, 32 Ky. Law Rep.
1272, 17 L. R. A. (N. S.) 224, where there was testimony by bystanders as to what occurred when the
woman was struck showing just how the accident occurred, and it was insisted that a peremptory instruction should have been given the jury to find for the defendant, this court said: "The woman manifestly could
have seen the train if she had looked in that direction
just before she went on the track, but she had a right
to assume that notice of the approach of a train would
be given and where proper signals are not given, this
court has held in a number of cases that the question
whether the traveler used ordinary care is for the
jury—(citing authorities). To hold as a matter of law
that the footman is guilty of contributory negligence

barring a recovery for his injury whenever he goes
upon a railroad track, without stopping, looking, or
listening would be practically to exempt railroads
from all responsibility in cases of this sort." The rule,
stop, look and listen is not applied. There is nothing
to show negligence on the part of the child except that
he was riding along the road and did not look behind
him. He had not reached the crossing. If his horse
was gentle and did not usually take fright from the
cars, this was at least not a reason for requiring unusual precautions on his part. If his horse had, when
frightened, run back and not forward, to the crossing,
he would have the same right of action if hurt as he
now has. The gist of his action is that the signals to
which he was entitled were not given, and it is not
material whether his horse was thus frightened at
the crossing or a few yards from it. He cannot recover unless he used ordinary care, but what would be
ordinary care for a child 11 years old might not be
ordinary care for an adult. In City of Owensboro v.
York's Adm'r, 117 Ky. 300, 77 S. W. 1130, 25 Ky. Law
Rep. 1397, this court quoted with approval from 7
Am. & Eng. Enc. of Law, 408; "As the standard of
care thus varies with the age, capacity, and exper-
ence of the child, it is usually, if not always, where
the child is not wholly irresponsible, a question of fact
for the jury whether the child exercised the ordinary
care and prudence of a child similarly situated; and,
if such care was exercised, a recovery can be had for
an injury negligently inflicted, no matter how far the
care used by the child falls short of the standard
which the law erects for determining what is ordinary
care in a person of full age and capacity." The same
rule is thus stated in 29 Cyc. 642: "It is also a question for the jury to determine under all the facts

whether a child exercised such care and discretion as might reasonably be expected of one of his age, capacity, and experience situated as he was." In United States Natural Gas Co. v. Talmage Hicks (decided May 19, 1909) 119 S. W. 166, this court said: "The general rule is that, when a child reaches the age of 14 years, the legal presumption is that it knows right from wrong, and it is responsible for its acts. Between that age and seven years the legal presumption is with the child, and, to make it responsible, it must be shown by the testimony that it had sufficient intelligence and discretion to realize and to know what would be the result of its acts. Hence it is always proper to submit the question of contributory negligence in such cases to the jury." See also, 1 Shearman and Redfield on Negligence, Sec. 73. When the plaintiff is placed in a position of peril by the defendant's negligence, and thus suffers an injury, the rule is that he may recover unless at the time he failed to exercise ordinary care for his own safety, and but for this would not have been injured. Here by the defendant's negligence the plaintiff was placed in a position of peril and was injured: and, under the rule heretofore laid down by this court, he may recover unless he failed then to exercise ordinary care for his own safety. What he would have done if the defendant had not been negligent is only material on the question of proximate cause. Western Union Telegraph Co. v. Caldwell, 126 Ky. 42, 102 S. W. 840, 31 Ky. Law Rep. 497, 12 L. R. A. (N. S.) 748; Sutton v. Western Union Tel. Co., 110 S. W. 874, 33 Ky. Law Rep. 577.

The rule in this state is that, if there is any evidence, the question is for the jury. The scintilla rule has been so often upheld that the question is no long-

er open. The proof is abundant that no signals of
the approach of the train were given, and that the
child was thus caught in a trap. By reason of the
want of the signals he had no opportunity to protect
himself as he would have had if the signals had been
given. The facts show that, if proper signals were
given, a person of ordinary care could have protected himself. It cannot be presumed that the child would
not have used ordinary care for one of his age; and,
it being conceded that the defendant was negligent in
the discharge of a legal duty required of it for his protection as a traveler on the highway, it was a question
for the jury whether this negligence was the proximate cause of his injury, and whether he exercised
such care as may be reasonably expected of a child
of his age under the circumstances. The opinion of
the court refers to L. & N. R. R. Co. v. Smith, 107 Ky.
178, 53 S. W. 269, 21 Ky. Law Rep. 848; C., N. O.
& T. P. R. R. Co. v. Bagby, 29 S. W. 320, 16 Ky. Law
Rep. 533; L. & N. R. R. Co. v. Bowen, 39 S. W. 31,
18 Ky. Law Rep. 1099; C. & O. R. R. Co. v. Pace,
106 S. W. 1176, 32 Ky. Law Rep. 806, and L. & N. R.
R. Co. v. McCandless, 123 Ky. 121, 93 S. W. 1041, 29
Ky. Law Rep. 563, but these were all cases where
crossing signals were not involved. The gist of this
case is that the plaintiff was entitled to the crossing
signals, and these were not given. To say that the
child cannot recover because on the facts shown he
was as a matter of law guilty of contributory negligence is to adopt in this state the rule, stop, look
and listen before the traveler reaches the crossing and
to make it apply to a child eleven years old. Under the
opinion, the rule would apply equally if the child had
been on the crossing. If not, why not? For he was

equally entitled to the crossing signals as he approached the crossing as when he was on it.

I therefore dissent from the opinion.

NUNN, C. J., concurs in this dissent.

———————

CASE 31.—ACTION BY CHARLES A. HAHN'S ADMINISTRA-
TOR AGAINST THE LOUISVILLE & NASHVILLE
R. R. CO. AND ANOTHER.—November 9, 1909.

L & N R R Co, &c v. Hahn's Adm'r

Appeal from Nelson Circuit Court.

GEORGE W. STONE, Special Judge.

Judgment for plaintiff, defendant appeals.—Affirmed.

1. Master and Servant—Injury to Servant—Negligence—Evidence.—In an action for the death of a locomotive fireman, evidence held to support a finding that decedent was struck by a semaphore pole maintained at a point so close to the track as to be a source of great danger to trainmen, authorizing a recovery.

2. Master and Servant—Injury to Servant—Assumption of Risk.—Where a railroad maintains obstructions near its tracks, it is liable for injuries occasioned by its neglect of duty, and a trainman knowing of them does not assume the risk.

3. Master and Servant—Injury to Servant—Contributory Negligence.—Whether a locomotive fireman charged with the duty of keeping a lookout in front of the locomotive and to the rear of the train, who was struck by a semaphore pole near the track and killed was guilty of contributory negligence, held, under the evidence, for the jury.

JOHN S. KELLEY, TRABUE, DOOLAN & COX and BENJA-
MIN D. WARFIELD for appellants.

POINTS DISCUSSED AND AUTHORITIES CITED.

The trial court erred in refusing to peremptorily instruct the jury to find for appellants. Plaintiff's theory is that decedent, a fireman for the L. & N., was knocked from his engine, while in motion, by a semaphore pole alongside of, and negligently close to, the track. But no one saw the accident. We are left wholly to conjecture as to where decedent was or what he was doing at the time he was hurt and as to the manner in which he received his injuries. The jury could not have done any more than guess as to whether he was struck by the pole, and defendants' rights should not be guessed away in behalf of one on whom the burden rests to establish a cause of action against them. Further more, they are not liable, even if decedent was struck by the pole, for the reason that it conclusively appears from the evidence that he had no duty to perform that required him to protrude any portion of himself beyond the engine, which it was necessary for him to do in order to be struck by the pole. If he was leaning out, it was for his own purposes, and not in furtherance of defendants' business. Again, even if it satisfactorily appeared from the evidence that decedent was struck by the pole while discharging a duty which made it necessary for him to assume a position of danger, still defendants would not be liable. The semaphore pole was absolutely necessary for the safety of employees and passengers of certain cars which used the elevated tracks where the accident occurred, and was properly placed to serve its purpose. Therefore, its construction and maintenance in that position was not negligence in defendants. The court erred in admitting incompetent evidence for plaintiff and in rejecting competent evidence offered by defendants. And also erred in instructing the jury on plaintiff's motion and in refusing instructions asked by defendants.

AUTHORITIES CITED.

Wintuska's Adm'r v. L. & N. R. R. Co., 14 R., 579; Caldwell's Notes to Kentucky Reports, Vol. 2, p. 1522; L. & N. R. Co. v. McGary's Adm'r, 104 Ky. 509; Hughes v. Cincinnati, etc., R. Co., 91 Ky. 526; L. & N. R. Co., v. Scalf, 110 S. W., 862; L. & N. R. R. v. Milliken's Adm'r, 21 R., 489; Randall v. B. & O. R. Co., 109 U.S., 478; Tuttle v. D. G. H. & M. Ry., 120 U. S., 189; 4 Thompson's Commentaries on the Law of Negligence, Secs. 4755, 4756; Scid more v. M. L. S. & W. Ry. C., 61 N. W., 765, 89 Wis., 188; Thain v. Old Colony R. Co., 161 Mass., 353, 37 N. E. 309; Pennsylvania Co. v. Finney, 42 N. E. 816 (Ind.); Wilson v. L. S. & M. S. Ry. Co., 108 N. W., 1021 (Mich.); Mize v. L. & N. R. Co., 127 Ky. 496; L. & N. R. Co. v. Daniel, 122 Ky., 256; Schlaff v. L. & N. R. Co., 14 Sou., 105 (Ala.); L. & N. R. Co. v. Hall, 87 Ala., 708, 4 L. R. A., 710; Hughes v. General Electric Light & Power Co., 107 Ky., 485; Mayer v. Building Co., 116 Ala., 634; 22 Sou., 859; Martinez v. Planel, 36 Cal., 578; Hudson v. Railroad Co., 59 Ia.,

L. & N. R. R. Co., &c. v. Hahn's Admr.

581, 13 N. W., 735; Hubbard v. Railroad Co., 39 Me., 506; Parker v. Publishing Co., 69 Me., 173; Branch v. Libbey, 78 Me., 321; Wise v. Ackerman, 76 Md., 375, 390, 25 Atl., 424; Collins v. Dorchester, 6 Cush., 396; Bridger v. Railroad Co., 27 S. C., 456, 3 S. E., 860; Snowden v. Coal Co., 16 Utah, 366, 52 Pac., 599; Phillips v. Willow, 70 Wis., 6, 34 N. W., 731; Barrett v. Hammond, 87 Wis., 654, 657, 58 N. W., 1053; Kreider v. W. R. P. & P. R. Co., 110 Wis., 645, 86 N. W., 662; L. & N. R Co. v. Mulloy's Adm'r, 122 Ky., on pp. 335-6; C., N. O. & T. P. Ry. Co. v. Zachary's Adm'r, 32 R,678, 680.

NAT HALSTEAD for appellee.

CHARLES OGDEN, D. A. McCANDLESS and F. E. DAUGHERTY of counsel.

AUTHORITIES CITED.

Shoulder's Domestic Relations, Sec. 230; Civ. Code, Sec. 73; L. & N. R. R. Co. v. Hoskin's Adm'r, 32 Ky. Law Rep., p. 1263; I. C. R. R. Co. v. Smith's Adm'r, 27 Ky. Law Rep., 598; Turner's Adm'r v. L. & N. R. R. Co., 23 Ky., p. 340; L. & N. R. R. Co. v. Gilliam's Adm'r, 24 Ky. Law Rep., p. 1536; Sherill v. C. & O.. S. W., 11 Ky., p. 502 and 89 Ky., 302; Home Tel. Co. v. Beeler's Adm'x, 31 Ky., p. 19; Elliott on Railroads, 2nd edition, vol. 1, Sec. 477; Vol. 1, Sherman & Redfield on Law of Negligence, 5th Edition, Sec. 225; Shulte v. L. & N. R. R. Co., &c., 31 Ky., p. 34; C. & O. R. R. Co. v. Osborne, 97 Ky., p. 112; L, H. & St. Louis R. Co., v. I. C. R. R.Co., 29 Ky., p. 265; L, H. & St. Louis R. Co. v. Kessee, 31 Ky., p. 617; Clinger's Adm'r v. Chesapeake & Ohio, of Ky., &c., 33 Ky., 88; Pugh v. C. & O. R. R. Co., 101, Ky., p. 77; L. & N. R. R. Co. v.Gilmore's Adm'r, 33 Ky., p. 76; L. & N. R. R. Co. v. Creighton, &c., 106 Ky., p. 42; Finley v. Louisville Railway Co, 31 Ky., p. 743; Derby's Adm'r v. Ky. Central R. R. Co., 9 Ky., p. 153; Houston Ry. Co. v. Oran, 49 Texas, p. 341; Cincinnati, &c., R. R. Co. v. Sampson's Adm'r., 16 Ky., p. 819, and 97 Ky., p. 65; Chicago, &c., R. R. Co., v. Johnson, 116 Ill., 206; Cincinnati R. R. Co., v. Sampson's Adm'r, 97, Ky., p. 73; Hugh's Adm'r v. L. & N. R. R. Co., 104 Ky., p. 774, and 32 Ky., p. 13, 14.

OPINION OF THE COURT BY WM. ROGERS CLAY, Commissioner—Affirming.

This action was instituted in the Nelson circuit court by W. G. Hahn, as administrator of Charles A. Hahn, deceased, against the Louisville & Nashville

Railroad Company, the Illinois Central Railroad Company, and the Kentucky & Indiana Bridge & Railroad Company to recover damages for the destruction of the life of Charles A. Hahn. The trial court gave a peremptory instruction in favor of the Kentucky & Indiana Bridge & Railroad Company. The jury returned a verdict against the Louisville & Nashville Railroad Company and the Illinois Central Railroad Company for the sum of $5,000. From the judgment based thereon, this appeal is prosecuted.

While several alleged errors are assigned as grounds for reversal, counsel for appellants state in their brief that they do not care to have the judgment reversed unless this court shall hold that plaintiff made no case to submit to the jury, and that the trial court erred in refusing to award appellants a peremptory instruction. We shall therefore discuss the case from the standpoint of the question thus presented. Decedent, Charles A. Hahn, at the time of his death was in the employ of the Louisville & Nashville Railroad Company and engaged in the capacity of locomotive fireman. The accident occurred on the south track of the Short Route Railway in the city of Louisville. The railway referred to extends from near Floyd street to Thirteenth street, in the city of Louisville. It consists of a double track and passes over a trestle commencing at Floyd and First streets. The grade between Floyd and First streets is very steep. Located about 120 feet west of Floyd street is a semaphore pole which was used for signal purposes for the benefit of all the trains of the different companies using the Short Route Railway track. The Short Route Railway was maintained, controlled, managed, and operated by the Illinois Central Railroad Company as a part of its sysem, under and by virtue of a lease for a period of 99 years. The Louisville & Nashville Railroad Co. had for a long time prior to the death of the decedent been using the Short Route Railway track daily for the purpose of passing its trains over it, and was so using the track on the occasion of the accident. On the day the decedent was killed the Louisville & Nashville Railroad Company was taking a train consisting of 32 cars to the Big Four Railroad. This train was in charge of two engines. The Louisville & Nashville engine was in front, while the Big Four engine was in the rear. At the time of the accident, the train was passing over the south track of the Short Route Railway. The Louisville & Nashville engine was backing. The decedent was thus placed on the side next to the semaphore. The negligence charged is that the defendants suffered and permitted the semaphore pole to be and remain so close and in such dangerous proximity to the track of said Short Route Railway, over which the engine on which the decedent was fireman was passing, as to render same unsafe and dangerous to the decedent in the discharge of his duties as such fireman, and dangerous and unsafe to the employes of the company in operating trains along and over said track. When decedent was last seen he was in the engine at Jackson street. He then had a conversation with the engineer, O'Hern, who told him to have his fire hot as it was a heavy pull up that hill. Some time after passing the semaphore pole, decedent was missing. His body was afterwards found some 30 or 40 feet west of the pole. An examination of the pole showed that there was a fresh mark on it at about the height of a man's head seated in the engine cab or standing in the gangway. Decedent's cap was found

at the foot of the pole. A portion of his brain was
also found about five feet from the pole. There was
no blood or clothing found upon the wheels of the
engine. Blood was found upon the wheels of the
other cars beginning with the car next to the engine.
The top of decedent's head was knocked off. One of
his hands was found about 12 feet west of the semaphore pole. His body was cut in two. Blood and
flesh were found strung along the track from about 12
feet west of the semaphore pole, where the body was
found, a distance of 30 or 40 feet.

The accident occurred on July 4, 1907. It took place
about 4:15 a. m. While the evidence for appellants is
to the effect that it was then broad daylight, the evidence for appellee is that it was barely day, and the
morning being a hazy one, it was necessary in signal-
ing to use lighted lanterns. According to appellee's
testimony, the semaphore pole was located at a point
from 14 to 18 inches distant from a passing engine
or car. The position of the pole was such as to be
a source of danger to the men operating the trains.
According to the evidence for appellants, the pole
was some distance further from a passing engine or
car, and it was necessary that it should be placed at
that point. It was a permanent structure, and had
been there during all the time that decedent was in
the employ of the Louisville & Nashville Railroad
Company, a period of eight or nine months. While
appellants' witnesses testify that it was necessary
that the semaphore pole be located at the point where
it was located, the witnesses for appellee say that it
should have been placed upon the side of the tracks
at a point where its presence would not be dangerous
to trainmen, and in this position it would have been
just as serviceable for the purposes required. It was

shown by various witnesses that it was decedent's duty while not engaged in the actual act of firing, to assist the engineer to keep a lookout. To this end it was necessary for him, not only to look in the direction in which the train was moving so as to avoid coming in contact with people or objects on the track, but also to look to the rear of the train in order to take signals from brakemen. On the other hand, there was testimony to the effect that at the particular time the decedent was killed the engineer could see the head brakeman and take all the necessary signals from him.

It is first insisted by appellants that, under the facts of this case, the jury could do nothing more than guess; that there was no evidence tending to show that decedent was actually struck by the semaphore pole; that he might have fallen out of the engine and the same result followed. While it is true that no one saw the accident, and that whatever conclusion is reached in regard to the cause of the accident is deducible only from the circumstances, in our opinion, all the facts point unerringly to the conclusion that decedent was struck by the semaphore pole. It is altogether improbable that a fall from an engine would have knocked off a portion of decedent's skull. The presence of his cap at the semaphore pole, the fact that the pole was marked at a place where his head would likely come in contact with it, the character of the blow on the head, and the further fact that a portion of his brains were found at that particular point, when considered in connection with the improbability of his death having occurred in any other way, removed the case from the field of speculation, and were sufficient to authorize the finding of the jury that the decedent's head was actually struck by the pole.

But it is insisted that decedent in projecting his head from the engine was acting solely for himself, and not in the performance of any duty in the capacity of fireman. The proof, however, shows that it was the decedent's duty, not only to look in ·front of the engine, but to the rear of the train. If it was a hazy morning, as some of the witnesses testify, it is certainly true that decedent could get a better view, not only of the track, but of the train, by projecting his head out of the engine. Where it is the duty of the fireman to keep a lookout, we will not say that it is negligence upon his part to attempt to perform this duty in a manner that will render it most effective. Nor can we say he was acting merely for his own convenience when his purpose was to serve his master in a most commendable way.

Lastly, it is insisted that the semaphore pole was a permanent structure and necessary for the operation of trains; that the decedent had passed it daily for several months, and he must assume the risk of being injured thereby. In support of this conclusion, we are cited to 4 Thompson's Commentaries on the Law of Negligence, Sec. 4755. It is undoubtedly true that this doctrine has been recognized in certain jurisdictions, but it is not the law of this state. Thus in the case of Cincinnati, etc., R. Co. v. Sampson's Adm'r, 97 Ky. 65, 30 S. W. 12, 16 R. 819; this court used the following language: "It is contended that this bridge has been constructed for many years, and, no employe having been injured or killed by reason of its construction, it must be assumed that it is such a structure as is reasonably safe for its employes. We cannot adopt this view of counsel, but, on the contrary,

it is plain from the record before us that this overhead structure was in no such condition as enabled
this employe to discharge the duty he owed the company, and at the same time however careful, protect
himself from the danger impending by reason of the
unsafe condition of the bridge. The employe assumes
the ordinary risks pertaining to an employment that
is often and necessarily attended with much danger,
but this does not exempt the railroad company from
liability when reasonable precaution on its part would
save its employes from harm, and in a case like this
where the exercise of the slightest care would have
prevented the accident. There can be and has been
no reason assigned in this case why a corporation
with the means to construct a railway would in the
construction of all or large bridges leave them in
such condition as involves its employes, brakemen, in
imminent peril when passing through them, when
with a small expenditure such structures in this regard could be made perfectly safe. We are aware of
many reported cases, some of which have been referred to by counsel, where the absence of ordinary care and the means of knowing the condition of
the bridge by the employes have been held as relieving the railway company from responsibility in such
cases. This court, however, has not followed or approved those decisions in reference to such structures, but, on the contrary, in the case of Derby's
Admr. v. Kentucky Central Railroad Company, 9 Ky.
Law Rep. 153, 4 S. W. 303, plainly intimated that if
the intestate in that case had been required to be on
top of the car as it passed through the structure in
discharge of his duty, and was killed by reason of its
being too low for the cars to pass under, the brakeman, standing erect upon them, a recovery would
have followed.''

In the case of Finley v. Louisville Ry. Co.,
31 Ky. Law Rep. 740, 103 S. W. 343, this court said:
"We are unable to percieve any difference in the
the principles governing the liability of the master
for injuries to a servant caused by an obstruction
overhead and one caused by an obstruction at the
side or any other place."In the same connection the
court uses the following language: "From these authorities it is perfectly manifest that the rule in the
state of Kentucky is that the master is required to
furnish the servant a reasonably safe place to work;
and unless it is in the line of the servant's duty, he
is not required to make an inspection of the place of
work to discover the defects and the danger incident thereto; and he is not precluded from recovering of the master when he is injured by defects or
dangerous obstructions, unless he knows of them or
they are patent to persons of his experience and understanding." In 26 Cyc. 1130, the rule is thus stated: "A railway company is bound to exercise reasonable care and diligence to prevent obstructions or
erections on or over or near its tracks which are a
source of danger to its servants, and will be held liable for injuries occasioned by its neglect of duty."
Many cases are there cited to support the doctrine of
the text.

Under the facts of this case, there can be no doubt
that the presence of the semaphore pole at the point
where it was located was a source of great danger to
men operating the trains along the Short Route Railway. We cannot say as a matter of law that decedent
was guilty of contributory negligence in projecting
his head for the purpose of keeping a lookout at a
time when it would come in contact with the semaphore pole. That was a question for the jury.

We therefore conclude that the court did not err in refusing appellants a peremptory instruction.

Judgment affirmed.

CASE   32.—ACTION BY THE CITY OF LOUISVILLE AGAINST H. B. COOKE AND ANOTHER TO RECOVER CITY TAXES.—November 9, 1909.

City of Louisville v. Cooke, &c.

Appeal from Jefferson Circuit Court (Chancery Branch, Second Division).

Samuel B. Kirby, Judge.

Judgment for defendants, plaintiff appeals.—Reversed.

1. **Wills—Creation of Life Estate—Conditions—Creation of Debts.**—A will devising a life estate to testator's son on condition that, if a judgment was entered against him subjecting his interests in the property or its use or income for his debts, the estate would cease at the date of the judgment, though appealed from, is valid.

2. **Wills—Construction——Judgment for Taxes.**—Under such will that a judgment was entered against the life estate for taxes and the estate ordered sold was not such a debt as determined the estate as it was testator's intention that only debts created by the act of the son himself could have that effect.

C. B. BLAKEY and J. M. CHILTON for appellant.

C. B. SEYMOUR for appellees. No briefs in the record.

Opinion of the Court by Judge Hobson—Reversing.

The will of George G. Cooke, made in the year 1893, contained among other things the following provision: "All the balance of my estate of every character and description, real, personal and mixed, and including the estates in remainder heretofore mentioned in this will, I hereby devise in equal parts to my two sons, H. Brent Cooke and J. Esten Cooke upon the following trusts and with the following limitations, to-wit: The part devised to each of them shall be held by him for his own benefit for the period about to be mentioned, but without any power in him to sell or encumber the same, or to anticipate its income or in any way subject same to his debts, for and during his natural life or until a court of competent jurisdiction shall by a judgment hold that his interest in said property, or its use or income is liable to be subjected to his debts or liable to be sold or encumbered by him, or to have its rents and profits anticipated by him, with remainder after such death or judgment to my grandchildren now born or to be hereafter born, per capita and not per stirpes, but in case of the death of any such grandchild, leaving descendants, before the termination of the particular estate, the interest he or she would have taken shall go to his or her descendants. And though such judgment should be appealed from, still it is my will that said beneficial interest of that son against whom such judgment shall be entered shall cease and determine at the date of the judgment appealed from." The city of Louisville instituted this action against H. Brent Cooke and J. Esten Cooke to recover the city taxes for the years 1906 and 1907 on property which they had received under this clause. They filed an answer, in which they claimed to have a defeasible life estate in the property. Thereupon the city filed an amended petition setting up the conditions under which they held the life estate in the land, and asked for a sale of their life estate to satisfy the payment of the taxes. They demurred to the amended petition. Their demurrer was overruled, and a judgment was rendered against them for the taxes, adjudging that their life estate was subject to the payment of the debt; that under the will their life estate thereupon ceased, and the title to the property vested in their children. Leave was given to the city of Louisville to proceed against the grandchildren of George E. Cooke for the taxes and a sale of the property. The city of Louisville appeals.

It was held in Bull v. Ky. Nat. Bank, 90 Ky. 452, 14 S. W. 425, 12 Ky. Law Rep. 536, 12 L. R. A. 37, that a provision in a will such as that before us is valid. By section 2998, Ky. Stat., all taxes remaining uncollected on the first day of May shall be deemed a debt from the taxpayer to the city, arising as by contract and may be enforced as other contract debts, where the taxpayer is under no disability; but this statute was passed long after the will in question was made. The thing that the testator had in mind was to provide against his two sons selling or incumbering the property in any way or making it subject to debts of their own creation. He had in mind debts voluntarily created by them, not charges created by law without their volition. He had in this provision of his will no reference to the taxes required for the support of the state or municipal government. Their life estate may be sold to pay the taxes without its being terminated as provided in the will. The testator had no intention to so fix the estate as to shield it from taxation or to provide that, if his sons did not pay the taxes on the estate, it should go to his grandchildren.

Under the pleadings the court should have entered a judgment subjecting the life estate of the defendants in the property to the tax claims.   If this
fails to pay the taxes, the city may be allowed to
amend its petition and bring the grandchildren before the court and subject the remainder.

Judgment reversed and cause remanded for further proceedings consistent herewith.

CASE 33.—ACTION BY ROSE SMITH AGAINST MARGARET
    RUEHL.—November 9, 1909.

Smith v. Ruehl

Appeal from Campbell Circuit Court.

Judgment for defendant, plaintiff appeals.—Reversed.

1. Insane Persons—Insane Husband—Lands—Sale by Wife—
    Proceedings.—Ky. St. Sec. 2131, provides that when a hus-
    band has become permanently deranged the wife may be em-
    powered by decree to convey by her own deed any of her
    real estate freed as to it and its proceeds from any claim of
    her husband, providing that the husband shall have been ad-
    judged a lunatic by a court of competent jurisdiction. Held,
    that where a wife, whose husband has been duly declared in-
    sane, filed an ex parte petition in the circuit court stating
    the facts and with it an authenticated copy of the record
    showing the lunacy adjudication and prayed for a decree au-
    thorizing the sale of her land free from any claim of her hus-
    band, and a guardian ad litem was appointed, a decree grant-
    ing the relief prayed without any evidence other than the
    record of the inquest, and without having before the court
    any person representing the husband, was not objectionable
    for failure to make the husband's committee or guardian, if
    any, a party defendant.

2. Insane Persons—Adjudication of Insanity—Conclusiveness.
    A judgment of the circuit court adjudging a husband a luna-

tic was conclusive in a subsequent proceeding by the wife to obtain a decree authorizing a sale of her land free from any interest of the husband as provided by Ky. St. Sec. 2431.

FRANK V. BENTON and HENRY A. FABER for appellant.

WILLIAM U. WARREN for appellee

No briefs. Record misplaced.

OPINION OF THE COURT BY JUDGE CARROLL—Reversing.

In a suit by the appellant to enforce specifically a contract for the sale of real estate purchased from her by the appellee, the appellee defended upon the ground that the appellant could not make a good title. The lower court sustained her defense, and the appellant has brought the case here.

The appellant's immediate vendor obtained the land from a Mrs. Puff, and the only question in the case is whether or not Mrs. Puff conveyed a good title. In 1906 Henry Puff, the husband of Mrs. Puff, was adjudged by the circuit court of Campbell county, in a proceeding instituted for that purpose, to be a person of unsound mind and a lunatic, and he was ordered to be and was confined in one of the state institutions for the insane. Afterwards his wife filed her *ex parte* petition in the Campbell circuit court, in which she set out that she was the owner of certain described land, and that her husband, who had been adjudged a lunatic, was incurable and confined in the state asylum for the insane, and she prayed for a decree that she have the right to dispose of any real estate that she then owned or might thereafter acquire, free from any claim of her husband. Although neither the husband, nor any person, was made a party to the pe-

tition, a summons was issued against him and executed as provided in section 53 of the Code upon the
superintendent of the asylum in which he was confined. Thereafter a guardian *ad litem* was appointed
and when his report was filed the court, without
hearing any evidence, except the record of the inquest, or having before it any person representing
the husband, entered a judgment decreeing that "the
petitioner, Kate Puff, may by her own deed sell and
convey any of her real estate freed as to it and its
proceeds from any claim of her husband."

It is insisted that this proceeding was void, upon
the ground that it was necessary under the statute
that the husband, and his committee or guardian,
if he had one, should be made a party defendant to
the action, and a summons executed upon either the
committee, father or guardian. Secton 2131 of the
Kentucky Statutes, under which the proceeding by
Mrs. Puff was instituted, reads as follows: "When
the husband abandons the wife and lives separate
and apart from her, or abandons her without making sufficient provision for her maintenance, or when
he is confined in the penitentiary for an unexpired
term of more than one year, or when he becomes
permanently deranged in his mind, the wife, by
judgment of a court of equity, may be empowered
to sell and convey by her own deed any of her real
estate freed as to it and its proceeds from any claim
of her husband; provided, that in case of insanity he
shall have been adjudged a lunatic by a court of competent jurisdiction." Under this statute it is not,
in our opinion, necessary that the wife shall do
more, in a case like the one before us, than file her
ex parte petition in the circuit court, stating the facts,
and with it file an authenticated copy of the record

showing that the husband has been adjudged a lunatic by a court of competent jurisdiction. The manner in which a husband may be divested of his interest in the estate of his wife is entirely within the
control of the legislative department of the state,
and it seems that the Legislature only deemed it necessary that the wife should bring to the notice of the
chancellor by her petition the disability under which
her husband was laboring, and that then the court
might make such orders as were necessary to grant
the relief desired without service of process upon
any person or the appointment of a guardian *ad
litem.* It would probably have been better if the
Legislature had prescribed more definitely the practice or method of procedure, or have directed that the
committee or guardian or some person interested in
the person and estate of the person of unsound mind
should be brought before the court to represent his
interests; but it did not see proper to do this, and
we do not feel authorized to supply by judicial interpretation a system of practice and procedure that
the legislative department did not deem it necessary
to incorporate in the statute.

We are confirmed in the correctness of our construction of the statute by the fact that sec. 2145 in
the same chapter in the statute, directing how the
inchoate right of dower of an insane married woman
may be divested upon the petition of her husband,
provides that: "The wife and her committee, if she
have one, shall be made defendants to said action;
if she have no committee, the court shall appoint an
attorney to defend for her, * * * and if the court
be satisfied by the proof that the wife is a confirmed
lunatic, it may adjudge the sale and conveyance of
her inchoate right of dower in said land; and if she

has a committee, the court may direct that he unite with the husband in the deed conveying said land; or if she has no committee, the court shall appoint a commissioner, who shall unite with the husband in such conveyance. A deed so executed shall pass such wife's inchoate right of dower. Before any judgment pursuant to this section shall be rendered, the husband, with at least two good sureties, shall execute, before the court, a covenant to the commonwealth for the benefit of the wife, to be approved by the court, that she shall be paid the value of her right of dower in said land should such right thereafter become complete.'' It will thus be seen that, in providing for the sale of land in which an insane wife has an inchoate right of dower, particular care is taken to protect her interest, and if the Legislature had intended that the same or a similar practice should be followed in a. proceeding to divest the husband of his interest it would have so declared. Why the Legislature did not see proper to guard as carefully the interest of the husband as that of the wife, we are unable to say; but that it did not is manifest from the sections of the statute quoted.

This view of the case renders it unnecessary to consider the regularity of the process served upon the husband. Mrs. Puff filed with her petition copies of the records of the Campbell circuit court showing that her husband was in that court adjudged to be a lunatic. The judgment of that court and the orders appearing are conclusive in this action of the question that the proceedings in the Campbell circuit court by which the husband was adjudged a lunatic were regular. Crown Real Estate Co. v. Rogers (Ky.) 117 S. W. 275.

Wherefore the judgment of the lower court is reversed for proceedings in conformity with this opinion.

CASE 34.—PROCEEDINGS TO APPOINT AN ADMINISTRATOR WITH THE WILL ANNEXED OF J. G. PHILLIPS, DECEASED.—November 4, 1909.

Phillips v. Hundley, &c.

Appeal from Marion Circuit Court.

I. H. THURMAN, Circuit Judge.

From a judgment of the circuit court dismissing an appeal from the county court, Phillips appeals.—Affirmed.

Executors and Administrators — Administrators C. T. A.— Void or Erroneous Appointment—Time for Review.—The appointment, as an administrator with the will annexed, of another than the one entitled to, and asking for, the appointment, governed as provided by Ky. St. Sec. 3891, by sections 3896, 3897, as to appointment of administrators, is not void for want of jurisdiction, but only erroneous; so that it can be reviewed only by an appeal from the county court to the circuit court within 60 days of the order, and not by an appeal from an order denying a motion made at a subsequent term to set aside such appointment and appoint the one entitled to it.

LINDSAY & EDELEN and HUGH P. COOPER for appellant.

1. In conclusion we most respectfully submit that under a fair construction of Sections 3891, 3896, and 3897 of the Kentucky Statutes (Sections 3937, 3919 and 3920 of the Statutes of Kentucky), the family of the deceased have a right until and including the second term of the county court to qualify as personal representatives of the decedent. Buckner's Adm'r v. Buckner, 120 Kentucky, 596.

2. That while the appointment of a creditor or other person is not a nullity where the question arises collaterally, it will never

be held to prevent the appointment of a person specifically named by Section 3896, where the application for such appointment is seasonably made. Young's Adm'r v. Louisville & Nashville R. R. Co., 121 Kentucky, 483; Buckner v. Louisville & Nashville R. R. Co., 120 Kentucky, 600.

3. The question of the validity of the appointment of Kelly and Rogers does not properly arise in this case, because such appointment was not pleaded in the county court when Bird Phillips applied for the appointment at the February term, 1908.

W. W. SPALDING, W. C. McCHORD and SAMUEL AVRITT for appellees.

AUTHORITIES.   .   .

1. The Marion County Court on January 22nd, 1908, had jurisdiction of the subject matter and of all the parties in interest. On this date it entered a judgment defining the rights of the parties. Appellant was before the Court and made her motion to be appointed administratrix. No objection was made to the jurisdiction of the Court. The judgment has never been vacated. Having been rendered by a court of competent jurisdiction it is a complete bar to this action. The issues herein made have become res adjudicata.   Section 1057, Ky. Statutes; Jacobs v. L. & N., 10th Bush. 263; Miller v. Swan, 91 Ky., 36; Kimbraugh v. Harbert, 110 Ky., 94; Sections 3991 and 3894 Ky. Statutes; Underwood v. Underwood's Adm'r, 111 Ky., 966; Section 3905, Ky. Statutes; Underwood v. Underwood, supra; Section 3891, Ky. Statutes; Buckner's Adm'r v. L. & N., 120 Ky., 600; Section 3890, supra; Young's Adm'r v. L. & N., 121 Ky., 483; Spayd's Adm'r v. Brown, (Ky.) 102 S. W., 823; Cunningham v. Clay's Adm'r (Ky.) 112 S. W., 853; McFarland's Adm'r v. L. & N. (Ky.) 113 S. W., 83; Section 978, Ky. Statutes; Penn v. Emerson, 2 Ky. (Sneed) 292; Ward v. Lee, 3 Ky. (Bibb) 18; Com. v. Shanks, 49 Ky. (10 B. Mon. 304.); Daviess County v. Howard, 13 Bush, 101; Seiter v. Northern, 86 Ky., 128; Ayers v. Fuqua (Ky.) 48 S. W., 15; Lovelace v. Lovell, 107 Ky., 676; Kimbraugh v. Harbett, supra.

2. The right to appeal from orders and judgments of the county court to the circuit court is limited to 60 days after the judgment of the lower court was entered. Appellant did not appeal within sixty days after the judgment appointing the personal representative was entered, nor within sixty days after her motion to set aside as void their appointment and to appoint her was made. Her right of appeal was therefore lost. Section 978, Ky. Statutes; Chapters 1 and 2 of Title 16, Civil Code of Practice. Sections 625, 726, 727, 728, 729, 763, 927, 978, and 724.

3. In cases of testacy it is not mandatory upon the County Judge that he should appoint any of the relatives of the decedent as personal representative. In intestacy cases, the rule is different. Therefore the County Judge in appointing appellees Rogers and Kelly as administrators was exercising a sound judicial discretion which the law has reposed in him. Consequently, his action in appointing them was not even erroneous. Chapter 93, Ky. Statutes, Sec. 3891, 3866 Buckner's Adm'r v. L. & N., supra (120 Ky. 600.); Taylor v. Tibbatts, 13 Ben Monroe, 183.

4. The ends of justice do not require a reversal of this case. If it were reversed all that this court upon this record could hold would be that the lower court erred in sustaining appellee's motion to dismiss appellant's appeal from the county court. Upon a return of the case the nominated executors, the widow, and possibly the older children of J. G. Phillips would have precedence over appellant in the appointment of the personal representative.

OPINION OF THE COURT BY JUDGE CARROLL—Affirming.

J. G. Phillips died testate in Marion county in December, 1907. In his original will he nominated E. N. Hundley as executor, but by a codicil John B. Phillips and Owen D. Thomas were substituted as executors in place of Hundley. The decedent left surviving him his widow and four children; one of the children being the appellant, Bird Burton Phillips. The first regular county court day after the death of Mr. Phillips occurred on January 6, 1908. The county court that convened on this day was adjourned until January 10th, when the executors, Thomas and Phillips, offered the will for probate, to which Hundley objected. For various reasons not necessary to mention the disposition of the case was continued until January 22d, when the county court met and probated the will; all opposition to it having been withdrawn. After the probate the nominated executors stated to the court that, if W. C. Rogers and J. A. Kelly were appointed administrators with the will annexed, they would relinquish their right to qualify. In this arrangement the widow and children, except appellant, also concurred. Thereupon the appellant demanded the right to be appointed administratrix, but the court appointed Rogers and Kelly, and on that day they qualified and entered upon the discharge of their duties. The record shows that when the parties appeared in court on the 22d day of January, and announced their desire that Kelly and Rogers be appointed, "Bird Burton Phillips, a daughter of J. G. Phillips, deceased, thereupon by attorney demanded that she be appointed and qualified as administratrix with the will annexed in lieu of the said J. A. Kelly and W. C. Rogers, and in lieu of all other persons," which motion the court overruled; and on the same day the following order was entered: "In the Matter of the Estate of J. G. Phillips. Bird Burton Phillips by attorney moved the court to set aside so much of the order this day entered as appoints J. A. Kelly and W. C. Rogers administrators with the will annexed of J. G. Phillips, and refused to appoint her, Bird Phillips, as a void order; and, the court being advised, overruled said motion, to which Bird Burton Phillips objected and excepted, and prayed an appeal to the circuit court." The county court record also shows that on February 3, 1908, which was the first day of the second regular term of the county court after the death of Mr. Phillips, the following order was entered: "In the Matter of the Estate of James G. Phillips. This day came Miss Bird Phillips, by attorney, and moved the court to appoint her administratrix with the will annexed of the estate of her father, J. G. Phillips, deceased. The court, for reasons sufficient to itself, declined to take action of any kind upon said motion.'' And again, on the 2d day of March, 1908, Miss Phillips appeared in court and renewed her motion, which was continued until March 11, 1908. On May 4, 1908, Miss Phillips filed her affidavit in the county court, setting out her qualifications for and right to the office of administratrix, and ''moved the court to set aside as void the former order of this court appointing W. C. Rogers and J. A. Kelly as administrators of the estate of her father, J. G. Phillips, and to appoint her as administratrix of her said father's estate with the will an-nexed; and the court, being sufficiently advised, over-ruled each of said motions, and on account of the said former appointment refused to grant letters of administration to Bird Phillips, to all of which Bird Phillips objected and excepted and prayed an appeal to the Marion circuit court, which is granted.'' On May 26th Miss Phillips filed and perfected her ap-peal in the circuit court, and when the case came up for hearing, the appellees moved to dismiss the ap-peal, because it was not prosecuted in time. The cir-cuit court sustained this motion, and Miss Phillips appeals.

It will be observed, as shown by the records of the county court, that Miss Phillips appeared in the county court when Kelly and Rogers were appointed ar administrators, and asked to be appointed in their place, and that when her motion was overruled, she prayed an appeal to the circuit court, but did not per-fect it. Appeals in matters like this must be prose-cuted from the county court to the circuit court with-in 60 days after the order appealed from is made in the county court. The order of the county court, made in January appointing Kelly and Rogers administrators and refusing to appoint Miss Phillips, was a final and appealable order. And if she desired to have this order reviewed in the circuit court, an appeal should have been taken and perfected in that court within 60 days thereafter. It is evident however, that the appeal to the circuit court was prosecuted, not from the orders of the county court made in January, but from the order made in May. In support of the right to appeal from the order made in May it is argued that the appointment of Kelly and Rogers under the circumstances stated was void, and hence the county court should have set it aside at any time; and, if it refused, the circuit court should set it aside on appeal. That being a void order, it was not important whether the motion to vacate it was made during the term—that is, before the regular term of the county court in February—or afterwards, and that when Miss Phillips moved the court in May to revoke the appointment of Kelly and Rogers and substitute her, she had the right, within 60 days thereafter, to appeal from the order overruling her motion, and have the matter of the appointment of Kelly and Rogers, and the refusal to appoint her, inquired into. In this view of the case we are unable to agree. If the order appointing Kelly and Rogers was void upon the ground that the court had no jurisdiction to appoint them, there would be much force in the argument presented by her counsel. But the appointment of Rogers and Kelly was not void. It was only erroneous. We may concede that under section 3896, of the Kentucky Statutes, Miss Phillips was entitled to be appointed at the time Kelly and Rogers were, if the widow had declined the appointment; but, as their appointment was only erroneous, and the court had jurisdiction to appoint them, Miss Phillips, who objected to their appointment, should have prosecuted within 60 days thereafter an appeal to the circuit court, and failing to do this, she lost her right to complain about the appointment. In Underwood v. Underwood, 111 Ky. 966, 65 S. W. 130, 23 Ky. Law Rep. 1287, the court held that the appointment of a public administrator before the expiration of three months after the death of a decedent was void—holding that under section 3905 of the Kentucky Statutes the court had no juris- diction to make the appointment until the three months had expired; but this rule has never been ap- plied to the appointment of administrators under sections 3896, 3897 (Russell's St. 3919, 3920), of the Kentucky Statutes; and the appointment of an ad- ministrator with the will annexed is, as provided in section 3891, of the Kentucky Statutes (Russell's St. sec. 3937), regulated by these sections. On the con- trary, we held in Buckner v. L. & N. R. Co., 120 Ky. 600, 87 S. W. 777, 27 Ky. Law Rep. 1009, Young's Admr. v. L. & N. R. Co., 121 Ky. 483, 89 S. W. 475, 28 Ky. Law Rep. 451, Spayd v. Brown, 102 S. W. 823, 31 Ky. Law Rep. 438, Cunningham v. Clay (Ky.) 112 S. W. 852, and McFarland v. L. & N. R. Co. (Ky.) 113 S. W. 82, that the appointment of an administra- tor, not of kin to the deceased, before the second county court day after the death of the intestate, was erroneous, but not void. It, therefore, follows that as the order of the county court appointing Rogers and Kelly was erroneous, the only way to correct it was by an appeal to the circuit court within sixty days from the date of the order making the appointment.

Wherefore the judgment of the lower court is af- firmed.

· CASE 35.—ACTION BY R. A. HURST AGAINST G. P. GOFF.—
November 5, 1909.

Goff v. Hurst

Appeal from Breathitt Circuit Court.

· J. P. Adams, Circuit Judge.

Judgment for plaintiff, defendant appeals.—Reversed.

Brokers—Right to Commissions—Efficient Agent—Procuring Cause of Contract.—Where a real estate broker who had been authorized to sell the timber on a tract of land merely informed the purchaser, who had been negotiating with the owner for some time in regard to purchasing the land, that he had the land·for sale, but did nothing further, and knew nothing of the subsequent negotiations which led up to the sale, which was not made until the vendor agreed that a mill and the down timber would be included, and also agreed to the purchaser's terms as to time of payment, he was not the efficient agent in, or the procuring cause of the contract, so as to entitle him to a commission.

E. C. HAYDEN, W. W. McGUIRE and O. H. POLLARD for appellant.

J. J. BACH for appellee.

Opinion of the Court by Judge Settle—Reversing.

R. A. Hurst brought this suit against C. P. Goff. He alleged in his petition that Goff had employed him to procure for him a purchaser for the timber on a tract of 1,076 acres of land known as the Ware Cannel Coal tract, and had agreed to pay him $500 upon condition that he would procure him a purchaser for the timber at the price of $10,000; that he procured such a purchaser who bought the property, and that Goff had refused to pay him the $500. Goff filed an answer in which he denied that Hurst had procured a purchaser of the timber, or that the sale was in any wise induced by him. There was a trial of the issues thus joined resulting in a verdict and judgment in favor of the plaintiff. Goff appeals.

The evidence introduced by Hurst on the trial was in substance as follows: Samuel E. Patton, in the spring of 1906, had some correspondence with Goff relative to the purchase of the timber, but they came to no agreement. In October the negotiations were renewed, and in December no agreement between them had been reached. At this time Hurst met Goff in Jackson and had a talk with him about finding him a purchaser for the timber. On December 6th he wrote Goff the following letter: "Jackson, Ky., Dec. 6, 1906. Cas. Goff, Esq., Paris, Ky. Dear Sir: I had a talk with you about the property you were in- terested in in this county last fall and you indicated to me that if I found a purchaser to let you know and you would give me the right to sell same. I have a purchaser and he will act promptly. Please put the lowest price on the timber of each tract and give me the number of acres and the location of each tract and at once, and write me by return mail and oblige, Respectfully, R. A. Hurst." On December 10th Goff wrote Hurst as follows: "Paris, Ky., Dec. 10, 1906. Mr. R. A. Hurst, Jackson, Ky. Dear Sir: The only piece of timber we are offering now for sale is a boundary of 1,076 acres at the mouth of Troublesome Creek, known as the Ware Cannel Coal Co.'s boun- dary. The standing timber on this boundary I offer

for $10,000.00. If you can find a buyer at the price
will allow you 5 per cent or $500.00. Very Resp.,
C. P. Goff.''

Hurst immediately upon receiving this letter from
Goff saw Patton and informed him that he had the
tract of land for sale, and that it could be purchased
for $10,000. He asked him to take the matter up
with Goff. Patton said he would examine the timber, and take the matter up with Goff. He did make
an examination of the timber, and on the 31st of
December he closed a trade with Goff, by which he
paid Goff $10,000 for the timber on the land standing
and down and a mill Goff owned. Hurst did not notify Goff that Patton was the man he was furnishing
as a buyer. He did not introduce Patton to Goff. He
knew nothing of the correspondence carried on between them for the sale of the timber. He was not
present at any of the meetings they had, and knew
nothing of them. He did not notify Goff at any time
that he had seen Patton about the timber, and Goff
did not know that Hurst claimed to have had any
thing to do with the matter until a month after the
trade was made. Patton did not buy the timber
through Hurst, but bought it independently of him of
Goff, and he did not make the trade with Goff until
Goff agreed to put in the mill and down timber, and
also agreed to his terms as to the time of payment
of the price. The rule is that, to be entitled to a commission, a broker must be an efficient agent in, or the
procuring cause of the contract, or it is sometimes
expressed he must be the primary procuring cause or
controlling cause. Collier v. Johnson, 67 S. W. 830,
23 Ky. Law Rep. 2453, and cases cited. In the case
at bar Hurst was in no sense the efficient or procur-

ing cause of the contract. At the time that Hurst
saw Patton, he had been negotiating for some months
with Goff for the purchase of the timber, and Goff had
priced it to him at $10,000. Hurst did nothing except
to see Patton and inform him that he had the tract of
land for sale, and ask him to take the matter up with
Goff. He gave Patton no information that he did
not already have except to inform him of his agency.
After telling Patton this, he did not see Patton any
more and had nothing to do with the matter; but Goff
went on and made the trade with Patton without
any help from Hurst. To say on this proof that
Hurst was the primary controlling cause of the contract would be to make the rule mean nothing and
to ignore the principle on which the rule rests. On
the admitted facts the court should have instructed
the jury peremptorily to find for the defendant.
Alexander v. Breeden, 14 B. Mon. 154, is not like this
case. There the agent procured the purchaser, and
the owner of the property prevented him from selling it for the price named as he would have done but
for the owner's interference. In Coleman v. Meade,
13 Bush, 358, the broker procured the purchaser, and
he was accepted by the owner of the property.

Judgment reversed and cause remanded for further
proceedings consistent herewith.

CASE 36.—ACTION BY GEORGE L. GILLUM & SON AGAINST
JOHN W. MILLIKIN AS TREASURER OF LOGAN
COUNTY AND ANOTHER.—November 5, 1909.

Millikin, Treasurer, &c. v. Gillum, &c.

· Appeal from Logan Circuit Court.

W. P. SANDIDGE, Circuit Judge.

Judgment for plaintiffs, defendants appeal.—Affirmed.

1. Counties—Allowance of Claim—Order—Indefiniteness.—An
    order of the fiscal court that "the following claims were al-
    lowed and made payable out of the county levy for 1906;
    'Roads.' Flowers, J. S. Commissioner at Duncan's on Muddy
    River $1,650.00," held void for indefiniteness it being impos-
    sible to determine from the language of the order whether
    he was appointed commissioner to construct a bridge, public
    road or some other public improvement not described.

2. Evidence—County Records—Extraneous Evidence—Admis-
    · sibility.— The fiscal court, like other courts, must speak
    through its records, and extraneous evidence is not admissi-
    ble to show the meaning of its orders.

3. Bridges—Fiscal Courts—Delegation of Discretion.—Although
    the fiscal court cannot delegate to an agent the discretion
    with which the law clothes it, it may after determining the
    necessity therefor appoint a commissioner, not a member of
    the court, to construct a bridge or contract for its construc-
    tion, but it should in advance direct through its records the
    character of the bridge and its cost, and not allow the com-
    missioner a round sum for the work, or leave to his judgment
    the character of the work and the cost, or allow him to ob-
    tain the money in advance for the doing of the work, either
    by a sale or assignment of the warrants therefor, or collect-
    ing it from the county treasurer.

4. Counties—Funds—Disposition.—The fiscal court has no power
    to order the county treasurer to pay into the hands of a
    third person the county's money, to be paid out by him
    months later in satisfaction of county indebtedness created

by him, nor does the fact that such method is customary sanction or legalize the method.

5. Counties—Fiscal Courts—Void Appointments.—An order of the fiscal court appointing one of its members a commissioner to do certain county work was void.

6. Counties—Fiscal Courts—Void Orders—County Warrants—Equity.—Plaintiffs discounted two warrants issued to a bridge commissioner upon a void order of the fiscal court of L county. Both parties acted in good faith. The parties to the transaction only followed a custom which, though unsanctioned by law, had long obtained in the county. The bridge constructed with part of the money received from plaintiffs was of excellent material and workmanship, and its cost was less than expected by the fiscal court. The fiscal court accepted the bridge, which was used regularly by the people, and is worth the cost of construction. Held, that equity required that defendant county should pay plaintiffs the amount they furnished to construct the bridge.

7. Counties—Fiscal Courts—Void Orders—County Warrants—Equity.—Since the bridge commissioners sold plaintiffs void warrants he is liable to them for the difference between what they paid him for the warrants and the amount for which they were given judgment against the county.

R. W. DAVIS and S. R. CREWDSON for appellants.

BROWDER & BROWDER for appellees.

OPINION OF THE COURT BY JUDGE HOBSON—Affirming.

The fiscal court of Logan county during its regular October term, 1905, allowed numerous claims, including one of $1,650 involved in this action. That part of the order allowing this claim is as follows: "The following claims were allowed and made payable out of the county levy for 1906: 'Roads.' Flowers, J. S. Commissioner at Duncan's on Muddy River $1,650.00." Soon after the allowance of the claim, Flowers, who was a magistrate of Logan county and therefore a member of the fiscal court, procured of the clerk of the Logan county court two warrants covering the amount named; one of them being for $450 and the other for $1,200. In November, 1905, he assigned the two warrants to appellees, George L. Gillum & Son, a firm composed of George L. Gillum and Perry Gillum, engaged in the hardware business in Russellville, and received of them $1,552.40 therefor. Of the amount thus received, Flowers expended $1,108.17 in constructing an iron bridge on Muddy river, where it is crossed by the Russellville and Morgantown road near Duncan's in Logan county. Following the completion of the bridge, the appellees, George L. Gillum & Son, demanded of the appellant John W. Milliken, treasurer of Logan county, payment of each of the warrants assigned them by Flowers, but that officer refused to pay them, and appellees thereupon brought suit against him in his official capacity and against Logan county and also against J. S. Flowers to recover the $1,650 claimed to be due them upon the warrants.

The answer filed by the treasurer for himself and Logan county denies any liability on their part upon the warrants, claims that both are void for uncertainty, that the fiscal court was without power to appoint Flowers commissioner to construct the bridge, and that the assignment of the warrants by the latter to appellees was unauthorized and void, as were his acts in constructing the bridge and expending therefor such part of the money he received from appellees as was applied to that purpose. The answer of Flowers alleged the bona fides of the assignment of the warrants to appellees, and of his acts in constructing the bridge and expending therefor the money received of appellees, and also alleged that out of the balance of $444.23 he claimed was left in his hands after paying for the bridge he paid $260 for road work in the Russellville magisterial district which the fiscal court had directed him as commissioner to have done, but later refused to pay him for, and was entitled to $42 for his services in superintending the building of the bridge, and these sums, which, it was averred, he was entitled to be paid out of the $444.23, left in his hands, but $184.23, and the latter sum he was, as alleged, entitled to retain for services rendered by him as commissioner of public roads by order of the fiscal court. Responsive pleading controverting both answers was filed by appellees.

The circuit court on the issues thus made, and following the taking of proofs by the parties, rendered the following judgment, viz.: "These consolidated causes coming on to be heard upon the pleadings and testimony and the court being advised, it is now adjudged by the court that the plaintiffs, George L. Gillum and Perry Gillum, partners trading as George L. Gillum & Son, recover of the defendant, Logan county, the sum of $1,108.17, with interest thereon at the rate of 6 per cent. per annum from the 1st day of January, 1907, and two-thirds of their costs in these actions expended, for which execution may issue after 10 days. To which judgment the defendant Logan county objects and excepts, and prays an appeal to the Court of Appeals, which is granted. It is further adjudged by the court that the plaintiffs as above named recover of the defendant J. S. Flowers, the sum of $454.83, with interest thereon from January 1, 1907, until paid at the rate of 6 per cent. per annum, and one-third of their costs in these actions expended, for which execution may is-

sue after 10 days. To all of which judgment against
him the defendant J. S. Flowers objects and excepts,
and prays an appeal to the Court of Appeals, which
is granted. The court delivered a written opinion
in these actions, which is hereby filed and made a
part of this record, and these cases are hereby continued.'' We concur in the conclusions expressed in
the written opinion of the circuit court that the order
allowing Flowers the $1,650 was and is void, because
of its indefiniteness and the want of authority on
the part of the fiscal court to appoint Flowers, one of
its members, a commissioner to construct a bridge.
It is impossible to determine from the language of
the order for what purpose Flowers was appointed
a commissioner, whether to construct a bridge. public
road, or some other public improvement not described.

The fiscal court, like other courts, must speak
through its records. Extraneous evidence to show
the meaning of its orders will not be allowed. As
the fiscal court, though a court of record, is one of
limited jurisdiction and powers the greater reason
exists for applying to its records the rule referred
to, otherwise the counties of the state could not conduct their monetary affairs with safety, or protect
themselves from expensive and unnecessary litigation. The fiscal court cannot delegate to an agent
the discretion with which the law clothes it. It may,
after determining the necessity therefor, appoint a
commissioner, not a member of the court, to construct a bridge or contract for its construction, but
in doing so it should in advance direct through its
records what character of bridge it should be and
its cost, instead of allowing him a round sum with

which to do the work and leaving to his judgment
what shall be the character of the work and its cost,
or allowing him to obtain the money in advance of
the doing of the work, either by a sale and assignment of warrants therefor, or collecting it from the
county treasurer.

The treasurer of the county is the legal custodian
of its money and responsible upon his official bond
for its safe-keeping and payment, and the fiscal court
has no power to order the county's money paid by
the treasurer into the hands of another person to be
paid out by the latter some months later in satisfaction of the county's indebtedness created by the person receiving the money. Nor can the fact that such
a method of building and paying for roads and
bridges had long been a matter of custom in Logan
county sanction or legalize the method. In the in-
stant case the warrants embracing the sum allowed
for the construction of the bridge were assigned to
and discounted by appellees in November or December, 1905, when the commissioner had not made a
contract for the construction of the bridge, and did
not know what it would cost. The money he received upon the warrants he held until the summer of
1906, when about two-thirds of it was paid on the
bridge, leaving the remainder in his hands, which, it
is claimed for the county, has not since been expended as contemplated by the fiscal court. Such methods of conducting the business of a county cannot receive our approval. In no event had the fiscal court
the power to appoint Flowers commissioner to construct the bridge in question, as he was a magistrate
of Logan county, and, by virtue thereof a member
of the fiscal court of the county. In the case of

Pulaski County v. Sears, 117 Ky. 249, 78 S. W. 123, 25 Ky. Law Rep. 1381, it was held that an order of the fiscal court investing the county judge with the general supervision of the roads of the county and making the magistrate in each magisterial district his assistant was void. In Boyd County v. Arthur, 118 Ky. 932, 82 S. W. 613, 26 Ky. Law Rep. 906, it is said: "The statutes that we have referred to have the same end in view when they forbid members of the fiscal court being interested in any contract or work. * * *'' Vaughn v. Hulett, 119 Ky. 380, 84 S. W. 309, 27 Ky. Law Rep. 35; Daviess County v. Goodwin, 116 Ky. 891, 77 S. W. 185, 25 Ky. Law Rep. 1081. It is patent, however, from the record that the warrants issued to Flowers were discounted by appellees in good faith, and that Flowers also acted in good faith in so disposing of the warrants. Indeed, the record casts no reflection upon the character of any of the parties to the transaction, but, on the contrary, shows that they but followed a custom which, though unsanctioned by the law, had long obtained in Logan county. It conceded that the bridge constructed across Muddy river near Duncan's, under the supervision of Flowers, was of excellent material and workmanship, and that its cost was less than was expected by the fiscal court. As before stated, the bridge cost $1,108.17, and this sum was admittedly paid by Flowers out of the $1,552.40 obtained from appellees upon the warrants. As the fiscal court of Logan county seems to have accepted the bridge and it has been in use by the people of the county since its completion and is conceded to be worth the amount expended by Flowers in its construction, we think equity requires that Logan county should pay appellees the $1,108.17 they furnished to construct the bridge.   Therefore in so adjudging the circuit court did not err.   As Flowers, however innocent of any purpose to wrong them, sold and assigned appellees, the two void warrants, he is liable to them for the difference between what they paid him for the warrants and the amount for which they were given judgment against Logan county; that is, they were entitled to recover of him $454.83, with interest from January 1, 1907, and for this sum and interest the circuit court very properly gave appellees judgment against Flowers.

The circuit court did not pass upon the credits and demands asserted against the claim of appellees and against Logan county by the answer of Flowers, nor will we do so, as it appears that these matters cannot be relied on to defeat appellees' claim, and besides they, with other like demands, are involved in another action between Flowers and Logan county, pending in the Logan circuit court.

Finding no error in the judgment appealed from, it is affirmed both as to Logan county and J. S. Flowers.

CASE 37.—ACTION BY JOHN WICKHAM'S ADMINISTRATOR AGAINST THE LOUISVILLE & NASHVILLE RAIL- ROAD COMPANY FOR CAUSING THE DEATH OF PLAINTIFF'S INTESTATE.—November 10, 1909.

Wickham's Adm'r v. Louisville & Nashville R R. Company

Appeal from Spencer Circuit Court.

CHAS. C. MARSHALL, Circuit Judge.

Judgment for defendant, plaintiff appeals.—Affirmed.

1. Master and Servant—Injuries to Servant—Contributory Negligence.—Where a watchman employed to keep trespassers on a railroad track from being injured by trains suddenly stepped without looking from a place of safety before an approaching train, which he knew was due, he was negligent as a matter of law barring a recovery for his death.

2. Master and Servant—Injuries to Servant—Care Required of Master.—A railroad does not owe to its watchman employed to keep trespassers on the track from being injured by trains the duty of regulating the speed of its trains, and it is not liable for the death of the watchman struck by a train merely because it operated the train at a negligent speed, because of the fact that the public customarily used the track at that point, which was within an incorporated town.

REASOR & CRUME and EDWARDS, OGDEN & PEAK and PEAK & HOLLAND for appellant.

We assert that we were entitled to have the jury pass upon the question as to whether thirty-five miles an hour under the circumstances proven in the case at bar was a negligent rate of speed which was the proximate cause of Wickham's death.

The same rule, that is, that it is the duty of the railroad to moderate the speed of its trains in such localities, has been announced by this court in a number of cases, of which are the following: L. & N. R. R. Co. v. Schuster, 10 Ky. Law Rep., 65;

Connelly's Admr. v. Cin., etc., R. R., 89 Ky. 402; Gunn v. Felton's Receiver, 22nd Ky. Law Rep., 268; 108 Ky., 561; C. & O. R. R. Co. v. Perkins, 20th Law Rep., 608; L. & N. R. R. Co. v. McComb, 21st Law Rep., 1233; C. & O. R. R. Co. v. Keelin's Adm'r, 22nd Ky. Law Rep., 1942.

LUTHER C. WILLIS and BENJAMIN D. WARFIELD for appellee.

·   POINTS DISCUSSED AND AUTHORITIES CITED.

In this action to recover damages for the killing of a yard watchman by being struck by a fast train, while said watchman was on duty, and when he knew the train was coming, the trial court properly instructed the jury to find for defendant. No negligence was proven against it. But even if it could be said that the train was run at a negligent rate of speed, that negligence was not the proximate cause of the accident. Decedent was at a safe place until the engine of the train had almost overtaken him, when he suddenly stepped closer to the track the train was on, and was struck and killed before there was time to do anything to avert the accident after he assumed a perilous position. Furthermore, even if the speed of the train was negligence, decedent's stepping on the track immediately in front of the train was also negligence, and if the negligence of both parties concurred to produce the accident, plaintiff cannot recover, as tne doctrine of comparative negligence does not prevail in Kentucky, but the doctrine is that contributory negligence bars a reeovery. L. & N. R. Co. v. Redmon's Adm'rx., 122 Ky. 385; I. C. R. Co. v. Willis' Adm'rx., 123 Ky. 636; I. C. R. Co. v. Dick, 91 Ky. 434; Coleman's Adm'r v. P. C. C. & St. L. R. Co., 23 R. 401; C. N. O. & T. P. R. Co. v. Harrod's Adm'r, 115 S. W. 699; Johnson's Adm'r v. L. & N. R. Co., 91 Ky. 651; Givens, by etc., v. L. & N. R. Co., 24 R. 1796; I. C. R. Co. v. Hocker, 21 R. 1398; Ford's Adm'r v. Paducah City Ry., 124 Ky. 488; L. & N. R. Co. v. Tower's Adm'r, 115 S. W. 719; Hummer's Extrx. v. L. & N. R. Co., 128 Ky. 486; L. & N. R. Co. v. Mounce's Adm'r, 28 R. on . 937.

OPINION OF THE COURT BY WM. ROGERS CLAY, COMMISSIONER—Affirming.

Appellant, J. W. Crume, as administrator of John Wickham, instituted this action against appellee, Louisville & Nashville Railroad Company, to recover damages for the destruction of the life of John Wickham. At the conclusion of all the testimony the court awarded appellee a peremptory instruction.

The deceased, John Wickham, was killed on April 29, 1908. At the time of his death he was 53 years of age. He was then in the employ of appellee in its South Louisville yards as day watchman, and had been working in that capacity for about six months. He was earning $40 per month. His duties as watchman were to protect the property of appellant in its yard at the point where he was stationed, and to see that school children and other trespassers were kept off the track and not injured by passing trains. The deceased was killed in Highland Park, an incorporated town of about 2,000 inhabitants. Highland Park is situated about one-half mile south of the southern limits of the city of Louisville. Its principal thoroughfare is Ottawa street, which crosses the tracks of appellee about 150 feet north of the station at Highland Park, about 680 feet south of the "FX" tower, and about 700 feet south of the point where decedent was killed. At the "FX" tower, the point near which decedent lost his life, appellee had three tracks, namely: North Main, South Main, and "Drill track." Just north of the "FX" tower the tracks became numerous and constitute appellee's yards; there being 12 tracks in all. There is a street on each side of the yards, one on the east and one on the west, running north from Ottawa street. They run for a short distance only. At the place where decedent was killed, appellee's right of way was about 80 feet wide. There was proof tending to show that a number of persons passed across the track at this point. Appellant was struck by train No. 4, which is a fast passenger train running between Nashville and Cincinnati. It was due at the

"FX" tower just north of Highland Park at 8:43 a. m. It was on time on the morning of April 29, 1908. It was then running between 25 and 30 miles an hour. Its speed was a little less than its usual rate.

Just prior to the accident the decedent was in the tower house talking to one Harry Barker. In the presence of decedent, and at a time when decedent was close enough to hear, Mr. Daniels, the tower operator, told Barker that No. 4 was approaching. Barker and decedent then left the tower house. Train No. 4 did not stop at the tower house. When it arrived it gave the usual signals of its approach by blowing the whistle and continually ringing the bell. The decedent went to a point between North Main track, that on which No. 4 was running, and track No. 1. At that time he was in a safe place. These tracks were about 10 feet apart. He then walked a distance of about 25 feet between these two tracks until he got where the switch target was located. As decedent approached the switch target, the yard engine was coming toward the switch target with a number of freight cars attached, and was making the usual and customary noises incident to a moving freight train. When decedent reached the switch target, he turned to pass between it and the North Main track. This brought him in dangerous proximity to train No. 4, which was then passing. Up to that time he had been in a safe place. When he attempted to step between the switch target and the North Main track, train No. 4, was right on him, and he was struck by the engine and killed.

It is not charged that there was any negligence in failing to give the usual, customary, and timely warning of the approach of the train. It is not alleged that those in charge of the train saw, or by the exercise of ordinary care could have seen, decedent in time to avoid injuring him. The only negligence relied upon is the speed of the train. To sustain this contention it is argued that it was shown that there was a customary use by the public of appellee's tracks at that point, and, as the accident happened in an incorporated town, appellee should have run its train with reference to the presence of such persons, and that it was negligence on its part to pass that point at a speed of 25 or 30 miles an hour. In considering this question, it must be remembered that there was some evidence tending to show that decedent had actual notice of the approaching train. Whether this be true or not, it is certainly true that decedent was employed to keep trespassers on the tracks from being injured. He had been employed as watchman for six months. It was his duty to know the time of the arrival and departure of trains at that point. What, then, was the duty of appellee towards decedent?

In the case of Conniff v. L. H. & St. L. Ry. Co., 124 Ky. 736, 99 S. W. 1154, 30 Ky. Law Rep. 982, where damages were sought for the death of a flagman who was stationed by the railroad company at a street crossing in Louisville to warn persons of the approach of trains, this court said: "It was as much the duty of Conniff to keep a lookout for trains approaching the crossing, and give warning to travelers, when he was arranging to switch targets, as it was when he had finished his task and was engaged in no other way than as flagman. Resting the case upon this ground, appellee did not owe Conniff any lookout duty, and was under no obligation to give him warning of the approach of its trains; in fact, owed him no duty, until, as the court said in the instruction, he was discovered to be in peril.

In the case of Cincinnati, N. O. & T. P. Ry. Co. v. Harrod's Adm'r (Ky.) 115 S. W. 699, the distinction between the duty owing by railroad companies to a licensee and to those whose duty it is to know of the time of the arrival of trains is clearly pointed out. There the decedent was a brakeman in the employ of the Southern Railway Company. He was at work in the railroad company's yards at Georgetown, Ky., and was engaged with others in shifting cars. This court, in discussing the question of excessive speed said: "If Harrod had been a section workman in the yards at Georgetown, his case would not have been less than it is. Section men work in railroad yards, as well as in the country, at all times, and may reasonably be expected there at any time. They must be aware of the time of the running of the trains over the track on which they are at work. Even though those in charge of a fast train knew they were working at that point, or might reasonably be expected to be working there, they also knew it was their duty to maintain a clear track for that train and to themselves keep out of its way, as they well could. Would the speed of the train, even though negligence to the passengers or licensees, have been negligence as to them? We think not, and it would make no difference whether they were in the yards at Georgetown, at Kincaid, or in the country where there was no station, for it must always be borne in mind that negligence toward a person is the antithesis of a duty owing to that person.

But the facts of this case carry us one step further. Decedent actually knew that train No. 4, a fast through passenger train, was due to pass that point at 6:50. He obtained the knowledge for the very purpose of keeping out of its way. When it came along at the very moment that it was due to come, it were as if he had at that moment notice of the fact. Why do trains whistle and ring their bells? Obviously to notify people, whom they owe a duty to, of their approach. If, then, the person to be notified already knows the fact, why again notify him? L. & N. R. R. Co. v. Taaffe's Adm'r, 106 Ky. 535, 50 S. W. 850, 21 Ky. Law Rep. 64; Helm v. L. & N. R. R. Co., 33 S. W. 396, 17 Ky. Law Rep. 1004; Craddock v. L. & N. R. R. Co., 16 S. W. 125, 13 Ky. Law Rep. 18. And why are trains required by common law to slacken their speed when passing through populous settlements? Because it is far more probable that one or more persons from among so great a number may be, and probably will be, rightfully using the tracks of the railroad at that point at that moment unaware of the train's approach, and, if the too high rate is maintained, they will be run over and killed or injured before they could get out of the way, even after learning that the train was coming. But those who know that the fast train is due and coming in cannot rely upon its duty towards others ignorant of the fact, so as to charge its operatives with negligence in running it at high rate of speed, for with their knowledge, by keeping off the track, the speed of the train would be harmless to them.

But the facts here carry us still another step. Decedent unnecessarily went from a place of safety to one of great hazard to serve his own convenience alone, and thereby put himself in a position where no amount of care in operating train No. 4 would have saved him. They could not see him until he sud-

denly stepped out on the track immediately in front
of their engine. Whether running 20 or 50 miles an
hour then, the train could not have been stopped in
time to avoid striking him. Between the tracks was a
safe place in which to do his work. On the west side
was safer, though not quite so convenient. To step
into the middle of the main track, at the moment a
fast, heavy train was due, and which he knew was
due, without looking, is such an act of negligence
that its quality is not debatable. Nor can it be ignored in law. Being established without question, its
legal effect is a pure question of law.

The rule laid down in I. C. R. R. Co. v. Murphy's
Adm'r, 123 Ky. 787, 97 S. W. 729, 30 Ky. Law Rep.
93, 11 L. R. A. (N. S.) 352, is not applicable to this
case. There Murphy was one of the public, and a
licensee. In this case the decedent was an employe
whose duty it was, not only to keep others out of the
way of approaching trains, but himself likewise. Furthermore, Wickham, who had been in a place of
safety, suddenly stepped before the approaching
train, which he knew was due, and without looking.
As said in the case of Cincinnati, N.O. & T.P. Ry. Co.
v. Harrod's Adm'r, supra, this was such an act of
negligence that its quality is not debatable.

In view of the foregoing authorities, we conclude
that the speed of the train at the time of the accident
was not negligence as to the decedent. It would be
a strange rule, indeed, that would require a railroad
company to regulate the speed of its trains with
reference to the presence of a watchman, whose duty
it was to know when the train would arrive and keep
others and himself from being injured by it. As no
other negligence is relied upon, we conclude that the
court properly directed a finding in favor of appellee.

Judgment affirmed.

CASE 38.—CONSOLIDATED CROSS ACTION BY ED. DOYLE, A
DEFENDANT IN SEVERAL ACTIONS, AGAINST OF-
FUTT & BLACKBURN.—October 29, 1909.

Doyle v. Offutt & Blackburn

Appeal from Scott Circuit Court.

R. L. STOUT, Circuit Judge.

From the judgment the defendants appeal.—Reversed.

1. Appeal and Error—Consolidation of Actions—Discretion of
    Trial Court—Review.—The action of the court in directing
    that an original cause of action and a cause of action pre-
    sented by cross-petition shall be heard together by the same
    jury will not be disturbed unless it appears that, in the ex-
    ercise of a sound discretion, the court should have ordered
    separate trials before separate juries.

2   Jury—Competency of Jurors—Prior Service—Similar Cause
    —In actions by buyers of seed wheat based on the seller's
    warranty that the wheat was good, and the fact that it did
    not germinate, the seller made his pleading a cross-petition
    against a warehouseman alleging that he had stored the
    wheat in the latter's warehouse, and that the latter violated
    his agreement. Some of the actions by the buyers were tried
    before juries without the issues made by the cross-petition be-
    ing heard. Thereafter the actions on the cross-petitions were
    consolidated, and were called for trial at the same term of
    court. Held, that the refusal of the court to continue the
    consolidated action or to impanel a new jury to try it on
    the ground that the jurors on the regular panel had served
    in trying the issues in the original actions was proper; the
    actions being entirely different, though in relation to the
    same subject matter.

3. Evidence—Parol Evidence—Receipts—Contracts.—A receipt
    issued by a warehouseman stating the receipt of a speci-
    fied quantity of wheat for delivery on the presentation of the
    receipt properly indorsed and the payment of the charges,
    and which provides that the wheat is held for the owner at

Doyle v. Offutt & Blackburn.

his risk as to fire or depreciation, that the grain may be mixed with grain of like quality and may be delivered from any bin containing like quality of grain, is more than a receipt, and is a contract fixing the rights of the parties, and parol evidence is admissible to vary its terms, in the absence of fraud or mistake, though a receipt may be contradicted by parol evidence without any averment of fraud or mistake.

4. Trial—Instructions—Evidence.—Where a written contract be-tween the parties to an action is set up or relied on in tne pleadings or is introduced in the evidence, the court should instruct on the writing, and, though there is evidence of mistake or fraud or want of consideration, the court should charge that the writing is the contract unless the jury believe that it was not executed, or that it was without consideration, or was procured by fraud or mistake.

5. Evidence—Parol—Admissibility.—Where there is a denial of the execution of a written contract relied on or an averment of want of consideration or of fraud or that by mutual mistake it does not contain the contract, parol evidence is admissible.

6. Trial—Instructions—Pointing Out Particular Evidence.—The rule that it is not proper to point out particular evidence in an instruction or to give undue prominence to any fact applies to parol evidence. and not to written evidence of a contract.

B. M. LEE, attorney for appellants.

CITATIONS.

1. The court should have continued the case or empaneled a new jury. Taylor, &c, v. Combs, 20 Ky. Law Rep., 1828; Herndon v. Bradshaw, 4 Bibb., 45; McKinley v. Smith Hard., 167; Pierce v. Bush, 3 Bibb., 347; Fitzpatrick v. Haris, 16 B. Mon. 564.

2. The court should have instructed the jury that if they believed that defendants only agreed to deliver No. 2 wheat and that plaintiff inspected and accepted as No. 2 wheat that offered by defendants they ought to find for defendants. Jones v. McEwan, 11 Rep., 138; Overman v. Nelson, 15 Rep., 92; Munford & Co. v. Kevil & Sons, 22 Rep. 730; 109 Ky., 246.

BRADLEY & BRADLEY for appellee.

We submit that in all cases where acceptance of an article has been held to bar recovery for a defect the defect was one discoverable by the inspection. This must necessarily be so for certainly the law is not so unjust as to estop a man because or

the use of a right which could do him no good in the particular
case.

So granting that the Court should have given any instruction
on this point the instruction would certainly not be more than
that the acceptance of the wheat by appellee barred him from
recovery if he discovered the defect by an inspection or could have
discovered it. The cases, which hold he is barred are limited to
this doctrine.

AUTHORITIES CITED.

1. The court properly refused to discharge the panel which
had tried the original issue. Smith v. Commonwealth, 100 Ky.,
133; Fowler v. Commonwealth, 7 Ky. Law Rep,. 529.

2. The Court properly instructed the jury as to the liability
of appellants. Pepper's Adm'x v. Harper, 20 Ky. Law Rep., 837;
Read v. Langford, 26 Ky. Law Rep. 420; Continental Life Ins. Co.
v. Randolph, 3 Ky. Law Rep., 188; Roundtree v. Glatt, 13 Ky. Law
Rep., 462; Pierce v. Brown, 12 Ky. Law Rep., 292; Anderson v.
Baird, 19 Ky. Law Rep., 444.

3. The Court properly refused to instruct that the appellee
was barred by his acceptance of the wheat.   W. F. Main & Co.
v. Fielder, 144 N. C., 307; Glucose Sugar Refining Co. v. The
Coffee & Baking Powder Co., 81 N. E., 589; Krunman v. Roush
Produce Co., 59 S. E., 320; North Baltimore Bottle Glass Co. v.
Alpeter, 113 N. W\, 435; Heath Dry Gas Co. v. Hurd, 108 N. Y
S., 410.

OPINION OF THE COURT BY JUDGE CARROLL—Reversing.

The appellants are seed warehousemen, and in
July, 1907, the appellee Doyle stored in their warehouse some 600 bushels of wheat. In the fall of the
same year the appellee sold this wheat to a number of
farmers, who wanted it for seeding purposes. The
farmers to whom the wheat was sold sowed it, and it
failed to germinate. Thereupon the farmers brought
suits against appellee for damages, and each of them
recovered judgment against him for the price paid
for the wheat. The suits of the farmers were based
on the ground that the wheat was bought to be used

as seed wheat, and for no other purpose, and that appellee warranted it to be good seed wheat.

In his answer to these various suits, which was in substance a traverse, appellee made his pleading a cross-petition against appellants, averring in the cross-petition: That, when he stored the wheat in the elevator of appellants, he informed them that it was to be sold as seed wheat, and they agreed to store the same in a separate bin or elevator and deliver to him, or the persons to whom he might sell, the identical wheat stored, and also to deliver No. 2 wheat. That in violation of their agreement appellants failed to keep the wheat in a separate bin or elevator and mixed it with other wheat, allowing it to become overheated, and also that they failed to deliver to him No. 2 wheat.

. He also averred that by mistake appellants issued to him the following receipt: "Received in store from Ed. Doyle, 601 bushels of wheat, grade No. 2, which we will deliver to Ed. Doyle, or order, upon presentation of this receipt properly indorsed, on payment of charges. This property is held for the owner in store at his risk as to fire or depreciation from any cause. This grain may be mixed with grain of like quality, and may be delivered from any bin containing like quality of grain." And that, when he learned the contents of the receipt, he notified them that a mistake had been made in its issual, and they told him to keep the receipt, and they would store his wheat in a separate bin or elevator. He asked judgment against them for the amount of any judgment that might be obtained against him by the farmers who had sued him. To this cross-petition the appellants filed an answer denying all its material allega-

tions, but they did not set up or rely on the receipt
as containing the contract between them.

It appears from the record that three of the suits
filed by the farmers against appellee were tried before juries without the issues made by the cross-
petition being heard or disposed of, and that after
verdicts had been returned in favor of the farmers in
these cases the actions of appellee against appellants
on his cross-petition in the cases in which the farmers had obtained judgments were by consent consolidated and called for trial at the same term of the
court at which the farmers who sued appellee had obtained judgments against him.   When the consolidated actions on the cross-petition were called for
trial, the appellants moved the court to continue the
case or impanel a new jury to try the issues upon the
ground that the jurors upon the regular panel had
served in trying the issues on the original petition
between the farmers and appellee. The court overruled the motion, and the record shows that the panel
of jurors who tried the case on the cross-petitions
of appellee against appellants was composed, with
one exception, of the same persons who sat as jurors
in the cases of the farmers against the appellee. We
are asked to reverse the verdict in favor of appellee
for the alleged error of the court in refusing to continue the case or select new jurors before whom it
might be tried, and for error in giving and refusing
instructions.

Although the record does not contain the evidence
heard in the cases of the farmers against Doyle, it
is entirely probable, and we so assume, that in those
cases the juries heard a good deal about the suits
pending on the cross-petition of Doyle against Offutt
& Blackburn and possibly they formed some opinion

as to the merits of the case pending between Doyle and Offutt & Blackburn. The issues in the two cases, however, were very different. In the suits between the farmers and Doyle there were really only two questions in dispute: One, whether the wheat was bought for and represented to be good seed wheat, the other whether or not it germinated; whereas, in the suit between Doyle and Offutt & Blackburn, the issues were first whether or not Offutt & Blackburn agreed to keep the wheat in a separate bin, or so that it would not become heated; and, second, whether or not they committed a breach of this agreement in putting it in bins with other wheat and permitting it to become overheated, and in failing to deliver No. 2 wheat.

But without respect to the similarity or difference in the facts in the cases between the farmers and Doyle, and those between Doyle and Offut & Blackburn, it is a sufficient answer to the argument of counsel to say that the court in its discretion might have directed the actions of Doyle against Offutt & Blackburn to be tried with the suits of the farmers against Doyle. Doyle's cause of action against Offut & Blackburn was affected by and grew out of the original cause of action against him. If his contention was true, the suits of the farmers against him were caused by the negligence or breach of contract on the part of Offutt & Blackburn. If the court had directed the original cause of action, and the cause of action arising on the cross-petition to be heard at the same time before the same jury, the jurors in place of hearing both cases at different times would have heard both of them together, and it is plain that the effect on their minds would be precisely the same. If the facts they heard in the cases of the farmers against Doyle operated to prejudice them in any way against Offutt & Blackburn, it would have affected them the same way if the cases had been heard together. And so we are unable to perceive how Offutt & Blackburn were prejudiced by the ruling of the court.

It is quite common practice for the trial court to order an original cause of action and a cause of action presented by cross-petition to be heard together by the same jury; and, although this practice may sometimes operate to the disadvantage of one of the litigants, it will not be ground for reversal unless it is made to appear that in the exercise of a sound discretion the trial court should have ordered separate trials and before jurors who did not sit in the first trial. It is, of course, of the highest importance that jurors who are called upon to decide issues of fact should be free from bias or prejudice for or against either of the parties to the litigation, and that their minds should be in such condition as to receive, free from former opinions or impressions, the evidence introduced in support of the respective contentions of the parties. But this much-desired end cannot in all cases be obtained; and in trials where cross-petitions are allowable, and the court in the exercise of a sound discretion   directs the issues on the original and cross-petition to be heard together, the jurors necessarily hear evidence in one branch of the case that may have a tendency to influence their judgment upon the other.

We may further add that, if a new jury had been impaneled, they would necessarily have learned all about the suits of the farmers in the trial of the case between Doyle and Offutt & Blackburn.   Doyle's cause of action against Offutt & Blackburn was rest-ed solely on the ground that he was obliged to pay damages to the farmers who sued him. And so, in the trial of his case against Offutt & Blackburn, the facts as to his loss and how it occurred and everything relating thereto would necessarily be brought to the attention of the jury.

Counsel for appellant requested the court to give an instruction saying, in substance, that the warehouse receipt was the written evidence of the contract between the parties, and the law presumed that it expressed the true agreement, and the jury should so find, unless they believed that the contract between the parties was that the wheat should be stored in a separate bin and kept as seed wheat, and that by mutual mistake this part of the agreement was omitted from the receipt. But the court refused to give this or any instruction based on the receipt. Offutt & Blackburn introduced evidence showing that the receipt contained the only contract they had with Doyle, while the evidence for Doyle tended to show that the receipt did not contain the contract, and that this fact was known to and in effect acknowledged by Offutt & Blackburn. There was also evidence conducing to show that Offut & Blackburn did not properly handle the wheat or deliver No. 2 wheat. The execution and delivery of the receipt was admitted; the only contention of Doyle being that it did not fully express the contract. In the absence of mutual mistake as to its contents, the receipt was the contract between the parties. It not only acknowledged the receipt of the wheat, but contained an agreement upon the part of Offutt & Blackburn to deliver it. Although called a warehouse receipt, it was more than an ordinary receipt, and must be treated as a contract fixing the right of the parties as to the matters it related to.

When there is a written contract between the parties engaged in litigation, and the contract is set up or relied on in the pleadings, or is introduced in evidence, the court should give an instruction based on the writing. A writing is the best evidence of what the parties agreed to do; and, when its execution is admitted, in the absence of fraud, want of consideration or mistake, their rights must be settled according to its terms. Where there is a denial of the execution of a paper, or an averment that it was obtained by fraud, or that by mutual mistake it does not contain the contract, or a want of consideration is pleaded, it is proper to admit oral evidence to sustain the pleas. But this does not change the rule that the court should instruct the jury that the writing is the contract, and they should so find, if it was executed, unless they believe from the evidence that it was executed without consideration or by fraud or mistake as the case may be. A writing like this does not stand on the same footing as parol evidence.

It has been ruled time and time again that it is not proper to point out particular evidence in an instruction, or to give undue prominence to any fact; but this practice applies to parol evidence, and not to written evidence of a contract. If in the trial of an ejectment case the plaintiff introduces deeds and records showing that he has a good paper title, the court should instruct the jury that the record evidence invests the plaintiff with a good title and they should so find, unless they believe it is avoided by some defense set up by the defendant that is supported by the evidence. And so in a suit on a promissory note, judgment, or other record, the law gives high regard to written contracts, and, when engagements or undertakings are reduced to writing, the legal presumption is that they express the true agreement between the parties.

It should, however, be noted that the rule stated with reference to written contracts, deeds, and records does not apply to an ordinary receipt acknowledging the payment of money or other thing, or to the recital in an instrument of the amount of the consideration paid or received. A receipt is only prima facie evidence of the truth of what it contains. It may be assailed and contradicted by parol evidence without any averment of fraud or mistake in its execution or delivery. The distinction in this particular between deeds, contracts, and other agreements and receipts is well pointed out in Gully v. Grubbs, 1 J. J. Marsh. 387, where, in discussing this question, the court said: "Wherever a right is vested or created or extinguished by contract or otherwise, and writing is employed for that purpose, parol testimony is inadmissible to alter or contradict the legal and common-sense construction of the instrument. But that any writing which neither by contract, the operation of law, nor otherwise, vests or passes, or extinguishes any right, but is only used as evidence of a fact, and not as evidence of a contract or right, may be susceptible of explanation by extrinsic circumstances or facts. Thus a will, a deed, or a covenant in writing, so far as they transfer or are intended to be evidences of rights cannot be contradicted or opposed in their legal construction by facts 'aliundi.' But receipts or other writings, which only acknowledge the existance of a simple fact, such as the payment of money for example, may be susceptible of explanation and liable to contradiction by witnesses.'' This principle has been approved in Caldwell v. Hardin, 3 T. B. Mon. 349; Peddicord v. Hill, 4 T. B. Mon. 370; Gordon v. Gordon, 1 Metc. 285; and many other cases.

If, therefore, the contract did express the agreement between the parties, Doyle was not entitled to recover unless Offutt & Blackburn failed to deliver to him No. 2 wheat, or were guilty of negligence in storing or handling the wheat. On another trial of the case the court will, in addition to the other instructions given, in substance, instruct the jury that the receipt was the contract between the parties unless by mutual mistake it failed to express the true agreement between them, and the jury should find for Offutt & Blackburn if they delivered to Doyle No. 2 wheat and were free from negligence in storing or handling it. There should also be incorporated in instruction No. 1 the idea that the receipt controlled, unless there was a mistake in it.

Wherefore the judgment is reversed with directions for a new trial in conformity with this opinion.

CASE 39.—ACTION BETWEEN W. T. PATRICK AND OTHERS
AND FANNIE PATRICK FOR THE CONSTRUCTION
OF THE WILL OF R. E. PATRICK, DECEASED.—
October 28, 1909.

Patrick, &c. v. Patrick

Appeal from Daviess Circuit Court.

T. F. BURKHEAD, Circuit Judge,

From the judgment plaintiffs appeal.—Affirmed.

1. Wills—Construction—Intention of Testator.—The court in
   construing a will should aim to ascertain testator's intention, and should, if possible, so construe the will as to uphold
   each item or clause thereof.

2. Wills—Construction—Creation of Trusts—Implication.—Testator devised all of his property to his son, providing he
   should pay a specified sum to each of his sisters, and declared
   that the property should be kept together until the death or
   remarriage of the wife, and that the son should remain with
   the family and manage the estate until the wife's death or
   remarriage, when the property should pass as provided for.
   Held, that the wife was the beneficiary of the entire estate
   for life or during widowhood, with remainder to the son, who
   took the title as trustee for the wife.

3. Wills—Charge on Property Devised—Nature.—A testamentary gift to testator's son, provided that he pay to each of
   his sisters a specified sum and that if any of the sisters
   should be dead at testator's death, the sum should be paid to
   her bodily heirs, was a gift to the son on condition that
   the payments to his sisters were made, which payments must
   be made at the death of testator, and the amount due each
   with interest from the end of the year succeeding testator's
   death, was a charge on the son's interest.

4. Wills — Construction — Trusts   Eliminated — Termination.—
   Where testator devised all his property to his son, provided
   that he pay to each of testator's daughters a specified sum, and
   declared that the property should be kept together until the
   death or marriage of testator's wife, and that the son
   should remain with the family and manage the estate until

the wife's death or remarriage, the fact that the son removed
from the property did not affect the trust created in favor
of the wife or the rights of the wife, where the son continued
to faithfully execute the trust.

5.   Trusts—Testamentary Trusts—Compensation of Trustee.—
Where the will creating a trust does not declare that the
trustee shall not be compensated for the services rendered in
executing the trust, the court may allow him a reasonable
compensation therefor.

6.   Wills—Construction—Estates Created.—Testator devised all
his property to his son, providing he pay a specified sum to
each of testator's daughters, and declared that the property
should be kept together until the death or marriage of testator's wife, and that the son should remain with the family
and manage the estate until the wife's death or marriage and
that if the son should die without bodily heirs his share
should go to his surviving sisters or their bodily heirs. Held,
that the son acquired a fee in the entire estate, subject to
defeat by his death without living issue before the death or
marriage of testator's wife.

7.   Wills—Construction—Defeasible Fee—Time of Contingency
—The rule that where an estate is given by will which may
be defeated on the happening of a contingency, and there is
no other period apparent or intended in which the event shall
occur, it shall refer to an event happening within the lifetime
of the testator, does not obtain when the will shows on its
face with reasonable certainty that the event to which the
contingency refers is in contemplation of testator to occur
after his death.

MILLER & TODD and C. S. WALKER, attorneys for appellants.

SYNOPSIS.

1.   A testator, having given a devise in fee clearly manifested
in the earlier clauses of the will, is not presumed to have intended, by words subsequently used, to cut down this devise by a life
estate in another, unless the words used clearly indicate such
intent. A devise in fee clearly manifested in the earlier clauses
of the will is not cut down by subsequent words or later clauses.
Any other construction would be inconsistent with and repugnant to the fee clearly devised. 49 Cent. Dig., sec. 1341, pp. 1823.
1824, (e); p. 1824, (g); sec. 1324, p. 1827, (a); Becker v. Roth,
115 Ky. Dec. (in S. W.) 761.

2.   Where property, real or personal, is devised or bequeathed
to one in fee, nothing remains to be devised over, and a devise

or bequest over to others, if the devisee should die and leave no heirs, is void. Becker v. Roth, 115 Ky. Dec. (in S. W.) 761; 49 Cent. Dig., sec. 1342, p. 1827, (a).

3. A devise on condition that the devisee pay to another a certain sum, and upon such payment the fee becomes vested, is a conditional devise, and such payment cannot be compelled and its payment cannot be premature. The devisee may elect to comply with the condition and take the fee, or not to comply with it and not take the fee.

LAVEGA CLEMENTS and BEN D. RINGO for appellee.

POINT INVOLVED AND AUTHORITIES.

Under a proper construction of the will of R. E. Patrick, appellee, Fannie Patrick is entitled to a life estate in all the property that decedent owned at the time of his death. Hunt v. Johnson, 10 B. Mon. 344; Page on Wills, Sctions, 461-2-3; Allen, &c., v. VanMeters Devisees, 1st Met. 264; Axton v. Watson, 84 Ky. page 210.

OPINION OF THE COURT BY JUDGE SETTLE—Affirming.

R. E. Patrick died in Daviess county leaving a will which was duly admitted to probate. So much of the will as it will be necessary to consider is as follows:

"(1) I will all my property, real, personal and mixed, to my son, W. T. Patrick, after paying all my debts and funeral expenses, provided he shall pay each one of my daughters, to-wit, Maggie Bishop, Cora Jesse, Mollie Ayers, Minnie Patrick. Fannie Patrick, Annie Patrick, Luvena Patrick, $100.00. If any of my said daughters shall be dead at my death, then the $100.00 shall be paid to her bodily heirs, if any; if none, the $100.00 shall belong to said W. T. Patrick.

"(2) If my beloved wife shall survive me I will and desire my property be kept together just as it is until her death or marriage, my son, W. T., to stay with the family and manage the estate to the best possible advantage until her death or marriage when the property shall pass as in item one.

"(3) If my son shall die without bodily heirs his share of my estate shall go to his surviving sisters, or to their bodily heirs, if any shall be dead leaving bodily heirs."

The testator was survived by his widow and the son and seven daughters named in the will. The son resided on the real estate devised at the time of the testator's death, but has since removed to another home, acquired with means of his own. While the fact does not clearly appear from the record before us, we take it for granted that the widow and daughters of the testator, or such of the latter as are unmarried still reside on the land devised. By the present action brought in the court below the widow set up claim to an estate for life or during her widowhood in the property devised, asked a construction of the will, that the executor, W. T. Patrick, be required to settle his accounts as executor, and pay her the net income arising from the estate. The answer, in substance, denies that she owns any interest in the estate devised, asserts title in appellant to the whole estate and his right to certain credits in the settlement of his accounts as executor. The issues presented by the pleadings made a construction of the will necessary, and the construction given it by the circuit court was that the appellee as widow took, under its provisions, an estate for life, or during her widowhood, in the property devised, with remainder at her death or marriage to appellant. Therefore by the judgment rendered it required of appellant the accounting asked, and he, being dissatisfied with the judgment, has appealed.

A will should, if possible, be construed so as to uphold each item or clause thereof.. The end to be attained is the ascertainment of the testator's intention. Applying these well known rules to the will under consideration, we think its meaning is that appellee, after the payment of the testator's debts, takes or becomes the beneficiary of the entire estate devised, for life, or during her widowhood, with remainder to appellant. The title, however, to the estate which she takes is, by the will, vested in appellant as her trustee. In other words, so long as she lives and remains unmarried, appellant holds in trust for her the title to the property devised. At her death or marriage the trust will cease, and, if he is then living, the estate devised becomes his absolutely.

The requirement of the will that the property after the death of the testator shall be ''kept together just as it is until her death or marriage, my son, W. T., to stay with the family and manage the estate to the best possible advantage until her death or marriage,''means something more than that the support of the widow shall be a mere charge or burden upon the estate. Its meaning is an estate to her for life or widowhood in the property devised, although the son is to hold and manage it as her trustee, devoting the income of the estate to her use and to the support of such of the daughters as may live with her and constitute a part of the family. If such was not the intention of the testator, what meaning can be given the following language as to the disposition of the estate after the death of the widow, ''when property shall pass as in item one,'' namely, to the appellant, W. T. Patrick? While the language of the second clause of the will does not in express terms declare that appellant is to take and hold as trustee

for appellee, during her life or widowhood, the title
to the entire estate devised by the first clause of
the will, it obviously does so by implication, and as
obviously makes the widow of the testator the cestui
que trust.

It is not clear that the daughters are also to be regarded as cestui que trust, but such of them as may
remain with their mother, as a part of the family,
are, we think, to be supported from the estate as
long as she lives and continues a widow but, with her
death or marriage, the right of the daughters to live
upon or receive a support from the estate will cease,
as will the trust itself. Not only does appellant take
the property devised by the will subject to the life
estate or widowhood of appellee, though holding in
trust the title and possession thereof during that
period, but he also takes it upon the condition that he
shall pay each of his seven sisters $100. We think
it was contemplated by the testator that the $100 to
each of his daughters should be paid by appellant
at his death, not from the estate, but out of his
own means, for the will provides: "If any of my
said daughters shall be dead at my death, then the
$100.00 shall be paid to her bodily heirs, if any, if
none, then the $100.00 shall belong to said W. T. Pat-
rick." It appears that all the daughters were living
at the testator's death and are still living, but does
not appear whether they have been paid the $100.
If not, the amount due each should be a charge upon
appellant's remainder interest in the testator's estate with interest from the end of the year succeeding the testator's death.

Our conclusion that appellee took under the will a
life estate in the property of the testator seems to us
to be consistent with all of the provisions of that in-

strument, and not less consistent with its provisions do we regard the further conclusion as to the creation of the trust under which appellant is to preserve the estate and apply its net proceeds or income to appellee's use. The language of the will from which the trust is to be implied is not merely suggestive, recommendatory, or in the form of a request from the testator, with which appellant might or might not in his discretion have complied, but is of such a precatory character as to reasonably satisfy us from the language itself, taken in connection with its effect upon the disposition of the testator's property, that the latter's intention to create a trust beneficial to his widow is as complete as if he had given the property to hold upon a trust declared in express terms and in the customary manner. Pomeroy's Eq. Sec. 1016.

If correct in our conclusion that the property devised appellant in trust for appellee is an estate for life or during her widowhood, in all the property left by the testator, it would seem to follow that she is entitled to receive, year by year, from the trustee the entire net profits of the estate as long as she lives and continues a widow. The fact that appellant has removed from the property of which he is trustee does not affect the trust or the rights of appellee, if he continues to faithfully execute the trust. As the will does not declare appellant shall not be compensated for the services he renders in executing the trust committed to him, we think the circuit court should allow him reasonable compensation therefor, and, as appellee has not taken a cross-appeal from that part of the judgment declaring appellant entitled to a reasonable compensation, the question will not be considered by us.

The third clause of the will was not construed by
the circuit court; but, the entire will being before us,
we will give an interpretation of that clause, as it may
prevent further controversy between the parties. The
question suggested by the reading of the clause is:
At what time would the death of appellant without
"bodily heirs" cause "his share" of the testator's
estate to "go to his (appallant's) surviving sisters,
or to their bodily heirs, if any shall be dead, leaving
bodily heirs"? Numerous cases may be found in
which this court held that where an estate is given
by will which may be defeated upon the happening of
a contingency, and there is no other period apparent
or intended in which the event shall occur, it shall refer to an event happening within the lifetime of the
testator; but this rule does not obtain when the will
shows on its face with reasonable certainty that the
event to which the contingency refers is, in contemplation of the testator, to occur after his own death.
We think the clause under consideration has reference to the death of appellant before the death or
marriage of his mother, the life tenant.

If the testator had had in mind the death of appellant before his own death, he doubtless would have
said so in clause 3, as he did in clause 1 with respect
to the bequest to his daughters of $100 each to be paid
by appellant; it being therein declared: "If any of
my said daughters be dead at my death, then the
$100.00 shall be paid to her bodily heirs, if any; if
none, the $100.00 shall belong to said W. T. Patrick."
But the third clause simply provides: "If my son
shall die without bodily heirs his share of my estate
(i. e., the remainder) shall go to his surviving sisters," etc. In our opinion the testator here meant
that, if appellant should die childless before the death

or marriage of his mother, in that event his sisters, or the children of such of them as may then be dead, will take the estate devised him; that is, the will gives appellant a defeasible fee in the entire estate devised; in other words, the fee in remainder to the whole, subject to be defeated by his death, without living issue, before the death or marriage of his mother. Baxter v. Isaacs, 71 S. W. 907, 24 Ky. Law Rep. 1618; Lewis v. Shropshire's Trustee. 68 S. W. 426, 24 Ky. Law Rep. 332; Birney v. Richardson, 5 Dana. 424.

As the judgment of the circuit court in all essential particulars conforms to the conclusion herein expressed, it is hereby affirmed.

CASE 40.—SUIT BY THE COMMONWEALTH FOR THE USE OF THE CITY OF LOUISVILLE AGAINST HUNTER ROSS AND OTHERS FOR AN ACCOUNTING.—November 5, 1909.

Commonwealth, for City of Louisville v. Ross, &c.

Appeal from Jefferson Circuit Court (Chancery Branch, Second Division).

Samuel B. Kirby, Judge.

Judgment for defendants, plaintiff appeals—Reversed.

1. Statutes—Construction—Existence of Ambiguity.—The doctrine of practical construction cannot be applied unless the language of the statute is so ambiguous as to leave the judicial mind in doubt.

2. Statutes—Construction—Aid from Other Statutes.—To aid the construction of a statute as to when a bond recorder in a city should account, the court may look to all other statutes relating to public officers receiving public revenue for which they are required to account.

3. Municipal Corporations—Bond Recorders—Fees—Accounting —Statutes.—Ky. St. Sec. 2947, authorizes the appointment of a bond recorder in a city of the first class by circuit court judges for a term of four years; qualifications, oath and bond to be required as required of county clerks, compensation to be the same as allowed to justices of the peace in trials for breach of the peace, to be paid by the party to whom the services are rendered, two deputies to be appointed to be paid out of the fees collected, a record of bonds to be kept by him, and all moneys received over $4,000, exclusive of the deputy's salary, to be paid to the city treasury. Held, that since all other statutes relating to officers receiving public revenue required an accounting of moneys collected at least once a year, and the recorder's fees and expenses are on an annual basis, the bond recorder must make at least annual settlements with such officials as the city shall designate, keep an accurate record of all amounts collected by him, and, when he is shown to have collected enough to pay his salary and his deputies and other legal expenses for the current year, he must account to the city for the balance every month, if so desired by the city.

4 Statutes—Contemporaneous Construction—When Allowable.— Contemporaneous construction will not be allowed where to apply it will override a fixed legislative purpose.

5. Municipal Corporations—Bond Recorders—Compensation— Statutes.—Such section of the statute imports that the bond recorder is to receive $4,000 a year, and $1,000 a year for each deputy actually employed, not exceeding two.

JAS. BREATHITT, Attorney General, C. B. BLAKEY and J. M CHILTON for appellant.

KOHN, BAIRD, SLOSS & KOHN, ARTHUR B. BENSINGER and FAIRLEIGH, STRAUS & FAIRLEIGH for appellee.

OPINION OF THE COURT BY JUDGE O'REAR—Reversing.

This suit was instituted against appellees, Joseph Hunter Ross and his surety upon the former's bond as bond recorder for the city of Louisville, for an accounting by Ross of the fees collected by him during his term, and for judgment for balance in his hands. Ross was elected to his office in December of 1905, for a term of four years, and on December 2, 1905, executed the bond and entered upon the discharge of his official duties. The petition charges: That in the month of December, 1905, he collected as fees for accepting and recording appearance and peace bonds, at $2 for each bond, $430. That during the year ending December 31, 1906, he likewise collected as fees, $6,330; for the year ending December 31, 1907, $8,-050; for the year ending December 31, 1908, $9,663; and for taking other bonds in criminal proceedings (in the Jefferson circuit court), $1,619, during the three years and one month named. That he had upon demand by the city of Louisville for an accounting refused to account or pay over to the city any of these sums, or any part of them, but had taken his records from his office and concealed them, refusing to allow the city's authorities access to them. That he had collected large sums in addition as fees, which the plaintiffs were unable to state because of his conduct in secreting his records. The prayer was for a judgment for the sums stated, less his salary and deputies' salaries, and for a reference to the commissioner of the court to ascertain the further amount collected by him as fees, and for a full accounting by him. Interest at 6 per cent. per annum and penalties of 20 per cent. on the sums due the city at the end of each settlement period were also sought.

The statute under which appellee Ross was elected, which governs in fixing the times of settlement and payment by him, as well as fixes his salary, is section 2947, Carroll's Ky. St., a part of the act of 1893, governing cities of the first class, and is as follows: "There shall be appointed by a majority of the judges of the circuit court having jurisdiction in said cities, a bond recorder for said cities. He shall be appointed for a term of four years, and shall have the qualifications, take the oath, and give the bond required of the county clerks, and he shall be subject to the same fines and penalties to which they are subject and for neglect and violation of his duty he may be prosecuted, punished, or removed, in the same manner in which said clerks may be prosecuted, punished, or removed.

The bond furnished by said recorder, and the requisite surety thereon, must be approved by said judges. Said bond recorder shall have exclusive right to take all bonds required by law to be taken or given by persons arrested in the city in and for which he is appointed, for their appearance before the proper tribunal; also all bonds or recognizances required by law to be taken or given by or in the police court of said city; and no person in custody shall be released therefrom, before trial, unless bond be first given as herein required. Said bond recorder shall be allowed for his services the same compensation as now allowed by law to justices of the peace in trials for breach of peace, to be paid by the party for whom the services are rendered. He may appoint two deputies, and the salary of each of said deputies shall be $1,000.00 per annum, and shall be paid from the fees collected by the said bond recorder. Said deputies shall give bond the same as the recorder, and he is hereby given power to administer oaths to parties offering as sureties on bonds, and for all purposes necessary for the proper conduct of his office, to carry into effect the provisions of this act, and enable him to properly execute his duty.

And no officer or other persons shall have power to take any bond or administer any oath herein mentioned, except said recorder. Said bond recorder

shall keep a record of all the bonds taken by himself
or his deputy, showing the date, amount of bail, the
name of defendant, and the charge under which the
arrest was made; and all money received by the bond
recorder, over and above the amount of four thous-
and dollars, exclusive of the deputy's salary, shall
be paid into the treasury of the city for which the recorder is appointed.   Said recorder, or one of his
deputies shall be in the office at all hours, for the
purpose of taking bonds.   All bond and affidavits
shall be returned within twenty-four hours to the
proper tribunal.   In continued cases, the bond recorder may require a memorandum from the clerk of
the court, showing the charge, amount of bail, and
date of continuance.''

The defense to this suit is that it was brought pre-
maturely.   The answer is styled a ''plea in abatement.''   It assumes, as the proper construction of
the foregoing statute that the bond recorder of the
city of Louisville is not required to settle his accounts, or to pay over to the city any balance in his
hands from the fees of his office, except at the end
of his term.   The chancellor, in an opinion delivered
in overruling a general demurrer to the petition, indicated that, reading the statute alone, he could not
say that the time of settlement and payment was at
the end of the term, but, evidently in response to
argument, that the statute was ambiguous on that
point, and if the officers of the city had, by a practical contemporaneous construction during the 15
years since its enactment, construed it so, that was a
fact to be pleaded.   Thereupon the defendants filed
their answer, or plea in abatement, in which they asserted that such had been the practical contemporaneous construction by the city officials, and of ap-

pellee Ross and his predecessors in office. A demurrer to this answer was overruled. The city declined
to plead further, and its petition was dismissed. This
appeal is prosecuted from that judgment.

Before the doctrine of practical contemporaneous
construction can be applied to the interpretation of a
statute, the language of the enactment must be so
ambiguous as to leave the judicial mind in doubt
as to the legislative purpose. The statute in question deals with the duties and compensation of a
collector of public revenues. By the terms of the section he is placed on the plane of county court clerks
—public officials who are paid out of the fees of their
offices, and whose duties include the collection of public moneys. Turning to the statute bearing on the
duty and liabilities of county court clerks when their
duties are analogous to those to be performed by
the bond recorder, we find that by section 4242, Ky.
St., county court clerks are required on the first day
of each circuit court to make out and file with the
court an account showing all public money received
by them, and pay it over to the trustees of the jury
fund on the order of the court. By sec. 4248, a failure
is penalized by a fine of from $200 to $300. Section
4255 requires the clerks to keep a well-bound book in
their offices showing all money received by them for
the commonwealth. Sec. 1761 requires county court
clerks in all counties having a population of 75,000
or more to pay over to the auditor of public accounts
on the first of each month the money due the state
from them, and to file a statement showing the
amount due. Every officer who collects or holds
money for the state or county is required to make frequent settlements—none less often than once a year

—and to then, or oftener, pay over the public funds in their hands.

The State Auditor and Treasurer are required to have their accounts examined monthly (sec. 4630); the sheriff is required to settle annually (sec. 4143, Ky. Stat.); county court clerks and circuit clerks monthly (sec. 1761). The jailers are required to pay over monthly (sec. 1773); the clerk of the Court of Appeals and the assessor in counties having population of 75,000 or over, in January of each year; sheriffs, clerks, county judges, police judges, constables, justices of the peace, marshals, and other officers authorized to receive money due the commonwealth are required to report on the first day of each circuit court (three times a year). Section 4252, Ky. Stat. It appears the bond recorder collects money, which is due the city, amounting to $5,000 or more annually. The settled policy of the state is to require frequent settlements of all of its collecting officers. These various statutes may be looked to to ascertain the legislative purpose in the statute under examination, as to when the recorder should settle his accounts. The allusion in the statute to the duties and liabilities of county court clerks clearly meant to embody those provisions so far as applicable to the bond recorder. While the reports to and settlements with the same officers are not, of course, required, settlements with the proper officials of the city are as clearly indicated by the allusion; but his fees and office expenses are to be deducted from his collections. They are based upon an annual basis. It cannot be known before the expiration of the year, possibly, whether anything would be due from the office, as it is possible that for the first 11 months not enough would be collected to defray its expenses.

From the scope of the section, and its allusions to other statutes, so far as applicable, we think the proper construction is: That the bond recorder must make at least annual settlements with such officials as the city council may designate; that he must keep an accurate record at all times in the book in his office, which shall be a public record, of the amounts collected by him; that when he is shown to have collected as much as will pay his salary, and his deputies', and other legal expenses for the current year, the balance is due to the city, and may be required to be paid over each 30 days if the city council so demands; but that, until there is a demand and a failure to settle and pay, there is not a default, and no penalty could be attached till after such demand and default.

The plea of contemporaneous construction, one always of last resort, at least always deferred as a source of information until the interpretation put upon the language by the Legislature itself is applied, if it has given such interpretation, cannot avail in this case. To allow it would be to override the fixed legislative purpose, as indicated by a great number of provisions, applicable to every class of collecting officers, by a kind of sufferance of administrative officials. It is not probable—there is no reason for supposing it likely—that the Legislature intended to make an exception of this official and to allow him to hold in his hands many thousands of the public dues for four years, while the public was being taxed to pay indebtedness to which the fees on hand were applicable. Something more than mere passivity of the city officials, and of the course pursued by the predecessors in the office of the recorder, must concur to authorize the courts to adopt that construction as the one the Legislature intended.

As to the compensation of the bond recorder, we think that the language of the section imports that he is to receive $4,000 a year, and $1,000 a year for each deputy actually employed, not exceeding two.

The case should have been referred to the commissioner to ascertain the true amount due by the bond recorder for each year of his term, and the judgment should be for the balance found due each year after deducting the salaries alluded to, plus 6 per cent. per annum interest on each balance.

Reversed and remanded for proceedings consistent herewith.

CASE 41.—PROCEEDING BY THE COMMONWEALTH ON
RELATION OF AUDITOR'S AGENT AGAINST THE
LOUISVILLE GAS CO. TO ASSESS OMITTED PROP-
ERTY.—November 5, 1909.

Commonwealth, on Relation of Auditor's Agent v. The Louisville Gas Co.

Appeal from Jefferson Circuit Court (Chancery
Branch, Second Division).

SAMUEL B. KIRBY, Circuit Judge.

Judgment for Gas Co., and the Commonwealth
appeals.—Affirmed.

1.   Taxation—Uniformity—Taxation of Corporations and Individ-
     uals—"Property Tax"—"Privilege Tax."—Ky. St. 1909, Secs.
     4077, 4082, provide that certain corporations, including gas
     companies, shall in addition to other taxes, annually pay a
     tax on their franchise to the state and a local tax thereon to
     the county, town, etc., where a franchise is exercised; and
     each corporation shall report the amount of tangible property
     in the state, and where situated and assessed and the fair
     cash value thereof; and the board of valuation and assess-
     ment is required to fix the value of the capital stock of each
     corporation and from such amount deduct the assessed value
     of all tangible property assessed in the state; the remainder
     to be the value of its corporate franchise subject to taxation,
     etc. By another provision all the property of domestic cor-
     porations, including intangible property considered in deter-
     mining the value of the franchises, shall be subject to taxa-
     tion unless exempt by the Constitution. Held, that within
     Const. Sec. 174, requiring the property of corporations and
     natural persons to be similarly taxed, and allowing such fur-
     ther license, income and franchise taxes as the Legislature
     may deem proper, the tax on the franchise of a gas company
     was a "property tax" on the intangible property, and not a
     "privilege tax" for engaging in a business that natural per-
     sons could not, since under section 4082 natural persons en-
     gaged in such business are taxed as such corporations are.

2. Taxation—Uniformity—Taxation of Corporations and Individ-
    uals.—Held, also, that the franchise tax is not a privilege
    tax imposed on the right to be a corporation.

3. Taxation—Shares of Stockholders—Effect of Tax on Corpo-
    rate Property.—Under such statute, where the corporation
    does report and pay taxes on all its property as required,
    then the stockholders of the corporation are not required to
    list their shares in the company for taxation.

4. Taxation—Shares of Stockholders—Effect of Tax on Corpo-
    rate Property—Shares Owned by Other Corporation.—Where
    a gas company is a shareholder in an electric company, all
    the property of which has been reported and taxed, including
    its franchise under such statute, the gas company's liability
    for taxation on its shares are precisely as any other share-
    holder, and hence the shares are not assessable.

5. Taxation—Corporate Franchise—Mode of Valuation.—Held,
    also, that the bonds of the electric company owned by the
    gas company were to be computed in determining the value
    of the latter's franchise as any other property.

6. Taxation—Corporations—Omitted Property—Burden of Proof.
    —Under said statutes, in a proceeding to assess omitted prop-
    erty, the burden of proof is on the state to show that the
    bonds of the electric company held by a gas company were
    omitted from the latter's report of its taxable property.

7. Taxation—Corporation—Omitted 'Property—Sufficiency of Re-
    port.—Under such statutes, where the gas company reports
    what it claims to be all its taxable property, but the report
    does not specifically show that bonds of an electric company
    which the gas company owns are listed, the bonds cannot be
    taxed as omitted property, where the board of assessment
    does not require a further report.

8. Courts—Precedents—Stare Decisis.—Where ruling precedents
    as to the construction of a statute are long and definitely
    settled and the business of the state has become adapted
    to it, the construction will not be departed from.

M. J. HOLT for appellant.

HUMPHREY, DAVIE & HUMPHREY for appellee.

OPINION OF THE COURT BY JUDGE O'REAR—Affirming.

This is a proceeding begun in the Jefferson county
court to assess as omitted property certain stocks

and bonds of another corporation owned by appellee gas company. The judgment was for the taxpayer. Formerly the Louisville Gas Company operated in Louisville, in addition to its plant for the manufacture of gas, an electric light plant. In 1902 it sold the light plant, and took in part payment $1,500,000 5 per cent. bonds of the purchasing company, called the Louisville Lighting Company, and 16,667 shares of the capital stock of the latter company, of the par value of $100 a share. These bonds and stock were owned by appellee for the tax year of 1904. In August, 1904, it sold all the bonds except $670,000 worth, par value, since which date it has owned that amount of bonds and the stock named. The capital stock of appellee is $3,600,-000. The bonds of the lighting company had during the years in question (which are the years of 1904 and 1905) a market value of 102 and 103, and the stock paid regularly a dividend of 4 per cent. Appellee is what is called a "public service corporation." It is, by the provisions of section 4077, Ky. Stat., required to pay, "in addition to the other taxes imposed on it by law," "annually a tax on its franchise" to the state, and "a local tax thereon to the county, incorporated city, town and taxing district, where its franchise may be exercised."

The first question is, what is the franchise to be taxed? The second is, how is its value to be ascertained? The third is, has it been done in the manner provided by the statute?

Appellant contends that the franchise to be taxed is not the intangible property of the corporation, but is a privilege tax; that is, it is a tax imposed upon the privilege of engaging in a business that a natural person could not engage in. But that position cannot be maintained of the Kentucky Statutes. Natural persons may engage in the business of manufacturing and selling gas, as well as in some of the other business that is subjected to this tax. When they do, they are taxed upon the same principle as corporations are that are engaged in like business. Section 4082, Ky. Stat.; Providence Bk. Co. v. Webster Co., 108 Ky. 527, 57 S. W. 14, 22 Ky. Law Rep. 214. Nor is a tax imposed upon the right to be such a corporation. The organization tax imposed by sec. 4225, Ky. Stat., which is one-tenth of 1 per cent. of the authorized capital of such corporation, is the only tax exacted of a corporation for being and exercising the trade allowed by its charter. The Constitution requires taxes to be imposed alike upon the property of corporations and natural persons (section 174), and it allows in addition the imposition of a license tax, an income tax, and a franchise tax, as the Legislature may determine upon.

So far the Legislature of this state has not provided for an income tax, and license taxes are imposed upon certain kinds of business, but not upon that of serving the public as do corporations like appellee gas company. The assessing board created and empowered by the statute (section 4077, supra) to value the franchises subjected to the tax is given a large discretion in the manner of its procedure; but it is required of the property owner subjected to the tax to make a report showing, among other things, the amount of the capital stock of the corporation, the nature of its business, how its shares are divided, the amount of paid-up stock, its par and market values, the highest price at which the stock has been sold at a bona fide sale in the preceding 12 months, the amount of surplus fund and undivided profits, "and all other assets;" the total indebtedness as principal; the gross and net income, "and including interest on investments;" the value of its tangible property, "and such other facts as the Auditor may require" (section 4078, Ky. Stat.); the length of line of railroads and other common carriers, and other provisions especially applicable to corporations doing an interstate business. The direction to the board is then summed up (section 4079, Kentucky Statutes): "Said board from said statement, and from such other evidence as it may have, if such company, corporation, or association be organized under the laws of this state, shall fix the value of the capital stock of the corporation, company or association as provided in the next preceding section (4078), and from the amount thus fixed shall deduct the value of all tangible property assessed in this state, or in the counties where situated. The remainder thus found shall be the value of its corporate franchise subject to taxation as aforesaid."

It is thus made clear that the tax imposed is a property tax, pure and simple. It groups all the property of the corporation, and values it according to its earning or producing capacity. In a sense the capital stock of the corporation represents all its property; but it was known that sometimes the market value of such stock differs from its actual or earning value. The franchise value takes into consideration all these elements which go to make the real value of the corporation property considered as an entirety. It has been so construed and held in Henderson Bridge Co. v. Commonwealth, 99 Ky. 623, 31 S. W. 486, 17 Ky. Law Rep. 389, 29 L.

R. A. 73; Hager v. American Surety Co., 121 Ky.
791, 90 S. W. 550; 28 Ky. Law Rep. 782; Commonwealth v. Cumberland Tel. Co., 124 Ky. 535, 99 S.
W. 604, 30 Ky. Law Rep. 723; Henderson Bridge Co.
v. Kentucky, 166 U. S. 154, 17 Sup. Ct. 532, 41 L.
R. A. 953; Louisville Tobacco Warehouse Co. v.
Commonwealth, 106 Ky. 165, 49 S. W. 1069, 57 L. R.
A. 33; Aetna Life Insurance Co. v. Coulter, Auditor,
115 Ky. 803, 74 S. W. 1050, 25 R. 193; Marion National Bank of Lebanon v. Burton, Sheriff, 121 Ky.
876, 90 S. W. 948, 28 R. 864, 10 L. R. A. (N. S.)947;
Commonwealth v. Walsh's Trustee (Ky.) 117 S. W.
398. Had we doubt of the correctness of that construction, we should not feel at liberty to depart
from it after it has been so long and definitely settled, and the business of the state has become adapt-
ed to it.

The corporation in this state is required to pay
taxes on all its property not specifically exempt by
the Constitution from taxation. When the corporation does report and pay the tax on all
its property, as required by the statute, then
the stockholders of the corporation are not required to list their shares in the company for taxation. Section 4088, Ky. Stat.; Commonwealth v.
Walsh's Trustee, supra. The Louisville Lighting
Company is a domestic franchise-taxed corporation.
Appellee gas company is a shareholder in the lighting company. The gas company's liability to taxation upon the shares of the lighting company owned by it are precisely the same as on other shareholders. It is conceded that the lighting company
was assessed and paid its franchise tax. Being so,
the shareholders are not assessable. So appellee
was not required to pay upon so much of its in-

tangible property as was represented by those
shares, a fact doubtless taken into consideration by
the state board in fixing the value of appellee's franchise. Commonwealth v. Steele, 126 Ky. 670, 104 S.
W. 687, 31 Ky. Law Rep. 1033; Commonwealth v.
Ledman, 127 Ky. 603, 106 S. W. 247, 32 Ky. Law
Rep. 452; Commonwealth v. Ames, 106 S. W. 306,
32 Ky. Law Rep. 569. But upon the bonds appellee
was required to pay precisely as it did upon its
other intangible property; that is, the bonds, and
their market value and earning quality were pertinent facts to be reported to the state board, and in
estimating the value of appellee's franchise those
bonds were considered, or ought to have been, as
any other chose in action owned by appellee.

Appellee contends that the action of the State
Board of Valuation and Assessment in valuing a
franchise for taxation is one act, not severable, and
whether it considered all the evidence bearing upon
the value of the franchise, or omitted to take some
evidence that it might have required, cannot be reviewed by the courts in a proceeding to list omitted
property; that the thing being now considered, i. e.,
whether the bonds were included in the gas company's report and the board's estimate, might be
omitted evidence, but not omitted property, as there
was no warrant for the board to assess the bonds
in any event as property. This franchise tax is
new. It is substitutional as a method of valuation
only. Its like existed under the old statutes of this
state where choses in action and the like were
grouped as "miscellany." Then a taxpayer could
have reported, say, $10,000 in "miscellany," which
was supposed to embrace all his notes and accounts;
but suppose he had notes to the amount, and solvent,

of $20,000, not an erroneous valuation of those re-
ported as $10,000, but $10,000 in addition. It would
scarcely have been contended that the failure to list
C. D.'s notes for $10,000 was merged in the listing of
the A. B. notes.

The Legislature could have required corporations
to pay on each item of their intangible property, on
their notes, bonds, accounts, capital stock, and so
forth, in detail; but it allowed all these properties to
be grouped for purposes of taxation, as a more convenient and just method of assessing. It was not
contemplated that the privilege thus accorded the
taxpayer was to be a shield for his neglect or fraud
in omitting a material part of his property. If,
for example, a railroad corporation owns two different lines of railroad in this state, but reports only
one of them, and the earnings of but one, it must
be apparent that the failure to report the other is
something more than an omission of evidence. It
would be an omission of property. It is not true
that the bonds in appellee's hands are not taxable.
They are. The Constitution prohibits their exemption. Section 174. But the manner of assessing them
is to have them reported to the state board, and
there valued as a part of the owner's "franchise."
When they are omitted, property liable to taxation
is omitted. It may be brought in and assessed as
omitted property under section 424, Ky. Stat. (Russell's St. sec. 4815).

But were the bonds omitted? Appellant took the
burden of showing that they were. He produced
the reports, filed with the Auditor of State by the
gas company. The reports did not name the bonds;
but the reports did show that the company reported
its gross income from "coke, tar, ammonia, etc.,"

at $187,886.18 for one of the years, and approximately the same for the other, while it reported "gross earnings from gas" at $391,569.45. The reports did not disclose the facts as they should have done, and as the state board might have required. Appellee's bookkeeper testified that the bonds were reported by and included in that item. The books of the company would have shown. Appellant might have compelled their production; but it did not.

The evidence in the record then is that the bonds were not omitted from the report, and actually went into the consideration of the board in fixing the value of the franchise; that is to say, the income produced by the interest on the bonds was treated as part of the company's gross earnings, and, whether from bonds or the sale of gas, went to enhance the value of the company's money earning capital by that much. So that it appears that the bonds were in fact, though perhaps not in name, as effectually valued in making the franchise assessment as if they had been reported specifically as they should have been.

Finding no prejudicial error in the record, the judgment must be affirmed.

CASE 42.—ACTION BY JOSIE LOW AGAINST CHARLIE RAM-
SEY AND OTHERS.—November 10, 1909.

Low v. Ramsey, &c.

Appeal from Garrard Circuit Court.

W. C. BELL, Circuit Judge.

Judgment for defendants, plaintiff appeals.—Affirmed.

1. Wills—Charge on Devise—Care of Children—Lien on Land.—
   A provision in a will, charging a son to whom all the property was given with the duty of caring for two younger children of the testatrix till they reached a certain age, created
   a lien on the land in their favor for this purpose.

2. Wills—Liabilities of Purchaser from Devisee.—A purchaser
   from a devisee is charged with notice of provisions of the
   recorded will. and holds the land subject to the liabilities imposed on the devisee.

3. Wills—Construction—Vesting of Devise—Condition Precedent
   or Subsequent.—A provision in a will imposing on a son to
   whom all the property was given, the duty of supporting and
   caring for other children of the testatrix, was neither a condition precedent to the vesting of a devise in him, nor a condition subsequent, which by failure to perform would forfeit
   the estate.

4. Limitation of Actions—Accrual of Cause of Action—Infant's
   Rights Under Will.—Where an infant was entitled under the
   terms of a will to support and maintenance by a devisee, till
   she reached the age of 15, her cause of action thereunder to
   enforce a lien on the land first accrued when the devisee
   failed to furnish her support, and her full cause of action
   was protected when she reached that age.

5. Limitation of Actions—Computation of Period—Effect of Infant's Disability.—One who was an infant when a right of
   action accrued had the same length of time to sue after becoming of age that she would have had had she been of age
   when the cause of action accrued; Ky. St. Sec. 2525, expressly
   providing as to infants entitled to sue that action may be

brought within a like number of years after removal of their
disability that is allowed to a person having no such impediment.

6. Limitation of Actions—Limitations Applicable—Action
on Contract Not in Writing.—An action to enforce an undertaking to support a minor assumed by one accepting property
under a will providing therefor is governed by the five-year
limitation of Ky. St. Sec. 2515, as to actions on contracts not
in writing, and the mere fact that the acceptance of the devise charged the property with the liability undertaken by
him does not extend the time.

7. Limitation of Actions—Pleading—Demurrer Raising Defense.
—The statute of limitations must be pleaded, unless the petition shows not only a sufficient lapse of time, but non existence of any ground of avoidance; but when the petition
shows that the action is barred, and that plaintiff is not
within any exception contained in the statute which saved his
right to sue, the question may be raised by demurrer.

OPINION OF THE COURT BY JUDGE CARROLL—Affirming.

Mrs. Mary L. Low died, after making her last will,
which was probated in January, 1888. By this will
the testatrix gave her son, Wiatt Low, all of her personal and real estate, declaring that he should
pay $1.00 to each of her children, viz., Mary E.
Jordan, Harry, Josie, Aaron, Elgie, and Samuel.
The balance of her estate, both real and personal,
she devised and bequeathed to him "with the understanding that he is to take and raise my children
Harry and Josie until they are 15 years old." At
the time the testatrix died, Josie Low was between
seven and eight years old. Shortly after the probate of the will Wiatt Low sold the real estate devised to him to James Ramsey, and moved out of the
state, taking with him Harry Low. Ramsey remained in possession of the land from the time he bought
it from Wiatt until his death in 1908, when it descend-

ed to his widow and children, the appellees herein,
In 1908 Josie brought this suit against the Ramsey
heirs, charging that Wiatt Low immediately after
the death of the testatrix abandoned her, and did not
at any time provide her with food, clothing, money,
or property of any sort. She alleged that she was
entitled to a lien on the land for the reasonable cost
of her care and support from the time of her mother's
death until she became 15 years of age, and that the
reasonable cost of caring for and supporting her during this period would be $1000.She further alleged that
when Ramsey bought the land from Wiatt he had actual and constructive knowledge of the contents of
the will. She asked that she be adjudged the lien
on the land, and that it be subjected to the payment
of her demand of $1,000. The lower court sustained
a general demurrer to her petition as amended, and,
declining to plead further, her action was dismissed,
and she appeals.

In our opinion the provision in the will charging
Wiatt Low with the duty of caring for Josie and
Harry until they were 15 years old created a
lien upon the land in their favor and for this purpose, and as the will was put to record the vendee
of Wiatt was charged with notice of its provisions
and held it subject to the liabilities imposed upon
Wiatt.

It is insisted by counsel for appellant that the provisions in the will imposing upon Wiatt the duty of
supporting and caring for these children was either
a condition precedent to the vesting of the devise in
him, or a condition subsequent, that by his failure
to perform forfeited the estate; but in this view we
do not agree. Giving to the provision in the will the

same effect that 'was given to similar provisions in the wills construed in the cases of Pearcy v. Green-well, 80 Ky. 616, 4 R. 587 and Bryant v. Dungan, 92 Ky. 627, 18 S. W. 636, 13 R. 841, 36 Am. St. Rep. 618, we hold, as did the court in Pearcy v. Grenwell, that Wiatt took the estate subject to the charge upon it in favor of Harry and Josie.

Assuming then that it was the duty of Wiatt to support and care for these beneficiaries,.the question remains whether or not the appellant has not surrendered her claim by the long delay before attempting to enforce it. Her cause of action first accrued when Wiatt failed to furnish her support, and her full cause of action was perfected when she became 15 years of age. She might then, under the facts stated in the petition, have recovered everything that was due her under the will; but, as she was an infant when her right accrued, she had the same length of time after becoming of age to bring the suit that she would have if she had been of age when her cause of action accrued—section 2525 of the Kentucky Statutes, reading: "If a person entitled to bring any of the actions mentioned in the third article of this chapter, except for a penalty or forfeiture, was, at the time the cause of action accrued, an infant, * * * the action may be brought within the like number of years after the removal of such disability, * * * that is allowed to a person having no such impediment to bring the same after the right accrued."

The next question is: How many years did she have after becoming of age to bring the action? Section 2515 of the Kentucky Statutes provides in part that "an action upon a contract not in writing signed by the party * * * shall be commenced within

five years next after the cause of action accrued,''
and we have no question that this statute applies.
The contract attempted to be enforced was not signed
by Wiatt. He merely accepted the provisions of a
will that imposed upon him an obligation. The undertaking to support and care for appellant was assumed by Wiatt as a personal obligation when he
took the devise, and the mere fact that the acceptance
of the devise charged the property with the liability undertaken by him does not have the effect
of extending the time in which an action to enforce
it may be brought beyond five years. This point was
adjudged in Collings v. Collings, 92 S. W., 577, 29
Ky. Law Rep. 51. In that case Elisha Collings conveyed to his daughter certain lands in consideration
of her agreeing to pay specified debts then owing by
Collings. In the course of the opinion the court said:
''While it is true the deed imposed on the grantee
the payment of the debts named in it, which became
thereby a lien on the land in favor of the respective
creditors to whom owing, it was an express assump-
sit, barred by limitation after five years, so far as
the grantee was concerned, although as between the
original debtor, Elisha Collings, and his creditors,
the debts may not have been barred. When the debts
became outlawed, so far as they affected the grantee,
the lien was likewise discharged. It was not competent for Elisha Collings and his creditors by any subsequent agreement between themselves to prolong
the lives of these debts so as to affect Mrs. Alloway,
the grantee of the land without her consent.''

As the claim of appellant is barred by the statute,
can this defense be presented by a general demurrer? The rule is that the statute of limitations must

be pleaded, unless the petition shows not only a sufficient lapse of time but the non-existence of any
ground of avoidance; but when the petition shows
that the action is barred, and that plaintiff is not
within any of the exceptions contained in the statute
which saved his right to sue, the question may be
raised by demurrer. Stillway v. Leavy, 84 Ky. 379,
1 S. W. 590, 8. Ky. Law Rep. 321. The only relief
sought is the subjection of the land in the hands of
the appellees to the payment of appellant's claim.
There is no averment that the appellees in any manner or form assumed the payment of appellant's
claim or any part of it. The petition does not seek any
relief against the appellees personally, and so it follows that she could not be entitled to any of the exceptions contained in the statute of limitations that
would save it from running against her. Under these
circumstances we think the question that the claim
was barred by limitation could be raised by demurrer.

Wherefore the judgment of the lower court is affirmed.

CASE 43.—ACTION BY JOHN PATTERSON AND OTHERS
AGAINST JACOB S. PATTERSON AND OTHERS.—
November 9, 1909.

Patterson, &c. v. Patterson, &c.

Appeal from Fayette Circuit Court.

WATTS PARKER, Circuit Judge.

Judgment for defendants, plaintiffs appeal.—Reversed.

1. Perpetuities—Construction of Deed.—A deed conveying land
   to a turnpike company for a tollhouse, and providing that,
   when the house should cease to be used for such purpose,
   the land and building should revert to certain persons named,
   did not create a perpetuity in violation of Ky. St. 1909, Sec.
   2360, since the grantee might at any time with the sale
   of its turnpike convey the use of the tollhouse and ground
   to its vendee, and under section 2359 the reversioners might
   at pleasure sell their reversionary interest.
2. Deeds—Construction — Condition   Subsequent — Covenant.—
   Conditions subsequent are not favored, and, if it be doubtful
   whether a clause in a deed be a condition or a covenant,
   courts will incline to the latter construction.
3. Perpetuities—Conveyance for Highway.—The statute against
   perpetuities (Ky. St. 1909, Sec. 2360) does not apply to a
   conveyance of land for a public highway, or for its use in
   connection with the operation of a turnpike, which is a public
   highway.
4. Perpetuities—Reversions—Construction.—Where a deed conveyed land to a turnpike company for use for a tollhouse, a
   provision that on cessation of such use the land should revert to certain named persons, instead of herself, was valid.
5. Pleading—Demurrer—Effect.—On demurrer to the petition
   the facts therein alleged must be accepted as true.

G. ALLISON HOLLAND and WALLACE MUIR for appellants.

POINTS AND AUTHORITIES.

1. The land in question was not inalienable, the turnpike company having the power to convey, and it was not therefore taken out of commerce. The grantor reserved no right to herself and heirs to re-enter on the land and resume possession. Kentucky Statutes, Section 2360; Carroll County Academy v. Gallatin Academy, 20 Ky. Law Rep. 824; Trustees Gen'l Assembly Presby. Church in U. S. v. Alexander, 20 Ky. Law Rep., 391; Fuquay's Heirs v. Trustees Hopkins' Academy, 22 Ky. Law Rep., 744; McDaniel v. Watson, 4 Bush, 234; Morrow, etc., v. Slaughter, 5 Bush, 330; 22 A. & E. Ency Law, 2 Ed., 704; Lewis on Perpetuities; Lamb v. Lynch, 56 Neb. 135; Cowell v. Colorado Springs Co., 100 U. S., 55; 4 Kent's Commentaries, 12 Ed., 129-30; 3 Rapalge's Digest, Secs. 1095 and 1096; Rawson's School Digest; 83 Am. Decision, 670; Green v. O'Connor, 19 L. R. A., 264; Railey v' Umantillo County, 15 Oregon, 172.

2. The contingency matured during the lifetime of the grantor. A limitation that would have been void at the time the conveyance was executed will not affect its validity if it took place during the lifetime of the grantor, all parties being in esse at the time the deed was made and when its final conditions went into effect. 22 A. & E. Ency. Law, 709; Southern v. Wallaston, 16 Beav., 166; Peard v. Kekuvich, 15 Beav., 166 Gooch v. Gooch, 14 Beav., 565; Wallace v. Smith, 24 Ky. Law Rep., 139; Call v. Shewmaker, 24 Ky. Law Rep., 686; Davis v. Wood, 17 B. Mon., 86.

3. Statute against perpetuities does not apply to charitable uses or to public highways. Gass & Bonta v. Wilhite, etc., 2 Dana, 170; 23 Henry VIII, ch. 10; Porter's case, 1 Co. R., 24; Pullius, etc., v. Board of Education of Methodist Church, 25 Ky. Law Rep., 1715.

4. A turnpike road is a public highway. Roads created for public use under a charter of a corporation are public roads, though the charter gives the corporation the right to appropriate the tolls. Lexington & O. R. Co. v. Appelgate, 8 Dana, 289; Ware v. Clark's Run & S. R. Turnpike Co., 3 Ky. Law Rep. (Abstract) 325; Elliott on Roads and Streets, Sec. 69.

ALLEN & DUNCAN, attorneys for Fannie Hickey and John B. Smedley.

The decisions in our own state are sufficiently abundant, without citing authorities, and are conclusive of the question at issue.

It will be sufficient, we believe, to refer to the following recent cases: Ludwig v. Coombs, 58 Ky. (1 Met.) 128; Stevens v.

Stevens, 21 Ky. Law Rep., 1315, 54 S. W., 835; Coleman v. Coleman, 23 Ky. Law Rep., 1476, 65 S. W., 832; Fidelity Trust Co. v. Lloyd, 25 Ky. Law Rep., 1827, 78 S. W., 896.

.OPINION OF THE COURT BY JUDGE SETTLE—Reversing.

On October 27, 1891, Nannie C. Smedley, spinster, in consideration of $1 in hand paid, sold and by deed conveyed to the Ft. Spring & Pinkard Turnpike Company, a corporation owning and operating a turnpike in Fayette county, a quarter of an acre of ground "for the purpose of building a house for collecting toll for said pike." The deed also provides: "Now, it is further agreed that when said house ceases to be used for collecting toll for said pike, then and at that time the above tract of land with all buildings and fixtures to revert back to Jacob Smedley, Will Waltz, and John Patterson or their heirs." Jacob Smedley was a brother, John Patterson and Will Waltz, brothers-in-law of Nannie Smedley. On May 9, 1894, the turnpike company, grantee in the deed referred to, sold and conveyed its turnpike to the fiscal court of Fayette county, and that court at once made it a free turnpike and ceased to collect tolls thereon and to use the tollhouse on the lot conveyed by Nannie Smedley to the turnpike company.

Thereupon Jacob Smedley, Will Waltz, and John Patterson without objection from any source took possession of the tollhouse and ground in question, and they, or Patterson and the heirs at law of Jacob Smedley and Will Waltz, have since continuously had and held the actual adverse possession thereof, claiming it as against all others. Nannie Smedley, the grantor in the deed to the turnpike company, was living at the time Jacob Smedley, Will Waltz, and John

Patterson took possession of the tollhouse and for ten years thereafter, and all the while residing near the property in question. Nannie Smedley died in 1904, childless, but left a will which was duly probated, following which her estate was in due course settled and distributed as by the will directed. Jacob Smedley and Will Waltz both died after they and John Patterson took possession of the tollhouse and ground, but both left children who are their heirs at law, respectively. Some years after Nannie Smedley's death, and after the distribution of her estate, the appellees, Fanny Hickey and John B. Smedley, the former a sister and the latter a brother of the decedent, set up claim to the lot and tollhouse as her heirs at law, whereupon John Patterson and the heirs at law of Jacob Smedley and Will Waltz, deceased, brought this action in the Fayette circuit court to quiet their title to the tollhouse and lot, alleging their ownership and possession of same under the deed from Nannie Smedley to the turnpike company and its reversion to them by reason of the purchase and freeing of the turnpike by the fiscal court of Fayette county. The devisees and heirs at law of Nannie Smedley, deceased, were made parties defendant to the action, and were duly summoned. But only two of them, Fannie Hickey and John B. Smedley, made defense to the action. This they did by filing a general demurrer to the petition, and without waiving same, later filing an answer.

By the demurrer and answer they resisted appellant's right to the property in question on the ground that the deed from Nannie Smedley to the turnpike company, in so far as it provided that the tollhouse and lot should revert to and become the property of Jacob Smedley, Will Waltz, and the appellant, John

Patterson, upon the turnpike company ceasing to use it for collecting toll, was and is void for remoteness and by reason of the statute against perpetuities, and that, therefore, the title, following the abandonment of the use of the property for collecting toll reverted to the grantor, Nannie Smedley, upon whose death it descended to appellees and the other heirs at law of the decedent. Accepting this view of the matter, the circuit court sustained the demurrer to the petition and dismissed the action at appellants' cost. Appellants, being dissatisfied with the judgment have appealed.

For appellants it is urged that the circuit court erred in adjudging that the reversion or limitation over contained in the deed from Nannie Smedley to the turnpike company created a perpetuity in violation of section 2360, Ky. St. The section reads as follows: "The absolute power of alienation shall not be suspended by any limitation or condition whatever, for a longer period than during the continuance of a life or lives in being at the creation of the estate, and twenty-one years and ten months thereafter." Without entering upon a dissertation as to the meaning of the legal term, "perpetuity," it is sufficient to say that the purpose of the statute is not to compel the vesting of estates, but to prohibit unreasonable restraints upon alienation. Neither in law nor fact did the deed under consideration create or seek to create a perpetuity. It conveyed to the turnpike company for a specific purpose, namely, for use in the collecting of tolls on the pike, the ground described. The deed did not render the property inalienable, for the turnpike company, after receiving it, had at any time the right to sell its turnpike to an individual, company, or the fiscal court, and with

such sale convey the use of the ground and tollhouse
to its vendee, and that vendee to another ad libi-
tum, so long as the property was used for the single
purpose to which it was devoted by the Smedley deed.

On the other hand, appellants had like power to
sell and convey at any time the reversionary interest
in the tollhouse and ground conveyed them by the
deed. Section 2359,Ky. St. The deed contains no
language which imports that the grant was to become
void in case the purpose for which the land was
conveyed was not carried out, nor does it reserve
to the grantor the right, in that event, to re-enter
upon the land and resume possession of it as of her
former estate. On the contrary, its language leaves
no doubt of the intention of the grantor to give the
property to her brother and brothers-in-law named
therein when its use as a tollhouse shall cease. "It
is a rule of law that conditions subsequent are not
favored because they tend to destroy estates, and, if
it be doubtful whether a clause in a deed be a condition or a covenant, courts will incline to the latter
construction." Carroll County Academy v. Gallatin Academy, 104 Ky. 621, 47 S. W. 617, 20 Ky. Law
Rep. 824.

There is another thing aside from the deed itself
that has an inportant bearing on the case. The contingency entitling appellants to the land in controversy matured during the lifetime of the grantor. We
think it safe to say that a limitation that would have
been void under conditions existing when the deed
was executed will not affect the ability of such a
limitation, if by reason of circumstances happening
subsequent to the execution of the deed but before the
death of the grantor it does not offend the rule. The
facts averred in the petition and admitted by the de-

murrer are that the deed from Nannie Smedley to the turnpike company was made in 1891; that the turnpike company conveyed its road and property to the fiscal court of Fayette county May 9, 1894; that upon that day appellants took possession of the toll-house and ground by virtue of the reversionary interest conveyed to them by the deed from Nannie Smedley to the turnpike company and have ever since been in the actual, adverse possession thereof; and that the grantor, Nannie Smedley, died in 1904, 10 years after appellants took possession of the property, and during the whole of that time set up no claim that it had reverted to her. These facts show that she had knowledge of their taking possession of and retaining the property, and that it was done with her acquiescence, if not actual consent.

Finally, we are of the opinion that the statute against perpetuities does not apply to a conveyance of land for a public highway, or for use in connection with the operation of a turnpike, which is a public highway. Gass & Bonta v. Wilhite, etc., 2 Dana, 170, 26 Am. Dec. 446. If the deed from Nannie Smedley to the turnpike company had not provided for the reversion of the title upon the abandonment of the use of the land for tollhouse purposes, nevertheless, under the law of this state, it would in consequence of such abandonment have reverted to the grantor, and, this being true, neither the statute against perpetuities nor other obstacle stood in the way of her providing in the deed for its reversion to another or others instead of herself.

Accepting as true the facts alleged in the petition, and this we must do on demurrer, we think they entitled appellants to the relief asked. Therefore the circuit court erred in sustaining the demurrer.

For the reasons indicated, the judgment is reversed and cause remanded, with directions to the circuit
court to overrule the demurrer, and for further proceedings consistent with the opinion.

CASE 44.—ACTION BY G. M. GABBERT AGAINST THE CITY
OF OWENSBORO.—November 4, 1909.

City of Owensboro v. Gabbert

Appeal from Daviess Circuit Court.

T. F. BURKHEAD, Circuit Judge.

Judgment for plaintiff, defendant appeals.—Affirmed.

1. Master and Servant—Assumed Risk—Obvious Dangers.—A
    ditch two feet wide and six feet deep which, a servant was
    digging through sandy soil when the sides caved in and in-
    jured him, was not such an obviously dangerous place of
    work that one of common understanding would not have
    continued to work therein, though its walls were not sup-
    ported in any way.

2. Master and Servant—Place of Work—Assumption of Risk.—
    Where the place of work is not such as to impose upon the
    master the full duty of providing a safe place, and, though
    somewhat dangerous, it is not so obviously so that one of
    ordinary intelligence would not work there, and a servant
    is assured by the master or his representative that there is
    no danger, or is directed to continue the work, he may re-
    cover for injuries caused by the dangerous place of work,
    though the risk is as open to him as to the master; the
    doctrine of assumption of risk in case of equal knowledge of
    the danger not being strictly implied when the servant acts
    under the master's direction, as he may then rely on the
    master's judgment.

3. Master and Servant—Injuries—Assumption of Risk—Place of
    Work—Work Under Master's Direction.—Where a ditch
    which plaintiff was digging when it caved was not so obvious-
    ly dangerous for want of shoring up that one of ordinary

City of Owensboro v. Gabbert.

intelligence would have quit the work, the master was liabile for injuries caused by its caving, where he impliedly directed plaintiff to continue work after plaintiff had called his attention to the probable danger and necessity for bracing it, even if the place was such that plaintiff created the danger in the progress of the work, so that the rule as to a safe place of work would not apply.

4 Master and Servant—Injuries—Safe Place to Work—Duty to Make Safe—Excavating Work.—Whfle the rule requiring a master to furnish a safe place of work does not apply to many works of construction where the unsafe condition is necessarily made during the progress of the work, the master was bound to make reasonably safe, by shoring the walls, a ditch two feet wide and six feet deep which was being built through sandy soil; such precaution being possible at a slight expense, and the danger from working without it is not being obvious.

R. W. SLACK, City Attorney, for appellant.

CLASSIFICATION OF QUESTIONS DISCUSSED.

1. Where the work is one of construction, reconstruction, destruction or repair, the master is not charged with the duty of exercising care to discover dangerous or unsafe places, and the risks, incident to the places and kinds of work, are assumed by the servant. Kentucky Block Cannel Coal Co. v. Nanz, 165 Fed., 46, and citations; Armour v. Hahn, 111 U. S., 313, 4 Sup. Ct. 433, 28 L. E. 440; Ballard v. Lees Adm'r, 115 S. W. 732 and citations; Brown v. Electric Ry. Co., 101 Tenn., 252, 70 Amr. St. Rep. 666, and citations; Kranz v. Long Island Ry. Co., 123 N. Y., 1. 20 Am. St. Rep. 716, distinguishing cases where a workman makes the place where he is injured, from cases where the place is made for him.

2. If the work is in and of itself dangerous, the master does not insure against such danger, and the servant assumes the ordinary risks and hazards incident to the character of the work undertaken by him, with knowledge of its dangers, or the defective condition is so obvious that he could have known the danger by the exercise of ordinary care. Wilson v. Chess & Wymond Co., 117 Ky., 567; Shemwell v. Owensboro & Nashville R. R. Co., 117 Ky. 448; Duncan v. Gernert Bros. Lumber Co., 27 Ky. Law Rep. 1039; Chicago Veneer Co. v. Walden, 82 S. W., 294.

3. The court having instructed the jury to the effect that if appellee knew of the danger, or the danger was visible and ap-

City of Owensboro v. Gabbert.

parent to him, and he voluntarily continued at work, to find for defendant, the verdict was not sustained by the evidence, or by the law as given by the court to the jury. Appellees own evidence shows he saw the condition of the soil which caused the walls to cave in upon him, saw the walls were not braced, and that he voluntarily continued at work.

4. In this case, where it appeared appellee was constructing a ditch, it was error for the court to instruct the jury that it was the duty of the defendant to furnish him a reasonably safe place to do his work and that he had the right to assume such place was reasonably free from danger, and it was not his duty to look for danger. (Inst. No. 5. Rec. 13.)

5. Plaintiff's action is based upon the allegations in his petition that the ditch in question was dangerous, and its condition was known to defendant and its servants, "or could have been known to them by the exercise of ordinary care."

The court erred (1) in failing to instruct the jury upon that subject and (2) in failing to give the instruction offered by appellant to the effect that defendant is not an insurer of the safety of the place where plaintiff was put to work, and if the evidence does not show defendant, (or its servants, superior in authority to plaintiff,) knew of its dangerous condition, or could by the exercise of ordinary care, have discovered its dangerous condition, to find for defendant. (See Inst. X, Rec. 14-15.

LEVEGA CLEMENTS and BEN D. RINGO for appellee.

POINTS AND AUTHORITIES.

1. There being no dispute concerning the facts in this case this Court is left to determine the single question of whether or not the facts stated in plaintiff's pleadings and evidence as shown by the record entitle him to a judgment.

Plaintiff was working under the eye of the master and obeying an order, and in the place furnished him in which to work. The undisputed facts show that this place could have been made absolutely safe by the exercise of the smallest care on the part of the appellant. An ommission to do so was actionable negligence. Pfisterer v. Peter & Co., 117 Ky. 501; Cyc. Vol. 26, page 1117; Thompson's Law on Negligence, Vol. 4, sections 3912 and 3913.

2. The instructions of the trial Court are more favorable to the appellant than the law would warrant. Pfisterer v. Peter & Co., 117 Ky. 501; Norfolk, &c., v. Ward (Va.) 24 L. R. A. 717; I. C. R. R. Co. v. Keebler, 84 S. W., 1167; Ashland Coal & Iron Ry. Co. v. Wallace, 101 Ky., 626; Knoxville Iron Co. v. Pace, (Tenn.) 48 S. W., 235; 4 Am. and Eng. Ency. of Law, 857.

OPINION OF THE COURT BY JUDGE CARROLL—Affirming.

This appeal is prosecuted from a judgment in favor of appellee in an action brought by him against the appellant to recover damages for injuries sustained while in its employment as a laborer digging a ditch.

It appears from the evidence that appellee, under the direction of a superior servant of the city, was engaged in digging a ditch two feet wide and six feet deep in a sandy soil. The ditch was not braced or supported in any way, although it could have been shored up and made safe at little expense, and the sand in the side of the ditch gave way, causing the solid earth on the surface to cave in and fall on appellee. The argument is made in behalf of the city that appellee, who was a man of mature years and ordinary intelligence, knew, or by the exercise of ordinary care could have known, the dangers incident to the employment, which it is said were obvious and that he assumed the risk of being injured in the manner he was; and it is further insisted that, as this was a work of construction, and the dangerous place was being made by appellee in the course of his labors, the rule putting on the master the duty of furnishing reasonably safe places for the servant to work in does not apply. Complaint is also made of alleged errors committed by the court in giving and refusing instructions.

Excepting appellee and the physicians who testified in his behalf, no witnesses were introduced by either party. During the examination of appellee, he was asked the following questions: "Q. Now, Mr. Gabbert, at the time the walls of the ditch caved in, you knew it was going to cave in? A. Certainly not, or I would not have been in there. Q. Did you know the danger of its caving in? A. No, sir; I never worked in such sand and dirt as that before. Q. Upon whose judgment did you rely in that matter? A. Doc Woods. Q. You knew Mr. Woods well? A. Certainly. Q. And you had been working under him? A. Yes, sir. Q. You knew he was an experienced man? A. Yes, sir. Q.How long had you been digging ditches of that kind and depth? A. I don't know as I ever dug any besides that of that kind and depth. Q. How long had you been digging at six feet in that place? A. Something like two days, I guess. It was deeper out there where it caved in than where we commenced. Q. It hadn't caved in anywhere else, had it? A. No, sir; that was the first cave-in in that ditch. Q. Could you see anything more about that soil than the shape of that ditch, or know anything more about it than Mr. Woods could see? Was there anything he could see or know about it that you could not see or know? A. I can't say anything about that. Mr. Woods should have understood his business and known the disposition of the soil. Q. Did you see that sand crumbling? A. No, sir; I didn't see any sand crumbling. I was cleaning up the bottom of the ditch when it caved in, and I don't remember watching it. Q. You received all of your orders from Mr. Woods, did you? A. Certainly. Q. Did anybody else about the work have authority to give orders to the men except Mr. Woods? A. No, sir. Q. Did you have any warning at all before it caught you? A. No, sir; none at all. Q. What, if anything, had you said to the foreman about the ditch? A. I just remarked to Mr. Woods, who was 10 or 12 feet behind me, awhile before that happened, that I thought it ought to be braced, that there was sand there, and he said, 'Maybe we will get through without it,' and just went on that way.''

It thus appears that appellee, although not sure that the place was dangerous, felt some uneasiness about it and made the inquiry above set out to his foreman, Woods, who, in effect, assured him that there was no danger. It cannot be said that the place was so obviously dangerous that no person of common understanding would have continued to work in it, and so the principle announced in Wilson v. Chess-Wymond Co., 117 Ky. 567, 78 S. W. 453, 25 Ky. Law Rep. 1655, Shemwell v. Owensboro & Nashville R. Co., 117 Ky. 556, 78 S. W. 448, 25 Ky. Law Rep. 1671, Duncan v. Gernett Bros. Lumber Co., 87 S. W. 762, 27 Ky. Law Rep. 1039, and other like cases, does not apply. The rule in this state is that when the place in which the servant is engaged in working is not such as imposes upon the master the full duty of providing a safe place, but is somewhat hazardous or dangerous, although not obviously so, or the danger of continuing is not so apparent that a person of ordinary intelligence would not undertake it, and the servant is assured, in substance or effect, by the master, who is present, that it is reasonably safe or that there is no danger, or is directed by him to go on with the work, the servant may recover for injuries received, although the risk or hazard in prosecuting the work is as well known to the servant as it is to the master. When the master is present, the doctrine of equal knowledge and assumed risk, that is sometimes invoked in cases like this to relieve the master, should be sparingly applied. The position of the two is very different, and out of this difference grows the right of the servant to depend upon the master, if he be present directing the work, as he has a right to presume he will warn him of danger and save him from needless exposure to injury or death.

In Shearman & Redfield on Negligence, Sec. 186, this idea is well expressed in the following language: ''The true rule in this as in all other cases is that, if the master gives the servant to understand that he does not consider the risk one which a prudent person should refuse to undertake, the servant has the right to rely upon his master's judgment, unless his own is so clearly opposed thereto that in fact he does not rely upon his master's opinion. So, if the peculiar risk of the act commanded by the master is not obvious, the servant has the right to assume that he is not sent into any unusual peril, and is not bound to investigate into the risk, before obeying his orders. A servant is not called upon to set up his own unaided judgment against that of his superiors, and he may rely upon their advice, and still more upon their orders, notwithstanding many misgivings of his own.   * * *   The servant's dependent and inferior position is to be taken into consideration, and if the master gives him positive orders to go on with the work under perilous circumstances, the servant may recover for an injury thus incurred, if the work was not inevitably or immediately dangerous.'' So that, if we should put this case upon the ground that the servant was engaged in a work of construction, and was himself by his labor making the danger, and hence the strict rule for the protection of the servant in respect to safe places should not be applied we would yet feel obliged to say that the master in this case made himself liable by his implied direction to the servant to go on with the work after his attention was directed by the servant to the probable danger and the necessity for shoring or bracing. As said in Western Union Telegraph Co. v. Holtby, 93 S. W. 652, 29 Ky. Law Rep. 523, a case in many respects like the one at bar:

"There are exceptions to the rule that relieved the master from liability when the servant is injured by appliances or tools or unsafe places, when the danger is one that might have been discovered by the servant by the exercise of ordinary care. Among them, and applicable to the facts in this case, is the doctrine that, although an appliance, tool, or place may be unsafe, and the danger discoverable by reasonable or ordinary inspection, yet if the master is present and orders the servant to perform the duty, or the servant depends on the master's presumed knowledge of the defective appliance or unsafe place, or relies on the master's inspection of the premises, and acts under his immediate direction, the master will be liable."

But, aside from this, the character of the work, although constructive, was not such as to relieve the master from the duty of making it reasonably safe. There are a great many works of construction in which it would not be practicable for the master to keep a safe place in which the servant could work while engaged in the undertaking; the nature of the work being such that a continual change is going on with which the servant must familiarize himself and take such precautions as are necessary to avoid accident or injury. To this class of constructive work a lower standard of liability on the part of the master, and in many cases no liability, will be applied than in cases where the work has been finished and is being used in the ordinary conduct of the business. Bailey on Master & Servant, Sections 29, 267; Ballard & Ballard Co. v. Lee (Ky.) 115 S. W. 732.

But where an excavation like the one involved in this case is being made, and there is danger that the walls may cave in, and this is or should be in the exercise of ordinary care known to the master, and can easily and with little expense be obviated by shoring them up, there is no reason why the duty of the master to furnish the servant a reasonably safe place in which to work should not be applied in its fullest extent, unless the danger is so obvious that a person of ordinary intelligence would not undertake it. This doctrine is well supported by numerous authorities, among which we may mention Thompson on Negligence, Secs. 3912, 3913; Bailey on Master & Servant, Sec. 98; American and English Encyclopedia of Law, vol. 20, p. 59; 26 Cyc. 1178; Welch v. Carlucci Stone Co., 215 Pa. 34, 64 Atl. 392, 7 Am. and Eng. Ann. Cas. 299.

As the instructions given by the court conformed to our views of the law applicable to the case as we have expressed them in this opinion, and the verdict is not excessive, the judgment of the lower court must be affirmed, and it is so ordered.

CASE 45.—PROCEEDINGS BY E. B. ANDERSON TO SETTLE
    HIS ACCOUNTS AS ASSIGNEE FOR THE BENEFIT
    OF CREDITORS OF THE DAVIESS COUNTY BANK
    & TRUST CO.—November 9, 1909.

Burnes, &c. v. Daviess County Bank & Trust Co.

Appeal from Daviess Circuit Court.

T. F. BIRKHEAD, Circuit Judge.

From the judgment Edward Franke and Sam
Burnes appeal.—Affirmed.

1. Pledges—Delivery and Possession—Written Instruments—
   Bonds—Validity.—A bank issued to depositors certificates
   termed "mortgage certificates of deposit," which recited the
   deposit, and that the certificate was secured by an equal
   amount of bonds or lien notes. When such certificates
   were issued, the bank would indorse on one of its mortgage
   bonds or lien notes the fact that it was pledged as security
   for certificates issued, and the bond or note so indorsed was
   placed in a box retained by it with others similarly indorsed,
   and a similar indorsement was made on the register opposite the entry of such bond or note, and, when such indorsed bonds or notes were paid, another bond or note belonging to the bank was indorsed and placed in the box with
   the others. The indorsements were not dated and ordinarily
   not signed by the bank officers. Ky. St. Sec. 1908, makes
   every charge upon personalty, unless actual possession in
   good faith accompanies it, void as to any creditor prior to
   the recording of the charge. Held, that a pledge of personalty could only be created by actual or symbolic delivery of
   the property to the pledgee, and, while the pledge of the
   bonds, etc., was valid as between the bank and certificate holders, the statute made it void as to other creditors.

2. Assignment for Benefit of Creditors—Remedies of Assignee
   —Setting Aside Assignment—Right.—Under Ky. St. Sec.
   84, vesting in the assignee property fraudulently transferred by an assignor for the benefit of creditors
   before the assignment, if a transfer by the assignor is void
   as to his creditors, it is void as to the assignee, since he rep-

resents them, and holds the property in trust for their benent, so that the fact that a pledge of property by an assignor for the benefit of creditors without delivering possession was good as between it and the pledgees would not prevent the assignee from setting it aside as void against the assignor's creditors.

SWEENEY, ELLIS & SWEENEY, MILLER & TODD, J. D. ATCHISON and GEORGE W. JOLLY for appellants.

LEVEGA CLEMENTS, BEN D. RINGO, C. M. FINN, J. R. HAYS, W. F. HAYS and C. W. WELLS for appellees.

OPINION OF THE COURT BY JUDGE HOBSON—Affirming.

The Daviess County Bank & Trust Company began business in Owensboro, Ky., on August 7, 1900. On April 28, 1908, it made a general deed of assignment for the benefit of its creditors, and E. B. Anderson was appointed as trustee. He filed this action in the Daviess circuit court for a settlement of his accounts. There were a large number of depositors in the bank, some of whom held the ordinary certificates of deposit. Others held what is denominated in the record "mortgage certificates of deposit." The latter were in these words: "Owensboro, Ky., ——. $——. This is to certify that —— has deposited in the Daviess Bank & Trust Company — dollars payable to his order on return of this certificate properly indorsed twelve months after date with interest thereon at —— per cent. per annum, interest to cease on the —— day of ——, 19—. This certificate of deposit is one of a series of similar certificates and is secured by an equal amount of first mortgage bonds or lien notes on real estate in Daviess County, Kentucky, worth at least double the amount loaned."

These certificates were issued pursuant to an order of the board of directors made on March 26, 1903, which was as follows: "At a meeting of the directors of the Daviess County Bank & Trust Company held today in the directors' room there were present T. S. Venable, J. J. Griffin, and T. S. Anderson. T. S. Anderson laid before the board a plan for issuing certificates of deposit secured especially by first mortgage bonds or lien notes set aside for that purpose, all money coming in on said certificates to be invested in said class of securities and held as a special fund. Mr. Venable moved that the bank issue such certificates of deposit. His motion was seconded by Mr. Griffin and carried. Board adjourned."

The plan adopted by the bank for the issual of these mortgage certificates was this: The bank would issue a certificate of this kind to a person who deposited money with the bank, and it would take from among the mortgage bonds or lien notes a note or bond and indorse upon it in stencil these words: "This bond (or note) is pledged as security for the series of mortgage certificates of deposit issued by the Daviess County Bank & Trust Company." The bond or note thus stamped was then placed in a box with the others so stamped, and an indorsement in stencil was made on the register of the bank opposite the entry of this bond or note similar to the indorsement stamped on it. The indorsements were not dated, and were not ordinarily signed by the bank or any of the officers of it. When a bond or note thus stamped or an interest coupon was paid, it was paid to the bank in the regular course of its business and delivered to the payor, and another bond or note belonging to the bank was taken from the notes or bonds of the bank, stamped as above, and placed among those previously stamped in the box kept for that purpose.

At the time the bank failed it held bonds secured by mortgage of the par value of $206,066. It also held real estate notes to the amount of $28,084. On these mortgage bonds and real estate notes the holders of the mortgage certificates claimed a lien on $74,000 to secure their certificates, which amounted to the sum of $73,463.44. These bonds and notes were in the box referred to with indorsements as stated at the time they came to the hands of the assignee, and that they were placed there at the time the mortgage certificates were issued or when other notes previously placed there were withdrawn is conceded. In other words, it is conceded that the bank in good faith undertook to secure these depositors in this way at the time they deposited their money with it; and the only question we are to determine is whether a valid lien may be thus created on notes and bonds to the prejudice of other creditors.

Section 1908, Ky. Stat., is in these words: "Every voluntary alienation of or charge upon personal property, unless the actual possession, in good faith, accompanies the same, shall be void as to a purchaser without notice, or any creditor, prior to the lodging for record of such transfer or charge in the office of the county court for the county where the alienor or person creating the charge resides." Under this statute, it has been held in an unbroken line of decisions, that an absolute sale of personal property is per se void as to the purchasers and creditors unless the possession of the property accompanies the title, and that a lien on the property can only be created by a writing recorded in the county clerk's office where the owner retains possession. Enders v. Williams, 1 Metc. 346, and cases cited. In the case at bar the bank did not surrender possession of the notes and bonds put in the box to secure the mortgage certificates. These notes and bonds were not delivered to the holders of these certificates. If the maker of a note had a set-off against the bank, it was available against the note; but, if he had a set-off against the holder of a mortgage certificate, this could not have been asserted against the note in the hands of the bank and a payment to the holder of one of these certificates would have been no defense to an action by the bank on the note, if the bank had without notice of the payment, settled with the certificate holder. A pledge of personal property can only be created by actual or symbolic delivery of the property by the pledgor to the pledgee. If the property remains in the possession and under the control of the pledgor, the transaction falls within the statute, and is void as to creditors and purchasers. A bank has no greater rights than an individual, and to hold that an individual can create pocket liens upon his property in such a way as this that are valid against purchasers and creditors would be to nullify the statute and entirely defeat the legislative purpose in its enactment.

It is said that the assignee for the benefit of the creditors simply stands in the shoes of his assignor, and that the arrangement in contest was good as between the certificate holders and the bank; but by section 84, Ky. St., if the assignor before making the deed of assignment shall have made a fraudulent

transfer of his property, the property sold fraudulently transferred vests in the assignee. The assignee holds
the property for the benefit of the creditors and as
their trustee. If the transfer is void as to the creditors whom he represents, it is void also as to him as
their representative. A trustee may always assert
the rights of his cestui que trust, and take such steps
as are necessary to protect them in a court of equity.
Practically the same question we have before us was
before the Supreme Court of Louisiana in Succession
of Lanaux, 46 La. Ann. 1036, 15 South. 708, 25 L. R.
A. 580, and before the United States Supreme Court
in Casey v. Cavaroc, 96 U. S. 467, 24 L. Ed. 779, and
we concur in the reasoning of those opinions denying
a lien to creditors attempted to be created between
debtor and creditor by a private arrangement like
this.   See, also, Grand Avenue Bank v. St. Louis
Union Trust Co., 135 Mo. App. 366, 115 S. W. 1074.

It is insisted for the appellants that the bank held
the bonds and notes as trustee for the holders of the
mortgage certificates, and we are referred to a number of cases in which such trusts have been enforced as between trustee and cestui qui trusts; but it
will be seen from an examination of these cases that
in none of them were the rights of creditors or purchasers involved. The arrangement here was valid
as between the bank and the depositor if the bank had
remained solvent, and the rights of other creditors
were not involved; but it would entirely defeat the
statute to say that a trust of this sort could be enforced against purchasers or creditors. The purpose
of the statute was to declare inoperative and void
such transactions as to purchasers and creditors.

We therefore conclude that the circuit court properly held that the holders of the mortgage certificates

had no superior lien on the bonds and notes referred to.

Judgment affirmed.

CASE 46.—ACTION BY R. J. LEWIS AGAINST THE LOUIS
VILLE & NASHVILLE RAILROAD COMPANY FOR
LOSS OF GOODS BURNED IN DEFENDANTS'
WAREHOUSE.—November 10, 1909.

Lewis v. Louisville & Nashville R. R. Co.

Appeal from Bell Circuit Court.

M. J. Moss, Circuit Judge.

Judgment for defendant, plaintiff appeals.—Reversed.

1. Carriers—Loss or Damage to Goods—Nature of Liability.—
   A common carrier is an insurer of freight delivered to it
   for carriage and can only escape liability for loss or damage
   by showing it was caused by the act of God, or the public
   enemy, or by inherent defects in the goods.

2. Warehousemen—Nature of Liability.—A warehouseman is not
   an insurer of goods placed in his warehouse, and is only
   liable for such loss or damage thereto as is caused by his
   negligence for failure to exercise ordinary care.

3. Carriers—Delivery of Goods—Time for Removal by Consignee.
   —A consignee should have a reasonable time to remove
   goods after they have been in a carrier's warehouse at their
   destination.

4. Carriers—Transportation of Freight—Duty as to Carriage
   and Delivery.—The duty of a carrier accepting freight for
   transportation does not end by merely carrying the goods in
   its cars to the point of destination, but it must deliver them
   at such place in or about its station as will enable the consignee to conveniently get them.

5. Carriers—Carriage of Goods—Liability for Loss or Injury—
   Termination Thereof.—A carrier may keep goods in its cars
   or place them in its warehouse, but wherever it keeps them,
   except against loss or damage by act of God, or the public
   enemy, or by inherent defect, it insures their safety till the

consignee has a reasonable time to remove them after their arrival, as the delivery contemplated is not fully preformea till then.

6. Carriers—Carriage of Goods—Limitation of Liability.—In view of Const. Sec. 196, forbidding a common carrier to contract for relief from its common-law liability, a common carrier cannot by any stipulation in the contract or bill of lading, reduce its liability as an insurer of the safety of goods till the consignee has had a reasonable time to remove them after their arrival.

7. Carriers—Carriage of Goods—Removal by Consignee—"Reasonabe Time."—The period of reasonable time for the removal of goods begins when the consignee knows or, in the exercise of reasonable diligence should know, that they have arrived.

8. Carriers—Carriage of Goods—Actions for Loss or Injury—Questions for Jury.—Reasonable time for removal of goods by a consignee, and reasonable diligence on his part to inform himself of their arrival, are in general questions for the jury.

JAS. H. JEFFRIES and N. R. PATTERSON for appellant.

POINTS AND AUTHORITIES.

1. It was the duty of appellee as a common carrier upon receipt of appellant's goods at Pineville, to at once notify appellant by mail of such fact, and then to keep said goods safely, as a common carrier until appellant had received the notice of their arrival and then had reasonable time thereafter in which to remove the goods from the depot.

2. In view of the fact that one consignment of these goods was two days in being transported from Louisville to Pineville; that another consignment of the goods was twenty days in being transported from Louisville to Pineville; and that the third consignment of goods was seven days in being transported from Knoxville to Pineville, all over the same railroad system, it would be unreasonable and unfair to require appellant to be waiting at Pineville with his wagon and team, these indefinite and uncertain periods of time to receive his goods.

3. In view of the foregoing, the liability of the appellee, as a common carrier of and insurer of the safe delivery of these goods in question, continued until after they were destroyed by the fire. 2 Hutchison on Carriers (3rd Edition) Secs. 704, 707, 708; 2 Bush, 468, Jeffersonville R. R. Co. v. Cleveland; 92 Ky., 645,

Wald & Co. v. Louisville E. & St. L. R. R. Co.; 32 N. H., 523, Moses v. The Railroad (Quoted at length in 2 Hutchison, Sec. 704Supra.).

BENJAMIN D. WARFIELD, CHAS. H. MOORMAN and C. N. METCALF for appellee.

POINTS AND AUTHORITIES.

The liability of the defendant for the goods in question was that of a warehouseman, and, inasmuch as it was stipulated that the fire that destroyed them was not caused by the fault, wrongdoing, or negligence of the defendant or any of its agents or servants, the plaintiff is not entitled to recover, and the judgment should not be disturbed. Jeffersonville R. R. Co. v. Cleveland, 2 Bush, 468; Louisville, Cincinnati & Lexington R. R. Co. v. Mahan, 8 Bush, 184; Redfield on Railways, Section 171, Subsections 2 and 3,; Roth v. Buffalo & State Line R. R. Co., 34 N. Y. Reps., 548; Briant, &c., v. Louisville & Nashville R. R. Co., 9 Ky. Law Rep., 47; L. & N. R. R. Co. v. Jones, 10 Ky. Law Rep., 494; Wald & Co. v. L. E. & St. L. R. R. Co., 92 Ky., 645; Moses v. Boston & Maine, 32 N. H., 523; Moore on Carriers, page 267; Harris v. L. & N. R R. Co., 9 Ky. Law Rep. 392; L. & N. R. R. Co. v. Mink, 126 Ky. 337.

OPINION OF THE COURT BY JUDGE CARROLL— Reversing.

The questions presented by this record are: When does the duty and liability of a common carrier of goods as a carrier cease upon the arrival of the goods at the point of destination, and when does its duty and liability as a warehouseman begin?

It is agreed that there was shipped to the appellant Lewis over the road of the appellee company to Pineville, Ky., three packages of goods that were in its warehouse at Pineville on the night of September 16th, when the building and its contents, including this freight, was destroyed by fire; that the fire commenced at a late hour on the night of the 16th, or an early hour on the morning of the 17th, and was not caused either directly or indirectly by the negligence, fraud, or wrong-doing of the company or any of its agents, servants, or employes; that at the time of the fire, and for some five years prior thereto, Lewis was engaged in selling goods as a merchant at a point some 25 miles distant by the nearest traveled route from Pineville; that during that time all of the goods and merchandise that he sold was delivered to him by the company at its Pineville station, and this fact was known to its agent at Pineville, who also knew where Lewis lived and his postoffice address; that two of the packages of merchandise destroyed reached Pineville on the 13th of September, and were placed in the company's warehouse on that day, and the other package destroyed was placed in the warehouse at noon on September 16th; that neither Lewis nor any one for him made inquiry about or called at the warehouse for the goods, nor was any notice of the arrival of the goods or any of them sent or given by mail or otherwise to Lewis, and he did not at the time of the fire have any knowledge or notice that the goods or any of them were in the warehouse.

It is further agreed that, on account of the heavy traffic on the road, it was impossible for Lewis to know with reasonable certainty when the goods which were shipped from distant points would reach Pineville, and that the goods in question were transported without unreasonable delay, although it appears that one shipment that left Louisville on August 28th did not reach Pineville until September 13th, while another package that left Louisville on September 14th reached Pineville on September 16th, and that the package that was sent from Knoxville, which is only about half the distance from Pineville that Louisville is, did not arrive at Pineville until September

13th, although it was shipped on September 6th. Upon these facts the trial court held as matter of law that the company was not liable.

There is really no contrariety of opinion as to the difference between the liability of a common carrier and the liability of a warehouseman; it being everywhere agreed that a common carrier is an insurer of the freight delivered to it for carriage, and can only escape liability for loss or damage to the goods by showing that the loss or damage was caused by the act of God, or the public enemy, or by inherent defects in the goods. It is equally as well established that a warehouseman is not an insurer of goods placed in his warehouse, and is only liable for such loss or damage to the goods as is caused by his negligence or failure to exercise ordinary care.

From these rules it will be seen that, if the goods in controversy were in the custody of the company as a common carrier at the time of their destruction, it would nevertheless be liable for their value; while if they were in its custody as a warehouseman, it would not be liable, as the loss was not occasioned by its fault or negligence. Although the liability of a carrier and that of a warehouseman is well defined, and the distinction between them in this respect clearly pointed out in all the authorities, there is wide and irreconcilable conflict concerning when the liability of a common carrier as a common carrier ceases, and its liability as a warehouseman begins. In Massachusetts and other states the rule is that when the carrier has delivered the goods at the point of destination, removed them from its cars and placed them in its warehouse, its liability as a carrier immediately ceases, and thereafter it holds the goods as a warehouseman. In New Hampshire and other jurisdic-

tions the rule is that the carrier continues liable as
a carrier after the goods have reached their destination and have been placed in the warehouse, and for
a reasonable time thereafter, in which time the consignee must remove them or otherwise the carrier
will hold them as a warehouseman. While the Supreme Court of New York and other state courts of
last resort hold that unless the consignee is present
when the goods arrive, he must be notified of their
arrival and have a reasonable time after notice in
which to remove them before the liability of the carrier as a carrier ceases. Hutchinson on Carriers (3d.
Ed.) Secs. 701, 710; Elliott on Railroads (2d Ed.)
Sec. 1527; note to Denver, &c. R. Co. v. Peterson, 97
Am. St. Rep. 76; East Tenn., etc., R. Co. v. Kelly, 91
Tenn.. 699, 20 S. W. 312, 17 L. R. A. 691, 30 Am. St.
Rep. 902.

In this state we have no statute on the subject. but
the question we are considering has been before this
court in three cases. In Louisville, C. & L. R. Co. v.
Mahan, 8 Bush, 184, and Wald & Co. v. Louisville,
etc., R. Co., 92 Ky. 645, 18 S. W. 850, 13 Ky. Law Rep.
850, the point involved was what constituted a reasonable time in which a passenger might remove from
the depot the baggage that came on the train with
him. In Jeffersonville R. Co. v. Cleveland 2 Bush, 468,
the question presented was in many respects like the
one now before us, and the court in delivering the
opinion followed what may be called the New Hampshire rule. In that case suit was brought to recover
the value of goods shipped by freight and destroyed
by fire on the night of April 26th, while they were in
the warehouse of the carrier at the place of destination. The goods in the ordinary course of transportation should have arrived on the 20th, but on account

of delays, they did not arrive until the evening of the 25th; and the owner inquired at the warehouse for them on each day from the 20th to and including the morning of the 25th. On the morning of the 26th a notice to the owner of the fact that his goods had arrived, was deposited in the post office, but not received.

In the course of the opinion the court said: "Whether the responsibility of the company, after the arrival and storage of the goods in Detroit, was that devolved by law on carriers or only that of depositaries, it was not necessary in our opinion that the company should either give notice of the arrival of the goods or make actual delivery of them, as is now done by express companies, in order that the liability of carriers should cease after reasonable time had elapsed for the owner to attend and remove the goods. * * * But the liability of railroad corporations as common carriers for goods transported on their railroads continues until the goods are ready to be delivered at their place of destination, and the owner or consignee has had reasonable opportunity of receiving and removing them. * * * What such reasonable time should be must in the nature of the case when not provided for by express contract depend on the character of the freight, the distance to which it is to be carried, and the capacity and business of the road, with such other circumstances as would serve to notify the consignee of the probable time when the goods would reach their destination, so that, with proper watchfulness, he might receive them, and thus terminate the carrier's responsibility as soon as practicable."

Upon the facts stated, the court held the owner did not have a reasonable time in which to remove the goods after their arrival, and that the carrier at the time of their destruction was holding them as a carrier and hence liable. The liability was put upon the ground that the owner had exercised reasonable diligence to ascertain when the goods would arrive, and, as their arrival was delayed several days after the time when they should have reached their destination, the owner was not obliged to continue his inquiries as to when they would come, and the notice was not sufficient to enable him by reasonable diligence to remove the goods during the day on which the notice was sent.

Although disposed towards the view that the carrier should give notice if it desires to be relieved of its duty as a carrier, yet we are not fully prepared to overrule the Cleveland Case on this point. This being so, the only question left open is the one relating to reasonable time in which to remove the goods. That the consignee should have such time after the goods have been placed in the warehouse we have no doubt. When a carrier accepts freight for transportation, its duty as a carrier does not end by merely carrying the goods in its cars to the point of destination. It must deliver as well as carry, although by this we do not mean that it must deliver them as express companies do to the home or place of business of the consignee, but it must deliver them at such place in or about its station as will enable the consignee to conveniently get them. It may, if it desires, keep them in its cars or place them in its warehouse, but, wherever it keeps them, it insures their safety except against the causes mentioned until the consignee has reasonable time to remove them, as the delivery contemplated is not fully performed until the consignee has had this time after the arrival of the goods in

which to remove them. And this is true although the
bill of lading or contract for carriage, as in this case,
provides "property shall be at the risk of the owner
from the time of its arrival at destination whether
in the vessel, car, depot or place of delivery; if not
taken possession of and removed by the party entitled thereto within twenty-four hours thereafter, shall
be subject to a reasonable charge for storage, or at
the option of the carrier may be removed or otherwise
stored at the owner's risk and cost," as neither this
nor any other stipulation in the contract or bill of
lading will be allowed to reduce the liability of the
carrier below what it was at common law.

Our Constitution (section 196) provides in part
that "no common carrier shall be permitted to contract for relief from its common-law liability;" and,
under the common law, the duty and liability of the
common carrier was not terminated until the goods
after the carriage were delivered to the consignee. 2
Kent, Com. 604; Moses v. Boston & Maine R. Co., 24
N. H. 71; 55 Am. Dec. 222. But, as it is not deemed
reasonable to require a railway carrier of freight to
deliver the goods to the consignee at his residence or
place of business, the rule of the common law in the
interest of and for the convenience of this class of
carriers has been modified, and now it is only required that the delivery shall be at the point of destination, and at this place the consignee must come for
and remove his goods within a reasonable time after
their arrival during which time the common-law liability of the carrier continues.

The question then comes up: What is a reasonable time? How it is to be determined? Is it to be
decided by the court as a matter of law or by the jury
as a matter of fact? Some courts hold that a reason-

able time for the consignee to remove the goods is
not to be measured by any peculiar circumstances in
his own condition or situation rendering it necessary
for his own convenience and accomodation that he
should have a longer time or better opportunity than
if he resided in the vicinity of the warehouse and
was prepared with the means and facilities for taking
the goods away; or, to put it in another way, a reasonable time is such as will enable one living in the vicinity of the place of delivery in the ordinary course of
business and in the usual hours of business to remove
the goods. Moses v. Boston & Maine R. Co., 32 N.
H. 523, 64 Am. Dec. 381; L. L. & G. R. Co. v. Maris,
16 Kan. 333; Wood v. Crocker, 18 Wis. 363, 86 Am.
Dec. 773; United Fruit Co. v. New York Transportation Co., 104 Md. 567, 65 Atl. 415, 8 L. R. A. (N. S.)
240, 10 Am. & Eng. Ann. Cas. 437; Columbus R. Co.
v. Ludden, 89 Ala. 612, 7 South. 471; 5 Am. & Eng.
Ency. of Law, pp. 263-274; 6 Cyc. 445.

It must be conceded that this rule has at least the
merit of easy application, and that its adoption would
solve the question of what is a reasonable time with
little difficulty. Under it the only issues of fact left
open would be the time of day the goods arrived at
the station, as, if they arrived in time to remove
them on that day in the usual hours of business, then
they must be removed on that day or afterwards the
carrier would hold them as a warehouseman; and so,
if they arrived in the night, they must be removed in
the hours of business on the following day. And it
is manifest that, if this rule should be applied to the
case before us, the carrier would be relieved of responsibility, even as to the package of goods that arrived at noon on the 16th, as a person living in the
vicinity of the depot could have removed this package

as well as the ones that came on the 13th, during the afternoon of the 16th. But we do not feel disposed to follow the rule announced. Nor was it observed in the Cleveland Case, supra. There the goods, although they arrived on the 25th, were not destroyed until the night of the 26th, and yet, notwithstanding the fact that the consignee had the entire day of the 26th in which to remove them, the carrier was held liable as a carrier.

In our opinion the true test of what is a reasonable time depends, not on whether the consignee lives in the vicinity of the station, or whether he could remove the goods in the usual hours of business on the day of their arrival, but on the question whether or not he exercised reasonable diligence to ascertain when the goods would or did arrive, and reasonable diligence in their removal, or in the exercise of reasonable care should have received notice of their arrival. If the consignee is present, or if he has notice of the time of the arrival of his goods, or if he is notified by the consignee that his goods have been shipped on a certain day, and the train upon which they are shipped arrives on schedule time, he should remove them within reasonable time thereafter, and, if he fails to do so, the liability of the carrier will be reduced to that of a warehouseman. On the other hand, if he is not present, and has no notice of when they arrive, or there is delay in the transportation of the goods, he should exercise reasonable diligence to inform himself of their arrival and have a reasonable time thereafter to remove them. In other words, the period at which the reasonable time for removal begins is when the consignee knows or in the exercise of reasonable diligence should know that his goods have arrived.

In every state of case the consignee must exercise reasonable diligence to inform himself of the arrival of the goods, and, if he wishes to hold the carrier liable as a carrier, must remove them within a reasonable time thereafter, whether it be a day or a week. What is reasonable diligence being, like reasonable time, a question of fact varying with each case, it is manifest that no fixed rule can be laid down to measure reasonable time or reasonable diligence. What would be reasonable in one instance would be unreasonable in another, and so in these particulars each case must be adjudged upon the facts it presents. If the consignee is to have a reasonable time in which to remove the goods, then it is not just that this should be measured by his proximity to the depot, or his ability to remove the goods on the day of their arrival. All consignees should be treated alike, no matter whether they live close to or far from the depot. If the consignee has exercised reasonable diligence in ascertaining when his goods arrived and in removing them, then he has removed them in a reasonable time. If he has not exercised reasonable diligence in finding out when his goods have or should have arrived, and in removing them, he has not removed them in a reasonable time. This, notwithstanding the respect we have for the courts that define reasonable time in the manner before stated, is, we submit, the true rule, and that the other definition is both illogical and unsound.

How can it be said that a consignee who does not know, and in the exercise of reasonable care, cannot know, that his goods had arrived, has had a reasonable time to remove them? How can it be said that a person has failed to do a thing within a reasonable time when he has no notice that he will be required to do it? It would be just as well to abolish the rule of reasonable time as to say that the time when reasonable time commences to run is the time when the consignee had not and could not in the exercise or reasonable diligence know of its beginning. The test of reasonable time should not be made to turn on whether or not the consignee might remove them on the day of their arrival if he can do this in the business hours of that day. To illustrate, under this rule if a box of goods arrived at noon, and the warehouse was open in the afternoon, the consignee, if present, or notified, that his goods would be sent on the train that arrived at noon, and the train reached the station on schedule time, and would have a reasonable time in the business hours of that day to remove them.

But, let us suppose that he is not present, and has no notice that his goods have arrived, or are expected to arrive, how can it be said that he has had a reasonable time to remove them on the day of their arrival, when he does not and by the exercise of reasonable diligence, could not learn of their arrival until the following day or the day thereafter? Or let us suppose that the consignee has notice that his goods have been shipped at a certain time, and that in the ordinary course will reach their destination at a certain hour, and the consignee is at the station when the train is due, but it is delayed and does not come until the next day or the day following, must the consignee wait until its arrival? Or let us suppose that the goods in the course of shipment are in some way delayed and do not come for a week, must he wait in attendance at the depot? These examples, which are of common occurrence, illustrate that the rule requiring the goods to be removed on the day of their arrival, if this can be done in the usual business hours, is not the proper

test of what constitutes a reasonable time in which
the consignee must remove his goods after their arrival. Nor are we wanting in authority for the views
we have expressed as to what constitutes reasonable
time. In Redfield on the Law of Railways (6th Ed.)
Sec. 175, the learned author, speaking upon this point,
says: "Upon principle it seems more reasonable to
conclude that the responsibility does not terminate
until the owner or consignee, by watchfulness, has
had, or might have had, an opportunity to remove
them. * * * There is then no very good reason, as
it seems to us, why the responsibility of the carrier
should not continue until the owner or consignee by
the use of diligence might have removed the goods.
The warehousing seems to be with that intent, and for
that purpose.

And, if we assume, as we must, we think that there
is no obligation upon railway carriers to give notice of
the arrival of the goods, there does still seem to be
reason and justice in giving the consignee time and opportunity to remove the goods by the exercise of the
proper watchfulness, before the responsibility of the
carrier ends." We appreciate the fact that the rule
we have announced is open to objection on account of
its uncertainty and the difficulty of its application;
but it is not more uncertain or difficult of application
than any other matter involving like questions of fact.
The decisions of many of the most important business
affairs that come before the court turn upon the question of what is reasonable time, and what is reasonable diligence. These two factors enter into cases
that come up every day. Nor does the rule impose
any particular hardship on the carrier, as it can, by
giving notice to the consignee of the arrival of his
goods, reduce its liability to that of a warehouseman,

if the consignee within a reasonable time after the reception of the notice does not remove them. We may also add that what is reasonable time and reasonable diligence is, except in rare cases, a question for the jury, although it might become, as any other question of fact about which there was no dispute, an issue to be decided by the court.

In conformity with these views, the court should on another trial of the case submit the issues of fact to a jury, and instruct them in substance that if they believe from the evidence that Lewis knew, or in the exercise of ordinary diligence could have known, when his goods arrived, they should find for the railroad company, if he failed to remove them from the warehouse within a reasonable time after he knew or by the exercise of reasonable diligence could have known of their arrival. But if he did not, or in the exercise of reasonable diligence could not have known the time of the arrival of the goods, and did not fail to remove them within a reasonable time after he so knew or could have known, they should find for Lewis.

In the trial each party should be permitted to introduce all pertinent evidence throwing light upon the question of whether or not Lewis exercised reasonable diligence, and failed to remove the goods in a reasonable time.

The judgment of the lower court is reversed, with directions to grant appellant a new trial in conformity with this opinion.

CASE 47.—PROCEEDINGS AGAINST THE SEELBACH HOTEL
     COMPANY FOR SELLING LIQUORS ON SUNDAY.—
     November 11, 1909.

Seelbach Hotel Co. v. Commonwealth

Appeal from Jefferson Circuit Court (Criminal Division).

JOSEPH PRIOR, Judge.

Defendant convicted and appeals.—Affirmed.

Intoxicating Liquors—Sunday Sales—Inkeepers.—An inkeeper,
    not being exempt from Ky. St. Sec. 1304, by which no one can
    sell intoxicating liquors without a license, violates section
    1303, declaring it an offense to sell such liquor on Sunday by
    serving it with a Sunday meal, though an inkeeper's ordinary
    business is one of necessity within Sunday closing acts.

GIBSON, MARSHALL & GIBSON and KOHN, BAIRD, SLOSS
& KOHN for appellant.

JAMES BREATHITT, Attorney General, and TOM B. McGRE-
GOR, Assistant Attorney General, for Commonwealth.

No Briefs—record misplaced.

OPINION OF THE COURT BY JUDGE O'REAR—Affirming.

This is an appeal from a judgment of conviction
against appellant in a penal action instituted for four
alleged violations of section 1303, Ky. St., which section reads as follows: "Any person who shall, on
Sunday, keep open a barroom or other place for the
sale of liquors, or who shall sell or otherwise dispose
of such liquors, or any of them on Sunday, shall be
fined not less than ten nor more than fifty dollars

for each offense. The case was submitted and decided in the circuit court upon an agreed state of facts, disclosing: That the appellant was at the time mentioned in the petition (on a Sunday) a duly licensed hotel and inn keeper in the city of Louisville, and operating its hotel in good faith, having all the essentials and conveniences to enable it to do, so. That appellant also had a bar attached to its hotel, but that on the occasion named the bar was closed. That appellant furnished a guest at its hotel, who was a citizen of Louisville and came to the hotel for his dinner, a quart of champagne as a part of his dinner, partaken of by him and his friends who accompanied him; to another guest, who was a traveling salesman from New York, a cocktail and a pint of white wine as a part of his dinner; to another guest, who was then living in the hotel, as part of his dinner. a pint of claret; to another guest, then living in the hotel as a guest, as a part of his supper, a mug of beer. That the liquors were ordered by the guests as parts of their meals and were served to them in good faith as parts of their entertainment, "and that said persons, according to their mode of living, manner, and habits, required and generally took for and as a part of their meals as a beverage liquors, and they had acquired the habit of drinking, instead of coffee or tea, such liquors with their meals, and it was necessary for them to have the same for their comfort and habits."

It was further agreed that such habits and customs existed with a large number of people who patronized that hotel, became its guests, and took their meals therein. This additional statement was incorporated in the stipulation of facts: "That there has been a statute in this state, differing in character, forbidding labor and doing business on the Lord's Day, or Sunday, for more than 100 years, and that under all the statutes in this state, during all of said time, hotels and innkeepers have been permitted to serve their guests with liquors at their meals, and it was never attempted to enforce any statute against them, exercising such rights, although several statutes of this state on this subject has been enforced at various times that they never have been considered as applicable to hotels and innkeepers and never have been sought to be enforced against them until recently within a year or 18 months past.''

That the sale of intoxicating liquors is a subject for the state's police regulation is no longer an open question. Anderson v. Commonwealth, 13 Bush, 485. In this state no person has the right to sell such liquors at all as a matter of right, nor until they shall have been granted a license by the state to do so.   Section 1304, Ky. St. This regulation applies as well to innkeepers as to other people.   If the state may regulate the sale and to that end may require a license to be obtained by the vendor as a prerequisite to his engaging in the business, it is equally competent for the state to regulate the times during which the privilege secured by the license may be exercised, and the places where liquors may be sold, and the persons to whom they may not be sold.   It is probably true that the reason Sunday is excepted from the times when liquors may be sold in this state was in deference to the religious views of a vast number of people; but whether that was the reason, or not, or whether it was to enforce a day of rest and quiet as tending to enhance public health and peace, or whatever the reason, it was competent for the Legislature to prohibit the sale on that day in the exercise of the police power of the state.

For that matter it was equally competent to have prohibited the sale on Monday or Saturday, or election days, as is done (section 1575, Ky. St.), or to require the selling to cease at midnight of every day (McNulty v. Toof, 116 Ky. 202, 75 S. W. 258, 25 Ky. Law Rep. 430). Sales to minors are .forbidden (Section 1306, Kentucky Statutes), as are sales to inebriates (Sec. 1307). Could it be successfully urged that these provisions against selling to minors and in ebriates are not applicable to tavern keepers? In this state local option may be voted by any town, county, or precinct. Section 61, Const. If such territory votes "dry," and if by the term of the vote druggists are included, then no one can sell liquor in such territory by retail. Such is the unqualified prohibition of the statute. Section 2557a, Ky. St. In none of these statutes are innkeepers excepted. Wholesale dealers selling their own product at place of manufacture by wholesale and physicians are expressly excepted. If the Legislature had intended to except others, they would have been named.

It is idle to argue that as some people habitually drink wines, beer, or other liquors with their meals, instead of coffee or tea the innkeeper must provide these guests with what they demand. Unless the innkeeper is licensed to sell liquors, he cannot lawfully do it, no matter what the tastes or habits of his guests may be; and, if his license does not permit him to sell liquors on Sunday (and it does not), it is as unlawful for him to do so as it would be to sell them on Monday without any license. Appellant's contention is, in short, that innkeepers are, by reason of the customary requirements of their calling, excepted from the operation .of the Sunday statute (section 1303, supra), because their guests are themselves not prohibited from drinking liquors at their own tables on Sunday; but it does not follow. Granted that a man may drink what he pleases at his own table on Sunday, nevertheless sales to him of liquors on that day are prohibited. Whether he buys from the bar, or the merchant, or the druggist, or the tavern, the sale is forbidden. The drinking is not. When the tavern keeper sells his guest a mug of beer on Sunday, the act is as clearly within the prohibition, of the letter and terms of the statute as if the sale had been by the barkeeper.

Nor do we regard the act set out in the stipulation as to the construction of the Sunday closing statute for the past hundred years of any significance in this case. If one's ordinary business is a necessity (which a tavern keeper's is), he is not within such statute. If his business is not prohibited, the statute would not apply at all. For example, some sorts of traveling on Sunday are regarded as necessary. On that ground the operation of a railroad train was allowed as not contravening the Sunday closing statute. Commonwealth v. L. & N. R. R. Co., 80 Ky. 298, 3 R. 788, 44 Am. Rep. 475. But if the railroad company carried passengers upon whom there was no urgency for going on that day, it would not be liable under the statute. If innkeepers are, by virtue of their calling and the habits and wants of their customers, bound to furnish their guests food and drink as called for, and on that ground, and that the usage and customs of hospitality here and abroad in the past have included the furnishing of intoxicating drinks as part of the entertainment of hotel guests, exceptions by implication to the sweeping prohibition of our liquor statutes, then, on the same ground, it would follow that they are excepted from the statutes requiring license to liquor sellers, and from the statutes forbidding sales to minors (who may also be guests at inns) and that in local-option territory they would be excepted from the operation of the vote, and that dining-car companies, pullman-car companies, restaurants, cafes, lunch counters and all places where eating is provided, drinking also might be provided, regardless of license, Sunday closing, or any other regulation.

We find no warranty for such sweeping construction. The Legislature did not intend to except hotel keepers from the operation of the statutes aimed to stop the liquor traffic for one day in seven. At least no such intention is manifested.

The judgment is affirmed.

CASE 48.—ACTION BY JUSTUS CRUTCHER AGAINST THE LOUISVILLE & NASHVILLE RAILROAD FOR PERSONAL INJURIES.—November 10, 1909.

Louisville & Nashville R. R. Co. v. Crutcher

Appeal from Franklin Circuit Court.

R. L. STOUT, Circuit Judge.

Judgment for plaintiff, defendant appeals.—Reversed.

1. Master and Servant—Injuries—Action—Jury Questions—Gross Negligence.—In a switchman's action for injuries caused by being thrown from a switch engine cab, whether plaintiff was thrown from the engine by the gross negligence of the engineer in running at a dangerous rate of speed held for the jury.

2. Release—Validity—Mistake.—If an injured servant signed a release of a claim for injuries believing it to be a receipt for wages due him, and the question of a settlement was not mentioned at the time, the release was invalid as being obtained by fraud or mistake.

Louisville & Nashville R. R. Co. v. Crutcher.

3. Release—Jury Question—Conflicting Evidence.—Where the testimony was conflicting as to whether a release was signed under the belief that it was a receipt for wages, as claimed by one party thereto, the question was for the jury.

4. Release—Actions—Burden of Proof.—A written release of all claims for injuries, signed by plaintiff, made out a prima facie defense when introduced in a personal injury action, and the burden was on plaintiff to avoid the release by showing its invalidity.

5. Master and Servant—Instructions—Concrete Instructions—Sufficiency.—In a switchman's action for injuries by being thrown from a switch engine cab, where plaintiff claimed that the engine swayed violently when running at a high speed, and was being so run when he was thrown out, an instruction that if plaintiff was injured by gross negligence of defendant's engineer in operating a certain engine in its yards, by which negligence plaintiff was thrown from the engine and injured, the jury should find for him in such sum as would compensate him for pain and mental anguish suffered, if any, and which it is reasonably certain that he will suffer hereafter, and for impairment of his earning power, if any, was not sufficiently concrete as to plaintiff's contention, and the court should have instructed that, if the jury believed that by the engineer's gross negligence in operating the engine at a high and dangerous rate of speed plaintiff was thrown from the engine and injured, they should allow him such sum as would compensate him for pain of body and mind suffered, if any, or which he is reasonably certain to suffer hereafter, and for impairment of earning power, if any, resulting directly and proximately from the injury, not exceeding the amount demanded.

6. Release—Instructions—Sufficiency—Concrete Instructions.—In a switchman's action for injuries by being thrown from a switch engine cab, in which defendant offered a release, which plaintiff claimed was signed by him under the belief that it was a receipt for wages, an instruction that if the jury believed the paper relied on by defendant as a release was executed by the parties, each understanding that it was a release of all of plaintiff's claims against defendant on account of the injury, they should find for defendant, but, if they believed that it was executed by the parties under a mutual understanding that it was for the time lost by plaintiff for 12 days on account of his injuries, the jury should regard the paper as a release, was not sufficiently concrete, and the court should have instructed, in connection with an instruction authorizing a recovery if plaintiff was thrown

Louisville & Nashville R. R. Co. v. Crutcher.

from the engine by the gross negligence of defendant's engineer, that plaintiff could recover if the jury believed that the paper read in evidence as the release was executed upon the mutual understanding of both plaintiff and defendant that it was for time lost by the plaintiff for 12 days on account of his having been injured, and that plaintiff executed the release by mistake, or fraud of defendant.

7. Master and Servant—Injuries—Assumption of Risk—Concrete Instructions.—In a switchman's action for injuries by being thrown from a switch engine cab, where plaintiff claimed that the accident was caused by the swaying of the engine while it was running at a dangerous speed, an instruction that when plaintiff entered defendant's service he assumed all the risks ordinarily incident to his employment, and, if the injury received by him was in his ordinary employment and in the ordinary operation of the engine he was on, the jury should find for defendant, was not sufficiently concrete, and the court should have instructed that when plaintiff entered defendant's service he assumed all risks ordinarily incident to the business conducted with ordinary care, including the danger from operating the engine on which plaintiff was injured, unless the engineer was guilty of gross negligence in running it at a dangerous rate of speed.   •

8. Master and Servant—Injuries—Instructions—Contributory Negligence—Concrete Instructions.—In a switchman's action for injuries by being thrown from an engine cab, where defendant claimed that the engine was running at an ordinary rate of speed, and plaintiff was starting to get off when he fell and his foot turned on a lump of coal, but plaintiff claimed that he was thrown out by the swaying motion of the engine, which was running at a high speed, an instruction that, though defendant's agents were negligent, yet, if plaintiff was himself negligent, and such negligence, if any, contributed to the injury, which would not have occurred without it, the jury should find for defendant, was not sufficiently concrete upon the issues, and the court should have instructed that if plaintiff's fall was caused by his negligently undertaking to step from the engine when it was running at a dangerous speed, or by stepping upon a lump of coal and losing his balance, and not by the speed of the engine, or if he failed to exercise such care for his own safety as a person of ordinary prudence similarly situated would usually exercise, and but for which omission he would not have been injured, the jury should find for defendant.

McQUOWN & BECKHAM, CHARLES H. MOORMAN and BENJAMIN D. WARFIELD for appellant.

Louisville & Nashville R. R. Co. v. Crutcher.

POINTS DISCUSSED AND AUTHORITIES CITED.

The judgment appealed from must be reversed for any one of the following reasons:

1. If defendant was ever liable to plaintiff on account of the accident sued for, plaintiff made a free, voluntary and complete settlement of his claim therefor with defendant long before this suit was brought he has shown no sufficient reason for the disaffirmance of that settlement; he has never tendered or offered to defendant the amount it paid him in settlement; and he has not shown that defendant practiced any fraud upon him in making the settlement. Wells v. Royer Wheel Co., 114 S. W., 737, and cases there cited; The Addiston Pipe & Steele Co. v. Coppple, 94 Ky., 292; I. C. R. Co. v. Vaughn, 33 R., 906; Same v. Edmunds, 33 R. 933, distinguished.

2. The amount paid plaintiff in settlement of his claim was for such sum as shows conclusively that it could not have been for wages—for time lost while he was off-duty on account of the accident.

3. Plaintiff's sole excuse for executing the release, which is made part of the pleadings and the evidence and which is quoted in the brief, without reading it (if he did not read it) or having it read to him before he signed it is that he believed it was for wages. It was plaintiff's legal duty to know the contents of the paper before he executed it, and the law will not permit him to say that he did not do so. Hazard v. Griswold, 21 Fed. 178, 180; Standard Mfg. Co. v. Slot, 98 N. W., 923; Bonnot Co. v. Newman, 78 N. W., 817; Bannister v. McIntire, 84 N. W., 707; Dellinger v. Gillespie, 24 S. E., 538; Gulliher v. C. R. I. & P. R. Co., 13 N. W., 429; Wallace v. C. St. P. M. & O. R. Co., 25 N. W., 772; Dunham Lumber Co. v. Holt, et al., 26 Sou., 663; Georgia Home Ins. Co. v. Warten, 22 Sou., 288; Lanham v. L. & N. R. Co., 27 R., 773, 120 K., 351; Taylor v. Fleckinstein, 30 Fed., 99; Gibson v. Brown, 24 S. W., 574; Reid, Murdock & Co. v. Bradley, et al., 74 N. W., 896.

4. In three written papers signed by him after the accident, and before the suit was brought, and in statements other persons heard plaintiff make, he stated that the accident happened for a cause for which defendant would not be liable. The judgment in his favor cannot be supported upon his testimony on the witness stand that it happened from a cause different from that by which he had previously repeatedly stated, both in writing and orally, it happened.

5. Under the well settled principle of the law that a written contract is not to be varied from or contradicted by cotemporaneous parol testimony ; it was improper to permit plaintiff to testify   to   an   alleged   conversation   between   him   and

Louisville & Nashville R. R. Co. v. Crutcher.

Yard-master Wilder in connection with the settlement voucher that Wilder furnished plaintiff. Lanham v. L. & N. R. Co., 120 Ky. on p. 356; C. N. O. & T. P. R. Co. v. Zachary's Adm'r, 32 R. on p. 680.

6. Plaintiff claimed that the engine was dangerous by reason of certain characteristics described by him. He admitted that he knew all about this condition for a long time before the accident happened. There is no pretense that he made any objection to working with the engine; asked to have it repaired, or that another engine be substituted or that he had ever had any promise to repair it or be furnished with a better engine. Under these circumstances plaintiff took the risk, if any there was, of injury while working with that engine. L. & N. R. Co. v. Stanfill, 33 R. on p. 1044, and cases there cited; Reiser v. Southern Planing Mill & Lumber Co., 114 Ky., 1; Kirby v. Hillside Coal. Co., etc., 22 R., 519; Avery & Sons v. Lung, Id. 702.

7. Even if the engine was running faster than the defendant's rule permitted, the rule was not made for plaintiff's benefit, and the violation of the rule, if it was violated, was not negligence as to him and had no connection with his injury. Hummer's Extrx. v. L. & N. R. Co., 32 R., p. 1318; Thompson's Commentaries on the Law of Negligence, p. 5.

8. The court should have peremptorily instructed the jury to find for defendant, both on the ground that the plaintiff assumed the risk of whatever injury he received, and on the ground that defendant's liability, if any, to him was fairly, fully and freely compromised between plaintiff and defendant before this suit was brought and plaintiff never disaffirmed that settlement, or took any steps toward doing so.

9. The instructions which the court on its own motion gave to the jury were prejudicial to the defendant in numerous particulars, L. & N. R. Co. v. Veach's Adm'n, 112 S. W., 869, 872; L. & N. R. Co. v. King's Adm'r, 115 S. W., 196.

10. The court erred in refusing to instruct the jury as requested by defendant.

LINDSAY & EDELEN for appellee.

No point is made that the verdict was excessive, or that there was not very substantial testimony that plaintiff has acquired tuberculosis as the direct result of the injury. Aside from the testimony of Drs. Roemele and Kenney, two very high class physicians, that the plaintiff's condition was the direct result of the accident, we have the latest word of science in dealing with pathological conditions in confirmation. The accepted germ theory of disease is that the development of any zymotic disease is due to the concurrence of a germ and a favorable enviroment for its development. Any number of tubercular germs might be present upon a perfectly healthful, normal tissue and the disease would not manifest itself. Conversely the tissue favorable for the development of such a disease might be in a weakened condition and favorable to the development of the germ, but in the absence of the germ, of course no disease results. Let the tissue, however, be weakened or enfeebled by a blow or other external cause, and the presence of the germ inevitably produces the disease.

We most respectfully submit to Your Honors that this is the latest word of science upon the subject and so the parable of the seed, some of which fell upon stony ground, others upon thorny ground and still others upon suitably prepared soil, finds its confirmation in the modern theory of the development of zymotic diseases. The testimony of these eminent physicians abundantly demonstrated this as the result of modern science. The jury believed their testimony and the verdict was rendered in mercy rather than in strict justice.

OPINION OF THE COURT BY JUDGE HOBSON—Reversing.

Justus Crutcher was a switchman in the service of the Louisville & Nashville Railroad Company in its yard at Paris, Ky. The crew to which he belonged used an engine known as "No. 603." It was a road engine and had been converted into what is known as a "yard engine." When used as a road engine it had three driving wheels on each side, and a truck composed of four small wheels supporting the front of the engine. To change it from a road engine to a yard engine, the pilot was taken off, a step being put in its place, and the truck of four small wheels was removed. These small wheels served to steady the engine when running, and, to compensate for taking them out, the position of the boiler was changed to balance the machinery upon the three pairs of driving wheels so as to steady it for use in the yards.

In January, 1908, the crew were going with the engine up in the yard to move a car, Crutcher being in the cab of the engine. As to what happened the proof is conflicting. The proof for him is to the effect: That the attempt to steady the engine had been unsuccessful. That it rocked as it went to such an extent that it had acquired the name "Ocean Wave," and this was known to all of them. That the engineer, as they were going up after this car, being in a hurry to get out of the way of a train that was about due, was running about 15 or 20 miles an hour. This caused the engine to oscillate violently, and by reason of this oscillation Crutcher was thrown from the cab. He caught the handhold as he was thrown out, which caused him to swing around with great violence against the step, which struck him in the side, causing violent hemorrhages from the lungs, and by reason of his injuries his capacity to earn money was practically destroyed. The proof for the defendant is to the effect that the engine was running only at its ordinary rate of speed at 4 or 5 miles an hour, that Crutcher started to get down off the engine for the purpose of throwing the switch while the engine was in motion and, that as he stepped his foot turned on a lump of coal, and he lost his balance and fell for this reason.

After he had been laid up for 12 days with his injuries, and when they were not regarded as serious, as they afterwards appeared, the defendant paid him $28.80 and he executed to it a release of all claims on account of his injuries. Afterwards he brought this suit to recover damages, and the defendant pleaded the written release in bar of a recovery. It also traversed the allegations of the petition and pleaded contributory negligence. A reply was filed by him, and the issue was made up. The case was submitted to a jury, who found a verdict for him in the sum of $6,000, and the defendant appeals.

The court did not err in refusing to instruct the jury peremptorily to find for the defendant. If this engine wobbled as much as the proof for the plaintiff tends to show when run over six miles an hour, there was evidence of gross negligence on the part of the engineer in running it 15 or 20 miles an hour; and, if by reason of this dangerous speed Crutcher was thrown from the engine, the question of gross negligence should be submitted to the jury.

Crutcher was making $2.40 a day. He had been unable to work for twelve days, and he was paid $28.80. This he testified was paid him for his lost time, and that the question of a settlement for his injuries was not mentioned. He signed the paper in ignorance of its being a release, and believing it to be simply a receipt for his wages. If his evidence was true, the settlement was obtained by fraud or mistake, and this question was for the jury.

The court, at the conclusion of all the evidence, gave the jury these instructions:

"Instruction No. 1. The court instructs the jury that if they believe from the evidence that the plaintiff was injured on January 11, 1908, by the gross negligence of the defendant's engineer in the operation of engine No. 603, in the yards at Paris, by which negligence, he, the plaintiff, was thrown from the said engine, injuring him, then they will find for the plaintiff such sum as will compensate him for his pain and mental anguish, if any, which he has heretofore suffered, and which from the evidence it is reasonably certain that he will hereafter suffer, if any, for the impairment of his power to earn money, if any, not exceeding in all $10,000, and, unless they so believe, they will find for the defendant.

"Instruction No. 2. The court instructs the jury that if they believe from the evidence that the paper relied on by the defendant as a release was executed both by the plaintiff and the defendant, each understanding and agreeing that the said paper was a release for all claims which the plaintiff had or might have against the defendant on account of the injury received by the plaintiff, then the jury are instructed to find for the defendant; but, if they believe that the paper produced in evidence was signed and executed both by plaintiff and defendant with the mutual understanding that it was for the time lost by plaintiff for 12 days on account of his having received the injury complained of, then the jury shall not regard the paper as a release of all claims by the plaintiff against the defendant, but it shall be wholly disregarded by them.

"Instruction No. 3. The court instructs the jury that, when the plaintiff entered the services of the defendant, he assumed all the risks which are ordinarily incident to his employment, and if the jury believe that the injury received by the plaintiff was received in the ordinary employment of the plaintiff by the defendant, and in the ordinary operation of engine No. 603, then they ought to find for the defendant.

"Instruction No. 4. Even though the jury may believe that the defendant, by its agents and servants then in charge of the engine mentioned herein, was

careless and negligent, yet, if they further believe that
the plaintiff himself was careless and negligent, and
that such carelessness and negligence on his part, if
any, contributed to the injury received by him, but
for which contributory negligence on his part, if there
was any, the injury would not have been received, then
the jury ought to find for the defendant.''

The defendant, among others, asked this instruction: ''The court instructs the jury that if they shall
believe from the evidence that the plaintiff, Crutcher, while riding on defendant's engine leaped or
stepped from said engine while it was in motion, and
thereby received the injury complained of, the jury
should find for the defendant.''

The written release barred the plaintiff's action
unless the evidence offered by the plaintiff was sufficient to relieve him from it. It made out prima
facie a defense for the defendant. The instructions do not so present the matter. The defendant
was not required to offer any evidence except the
writing to make out its defense. The burden was on
the plaintiff to avoid the writing, and the instructions of the court should be so framed as to show
this. Another objection to the instructions is that
they do not present to the jury in a sufficiently concrete form the plaintiff's case or the defendant's defense. L. & N. R. R. Co. v. King (Ky.), 115 S.
W. 196.

In lieu of instructions No. 1 and No. 2, the court
should have told the jury that if they believed from
the evidence that, by the gross negligence of the engineer in the operation of the engine at a high and
dangerous rate of speed, the plaintiff was thrown
from the engine and injured, and if they further be-

lieve from the evidence that the paper read in evidence as a release was executed upon the mutual understanding of both the plaintiff and the defendant that it was for the time lost by the plaintiff for 12 days on account of his having been injured, and that the plaintiff executed the release by mistake, or by fraud of the defendant, then they should find for the plaintiff such sum as would compensate him for the pain of body and mind, if any, which he has heretofore suffered, or which it is reasonably certain he will thereafter suffer, if any, and of the impairment of his power to earn money, if any, resulting directly and proximately from his said injury, not exceeding in all $10,000, and unless they so believe they will find for the defendant.

In lieu of instruction No. 3, the court should have told the jury that when the plaintiff entered the service of the defendant he assumed all the risks which were ordinarily incident to the business conducted with ordinary care, including the danger from the operation of engine No. 603, unless the engineer was guilty of gross negligence in running at a high and dangerous rate of speed as set out in No. 1.

In lieu of instruction No. 4, the court should have told the jury that if they believe from the evidence that the plaintiff, Crutcher, while riding on the engine, negligently undertook to leap or step from it when it was running at a rapid and dangerous rate of speed, or if he stepped upon a lump of coal, and his foot slipped, and he thus lost his balance, and this, and not the speed of the engine, was the proximate cause of his fall, or if while riding on the engine he failed to exercise such care for his own safety as a person of ordinary prudence, situated as he was would usually exercise, and but for this would not have been injured, then, in any of these events, they should find for the defendant.

We see no other error in the record.

Judgment reversed, and cause remanded for a new trial.

CASE 49.—PROCEEDING BY THE COMMONWEALTH BY THE AUDITOR'S AGENT AGAINST MARGARET HELM'S TRUSTEE TO LIST OMITTED PROPERTY FOR TAXATION.—November 18, 1909.

Helm's Trustee v. Commonwealth

Appeal from Fayette Circuit Court.

WATTS PARKER, Circuit Judge.

From a judgment for the plaintiff in the circuit court reversing a judgment for the defendant in the county court, defendant appeals.—Reversed.

1. Domicile—Intent.—The question of domicile is usually one of intent; slight circumstances often being sufficient to determine the question.

2. Domicile—Necessity.—Every person has a legal domicile.

3. Domicile — Abandonment — Intention — Evidence.— Where a domicile is once established, intent to abandon it and adopt a new one must be satisfactorily shown.

4. Domicile—Evidence—Admissibility.—In determining the domicile of a person, her sex, status as married or single, and all surrounding circumstances which tended to influence or explain her acts by which her residence is sought to be established, such as the fact that it was unnecessary for her to own a home because she was single and without family ties, or to engage in business because she was wealthy, should be considered.

5. Domicile—Evidence—Sufficiency.—In a proceeding to require personalty to be listed for taxation in a certain county on

the ground that the owner was there domiciled, evidence held to show that she was a resident of another county.

GEORGE B. KINKAID and WALLACE & HARRIS for appellant.

D. C. HUNTER and GEORGE C. WEBB for appellee.
No briefs—record misplaced.

OPINION OF THE COURT BY JUDGE BARKER—Reversing.

This is a proceeding commenced in the county court of Fayette county to require the appellant, as trustee for Margaret Helm, to list the personal property of the cestui que trust for taxation as omitted property for the years 1904, 1905, 1906, 1907 and 1908. The merits of the question involved here turn upon whether or not Margaret Helm was domiciled in Fayette county, Ky., during the years mentioned, as is claimed by appellee, or whether her domicile was in Woodford county, as claimed by appellant. The question is one wholly of fact, and is not altogether free from doubt.

Margaret Helm's father and mother resided on a large farm in Woodford county, Ky., up to the time of the death of the father. After his death the mother, Mary L. Helm, and her daughter, Margaret, continued to reside in Woodford county, although they were absent therefrom a large part of the time. The farm was rented out, but the mother retained a room in the house which she kept furnished and occupied from time to time. After the death of her mother, Margaret Helm did not continue to keep a room in the house on the farm, but boarded in Lexington, Ky. She was unmarried, and able financially to live how and where she pleased. Her mother died in 1903, and since that time she has for the most part boarded in

Lexington. Whether or not that was her domicile is the question for adjudication.

The will of the mother, Mary L. Helm, was probated in Woodford county, and the Security Trust Company was appointed and qualified there as trustee under the will for the daughter, Margaret. It is conceded that each and every year since the appointment of appellant as trustee it has paid state and county taxes on the trust estate in Woodford county, Ky. The question of domicile is nearly, if not always, one of intent, and often very slight circumstances will serve to turn the judgment in favor of one or another of the different places claimed to be the domicile. It is a firmly settled rule of law that every person has a legal domicile somewhere; and it is .equally well settled that, where the domicile is once established, an intent to abandon it and adopt a new one must be satisfactorily shown. Now, in the case before us, it is conceded that, up to the time of the death of her mother in 1903, the domicile of the mother and daughter was in Woodford county. To establish the fact that the daughter, after the death of the mother, changed her domicile from Woodford to Fayette county, the commonwealth proved that for the larger part, if not all, of the time since the death of the mother, the daughter has lived in a boarding house in Lexington, and evidence is given of certain statements of the cestui que trust relative to a proposd change of residence to avoid taxation; but this was after this procedure was commenced and had reference to escape from city taxation.

On the other hand, we have the undisputed fact that the trustee has regularly listed the whole estate for taxation in Woodford county, and paid the taxes due thereon each year. We find, also, that Margaret Helm retained her membership in the Episcopal church at Versailles, and has never changed it to a church in Lexington; and it is shown that she told the officers of the trust company that she resided in Woodford county, she having been asked this question for the purpose of ascertaining where her estate should be taxed, and this long before any question of taxation in Fayette county arose. In reaching the proper conclusion as to the domicile of the cestui que trust, her sex and status and all her surroundings should be taken into consideration. Being single, with no family ties it was not necessary for her to own a house; being wealthy, she was not required to go into any business; and, being a female, she might feel a delicacy in keeping a room in the home of her tenant. On the whole, we think that the fact that the estate was listed for taxation during all of the years involved herein in Woodford county, Ky., ought to establish, in the absence of stronger evidence, that Margaret Helm resides in Woodford county.

In the case of City of Lebanon v. Biggers, 117 Ky. 430, S. W. 213, 25 Ky. Law Rep. 1528, the question we have here was discussed at considerable length. In the opinion it is said: "It is a maxim of the law that every person must have a domicile, and also that he can have but one, and that, when once established, it continues until he renounces it and takes up another in its stead. Nor can there be any question that a domicile is not lost by temporary absence. The question is one of fact, and it is often difficult to determine. The rule is laid down by Mr. Justice Cooley, in volume one of his work on Taxation (3d Ed.) p. 641, quoting Shaw, C. J., as follows: 'No exact definition can be given of domicile. It depends upon no one fact or combination of circumstances, but from the whole, taken together, it must be determined in each particular case. It is a maxim that every man must have a domicile somewhere, and also that he can have but one. Of course, it follows that his existing domicile continues until he acquires another, and, vice versa, by acquiring a new domicile he relinquishes his former one.'

· "From this point of view it is manifest that very slight circumstances must often decide the question. It depends upon the preponderance of evidence in favor of two or more places; and it may often occur that the evidence of fact tending to establish the domicile in one place would be entirely conclusive were it not for the existence of facts and circumstances of still more conclusive and decisive character, which fixes it beyond question in another. So, on the contrary very slight circumstances may fix one's domicile, if not controlled by more conclusive facts fixing it in another place." So, in this case, taking the evidence for the Commonwealth and looking from that point of view, it would appear that Margaret Helm was domiciled in Lexington. Taking that for the appellant, it seems to us that her domicile was in Woodford county. Certain it is that she so believed and intended, and her trustee acted upon this view in giving in the estate for taxation.

For these reasons, the judgment is reversed, with directions to the circuit court to affirm the judgment of the county court dismissing the proceeding of the auditor's agent.

CASE 50.—ACTION BY FAIRBANKS, MORSE & CO. AGAINST
S. W. HELTSLEY & CO.—November 17, 1909.

Fairbanks, Morse & Co. v. Heltsley

Appeal from Todd Circuit Court.

W. P. SANDIDGE, Circuit Judge.

From a demurrer by defendants, plaintiff appeals.
—Affirmed.

1. Sales—Contract—Breach—Action for Price.—Where the buyer
    of an engine from a manufacturer notified the seller before
    the engine had been seen, tendered, or delivered that he
    would not accept it, and for this reason there was no delivery
    and the title at all times remained in the seller, he could not
    maintain an action for the price.

2. Judgment—Res Judicata—Dismissal—Insufficiency of Plead-
    ing.—Dismissal of a seller's action for the price because the
    petition was demurrable for want of facts was no bar to
    another action for breach of contract.

TRIMBLE & MALLORY, GIFFORD & STIENFELD and CHAS.
H. GOWEN for appellant.

C. A. DENNY for appellees.
No briefs—record out of office.

OPINION OF THE COURT BY JUDGE HOBSON—Affirming.

Fairbanks, Morse & Co. brought this suit against
S. W. Heltsley & Co. in the Todd circuit court. The
defendants demurred to the petition; their demurrer
was sustained. The plaintiff filed an amended petition. The defendants demurred to the petition as
amended. The demurrer was sustained, and, the

plaintiff failing to plead further, the petition was dismissed. The plaintiff appeals.

The facts stated in the petition are briefly these: The plaintiff is a corporation created by the laws of Illinois. On July 30, 1908, it entered into a written contract with the defandants by which it agreed to deliver on board the cars at Elkton, Ky., one 15 horse power gasoline engine, for which the defendants agreed to pay $660. The plaintiff immediately proceeded to build and equip an engine in compliance with the terms of the contract, and crated and prepared it for shipment from its factory to Elkton; but before it was shipped the defendants notified the plaintiff that they would not receive the engine if shipped, or pay for it, and for this reason it did not ship the engine, although ready and willing to do so. No part of the contract price was paid, and on these facts the plaintiff asked judgment for the contract price, $660 and costs.

In Cook v. Brandeis, 3 Metc. 555, the plaintiff sold certain wheat to the defendants to be thereafter delivered, but the defendants, when the time came for delivery, refused to receive it. The plaintiff thereupon sold the wheat for less than the contract price, and brought a suit to recover damages. In defining his rights the court said: "In such case—that is, where the vendee refuses to receive the thing bargained for—the vendor may consider it as his own, as if there had been no delivery, and recover the difference between the value at the time and place of delivery and the contract price; or he may sell it with due precaution and diligence to satisfy his lien for the price, and then he may sue and recover only the unpaid balance of the contract price, or he may consider

it as the property of the vendee subject to his call or
order, and then he recovers the full price which the
vendee was to pay. In either case the election rests
with the vendor; the vendee having violated his contract." In the subsequent case of Bell v. Offutt, 10
Bush 632, Bell had sold certain hogs to Offutt to be
thereafter delivered, and Offutt declined to take the
hogs when tendered. Bell thereupon sold the hogs
for less than the contract price, and brought suit for
damages. The court there laid down the same rule
as in Cook v. Brandeis.

But it will be observed that in both of these cases
the seller had sold the property in the open market
for the best price attainable, and the court did not
have before it the question what he must do to recover the contract price in order that the thing sold
might be regarded as the property of the purchaser.
This question was presented in Webber v. Minor, 6
Bush, 463, 99 Am. Dec. 688. In that case, the plaintiff had sold a lot of wood, which defendant refused
to receive, and brought an action for the price while
he still had the wood. The court, holding that he
could not recover the price, said: "According to the
case of Cook v. Brandeis and Crawford, 3 Metc. 555,
relied on for the appellee, and the authorities therein
cited, the appellee might on the refusal of the appellant to receive and pay for the wood, if he was bound
to do so by the contract, have either kept the wood and
recovered by proper action the difference between
its value at the time and place of delivery and the
contract price, or he might have sold it with due precaution and diligence, and then have sued for and
recovered the difference between the price received
and the contract price, or he might upon making an

actual or constructive delivery of the wood have recovered the full contract price, the measure of relief sought in this action.

But, although the evidence conduces to sustain the plaintiff's averments of the contract, and his readiness and offer to deliver the one hundred and fifty-four cords of wood, and the refusal of the defendant to receive it, these facts do not in our opinion constitute, actually or constructively, a complete performance of the contract; for, conceding that a substantial compliance with his undertaking did not require that he should place the wood upon the brickyard against the will of the defendant, he should have set it apart for the defendant, and relinquished his own control of it at or as near to the place of delivery as was reasonably practicable. This would have been a constructive delivery of the wood, not merely an offer or tendency of delivery. Duckham v. Smith, 5 T. B. Mon. 372; 2 Story on Contracts, Sec. 800. And, as there would have remained nothing more for the plaintiff to do to vest the property in the defendant and render the sale absolute, he might then have recovered the contract price of the wood. But he was not entitled to a recovery to that extent upon the allegation and proof only of a tender or offer of delivery, which, if true, neither divested him of the legal title nor the possession of the wood.''

This case followed the rule which had been previously announced in Williams, etc., v. Jones, etc., 1 Bush, 621, and it has been followed in Wells v. Maley, 6 Ky. Law Rep. 77; Miller v. Burch (Ky.) 41 S. W. 307, 19 R. 629; Singer Mfg. Co. v. Cheney (Ky.) 51 S. W. 813, 21 R. 550; Hauser v. Tate, 105 Ky. 701, 49 S. W. 475, 20 Ky. Law Rep. 1716. A contrary rule was not laid down in Jones v. Strode, 41 S. W. 562, 19 Ky. Law Rep. 1117, or in Hollerback and May Contract Company v. Wilkins (Ky.) 112 S. W. 1126. In each of these cases the action was brought to recover damages for the breach of the contract. In Benjamin on Sales, Sec. 1117, the rule is thus stated: ''When the vendor has not transferred to the buyer the property in the goods which are the subject of the contract as has been explained in Book 11, as where the agreement is for the sale of goods not specific, or of specific goods which are not in a deliverable state, or which are to be weighed or measured before delivery, the breach by the buyer of his promise to accept and pay can only affect the vendor by way of damages. The goods are still his. He may resell or not at his pleasure. But his only action against the buyer is for damages for nonacceptance. He can in general only recover for the damages that he has sustained, not the full price of the goods.

The law with the reason for it was thus stated by Tindal, C. J., in delivering the opinion of the Exchequer Chamber in Barrow v. Arnaud: ''Where a contract to deliver goods at a certain price is broken, the proper measure of damages in general is the difference between the contract price and the market price of such goods at the time when the contract is broken, because the purchaser, having the money in his hands may go into the market and buy. So, if a contract to accept and pay for goods is broken, the same rule may be properly applied, for the seller may take his goods into the market and obtain the current price for them.' ''

Here there was a contract to make a gasoline engine, and deliver it on board the cars at Elkton, Ky.

Before the manufacturer had shipped the engine, and before it had been seen, tendered, or delivered to the purchaser, he notified the seller that he would not take it. The property in the engine had not passed. The engine remained at the manufacturer's factory. It was its property, and was subject to its control. The plaintiff had in no manner released its control of the engine. If the engine had been destroyed, it would have been at the plaintiff's loss, and any insurance upon it would have belonged to the plaintiff. That in such a state of case an action for the price cannot be maintained is sustained by the great weight of American authority. Mechem on Sales of Personal Property, Secs. 1091, 1092; Newmark on Sales, Sec. 391; 24 Am. & Eng. Ency. of Law, 1118; Note to Gardner v. Deeds, 7 Am. & Eng. Ann. Cas. 1175, 1176; Oklahoma Vinegar Company v. Carter, 116 Ga. 140, 42 S. E. 378, 59 L. R. A. 122, 94 Am. St. Rep. 112; McCormick v. Belfany, 78 Minn. 370, 81 N. W. 10, 79 Am. St. Rep. 393, and cases cited.

The plaintiff's petition states no facts to constitute a cause of action for damages for the breach of contract. It is simply an action for the price; no facts being stated upon which a judgment for damages could be rendered. The dismissal of this action will not bar another action for damages for the breach of the contract, as a judgment upon an insufficient petition is never a bar to another action.

Judgment affirmed.

CASE 51.—SUIT BY MARY F. MADDOX AND ANOTHER
    AGAINST MATTIE MADDOX AND OTHERS TO
    SET ASIDE A DEED.—November 18, 1909.

Maddox v. Maddox, &c.

Appeal from Ohio Circuit Court.

T. F. BIRKHEAD, Circuit Judge.

From the judgment plaintiff appeals.—Reversed.

Deeds — Failure of Consideration — Support. — Grantors con-
    veyed to their two sons their property, in consideration of
    support and payment of $200 to another brother, which
    payment was made. After supporting grantors for a time
    one of the sons died, and the other was unable to support
    them without the aid of the heirs of the other brother, who
    were also unable to furnish any support. Held, that, as the
    grantees could not comply with the covenants of the deed,
    the deed should be set aside, on repayment to the grantees of
    the money paid and expense of support.

J. P. SANDERFER and J. E. FOGLE for appellants.

GLENN & SIMMERMAN for appellees.

OPINION OF THE COURT BY JUDGE BARKER—Reversing.

The appellants, J. L. R. Maddox and Mary F. Maddox, his wife, are very old people, who live in Ōhio
county, Ky. On the 30th day of July, 1900, they conveyed by deed to their two sons, Moses R. Maddox
and J. L. R. Maddox, Jr., a tract of land in Ohio
county, containing 243 acres, more or less, and which
is set out by metes and bounds in the petition. The
consideration for the conveyance was that the two

sons agreed and undertook, first, to pay W. P. Maddox, a brother, $200 for his interest in the land conveyed: and, second, that the grantees would support their father and mother during their declining years and decently bury them after their death.

It appears that the $200 was paid to the brother, and the sons undertook to, and did for a while, support their parents. One of the sons, J. L. R. Maddox, Jr., afterwards became insane and was sent to the asylum, where he has since died, leaving a wife and two children, who are the appellees. After the death of J. L. R. Maddox, Jr., this suit was instituted by the grantors to have the deed set aside and annulled for a failure of consideration—it being alleged that J. L. R. Maddox, Jr., was dead; that the infant defendants and their mother, Mattie F. Maddox, were unable to support the grantors or carry out the covenant made by the husband and father; that they were without means of any sort, and had abandoned the place, and done nothing towards the support or maintenance of the grantors for two years. The other son, Moses R. Maddox, in his pleading expressed a willingness to carry out the covenant in the deed so far as he is able, but alleges that he is unable to support his parents by himself without the aid of the other covenantor. He states that he is willing to pay his brother's children $450, and then take the whole land and carry out the covenant, and alleges that he has already paid to his brother, W. P. Maddox, the $200 stipulated in the deed from his father and mother. To the petition a general demurrer was interposed, and sustained by the court; and, the plaintiffs having declined to plead further, the petition was dismissed.

We are of the opinion that the court erred in sustaining the demurrer to the petition. So far as the defendants were concerned, it appears that they are not able to carry out the covenant of their deceased father and husband. They cannot, therefore, have the land without paying the consideration, and the old people are clearly entitled to their land back, unless the grantees are able and willing to comply with the convenant to support and maintain them throughout their lives and bury them at their death. But, inasmuch as J. L. R. Maddox, Jr., has paid a part of the consideration for the conveyance, it would be inequitable that his wife and children should lose the whole of that for which he had in part paid. The court should have overruled the demurrer, and required the defendants to plead, and, if it appeared that they were unwilling or unable to perform the covenant of J. L. R. Maddox, then the case should have been referred to a commissioner for the purpose of ascertaining what proportion of the whole consideration the father had paid, either in money or service, to be credited of course by the value of the use of the land, if any, during the time the service was being rendered, and the balance so ascertained should be refunded to the widow and children of the dead grantee.

For these reasons the judgment is reversed, for further procedure in accordance with this opinion.

CASE 52.—ACTION BY JOHN TROSPER AGAINST THE EAST
JELLICO COAL COMPANY.—November 18, 1909.

Trosper v. East Jellico Coal Co.

Appeal from Knox Circuit Court.

E. E. Hogg, Circuit Judge.

From a directed verdict for defendant, plaintiff appeals.—Affirmed.

1   Master and Servant—Safe Place to Work.—A servant cannot
    recover for injuries if he knows of a danger and does not
    exercise ordinary care for his own safety; and, where a
    servant engaged in hauling rails on a car in a mine knew that
    certain cross-beams were not high enough to permit him to
    pass without stooping while riding on the car, and neglected
    to do so when passing under one of them, which he could
    have seen if he had looked, he could not recover for injuries
    resulting from such negligence.

2. Master and Servant—Permanent Structures Near Track—
    Application of Rule.—The rule applicable to permanent struc-
    tures by the side of railroad tracks or overhead bridges
    does not apply to employes in a mine who either walked or
    rode slowly behind a mule.

EDWARD W. HINES, B. B. GOLDEN and McCHORD, HINES
& NORMAN for appellant.

PITZER D. BLACK, JAS. D. BLACK and WM. R. BLACK for
appellee.

Opinion of the Court by Wm. Rogers Clay, Commissioner—Affirming.

Appellant, John Trosper, instituted this action
against appellee, East Jellico Coal Company, to recover damages for personal injuries. Upon the conclusion of the evidence the court gave a peremptory
instruction to find for appellee. To review the propriety of this ruling this appeal is prosecuted.

At the time appellant was injured he was employed in removing some steel rails and air pipe from ap-

pellee's mine and was struck by an overhead timber.
He had been in appellee's employment for seven or
eight years, but during the greater part of that time
he worked outside of the mine. While so employed
he ran the locomotive engine for a while, and also
a small dinky engine. He also ran the drum which
pulls the coal up and down the hill, and the compressor which forces the air into the mine. A few days
prior to the accident Trosper and an employe by the
name of Frank Burch exchanged jobs. Burch was
employed on the inside of the mine in some capacity
necessitating the use of a car and mule in hauling water, slate and other things. The exchange was made
at the request of Trosper and Birch and was approved by the mine foreman. The accident occurred
in what is known as the "7th left entry" of the mine.
The coal had been practically exhausted when the
work of "robbing the mine" (i. e., pulling the stumps,
removing the rails, etc.) had commenced at the head
of the entry. In order to save the piping and steel
rails in said entry, it became the duty of appellant,
his brother, Milton Trosper, and another employe of
the name of James Curtis, to remove the piping and
rails to the outside of the mine.

It was in the performance of this duty that appellant was injured. The place at which he was injured was about midway between the two ends of the
entry, which was several hundred feet in length.
There were arranged in the mine certain cross-
beams which were located $1\frac{1}{2}$ to 2 feet from the top
of the mine. These cross-beams were set in hatches
cut into the slate and supported the pipes which conveyed air from the compressor on the outside. At
first appellant and his fellow workmen dragged the

rails out on the ground. He then claims he was instructed by the mine foreman to use a car for that purpose. The steel rails were placed on the back of the car and fastened there with a chain; four rails being hauled at a time. It became necessary, according to the evidence for appellant, for him and his two fellow workmen to stand on the bumper in front of the car in order to hold it on the track. The bumper was about 10 inches above the rails of the track. While standing on the bumper, appellant claims that he turned his head to see whether or not the rails were going to catch in the ties behind the curve, and, as he did so, Curtiss hallooed for him to look out. Appellant started to throw his head under the timber, but the timber struck his head and pressed him over the car, thus causing the injury complained of.

According to the evidence for appellant, the cross-beams were located about five feet and a half or a little over above the track. According to the testimony for appellee, the cross-beams were more than six feet distant from the track. Appellant is six feet three inches tall. While he had worked on the outside of the mine his evidence shows that he has frequently been in the mine. The evidence shows that Curtis and appellant's brother always stooped when walking under the cross-beams. On the evening of the accident appellant and his companions had made at least two trips into the seventh left entry, and had passed the cross-beams not less than four times. The mine was sufficiently lighted to enable appellant to see a distance of from 30 to 35 feet. Appellant was engaged as driver, and it was his duty to look after the mule. He was in charge of the work that was then being done. In answer to the question, "You knew as a matter of fact that there were cross-beams along different places in the seventh entry?" Appellant answered, "Yes." The further question was asked: "Then, if you had looked up there, you could have seen that cross-beam with which you came in contact? A. Yes." It is manifest from this evidence that appellant knew the cross-beams were there. They were right before his eyes and could be readily seen. All he had to do was to bend his head and avoid coming in contact with them.

While it is the duty of the master to furnish the servant a reasonably safe place in which to work, yet the servant cannot recover if he knows of a danger, and does not exercise ordinary care for his own safety. Knowing of the location of the cross-beams, appellant could have escaped injury by the exercise of the slightest degree of ordinary care.

Appellant insists, however, that the rule applicable to permanent structures by the side of railroad tracks or overhead bridges should be applied in this case. There is, however, a wide distinction between the two cases. A train moves along at a high rate of speed. A trainman while engaged in the performance of his duty on the top or side of a car may be caught unawares. While his attention is fixed upon the performance of his duties, he may be suddenly carried under a bridge and thrown from the train. Here the employes either walked or rode slowly behind a mule. The cross-beams were a part of the general plan of the mine.

Entries in mines are necessarily low, as there must be economy of space. This is not the case with reference to overhead or side structures along a railroad. There is plenty of room for them. There was no danger of being caught unawares by being carried rapidly beneath one of the cross-beams. Being there as a permanent part of the mine, it was necessary for appellant in the exercise of ordinary care to recognize their presence and avoid coming in contact with them. If it was necessary to stoop while walking in order to avoid the timber, as appellant's companions testified, it was all the more necessary to stoop when standing on the bumper, which was 10 inches above the track. As the proof shows the mine was well lighted, the cross-beams were right before their eyes. He could not close his eyes to their presence, and then recover for an injury which was entirely due to his failure to observe them.

The fact that the pipe had been removed from the cross-beams at the time of the accident has no bearing upon the case. Appellant knew this fact, because he was engaged at that very time in taking the air pipes out of the mine; and he knew from whence the air pipes had come. Having stated that he knew the cross-beams were there, it is immaterial that the air pipes were not resting on the cross-beams. Even though the place where appellant was working may not have been reasonably safe for a person who did not know of the presence of the cross-beams, it cannot be said that the place was not reasonably safe for one who actually knew the cross-beams were there. We therefore conclude that the trial court properly instructed the jury to find for appellee.

Judgment affirmed.

CASE 53.—ELECTION CONTEST BY JOHN T. MAY AND
OTHERS AGAINST J. B. FERGUSON AND OTHERS.
—November 18, 1909.

May, &c. v. Ferguson, &c.

Appeal from Muhlenberg Circuit Court.

W. P. SANDIDGE, Circuit Judge.

From the judgment, contestants appeal.—Reversed.

1. Intoxicating Liquors—Local Option Elections—Statutes.—Under the Cammack act (Act March 14, 1906 (Acts 1906, p. 86, c. 21)), providing for local option elections for entire counties, except that cities of the first, second, third, or fourth class may hold an election on the same day, the county is absolute unit except in counties in which a city of the first, second, third, or fourth class is situated, and in such counties all of the territory outside of the city limits is an absolute unit, and the city is a separate unit, and, where a vote is offered for an entire county in which there is situated a city of the first, second, third, or fourth class, unless a separate vote is asked for and had within the limits of the city, it is bound by the result of the election in the entire county, and it is only where the citizens of the city seek and are granted a separate vote on the same day that its right to be treated as a separate unit is recognized.

2. Intoxicating Liquors—Local Option Elections—Statutes.—Where prohibitory laws are not in force in a county, any magisterial district, voting precinct, or town of any class may vote to establish prohibition within the limits of such district, precinct, or town, but, where prohibition has been established in the entire county pursuant to the Cammack act (Act March 14, 1906 (Acts 1906, p. 86, c. 21)), a unit has been established, and the vote cannot again be taken in any subdivision of the county other than in a city of the first, second, third, or fourth class situated in the county, unless it is taken in the entire county, and, so long as a city of one of the designated classes in a county preserves its identity by taking a vote on the same day that the vote is taken in the

entire county, its status is not changed by the will of the majority of the voting population of the county or of a magisterial district therein.

WILLIS & MEREDITH, BETCHER & SPARKS and J. K. FREEMAN for appellants.

POINTS AND AUTHORITIES.

1. The petition asking for an election in a magisterial district No. 1 was insufficient and fatally defective.   Kentucky Statutes, Section 2554; Nall v. Tinsley, 54 S. W., 187; Davis v. Henderson, 104 S. W. 1009; 8th Kentucky Law Rep. (abstract), 463; Napier v. Cornett, 68 S. W., 1076. '

2. The status of the territory to be affected was such that the magisterial district could not compel Central City to vote upon the local option question.

3. The voters residing in the city of Central City were not permitted to vote in the election for the magisterial district, and therefore the election in said district is and was void.

4. No election officers were appointed or elected to hold the elections in Central City and magisterial district No. 1, and therefore the elections were void.   Kentucky Statutes, Section 2555; Kentucky Statutes, Section 1596a, subsec. 3; Erwin v. Benton, 87 S. W., 291.

WALTER WILKINS and TOM B. McGREGOR, Assistant Attorney General, for appellees.

POINTS AND AUTHORITIES.

1. No notice of contest, such as the statutes contemplates has been given by appellants in this case.   Sub-section No. 2 of Sec. 2566 Ky. Stat.; Vol. 23 page 468 Am. & Eng. Encyc. of law, First Ed.; Russell v. Muldraugh's Hill & etc., 13 Bush 307; Ky. River Navigation Co. v. Commonwealth, 13 Bush, 436.

2. Petition asking for election in the magisterial district sufficient.   Sec. 2554 Ky. Stat.

3. The magisterial district was entitled to a vote.   Eggen v. Offutt, 128 Ky. 314; Trustees & etc., v. Scott, 125 Ky. 545; Sec. 2563. Ky. Stat.

4. City election not invalid because voters residing in Central City did not vote in magisterial district election.

5. Elections not invalid because same were held by regular election officers.   Sec. 2555 Ky. Stat.; Cyc. Vol. 15, page 362; Vol. 23, page 458, Am. & Eng. Encyc. of Law, First Ed.; Varney v. Justice, 86 Ky., 596; Fidelity Vault & Trust Co. v. City of Mor-

ganfield, 96 Ky., 563; Anderson v. Winfree, 85 Ky. 597; Lunsford v. Culton (unreported) 23 S. W., 946.

6. The officers who held elections were de facto officers and their acts in holding elections are valid. Justices of Jef. Co. v. Clark, Mon. 82; Wilson v. King, 3 Littell, 459; Rodman v. Harcourt & Carrico, 4 B. Mon., 224.

OPINION OF THE COURT BY JUDGE LASSING—Reversing.

In August, 1903, a local option election was held under the law then in force for the entire county of Muhlenberg. At that election a separate vote was had within Central City. The county voted dry and the city wet. No election has been held in the entire county since that time. October 6, 1906, another election was held in Central City, and the city again voted wet. In July, 1908, petitions were filed with he county judge, signed by the requisite number of voters residing in magisterial district No. 1, which is composed of six voting precincts, including Central City, asking for local option election in said magisterial district. Petitions were thereafter filed, signed by the requisite number of citizens of Central City, asking for a separate vote at the same time.

The election was on August 31st ordered to be held on December 7th, and it was so held; the officers who officiated at the regular November election, 1907, acting as the officers of this election, except in cases where they had removed from the precinct or otherwise disqualified themselves. In this election on December 7th the district went dry by something like 400 and the city by 23. The residents of the city were with few exceptions denied the right to participate in the election for the district; separate ballots being furnished to the voters for the district election from those for the city election. The wets contested the validity of the election before the county board, and, its decision being adverse to their contention, they prosecuted an appeal to the circuit court, where they were again unsuccessful, and the case is brought before us for review.

Many reasons are assigned why the election should be set aside, the principal of which is that there was no authority of law to warrant the county judge in ordering a local option election in magisterial district No 1, and from the conclusion which we have reached this is the only question which we will consider.   Under the Cammack act, which became a law March 14, 1906 (Acts 1906, p. 86, c. 21), the county is the absolute unit in all counties save those in which there is situated a city of the first, second, third, or fourth class, and in such counties all of the territory outside of such city limits is an absolute unit, and the city is made a separate unit.   This was a complete reversal of the order of things that had theretofore existed, for under the law in force prior to the adoption of this act the precincts and incorporated town of whatever class were recognized as sparate units, and might take a separate vote upon the question as to whether or not local option should be enforced within a given boundary or territory.

The old law was not satisfactory to the temperance or local option adherents, and, in order that the citizens in one part of a county might have a voice in determining whether or not prohibition should be enforced in another part of the county, the law was amended as above indicated so as to make the county the unit, and the only exception which the act recognizes is that cities of the first, second, third, and fourth class are made separate units, but in order for them to avail themselves of the right to be recognized as separate units, it is necessary that they should vote upon the same day upon which the vote is taken in the entire county when the question is submitted as to whether or not prohibition shall prevail in the county. So that, where a vote is ordered upon this question for the entire county in which there is situated a city of the first, second, third, or fourth class, unless a separate vote is asked for and had within the territorial limits of such city, it is bound by the result of the election in the entire county, and it is only where its citizens seek and are granted a separate vote on the same day that its right to be treated as a separate unit is recognized. Yates, County Judge, v. Nunnelly, 125 Ky. 644, 102 S. W. 292, 30 Ky. Law Rep. 984.

Central City is a city of the fourth class. It had on the 6th day of October, 1906, voted wet. The entire county outside of said city was at that time dry. No vote had been taken in the entire county since 1903, at which time it voted dry. It is most earnestly insisted for appellant that, inasmuch as the law expressly provides that no election can be held upon this question oftener than once in three years, the county judge had no right to order an election upon this question at all unless he has ordered it for the entire county; that there is no authority in law whatever for ordering a vote in a subdivision of the county other than a city of the first, second, third, or fourth class where such county has theretofore voted dry. The whole object of temperance legislation has been to bring about prohibition and create dry territory, and courts in dealing with this class of legislation have borne in mind this primary object of the Legislature, and have construed such acts as far as possible so as to carry out this legislative intent. Hence it

has been held that where territory is wet where
prohibition has not theretofore been enforced, any
subdivision of a county may vote upon the question
of establishing prohibition therein, but no subdivision
of a county, other than cities of the first, second, third
or fourth class may take a vote upon the question at
all when prohibition is already enforced within such
territorial limit. .

In other words, where no prohibitory laws are in
force in the county, any magisterial district, voting
precinct, or town of any class may vote to establish
prohibition within the limits of such magisterial district, voting district, voting precinct, or town; but,
where prohibition has been established in the entire
county, a different rule obtains. A unit has been
established, and the vote can never again be taken in
any subdivision of that county other than in some one
of the cities belonging to the excepted class, unless
it is taken in the entire county. So that, where a
precinct or magisterial district has once been made
dry by by a vote of the county, it must forever remain
dry, unless the bond is lifted by the people of the entire county. Egen, etc., v. Offutt, etc., 128 Ky. 314,
108 S. W. 333, 32 Ky. Law Rep. 1350. It is true, in
the case to which we have just referred this identical question was not before the court, but just the
converse of the conditions with which we are dealing
were under consideration.

There the county was wet, and the precinct had tak-
en a vote upon the question as to whether or not prohibition should be enforced within its limits and had
voted dry, and the court held that it might do so, but
in the same opinion distinctly stated that, if the county in which this precinct was situated had thereto-

fore voted dry, the election would have been invalid, for prohibition having been established in the county, the unit, the will of the people therein could not be overthrown by the voters of any part of that unit.

Applying the rule announced in that case to the case at bar, we find that there are in Muhlenberg county two units of equal dignity, one including all of the county outside of the limits of Central City, the other including the territory within the limits of Central City, and, so long as the city preserves its identity by taking a vote upon the same day that the vote is taken in the entire county, its status cannot be changed by the will of the majority of the voting population of Muhlenberg county, much less of a magisterial district therein, and, the precinct or magisterial district in dry territory no longer being recognized as a unit, there was no authority under which the county judge could legally order the election in magisterial district No. 1, and, as a vote had been taken in Central City within less than three years from December 7, 1908, the county judge was without authority to order an election in said city on said date, and for these reasons both of said elections were illegal and absolutely void. This being true, it is unnecessary to consider the other questions raised upon this appeal.

The judgment is reversed, with directions to the lower court to enter a judgment in conformity with this opinion, declaring each of said elections null and void.

Shallcross v. Shallcross

Appeal from Jefferson Circuit Court (Chancery Branch, Second Division).

SAMUEL B. KIRBY, Judge.

From an order modifying a divorce decree as to the custody of the children defendant appeals.—Affirmed.

1. Divorce—Custody   of   Children—Judgment—Modification—
Statutes.—Ky. St. 1909, Sec. 2123, provides that the court
in divorce proceedings, may make an order for the care,
custody, and maintainance of minor children, and at any time
afterward, on the petition of either parent, may revise the
same, having, in all cases, the welfare of the chidren principally in view. Held, that such section did not deprive the
court, after granting a divorce decree, from modifying the
same after the term, on its own motion, in so far as it granted the father the right to visit a child, the custody of which
was granted to the wife, nor to limit such action to a case
instituted for that purpose by petition of either parent.

2. Divorce—Custody of Children.—Where a child of divorced parents has reached years of discretion, its wishes as to its custody will be considered, but are not controlling.

3. Divorce—Custody of Children—Rights of Parents.—On the
granting of a divorce, the custody of very young children
will generally be awarded to the mother.

4. Divorce—Custody of Children—Modification of Decree.—
While the circuit court should not modify a divorce decree in
so far as it affected the custody of children, without notice
to the parents, a divorced husband, having applied for a rule
on his divorced wife to show cause why she did not comply
with the decree in so far as it granted the husband a right
to have visits from his child, could not object to a modifica-

Shallcross v. Shallcross.

tion of the decree denying him the right to further visits because he was not served with a written notice of an application to modify the decree.

5. Divorce—Custody of Children—Visitation.——Where a father, by reason of inebriety and profligacy, was not a proper person to associate with his infant son, the court properly modified a prior divorce decree granting the father the right to visit his son and have him with him under certain circumstances, by withdrawing such right of visitation; benefit to the child being the chief concern.

GIBSON, MARSHALL & GIBSON for appellant.

THE LAW OF THE CASE.
ACCESS TO CHILD BY PARENT DEPRIVED OF CUSTODY.

1. As to the right of a husband who drinks to excess, becoming quarrelsome and abusive at times, to see his children: Hoskins v. Hoskins, 28 Ky. Law Rep., 435.

2. As to the right of a mother addicted to the use of opium and who is unfit to have the custody of the child: Finley v. Finley, 8 Ky. Law. Rep. 605.

3. As to right of parent deprived of custody to see child, although divorce was granted for his habitual drunkenness: Bates v. Bates, 166 Ill., 448.

4. Access should be granted to the guilty party: Oliver v. Oliver, 151 Mass., 349; McGown v. McGown, 22 Misc. Repts. (N. Y. Supreme Ct. Special T. 307.) Bailey v. Bailey, 17 Ore, 114.

R. A. McDOWELL and CHAS. H. SHIELD attorneys for appellee.

AUTHORITIES CITED.

1. Court of Appeals will not review question of contempt or no contempt. Brown v. Brown, 96 Ky. 505; Johnston v. Commonwealth, 1 Bibb., 598; Watson v. Thomas, Litt. Selected Cases (16 Ky.) 248; Bickley v. Commonwealth, 2 J. J. Mar (25 Ky.) 572; Turner v. Commonwealth, 2 Metc. (59 Ky.) 619; Urton v. Downey, 3 Ky. Law Rep. (abstract) 592.

2. Paramount duty of the Court is to look to the interest and welfare of the infant children regardless of wishes of either or both parents. Adams v. Adams, 62 Ky. 169; Masterson v. Masterson, 24 Ky. Law Rep., 1352; Fletcher v. Fletcher, 21 Ky. Law Rep., 1304; Hoskins v. Hoskins, 28 Ky. Law Rep. 435; McBride v. McBride, 1 Bush 15; Irwin v. Irwin, 105 Ky. 641; Crabtree v. Crabtree, 27 Ky. Law Rep., 435; 2 Bishop on Marriage & Divorce, Sec. 1161-2.

3. Power of the Court to control the custody and control of children. Bristow v. Bristow, 21 Ky. Law Rep., 585; Conrad v. Conrad, 23 Ky. Law Rep., 1066.

OPINION OF THE COURT BY JUDGE SETTLE—Affirming.

On April 29, 1907, the appellee, Sarah Shelby Shallcross, was, by a judgment of the Jefferson circuit court, chancery branch, second division, divorced from her husband, the appellant, Harry M. Shallcross, and given the custody of their son and only child, Vernon Lewis Shallcross, an infant of tender years.

The judgment in question is as follows: "This action having been heard and submitted upon the plaintiff's petition and defendant's answer herein and upon the proof, and the court being advised, it is adjudged that the plaintiff, Sarah Shelby Shallcross, be and she is hereby divorced from the bonds of matrimony with Harry Mason Shallcross, and it is further adjudged that the said plaintiff is given the custody and control of her son, Vernon Lewis Shallcross, and it is further adjudged that the defendant, Harry Mason Shallcross, shall have the privilege of seeing his child at such reasonable times as will not interfere with the education of the child and that he shall have the privilege of having the child with him at least two days during each month during school season, and shall have the privilege of having the child with him during vacation for periods ranging from one to two weeks at a time such periods of visit to his father to be, however, at such times as shall be mutually agreed on between the plaintiff and the said defendant, and will not in any wise interfere with the health or welfare of the said child. It is further adjudged that the final custody of said child, in case of the death of Sarah Shelby Shallcross during the minority of said child, shall not now be determined, but left open, and this action is reserved for such proceedings as may then be had. It is further adjudged that the defendant shall be charged with the reasonable and proper clothing and education of such child, and that the question of alimony to his wife be reserved for future determination, and this action is reserved for said purpose. It is further considered and adjudged by the court that each party shall restore to the other such property not disposed of at the commencement of this action as either may have obtained, directly, or indirectly from or through the other, during marriage in consideration or by reason thereof.''

It does not appear from the foregoing judgment, or any subsequent order found in the record before us, that the case was ever stricken from the court's docket. At any rate on June 30, 1909, the same court on motion of the appellant, Harry M. Shallcross, based on his affidavit then filed, granted and issued a rule against appellee, Sarah Shelby Shallcross, returnable July 5, 1909, requiring her to show cause, if she had any, why she should not comply with the judgment of April 29, 1907, by permitting him to see and be with their infant son as provided therein. In the affidavit for the rule appellant stated that the appellee had not, since November 26, 1908, permitted him to see his son, Vernon Lewis Shallcross, and had repeatedly refused him the right to do so, or to have the child with him at any time, and had announced that she did not intend, in the future to permit appellant to see or have him in custody.

Appellee, on the day the rule was returnable, filed a response thereto, in which it was admitted that she had refused appellant the privilege of seeing or hav-ing their child, and had announced her purpose to persist in such refusal as charged in appellant's af-fidavit for the rule, but stated, in substance, that she was constrained to so act because of the drunken and debauched habits and life of appellant from the ex-cessive use of whisky and cigarettes; many instances being given of intoxication and boisterous and other unseemly conduct on his part in hotels, saloons, and other public places in the city of Louisville, some of which occurred when appellant had his son with him. It was further in substance, stated in the re-sponse that appellant constantly kept whiskey in his apartments, which he regularly drank in excessive quantities in the presence of his son, when the latter would visit him; and by indulging the whims of the child, and otherwise improperly influencing him, ap-pellant attempted to wean his affection from appellee and make him disobedient to her; that the intem-perance, profligacy, and evil example of. appellant, manifested as stated, were well calculated to corrupt the mind and morals and ruin the life of the child, and that to avert such a catastrophe appellee believed it her duty to prevent further association between the father and son, for which reason alone she had for some time as complained by appellant refused his requests to have the child visit him as he had been accustomed to.

Appellant by a pleading entitled an answer con-troverted all the affirmative statements of the re-sponse. Thereupon the court heard all the evidence introduced by the parties and thereafter rendered the following judgment: "The court being sufficiently advised, it is considered and adjudged that said response of the plaintiff is sufficient, and the rule awarded against her is hereby discharged at defendant's costs. It is further considered and adjudged that by the original judgment the plaintff is given the custody and control of the child, Vernon Shallcross, and the defendant is not entitled thereby to any custody or control over said child, and the plaintiff's motion is therefore unnecessary and overruled. The court on its own motion sets aside as much of the provision in said judgment as gives the defendant the privilege of seeing his child at his home, and it is hereby ordered that the plaintiff shall send the child to the home of Henry T. Shanks at No. 619 Floral Terrace, in the city of Louisville, at 2 o'clock, p. m. on the 1st and 3d Saturday afternoons of each month, to remain until 6 o'clock of said day, where the defendant may visit and see said child according to the opinion filed herein. Such visits, however, not to interfere with the welfare, health, and education of said child. Exceptions reserved to both parties, appeal to the Court of Appeals granted to the defendant, and a cross-appeal granted to the plaintiff." Being dissatisfied with the judgment appellant prosecutes this appeal.

His able counsel earnestly insists that the judgment complained of is but a modification of the first judgment, rendered in the action for divorce at a previous term, and that the court was without jurisdiction, and had not the power, upon mere motion, to modify or vacate the former judgment after the expiration of the term at which it was rendered. Section 2123, Ky. St. (Carroll Edition 1909), provides: "Pending an application for divorce, or on final judgment, the court may make orders for the care, custody and maintenance of the minor children of the parties, or children of unsound mind, or any of them, and at any time afterward, upon the petition of either parent, revise and alter the same, having in all such cases of care and custody the interest and welfare of the children principally in view; but no such order for maintenance of children or allotment of favor of the wife shall divest either party of the fee-simple title of real estate.''

It is not denied by counsel that the court rendering such a judgment as that referred to can modify or vacate it, after the expiration of the term at which it was rendered, but contended that, in order to enable it to do so, the power to that end must be reserved in the judgment itself, or its exercise invoked by the petition of a parent of the child to be affected. In all cases respecting the custody of a child the welfare of the child is the governing principle with the courts. The right of the father to have the custody of his child is, in its general sense, admitted, but, this is not on account of any absolute right of the father, but for the benefit of the infant; the law presuming it to be for its interest to be under the care of its natural protector, both for maintenance and education.

Neither the father nor mother, however, has any right that can be allowed to seriously militate against the welfare of the child. If the father be unfit to have the custody of his child, the courts will promptly declare his rights forfeited. The same is true of the mother, and neither parent is entitled to the custody, if it is manifestly against the child's welfare. In such a case the custody of the child will be awarded to a third person. If the child has reached years of discretion, its wishes will be considered, but will not always control. As between the parents, the tendency of the courts is to give very young children to the mother, especially in cases of divorce. Our meaning has been admirably expressed by Judge Robertson in the opinion in Adams v. Adams, 1 Duv. 167, as follows: ''The welfare of infancy, involving that also of the commonwealth, defines the sphere of parental duties and rights, and these preferred rights and duties are correlative. The character and destiny of the citizen are molded by the domestic tutelage of the nursling. Therefore, whenever the parents are separated by divorce, although prima facie the abstract right and duty of the father are superior to those of the mother, yet the court dissolving the union should confide the care and custody of their infant child to the parent most trustworthy and capable, and if neither of them shall be worthy of such a delicate and eventful trust, the interest of the child and the public may authorize the transfer of the custody to a stranger.''

In this state courts of equity are given practically exclusive jurisdiction over the persons and property of infants, and the jurisdiction attaches from the very fact of the institution of an action or proceeding affecting the person or property of an infant, and at once makes him a ward of the court. When such jurisdiction is invoked in the infant's behalf, there are few, if any, inflexible rules of procedure. Even section 2123, Ky. Stat., which gives to the parent of an infant the right to apply by petition to a court of equity for the vacation or modification of a judgment with respect to the custody of the infant, rendered at a previous term, should not be so interpreted. as to exclude any other remedy or course of procedure allowed under the rules of chancery, or that might be invoked or followed in a court of equity for such relief, unless the language of the statute sufficiently indicates that such was the legislative intent. On the contrary, it should, if such a meaning can reasonably be given its language, be construed as intended to add to the jurisdiction and power already possessed by courts of equity, or as affording an additional remedy to either divorced parent. At any rate, we are unwilling to hold that the statute, supra, ties, or was ever intended to tie, the chancellor's hands until a parent acts in the matter. Besides, the language of the statute itself recognizes and emphasizes the paramount duty of the court, which is to look to the child's welfare regardless of both parents, or, to quote from the statute, "having in all such cases of care and custody the interest and welfare of the children in view."

Exercise of the power possessed by a court of equity with respect to the custody of an infant in such a case is not therefore dependent upon action upon the part of either of the divorced parents, or upon a reservation in the judgment of authority to subsequently change or modify it. The court need not have waited for either parent to take the initiative, but possessed the power to modify, upon its own motion, the previous judgment as to the custody of the infant, upon the state of facts appearing in the response and established by the proof. We do not mean to say that the circuit court should at any time enter a judgment, or change one rendered at a previous term, as to the custody of a child without notice to the parents. In this case, however, both had notice.

It does not lie in the mouth of appellant to complain that he was not served with a written notice of the proceedings resulting in the modification of the original judgment as to the custody of his son; for he instituted the proceeding by taking the rule against appellee, and thereby gave cause and opportunity for the filing of her response, the statements of which, together with the evidence introduced to support them, convinced the court of the necessity for modifying the first judgment to the extent that would prevent appellant from having the custody of his son at all. In this view of the matter we think appellant is estopped to complain of the want of previous formal notice of the action of the court in modifying the judgment, and likewise estopped to complain that the modification resulted without the filing of a petition therefor by appellee or himself.

We deem it unnecessary to discuss in detail the evidence upon which the circuit court acted in modifying the judgment as to the custody of the child, but we think it was sufficient to show that appellant is unfit to have the custody, even temporarily, of his son.

The circuit court did what it could and was authorized to do to protect the child. Wherefore the judgment is affirmed.

CASE 55.—ACTION BY THE CRANE & BREED MANUFACTUR-
.ING COMPANY AGAINST MATILDA STAGG'S AD-
MINISTRATOR.—November 17, 1909.

Crane & Breed Mfg. Co. v. Stagg's Adm'r

Appeal from Mercer Circuit Court.

W. C. BELL, Circuit Judge.

Judgment of dismissal and plaintiff appeals.—Reversed.

1. Pleading—Affidavits—Pleadings Executed in Another State—
    Sufficiency.—A pleading or affiadavit to be used in Kentucky
    must be made and verified as required by the laws thereof,
    though executed in another state.
2. Executors and Administrators—Actions Against—Verification
    of Claims.—Ky. St. Sec. 3870, provides that all demands
    against the estate of a decedent shall be verified by the claim-
    ant's written affidavit. Civ. Code Prac. Sec. 544, defines an
    affidavit as a written declaration under oath made without
    notice to the adverse party. Sec. 550, subsec. 1, provides that
    any affidavit by law may, unless otherwise expressed, be made
    by his agent or attorney if he be absent from the county.
    Section 117 provides that an affidavit of a private corporation
    must be verified by its chief officer or agent, etc., or if it
    have no such officer or agent in the county in which the ac-
    tion is brought, that it may be verified by its attorney. Sec-
    tion 549, subsec. 2, provides that an affidavit may be made
    out of the state before any officer or person who may be
    authorized pursuant to section 564 to take depositions and sec-
    tion 564 authorizes the taking of depositions out of the state
    before a notary public, etc. Held, that the affidavit of a non-
    resident corporation claimant against the estate of a decedent
    may be made before a notary at its chief office or principal
    place of business in the state of its residence by its chief
    officer, or in his absence from the county of its principal place
    of business, by its treasurer or other authorized agent, the
    affidavit in the latter case to show the official title of the chief
    officer, his absence from the county, and the authority of the

treasurer or other agent to make the necessary affidavit, and such an affidavit which does not purport to have been made by the corporation's chief officer, or state that he was absent from the county, or that the corporation's treasurer, in the absence of its chief officer from the county, was authorized to make the affidavit is insufficient.

3   Executors and Administrators—Actions Against—Affidavit of Claim—Sufficiency.—Under Ky. St. Sec. 3871, providing that, if any part of the demand of a claimant against a decedent's estate has been paid, the affidavit of claim shall state the payment, and, when it was made, to the best of affiant's knowledge and belief, an affidavit of claim upon an account which embraces sales of merchandise from claimant to decedent covering a period of four years, aggregating $1,463.71, upon which decedent had made during that period numerous payments, all credited on the account, amounting to $1,062.91, leaving a balance due of $400.80, which affidavit treated the balance, not as a balance, but as representing decedent's entire indebtedness from start to finish, was insufficient.

4   Executors and Administrators—Actions Against—Affidavit of Claim—Sufficiency.—Under Ky. St. Sec. 3870, which requires that, when a person other than the claimant against a decedent's estate makes affidavit to the claim, he shall state in his affidavit that he believes the claim to be just, and shall give the reason why he so believes, an affidavit by an employe of a claimant on an account against an estate giving as the only reason for his belief as to the correctness of the account that he had examined plaintiff's books, and found that the account against decedent appeared on the books as on the copy of the account to which his affidavit was attached, is insufficient.

5.   Executors and Administrators—Suit to Compel Settlement by Administrator—Necessity for Verified Affidavits of Claims.—Where a creditor sued in equity to compel the settlement of an estate by an administrator, under Civ. Code Prac. Sec. 428, and the payment of debts, including plaintiff's claims, making the administrator, decedent's heirs, and such of the creditors as were known to plaintiff, defendants, and the petition charged that the administrator was delaying settlement, stated the amount of the estate's indebtedness, the value of its property, that the personal property was not sufficient to pay the debts, alleged the necessity for a sale of realty for such purpose, asked a reference of the case to a master commissioner for taking proof as to creditor's claims, and reporting assets and liabilities of the estate, and closed with a prayer for personal judgment for plaintiff's debt, with

interest, and for a settlement of the estate, etc., it was unnecessary that payment of plaintiff's claim should have been
demanded of the administrator before the institution of the
action, and it was error to dismiss the suit because of a failure of plaintiff to present such affidavit, the object of the statute requiring the claimant, before bringing an action on his
claim to make demand of payment, being to afford the personal representative an opportunity to pay it without cost of
suit, which would not be necessary where there are no assets
in the bands of the personal representative with which to
pay decedent's debts, or such as he may have are insufficient
for that purpose, and decedent left real estate liable for such
debts.

B. F. ROACH for appellant.

AUTHORITIES CITED.

Kentucky Statutes, Section 3872; Hoffman v. Moore's Adm'r,
101 Ky., 1290; Howard v. Leavell, 10 Bush, 481; Thomas Exr.
v. Thomas, 15 B. Mon., 182; Stix, &c., v. Eversole's Adm'r, &c.,
106 Ky., 517; Civil Code, Section 428; Civil Code, Section 429;
Brand v. Brand, 22 Ky. Law Rep., 1366; Holland v. Lowe's Adm'r,
101 Ky., 289.

THOMAS H. HARDIN for appellee.

AUTHORITIES CITED.

Rogers v. Mitchell's Executor, 1 Met., 22; Carroll's Code, Sec.
733, subsec. 33 (Edition 1906); Ky. Statutes, Secs. 3870 to 3872
(Edition 1905); Bullitt's Code, Sec. 437 (Edition 1895); Leach v.
Kimball's Adm'r, 13 Bush, 424; Tichenor v. Wood, 24 Ky. Law
Rep., 1100; Thomas' Executor v. Thomas, 15 B. Mon., 184; Nutall's
Adm'r v. Brannen's Exr., 5 Bush, 17 to 20; Holland v. Levi's Adm'r,
101 Ky., 103.

OPINION OF THE COURT BY JUDGE SETTLE—Re-
.versing.

This is an appeal from a judgment of the Mercer
circuit court dismissing appellant's action upon the
grounds that the account of $400.80 against the es-
tate of Matilda Stagg, deceased, sued on, had not
been verified, or its payment demanded of the ad-

ministrator before suit, as required by sections 3870-3872, Ky. Stat. Attached to the account filed with the petition were two affidavits; the first being that of appellant's treasurer, and the second that of another person, presumably an employe of appellant, who made oath as to the correctness of the account from a comparison of it with the original entries contained in appellant's books. The first affidavit was insufficient. In the first place, it did not purport to have been made by appellant's chief officer, or state that such chief officer was absent from the county in which appellant's chief office is situated at the time the affidavit was made, or that appellant's treasurer, in the absence of the chief officer from the county, was authorized to make the affidavit. Appellant is a corporation created and doing business as such under the laws of Ohio, and its chief office or place of business is in that state, as is the residence of its chief officer.

A pleading or affidavit to be used in Kentucky must, though executed in another state, be made and verified as required by the laws of Kentucky. Section 3870, Ky. Stat., provides: "All demands against the estate of a decedent shall be verified by the written affidavit of the claimant, or in his absence from the state, by his agent, or if dead, by his personal representative, stating that the demand is just, and has never to his knowledge or belief been paid, and that there is no off-set or discount against the same, or any usury therein; and if the demand be other than an obligation signed by the decedent, or a judgment, it shall also be verified by a person other than the claimant, who shall state in his affidavit that he believes the claim to be just and correct and give the reasons why he so believes."

Civil Code Prac., sec. 544, thus defines the word
"affidavit": "An affidavit is a written declaration
under oath, made without notice to the adverse party." Subsection 1, section 550, provides: "Any affidavit which this Code requires or authorizes a
party to make máy, unless otherwise expressed, be
made by his agent or attorney, if he be absent from
the county." By yet another provision of the Civil
code of Practice, viz., section 117, a pleading or affidavit of a private corporation "must be verified by
its chief officer or agent upon whom a summons in
the action is lawfully served, or might be lawfully
served if it were a defendant; or if it have no such
officer or agent in the county in which the action is
brought, or is pending, it may be verified by its attorney."

It will be observed that neither the sections of the
statutes nor those of the Code, supra, offer any obstruction to the right of appellant to make or execute the affidavits in verification of its claim in the
state of Ohio. They merely provide how the verification shall be effected if made or to be used in this
state. The Code (section 549, subs. 2) does, however, provide: "That an affidavit may be made * *
out of this state, before any officer or person who
may be authorized, pursuant to section 564, to take
depositions." And section 564 authorizes the taking of depositions out of this state "before a commissioner appointed by the Governor thereof; or before
any other person empowered by a commission directed to him by consent of the parties, or by order
of the court; or before a judge of a court, a justice
of the peace, mayor of a city, or notary public."
Therefore the claimants' affidavit, in proof of appel-

lant's demand against appellee, might have been made before a notary at its chief office or principal place of business in Ohio by its chief officer, or, in his absence from the county in which such chief office or principal place of business is situated in that state, by its treasurer, or other authorized agent. In the latter case, however, the affidavit should, by an appropriate statement, be made to show the official title of the chief officer, his absence from the county, and the authority of the treasurer or other agent to make the necessary affidavit. None of these essential facts appear in the affidavit made by the treasurer, and their omission, as we have already intimated, rendered it fatally defective.

We think the affidavit defective in another particular. It fails to state the decedent's full indebtedness to appellant according to the account as originally rendered, or to indicate the payments for which the account on its face shows she was given credit. In other words, the affidavit treats the $400.80 balance due on the account, not as a balance, but as representing the decedent's entire indebtedness to appellant from start to finish; whereas, according to the account itself, it embraced sales of merchandise from appellant to the decedent covering a period of four years, aggregating $1,463.71, upon which she made, during the same period, numerous payments, all credited on the account and amounting in the aggregate to $1,062.91, which, subtracted from the total indebtedness, left a balance due appellant of $400.80. In addition to what section 3870, Ky. Stat., directs to be stated in the affidavit of the claimant, section 3871 requires: "If any part of the demand has been paid, or there be any set-off or

vol. 135—28

discount against   the same, or any   usury therein,
the affidavit shall state the payment or usury, when
the payment was made, and when the set-off or discount was due, to the best of the affiant's knowledge and belief.   *   *   *"

The second affidavit accompanying the account,
made doubtless by an employe of appellant, appears to be defective in one particular. It gives but
a single indefinite reason for the affiant's belief as
to the correctness of the demand sued on, viz., that
he had examined appellant's books and found that
the account against the decedent appeared on the
books as on the copy of the account to which his
affidavit was attached. Though without personal
knowledge of the sales to the decedent of any of the
merchandise set forth in the account, if, in addition
to what is said in his affidavit, this employe had
therein stated he was familiar with the merchandise
described in the account as having been sold the decedent and its market value during the period covered by the account, that the various sums charged
in the account therefor were reasonable and the customary prices for such goods, and that it appeared
from the original entries that the merchandise therein described was sold the decedent as of the dates
respectively therein specified—it would have made
the affidavit sufficiently conform to section 3870 of
the statute, supra, which requires that the person
other than the claimant "shall state in his affidavit
that he believes the claim to be just and correct, and
give the reason why he so believes." Dewhurst v.
Shepherd, 102 Ky. 239, 43 S. W. 253, 19 Ky. Law
Rep. 1260. But, notwithstanding the conclusions we
have expressed as to the insufficiency of the affidavits

furnished by appellant in proof of its claim, we are, nevertheless, of the opinion that the circuit court erred in dismissing the action on that ground, or because of the alleged failure of demand.

We find from the record that the action was one in equity brought under section 428, Civ. Code Prac., by appellant as a creditor of the decedent to compel a settlement by the administrator of her estate and the payment of the estate's indebtedness, including its claim of $400.80. The administrator, heirs at law of the decedent, and such of the creditors as were known to appellant were made defendants, and the petition, as amended, charges that the administrator is delaying the settlement of the decedent's estate in order to obtain profit in its business from the interest realized on the money belonging to the decedent's estate it has received; states with particularity the amount of the estate's indebtedness, the nature and value of the property, real and personal, left by the decedent; that the personal property is not sufficient to pay the debts; and alleges the necessity for a sale of the real estate or such part thereof as will realize an amount, which together with the proceeds of the personalty will be sufficient to pay the decedent's debts. The petition also fully described the real estate, asks a reference of the case to the master commissioner for taking proof as to the claims of creditors and reporting the assets and liabilities of the estate, and closes with the prayer for a personal judgment against the administrator for appellant's debt with interest, for a settlement of the estate, and all necessary general and equitable relief.

In view of the object of the action and the fact that appellant's claim, as well as those of all other creditors of the estate, must be properly proved as required by the statute before they are filed with and allowed by the commissioner, it was unnecessary that payment thereof should have been demanded of the administrator before the institution of the action by the presentation to him of the claim accompanied by the necessary statutory affidavits. Huffman v. Moore's Admr. 101 Ky. 288, 41 S. W. 292, 19 Ky. Law Rep. 461; Grey v. Lewis, 79 Ky. 453; Hamilton v. Wright, 87 S. W. 1093, 27 Ky. Law Rep. 1144.

The object of the statute in respect to the verification of claims against decedent's estates is to protect them against unjust or fraudulent claims, and the reason for requiring the claimant, before bringing an action on his claim, to make demand of payment, is to afford the personal representative an opportunity to pay it without cost of suit, and at the same time have a legal voucher of such payment. If, however, there are no assets in the hands of the personal representative with which to pay the decedent's debts, or such as he may have be insufficient for that purpose, but the decedent left real estate liable for such debts, there can be no reason or necessity for a creditor's presenting his claim, accompanied by the statutory affidavit, to the personal representative, in order to entitle him (the creditor) to bring suit for the purpose of subjecting such real estate to the payment of the decedent's debts, including his own.

As was well said in Huffman v. Moore's Admr., supra: "Indeed, the right to bring an action such as this is expressly given to a creditor by section 428, Civil Code Prac. And that right is not thereby made conditional upon compliance by the creditor with the terms prescribed by the statute in order to maintain an action ordinary to recover personal judgment against the administrator or executor. Of course, an action such as this involves a reference to the master commissioner of court to pass upon and report, subject to approval of court, in regard to every claim or demand that may be presented, each of which must be verified, and approved as required by statute before being allowed." When appellant's claim against the decedent's estate is presented to the commissioner, it can then be, and should be, verified and proved in the statutory manner.

On account of the error committed by the circuit court in dismissing the action, the judgment is reversed, and cause remanded for further proceedings consistent with the opinion.

CASE 56.—ACTION BY G. W. GUNTERMAN AGAINST THE
ILLINIOS CENTRAL RAILROAD COMPANY FOR
DAMAGES FOR PERSONAL INJURIES —November
23, 1909.

Ill. Central Ry. Co. v. Gunterman

Appeal from Muhlenberg Circuit Court.

W. P. SANDIDGE, Circuit Judge.

Judgment for plaintiff, defendant appeals.—Reversed.

1. Carriers—Passengers—Injuries by Carrier's Agent—Question
for Jury.—In an action for injuries to a passenger from a
shot fired at a third person by a carrier's flagman, evidence
held to warrant submission to the jury.

2. Carriers—Passengers—Injuries.—It is the duty of a carrier
to protect its passengers not only on the train, but while
they are alighting, and until they have a reasonable time to
leave the platform.

3. Carriers—Passengers—Protection from Third Persons.—It is
a carrier's duty to protect passengers from unruly persons.

4. Carriers—Passengers—Injuries from Acts of Flagman.—
Where trainmen were attacked, and the flagman in the performance of his duty while repelling the attack shot and injured an innocent passenger, tne carrier was liable if the act
was wrongful.

5. Carriers—Injury to Passenger—Act of Flagman—Proximate
Cause.—Where a conductor, hearing a disturbance in a car,
entered and quieted the passengers causing the trouble, his
failure to eject such passengers was not the proximate cause
of injury to an innocent passenger from a renewal of the
difficulty after reaching a station.

6. Trial—Instructions—Applicability to Proof—Injury to Passenger—Act of Carrier's Agent.—In an action by a passenger
for an injury from being shot by a flagman, who attempted to
shoot another who had attacked him, there being no
question of negligence, an instruction using the word "negligently," instead of the words "not in the necessary or ap

parently necessary defense of himself and associates," was erroneous.

7. Carriers—Injury to Passenger—Shooting by Trainman—Instructions.—In an action by a passenger for injury from being shot by a trainman, who shot at another person, an instruction to find for defendant unless one of defendant's agents while attempting to shoot another person negligently shot plaintiff, should have stated that if defendant's trainman, when he fired the shot, believed and had reasonable ground to believe that it was necessary to fire the same to protect himself or associates from death or harm, and he so fired the shot to protect himself or associates, they should find for defendant.

8. Carriers—Injury to . Passenger—Instructions—Evidence.—In an action for injury to a passenger from being shot during a disturbance between the trainmen and disorderly passengers, where the evidence was conflicting as to whether the shot injuring plaintiff was fired by a trainman or a passenger, the court should have instructed that defendant was not liable if the shot was fired by a passenger.

R. Y. THOMAS for appellant.

TAYLOR & EVANS, TRABUE, DOOLAN & COX, and BLEWETT LEE of counsel.

I am confident that the Court will have no hesitancy whatever in reversing this case and I believe it ought and will say that the instruction should have been given the jury to find for the defendant, appellant herein. The court should have instructed the jury to find for appellant:

1. Because the proof in this case shows that the train crew acted courageously and circumspectly under the circumstances in quelling the disturbance on the train created by the disorderly persons.

2. Because the proof in this case shows that these disorderly persons while on the train did not insult or offer to insult, and did not harm or offer to harm Gunterman or any other passenger on the train or on the platform.

3. Because all the evidence of appellee shows that this difficulty took place on the platform after the train had stopped and most of the passengers had alighted, and came up suddenly and was brought on by persons on the platform assaulting the porter and flagman.

Ill. Central Ry. Co. v. Gunterman.

AUTHORITIES CITED.

Kinney v. L. & N. R. R. Co., 99 Ky., 59; 6 Cyc. 542; South Covington & C. St. Ry. Co. v. Beatty, (unreported) 50 S. W., 239; Winnegar's Adm'r v. Central Passenger Ry. Co., 85 Ky., 547; Sullivan v. L. & N. R. R. Co. 115 Ky., 447; Smith v. L. & N. R. R Co., 95 Ky., 11; Ferguson v. Terry, 1 Ben Monroe, 96; Crabtree v. Dawson, 119 Ky., 148; 1st Joyce on Damages, page 427, section 363; Robertson's Criminal Law and Procedure, Section 542, page 752.

WILLIS & MEREDITH for appellee.

POINTS AND AUTHORITIES.

1. When the relationship of carrier and passenger is once established it does not cease until the passenger has had a reasonable opportunity to leave the station platform and the premises of the carrier at the termination of his journey, and the question as to whether or not he has had a "reasonable opportunity" to leave its premises is one for the jury. L. & N. R. R. Co. v. Keller, 47 S. W., 1072, (unreported).

2. A carrier of passengers for hire obligates itself to use a high degree of care to transport the passenger safely to his destination, and it will be liable for any breach of this contractual duty to him. 71 Ky. 147; 41 S. W. 580, (unreported); Cyc. Vol. 6, page 592.

3. A carrier of passengers for hire is liable to the passenger for injury done him by the carrier's servants whether the servant is acting within the scope of his employment, or maliciously, or from motives purely his own. Cyc. Vol. 6, page 600; Chicago & Eastern R. R. Co. v. Flexman, (Ill.) 42 American Reports, 33; 85 Ky., 547.

4. The carrier is also responsible for injury to the passenger by a fellow passenger if it fails to use that degree of care required of it to protect the passenger from injury after it knows or by the exercise of the proper care it could know the fellow passenger's dangerous condition, and the impending peril of the passenger. Cyc. Vol. 6, page 602; L. & N. v. McEwin, 51 S. W., 619, (unreported).

5. When a passenger is injured either by the carrier's servants, or a fellow-passenger, it is a question of fact for the jury to say from all of the evidence and surrounding circumstances of the case whether or not in either event the carrier exercised that degree of care required of it to protct the passenger. (Authorities above cited.)

6.   Where a passenger is injured by the carrier's servant an instruction authorizing a recovery, if the jury believed that the servant "negligently" injured the passenger, was proper.

7.   Plaintiff is not required to anticipate and meet on his direct proof the proof that may be offered by the defendant on a matter plead affirmatively by the defendant as a defense, but is only required to meet such proof as is offered by the defendant thereon.

OPINION OF THE COURT BY JUDGE HOBSON—Reversing.

G. W. Gunterman was a passenger on the accommodation train of the Illinois Central Railroad Company running from Central City westward.   The train was much crowded, and Gunterman rode upon the platform of one of the cars, as his destination was a station known as Mercer, about three miles from Central City.   The proof for him tends to show these facts: After the train pulled out from Central City, a crash was heard in the smoking car, and there was some disturbance in there.   The conductor went forward hurriedly to the car, and soon he and the flagman came out bringing with them a man named Jackson, whom the conductor said he was going to put off; but he then decided not to put him off, but to take him on to Greenville, and allowed him to go back into the car.   After Jackson returned to the car, there was still a disturbance in there.   When the train reached Mercer, Gunterman got off and was standing on the platform, while the flagman was helping a lady off. At this juncture a man named Laswell, who had gotten off the train, picked up a rock and knocked down the porter, who was by the side of the car, and struck Langley, the flagman.   The proof for the plaintiff shows that at this point the conductor and Langley took out their pistols and Langley began shooting; one of the balls from Langley's pistol striking Gunterman in the back of the neck.

The proof of the railroad company is to the
effect that, when the conductor went forward into the
smoker, he found that Jackson and Laswell had
kicked down the door to the water-closet, claiming
that someone had locked them in there, although the
fact was that they simply had failed to turn the lock
the right way.   The conductor undertook to quiet
them, and, Jackson being unruly, the conductor
struck him.   He thereupon quieted and took a seat;
and the conductor left the car and went back to the
ladies' car to take up his fares.   After the conductor
left, Laswell, who was with Jackson in the water-
closet, became boisterous again, and the flagman, who
was in the car, undertook to quiet him, and struck him
on the head, from which he bled considerably.   He
then became quiet, and soon the train pulled into Mercer, where Jackson, Laswell, and a man named Hopkins, among others, left the train.   As soon as Laswell got on the ground, he began hunting for a rock,
with which he knocked down the porter who had his
back to him, and then struck Langley, the flagman,
and Langley drew his pistol and snapped it.   At this
juncture Hopkins drew his pistol and fired two shots
at Langley, the first of which struck Gunterman in
the neck.   The conductor was standing on the platform of the car, but had not gotten off the car when
the difficulty took place.   There was testimony for
the plaintiff to the effect that Hopkins had drawn his
pistol in the car before he reached Mercer; but there
was no proof that any of the railroad men saw this, or
that he was in any way connected with the difficulty
that had taken place in the car.   The proof for the
railroad company was to the effect that Hopkins had
done nothing until after the difficulty began on the

ground. On this conflicting testimony the circuit court instructed the jury as follows:

"(1) The court instructs the jury that if they believe from the evidence that the plaintiff was a passenger on the defendant's (railroad company's) train from Central City to Mercer station, and that when the plaintiff was on the station platform at Mercer Station on the occasion of his leaving the cars after he had been carried from Central City to Mercer Station, and before he had had a reasonable opportunity to leave said station platform after getting off the cars, the agents of defendant railway company, or any of them in charge of said passenger train, while attempting to shoot another person, unintentionally but negligently shot and wounded the plaintiff upon his body and person with a pistol, then, and in that event, the jury should find for the plaintiff such compensatory damages, if any, as were thereby caused to the plaintiff, and which were the direct and natural result of the negligence aforesaid, not exceeding $1,999 the amount claimed.

"(2) The jury should find for defendant unless they should believe from the evidence that some one of the defendant's agents in charge of said train while attempting to shoot another person negligently shot and wounded the plaintiff while he was on the station platform, and before he had had a reasonable opportunity to leave the platform after getting off the cars."

"(4) Negligence as used in the instructions means the failure to use ordinary care, and ordinary care is such care as an ordinarily prudent person would usually exercise under similar circumstances in matters involving his own interest.

He refused to give this instruction, which was
asked by the defendant: "The court instructs the
jury that, although they may believe from the evidence that one of the defendant's agents fired the
shot which struck and injured the plaintiff, but should
further believe from the evidence that the said agent
who fired said shot, if he did so fire it, was being attacked by some other person, and at the time believed
or had reasonable grounds to believe that it was
necessary for him to fire same to protect himself from
death or great bodily harm at the hands of said person, then the law is for the defendant, and they will
so find.''

The jury found for Gunterman, and fixed his
damages at $1,000.   The railroad company appeals.

The court did   not err in refusing to instruct the
jury peremptorily to find for the defendant, for in
helping the passengers from the train the flagman
was discharging a duty assigned him by the defendant.   It was the duty of the defendant to protect its
passengers, not only on the train, but while they were
alighting from it, and until they had had a reasonable
time to leave the platform.   It was incumbent upon it
to protect its passengers from unruly persons as they
alighted from the train no less than while they were
on the train.   If the flagman was attacked while he
was performing the duty assigned him by the defendant, he had a right to stand his ground and meet
force with force, and to use as much force as was
necessary to protect him or his associates from death
or great bodily harm at the hands of their assailants.
In doing all this he was acting for the company, and
therefore it is responsible for his acts.   Gunterman
had just alighted from the train, and a reasonable
time had not elapsed when the shooting was done.

The court also properly refused to submit to the jury the question whether the conductor in the exercise of ordinary care should have put Jackson and Laswell off the train before they reached Mercer.' When the conductor went to Jackson, he quieted down, and it does not appear that he was afterwards disorderly on the train. There was nothing in the conduct of Laswell and Jackson that should have made the conductor anticipate that after they reached Mercer and got upon the ground they would make an attack upon the trainmen. As what happened at Mercer was not to be reasonably anticipated from what had taken place in the presence of the conductor on the train, it cannot be said that his failure to put Laswell and Jackson off before they reached Mercer was the proximate cause of this trouble.

The fact is that the difficulty at Mercer seems to have followed the flagman striking Laswell after the conductor had left the car and without his knowledge; for it is evident that Laswell got the rock and began the assault at Mercer to avenge himself for the blow which the flagman had given him on the train. This occurred just as the train was pulling into Mercer, and the conductor had no opportunity to do anything before the train reached Mercer. He was then taking up the tickets in the ladies' car, and had no knowledge of it until after the difficulty at Mercer. There was no evidence in the case that any one of the trainmen but Langley, the flagman, did any shooting. In instruction No. 1, in lieu of the words "the agents of defendant railroad company or any of them in charge of said passenger train," the court should have used the words, "the defendant's flagman, Langley."

There is no question of negligence in the case.
If Langley drew his pistol and fired it into the crowd,
shooting the plaintiff, the company is responsible
unless he acted in self-defense. In lieu of the words
in the first instruction "but negligently," the court
should have used the words "and not in the necessary
or apparently necessary defense of himself or his
associates on the train." In lieu of instruction No.
2, the court should have told the jury that it was the
duty of the defendant's agents in charge of the train
to protect the passengers while they were alighting
from the car, and that, if they were attacked, they
had a right to stand their ground and meet force with
force, and that, though they should believe from the
evidence that Langley fired the shot which struck the
plaintiff, yet, if they further believe from the evidence that when he so fired it he or his associates on
the train were being attacked by some other person
or persons, and he believed, and had reasonable
grounds to believe, that it was then necessary for him
to fire same to protect himself or them from death or
great bodily harm at the hands of such person or
persons, and he so fired the shot to protect himself
or one of his associates from the said danger real or
to him apparent, they should find for the defendant.
Crabtree v. Dawson, 119 Ky. 148, 83 S. W. 557, 26 Ky.
Law Rep. 1046, 67 L. R. A. 565, 115 Am. St. Rep. 243.
By another instruction the jury should have been told
that the defendant was not liable if the shot which
struck the plaintiff was fired by Hopkins.

The other objections urged are as to matters
which will probably not occur on another trial. In
view of all the evidence, we conclude that there
should be a new trial.

Judgment reversed and cause remanded for further proceedings consistent herewith.

CASE 57.—TWO INDICTMENTS AGAINST JAMES WYNN FOR ROBBERY TRIED TOGETHER.—November 23, 1909.

Wynn v. Commonwealth.

Appeal from Hopkins Circuit Court.

J. F. GORDON, Circuit Judge.

Defendant convicted and appeals.—Reversed.

1. Robbery—Evidence—Sufficiency.—In a prosecution for robbery, evidence held to sufficiently identify accused as the perpetrator of the robbery to warrant a verdict of guilty.

2. Criminal Law—Credibility of Witnesses—Questions for Jury. —Where the prosecuting witnesses identified accused as the perpetrator of the crime, the jury had the right to accept their testimony as against that of accused and his witnesses.

3. Robbery—What Constitutes—Search of Persons Under Arrest—Right of Officer.—Though a deputy marshal had the right to arrest, without a warrant, persons who were drunk and disorderly, and following such arrests to search them to ascertain whether they possessed weapons or other means of resisting his authority, or affecting their escape if imprisoned, if in making search he obtained money from them, it was his duty to return it upon discharging them from arrest, and if, after making the arrest he took advantage of the duress under which such arrest placed them, and by force or putting them in fear took from them money in their possession feloniously, intending at the time to convert it to his own use, his act was robbery.

4. Larceny—Petit Larceny—What Constitutes—Money Taken From Persons Under Arrest.—In a prosecution for robbery, where it appeared that accused, a deputy sheriff, arrested the complaining witnesses for being drunk and disorderly, and after making the arrests searched their persons and obtained an amount of money, which he did not return upon releasing them, it was error not to charge the jury on petit larceny,

since, if accused made the search in good faith, and not for the purpose of robbing them, but after thus getting the money feloniously kept and converted it to his own use, his act in so doing was petit larceny.

JOHNSON & JENNINGS for appellant.

JAS. BREATHITT, Attorney General, and TOM B. McGREGOR, Assistant Attorney General, for Commonwealth.

OPINION OF THE COURT BY JUDGE SETTLE—RE-VERSING.

This is an appeal from two judgments of the Hopkins circuit court, each convicting the appellant, James Wynn, of the crime of robbery. By agreement he was tried under the two indictments at the same time, and by the single verdict of the jury his punishment under one of the indictments was fixed at three and under the other at two years' confinement in the penitentiary.

According to the commonwealth's evidence, the alleged robberies were committed by appellant in the village of Nortonville, at night, in August, 1907, under the following circumstances: Naaman Wilson and J. L. Kenny, who were going from Central City to Crofton, reached Nortonville upon a train of the Illinois Central Railroad, at which place they had to await a later train of the Louisville & Nashville Railroad upon which to go to Crofton, situated upon the last-named railroad. Having severa' hours to wait at Nortonville, Wilson and Kenny visited one or more saloons and took two drinks of beer and one of whisky each, and then went to the depot, intending to take the Louisville & Nashville Railroad train upon its arrival. While in the depot, Kenny became sick from intoxication or the mixture of drinks he had taken, and vomited upon the floor, which displeased the ticket agent in charge of the depot, who ordered both Kenny and Wilson from the building.

At this juncture, appellant, who claimed to be acting as deputy marshal of Nortonville, appeared on the scene and arrested Wilson and Kenny, and ostensibly started with them to the town prison. They both testified that appellant upon reaching a point on the railroad track about 75 yards from the depot stopped and told them he would have to search their persons, to which they objected, but that he nevertheless proceeded with the search, and took from the pocket of Wilson two $5 bills, after which he told Wilson and Kenny that if they would go to an adjoining woodland, which he pointed out to them, and quietly remain there until the time arrived for reaching the depot to take the train upon which they expected to go to Crofton, he would release them from arrest, whereupon they agreed to follow appellant's commands and were discharged by him, but that he retained the money he took from Wilson, and did not thereafter return it. Wilson and Kenny further testified that they went to the woods as directed by appellant, but there encountered some negroes who "bummed" them for money, and that, to avoid the negroes, they returned to the depot, and were again arrested by appellant, who took them to the place of the first search, and again searched their persons, taking at that time from Kenny $2, which he appropriated as he had done the $10 of Wilson, after which appellant turned them loose, and again ordered them to the woods.

In addition to the testimony of Wilson and Kenny, the commonwealth proved the flight of appellant to Indiana after his indictment for the robberies, and the forfeiture of the bail bonds executed to secure his appearance for trial under the indictments. Appellant in testifying admitted his escape from jail and flight to Indiana, but claimed that he was confined to jail for a misdemeanor, and that the escape and flight were caused by the need of his services by his family in Indiana, some of whom were then ill. It does not appear from the evidence, however, whether his return from Indiana for trial was voluntary or because of his arrest for that purpose; but it does appear that his bail in the robbery cases, following his escape and flight, procured of the clerk of the Hopkins circuit court copies of the bail bonds, with a view to his arrest and return to answer the indictments.

Appellant, upon being introduced as a witness in his own behalf, admitted that he twice arrested Wilson and Kenny as stated by them, but denied that he searched or took any money from either of them. He was corroborated as to what took place at each arrest by three companions who claimed to have been with him at the time, one of whom was a saloon keeper who seemed to have been considerably under the influence of intoxicants. In addition, appellant proved by the ticket agent that Wilson and Kenny after their arrest accused him of being the person who robbed them, but later retracted the accusation, apologized to him therefor, and informed him that appellant was the guilty party. It also appeared from the evidence that the ticket agent resembled appellant in figure, and wore clothing of the same fashion and color. Appellant also proved by one of the town trustees that Wilson and Kenny on the morning following the robberies claimed that they had been robbed by a man who had arrested them as marshal, but that they failed to identify appellant as the guilty party when he was called to them.

Appellant contends that he should have been granted a new trial, and is entitled to a reversal of the judgments of conviction, because the verdict was contrary to and unauthorized by the evidence. This contention cannot prevail, for the reason that the testimony of both Wilson and Kenny make it appear that he was the guilty party, both identified him as the perpetrator of the crimes, and related with particularity the facts and circumstances tending to establish his guilt, and the jury had the right to accept their testimony as against that of appellant and his witnesses. And the trial court, even if of opinion that the weight of the evidence conduced to prove appellant's innocence, could not have usurped the powers of the jury by determining the matter of his guilt or innocence.

It is further contended by appellant that the trial court in addition to the instructions given should have given one under which the jury might have found appellant guilty of petit larceny. We are disposed to sustain this contention. If Wilson and Kenny when found by appellant were drunk or disorderly, he had the right as deputy marshal of Nortonville to arrest them without a warrant, and following such arrest, to search their persons for the purposes of ascertaining whether they were in possession of weapons or other means of resisting his authority as an officer, or of effecting their escape if imprisoned, but, if in making such search appellant obtained from their persons money, it was his duty to return it upon discharging them from arrest. If, however, after making the arrest, he took advantage

of the duress under which such arrest placed them,
and by force or by putting them in fear took from
them money in their possession, feloniously intending
at the time to convert it to his own use, his act in
doing so was robbery. On the other hand, if appellant searched Wilson and Kenny in good faith, and
not for the purpose of robbing them, but after thus
getting the money feloniously kept and converted it
to his own use, his act in so doing constituted petit
larceny.

We are of opinion, therefore, that on a retrial of
the case the circuit court in addition to the instructions given on the former trial should give another
or others embodying substantially in terms as above
indicated the law as to petit larceny.

On account of the error of the trial court in instructing the jury, the judgments are reversed and
cases remanded for a new trial in conformity to the
opinion.

CASE 58.—ACTION BY JAMES MATT SANDIDGE'S COMMIT-
TEE FOR THE SALE OF LAND TO PAY DEBTS.—
November 23, 1909.

Brandenburg v. Sandidge's Comittee.

Appeal from Hardin Circuit Court.

W. S. CHELF, Circuit Judge.

From a judgment requiring the purchaser, Brandenburg, to pay for the land he appeals.—Reversed.

Insane Persons—Sale of Real Estate—Validity.—Where the appointment of a committee for a lunatic was void, and an order for the sale of the lunatic's real estate to pay debts made in a suit by the committee against the lunatic confined in an asylum and his creditors was void, the court could not compel the purchaser to accept a deed from the lunatic while in the asylum on the mere ex parte affidavit of the asylum physician, averring that the lunatic had been restored to reason.

H. L. JAMES for appellant.

LAYMAN & HOLBERT and L. A. FAUREST for appellees.

No briefs—record misplaced.

OPINION OF THE COURT BY CHIEF JUSTICE NUNN—
Reversing.

Prior to May 25, 1908, one James Matt Sandidge owned about 185 acres of land in one body in Hardin county, Ky. He was indebted to the Leitchfield Deposit Bank in the sum of about $2,300, which was secured by a mortgage on the land and to C. Z. Aud something over $100, which was also secured by a mortgage on the land. He owed two or three merchants' accounts which were unsecured. All of his indebtedness amounted to something like $2,700. On the date above named Sandidge was given a form of trial as to his sanity in the county court. The jury found him of unsound mind and to be a lunatic. The court so adjudged him, and directed his immediate conveyance to the asylum in Lakeland, Ky., which was done. W. H. Gardner was appointed his committee, and he instituted this action, alleging that Sandidge was a lunatic and then confined in the asylum in Lakeland, and made him a defendant with the creditors of Sandidge, and asked that the land be sold to satisfy the creditors.

The case was referred to a master commissioner to take proof of and report claims against Sandidge's estate. He reported the amount thereof, which was, in substance, as stated. The court directed a sale of all the land for the reason that it could not be divided without materially impairing its value, and directed that the creditors of Sandidge be paid out of the purchase price. The land was sold by the commissioner, and appellant, Brandenburg, bid the sum of $4,450, about $1,200 or $1,400 more than the proof shows that it was worth. The sale was reported by the commissioner to the court, and at the first term after the sale, a guardian ad litem for Sandidge's infant children filed exceptions to the sale of the whole of the land, stating that Sandidge and his children were entitled to a homestead, which should be set apart and the balance sold to pay the debts. Brandenburg appeared at the same time, and filed exceptions to the report of sale, making the point that the whole proceeding by which the land was sold was void; that the confinement of Sandidge in the asylum was without legal authority because he had not been lawfully adjudged to be a lunatic.

Both parties agree that these contentions are true, and the court so stated in its judgment, but compelled Brandenburg to take the land at his bid for the following reasons: After it was discovered that all the proceedings leading up to the sale of the land by an order of the court were void, a deed was prepared from James Matt Sandidge to appellant, Brandenburg, the purchase price being fixed at appellant's bid, which contained a clause of general warranty, and was sent or carried to Jefferson county, where the asylum is situated, and was signed and acknowledged by J. Matt Sandidge before Victor Swope, a notary public for that county, who certified that Sandidge freely ratified and confirmed the sale to Brandenburg. On the same day one W. E. Gardner made an affidavit stating, in effect, that he was the first assistant physician at the Central Kentucky Asylum for the Insane in Lakeland, Ky.; that as such physician J. Matt Sandidge was placed under his care when sent to the asylum; that he had been restored to his right mind, was then, and had been for several months, of sound mind, and thoroughly capable of attending to his own business, although somewhat physically disabled; that he had mind and capacity to understand a contract to sell and convey his real estate and other property. This affidavit was filed in court, and the court directed its commissioner who made the sale of the land to join Sandidge in the deed to appellant, and from this order the appeal was prosecuted.

The only question to be considered is whether the court erred in compelling appellant to accept the deed so made and tendered and pay the purchase price.

Appellees' counsel concedes in his argument that the lower court had no jurisdiction to make the sale of the land, but as Sandidge, when in his right mind, as shown by the affidavit of the assistant physician, ratified and confirmed the attempted sale of the land by the court and executed a deed of general warranty, appellant should be required to take the land and pay the purchase price. In support of this contention, counsel refer to some authorities to the effect that, when an agent makes a sale of land without disclosing his agency, the purchaser was compelled to take the land when the principal made a good title.

The case at bar is not like those cases. We have found no case where the purchaser of land who believed that he was getting a good title from the person who sold it to him was compelled to take the land when he discovered that the seller did not own it and his principal was an infant, idiot, or lunatic, or there were reasonable grounds to believe that the principal was laboring under any one of these difficulties. Brandenburg knew the owner of the land was in the asylum, and believed that the court had jurisdiction to make a sale and pass a good and perfect title to the land, and he should not have been made to accept the deed from Sandidge made while he was in the asylum; the only evidence of his having been restored to his right mind being an ex parte affidavit of the assistant physician of the asylum.

While it is agreed that all the proceedings which led up to the placing of Sandidge in the asylum were void, yet the record shows that a jury was impaneled, the proper oath administered, and a verdict returned to the effect that Sandidge was of unsound mind and a lunatic, and that he was immediately sent to the asylum, where he remained until after the court ordered appellant to accept the deed. Appellant traded with the court and expected a good title from it, and the court had no power to compel him to accept a deed from another vendor, especially when that vendor's sanity was in doubt, and appellant might be put to the expense and trouble in maintaining his title against the claim of Sandidge's heirs. If the creditors of Sandidge had made their answers to the petition a cross-petition against Sandidge and had him served with process before the sale of the land, it would have been valid, but they did not do that. Sandidge was before the court only upon the petition of Gardner, his alleged committee, whose appointment was void, wherefore Gardner had no right to institute the action.

For these reasons, the judgment of the lower court is reversed and remanded, with directions to set aside the sale and to dismiss the petition.

CASE 59.—ACTION BY THE CLEAR SPRING DISTILLLING
    COMPANY AGAINST BARDSTOWN GRADED COM-
    MON SCHOOL DISTRICT.—November 23. 1909.

Clear Spring Distilling Co. v. Bardstown Graded School District.

Appeal from Nelson Circuit Court.

SAMUEL E. JONES, Circuit Judge.

Judgment for defendants, plaintiff appeals.—Reversed.

Schools and School Districts—Graded Common School District—
    Boundaries.—Ky. St. 1909, Sec. 4464, providing that no point
    on the boundary of a proposed graded common school district
    shall be more that 2½ miles from the site of its proposed
    schoolhouse, etc., when considered in connection with sec-
    tion 4481, authorizing the trustees to order an election to
    submit the question of the issuance of bonds to provide
    grounds, buildings, etc., and section 4439, authorizing proceed-
    ings to condemn a site for a schoolhouse not exceeding one
    acre, requires that the 2½-mile boundary for a graded com-
    mon school district shall be measured from the outer boun-
    dary of the site of the school building, provided the site does
    not exceed one acre.

JOHN D WICKLIFFE for appellant.

REDFORD C. CHERRY and JOHN S. KELLY for appellees.

OPINION OF THE COURT BY CHIEF JUSTICE NUNN.—
Reversing.

The county court of Nelson county recently established a graded common school district in the city of
Bardstown, the boundary of which included several
ware-houses containing 15,000 barrels of whisky, upon
both of which the trustees claim the school district

is entitled to taxes. The trustees obtained 8 or 9 acres of land and erected a schoolhouse upon it, and the county court, in establishing the outside boundary line of the district 2½ miles from the outer boundary of the eight or nine acres survey, included the warehouses and whisky. We copy an excerpt from the facts as agreed by the parties, which is as follows: "If a straight line is run from the northwestern portion of said school site in a northwesterly direction towards plaintiff's distillery warehouses, the line described by this radius will include the whisky and warehouses in controversy; while, if such line is run from the main school building, said whisky and warehouses will be excluded from the 2½-mile boundary line of said district."

The only question to be determined is: From what point should the measurement begin to arrive at the outer boundary 2½ miles from the school site? It is provided in section 4464, Ky. St. under title of "Graded Common Schools," as follows: "No point on the boundary of any proposed graded common school district shall be more than two and one-half miles from the site of its proposed schoolhouse, and that the location and site of said schoolhouse in said district are set out with exactness in said petition to the county judge." Sec. 4481 of the Statutes (Russell's St. Sec. 5758) provides that the trustees of graded common school districts may order an election, and submit to the voters of the district the question whether or not the trustees thereof shall issue bonds for the purpose of providing suitable grounds, school buildings, furniture, and apparatus for the proposed graded common school district. It is further provided in this section that: "Said board of trustees shall provide funds for purchasing suitable grounds

and buildings, or for erecting or repairing suitable
buildings, and for other expenses needful in conducting a good graded common school in their graded
common school district.'' There is no direct and
positive authority given the trustees in graded common school districts to purchase suitable grounds,
etc., for the erection of school buildings, but this must
necessarily be inferred from the language quoted
from section 4481, and it would be unreasonable to
construe the statute as confining the trustees to a site
only sufficient to erect a building upon.

It is our conclusion that the General Assembly
never contemplated that the measurement of the 2½
miles should begin at the building. We are also of
the opinion that it did not contemplate that such
measurement should begin at the outer boundary of
any survey of land that the trustees might procure
by purchase or gift for school purposes, for the trustees might procure 100 acres or more, and thereby
enable their district to obtain an advantage for educational purposes over the surrounding districts, and it
would enable them to tax persons in that district who
would be unable to derive any benefit from the school
by reason of the great distance therefrom. As stated,
under the title of ''Graded Common Schools,'' article
10 of the General Statutes, the General Assembly, by
inference only, authorized the trustees to purchase
a site for a school building, but did not authorize
them to take steps in the county court to condemn
land for such purposes, in case they could not agree
with the owner of the land for its purchase. The
General Assembly, when it enacted the sections of the
statute included in article 10, and which have special
reference to graded common schools, knew that it had
enacted section 4439 under the head of ''Common

Schools," applying to all common schools, which includes graded common schools. By that section the trustees are authorized to condemn a site for a school house when they cannot agree with the owner on the price. It is also provided by that section that "the quantity of land thus condemned shall not in any case exceed one acre.'

Our conclusion is that the General Assembly, in enacting section 4464 of the Statutes, intended that the 2½-mile boundary of graded common school districts should be measured from the outer boundary of the site of the school building, provided the site does not exceed one acre. It was not intended to confine the trustees of a graded common school to one acre of land if they saw proper to procure more, but it was meant to confine the taxing district within the above limits.

This, in our opinion, is the only reasonable construction that can be given the statutes upon this subject. The following authorities, while not exactly in point, throw some light upon the subject: Trustees Paintsville School District v. Davis, 64 S. W. 438, 23 Ky. Law Rep. 838, Jackson v. Brewer, etc., 112 Ky. 554, 66 S. W. 396, 23 Ky. Law Rep. 1871, and Hundley etc., v. Singleton, Supt. etc., 66 S. W. 279, 23 Ky. Law Rep. 2006. The agreed state of facts is insufficient to enable us to settle this case. We cannot tell whether the warehouses and whiskey will be included when the measurement is made to begin at the outer boundary of an acre, considering the school building as in the center of the acre.

For these reasons, the judgment of the lower court is reversed and remanded for further proceedings consistent herewith.

CASE 60.—ACTION BY L. W. SMITH AGAINST THE LOUIS-
VILLE & NASHVILLE RAILROAD COMPANY FOR
DAMAGES FOR PERSONAL INJURIES.—November
26, 1909.

Louisville & Nashville R. R. Co. v. Smith

Appeal from Jefferson Circuit Court (Common
Pleas Branch, First Division).

EMMET FIELD, Judge.

Judgment for plaintiff, defendant appeals.—Affirmed.

1. Appeal and Error—Review—Weight of Evidence.—The jury
   has the exclusive right to weigh conflicting evidence.
2. Railroads—Injury at Crossing—Right of Action—What Law
   Governs.—The right of recovery for injuries at a railroad
   crossing in another state is, in the absence of a statutory
   provision, to be determined by the laws of that state as declared by its Supreme Court.
3. Carriers—Injury at Station—Contributory Negligence.—A
   person going to a train then due to meet a friend, who exercised due care to observe the situation in passing from the
   depot to the train, was not so negligent in undertaking to
   pass between cars three feet apart on an intervening track
   as to prevent his recovery for injuries by one of the cars
   suddenly closing the space under the rule in Alabama that
   the failure to stop, look and listen before crossing a railroad
   track is such contributory negligence as will defeat a recovery for injuries, in the absence of evidence that the
   company was guilty of reckless or wanton negligence.
4. Carriers—Care of Persons Accompanying Passenger.—
   Though a carrier does not owe a person going to a train to
   meet a friend the degree of care due a passenger, it must
   exercise ordinary care for his safety.
5. Carriers—Care of Persons Accompanying Passenger.—A person going to a train to receive a passenger need not wait until the train has actually arrived before going to the platform
   in order to avail himself of the rule of law that requires a
   carrier to exercise ordinary care for his safety.

6. Carriers—Injuries at Station—Care Due Travelers.—Where an opening in a train at a station has been made for the passage of persons, the duty to give warning before closing the space is not satisfied by merely ringing the engine bell or sounding the whistle.

7. Carriers—Injuries at Station—Negligence—Question for Jury. —Whether sufficient warning was given before closing the space left for the passage of persons between cars at a station is a question for the jury.

8. Carriers—Injury at Station—Instruction.—Where the evidence is conflicting as to whether defendant exercised sufficient care to give warning before closing the space left for the passage of persons between cars at a crossing, it is proper to instruct to find for defendant, if plaintiff would not have been injured except for his contributory negligence, unless when he came in peril defendant's employes could, by the exercise of ordinary car, have discovered his peril and prevented the injury.

9. Damages—Punitive Damages—What Law Governs.—The laws of the state wherein a personal injury occurred govern the question whether punitive damages should be awarded.

10. Evidence—Presumptions—Law of Other State.—In the absence of proof of the law as to punitive damages for personal injuries in the state where the personal injuries occurred, the law of that state is presumed to be the same as that of the forum.

11. Negligence—"Gross Negligence."—"Gross negligence" is the absense of slight care.

12. Damages—Punitive Damages—Personal Injuries.—Where the negligence from which a personal injury results is gross, punitive damages may be awarded.

13. Carriers—Injury at Station—Negligence—Sufficiency of Evidence.—Evidence, in an action for injuries at a station, held to show that plaintiff was injured by defendant's reckless disregard of its duty to plaintiff.

14. Appeal and Error—Harmless Error—Punitive Damages—Instructions.—The objection to an instruction on punitive damages that the words "or may not" should have been inserted after the words "then you may" in the clause allowing an award of such damages is too technical for consideration.

15. Damages—Propriety of Instructions on Punitive Damages.— Where there is evidence that the injury at a crossing was caused by a reckless disregard of human life, an instruction on the subject of punitive damages is proper.

16. Damages—Excessive Damages—Personal Injuries.—Verdict for $12,500 for permanent personal injuries held not excessive.

HELM & HELM and B. D. WARFIELD for appellant.

POINTS AND AUTHORITIES.

The defendant on this appeal contends that the following were errors prejudicial to the defendant's substantial rights:

1. That under the law of Alabama as proven in this case and as it exists, the plaintiff was as a matter of law guilty of contributory negligence in endeavoring to pass between the ends of cabooses or cars which were attached to engine with steam up, and that therefore the defendant's motion for a peremptory instruction should have been sustained. Glass v. Memphis & C. R. Co., 94 Ala., 591, 10 So. Rep., 215; Ga. Pac. R. Co. v. Lee, 92 Ala., 262, 9 So. Rep., 232; L. & N. R. Co. v. Crawford, 98 Ala., 220, 8 So. Rep., 242; Leak v. Ga. Pac. R. Co., 90 Ala., 161, 8 So. Rep., 245; Pannell v. Nashville F. & S. R., 97 Ala., 289, 12 So. Rep. 263; E. Tenn., Va. & Ga. v. Kornegay, 92 Ala., 228, 9 So. Rep. 537; L. H. & St. L. R. Co. v. Jolly's Adm'r, 28 R., 992; Elliott on Railroads, Vo. 4, Sec. 1793; So. Ry. v. Clark, 32 R., 69; Sou. Ry. v. Thomas, 29 R., 79; Brackett's Adm'ra v. L. & N. R. Co., 111 S. W.,(710.

2. That the third instruction given by the court was erroneous and prejudicial in that it permitted the jury to find for the plaintiff notwithstanding his contributory negligence if they believed that "when the plaintiff came in peril from the train, the employes of the defendant in charge of the train could by the exercise of ordinary care have discovered his peril, and by ordinary care have prevented his injury," because it tendered a false issue to the jury, which confused and misled them, and upon which there was not a scintilla of evidence in the record to support a finding by them. 11 Ency. Pleading Practice, p. 170; L. & N. R Co. v. Joshlin, 33 R., 516; L. & N. R. R. Co. v. McCoombs, 21 R. 1232; L. & N. R. R. Co. v. Veach's Adm'r, 112 S. W., 869; (to be officially reported.).

3. That the fourth instruction on the measure of damages was erroneous and prejudicial in allowing the jury to award the plaintiff punitive damages if they found the defendant guilty of gross negligence. This instruction is erroneous for several reasons: A. Because in a form which this court has held to be bad and cause for reversal. I. C. v. Houchins, 121 Ky., 526-535. B. Because there is not a scintilla of evidence upon which to base a charge of gross negligence. L. & N. R. Co. v. Kingman, 18 R.,

Louisville & Nashville R. R. Co. v. Smith.

83; Andrews v. Singer Mfg. Co., 20 R., 1089; Lex. Ry. Co. v. Fain. 25 R., 2243; Sou. Ry. v. Goddard, 121 Ky., 567; Sou. Ry. v. Hawkins, 121 Ky., 415; L. & N. R. Co. v. Mount, 125 Ky., 599; Ill. Cen. R. Co. v. Lence, 30 R. 988; Sou. Ry. v. Brewer, 32 R., 1374; Pollock on Torts, p. 157; Jaggard on Torts, p. 392 (and other text books); Covington Saw Mill v. Drexilius, 120 Ky., 493. C. Because the law of the place of the injury, and which governs the plaintiff's rights, does not award punitive damages for so-called gross negligence.

4. Because the defendant's theory of the case was not submitted to the jury, and the instructions given are involving and confusing. L. & N. R. Co. v. King, 115 S. W., 196 (to be officially reported).

W. O. BRADLEY and SNODGRASS & DIBRELL for appellee.

POINTS AND AUTHORITIES.

1. Action based on Section 5476, Alabama Code, which places burden of proof on railroad to show no negligence.

2. Reply to plea of negligence sets up affirmative matter in avoidance which was not denied, hence, must be taken for confessed. Section 126, Ky. Civil Code. This renders affirmance absolutely certain.

3. Answer in attempting to plead law of Alabama governing contributory negligence fails to specifically mention the authority and page, hence, not good. Law of foreign State must be plead with same minuteness as any other fact. Therefore there is. in reality, no plea of contributory negligence. Roots v. Merriweather, 8 Bush, 401-2.

4. The answer does not reply upon any law of Alabama which disallows punitive damages (appellee contending that there is no such law), and, hence can not now be relied on. Chesapeake & N. R. v. Venable, 111 Ky., 47.

5. The ringing the bell or sounding of the whistle is no answer to charge of negligence, as those signals are not intended as signals to passengers seeking to get on the train, and not likely to be noticed in the confusion of two trains passing each other. Terry v. Louett, 78 N. Y., 378.

6. Protecting friends who go to meet travelers leaving a train are entitled to protection, and railroads owe special obligations to them different from those due the general public. Montgomery & Eufala R. Co. v. Thompson, 77 Ala., 457, and authorities therein cited. See also M. R. R. Co. v. Thompson, 77 Ala.. 448, (54 Am. Rep., 73; McKee v. Mich Cent., 51 Mich., 601, (47 Am. Rep., 596; Galloway v. C., M. & St. Paul R. R., 56 Minn., 346.

Louisville & Nashville R. R. Co. v. Smith.

7. A common duty rests on all persons, artificial and natural, who own real estate on which the public is expressly or impliedly invited to enter, to keep it free from traps or pitfalls. Persons suffering from neglect of such duty is entitled to damages. Montgomery & Eufala R. Co. v. Thompson, 77 Ala., 456.

8. Doctrine of "stop, look and listen" does not apply here, because appellant was under special obligation to protect appellee. Fetter on Carriers, 348, 397, and authorities cited; Warfield v. N. Y. & S. E. R., 8 App. Div. 479, s. c. 40 N. Y. Sup., 783; Pennell v. Nashville S. R., 97 Ala., 298, s. c. 12 Sou., 236; Memphis & R. Co. v. Copeland, 61 Ala., 376.

9. The cases cited by appellant concerning contributory negligence and decided by the Alabama court have reference to persons to whom the company owed not special duty, and who attempted to cross at public highways, etc.

10. The Kentucky cases cited by appellant that appellee was guilty of negligence are inapplicable, except the cases of Brackett's Adm'r v. L. & N. R. Co., 111 S. W., 710, which supports the contention of appellee.

11. Doctrine of Contributory negligence is not applicable, because the contributory negligence pleaded was not the proximate cause of the injury. Fraser v. So. & N. Ala., R. R., 1 Sou. 89-90 (Ala.); Thompson v. Duncan, 76 Ala., 334; Cent. of Ga. R. Co. v. Hyatt, 151 Ala., 363; Sou. R. R. Co. v. Jones, 143 Ala., 334; 7 Am & Eng. Enc. of Law, 2nd Ed., 381; Sav. & Mem. R. R. Co. v. Shear, 58 Ala., 672; Wilson v. L. & N. R. R., 85 Ala,, 269; C. & W. R. R. Co. v. Bradford, 86 Ala., 574; N. B. S. T. R. Co. v. Calderwood, 89 Ala., 274; So. & N. Ala. R. R. Co. v. Donovan, 4 Sou., 142 (Ala.); Kan. City, M. & B. R. Co. v. Lackey, 21 Sou. 447; Beach on Contributory Negligence, Secs. 24 and 31; Fairbanks v. Kerr, 70 Penna. State, 86 (10 Am. Rep. 664.).

12. Gross negligence has been in Alabama held to be equivalent to wantonness or willfulness. Birm., L. & P. Co. v. Nolan, 134 Ala., 329; A. G. S. R. v. Arnold, 63 Ala., 226; Seeds Case, 115 Ala., 670.

13. Where negligence is gross, wanton, reckless or willful, contributory negligence does not excuse the company. A. G. S. R. Co. v. Guest, 144 Ala., 373; A. P. R. Co. v. ——————, 9 Sou., 231 (Ala.).

14. Where the company knows that persons are in the habit of congregating at, or near, a depot platform, or that there is a likelihood of persons congregating on the track, it is its duty to guard against conflicting injury or death. A. G. S. R. Co. v. Guest, 144 Ala., 379; L. & N. R. Co. v. Lowe, 80 S. W., 769, and authorities cited (Ky.); L. & N. R. Co. v. Brown, 107 S W., 312 (Ky.);

Louisville & Nashville R. R. Co. v. Smith.

C. & O. R. Co. v. Nipp's Adm'r, 100 S. W., 247 (Ky.); Rader's
Adm'r v. L. & N. R. R. Co., 104 S. W. 774 (Ky.); L. & N. R. R.
Co. v. Schuster, 10 Ky. Law Rep.. 65; Conley v. C. R. R., 89 Ky.,
402; S. W. R. R. Co. v. Meadows, 95 Ala., 137; L. & N. R. R. Co.
v. Popp, 96 Ky., 99.

15. Necessary to keep a lookout at all such places. Shelby's
Adm'r v. Cin'ti, etc., R. Co., 85 Ky., 224; L. & N. R. R. Co. v.
Lowe, 80 S. W, 769 (Ky.); L. & N. R. R. Co. v. Popp, 96 Ky., 99;
Same v. Veech, 112 S. W., 870 (Ky.); C. & O. R. Co. v. Nipp's
Adm'r, 100 S. W., 274 (Ky.); Rader's Adm'r v. L. & N. R. R.
Co., 104 S. W., 774 (Ky.).

16. Where company knows public habitually uses its track in
populous community as a footway, so that at any moment persons
may be expected to be found thereon, such knowlede is equivalent to seeing them there. I. C. R. Co. v. Murphy, 97 S. W., 730
(Ky.); L. & N. R. Co. v. McNary, 108 S. W., 899 (Ky.).

17. The railroad company's acting, or failing to act, under
circumstances known to it that its conduct is likely to result
in injury, held to be reckless, indifferent, and the injury wantonly inflicted. Mobile, J. & R. C. R. Co. v. Smith, 151 Ala., 131

18. If likelihood to safty of passerby is known to person in
control of train, and through reckless indifference he consciously
and intentionally causes a train to run over a crossing at a reckless rate of speed, same amounts to wantonness, and has been
uniformly so held. M. & C. R. Co. v. Martin, 117 Ala., 376. 382
(23 Sou., 231); L. & N. R. Co. v. Webb, 97 Ala., 308 (12 Sou.
374); Birm. R'y & Elec. Co. v. Baker, 132 Ala., 507 (31 Sou.
618); Highland Ave. & Belt R. Co. v. Robbins, 124 Ala.. 113 (27
Sou., 432, 82 Am. State, 135); Sou. R. Co. v. Crenshaw, 136 Ala.,
573 (34 Sou., 913); Haley v. K. C. & M. B. R. Co., 113 Ala.. 640
(21 Sou., 357).

19. All that is meant by wanton, willful or intentional negligence is the conscious failure on the part of the defendant's
servants to use reasonable care to avoid injury after discovering
the danger of plaintiff. An intent to injure is not essential on
the part of defendant's servants, notwithstanding contributory
negligence. It is enough if such wantonness and recklessness as
to probable consequences on the part of the servant as implies
willingness to inflict, or indifference as to whether injury is inflicted A. G. S. R. Co. v. Williams, 104 Ala., 230.

20. That appellant is responsible, and that contributory negligence can not be pleaded in this case, see positive opinions in
C., N. O. & T. P. R. Co. v. Thompson, 64 Miss., 589; Nichols' Adm'r
v. W. O. & W. R. Co., 83 Va., 9 (55 S. E., 117); Brackett's Adm'r
v. L. & N. R. Co., 111 S. W., 710.

21. To constitute contributory negligence the plaintiff must have a knowledge of the danger to which he is expcsed. Beach on Contributory Negligence, Sec. 36; City of Henderson v. O'Haloran, 70 S. W., 664 (Ky.).

22. It was duty of appellant to provide appellee reasonably safe approach to passenger train, and operating cars on a switch between depot and assenger train is negligence. The road should be free from all obstruction when a passenger train stops at a station. A. T. & S. F. R. Co. v. Holloway, 80 Pac. Rep. 31; Terry v. Joulett, 78 N. Y., 378.

23. That punitive damages are authorized in this case by the law, see Thompson on Negligence, Secs. 19, 20, 22 and page 899; Columbus R. Co. v. Bridges, 86 Ala., 448; Patterson v. So. & R. Co., 89 Ala., 318; Ala., etc., Co. v. Arnold, 80 Ala., 600; Kilkinson v. Searcy, 76 Ala., 176; 86 Ala., 406; 63 Ala., 266; 99 Ala., 314.

24. In the latter case it was held that the injury need not be willful. Ala., etc., Co. v. Hill, 90 Ala., 71; 125 Ala., 384; Sou. R'y Co. v. Hawkins, 28 Ky. Law Rep., 366; I. C. R. Co. v. Lence, 30 Ky. Law Rep., 988; MeHenry Coal Co. v. Snedden, 98 Ky., 686; L & N. R. Co. v. Kingman, 18 Ky., 836; Sou. R'y Co. v. Brewer, 32 Ky. Law Rep., 1374; Sutherland on Damages, Vol. 1, 724; Hutchison on Carriers, Sec. 1436; Sherman & Redfield on Negligence, Vol. 2, Sec. 748.

Opinion of the Court by Judge Carroll— Affirming.

The appellee, Smith, at Blount Springs, Ala., while on his way to the depot from which passengers got on and off trains, was caught between the bumpers of the cabooses on two trains on the siding between the depot and the passenger platform. Both of his hands were crushed so badly that his right hand had to be amputated and his left hand is practically useless. To recover damages for the injuries sustained he brought this action, and upon a trial before a jury was awarded $12,500.

A reversal is asked upon four grounds: First, that under the laws of Alabama the plaintiff was guilty of contributory negligence in endeavoring to pass between the trains, which were attached to engines with steam up, and therefore the defendant's motion for a peremptory instruction should have been sustained; second, that the court erred in instructing the jury that they might find for the plaintiff, Smith, notwithstanding his contributory negligence, if they believed that when he came in peril from the trains the employes of the company in charge of the trains could, by the exercise of ordinary care, have discovered his peril and by ordinary care have prevented his injury; third, that the court erred in allowing the jury to award punitive damages if they found the defendant guilty of gross negligence; fourth, that the company's theory of its defense was not submitted to the jury, and the instructions given are involved in confusion.

The evidence upon all material points is conflicting but with the weight of it on any issue we are not particularly concerned, as the jury have the exclusive right, in cases like this, to decide controverted questions of fact. Therefore, having in mind only the controlling facts, and without attempting to set out the testimony in detail, we may say that the evidence is, in substance, as follows: Blount Springs is a small village immediately on the line of the appellant's railroad, and at the time of the injuries complained of it was frequented by a number of people who went there to visit the springs in the neighborhood. The appellee, a native of Texas, arrived in Blount Springs for the first time on the morning of July 22, 1907, and spent the day in and around the hotel and the village. About 5:40 in the afternoon he started on his way to the passenger platform for the purpose of meeting a friend he was expecting on the northbound Decatur passenger train that was due to arrive about the time he went to the station. The railroad

at Blount Springs runs north and south, and on the
east side of the road is situated the depot, the houses
that constitute the village, and the springs. The
track nearest to the depot is a long siding, and between this siding and the main track is the platform
used by passengers in getting on and off trains standing on the main track.

At the time appellee started to go to this platform
there were on the siding four trains. One of these
trains, known as No. 12, was a long freight, headed
north, that went in on the south end of the siding,
and pulled up until its caboose was opposite the depot
and then stopped. Soon thereafter No. 21, known as
the "water train," consisting of an engine, two cars,
and a caboose, backed in on the siding from the south
end, and stopped with its caboose some 30 to 60 feet
from the caboose of train No. 12 thereby leaving a
space of that distance between the two cabooses immediately in front of the depot, through which persons going to and from the passenger train to the
depot might pass. Shortly after the water train
had backed in, a long freight train, known as No. 19,
going south, also backed in on the south end of the
siding, and stopped with its caboose some 40 to 80
feet from the engine of the water train. After this,
passenger train No. 8, going north, also ran partially
in on the south end of the siding, but could not go
far enough to clear the main track on account of the
freight trains. About the time that passenger train
No. 8 went in on the siding, passenger train No. 5,
going south, came up on the main track, and stopped
in front of the depot to permit passengers to get on
and off.

With the four trains on the siding, and the spaces
before mentioned that had been left between them,

passenger train No. 5 going south could not pass passenger train No. 8 standing partially on the south end of the siding and partially on the main track. So that, when passenger train No. 5 started on its journey south, signals were given to the engineers on the water train and on train No. 19 to close up the spaces, in order that passenger train No. 8 might pull far enough in on the siding to allow passenger train No. 5 to pass in safety. But before the space between the cabooses in front of the depot was closed at all by the moving of the water train, a number of passengers and people had passed between the cabooses going to and from the train and the platform. Appellee was not at the depot or observing the trains when the space between the cabooses was 30 to 60 feet, or when the signals to close the space were given, or when the water train started back, but about the time he reached the depot on his way to the platform the caboose of the water train had been backed to within 3 to 10 feet of the caboose of train No. 12, and was standing still, and the caboose of train No. 19 had been backed close to the engine of the water train.

Just as appellee, who stopped, looked, and listened to ascertain if the passage was safe, stepped on the siding, the water train suddenly backed, and he was caught between its caboose and the caboose on train No. 19, which had never moved its position after going on the siding. The evidence is very satisfactory that when the water train by backing closed up the original space of 30 to 60 feet between it and train No. 19 to a distance of from 3 to 10 feet, it stopped for a few minutes, and it may be inferred from the testimony that the trainmen did not intend, at this time, to run it any closer to the caboose of train No. 19, and that

·the sudden movement of the water train that caught
appellee was caused by the slack running out of train
No. 21, the caboose of which had been stopped within
a few feet of the engine of the water train, and striking the engine of the water train, thereby shoving it
and its cars back.

At the moment appellee was injured the trainmen
who were giving the signals that moved the water
train and train No. 19, were standing between the siding and the main track, but before this, and when the
passengers from No. 5 were being discharged and the
signals to close the space were about to be given,
these trainmen, and probably others, notified people
to get out of the way; that the space would be closed.
Whether or not any persons were on the rear platform of the caboose of the water train, or the caboose
of train No. 12, when appellee was injured is sharply
disputed; the evidence for the company being that one
brakeman was on the rear platform of the water train
caboose, and one brakeman on the rear platform of
the caboose of train No. 12, while the evidence for the
appellee is that there was no brakeman at that time
on either of these cabooses. The evidence also conduces to show that, just as the cabooses came together
one of the trainmen, and probably a spectator,
holloed at appellee in an effort to warn him of his
danger, but it was too late.

From this statement it may be summarized that
there was evidence sufficient to sustain the verdict
conducing to show: (1) That when the trains were
put on the siding, and until passenger train No. 5
started, there was a space of from 30 to 60 feet in
front of the depot between the cabooses, left for the
purpose of permitting persons to go to and from
the depot to the passenger train; (2) that when pas-

senger train No. 5 started, it was intended to close the space of 40 to 80 feet between the caboose of train No. 19 and the engine of the water train, and to partially at least close the space in front of the depot between the caboose of the water train and the caboose of train No. 12, so that No. 8 might clear the main track and allow No. 5 to pass; (3) that when the caboose of the water train came within 3 to 10 feet of the caboose of train No. 12, the water train stopped, and after stopping for a few minutes it was put in motion, and its caboose caused to hit the caboose of train No. 12; (4) that at the time Smith was injured the bells on the engine of train No. 19 and on the engine of the water train were ringing; (5) that train No. 8, on which appellee expected the person he went to the depot to meet, would have reached the depot platform a few min-utes after he started to go to the platform; (6) that appellee did not know anything about the movements of the trains until he went to the depot to cross, and then there was a space in front of the depot of 3 to 10 feet between the cabooses of train No. 12 and the water train, both of which were standing still; (7) that before appellee went between the cabooses, he stopped, looked, and listened to ascertain if it would be safe to cross, and had no warning or notice that it would not.

Upon these facts the court gave to the jury the following instructions:

"No. 1. The court instructs the jury that the law is for the plaintiff, and they should so find, unless they shall believe from the evidence that, before the defendant moved its trains, or either of them, which were standing on the passing switch at Blount Springs, Ala., at the time mentioned in the petition

to close the passageway across the said switch between the ends of its two freight trains then standing
on said switch track, the employes of the defendant
in charge of the train by which plaintiff was injured
exercised ordinary care to give timely and reasonably
sufficient notice that the train was about to be moved
to close the said passageway, and exercised ordinary
care to prevent injury to the plaintiff from the moving train, unless they shall further believe from the
evidence that the plaintiff himself was negligent, and
thereby helped to cause or bring about his injuries;
that but for his own negligence, if any there was, he
would not have been injured.

"No. 2.   But if the defendant did give timely and
reasonable notice, as mentioned in instruction No. 1,
that the passway between the said trains was about
to be closed by backing one or both of said trains,
and did exercise ordinary care to prevent injury to
the plaintiff from the moving train, the law is for the
defendant, and so they should find.

"No. 3.   It was the duty of the plaintiff, before he
entered upon the passway between the said two trains,
to exercise ordinary care for his own safety, and to
stop and look and listen to ascertain whether he could
cross the track without injury from the said trains;
and, if he failed to discharge either of these duties,
and by reason of such failure he helped to cause or
bring about the injuries of which he complains, and
he would not have been injured but for his contributory negligence in that respect, then the law is for
the defendant, and so they should find, even though
you may believe from the evidence that the defendant
was negligent in failing to give notice of the fact
that the train was about to be backed to close the
passageway, if such is the fact, unless you shall

further believe from the evidence that when the plaintiff came in peril from the train, the employes of the defendant in charge of the train could, by the exercise of ordinary care, have discovered his peril, and by ordinary care have prevented his injury.

"No. 4. If you find for the plaintiff, you should find in such a sum as will reasonably and fairly compensate him for any pain and suffering, mental and physical, caused him by his injuries, and for any pain and suffering which it is reasonably certain from the evidence he will endure in the future as a result of his injuries, and for any permanent reduction in his power to earn money directly resulting from his injuries; and, if you shall believe from the evidence that his injuries were caused by the gross negligence of the defendant, then you may in your discretion find in such a further or additional sum as you may think right and proper under the evidence, and on these instructions, not exceeding in all the sum of $50,000, the amount claimed in the petition. If you find for the defendant, you will say so, and no more.

"No. 5. Ordinary care means the degree of care usually observed by ordinarily careful and prudent persons under the same or similar circumstances. Negligence means a failure to observe ordinary care. Gross negligence means a failure to observe slight care. Contributory negligence means a failure upon the part of the plaintiff, if he did so fail, to observe care for his own safety, as mentioned in instruction No. 3, and by reason of such failure he helped to cause or bring about his injuries, and when but for such failure he would not have been injured."

Under the law of this state, as settled in more than one opinion of this court, the facts of this case authorized the trial court to instruct the jury as it did, and warranted the jury in finding a verdict in favor of Smith and assessing the damages at the amount awarded. But, as the injuries occurred in the state of Alabama, the right of Smith to recover, and the propriety of the instructions given, is, in the absence of any statutory law in that state on the subject, to be determined by the laws of that state as declared by its Supreme Court. L. & N. R. Co. v. Whitlow, 43 S. W. 711, 19 Ky. Law Rep. 1931, 41 L. R. A. 614; Illinois Central R. Co. v. Jordan, 117 Ky. 512, 78 S. W. 426, 25 Ky. Law Rep. 1610; L. & N. R. Co. v. Graham, 98 Ky. 688, 34 S. W. 229, 17 Ky. Law Rep. 1229; L. N. R. Co. v. Harmon, 64 S. W. 640, 23 Ky. Law Rep. 871; L. & N. R. Co. v. Wyatt, 93 S. W. 601, 29 Ky. Law Rep. 437; L. & N. R. Co. v. Keiffer, 113 S. W. 433. That court has frequently considered questions like the one involved in this case, and counsel in support of their respective contentions have furnished us with an ample array of authorities. And so we will proceed to examine these decisions and apply them to the evidence and the law as given by the trial judge, for the purpose of ascertaining whether or not the errors assigned are well taken.

Taking up, first, the question of contributory negligence:

The theory of the company is that at the time appellee went through the opening the space between the two cabooses was not over three feet, and that if the water train was not at that time moving, it had only stopped a moment before, and appellee from his position could and should have known that the trains were closing up the space; that as there was then no passenger train at the platform, and the passenger train upon which appellee expected his friend to arrive was on the siding some distance off, appellee in attempting to cross as he did went into an obviously dangerous place, which, if he desired to cross, he could have avoided by crossing on the platform of one of the cabooses. It may be conceded that, if we should accept as true this view of the case, there would be much force in the argument that the appellee was guilty of such contributory negligence as authorized a direction to the jury, under the law as expounded by the Supreme Court of Alabama, to find a verdict for the company.

In Pannell v. Nashville, F. & S. R. Co., 97 Ala. 298, 12 South 236, the facts were as follows: Several parrallel tracks crossed streets in a town, and on one of these tracks cars had been placed for the purpose of being loaded and unloaded, but at the crossing a space of 15 or 20 feet was left between the cars for the use of the public. The cars had been placed in this way on the day preceding the accident, and Pannell, the injured party, who resided near the crossing, was entirely familiar with the location of the cars. On the day after the cars had been so placed, he passed through this opening, but on his return in about 30 minutes the opening had been materially diminished by an engine that was moving the cars, and in attempting to pass through he was caught between the drawheads and crushed. At the time the cars were placed on the track they were not connected with any engine, nor in charge of any employe, and no notice that the company intended to move them was given until shortly before the accident, when an engine was attached to the cars, and they were shifted about. In the course of the opinion the court said: "When Pannell crossed the track going west, the opening at the crossing was 15 or 20 or more feet, and the cars on either side were stationary. Everything about the crossing indicated perfect security in traveling the highway. When he returned appearances had greatly changed. The lumber cars left on the north side of the crossing had been moved so as to nearly block up the highway. Only a small opening was left. This should have been a warning to him that all was not well. He should have looked and listened. He was clearly guilty of contributory negligence in attempting, under the circumstances, to pass through the narrow opening. Had he looked at any time after passing the main track, save a narrow space hidden by a stack of shingles, he could not have failed to see the engine on the spur track with steam up.''

In L. & N. R. R. Co. v. Crawford, 89 Ala. 244, 8 South. 243, 244, 245, a watchman while in the discharge of his duties was injured by a switch engine pushing a box car. In announcing the general rule the court said: ''It is culpable negligence to cross the track of a railroad at a highway crossing without looking in every direction that the rails run to ascertain whether a train is approaching. If a party rushes into danger which by ordinary care he could have seen and avoided, no rule of law or justice can be invoked to compensate him for any injury he may receive. He must take care, and so must the other party. * * * We regard the question as settled in Alabama by our rulings cited above, and that a failure to employ the senses on approaching a railroad crossing, when such employment would insure safety, is as a matter of law contributory negligence, and a complete defense to a suit for injuries sustained by the negligent handling of a railroad train, unless such negligence was so reckless or wanton as to be in law the equivalent of wilful or intentional. * * * No man should put himself in peril; and, if he negligently does so, the duty of active effort to avert injury is as binding on him as is the defendant corporation's duty to do all in its power to extricate him.   If he fails in this, when such effort would probably save him from harm, he cannot be heard to complain that the defendant failed to do for him what he neglected to do for himself.   We have stated the duty required of mere travelers.''

In East Tennessee, Virginia & Georgia R. Co. v. Kornegay, 92 Ala. 228, 9 South. 557, Kornegay was injured while on his way to a depot to see a person who was a passenger on an east-bound train that had just come in.   This train stopped on the main track, and a west-bound train took the side track, and its engine was standing still across a dirt road.   Kornegay passed by the side of the engine and walked parallel with the track, and then turned and stepped on the side track in the direction of the east-bound train, which was still standing on the main track.   Just as his foot touched the crossing on the side track, he was knocked down by the engine of the west-bound train and injured.   The court said: ''It appears from Kornegay's own testimony that he was guilty of negligence proximately contributing to the injury.   It is plain that he undertook to cross the railroad track without stopping or looking or listening to ascertain if a train was approaching.   He says himself that he did not stop or look.   When he passed the engine, it was standing still on a downgrade.   It appeared from the testimony that the engine could not have been put in motion without making a noise, which the plaintiff must have heard if he had been listening.   He was not in apparent danger until he turned and stepped on the side track.   He was bound to look and listen before attempting to cross the track.   His neglect of this duty avoids his right of recovery, in the absence of evidence tending to show that the defendant was guilty of negligence so reckless or wanton as to be in law the equivalent of wilful or intentional wrong."

In each of these cases the rule is announced that the failure to stop and look and listen before crossing a railroad track is such contributory negligence as will defeat a recovery, in the absence of evidence showing that the company was guilty of reckless or wanton negligence. But in neither of them are the facts similar to those upon which the appellee rests his case. If we should assume that the railroad company in Alabama owed no higher duty to passengers or persons occupying the relation of appellee than it does to travelers at a public crossing, we should nevertheless feel obliged to hold that under the Alabama rule the appellee was not guilty of such contributory negligence as would defeat a recovery. The evidence introduced in his behalf shows that he was not negligent or inattentive, but that, on the contrary, before attempting to cross, he exercised ordinary care for his own safety by stopping and looking and listening. The appellee in attempting to go to the passenger platform was not a trespasser. He had a right to go there; and, although the company did not owe him the high duty attaching to a passenger, it did owe him the duty of exercising ordinary care for his safety. Montgomery & Eufaula Ry. Co. v. Thompson, 77 Ala. 448, 54 Am. Rep. 72; Berry v. L. & N. R. Co., 109 Ky. 727, 60 S. W. 699, 22 Ky. Law Rep. 1410; C. & O. Ry. Co. v. Meyer, 119 S. W. 183; Hutchinson on Carriers (3d Ed.) Sec. 991; Thompson on Negligence, Sections 2685, 2686.

The fact that the train upon which he was expecting his friend was not then standing on the main track at the depot for the purpose of discharging passengers is a matter of small moment, as it was only a short distance off on the siding, and might reasonably be expected to reach the depot in a few minutes, and was in fact due to arrive. A person going to the train to assist or accompany or receive a passenger need not wait until the train actually arrives before going on the platform, in order to avail himself of the principles of law that require the carrier to exercise ordinary care for his protection and safety. He may go to the platform when he sees the train approaching, or when it is reasonably near, or at the time he believes it should arrive. This being so, when appellee went to the depot, and saw an opening between the two cabooses amply wide for passage to the platform; saw other persons going through it; saw the trains standing still—he had the right to assume that the opening through which he attempted to pass had been purposely left there to permit persons to go to and from the depot and platform. The fact that the opening was there was an invitation to avail himself of it to cross. When an opening like this is left in a place like this, it is the duty of the railroad company to exercise ordinary care to prevent injury to persons rightfully using it, and this duty, under circumstances like those proven in this case, is not fulfilled by ringing engine bells or sounding whistles.

The duty of the company in this respect is not discharged until, or unless, it has given reasonably sufficient warning to the public having the right to use the passway that it is about to be closed; and whether or not it performed its duty in this particular was in this case a question for the jury. Tested by the Alabama rule, the appellee was not guilty of such contributory negligence as would defeat a recovery, and under the facts it was not necessary to show that the company was guilty of reckless or wanton conduct that would be in law the equivalent of willful or intentional wrong. This principle is only to be applied when it is attempted to. avoid the consequences of a state of facts that would amount to such contributory negligence as would defeat a recovery in the absence of willful or intentional wrongdoing on the part of the company. When the injured person has not been guilty of this character of contributory negligence, it is not essential under the Alabama law that the company should be guilty of willful or intentional wrongdoing before he can recover. The Kentucky Cases of Southern Railway Co. v. Clarke, 105 S. W. 384, 32 Ky. Law Rep. 69, 13 L. R. A. (N. S.) 1071, Southern Railway Co. v. Thomas, 92 S. W. 578, 29 Ky. Law Rep. 79, and Brackett's Adm'r v. L. &. N. R. Co., 111 S. W. 710, 33 Ky. Law Rep. 921, 19 L. R. A. (N. S.) 558, cited by counsel, are not in conflict with the views we have expressed on the subject of contributory negligence. On the contrary, they are in harmony with them.

The next argument presented as grounds for reversal is that the court erred in instructing the jury that, if they believed appellee would not have been injured except for his contributory negligence, they should find for the company, "unless they further believe from the evidence that when he came in peril from the trains, the employes of the defendant in charge of the train could, by the exercise of ordinary care, have discovered his peril, and by ordinary care have prevented his injury." The objection raised to this instruction is that there was no evidence upon which to base the qualifying clause relating to the discovery of the peril in which appellee was placed.

This objection is not well taken. Looking at the instruction from the viewpoint that it was the duty of the company to give reasonably sufficient notice to warn persons not to use the passway, the instruction was proper. We have found that the ringing of the bells was not sufficient notice, and in effect that the full measure of the company's duty required that some of its employes should have been stationed at the opening to notify appellee and others not to use it. It is true that the evidence for the company shows that it did have employes stationed at suitable places to perform this duty, but on the other hand the evidence for appellee shows that it did not.

With this conflict in the evidence it was the duty of the court to submit to the jury the theory of each of the litigants, and to do this the court gave this instruction. If the company had exercised the degree of care required under the circumstances, the peril of appellee could have been discovered in time to prevent the injury, as the employes, if located where they should have been, could have warned appellee not to cross. This view of the law was expressed in Louisville Railway Company v. Hudgins, 124 Ky. 79, 98 S. W. 276, 30 Ky. Law Rep. 316, 7 L. R. A. (N. S.) 152, where it was said, in answer to a similar objection to a like instruction: "It was the duty of appellee when she started to cross the tracks to exercise ordinary care for her own safety; but, although she failed to do this, and her failure may have contributed to such an extent to bring about the injury of which she complains that it would not have happened except for her failure to exercise this degree of care, this will not relieve the appellant of liability if the persons in charge of the car that struck her could, by the exercise of ordinary care, have discovered the peril appellee was in, and by the exercise of ordinary care have prevented the injury to her. It was the duty of the motorman in charge of the car at this point and place to keep a sharp lookout for persons alighting from the car, and who might be expected to cross the street immediately behind it, and to have his car under such control as that he might stop it at a moment's warning; and it is manifest that, if the motorman had exercised this degree of care, he could and should have discovered the appellee's peril in time to have prevented injuring her. It was therefore entirely proper, under the facts of this case, to qualify the instruction as to contributory neglect as was done.''

Did the court err in allowing the jury to award punitive damages if they found the defendant guilty of gross negligence? A careful examination of the Alabama cases introduced in evidence by appellant fails to disclose that that court has ever considered the question when punitive or exemplary damage may be awarded. The question of what constitutes gross negligence is presented in more than one decision, but it always came up in a discussion of the law of contributory negligence, and when the court was indicating the character of negligence on the part of the defendant that would authorize a recovery by the plaintiff notwithstanding he was guilty of negligence. If the Alabama court had defined the class of cases in which punitive damages might be allowed, and the character of negligence that would authorize a jury to award it, we would feel bound to follow its ruling, although it might not conform to our decisions on the subject, as the measure of damages recoverable under the law of the place where the injury occurred must control.

But, in the absence of decisions from the Alabama court, we will assume that the rule adopted in this state applies in Alabama, or would be applied if the question came up. This principle was laid down in Chesapeake & Nashville R. Co. v. Venable, 111 Ky. 41, 63 S. W. 35, 23 Ky. Law Rep. 427, where the court said: "Where a party seeks to recover or defend under a foreign law, such law must be pleaded and proved like any other fact; but, in the absence of averment and proof, the rule is that foreign states, whose system of jurisprudence is derived from the same source as our own, are presumed to be governed by the same law." To the same effect is Murray v. L. & N. R. Co., 110 S. W. 334, 33 Ky. Law Rep. 545. Conceding that the law is as we have announced, the argument is yet made that, under the law as declared and administered in this state, the evidence did not warrant exemplary damages, and the instruction submitting this issue was not only unauthorized, but defective in form. This court has repeatedly ruled that gross negligence is the absence of slight care, and that, in personal injury cases where the negligence from which the injury results is gross, punitive damages may be allowed.

Without again stating the facts, it is sufficient to say there was ample evidence that the appellant failed to exercise the slightest degree of care for the safety of appellee, and that he was injured by its reckless disregard of the duty it owed him. Nor is the instruction upon this subject open to meritorious criticism. It told the jury that they might in their discretion allow punitive damages. The argument that the words "or may not," after the words "then you may," should have been inserted is entirely too technical to be seriously considered; nor is it sustained by the opinion in Illinois Central R. Co. v. Houchins, 121 Ky. 526, 89 S. W. 530, 28 Ky. Law Rep. 499, 1 L. R. A. (N. S.) 375, 123 Am. St. Rep. 205. The addition of these words might slightly improve the verbiage of the instruction, but would make no change in its substance. Whether or not an instruction upon the subject of gross negligence or exemplary damages should be given is often a close one. Frequently, when the verdict appears to be excessive, or the evidence of gross negligence is not satisfactory, we have, as in the Houchins Case, ordered a new trial, and pointed out the impropriety of submitting this question. But when there is evidence that the injury was caused by conduct that amounted to a reckless disregard of human life, it is the settled law in this state that an instruction upon this subject is proper. Lexington R. Co. v. Fain, 80 S. W. 463, 25 Ky. Law Rep. 2243; Southern Ry. Co. v. Goddard, 121 Ky. 567, 89 S. W. 675, 28 Ky. Law Rep. 523; L. & N. R. Co. v. Mount, 125 Ky. 599, 101 S. W. 1182, 31 Ky. Law Rep. 210.

But, aside from all this, it is apparent that the jury did not award appellee more than fair compensation. At the time of his injury he was 44 years of age, a strong vigorous man of good health and industrious habits, in the prime of life and usefulness, earning by his labor and brains an annual income of as much as $2,000. But now he is virtually a physical wreck. One hand is gone; the other is useless. He cannot follow any wage-earning occupation or business in which the hand is an essential member of the body—and there are few in which it is not. So that, taking into consideration his age, physical condition, and earning capacity, it cannot be said that the amount awarded was more than reasonable compensation for the mental and physical suffering that he has already undergone and the permanent impairment of his power to earn money.

The contention that the instructions are involved and difficult to understand is not well founded. They presented to the jury the law of the case in simple and concise language.

Nor did the court fail in the instructions to submit appellant's defense. It was fully set out in instruction No. 3.

A careful examination of the record and the reasons urged for reversal convince us that no substantial error was committed to the prejudice of the appellant, and the judgment of the lower court is affirmed.

CASE 61.—ACTION BY THE BOARD OF TRUSTEES OF THE
COLUMBIA GRADED COMMON SCHOOL AGAINST
W. F. JEFFRIES AND OTHERS IN WHICH CERTAIN
OTHER PERSONS INTERVENED.—November 19,
1909.

Jeffries, &c. v. Board of Trustees, &c.

Appeal from Adair Circuit Court.

H. C. BAKER, Circuit Judge.

Judgment for plaintiffs, defendants appeal.—Affirmed.

1. Schools and School Districts—"Common Schools"—Graded
    schools are "common schools."
2. . Elections—Qualification of Voters—Sex—School Elections.—
    Ky. St. 1909, Secs. 4464-4500a, relating to graded common
    schools, provides no qualification for voters in graded school
    district elections except the qualification provided generally
    for school elections, in view of which it has been held that
    the qualifications are the same, and that under section 4458,
    providing that, in a common school district election to levy
    a district tax for common schools, any resident widow or
    spinster, who is a taxpayer, or who has children within school
    ages, may vote, such persons may vote upon the question of
    tax for a graded school in a proposed graded common school
    district. Act March 24, 1908 (Acts 1908, p. 133, c. 56), estab-
    lishes in some particulars a radical departure from the pre-
    existing system, but without any design to render the sys-
    tem as a whole inharmonious. and provides that graded com-
    mon school districts operating under special charter or es-
    tablished by popular vote in school districts operating in mu-
    nicipal districts established under special charter, and supple-
    menting the state school fund by a local tax of a certain
    amount, shall retain their present boundaries and be exempt
    from the provisions of the act. Held, that the effect of the
    prohibition of the act of 1908 was to re-enact sections 4464-
    4500a as part thereof, and the graded common school districts
    operating under special charter or established by popular vote

remained unaffected by the later law in their boundaries, government, and regulation; but the later act, providing that all resident males over 21 years of age shall have the right to vote at elections, women are no longer entitled to vote in graded common school elections.

3. Schools and School Districts—Levy of Tax—School Election—Manner of Voting.—Ky. St. 1909, Sec. 4467, relating to the voting upon the question of establishing a graded common school and a tax to maintain it, provides that on the day set apart for the election the officers shall open a poll and propound to each voter the question, "Are you against or for the graded common school tax?" and his vote shall be recorded for or against the same as he may direct, which has been held to require a viva voce vote on the subject of taxation. Act March 24, 1908 (Acts 1908, p. 133, c. 56), which in effect re-enacted the former act, as a part of the latter act, makes no provision as to how the votes shall be taken, whether by ballot or otherwise though in an election for trustees, voting by special ballot and the manner of preparing and furnishing the ballots are all provided for. Held, that the intent was that the vote on the question of the tax should be viva voce.

4 Schools and School Districts—School Election—Irregularities. —Ky. St. 1909, Sec. 4467 (Russell's St. Sec. 5739), provides that an election upon the question of a tax for the establishing and maintaining of a graded common school there shall be one judge and a clerk. Act March 24, 1908 (Acts 1908, p. 133, c. 56), for the government and regulation of common schools, which re-enacted in effect the former act as a part thereof, provides that two judges and a clerk shall be appointed by the county election commissioners. At such an election the sheriff appointed a judge and clerk, and the county election commissioners ratified the appointment and appointed one additional judge. He failed to act, and his place was filled by another. Held, that, as nothing done by the substitute affected the result, and there being no claim that the regular judge and clerk did not of their own judgment and action do all that the substitute is claimed to have attempted to do, his participation was, at most, a harmless irregularity.

5. Evidence—Judicial Notice—Location of High School.—The court will take notice of the location of the Columbia Male and Female High School building in the town of Columbia.

6 Elections——School Elections—Petition—Sufficiency.—Ky. St. 1909, Sec. 4464, relating to elections upon the question of a tax for the establishing and maintaining of a graded common school, provides that the petition for the election shall indi-

cate with exactness the location and site of the schoolhouse, meaning the schoolhouse that will be provided for the proposed graded common school. Held, that the intent was to settle as nearly as might be the location of the proposed building, and a petition, stating that the 'location of the school house * * * shall be at the building known as the Columbia M. & F. High School, if it can be secured upon terms satisfactory to the trustees who may be elected in said proposed district, or at some other suitable point within the corporate limits of the town of Columbia," was sufficient; the other words of the description being treated as surplusage.

7. Elections—School Elections — Petition—Sufficiency—"Other Expenses Needful in Conducting a Good Graded Common School."— Ky. St. 1909, Sec. 4464, provides for an election upon the question of levying a tax to maintain a graded common school and for erecting or repairing suitable buildings therefor, if necessary. Section 4481 (section 5758) makes it the duty of the district trustees to provide funds for purchasing suitable buildings, or for erecting or repairing them, and for other expenses needful in conducting a good graded common school, and permits them to use such part of the proceeds of the tax as they may deem necessary. Held, that the phrase "and for other expenses needful in conducting a good graded common school" implies the power to rent a suitable building temporarily and until one can be secured or built by the trustees, and a petition for the election, reciting that the proposed tax was to be used for the purpose of maintaining a graded common school and for the erecting, purchasing, leasing, and repairing of suitable buildings therefor if necessary, was no more than the two sections of the statute authorized, meaning that the trustees were to buy a building, if they could, and, if not, to buy a lot and build a house, to repair any buildings bought or built by them, and in the meantime to lease a suitable building for the continuation of the school, and did not render the petition insufficient.

8. Schools and School Districts—District Property—Power of State.—The maintenance of public schools is a state question done in the exercise of the state's sovereign power, and where the state authorized the application of public lands to build an academy for public education, and subsequently let the town sell the academy and lot and use the proceeds in paving its streets, the Legislature could require the town to reimburse the state by buying another lot for common school purposes, and, the town having done so without complaint, its subsequent holding of the title, as required by

Jeffries, &c. v. Board of Trustees, &c.

the Legislature, was a naked trust which the Legislature could end at its will, and it having provided by Ky. St. 1909, Sec. 4484, that the title of all common school property in the limits of a graded common school district organized under the provisions of the act shall be vested in the board of trustees of the school dictrict and empowered them to sell the same if they should think it best, the trustees could convey a good title thereto to their grantees.

9. Schools and School Districts—Purchase of Property—Discretion of Trustees.—The discretion of trustees elected upon the establishment of a graded common school district, as to buying a particular property for the school, which property the petition for election specified should be procured, if expedient, will not be interfered with by the courts, at least in the absence of such proofs of abuse as would be tantamount to fraud.

ROLLIN HURT for appellants.

JAS. GARNETT and W. W. JONES of counsel.

CLASSIFICATION.

1. The location and site of the proposed school house in said district must be stated with exactness in the petition to the County Judge and if this is not done the Court had no jurisdiction to order an election and such an election is void. Kentucky Statutes, Section 4464.

(a) The power to tax is a high Govermental power and where the Legislature grants this power to another tribunal it can only be exercised in strict conformity to the terms in which the power is granted and a departure in any material part will be fatal to the attempt to exrcise it. Campbell County Court v. Taylor, 8 Bush, 208; B. G. & M. R. R. Co. v. Warren County Court, 10 Bush, 724; Doores v. Varnum, &c., 94 Kentucky, 508.

2. The statute confers no power to levy a tax for the purpose of leasing buildings for graded common school purposes. Kentucky Statutes, section 4464; Kentucky Statutes, section 4437.

3. The officers and pretended officers of the election and the partisans of the tax conspired together and fraudulently permitted 8 persons who were not legal voters to vote for said tax and prevented 30 widows and spinsters who were legal voters from voting against the tax—a number more than sufficient to have entirely changed the result and in that way made a false return of the result.

(a)   The ascertainment of the will of the people of a district in relation to a tax proposed to be levied for school purposes is not an election but merely the action of the agency selected by the Legislature to determine when and to what extent the conditional statute shall become operative in the District. Marshall v. Donovan, &c., 10 Bush, 68.

MONTGOMERY & MONTGOMERY attorneys for appellees.

PROPOSITIONS SUBMITTED AND AUTHORITIES CITED.

1.   An election establishing a graded school can not be contested, and technical irregularities will not vititate it.   Patterson v. Knapp, 128 Ky., 474; Clark v. Rogers, 81 Ky., 43.

2.   Such elections can not be questioned collaterally as is attempted here. Hopkins v. Swift, 100 Ky., 14; 98 S. W., 1002.

3.   Burden is on party attacking such election to show that it was void, and necessary facts must be stated.   Trustees Common School District No. 88 v. Garner, &c., 80 Ky., 159; 14 Ky. Law Rep., 240; 24 Ky. Law Rep., 576.

4.   The election was not void. The law was complied with in letter and spirit.   Ky. Statutes, sections 4464, 4467, &c.; Grabbs Amended School law, subsec. 3, section 93, page 58; Grider v. Farmers' & Drovers' Bank, 12 Bush, 333; Anderson v. Winfrey, 85 Ky., 597; 1 Ky Law Rep., 199-274; 10 Ky. Law Rep., 167; 3 Dana, 160; 4. B. M.. 394; Hardin, 104; 1 Monroe, 140; 108 S. W., 289.

5.   The school house and lot involved in this action known as school house in district No. 29, is common school property. The trustees of the town of Columbia have no interest in it. The deed from C. J. Taylor and wife vested the title in the Common School District, No. 29. That part of section 4484, Ky. Statutes, that relates to Seminary property vested in trustees for the purpose of education has no application to this case.

OPINION OF THE COURT BY JUDGE O'REAR—Affirming.

This action was brought by the trustees of the Columbia Graded Common School against the town of Columbia, its trustees, and the board of education of Adair county, to quiet the title of the plaintiffs to the school house and lot in Columbia, which was known as "common school district No. 1" (formerly

No. 29). The town of Columbia is of the fifth class. It was embraced in parts of two school districts. A petition of the requisite number of electors and property holders resident of the two school districts was presented to the county court, asking the submission of the proposition whether the two districts would avail themselves of the provisions of the statutes allowing them to establish, in lieu of the district common school therein, a graded common school, and whether a tax necessary to procure a suitable building should be voted by the electors of the proposed graded school district. The proposition was ordered submitted.

At the election the officers returned, and the canvassing board certified, that both propositions had carried by a majority of the votes cast, and that appellees were elected trustees of the graded school district. The newly elected trustees, deeming the old school building in district No. 1 inadequate, proposed to sell the building, and to buy another. Certain citizens opposed the proposition, claiming that the vote by which the graded school was established was void, as was the vote by which the tax was authorized, and that the election of the trustees was void. They also denied that the trustees, even if the elections were valid, took the title to the school building and lot, or had power to sell it, or to invest the proceeds or any taxes raised to the purchase of the proposed site. The result was that the title of the plaintiffs to the lot they proposed to sell was so clouded that purchasers were deterred from bidding, and the contention of the dissident taxpayers clogged the action of the trustees so as to defeat their purposes. The plaintiffs asked that their title to the lot in question be quieted by the judgment of the court, and inasmuch as the legal title appeared to be vested in the trustees of the town of Columbia, who refused to join in the sale and conveyance, that the lot be sold by the court's commissioner, and the proceeds turned over to the plaintiffs.

The board of education disclaimed any property interest in the subject of controversy, as well as any denial of the plaintiff's title and authority in the premises. The trustees of the town by demurrer raised the question of their title; the facts being set out in the petition. Certain citizens and taxpayers of the proposed school district, who are appellants here, filed their intervening petition, alleging that the trustees of the town would not defend the action, being favorable thereto, and asked permission to defend on behalf of themselves and all other taxpayers concerned. Their petition was allowed. As defense they relied upon certain facts as showing that the elections were void, and that in any event the graded school trustees were not invested with the title to the lot in question. They also assailed the wisdom of the contemplated purchase of the other lot. A general demurrer was sustained to their answer because the facts stated did not present a defense to the cause of action set up in the plaintiff's petition, and, as they declined to plead further, the allegations of the petition were taken as true, and judgment rendered in conformity to its prayer. The trustees of Columbia and the interveners appeal from that judgment.

It is contended by appellants that the election by which the graded school proposition, including the tax proposition, was voted, was so irregular as that it was void. The irregularities relied on are: (1) That the petition of the county court did not show the location of the site of the graded school building with exactness, as required by the statute; (2) that the tax proposition included the leasing of a building, whereas the statute allows only the purchase or erection of a building; (3) that the election submitting the tax and district propositions was not held by secret ballot, whereas it should have been; (4) that the election of trustees was by secret ballot, whereas it should have been viva voce; (5) that one acted as judge of the election without appointment or authority and fraudulently interfered in its conduct; (6) that legally qualified voters were prevented by fraud of the officers of election from voting, who would have voted against the propositions, and others not legally qualified voters were permitted to vote who voted for the propositions, the result of the election being changed by the combined actions referred to. As the facts were pleaded, either in the petition of the plaintiffs, or the answers of the interveners, the question presented was one of law; no issue of facts being raised by the pleadings.

The elections were held under the provisions of article 10 of chapter 113, Ky. St., relating to graded common schools (section 4464 et seq., Carroll's Ky. St. The provisions of that article are part of the common school law of the state, and are part of the original act of 1893 for the government of common schools. Graded schools are common schools. Riggs v. Stevens, 92 Ky. 393, 17 S. W. 1016, 13 Ky. Law Rep. 631; Trustees Harrodsburg v. Harrodsburg Ed. District, 7 S. W. 312, 9 Ky. Law Rep. 605; Williamstown Graded F. S. District v. Webb, 89 Ky. 264, 12 S. W. 298, 11 Ky. Law Rep. 456. In 1908 the Legislature adopted new provisions concerning the establishment of district schools. Act March 24, 1908 (Acts 1908, p. 133, c. 56). Much of the confusion in this case has arisen out of what is conceived to be the different methods of holding elections in common school matters, and the qualifications of voters at elections affecting graded schools. We will consider that question first. The statute does not define the qualifications of the voters at graded school elections. They are alluded to merely as "the legal white voters in said proposed graded common school district." In section 4469, Ky. St. (Carroll's), it is provided: "The graded common schools, when organized as aforesaid, are hereby incorporated, and each of them shall be under the management and control of a board of six trustees. The first board to be elected at the same time and place, and by the same persons who vote at the election for the tax, as provided in sections 4464 and 4467 of this law, and the six persons receiving the highest number of votes shall be declared elected." The allusion to the qualifications of voters contained in section 4464 has already been quoted above. In section 4467 the reference is merely to "each voter who may vote." Under these provisions it was held, in Sisk v. Gardiner, 74 S. W. 686, 25 Ky. Law Rep. 18, that women who were spinsters or widows were legally qualified voters in graded school elections. Nothing in the article concerning graded common schools expressly gave women the right to vote in those elections. The provision of section 4458, Ky. St., was looked to. That provision is contained in the subdivision of article 94 of chapter 113, relating to "district taxation."

In Lee v. Trustees Shepherdsville Graded Common School District No. 4, 88 S. W. 1071, 28 Ky. Law Rep. 55, it was held that an election for graded school trustees and for voting a bonded indebtedness, held between the hours of 1 o'clock p. m. and 6 o'clock

p. m., was a literal compliance with the law, yet there is nothing in article 10 on that subject. Section 4434, Ky. St., being part of article 8 of chapter 113, deal-ing with "district trustees," and as to the time and manner of their election, provides that the election should be viva voce, and held at the schoolhouse of the district between the hours of 1 o'clock p. m. and 6 o'clock p. m. on the day fixed, and that "at this election the qualified voters of the district shall be the electors; and any widow having a child between six and twenty years, and any widow or spinster having a ward between the ages of six and twenty years may also vote." See, also, Moss v. Riley, 102 Ky. 1, 43 S. W. 421, 19 Ky. Law Rep. 993.

It will thus be seen the qualification of voters in graded school elections is that of the electors in com-mon school elections; the term "common schools" be-ing used to designate those common schools which are not graded or high schools. The act of March 24, 1908, supra, entitled "An act for the government and regulation of the common schools of the state," es-tablishes in some particulars a radical departure from the pre-existing system. It relates more espe-cially to the formation and changing of districts, to the unification of the system, to its centralization, and to the maintenance of the schools by county taxation, as well as local and district taxation. It is a revision of important parts of the old system, but without any design to render the system as a whole inharmonious or unnecessarily complicated. In this view we are to consider this proviso in the second section of the act of 1908: "Provided, that any graded common school district that may exist in any educational division or that may hereafter be established accord-ing to law, whether operating under special charter, or established by popular vote, as provided for in the laws relating to the graded common schools, and school districts now operating within municipal districts established and incorporated under special charter and supplementing the state school fund by a local tax of not less than twenty cents on each hundred dollars of assessed valuation of property, shall retain their present boundaries and be exempt from the provisions of this act." That means, we think, that in their boundaries, government, and regulation they are to be unaffected by the new statute. There is no qualification of voters provided for in graded school districts, except by reference to the qualification provided generally for school electors. When the Legislature changed the qualification in the revision of the law governing common schools in 1908, it must be deemed to have done so deliberately, and upon a careful study of the whole system. The effect of the proviso quoted above is the same as if the article on graded common schools (article 10, c. 113, Ky. St.) had been re-enacted as part of the act of 1908—and the special acts referred to in the proviso, also re-enacted, though their construction is not here involved. Sutherland on Statutory Construction, Sec. 154, thus states the rule: "A revision is intended to take the place of the law as previously formulated. By adopting it the Legislature say the same thing, in effect, as when a particular section is amended by the words 'so as to read as follows.' The revision is a substitute. It displaces and repeals the former law as it stood relating to the subjects within its purview. Whatever of the old law is restated in the revision is continued in operation as it may operate in the connection in which it is re-enacted."

The act of 1908 prescribes the qualifications of voters thus: "All male persons over 21 years of age, who shall have resided in a school subdivision for sixty days next before an election, shall have the right to vote at such election." Whatever other construction may be placed upon that language, it leaves no doubt that women are no longer entitled to vote in the general common school elections, however just might appear their claim to the right of suffrage. By the same act it is also provided: "All elections for school trustees shall be by ballot. * * * The officers of said election shall be a clerk and two judges, and shall be appointed by the regular election commissioners in each county." On the subject of voting upon the question of establishing a graded common school and a tax to maintain it, section 4467, Ky. St. (part of art. 10, supra) reads: "The said sheriff or other officer shall appoint a judge and a clerk of said election, who shall take and subscribe to an oath for the faithful performance of his duties.

On the day set apart for the election the officers shall open a poll, and shall propound to each voter who may vote the question: 'Are you against or for the graded common school tax?' and his vote shall be recorded for or against the same as he may direct." It was held, in Lee v. Trustees, supra, that that section required a viva voce vote on the subject of taxation. While the act of 1908 provides for a vote in school districts on the subject of local taxation, nothing is said as to how the vote shall be taken—whether by ballot or otherwise. In the election for trustees, voting by official ballot and the manner of preparing and furnishing the ballot are all provided for. From this, and the omission in the same act as to voting a tax, we infer that the Legislature intended the latter election should be viva voce. So, as there is nothing in the new act in conflict with the provision of section 4467, and particularly as the latter provides for a viva voce election on all questions except that of trustees, we must conclude that the elections in this case were regularly held, in the respect as to the manner of voting.

The act of 1908 provides that officers of election, two judges, and a clerk shall be appointed by the county election commissioners. Section 4467, Ky. St., provides for only one judge and a clerk. In this proceeding the sheriff appointed a judge and clerk. The county election commissioners met and ratified those appointments, and appointed one judge in addition. The latter failing to act, his place was filled by another. It is the last-named person whose presence it is claimed by appellants invalidated the election. We think he was properly there for the purpose of holding the trustee election. Even if he participated under a mistaken notion of authority in the other election, it is not averred that the regular judge and clerk did not of their own judgment and action do all that the outsider is claimed to have attempted to do. Nothing that he did affected the result. At most it would be a harmless irregularity.

The statute required (section 4464, supra) that the petition for the election shall indicate "with exactness" the "location and site of said schoolhouse," meaning the schoolhouse that will be provided for the proposed graded common school. The petition in this case stated on this point as follows: "That the location of the schoolhouse in said district shall be at the building known as the Columbia M. & F. High School if it can be secured upon terms satisfactory to the trustees who may be elected in said proposed district, or at some other suitable point within the corporate limits of the town of Columbia." The graded district proposed in the petition for the election embraced territory not within the town of Columbia, and included all the town. The Columbia M. & F. High School building is the Columbia Male and Female High School building in the town of Columbia, and is a well-known point, the location of which the voters and the court will take notice.

In the nature of things it is impossible to designate finally any point to be selected as the schoolhouse site, as it may not be possible to procure it at all, or upon reasonable terms. The idea is to settle as nearly as may be done the location of the proposed building. It is not contended by appellants that, if the designation had stopped at "M. & F. High School," it would not have been sufficient. That which was added was no more than what would have been implied if it had not been added, except that it indicated that in no event was the building to be located outside the corporate limits of the town. It is now insisted, as one of the grounds of this defense, by appellant, that the "M. & F. High School building" cannot and could not have been acquired by purchase, because the title is held in trust by the Transylvania Presbytery in special trust, the legal title being in divers individuals, some of whom are infants, and the reversion in still others.

If, then, the designation had been of that building as the site, which would confessedly have fulfilled the statute, it would have followed that the trustees could have procured another site as near as they could to the one indicated. Indeed, section 4481, Ky. St., requires: "Said board of trustees shall provide funds for purchasing suitable grounds and buildings, or for

erecting or repairing suitable buildings, and for other
expenses needful in conducting a good graded common school in their graded common school district;
and to this end they may use such part of the proceeds of the said tax as they may deem necessary."
The trustees are proceeding to acquire the identical
building named, and we have no doubt have the power
to do so. Unless insuperable obstacles arise, they
must do so, unless the people in the manner pointed
out by the statute require otherwise. If the title is
held as appellants say, still it may be acquired by
condemnation, it seems, if the proper parties are not
competent and willing to act in the premises. The
other words of the description may be treated as
surplusage.

The petition for election contained this clause with
respect to the use of the proposed tax: "For the purpose of maintaining a graded common school in said
proposed graded common school district, and for the
erecting, purchasing, leasing, and repairing suitable
buildings therefor if necessary." The language of
the statute allowing the tax to be valid is (section
4464, supra): "For erecting, purchasing or repairing
suitable buildings therefor if necessary." It will be
seen that from a reading of section 4481, Ky. St.,
quoted above, it is made the duty of the trustees to
provide a suitable building and to maintain a good
graded common school in their district. We think
the expression "and for other expenses needful in
conducting a good graded common school" implies
the power to rent a suitable building temporarily, and
until one may be bought or built by the trustees. Section 4481 expressly allows the tax voted to be so
applied. Its inclusion in the petition for the election
was nothing more than the two sections (4464 and

4481) read together authorized. It meant that the trustees were to buy a building, the one named, if they could, if not, to buy a lot and build a house in that vicinity; to repair any building bought or built by them; and in the meantime to lease a suitable building for the accommodation of the school. We conclude that the election was valid.

Prior to 1860, under the old seminary grants then in vogue in this commonwealth, there was established a school in Columbia known as "Robertson Academy." It was built with public funds, and for the purpose of public education. In 1860, by an act approved February 27th, of that year (Sess. Acts 1859-1860, p. 328, c. 674), the trustees of the town of Columbia were authorized to sell the Robertson Academy property and apply the proceeds to grading, graveling, and paving the public square of the town. On March 12, 1869, the Legislature passed another act (Acts 1869, p. 220, c. 1954), reciting the foregoing facts, and that the town had sold the Robertson Academy property for $346, and used the proceeds as authorized in the act of 1860, empowered the town to raise by taxation and appropriation of its public funds not exceeding $600 to the purchase of a lot and the building of a schoolhouse in the town "for common school purposes."

The act authorized the trustees of the town to take the title to the lot "to them and their successors in office as and for a common school house for said Columbia district." On April 23, 1869, C. J. Taylor and wife by deed referring to the above act conveyed to the persons named as trustees of the town of Columbia a lot in the town, in consideration of $140, "to have and to hold said lot of ground with all the appurtenances thereunto belonging to said persons,

named as trustees, and their successors in office as
and for the uses and purposes stated in said act."
The common school district comprising the town of
Columbia was then known as "District No. 29" in
Adair county. The Legislature, by an act approved
February 16, 1870 (Acts 1869-70, p. 274, c. 307),
authorized the citizens of district No. 29 in Adair
county to vote a tax to build a schoolhouse for said
district.

Whether the house on the lot now in question
(which is the lot conveyed by Taylor and wife) was
built by the town as a municipal corporation under
the act of 1869, or whether it was built by the tax
authorized to be raised by school district No. 29 by
the act of 1870, does not appear. Nor do we deem it
material. The maintenance of public schools is a
state question, done in the exercise of the state's
sovereign power. When it authorized the appropriation of public lands to build an academy for public
education, and subsequently let the town sell the
academy lot and use the proceeds in paving its
streets, it was competent for the Legislature to require the town to reimburse the state by buying another lot for common school purposes; and as the
town did so, without complaint, its subsequent holding of the title as required by the act was a naked
trust which the Legislature could end at its will. This
was done when the Legislature enacted section 4484,
Ky. St., reading:

"The title to all common school and all county
seminary property, the county court and the board
of trustees of said seminary consenting, in the limits
of any graded common school district organized under the provision of this law, shall be, and the same
is hereby vested in the board of trustees of said

graded common school district, and they are hereby
empowered to sell and convey same, or to use same
for graded common school purposes, as to them shall
seem best; but when county seminary property shall
be appropriated, all pupils of the county shall be permitted to attend such school at such reduced tuition
from what is ordinary as shall be equitable and made
good to them their interest in said seminary property.
It is further provided, that when any graded school
district shall embrace any school property owned or
held in trust by trustees, said trustees, by a majority
of their board, are hereby authorized and empowered
to convey their school property to the trustees of the
graded school, at such price and on such conditions
as may be agreed upon by the trustees of both
parties.''

This is not county seminary property, as that term
is used in the statute.   It was at one time, it seems;
but the Legislature, in the exercise of its power many
years ago, changed it into common school property.
It was not necessary then for the trustees (appellees)
to have the consent of the county court or of the
seminary trustees (there were none, so far as appears) to the vesting of the title in appellees.   The
town, as a corporation, had no beneficial interest in
the property.   Whether the trustees can or ought to
buy the M. & F. High School property from Transylvania Presbytery, or any other owner, if there are
others, is not presented in this record for decision.
The elections complained of being valid, the discretion of the trustees will not be interferred with by
the courts, certainly not upon less than such abuse
of it as would be tantamount to fraud.   No such case
is presented.   There need not have been a resort to

a sale by the court's commissioner; but of that unnecessary act appellants cannot complain.

We preceive no prejudicial error in the record, and the judgment is affirmed.

CASE 62.—ACTION BY WARDIE L. PATRICK, BY NEXT FRIEND, AGAINST THE CHESAPEAKE & OHIO RAILWAY COMPANY FOR PERSONAL INJURIES.— November 23, 1909.

Chesapeake & Ohio Ry. Co. v. Patrick
Same v. Picklesimer's Adm'r

Appeal from Boyd Circuit Court.

S. G. KINNER, Circuit Judge.

Judgment for plaintiffs, defendant appeals.—Affirmed.

1   Railroads—Crossing Accident—Questions for Jury—Evidence. —In an action for injuries in a crossing accident, whether plaintiff was negligent in standing on one track while a freight train was passing on another held, under the evidence, for the jury.

2   Railroads—Accidents at Crossings—Duty to Stop Before Crossing.—One having a right to cross a railroad track need not stop to look or listen, before crossing in order to discover whether a train is approaching.

3. Railroads—Crossing Accident—Instructions.—Where, in an action for injuries in a crossing accident, the whistle of the engine was not sounded, so that plaintiff could hear it, until the engine was within a few feet of, and in fact on, plaintiff, an instruction confining the signals to the ringing of the bell, which evidence showed was rung long before the engine struck plaintiff, was proper.

4. Trial—Cure by Other Instruction.—Error in an instruction, which is corrected by another instruction given, is cured.

WORTHINGTON, COCHRAN & BROWNING for appellant.

DINKLE & PRITCHARD for appellees.
No briefs in the record.

OPINION OF THE COURT BY JUDGE SETTLE—Affirming.

This is an appeal from a judgment of the Boyd circuit court, entered upon a verdict against the appellant, Chesapeake & Ohio Railway Co., in favor of the infant appellee, Wardie L. Patrick, for $2,000, in damages for injuries to his person from a collision with one of appellant's trains, alleged to have been caused by the negligence of its agents and servants in charge thereof. At the time of receiving his injuries appellee was 16 years of age, and the action was instituted by himself and next friend. The facts were that in December, 1905, appellee and a companion, Charles Picklesimer, a year his junior, went to the city of Ashland from their home in Magoffin county, seeking employment. After a few days' search they found work at the mill of the Herman Lumber Company. On account of a sleet and snow that fell, they were denied work one day at the mill, and upon again going to the mill in the afternoon, about 1 o'clock, they were advised that there would be no work for them there that day. After stopping for a while on Twenty-Seventh street, where a school building was being erected, they started to return to the house at which they were boarding on Thirty-Second street, going up what is known as Railroad alley, the usual and nearest route. On Railroad alley, which is a public street of Ashland, appellant has a double track, called the east-bound and west-bound tracks. The former, lying next to the hill, is used by appellant's trains running to Huntington, W. Va., and other points east, and the latter, lying next to the Ohio river, is used by its trains running to Cincinnati.

Appellee and his companion, after passing Thirty-first street, and upon reaching a point half way be-tween that street and Thirty-Second street, saw ap-proaching them on the west bound track a iong freight train, running at considerable speed and making a loud noise. They thereupon swerved their course sufficiently to keep out of the way of the freight train on the west-bound track, and proceeded in the direction of the boarding house on Thirty-Second street to which they had started; Thirty-Second street being then about 20 feet dis-tant. When they got to Thirty-Second street, the engine and a few cars of the freight train on the west-bound track had passed them. Upon appellee and his companion reaching Thirty-Second street, and while they were yet facing the east and in the act of turning to cross that street to get to the boarding house, a half square distant, an extra passenger train on the east-bound track, going at a high rate of speed, ran upon and against them, and dragged them under the engine tender some distance, thereby killing Pickle-simer and permanently injuring appellee upon his head and other parts of the body.

Appellant complains that the trial court improperly refused to peremptorily instruct the jury to find for it. We do not understand, from the brief of its able counsel, that it is claimed the peremptory instruction should have been given on the ground that appellee was a trespasser upon its track, for, when struck by the train, he and Picklesimer were on the crossing at Thirty-Second street, but because, it is insisted, he was guilty of contributory negligence in being upon the crossing and east-bound track at the time of the collision. Upon the facts furnished by appellee's testimony, the court could not, as a matter of law, hold that he was guilty of contributory negligence. Even before reaching the crossing at Thirty-Second street, he and his companion were walking along Railroad alley, a street or public way of the city, in constant use by its inhabitants, and when they got to Thirty-Second street, and on the crossing, they had, according to appellee's testimony, to stop until the freight train on the west-bound track passed them and the crossing to enable them cross the west-bound track to get to the boarding house. They had barely stopped, and were in the act of turning toward the freight train, but without having gotten their faces in line to see the approaching passenger train, when it struck them.

Under the circumstances, the mere fact that he was momentarily standing on the east-bound track was not of itself such evidence of contributory negligence on the part of appellee as would authorize the court to take the case from the jury. Whether, in thus situating himself, appellee exercised ordinary care for his own safety, was a matter to be determined by the jury. In view of the noise made by the freight train, to which his attention was particularly directed, because it was passing between him and the house to which he was going, and of the fact that the passenger train was an extra train, and, therefore, not expected, and the further fact that it was running, according to the testimony of three witnesses near by, at from 20 to 30 miles an hour without ringing its bell or giving other signal of its approach, it is not difficult to understand why the jury reached the conclusion that in the matter of receiving his injuries appellee was not guilty of such negligence as should defeat a recovery.

We do not overlook the fact that appellant's train crew, and other witnesses introduced in its behalf, furnished much evidence conducing to prove contributory negligence on the part of appellee, that he suddenly and unexpectedly to the engineer and fireman of the passenger train got upon the track in front of it, that the train was running at a moderate and reasonable rate of speed when the accident occurred, and that its approach was signaled by the usual and constant ringing of the bell; but, however contradictory this evidence may have been of appellee's, it all, with his, went to the jury, and we have no right to say that they should have given it more weight than appellee's was entitled to receive, or to direct that the verdict be set aside because they gave appellee and his witnesses the greater credence. Although repeatedly urged to do so, this court has never given its approval to the doctrine that one having a right to cross or go upon a railroad track shall, before doing so, stop, look, or listen, to discover whether a train is approaching or is so near at hand as to make it unsafe to himself to do so; for, as said in Ramsey v. Louisville, Cincinnati & Lexington Railway, 89 Ky. 104, 20 S. W. 163, 12 Ky. Law Rep. 559:

"It would be unreasonable to require of persons passing daily on foot or in vehicles along a public street in a populous, busy city or town, to stop at a railroad crossing in order to listen or look up and down a track, sometimes visible but a short distance, to ascertain whether a train is approaching, when they can without doing so have comparative security against inconvenience and injury by a reduction of the speed of trains, and easily and certainly warned of its approach by the bell or whistle." L. & N. R. R. Co. v. Lucas, 98 S. W. 308, 30 Ky. Law Rep. 359; Ky.

Central Ry. Co. v. Smith, 93 Ky. 449, 20 S. W. 392, 14 Ky. Law Rep. 455, 18 L. R. A. 63; L. & N. R. R. Co. v. Price's Adm'r, 76 S. W. 836, 25 Ky. Law Rep. 1033. We do not mean to be understood as holding that one, in crossing or going upon a railroad track, where he is entitled to go or be, should neglect the use of his faculties or fail to exercise any reasonable precaution that would enable a person of ordinary prudence under the circumstances to discover the approach or presence of a moving train and thereby prevent injury to his person, but simply to declare that he need not stop to look or listen before thus venturing, in order to discover whether a train is approaching.

The instructions of the circuit court gave to the jury the law applicable to the facts of this case, and were as follows:

"The court instructs the jury that it was the duty of the agents in charge of defendant's passenger train to use ordinary care to prevent collision with and injury to persons traveling the street where it intersects with defendant's railroad track by keeping a lookout in approaching said crossing, and in giving reasonably sufficient signals by ringing the engine bell to warn travelers of the approach of the train, and by running at such a rate of speed as was reasonably consistent with the safety of persons traveling the street. And if the jury believe from the evidence that on the occasion in controversy the defendant's agents in charge of its train failed in the performance of any or all of these duties, and by reason of such failure the collision occurred, then the jury should find for the plaintiff, unless they believe from the evidence the plaintiff failed to exercise ordinary care for his own safety."

No. 2: "The court instructs the jury, that it was the duty of the plaintiff, Wardie Patrick, on approaching the crossing mentioned in the evidence, to use such care as would be usually expected of an ordinarily prudent person to learn of the approach of the train and keep out of its way; and if he failed to exercise such care, and but for such failure would not have been injured, then the law is for the defendant and the jury should so find, even though they may believe from the evidence that the agents of defendant in charge of its train were negligent, as set out in instruction No. 1."

No. 3: "The court instructs the jury that if they believe from the evidence that, at the time and place of his injury, the plaintiff, Wardie Patrick, was not upon or traveling the Thirty-Second street crossing, but was walking upon defendant's tracks east of said crossing, then the law is for defendant, and the jury will so find."

No. 4: "If the jury find for the plaintiff under instruction No. 1, they will allow him such reasonable sum in damages as they may believe from the evidence will fairly compensate him for any suffering, mental or physical, which he has suffered as the direct result of said injury, and for any suffering they may believe from the evidence it is reasonably certain he will experience in the future as the direct result of said injury, and for all permanent reduction, if any of his power to earn money in the future as the direct result of said injury, not exceeding in the aggregate the sum of $2,000, the amount claimed in the petition."

No. 5: "Ordinary care is that degree of care which ordinarily prudent persons are expected to use under similar circumstances. Negligence is the failure to use ordinary care."

No. 6: "Nine or more of the jury concurring may return a verdict; but, if it is made by a less number than the entire jury, it must be signed by all the jurors thereto."

We do not think the instructions open to the objections made to them by appellant's counsel. It was not error for instruction No. 1 to confine the signals of the approach of the train by which appellee was injured to the ringing of the bell; for, according to appellant's evidence, no sounding of the engine whistle that could have been heard by appellee was done until the engine was within a few feet of, and in fact, upon him, which was too late to give notice of the coming of the train. Besides, nearly all of appellant's servants in charge of the passenger train testified that the bell rang as the train approached, and for a long distance before it struck, appellee. We fail to see that appellant was prejudiced by the instruction. The second objection to instruction No. 1 was removed by instruction 3, which in substance advised the jury that there could be no recovery unless appellee was upon the Thirty-Second street crossing when struck by the train. Instruction 2 could have been in no sense misleading or prejudicial, as the evidence showed that appellee was struck by the train upon reaching the Thirty-Second street crossing and as he was in the act of turning to cross the west-bound railroad track.

We have found no error in the admission or exclusion of evidence; and as, on the whole record, no reason has been shown for disturbing the verdict, the judgment is affirmed.

ACTION BY CHARLIE PICKLESIMER'S   ADMINISTRATOR
    AGAINST THE CHESAPEAKE & OHIO RAILWAY
    COMPANY.

Chesapeake & Ohio Ry. Co.v. Picklesimer's Admr.

Appeal from Boyd Circuit Court.

From a judgment for plaintiff, defendant appeals.
—Affirmed.

WORTHINGTON, COCHRAN & BROWNING for appellant.

DINKLE & PRITCHARD for appellee,

OPINION OF THE COURT BY JUDGE SETTLE—Affirming.

This case is a companion to that of Chesapeake & Ohio Railway Company v. Wardie Patrick,
by, etc., 122 S. W. 820, the opinion in which
was this day handed down. The questions of law and
fact in the two cases are the same, except that the
collision with appellant's train only resulted in great
bodily injury to Patrick, whereas appellee's intestate
was killed. The opinion in the Patrick Case, supra,
being conclusive of this case, an opinion herein, containing a further elaboration of our views upon the
questions involved, is deemed unnecessary.

Wherefore the judgment in this case is also affirmed.

CASE 63.—ACTION BY BESSIE KAY ENGLEMAN'S ADMINIS-
TRATOR AGAINST THE LOUISVILLE & NASH-
VILLE RAILROAD COMPANY FOR CAUSING HER
DEATH.—December 3, 1909.

Louisville & Nashville R. R. Co. v. Engleman's Adm'r

Appeal from Lincoln Circuit Court.

W. C. BELL, Circuit Judge.

Judgment for plaintiff, defendant appeals.—Reversed.

1   Railroads—Speed of Train Past Private Crossings—Signal—
Question for Jury.—A railroad company may run its trains
at any speed it pleases over private crossings, and it is not
required to give notice of their approach to such crossings
unless is has been customary for signals to be given there
which are relied on by persons using the crossing and whether, in a given case, the custom of giving signals for a crossing prevailed to an extent that persons using the crossing
could rely on the signals being given, is for the jury.

2. Railroads—Death at Crossing—Contributory Negligence—Presumptions.—There is no presumption that a person killed at a
private railroad crossing is guilty of contributory negligence;
that question being for the jury.

3. Railroads—Death at Crossing—Signals—Reliance Upon—
Question for Jury.—In an action for death of a person killed
at a private railroad crossing, whether the custom of giving
signals for a crossing prevailed to an extent that persons using the crossing could rely on the signals being given held,
under the evidence, a question for the jury.

4. Railroads—Death at Crossing—Instructions.—In an action for
death of a person killed at a private railroad crossing, an instruction that it was the duty of defendant's employes in
charge of the train, when approaching the crossing, to keep
a lookout for persons traveling over the crossing, and to give
reasonable signals of the movement of the train, and if defendant's employes negligently failed to perform these du-

ties, and by reason thereof plaintiff's intestate was killed, etc., was erroneous; a proper instruction being that if it was customary for trains to give signals of their approach to the crossing, and this custom prevailed to an extent that persons using the crossing had reason to rely on such signals being given, and the train in question failed to give such signals, and by reason of such failure decedent was struck, the jury should find for plaintiff.

5. Trial—Instructions——Conforming to Evidence.—In an action for death of a person killed at a private railroad crossing, it was error to charge that, although the jury believed that the employes on the train gave reasonable signals of the approach of the train, yet, if the employes discovered decedent's peril in time to have avoided the collision by the use of the available means and appliances at hand, to find for plaintiff; there being no evidence to support it.

6. Railroads—Crossing Accident—Duty of Engineer in Approaching a Crossing.—The engineer of a train approaching a private road crossing in the country is not bound to look away from the track to see if he can discover the top of any vehicle above the sides of the cut through which the road runs, but, on the contrary is bound to watch the track before him.

BENJAMBIN D. WARFIELD for appellant.

J. W. ALCORN of counsel.

POINTS DISCUSSED AND AUTHORITIES CITED.

1. Defendant did not owe decedent the duty of signalling, or slacking the speed of its train, for the private crossing where the accident happened. If it did not, then, obviously, defendant was not negligent as to decedent. L. & N. R. Co. v. Survant, 96 Ky., 197; Davis, adm'r, v. C. & O. Ry. Co., 116 Ky., 154; Johnson.s Adm'r v. L. & N. R. Co., 91 Ky., 651; Given's Adm'r v. L. & N. R. Co., 17 R. on p. 790; Hobacks Adm'r v. L., H. & St. L. Ry. Co., 30 R., 476; Parkerson's Adm'x v. L. & N. R. Co., 25 R. 2260; L. & N. R. Co. v. Cummin's Adm'r, 111 Ky. 333; L. & N. R. Co. v. Bodine, 109 Ky., 509, distinguished.

2. The jury were limited to finding compensatory damages for causing the death of a school girl, 16 years of age. They returned a verdict for plaintiff for $10,000. The verdict cannot stand in the absence of any sufficient averment, or any proof whatever, that decedent had any earning capacity, or that her estate suffered any pecuniary loss by reason of her death. The criterion of recovery of compensatory damages in such a sum as will

Louisville & Nashville R. R. Co. v. Engleman's Admr.

reasonably compensate decedent's estate for the destruction of
her power to earn money. In order to sustain a recovery on this
ground there must be both allegation and proof that decedent had
an earning capacity, and that her estate suffered a pecuniary loss
by reason of her death. There was no sufficient allegation, and
there was no proof whatever, that decedent had an earning
capacity or that her estate suffered any pecuniary loss by reason
of her death. Big Hill Coal Co. v. Abney's Adm'r, 30 R. on p.
1308; L. C. & L. R. Co. v. Case's Adm'r, 9 Bush, on p. 737; L. &
N. R. Co. v. Morris' Adm'r, 14 R. on p. 468; L. & N. R. Co. v.
Berry's Adm'r, 96 Ky., on p. 610; Cincinnati, etc., R. Co. v. Sampson's adm'r, 97 Ky. on p. 75; L. & N. R. Co. v. Ward's Adm'r,
19 R. on p. 1902; L. & N. R. Co. v. Eakin's Adm'r, 103 Ky., 479;
L. & N. R. Co. v. Taaffe's Adm'r, 106 Ky., on p. 541; L. & N. R.
Co. v. Sullivan's Adm'r, 25 R. on p. 875; L. & N. R. Co. v. Clark's
Adm'r, 105 Ky. on p. 585; So. Ry| Co. v. Barr's Adm'r, 21 R. on p.
1618; L. & N. R. Co. v. Schumaker's Adm'r, 112 Ky., on p. 437;
C. & O. Ry. Co., v. Lang's Adm'r, 100 Ky., on p. 230; L. & N. R.
Co. v. Milet's Adm'r, 20 R. on p. 533; L. & N. R. Co. v. Simrall's
Adm'r, 31 R. on p. 1273; L. & N. R. Co. v. Stock's Adm'r, 106 Ky.
42; C. N. O. & T. P. Ry. Co. v. Zachary's Adm'r, 32 R. on p. 680;
5 Encyc. Plead & Practic., p. 874; 13 Cyc., p. 343; Hurst v. Detroit
City Ry., 48 N. W. 44; Charlebois v. Gogebic & M R. Co., 51
N. W., 812; Rouse v. Detroit Electric Ry., 87 N. W., 68; L. & N.
R. Co. v. Orr, 91 Ala., 552; McHugh v. Schlosser, et al., 159 Pa.
St., 480, 28 Atyl., 291, 23 L. R. A., 574; Houston & T. C. R. Co. v.
Cowser, 57 Tex., 293; Consolidated Traction Co. v. Graham, 40
Atlantic, 773, 774.

3. It conclusively appears from the testimony that even though
there was negligence on the part of defendant's employes operating the train, decedent was also negligent, and that but for her
negligence the accident would not have happened. Therefore,
her administratrix is not entitled to recover damages for decedent's death, to which her own negligence contributed as the
proximate and efficient cause; and the trial court erred in not
peremptorily instructing the jury to find for defendant. Sou. Ry.
Co. in Ky. v. Barbour, 21 Ky. Law Rep., 266; L. & N. R. Co. v.
Cummin's Adm'r, 111 Ky., 338, supra; C. & O. Ry. Co. v. Riddle's
Adm'r, 24 Ky. Law Rep., 1687; P. & M. R. Co. v. Hoehl, 12 Bush,
44; I. C. R. Co. v. Dick, 91 Ky., 434-441; C. & O. Ry. Co. v. Gun-
ter, 108 Ky., 362; Johnson's Adm'r, v. L. & N. R. Co., 91 Ky.,
651-653; Wright v. Cincinnati, etc., R. Co., 94 Ky., 120; L. & N.
R. Co. v. Survant, 19 Ky. Law Rep. 1578; Rupard v. C. & O. Ry.
Co., 88 Ky., 280-5; L. & N. R. Co. v. Sights, 121 Ky., 203;
L. & N. R. Co. v. Cleaver, 28 Ky. Law Rep., 497; City of Maysville
v. Guilfoyle, 110 Ky., 674; L. & N. R. Co. v. Fox's Adm'r, 20 Ky.

Louisville & Nashville R. R. Co. v. Engleman's Admr.

Law Rep., 83; L. & N. R. Co. v. Mounce's Adm'r, 28 Ky. Law Rep.,
936; Jacobs v. O. & B. S. R. Co., 20 Ky. Law Rep., 190; Young v.
I. C. R. Co., 24 Ky Lew Rep., 789; Hummer's Extrx. v. L. & N.
R. Co., 32 Ky. Law Rep., 1315, "to be reported"; Ramsey v. L. C.
& L. Ry. Co., 89 Ky., 102; Ky. C. R. Co. v. Thomas, 79 Ky., on p.
163; Sou Ry. Co. in Ky. v. Clark, 32 Ky. Law Rep., 415; Sinclair's
Adm'r v. I. C. R. Co., 112 S. W. on p. 911.

4. Having improperly refused to give a peremptory instruction for defendant, the trial court erred in the insufficient manner
in which he submitted to the jury the issue as to decedent's contributory negligence. L. & N. R. Co. v. King's Adm'r, 115 S. W.
No. 1. "To be reported"; L. & N. R. Co. v. Cummins' Adm'r.,
111 Ky., 333; Sou. Ry. Co. in Ky. v. Winchester's executrix, 32
Ky. Law Rep., 19.

5. The instructions given to the jury on plaintiff's motion and
over defendant's objection and exception were erroneous in material respects and were prejudicial to defendant. L. & N. R. Co.
v. Joshlin, 32 Ky. Lew Rep., on pp. 516-517; L. & N. R. Co. v.
Veach's Adm'r, 112 S. W., 869.

6. The misconduct of counsel for plaintiff in closing argument
to the jury was prejudicial to defendant. L. & N R. Co. v.
Crom, 32 Ky. Law Rep., on p. 1146; L. & N. R. Co., v. Smith, 27
Ky. Law Rep., 257; L. & N. R. Co., v. Carter, 27 Ky Law Rep.,
748; I. C. R. Co. v. Jolly, 27 Ky. Law Rep., 118.

ROBT. HARDING for appellees.

E. V. PURYEAR, M. C. SAUFLEY, GREENE, VANWINKLE &
SCHOOLFIELD of counsel.

AUTHORITIES CITED.

L. & N. R. Co. v. Bodern, 109 Ky., 509; Earley's Adm'r v. L. H.
& St. L. R. R. Co., 24 Ky. Law Rep., 1810; Popp, Case 96 Ky., 99;
Bardswell v. N. O. & C. R. R. Co., 12 Ky. Law Rep., 180.

OPINION OF THE COURT BY JUDGE HOBSON—Reversing.

Bessie Kay Engleman, while driving a phaeton
across the Louisville & Nashville railroad track at a
private crossing known as ''Woods' crossing,'' about
2½ miles north of Stanford, Ky., was struck by the
north-bound passenger train and killed. This action
was brought by her administrator to recover for her

death, and, a recovery having been had in the sum of
$10,000, the railroad company appeals.

The pike ran on the opposite side of the railroad
from the home of the decedent.   To get out to the pike
from her home, she used a private road, and was
struck where this road crossed the railroad.   The
road was used as an outlet by persons living on the
farms of Samuel Harris and Eph Woods, including
their tenants and persons going to or from their
places on business or pleasure.   There was a gate
at the edge of the railroad right of way, 62 feet from
the track.   The private road passed through a cut
just before it reached the railroad, so that a person
driving a vehicle could not see an approaching train
until he was within a few feet of the track, and those
in charge of the train would be equally unable to see
him until about the same time, unless the top of the
vehicle was high enough to be visible above the cut
as it approached the track.   The evidence for the
plaintiff tended to show that the crossing was especially dangerous, that the railroad trains were accustomed to give signals of their approach to the crossing, and that no warning of the approach of this train
was given.   There was also much evidence tending to
show that the trains sometimes gave signals of their
approach, and sometimes did not, although the engineer of this train testified that he regarded it a dangerous crossing and always gave the usual crossing
signals as he approached it.   The evidence for the
defendant tended to show that the decedent drove on
the crossing without looking or listening when the
train was very close to it, and when it was too late
for those in charge of the train to avert the injury to
her.   It also showed that the train gave the usual
crossing signals as it approached.

On this evidence, the court, refusing to instruct the jury peremptorily to find for the defendant, gave the jury the following instructions:

"No. 1. If you believe from the evidence that the railroad crossing over the private passway, known and spoken of in the testimony as the 'Woods crossing,' is a dangerous crossing for persons traveling thereover in buggies in an ordinarily prudent manner, then it was the duty of the employes of defendant in control of the train that struck the deceased, when moving the train on that part of the track approaching said crossing, to keep a lookout for persons traveling over same in a vehicle or vehicles, and to give reasonable signals and warnings of the movement of its train when approaching said crossing, and if you believe from the evidence that the defendant's employes in charge of said train negligently failed to perform any of these duties in the movement of said train, and that by reason thereof the plaintiff's intestate while crossing, or attempting to cross, said crossing, was run against and killed by said train, and that the deceased was at the time using ordinary care for her own safety, then you will find for the plaintiff in damages such a sum as you believe from the evidence will reasonably compensate the estate of the deceased for the destruction of her power to earn money, not exceeding the sum of $30,000.

"No. 2. Although you may believe from the evidence that the employes on the train gave reasonable signals of the approach of the train to the Woods crossing, yet if you further believe from the evidence that the employes in charge of the movements of the train discovered the peril of the deceased in time to have avoided the collision by the use of the available

means and appliances at hand, then you should find
for the plaintiff."

"No. 5. Unless the defendant's employes in
charge of the train were negligent as defined in instruction No. 1 then you will find for the defendant;
and although you may believe from the evidence that
there was such negligence on the part of said employes, yet, if, in going on the track as she did, the
deceased failed to use ordinary care for her own
safety, and but for this would not have been injured,
then you will find for the defendant, notwithstanding
such negligence on its part."

It has been held by this court in a number of cases
that the railroad company may run its trains at such
speed as it pleases over private crossings, and that
it is not required to give notice of the approach of the
trains to such crossings, unless it has been customary
for the signals to be given, and they were relied on by
persons using the crossing. Johnson v. L. & N. R. R.
Co., 91 Ky. 651, 25 S. W. 754; 10 R. 227, 11 R.
118 Louisville, etc., R. R. Co. v. Survant, 96 Ky. 197,
27 S. W. 999, 16 Ky. Law Rep. 545; Davis v. C. & O.
Ry. Co., 116 Ky. 114, 75 S. W. 275; Hoback v. Louisville, etc., R. R. Co., 99 S. W. 241. On the other hand,
it has been held that where it has been customary for
signals to be given of the approach of trains to a private crossing, and these were relied on by persons
using the crossing, and a traveler on the crossing was
struck by reason of a failure to give the customary
signals, a recovery may be had. L. & N. R. R. Co. v.
Bodine, 109 Ky. 509, 59 S. W. 740, 23 Ky. Law Rep.
147, 56 L. R. A. 506; Early's Adm'r v. Louisville, etc.,
R. R. Co., 115 Ky. 13, 72 S. W. 348, 24 Ky. Law Rep.
1807. There was some evidence here that the trains
were accustomed to give the usual signals of their ap-

proach to this crossing, and that persons using the crossing relied thereon. This evidence was sufficient to submit the case to the jury under the rule referred to. No one saw the decedent as she approached the crossing. No one knows whether she stopped, looked, or listened, or what precautions she took. This being true, under a long line of decisions of this court, it is not presumed that she was guilty of contributory negligence, and the question is for the jury. The court therefore did not err in refusing to instruct the jury peremptorily to find for the defendant.

The rule that where it has been customary to give signals at a private crossing, and persons using the crossing have come to rely upon them, the signals may not be omitted without notice, obtains in other jurisdictions. Westaway v. Chicago, etc., R. R. Co., 56 Minn. 28, 57 N. W. 222; Nash v. N. Y. Cent. R. R. Co., 117 N. Y. 628, 22 N. E. 1128; 33 Cyc. 946, and cases cited. But there was in this case evidence that the train failed to whistle or give any signals for the crossing as often as they gave such signals. In view of this evidence, it was a question for the jury whether the custom of giving signals for this crossing prevailed to such an extent that persons using the crossing had a right to rely on the signals being given. It is not material that some trains passed this crossing without giving the usual signals, for some trains fail to give signals at public crossings. The case turns on whether there was such a custom to give the signals that persons using the crossing had the right to rely on it. In lieu of instruction No. 1, the court should have told the jury, in substance, that if it had been customary for trains to give signals of their approach to the Woods crossing, and this custom had prevailed to such an extent that persons using the crossing had reason to rely on such signals being given, and the train in question failed to give reasonable signals of its approach to the crossing, and by reason of such failure the decedent was struck and hurt, they should find for the plaintiff as set out in the instruction; otherwise for the defendant.

There was no evidence in the case to warrant the giving of instruction No. 2. It was not incumbent upon the engineer to look across the cut to see the tops of vehicles. It was his duty to watch the track. L. & N. R. R. Co. v. Onan, 110 S. W. 381, 33 Ky. Law Rep. 462. An instruction of this sort should never be given unless there is evidence to warrant it. L. & N. R. R. Co. v. Joshlin, 110 S. W. 383, 33 Ky. Law Rep. 513.

In Southern R. R. Co. v. Winchester, 127 Ky. 151 105 S. W. 167, where we had before us an instruction similar to No. 5, we said: "In lieu of the third instruction on another trial, the court will tell the jury that it was the duty of the intestate, on approaching the crossing, to use such care as may be usually expected of an ordinarily prudent person to learn of the approach of the train and keep out of its way; that, if the crossing was especially dangerous, it was incumbent on him to exercise increased care commensurate with the danger; and that if he failed to exercise such care, and but for this would not have been injured, then the law is for the defendant, and the jury should so find, even though they may believe from the evidence that the defendant or its employes were negligent as set out in No. 1 and No. 2." Instruction No. 6 given by the court, practically conformed to the rule thus laid down, but, for brevity, on another trial the court will give the one instruction indicated.

The two instructions we have outlined, with instruction Nos. 4 and 8, given by the court defining "reasonable signals" and "ordinary care," cover the whole law of the case. The other matters complained of will not, perhaps, occur on another trial.

Judgment reversed, and cause remanded for a new trial.

NUNN, C. J. I agree to the reversal, but do not assent to the opinion wherein it relieves the appellant from giving warning of the approach of the train to a known unusually dangerous private crossing. As decided by this court in the case of L. & N. R. R. Co. v. Bodine, 109 Ky. 509, 59 S. W. 740, 23 Ky. Law Rep. 147, 56 L. R. A. 506, the effect of the opinion is to give notice to railroad companies to cease to give warnings of the approach of their trains in such cases.

CASE 64.—ACTION BY FRANK WATERS AND OTHERS AGAINST J. H. KEENEY AND OTHERS.—December 2, 1909.

Keeney, &c. v. Waters, &c.

Appeal from Wayne Circuit Court.

M. L. JARVIS, Circuit Judge.

Judgment for plaintiffs, defendants appeal.—Affirmed.

1. Appeal and Error—Harmless Error—Amendment of Pleading.—Where a party gets the full benefit of a defense attempted to be pleaded by him, he can not complain, on appeal, that the answer pleading the defense was not permitted to be filed.

2 Frauds, Statute of—Parol Recission—Contracts Required to be in writing.—Though a contract is required by statue to be in writing, it may be rescinded by parol.

3. Contracts—Parol Rescission—Clearness of Evidence.—Where two witnesses testified to the parol rescission of a contract, neither of them being impeached, and where it was shown that a suit between the parties on the contract had been per-permitted to remain upon the docket without action ever being taken thereon by either party, the evidence of the oral rescission was sufficiently clear to authorize its admission in evidence by the trial court, and to warrant an instruction as to its effect if found to have been agreed on.

4. Champerty and Maintenance—Champertous Agreements.—Though a champertous agreement to sell land is void under the statutes, the cause of action which is the subject of the Champertous agreement is not destroyed thereby.

COOK & JONES for appellants.

HARRISON & HARRISON of counsel.

We submit that there is no merit in this case for the appellees, who are simply the tools of the Stearns Lumber Co. and W. A.

Kinnie, its agent, and this suit is the outgrowth of a champertous agreement between Kinnie, as the agent of said company, and the appellees, a contract that is condemned by our statutes and by the common law as well.

O. H. WADDLE & SON attorneys for appellees.

JOS. BERTRAM, J. N. SHARP of counsel.

POINTS AND AUTHORITINES CITED.

1. A mere usurper of land without color of title can only acquire title by adverse possession by actual enclosure continuously for the time required by statute. The actual possession of adjoining land can have no effect to entitle a person to the benefits of the constructive possession, and to secure title by naked adverse possession it must be shown that such adverse possession was so intended, and can only extend to the boundary intended to be occupied and claimed, and an accidental extension outside of such boundary does not enlarge the right beyond the boundary intended to be possessed. 1 Am. & Eng. Enc., 229 & 292; 2 Wood on Limitation, Sec. 267; Griffith v. Huston, 7 J. J. M., 385; Shackleford v. Smith, 5 Dana, 232; Brooks v. Clay, 3 A. K. M., 345; Haffendorfer v. Gault, 84 Ky., 124; Roy v. Barker, 1 B. Mon., 365; Croan v. Joyce, 3 Bush, 456; Smith v. Morrow, 5 Littell, 211.

2. While there may be a champertous agreement to divide the proceeds of litigation which can not be enforced, it does not render the existing cause of action void, for the statute to prevent champerty does not mean that when a party has a cause of action existing at the time he makes the champertous contract he shall forfeit his right to recover thereon, but that neither he nor the champetor shall have any right of action on such contract made in violation of the statute. Cumberland Tel. & Tel. Co. v. Maxberry, Mss., opinion filed october 1st, 1909.

3. Written contracts may be altered or discharged by subsequent parol agreement, even though the original contract is required, by the statute of frauds, to be in writing. Page on Contracts, Sec. 1346; 9 Cyc., 599; Cummings v. Arnold, 37 Am. Dec., 155; Gartland v. Connor, 22 Rep., 920; Hyden v. Perkins, 30th Rep., 583.

OPINION OF THE COURT BY WM. ROGERS CLAY, COMMISSIONER—Affirming.

The appellees, Frank Waters and others, instituted this action against J. H. Keeney and others to recover a tract of land in Wayne county, Ky., consisting of 50 acres. J. H. Keeney and others denied the title of appellees and pleaded title in themselves by adverse possession. The jury returned a verdict in favor of appellees. From the judgment based thereon, this appeal is prosecuted.

The 50-acre tract of land was patented by James Coffey on the 27th day of June, 1841. Coffey, in his lifetime, sold this land to G. W. Troxell, but did not convey the same by deed or other writing. On January 27, 1881, four out of the five heirs of James Coffey, who was then dead, together with his widow, made a deed to G. W. Troxell conveying the land in question. The deed recited that it was made in consideration of $200 paid to James Coffey in his lifetime. Before procuring this deed, G. W. Troxell, on October 3, 1880, sold by title bond to James H. Davis 300 acres of land in Wayne county, including the land in controversy. On April 26, 1888, G. W. Troxell instituted an action against James H. Davis, wherein he sought to recover a balance of $50 due as part of the purchase money for the land sold to Davis. To this action Davis filed an answer, in which he pleaded inability of Troxell to make title to a large part of the 300 acres mentioned in the bond. This action was never tried. The last order was made at the May term, 1889, of the Wayne circuit court.

In the year 1881 James H. Davis, who then held the title bond referred to, requested one John M. Foster, whom he had employed in removing the timber, to move upon the land and remain there until Davis told him to get off. Foster first moved upon the 50-acre track in controversy. He remained there for about two years. He then built a house on an adjoining

tract. A small portion of his garden extended into
the 50-acre tract. At the time Foster moved upon the
land, Davis was indebted to him in the sum of $70.
Foster claims that, as Davis failed to pay this
amount, he then began to claim the lands as his own.
In the year 1905 appellants purchased the land in controversy from Foster. On July 31, 1906, Sallie
Smith, the only remaining heir of James Coffey, deceased, together with her husband, conveyed her one-
fifth interest in the land in question to appellees,
Frank and Lile Waters. After the issues were made
up, appellants became aware of the institution and
pendency of the action of G. W. Troxell against James
H. Davis.

On January 28, 1909, they tendered an amended
answer, in which they pleaded the outstanding title
bond from G. W. Troxell to James H. Davis as a bar
to a recovery by appellees. The court did not permit
the amended answer to be filed. After the discovery
of the record in the case of G. W. Troxell against
James H. Davis, appellants went to the heirs of
James H. Davis and purchased from them all their
right, title, and interest in the 300 acres of land, including the land in controversy. Appellees are the
only heirs of G. W. Troxell, deceased. They introduced evidence to the effect that the written contract
of sale between G. W. Troxell and James H. Davis
was rescinded.

Upon the trial of the case, the court instructed the
jury to find for appellees the undivided one-fifth of
the 50-acre tract of land in controversy under the title
conveyed to them by the deed of Sallie and J. M.
Smith. As to the remaining four-fifths of said tract
of land, the court directed the jury to find for appel-

lants, unless they believed from the evidence that an
agreement was entered into between G. W. Troxell
and James H. Davis, whereby the title bond from
Troxell to Davis, introduced in evidence, should be
canceled and said tract of land remain the property
of Troxell, in consideration of Troxell releasing Davis
from the payment of the balance of the purchase
money due him from Davis for the land and in settlement of the controversy between them as to the payment of said purchase money and of the title to the
lands referred to in the title bond. If they so believed, they were told to find for appellees.

It is first insisted by appellants that the court erred
in refusing to permit the amended answer to be filed.
It is perfectly manifest, however, that appellants were
not prejudiced by this action of the court. They were
permitted to offer in evidence the title bond from
Troxell to Davis and all the record of the action instituted by Troxell against Davis. Appellants not
only received the benefit of this evidence, but the
court told the jury, in effect, to find for the appellants
unless they believed the contract of sale was rescinded. No instruction more favorable to appellants
could have been asked by them. Where a party gets
the benefit of a defense pleaded by him, he cannot
complain that the answer pleading the defense was
not permitted to be filed.

But it is insisted that the court erred in admitting
evidence of the parol rescission of the written contract of sale between Troxell and Davis. While there
is some conflict of authority upon the question whether or not a contract in writing, and which is required
by the statute to be in writing, can be rescinded by

parol agreement, this question has been decided in the affirmative by this court and by many other courts of this country. Davis v. Benedict, 4 S. W. 339, 9 Ky. Law Rep. 200; Hall v. Wright, 122 S. W.—; Stearns v. Hall, 9 Cush. (Mass.) 31; Beach v. Covillard, 4 Cal. 315; Morrill v. Colehour, 82 Ill. 618; Howard v. Gresham, 27 Ga. 347; Long v. Hartwell, 34 N. J. Law, 116; Wulschner v. Ward, 115 Ind. 219, 17 N. E. 273.

It is also insisted by appellants that the evidence of the parol rescission in this case does not come up to the standard set in the case of Davis v. Benedict, supra, where it is held that the proof must be clear and convincing. Two witnesses testified upon this point. Neither one of them is impeached. Their evidence is to the effect that, after the institution of the suit by Troxell against Davis, they agreed to leave the matter to Joe Roberts and Isaac Foster to settle. They compromised the matter by permitting Troxel to take back the 50-acre tract and Davis to keep the timber which he had gotten from the land. Both Troxell and Davis agreed to this settlement. Furthermore, the very fact that the suit instituted by Troxell against Davis was permitted to remain upon the docket without action ever being taken by either party is a circumstance tending to support the testimony of the two witnesses. We therefore conclude that the evidence of the oral rescission and compromise was sufficiently clear and convincing to authorize its admission by the court and to justify the instruction complained of.

There was some evidence to the effect that W. A. Finnie, agent of the Stearns Lumber Co., desired to purchase the Davis lands. He secured from Frank Waters and wife, two of the appellees, a contract empowering him, as their agent, to employ lawyers and institute suit for the purpose of establishing title to the land in controversy. By this contract Frank Waters and wife were to convey their interest in said lands to Kinnie in the event of a recovery. It also appears that Kinnie secured from Smith and wife a deed to their one-fifth interest in the lands in controversy. It is insisted by appellants that the above contract with Kinnie was champertous. However that may be, the law is well settled in this state that, by the terms of the statute, the champertous agreement to sell is rendered null and void—not the cause of action which is the subject of the champertous agreement. Cumberland Telephone & Telegraph Co. v. Maxberry, 121 S. W. 447; Wehmhoff v. Rutherford, 98 Ky. 91, 32 S. W. 288, 17 Ky. Law Rep. 659.

Upon the whole case, we are unable to find any error in the record prejudicial to the substantial rights of appellants, and the judgment is therefore affirmed.

*

CASE 65.—ACTION BY W. F. HUGHLEY AGAINST THE CITY
OF MAYFIELD.—November 30, 1909.

City Mayfield v. Hughley.

Appeal from Graves Circuit Court.

R. J. Bugg, Circuit Judge.

Judgment for plaintiff, defendant appeals.—Affirmed.

2. Municipal Corporations — Charter — Taxation—Liability for
Knowledge of.—The duty of a municipality to keep its streets
and sidewalks in a reasonably safe condition for persons traveling thereon extends to cases where the obstruction or unsafe condition of the street is brought about by persons
other than the agents of the city; but the party seeking to
recover for failure to perform such duty must show that the
city had knowledge of the defect, or might have had knowledge thereof by the use of reasonable care.

2. Municipal Corporations—Charter — Taxation —Liability   for
Defective Sidewalks.—It is no defense to an action against a
city of the fourth class for personal injuries from falling on a defective sidewalk that the territory where the accident occurred
had been annexed too late to be subject to taxation that year,
and that the taxes for subsequent years were sufficient to improve streets or sidewalks, since the charter of such cities
gives them the right to build sidewalks and assess the cost
against the abutting property, so that it was unnecessary for
the city to levy any general tax for such purposes.

3. Municipal Corporations—Defects in Sidewalks—Notice.—
Where it was shown that an excavation, which lowered a
sidewalk and allowed an obstruction to protrude, over which
the plaintiff fell, was .made about three months prior to the
accident, the city was chargable with notice of the obstruction.

M. B. HOLEFIELD for appellant.

HESTER & MARTIN for appellees.

OPINION OF THE COURT BY WM. ROGERS CLAY, COM-
MISSIONER —Affirming.

This action was instituted by appellee, W. F. Hughley, to recover damages for personal injuries occasioned by his falling over an obstruction in one of the
streets of the city of Mayfield. The jury returned a
verdict in favor of appellee for the sum of $250, and
the city appeals.

In the year 1907 the street on which appellee received his injuries, which is known as South First
street, was annexed to the city of Mayfield. At the
time appellee received his injuries, he was on his way
from his home to a union labor meeting. It was a
dark night, and there were no street lights in the immediate neighborhood. At the time he was engaged
in conversation with a friend. The accident occurred
in front of the residence of Caroline Armstrong. Having determined to build a sidewalk in front of her
property, she made an excavation in order to make
the grade of her walk conform to the grade of the
other walks which had been built. In doing this, she
lowered the ground and caused the stop box belonging
to the Mayfield Water & Light Company to project
above the ground to a height of about six inches.
While appellee had a general knowledge of the location of the stop box, he momentarily forgot its presence and stumped his toe against it and fell to the
ground.

Appellant filed an answer containing four paragraphs.,The first paragraph contained a general denial. The second paragraph contained a plea of contributory negligence. The third paragraph contained a plea to the effect that Caroline Armstrong,
without any notice to, or any order, permission, or

authority from, the city of Mayfield, undertook to
build a sidewalk in front of her premises, and made
the excavation which caused the stop box to project
high and thus cause the injuries complained of. The
fourth paragraph contained a plea to the effect that
the annexed territory where the accident occurred
was taken into the city when it was too late to subject
the same to taxation for the year 1907, and that in
the years 1907 and 1908 all the taxes were levied upon
property in the city that were permissible under the
charter of the city and the laws and Constitution of
the Commonwealth, and that the city could not in
either of said years improve the street or walkway
in question without expending more money than was
levied for public improvements.

It is first insisted by appellant that the court erred
in sustaining a demurrer to the third and fourth paragraphs of the answer. This contention, however, is
without merit. The rule is well settled that the duty
and consequent liability of a municipality to keep its
streets and sidewalks in a reasonably safe condition
for persons traveling thereon extends to those cases
where the obstruction or unsafe condition of the street
is brought about by persons other than the agents of
the city; but, to impose liability upon the municipality in such cases, it devolves upon the party seeking a
recovery to show that the city had knowledge of the
defect, or might have had knowledge thereof by the
use of reasonable care and watchfulness. 28 Cyc.
1353. Another statement of the rule is as follows:
"A municipal corporation is liable for injury resulting from an excavation or obstruction in one of its
public streets, made by an abutting owner for his own
purposes, if the corporation had actual or construc-

tive notice of the dangerous condition of the street for a sufficient length of time to enable it to guard the public safety.''   28 Cyc. 1354.

Nor did the fourth paragraph present any defense. The charter of cities of the fourth class gives to the city the right to construct or reconstruct its sidewalks and assess the cost thereof against the property of the abutting landowners.   It was unnecessary for the city to levy any general taxes for such purposes, and the fact that it did not have any funds levied for the purpose furnished no reason for not proceeding to have the sidewalk constructed or reconstructed as authorized by the charter.   The evidence shows that the excavation by Carolinê Armstrong was made about three months prior to the accident.   Thus the city had plenty of time to order the work done.

While it is not shown that appellee's injuries were at all serious, we cannot say that the sum of $250 is excessive.

The instructions are not complained of, and there was sufficient evidence to justify the submission of the case to the jury.

For the reasons given, the judgment is affirmed.

CASE 66.—SUIT BY THE STRAIGHT CREEK COAL & COKE
  COMPANY AGAINST THE STRAIGHT CREEK COAL
  MINING COMPANY.—November 30, 1909.

Straight Creek Coal & Coke Co. v. Straight Creek Coal Mining Co.

Appeal from Bell Circuit Court.

M. J. Moss, Circuit Judge.

·Judgment for plaintiff, defendant appeals.—Affirmed.

1. Carriers—"Common Carriers"—Switch Track of Coal Company.—One who constructs a railroad switch, under Ky. St. 1909, Sec. 815, authorizing the owner of a coal mine within three miles of a railroad to condemn a right of way for a railroad switch to get his product to market, and providing that the owner of such road shall be, so far as they are applicable, governed by the laws relating to other railroads, and shall have the same right and privileges granted to corporations owning and operating lines of railroads, is not a "common carrier," in contravention of Const. Sec. 210, providing that no corporation engaged in the business of common carrier shall own a mine, so that it can either ship or permit to be shipped by the lessees of its mine all products thereof free of charge.

2. Carriers—Discrimination in Rates.—A coal company, which constructs a railroad switch to its mine and allows the hauling over it of coal of its lessees and others, does not discriminate against such others, whom it charges five cents a ton trackage, by charging its tenants only eight cents a ton royalty; such charge to also cover transportation over the track.

3. Carriers—Discrimination—Lines Operated.—A railroad company, which has a mortgage on the switch road of a coal company coming into its road at P., and without charge puts its empty cars on the switch for the various mine-owners along it, and when they are loaded hauls them over the switch to P., making its charges from P., only, the same to all shippers does not operate the switch as a part of its general system,

so as to be subject to the charge of discrimination on account of the trackage charges made by the coal company owning the switch.

4. Carriers—Extortionate Charges.—A coal company', which con-
    structs a switch to its mine, and which is, under Ky. St. 1909,
    Sec. 815, subject to the general railroad laws, to the extent
    that it cannot make extortionate track charges to others,
    cannot, till it has been repaid its outlay for construction, be
    claimed by others to make such extortionate charges; the
    charges being such as were agreed on with them before
    the construction of the track as a consideration for the right
    of way.

5. Interest—Recovery—Pleading.—No claim of interest having
    been made in the pleadings by plaintiff, it cannot complain
    that none were allowed, even from the filing of tho suit.

T. B. ANDERSON for Appellant.

D. B. LOGAN and KOHN, BAIRD, SLOSS & KOHN for appellees.

B. D. WARFIELD and CHAS. METCALF for L. & N. R. R. Co.

OPINION OF THE COURT BY JUDGE LASSING—Affirming.

The Straight Creek Coal & Coke Company is a corporation owning large bodies of coal and timber lands
in Bell county, Ky.   For more than 10 years it has
operated a coal mine on a tract of its land on the
waters of Straight creek, about 2¼ miles eastwardly
from Pineville.   It also has a coke plant and a sawmill there.   In order to get its products to the market,
it owns and operates a railroad switch running from
its mines and coke plant to the Louisville & Nashville
Railroad at Pineville.   The corporation owns no rolling stock except a few logging cars on which it brings
its logs to its sawmill.   It rents an engine from the
Louisville & Nashville Railroad Company with which
to do the necessary switching of coal cars on the yards
at its mines.

In 1905 the corporation desired to develop a large body of its land which lays some four miles northwardly of its coal and coke plant. In order to do this, it entered into a contract with the Louisville & Nashville Railroad Company to build this four miles of additional switch from its mining camp to the property to be developed; the expenditure to be repaid to the Louisville & Nashville by the coal company's paying five cents per ton for every ton transported over the new switch. To further secure the payment of the cost of building the switch, the coal company executed and delivered to the railroad company a mortgage upon its whole railroad switch, and the railroad company agreed to maintain the switch during the existence of the mortgage, and to haul the coal company's coal from its mines to Pineville free of charge. In order to secure the right of way for the new switch, the coal company entered into contracts with the various landowners through whose lands it was proposed to run, by which it was agreed, among other things, that the owner conveyed a right of way 50 feet wide to the coal company, and the latter agreed that the landowner might have the use of the switch for transporting his coal to market at a trackage charge of five cents per ton.

Along the line of the proposed new switch, the Howards owned a tract of land, and they (except one infant to be hereafter noticed) conveyed to the appellee by deed a right of way through their land. The deed contains the agreement between the owners of the land and appellee concerning the trackage charges to be paid by the vendors to appellee for the use of its switch. So far as it is necessary to notice this contract, it may be stated that, as a consideration for the right of way, the owners of the land and their assignees were to have the use of the switch at a trackage charge of five cents per ton. One of the Howards was an infant, and, although his guardian offered to convey to appellee for the ward his interest in the right of way, it was thought better that a friendly condemnation suit should be instituted and carried to judgment in order to fully bind the infant; and this was done. With this exception the record shows that the appellee obtained its entire right of way for the new switch by contract.

During the pendency of the negotiations between appellee and the Howard heirs for the right of way, certain individuals, who afterwards organized themselves into a corporation called the Straight Creek Coal Mining Company, were negotiating with the Howards for a lease of their property for the purpose of opening and operating a coal mine thereon. This corporation is the appellant in this action. After the switch was built, the appellant opened its coal mine, and for some time shipped coal over the switch to Pineville under the contract made by appellee and the Howards, and during this period paid the trackage charges in accordance with the terms of the contract between appellee and appellant's lessors, the Howards. Afterwards, however, appellant refused to pay further trackage charges, asserting that appellee was a common carrier and was discriminating against it by not charging other coal miners on its switch any-thing for trackage, and that therefore it was not required to pay anything for the use of the switch.

This position is based upon the following state of facts: In order to induce the Louisville & Nashville Railroad Company to build the four miles of switch involved here, the appellee company found it necessary to insure the railroad company against loss by reason of its outlay in building the switch; and to do this it entered into a contract with the railroad that it would make certain developments of coal mines upon its land, which would insure a large haulage over the road and furnish to the railroad company a large quantity of freight from Pineville to the various coal markets of the country. In order to make good this contract with the railroad company, the appellee leased parts of its land, which was to be developed by the switch, to two coal mining companies, and agreed, among other things, that in consideration for the payment by its tenants of eight cents royalty on each ton of coal mined, it would haul, or cause to be hauled, the coal of its tenants to the Louisville & Nashville Railroad for the purpose of being transported to the market; it being especially agreed that the eight-cent royalty was to cover both payment for the coal and the transportation of it from the mine to the Louisville & Nashville Railroad.

So that the real questions here are: (1) Is the appellee, in the use of its switch, a common carrier? (2) If it be such, does the effect of the contract between it and its tenants result in an illegal discrimination in the trackage charges as between appellant and the tenants? It is not disputed by any of the parties to this record that, if appellee is a common carrier, it may not discriminate in trackage charges between its patrons, and that, if it allows any of its patrons to haul over its switch free, then it cannot charge trackage against any of its patrons; and therefore, if it be ascertained that appellee is a common carrier, the question at once arises: Is the contract with its tenants a discrimination in freight or trackage rates between them and the other patrons along its line?

Appellee, being a corporation engaged in the coal mining business, points out that under the Constitution it cannot be a common carrier; and in support of this position relies upon the provision of section 210 of that instrument, which is as follows: "No corporation engaged in the business of common carrier shall, directly or indirectly, own, manage, operate, or engage in any other business than that of a common carrier, or hold, own, lease or acquire, directly or indirectly, mines, factories or timber, except such as shall be necessary to carry on its business; and the General Assembly shall enact laws to give effect to the provisions of this section." It is obvious that the foregoing provision of the Constitution prohibits appellee, if it be a common carrier, from owning or operating a coal mine. Section 815 of the Statutes authorizes, among other things, the owner of a coal mine within three miles of any navigable stream or railroad to condemn a right of way, not to exceed 50 feet wide, for the purpose of building a switch or tracks in order to get his produce to market. We cannot presume that the Legislature intended by section 815 to authorize a coal mining corporation to violate the Constitution by becoming a common carrier, and therefore we must assume that when the owner of a coal mine or stone quarry, in order to develop his property, builds a railroad switch or track, he does not thereby become a "common carrier" within the meaning of section 210 of the Constitution. But under section 815 of the Statutes "the owner or operator of such road shall be, so far as they are applicable, governed and controlled by the laws relating to other railroads, and shall have the same rights and privileges granted to corporations owning and operating lines of railroad.''

Assuming, then, for the purpose of this case (but not deciding), that appellee built, or caused to be built, its railroad switch under the provisions of section 815 of the Statutes, does the contract with its tenants discriminate against appellant and the other independent mining companies along its lines who are charged five cents per ton trackage? We think not. In the first place, the very object and end of building the switch was to develop appellee's land, and for this purpose it obligated itself to lay out the round sum of about $90,000, and upon which it pays interest until the principal sum is repaid to the Louisville & Nashville Railroad Company. Appellee's tenants represent appellee and stand upon the same plane in the use of its switch, if appellee so desires, as does the appellee itself. The leases which appellee made to its tenants are the instrumentality for the development of the land and rendering it productive. If the appellee cannot lease its land, and is unable to open and operate mines for itself, then the whole purpose of the switch is frustrated. We therefore conclude that, as the switch was built to develop appellee's land, it has a right to either ship, or permit to be shipped by its tenants, all products of the land over the switch, free of charge.

But even if we felt less certain of this view than we do, there is nothing in this record to show that appellant has been discriminated against in favor of appellee's tenants. The tenants pay to appellee eight cents per ton, which by contract covers both royalty and trackage or freight charges. It must be con-

ceded that it has the right to make its royalty as low
as it pleases, even to giving its tenant the coal for the
mining of it; and, this being true, appellant cannot
claim to be discriminated against as long as the tenant is required to pay as much as five cents per ton
for both trackage and royalty. Upon this view appellant cannot say that it is discriminated against until
the tenant is required to pay less than five cents per
ton for the coal and its transportation to Pineville.
It is not disputed that the independent miners along
the line of appellee's switch are required to pay precisely the same trackage, five cents per ton; and the
only claim of discrimination is in regard to the two
mining companies which are the tenants of appellee.
It is not disputed that appellee owns the switch in
question; that is, it is not disputed that it has obligated itself to pay the Louisville & Nashville Railroad
Company for building it the round sum of $90,000,
that it pays part of this principle sum annually, and
pays legal interest on the unpaid balance until the
whole of the principal sum is finally discharged.

One of the contentions of appellant is that appellee
has leased its switch to the Louisville & Nashville
Railroad Company, and therefore that company is
operating it as a part of its general system, and that
it is discriminating against appellant. But the evidence in this case indubitably shows that, while the
first written contract drawn up between the Louisville & Nashville Railroad Company and appellee used
the word "lease," afterwards it was changed, and a
new writing drawn, which showed the real contract
between the parties to be that the Louisville & Nashville Railroad Company had a mortgage upon the
switch of appellee in order to more fully secure the

repayment of the funds expended by the railroad in the building of the switch; and the evidence further shows that the railroad company puts in its empty cars on the switch for the various mineowners along its line, and when these are loaded hauls them over the switch to Pineville free of charge. In other words, it makes no charge to any of the mining companies for what it does in the operation of the switch. The Louisville & Nashville Railroad Company has adopted Pineville as the general distributing point for all of the mines in that neighborhood, say, in a radius of 15 or 20 miles, and it has one common freight charge from that point to the various markets which it enforces against all the shippers alike. This is called in the record the "Pineville rate," and it is clearly established that this rate is enforced upon all shippers without any discrimination whatever.

The appellant also complains that the trackage rate of five cents per ton is extortionate. The evidence, however, does not bear out this contention. All of the evidence in the case bearing upon this point tends to show that five cents per ton is a reasonable rate under the circumstances. Moreover, it is the rate that was agreed upon by the lessors of the appellee company as a consideration for the grant of the right of way. This is fully set forth in the deed from the Howards to the appellee. The deed also contains a provision that the contract for the use of the appellee's switch redounds to the benefit of all assignees of the owners of the land. It was under this contract that appellant began the use of the switch, and it paid the charges in accordance with the terms of the contract for some time. We conclude therefore that, under the conditions now prevailing, five cents per ton

is a reasonable trackage charge. If, after the appellee company has been repaid its whole outlay, it
should be ascertained that five cents per ton is too
great a charge, then, upon a proper showing, the rate
may be reduced.

The appellee, while not a common carrier, is regulated by the general laws concerning railroads in so
far as they are applicable, and therefore the appellee
cannot prevent persons along its line from using its
switch upon the payment of a proper charge; nor can
it make this charge so great as to be either prohibi-
tive or extortionate. But as the rate of five cents was
agreed upon in advance, and, acting upon this agreement, appellee has built the switch and incurred a
large indebtedness therefor, those who use it cannot
be heard to say that this charge is too great or extortionate until appellee has been reimbursed for its outlay. It has to repay the railroad company the original cost price and pay interest on the unpaid balance
until the whole is paid. It must also pay all taxes
that are assessed against the switch. And certainly
it would be inequitable to permit those along the line,
who have contributed nothing to the building of the
switch, who have no money invested in it, and who do
not have to keep it in repair, to use it free of charge.
This position would put the owner of the switch in a
worse position towards its use than a stranger, because, if the stranger may use the switch without
charge as freely as the owner, and pay nothing for
the cost of building it, or taxes or repairs, this position is infinitely preferable to that of the owner. We
conclude therefore: That the payment of the trackage charges is a condition precedent to the use of the
switch; that the amount of five cents per ton, under

present conditions, is not too great; and that appellant must pay it before it has a right to use appellee's property.

None of the cases cited by appellant are apposite to the question in hand. The appellee does not dispute that, if it is a common carrier, it may not discriminate between its patrons, and therefore it is not necessary to discuss any of the numerous cases cited to show that common carriers cannot discriminate in favor of, or against, any of those who ship over their lines. The case of Bedford Stone Co. v. Oman, 115 Ky. 369, 73 S. W. 1038, 24 Ky. Law Rep. 2274, did not involve the question we have here. There the Louisville & Nashville Railroad, under the evidence, owned the switch, and had absolute control of it as a part of its general system, and it was refusing to permit Oman to ship stone over the switch at any rate; in other words, it was refusing to serve him as a common carrier at all. And it was there held that the Louisville & Nashville Railroad, while it had such control and ownership of the switch, could not refuse to haul Oman's freight.

That is not the question here. The Louisville & Nashville Railroad hauls the freight of appellant from the mine to Pineville without any charge to it, and from Pineville to the market it charges appellant the same rate that it charges all other shippers to the same place under the same conditions. The question is not between appellant and the Louisville & Nashville Railroad, but between appellant and the Straight Creek Coal & Coke Company, the owner of the switch; that company being perfectly willing for appellant to use its switch, but asking from it a fair remuneration for its use. The Oman Case is the exact opposite of the case at bar. The case of Greasy Creek Co. v.

Jellico Co., 116 S. W. 1189, involved the constitutionality of section 815 of the Kentucky Statutes, which authorizes the condemnation of private property for coal switches. There was no question of freight rates involved or discussed. All that was decided there was that switches built under section 815 are governed by the railroad law in so far as it is applicable. The court said nothing in that case which would intimate that one mining company might use the switch of ancther mining company without paying a fair remuneration for its use.

There was no dispute between appellant and appellee of the proper amount which the latter should receive, if it had a right to recover at all; in other words, the number of tons shipped were not disputed, and applying the trackage charge of five cents for each ton would show the proper amount of recovery.

Upon the trial of the case before the circuit judge, he decided the issues herein involved in favor of the appellee, and gave judgment for the sum of $2,247.70, and this judgment is affirmed, both as to the Straight Creek Coal & Coke Company and the Louisville & Nashville Railroad Company.

On the cross-appeal brought by plaintiff, complaint is made that the court erred in failing to allow interest on its claim, at least from the date of the filing of the suit; plaintiff's suit being upon an open, running account. It was clearly within the discretion of the chancellor to allow interest or not; but, inasmuch as no claim for interest was made in the pleadings by plaintiff, it is in no position to complain that none was allowed, and for this reason the judgment is affirmed on the cross-appeal.

BARKER, J., not sitting.

CASE 67.—ACTION BY THE CITY OF LOUISVILLE AGAINST
    WILLIAM SPECHT.—November 30, 1909.

Specht v. City of Louisville

Appeal from Jefferson Circuit Court.   (Chancery
Branch 1 Div.).

SHACKELFORD MILLER, Judge.

Judgment for plaintiff, defendant appeals.—Affirmed.

1   Taxation—Enforcement—Uniformity.—Ky. St. 1909, Sec. 2998,
    providing that uncollected tax bills shall be deemed a debt
    and may be enforced as such, except those against persons
    under disability, by the remedies given for the recovery
    of debt, and that all unpaid tax bills shall draw a specified
    rate of interest, etc., exempts infants, married women, and
    lunatics from the method of procedure prescribed for the col-
    lection of unpaid tax bills, but makes all tax bills liable to the
    specified rate of interest, and is not invalid as making any dif-
    ference in the levy of taxes, and the fact that it authorizes a
    personal judgment against an adult under no disability does
    not render the act unconstitutional.

2   Taxation—Delinquent Taxes—Penalty—Validity—Usury.—Ky.
    St. 1909, Sec. 2998, providing that unpaid tax bills shall for the
    first year bear interest at the rate of one-half of 1 per cent.
    for every month or fraction thereof, and thereafter, of 1 per
    cent for every month or fraction thereof until paid, imposes a
    penalty on delinquent taxpayers, and it is not invalid as seek-
    ing to enforce the collection of a rate of interest in excess of
    6 per cent. established as the legal rate, by section 2218 (sec-
    tion 1814), and is not in violation of section 2219 (section
    1815), providing that contracts and assurances made for the
    loan or forbearance of money at a greater rate than the legal
    rate of interest shall be void as to the excess of the legal
    rate, since a tax is neither a contract nor a loan, nor a for-
    bearance of money, though it is treated as a debt for the
    purpose of defining its mode of collection.

Specht v. City of Louisville.

3. Municipal Corporations—Classification—Validity.—The laws providing for the organization and powers of the various classes into which cities may be divided under the Constitution, requiring the Legislature to assign the various cities to the classes in which they belong, are general laws, where they are made applicable alike to all cities falling within the designated class, and the laws governing cities of the first class are general laws, though they are applicable in fact to only one city.

HARRISON & HARRISON for appellant.

PROPOSITIONS SUBMITTED.

1. Section 4 of Chapter 57 of the Acts of 1906, giving cities of the first class the right to exact interest at the rate of twelve per cent. per annum on all tax bills after the expiration of one year from the time the same are due is unconstitutional and usurious.

(a) It is unconstitutional in that it affects only adult persons and does not apply to the property of infants, married women or those of unsound mind.

(b) It is usurious because the twelve per cent. is no part of the obligation to pay the tax, nor it is a penalty, but it is given or allowed "for forbearance" only. Chap. 57, Sec. 4, Acts of 1906; Sec. 2218 Ky. Stats.; M'Cann's Executor v. Bell, 79 Ky., p. 112; Sec. 3005, Ky. Statutes.

JOSEPH S. LAWTON for appellee.

CLAYTON B. BLAKEY of counsel.

PROPOSITIONS AND AUTHORITIES.

1. The provision excepting persons under the disability of infancy, coverture, and unsound mind applies to the remedy and not to the amount of interest to be charged on the taxes. This provision was a part of the original statute, the validity of which has often been recognized by this court. Walston v. City of Louisville, 66 S. W., 385, 23 Ky. Law Rep., 1852; Woolley v. City of Louisville, 114 Ky., 556, 71 S. W., 893.

2. "The giving of interest on unpaid taxes is no more than a penalty for their non-payment." "What penalties may be imposed upon delinquents in the several classes of cities is a matter of legislative discretion." Walston v. City of Louisville, 66 S. W., 385, 23 Ky. Law Rep., 1852; Woolley v. City of Louisville, 114 Ky., 556, 71 S. W., 893; Droege v. McInerey, 87 S. W., 1085. 27 Ky. Law Rep., 1137.

3. The Act of 1906, being section 212 of an act for the government of cities of the first class, is not local or special legislation in violation of Section 59, Sub-section 21 of the Constitution, prohibiting local or special acts regulating the rate of interest. Walston and Woolley cases, supra.

4. The penalty imposed upon delinquent taxes in cities of the first class by the act in question is less than the penalties imposed by the acts governing the same subject in other classes of municipalities. A penalty of one per cent. per month, to be attached one year after the taxes are due and payable, is just and reasonable. Cooley on Taxation, 2nd Ed., page 457; 3rd Ed., Vol. 2, page 901; Lacy v. Davis, 4 Mich., 140; Nance v. Hopkins, 10 Lea., 508; Myers v. Parks, 8 Heisk, 500; Scott v. Watkins. 22 Ark., 556; Potts v. Cooley, 56 Wis., 45; Evermann v. Blakesley, 9 Mo., App. 231; Sections of Ky. Statutes (Carroll Ed., 1909). 3184, 3400, 3392, 3644. 3677, 4156, 4174, 4091; Owensboro Water Works v. City of Owensboro, 74 S. W., 685, 24 Ky. Law Rep., 2530. Response to petition for rehearing, 75 S. W., 261, 25 Ky. Law Rep., 434.

OPINION OF THE COURT BY JUDGE LASSING—Affirming.

This litigation calls in question the constitutionality of section 2998, Ky. St. 1909. Its validity is assailed upon two grounds: First, that it affects only adult persons and does not apply to the property of infants, persons under the disability of coverture, or insane persons; and, second, because the rate of interest charged on tax bills is usurious and in violation of sections 2218 and 2219, Kentucky Statutes. Section 2998 of the statutes, which is as follows: "All tax bills, uncollected in whole or in part, and which remain in the hands of the tax receiver on the first day of May succeeding the date on which they were listed with him for collection against any person owning property in his own right, shall be deemed a debt from such person to said city arising as by contract and may be enforced as such (except those against the persons under the disability of infancy, coverture or unsound mind) by all remedies given for the recovery of debt in any court of this commonwealth otherwise competent for that purpose; and those bills assessed against an administrator, executor or trustee shall be a charge against the whole succession of trust estates and may be in either case enforced accordingly, this being in addition to the other remedies hereinafter given. All tax bills remaining unpaid on the first day of May, succeeding the date on which they were listed with the tax receiver for collection shall bear interest at the rate of one-half of one per cent. for every month, or fraction of a month, from date until the first day of the next succeeding May, and thereafter shall bear interest at the rate of one per cent. for every month, or fraction of a month, until paid''—was, prior to its adoption in 1906, section 2998 of the Kentucky Statutes of 1903, and from a comparison of the two acts it will be observed that, so far as the first objection raised by appellant is concerned, the acts are identical, in that in each act there is an express provision that the tax owing by the property owner shall be deemed a debt from such person to the city, arising as by contract, and may be enforced as such by all remedies given for the recovery of debt in any court of the commonwealth otherwise competent for that purpose.

There is an express provision in each act exempting from this method of procedure infants, married women, and lunatics. This exemption, however, is in their favor merely as to the method of procedure; whereas, the tax and interest charged for delay in its payment are the same against all property, whether owned by adults or infants, women, married or single, and per-

sons sane or insane. The statute makes no difference
whatever in levy of taxes or the rate of interest that
shall be charged. The only difference is that a personal judgment may be taken against an adult under
no disability; whereas, infants and persons under disability can, under the express provisions and terms of
the act, have no personal judgment rendered against
them, and the remedy must be a proceeding against
the property itself. There is no provision that the
property of an infant, or a married woman, or insane
person should not be held liable to the payment of
the same taxes and rate of interest as that of an
adult.

In the cases of Walston v. City of Louisville, 66 S
W. 385, 23 Ky. Law Rep. 1852, and Woolley v. City of
Louisville, 114 Ky. 556, 7 S. W. 893, 24 Ky. Law Rep.
1357, this court passed upon the constitutionality of
this act prior to its amendments in 1906, and held it
to be constitutional, and, so far as the first objection
raised by appellant is concerned, the acts are identical. No complaint can justly be made because the
Legislature saw fit to define a different mode of procedure in enforcing the payment of tax claims against
the property of infants and persons under disability
from that which should be applied in enforcing similar claims against adults under no disability, so long
as the tax sought to be collected against each is the
same; and the act in question is undoubtedly so drawn
as to apply equally to all property, for, in its concluding sentence, we find the following: "All tax bills remaining unpaid on the first day of May, succeeding
the date on which they were listed with the tax receiver for collection shall bear interest at the rate of
one- half of one per cent. for every month, or fraction

of a month, from date until the first day of the next succeeding May, and thereafter shall bear interest at the rate of one per cent. for every month, or fraction of a month, until paid.'' This is the only portion of said act which fixes the rate of interest that shall be paid, and it will be observed that it applies alike to all property without exception. We therefore conclude that the objection raised by appellant to the validity of this act, on the ground that it is not uniform in its application, is not well taken.

Appellant's next contention is that as the act raises the tax claims which the city holds against the property owners to the dignity of a debt, and then seeks to enforce the collection of a rate of interest thereon in excess of 6 per cent., which by section 2218 of the statutes is established as the legal rate, it is in direct violation of section 2219, which provides that all contracts and assurances made for the loan or forbearance of money or other thing of value at a greater rate than the legal rate of interest, as provided for by section 2218, shall be void as to the excess of the legal rate. The trouble with this argument is that a tax is neither a contract nor a loan nor a forebearance of money in the sense in which these terms are used in the statute referred to. It remains a tax, and it is treated as a debt merely for the purpose of defining its mode of collection. The interest charge is upon taxes remaining unpaid at a designated date and is in the nature of a penalty for their nonpayment, and it has frequently been held that it is a matter of legislative discretion as to what penalty shall be imposed by the Legislature for the nonpayment of taxes, and this legislative will has never been disturbed or interferred with so long as the penalty has not been fixed at a figure that could be considered unreasonable, unjust, or confiscatory.

In the two cases above referred to, of Walston v. City of Louisville, and Woolley v. City of Louisville, it was expressly held that the collection of an interest charge upon overdue taxes was in the nature of a penalty. It is true that the act in force when passed upon in those cases did not authorize the imposition and collection of 12 per cent. interest, but it did authorize the imposition and collection of interest at the rate of one-half of 1 per cent. for each month, or fractional part thereof, that the tax remained unpaid, which was a higher rate than authorized by section 2218, and the principle contended for by appellant in this case would therefore apply with equal force in those cases. The court having upheld the validity of the act, even though it authorized an interest charge in excess of 6 per cent., settled the principle for which the city here contends, to wit, that the imposition of an interest charge on overdue taxes is in the nature of a penalty, imposed upon the delinquent taxpayer because of his delinquency, and, being a penalty, the amount thereof is clearly a matter of legislative discretion. Nor does the fact that the act authorizes the imposition and collection of 12 per cent. interest on taxes remaining unpaid at a certain day in cities of the first class justify the charge that the act is special legislation, for the Constitution, by express provision, requires that the General Assembly shall assign the various cities and towns in the state to the classes in which they properly belong. For governmental purposes, the organization and powers of the various classes into which the cities are divided are defined by general laws, and, so long as these laws are made applicable alike to all cities falling within the designated class, they have uniformly been held to be general in their application. Louisville is a city of the first class, and is the only city in that class in this commonwealth. Hence, while all laws governing cities of the first class must necessarily be applicable to the city of Louisville alone, they are nevertheless general laws, and this court has so recognized and held in the case of Walston v. City of Louisville, supra.

In framing these general laws for the regulation and government of the various classes into which the cities and towns of the state are divided, the members of the General Assembly realized that it was necessary to impose upon the taxpayer a burden in excess of the legal rate of interest, in order to enforce the speedy payment by the taxpayer of the taxes, for it can readily be seen that, if only the legal rate of interest were imposed upon the taxpayer for the nonpayment of his taxes when due, it would merely have the effect of making the city a lender of money to the various taxpayers until such time as suited their convenience to pay, and the city would be without means to carry on the various departments of its government. Hence there is incorporated in the charters of the cities of the various classes a provision whereby the taxpayer is called upon to pay an interest charge in the nature of a penalty upon all taxes that remain due and unpaid after a given period. This interest charge varies. In cities of some classes it is more, while in others it is less, than in cities of the first class; but, being uniform in each class, it meets the requirements of the Constitution calling for uniformity.

The only appreciable difference between the act here complained of and the act which it amended and

superseded is that in the act under consideration the
rate of interést for the second year's delinquency is
increased from one-half of 1 per cent. for each month,
or fractional part thereof, that the tax remains unpaid, to 1 per cent. This change was found to be
absolutely necessary in order to enable the city to
collect its revenue. So long ᵃs the penalty for failure
to pay amounted to but little more than the rate at
which money could be borrowed, the taxpayer did not
pay his taxes, and the city was without means necessary to enable it to run its government. It became
apparent that a more severe penalty would have to be
imposed in order to speedily collect the taxes, and
hence the increase in the rate of the interest charge;
but this increase in rate called into play the application of no new principle, for the old rate was in excess
of the legal rate, and the only complaint is that this
present rate is usurious, not that it is inequitable, unjust, or confiscatory, and, this being true, the chancellor correctly held that the answer filed presented no
defense.

Judgment affirmed.

CASE 68.—CONTROVERSY OVER THE APPLICATION OF CLARENCE EWING FOR A LICENSE TO RETAIL LIQUOR.—December 2, 1909.

Commonwealth v Ewing

Appeal from Warren County.

JOHN M. GALLOWAY, Circuit Judge.

From an order of the County Court granting liquor license to Clarence Ewing, which was affirmed in the Circuit Court, the Commonwealth appeals.—Reversed.

Intoxicating Liquors—Licenses—Merchants—Evidence.—Evidence, on application for a retail liquor license, held to show, notwithstanding applicant's testimony to the contrary that he was not in good faith a merchant, and that he has assumed the business for the purpose of retailing liquor; so that under Ky. St. 1909, Sec. 4205, authorizing such a license only on satisfactory evidence to the contrary, the county court did not exercise reasonable discretion in granting him a license.

THOS. W. THOMAS, W. B. GAINES, JAS. BREATHITT, Attorney General, and TOM B. McGREGOR, Assistant Attorney General, for the Commonwealth.

OPINION OF THE COURT BY JUDGE CARROLL—Reversing.

This appeal is prosecuted by the commonwealth from a judgment of the Warren circuit court affirming a judgment of the county court granting Ewing a merchant's license to sell liquors under section 4205 of the Kentucky Statutes reading, in part, as follows: "License to merchants, druggists or distillers shall be granted only upon satisfactory evidence that the applicant is in good faith a merchant, druggist or a distiller and that the applicant has not assumed the name or the business for the purpose of retailing liquors.'' We are asked to reverse the judgment upon the ground that Ewing was not, at the time he applied for license, a merchant in good faith, and that he assumed the business of being a merchant for the purpose of obtaining a license to retail liquors.

The only evidence in the record is that of Ewing, and two other witnesses who testified that they had never heard anything against his moral character. From Ewing's testimony we gather the following facts: Delafield precinct, in Warren county, adjoins the city of Bowling Green, and is the only precinct in the county in which license to sell liquors may be granted. The remainder of the county, including the city of Bowling Green, has voted against the sale of liquors. In this precinct a short distance from the city there is a place called the ''boat landing'' on Barren river, and in the immediate neighborhood of this boat landing there are several groceries and a few people. In the entire precinct there are 230 voters. Ewing some time in February, 1909, leased a lot 40x50 feet near the boat landing for a term of one year with the privilege of renewing the lease. On this lot he put up, at a cost of some $300, a plain room 20x40 feet, and on March 1, 1909, opened a grocery store in it with a stock of goods worth about $250. Previous to this time he had never engaged in the grocery or any mercantile business. His principal occupation seems to have been clerking in places where whisky was sold.

On March 1st there were four other grocery stores in the immediate neighborhood of Ewing's place, and all of them had license to sell liquor under the statute

supra.   Twelve days after he opened his grocery, he
put up notices that he would apply for license, and on
the 22d of March made the application.   In the course
of his examination, he said that he was a merchant in
good faith and did not engage in the business for the
purpose of getting license to sell liquor; but his statement is not corroborated by any other fact or circumstance in the record.   On the contrary, we should say
that it appears at first blush that his sole purpose in
opening the grocery was to engage in the sale of
liquor, and that it affirmatively appears that Ewing
was not a merchant in good faith, and that he had assumed the name and the business for the purpose of
retailing liquors.   There is no evidence that the place
had any business attractions whatever for a person
who wished to engage only in the sale of merchandise,
and it is inconceivable that a person of ordinary intelligence, as we assume Ewing to be, should attempt
to establish himself in the grocery business at this
point unless his intention was to use his pretense of a
grocery for the purpose of getting license to engage
in the more profitable business of selling whisky.
That he was not a merchant in good faith, and that
he did assume the business as a mere subterfuge behind which to hide his real purpose, is apparent in
almost every line of his evidence.

We are not concluded by his statement that he was
a merchant in good faith, nor are we estopped by it
from looking into the truth of the matter as it appears
in the record.   Courts, in the interest of justice and
truth, may, and often do, look beneath the surface of
things to discover the real nature of the transaction
under investigation, and are frequently justified in
putting aside as unworthy of serious consideration
statements which, although apparently candid, are

really used as mere forms of expression to bring the
actor within the protecting circle of some rule of law
or statutory phrase. In the enactment of this statute,
the Legislature was careful to provide not only that
the applicant for license should establish by satisfactory evidence that he was a merchant in good faith,
but also that he had not assumed the name or the
business of a merchant for the purpose of obtaining
license. A person may be a merchant in good faith
in the sense that he is engaged in the business at a
place and under circumstances indicating his intention
to follow it as a business; but proof of this fact alone
would not entitle him to license to sell liquors. He
must, in addition, show that he did not engage in the
business for the purpose of obtaining license.

It was the legislative purpose that the evidence in
support of both these propositions should be clear and
convincing, and, when a person applies for license to
sell liquor, the question of his good faith and intent
should be carefully inquired into in order that the
statute may not be used as an instrument to enable
persons not bona fide merchants to sell liquor. It is
manifest that, in cases like this, no rule of general fitness can be laid down by which the lower court may
be guided in granting or refusing license. Each application must stand or fall on the evidence introduced concerning it; but it may safely be said that
in every case the previous occupation, as well as repu-
tation of the applicant, the length of time he has been
engaged in the business at the place where he applies
for license, the value of his stock of goods, the probability of it being a good location from a business
standpoint, the volume of business done by him, the
number of people in the neighborhood, and its prox-

imity to other similar places of business, are matters pertinent to be inquired into and considered by the court in arriving at a conclusion, and the burden is upon the applicant to establish that he comes within the class to whom license may be granted.

In disposing of this case we have not overlooked or underestimated the weight that should properly be given to the judgment of the court granting the license. In more than one like case we have held that the discretion vested in tribunals authorized to grant license will not be interferred with unless it has been abused, or, in other words, not reasonably exercised. And this well-settled practice we have no disposition to modify or depart from; but, in the case before us, we feel obliged to say that in our opinion the county court did not exercise a reasonable discretion in granting Ewing license.

Wherefore the judgment is reversed, with directions to proceed in conformity with this opinion.

CASE 69.—ACTION BY JULIUS H. ULRICH AND OTHERS
AGAINST FREDRICK KOUSTMER AND OTHERS.—
November 30, 1909.

Ulrich, &c. v. Koustmer, &c.

Appeal from Campbell Circuit Court.

C. W. YUNGBLUT, Circuit Judge.

Judgment for defendants, plaintiff appeals.—Affirmed in part and reversed in part.

1. Municipal Corporations—Police and Fire Commissioners—
    Holding Over.—Ky. St. 1909, Sec. 3137, part of the charter of
    .cities of the second class, provides that four persons shall
    be appointed as police and fire commissioners for a term of
    one, two, three, and four years, respectively, and thereafter
    · yearly, as their terms of office expire, respectively, there
    shall be one appointed for a term of four years. Held, that
    such a commissioner does not hold over after expiration of his
    term till his successor is appointed and qualified, there being no provision therefor, and there being no such provision
    in section 3118 (section 1216), part of such charter, relative
    to the term of the superintendent of public works, while
    there is such provision in sections 3126 and 3143 (sections
    1028, 1080), also parts of such charter, relative to the terms
    of the auditor and commissioner of waterworks.
2. Municipal Corporations—Police and Fire Commissioners—
    Vacancy in Office—Appointment.—Under Ky. St. 1909, Sec.
    3137, part of the charter of cities of the second class, providing that the mayor, subject to the approval of the board of
    alderman, shall appoint four persons as police and fire
    commissioners; that they shall be appointed for a term of
    one, two, three, and four years, respectively, and every year
    thereafter as their terms of office shall expire, respectively,
    there shall be one appointed for a term of four years, and the
    mayor shall fill all vacancies—the mayor in making an original appointment (that is, appointing one, after the terms of
    the first four appointees have expired, to serve for four years)
    must submit the name of the appointee to the board of alder-

men for its approval, and, it having refused to approve the appointee, a vacancy, such as the mayor may fill without the approval of the board of aldermen, does not arise on expiration for the term of the outgoing member, but the mayor must submit another name for its approval.

THOMAS P. CAROTHERS, AUBREY BARBOUR, BRENT SPENCE and NELSON & GALLAGHER attorneys for appellants.

PROPOSITIONS DISCUSSED.

1. Injunction is a proper remedy for an officer interferred with or molested in the discharge of his duty. Poyntz v. Shackelford, 107 Ky., 546.

2. A member of the Police and Fire Commissioners of cities of the second class holds over until his successor is duly appointed and qualified. Dillion's Municipal Corporations, Sections 219, 220; Wier v. Bush, 4 Littell, 433; City of Louisville v. Higdon, 59 Ky., 526; McDermott v. City of Louisville, 98 Ky., 50; City of Wheeling v. Clock, 25 W. Va., 266; People v. Ferris (N. Y.) 16 Hun., 219; Sections 3137, 3118, 2143, Kentucky Statutes.

3. The expiration of the term of office of a member of the Board of Police and Fire commissioners of cities of the second Class does not create such a vacancy as is authorized to be filled by the mayor without confirmation by the Board of Aldermen. Ky. Statutes, Section 3137; Watkins v. Mooney, 24 Ky. Law Rep., 1469; People v. Tirrell, 87 Cal., 475; Lawrence v. Handley, 87 Mich., 399; People v. Lord, 9 Mich., 226; Miller v. Washington, Fed. Cas. No. 9, 593 A. (2 Hayn. & H.).

SAM E. ANDERSON for appellees.

GEO. H. AHLERING. C. T. BAKER, WM. A. BURKAMP and HARRY WEBER of counsel.

AUTHORITIES CITED.

1. Sections 3118, 3126, 3137, 3143 Kentucky Statutes on proposition that incumbent does not hold until his successor is appointed and qualified. Stevens v. Wyatt, 16 B. Mon., 594; Leeman v. Hinton, 1 Duvall, 44; Offutt v. Commonwealth, 73 Ky., 215; McDermott v. City of Louisville, 17 Ky. Law Rep., 617, all upon this same proposition.

2. State v. Blackmore, 104 Mo., 340; Opinion of the Justices, 45 N. H., 590. In re Supreme Court vacancy, 4 S. D., 532, upon what constitutes a vacancy in office.

3. Section 3143 of Kentucky Statutes upon the point that the mayor appoints to all vacancies in the office.

4. Watkins v. Mooney, 24 Ky. Law Rep., 1469, upon the propo- .
sition that the appointment to fill a vacancy need not be confirmed by the board of aldermen.

OPINION OF THE COURT BY CHIEF JUSTICE NUNN—
Affirming.

This controversy depends upon the construction of
section 3137, Ky. St., which is as follows: "The
mayor, subject to the approval of the board of aldermen, shall appoint four citizens and freeholders of the
city, who shall have been electors of the city for five
years preceding their appointment, and who shall not
be less than 30 years of age, and not related to the
mayor by blood or marriage, who, together with the
mayor, shall compose a board of police and fire commissioners. The mayor shall be ex officio chairman of
said board. Said commissioners shall be appointed for
a term of one, two three and four years, respectively,
upon the taking effect of this act; and every year
thereafter, as the terms of office of said commissioners shall expire, respectively, there shall be one commissioner appointed for a term of four years, and the
mayor shall fill all vacancies that may occur in said
board," etc.

This section is contained in the charters of second-
class cities. The city of Newport being one of that
class, the mayor on April 27, 1894, after the act became a law, appointed four persons to act as police
and fire commissioners, their terms of office to expire
in one, two, three, and four years, in accordance with
the statute, and on the same date each year thereafter
the mayor named a person to act in the place of the
one whose term expired, and sent the name to the
board of aldermen for confirmation. There seems to
have been no friction in the naming and confirming of

a person to hold the position until April, 1909, when the mayor, Edward L. Krieger, named one Bowman to fill the position, and sent his name to the board of aldermen for confirmation, which the board refused to do. The mayor failed to name another person in lieu of Bowman until after the term of Richard Pfingstag expired. He then declared a vacancy in the office, and appointed one Lindsay to fill the unexpired term.

This action was instituted, in which it was alleged, in substance, that Pfingstag was still a member of the board and had a right to hold the position until his successor was duly appointed, approved, and qualified; that the appointment by the mayor of Lindsay to fill the alleged vacancy was void, and that he, Pfingstag, had a right to act as a member of said board; that the mayor and one Koustmer, a member of the board, were threatening and about to induct Lindsay into office, and an injunction was sought to prevent it. The case was tried in the lower court, and judgment was rendered to the effect that Pfingstag's term of four years had expired, and that he had no right to hold the office until his successor was duly appointed and qualified, and that there was a vacancy in the position when the mayor appointed Lindsay and that the appointment of Lindsay was legal; that it was not necessary in such a case to submit his name to the board of aldermen for its confirmation. The injunction was dissolved, and this appeal prayed.

Immediately thereafter, and within the time fixed by law, the appellants moved a judge of this court to reinstate the injunction, and on June 9, 1909, W. E. Settle, at that time Chief Justice of this court, entered the following order, to-wit: "It is the opinion of this court, in which a majority of its members and all

who are present concur, that the injunction granted
appellants should have been continued in force until a
hearing of the case is had in this court upon the appeal and on the merits.   It is, therefore, adjudged
that the injunction dissolved by the circuit court be,
and it is, re-instated to continue in force during the
pendency of the appeal, and until the case shall be
decided by this court upon its merits.'' Counsel cite
several authorities which seemingly support their
contentions as to each of the questions involved.   We
will not take the time, however, to consider and discuss them in this opinion, as they construe statutes
different from ours, the one under consideration. We
have had no trouble in arriving at a proper construction of the section of the statute involved.   The charter for cities of the second class came from the Legislature as a whole, and it is not the province of the
court to add to it when the meaning is plain.   The
statute, in so many words, fixes the term each of the
persons appointed is to hold.

It was in the province of the General Assembly to
determine whether or not they should hold until their
successors were appointed and qualified.   Sections
3118, 3126, 3137, and 3143 of the Statutes throw much
light upon the question as to whether Pfingstag is authorized to hold the office of police and fire commissioner until his successor was duly appointed and
qualified.   Section 3118 relates to the appointment by
the mayor of a superintendent of public works, and
says that he shall be appointed, ''for a term of two
years,'' subject to the approval of the board of aldermen.   Section 3126 provides that the mayor shall appoint an auditor, subject to the approval of the board
of aldermen, to serve for two years, or until his suc-

cessor is duly appointed and qualified. Section 3137, the one under consideration, provides that four persons shall be appointed as police and fire commissioners, their term to expire in one, two, three, and four years, respectively, and thereafter, yearly, there shall be one appointment for a term of four years. Section 3143 fixes the term of the commissioner of the waterworks. ''Their terms of office shall be three years and until their successors are duly appointed and qualified.'' Here we have two instances expressly stating that the officers shall hold over until their successors are duly appointed and qualified, and in the other two no such power or right is conferred. The expression in the two instances that they should hold over and in the other two a failure to confer the right shows plainly that the General Assembly did not intend that the right to hold over should exist. This court has no power to add words to a statute when it is unambiguous. We are therefore of the opinion that Pfingstag's power as a police and fire commissioner ceased at the expiration of his term of four years.

The other question is also easy of solution. The statute unquestionably authorized the mayor to fill all vacancies in the office without submitting the names of such appointees to the board of aldermen for its approval. See the case of Watkins v. Mooney, 114 Ky. 646, 71 S. W. 622, 24 Ky. Law Rep. 1469. It was also decided in that case, with equal definiteness, that the mayor in making original appointments— that is, in appointing some one to serve for four years —should submit the name of the appointee to the board of aldermen for its approval, and this is in accord with the express terms of the statute. Our opinion is that, when Lindsey was appointed by the mayor, there was no such vacancy in the office as was contemplated by the General Assembly when it enacted the statute. The term of office succeeding Pfingstag had never been filled, so that it could become vacant, and the statute requires the mayor to appoint some one for the term and submit his name to the board of aldermen for approval. In our opinion there must have been some one duly appointed and qualified filling the office before a vacancy can occur as contemplated by the statute. It was the duty of the mayor to have submitted the name of Lindsay as his appointee to the board of aldermen for its approval before he could have been legally inducted into office.

In the case of Watkins v. Mooney, supra, this court said: "It is urged, and this we conceive to be the main argument for the appellee in his behalf, that there is no apparent reason, and, in fact, none, why the legislators should require the mayor's appointees, original and for full terms, always to be confirmed by the board of aldermen, and yet allow him to fill vacancies in the same board without such confirmation. The argument seems to us to be almost irresistible when presented to that body who make the law. But the consequences are not so much to be regarded in the construction of the statutes as the language employed, where the language is unambiguous. In fact, as long as the language of the statute is not ambiguous, the courts have no discretion as to the meaning they will give to it. * * * A distinction is obviously intended to be made between original appointments of members of the board and appointments to fill vacancies; otherwise, there is no sense or meaning in the provision directing and authorizing the mayor to fill all vacancies. If the Legislature had intended that appointments to fill vacancies should be submitted for confirmation to the board of aldermen, it would doubtless have put in after the word 'mayor,' as it expressly did when providing for the original appointment, 'subject to the approval of the board of aldermen.' '' Evidently the General Assembly intended that in selecting police and fire commissioners for a term of four years the mayor and board of aldermen should exercise their judgment in the matter, and the mayor alone could not have the power. To give the statute the construction contended for by appellees would thwart this object, as the mayor could fail to appoint and send in the name until after the term of the outgoing member had expired, or send in the name of a person that he knew was unfit, and that the board would reject, and then wait until the term of the outgoing member expired and declare a vacancy and appoint a person without submitting his name to the board for confirmation, and in this way govern and control the matter himself, and obtain a board of police and fire commissioners of his own selection and thus defeat the Legislature's will.

For these reasons, the judgment with reference to declaring that Pfingstag had no right to hold over beyond his term is affirmed, and that part declaring Lindsay duly appointed to fill the vacancy is reversed and remanded for further proceedings consistent herewith.

CASE 70.—ACTION BY S. J. SCHWALK'S ADMINISTRATOR AGAINST THE CITY OF LOUISVILLE.—December 1, 1909.

Schwalk's Adm'r v. City of Louisville

Appeal from Jefferson Circuit Court (Common Pleas Branch, Second Division).

THOS R. GORDON, Judge.

Judgment for defendant, plaintiff appeals.—Affirmed.

1. Municipal Corporations—Liability for Negligence—Governmental Duties.—A municipal corporation in maintaining a city hall for the use of its officers and agents as a place for transacting its business performs a public and governmental duty, and is not liable for the negligence of its agents and servants in the transaction of such business.

2. Taxation—Exemptions—Public Property Used for Public Purposes—City Hall.—Under Const. Sec. 170, which declares that public property used for public purposes shall be exempt from taxation, the city hall maintained by the city of Louisville, is exempt.

3. Municipal Corporations—Liability for Negligence—Governmental Duties.—In exempting municipal corporations from liability for defects in its public buildings used for public purposes or governmental purposes, or the negligence of its employes in their care, the law places them on the same footing with the state and counties thereof as to buildings owned and used by them in aid of government.

4. Municipal Corporations—Liability for Negligence—Governmental Duties—Exception to Rule.—That municipalities are liable for negligence in not keeping their streets in repair affords an exception to the general rule exempting municipalities from liability for negligence in the performance of a public governmental duty imposed upon them for public benefit, and for which they in their corporate capacity derive no pecuniary profit.

Schwalk's Admr. v. City of Louisville.

5.   Municipal Corporations—Persons Employed in City Hall—
Liability for Negligence—Respondeat Superior—"Public Officers."—Persons employed in a city hall in managing and
conducting the affairs of the municipality are public officers,
charged with the performance of public duties; and the
doctrine of respondeat superior does not apply to such employments.

6.   Courts—Previous Decisions as Precedents.—The appellate
court should be controlled by previous adjudications of the
court on the same question.

BENNETT H. YOUNG and MARION W. RIPY for appellant.
No brief in the record.

HUSTON QUINN for appellees.

CLAYTON B. BLAKEY and ELMER C. UNDERWOOD of counsel.

POINTS AND AUTHORITIES.

1.   In the maintenance and care of its public building or City
Hall, the appellee, City, is an arm of the State, and performs
certain State duties, and can not be held liable for the negligence
of an operator of the elevator in its City Hall.   The same rule
applies here as to a Court House, or to the Police and Fire Departments, etc.

(a)   What is a municipal corporation?   State v. Levy Court
(Del.), 43 Atl., 522; 1 Blackstone's Commentaries, 113-116; 2
Kent's Commentaries, 275; United States v. B. & O. R. R. Co.,
17 Wall. 322, 329; Marking v. Queen County, 49 N. E., 71.

(b)   A municipal corporation as defined by the Ky. Court of
Appeals.   City of Louisville v. Commonwealth, 1 Duv., 295; Taylor v. Owensboro, 98 Ky., 271; Lou. Bridge Co. v. City of Louisville, 81 Ky., 189, 212.

(c)   General rule as to municipal liability.   Sherman & Redfield
on Negligence, Sec. 253; Burdict's Law of Torts, page 109,
(Text.); Bigby v. United States, 188 U. S., 400 (Federal Bldg.);
Simons v. Gregory, etc., 120 Ky., 116 (Jeff. Co. Court House.);
Cunningham v. St. Louis, 96 Mo., 53, 8. S. W., 787 (Court House.).

(d)   State institutions and purposes.   Taxation, Constitution,
Sec. 170; City of Louisville v. Commonwealth, 1 Duv. 195. Schools:
Ernest v. West Covington, 16 Ky., 850.   Public Safety: Pollock's
Adm'r v. Louisville, 3 Bush, 221; Greenwood v. Louisville, 13
Bush, 226; O'Rourk v. Soulx Falls (S. D.), 19 L. R. A., 789; Wil-
cox v. Rochester, 190 N. Y., 131, 82 N. E., 1119.   City Court:

Constitution, Sec. 143; Kentucky Statutes, Secs. 2912, 2915, 2916, 2936, 2943. Health Department.

2. The erection, care and maintenance of the City Hall of Louisville is within the exercise of a purely governmental function, and this being true, the appellee, City, can not be held liable for any acts of negligence on the part of its employes enagaged therein.

(a) Organization. Constitution of Kentucky, Sec. 156; Kentucky Statutes, Sec. 2742.

(b) Governmental division. Cyc. Vol. 28, p. 1257.

(c) Application. Smith on Modern Law of Municipal Corporations, Sec. 157, etc.; Wright v. City of San Antonio (Texas). 50 S. W., 406; Dillon on Municipal Corporation, Sec. 30.

(d) School buildings. Ernest v. West Covington, 116 Ky., 850, etc. Clark v. Nicholasville, 27 Ky. Law Rep., 974; Dillon on Municipal Corporations, 965; Hill v. Boston, 122 Mass., 344.

(e) Prisons. Jones v. Corbin, 98 S. W., 1002; Gray v. Griffin, 111 Ga., 361, 51 L. R. A., 131.

(f) Bridges. Corning v. Saginaw (Mich.), 40 L. R. A., 526 French v. Boston, 129 Mass., 592.

(g) Hospitals. City of Richmond v. Long's Adm'r, 17 Gratt., 378; Maxmilian v. New York, 62 N. Y., 164, 20 Am. Rep., 468.

(h) Pesthouses. Twyman's Adm'r v. Board of Councilmen of Frankfort, 78 S. W., 466; Having v. Covington, 78 S. W., 431.

(i) Workhouses. Ulrich v. City of St. Louis, 20 S. W., 466.

(j) School of Reform. Williamson v. Louisville Industrial School of Reform, 95 Ky., 251.

(k) Parks. Board of Park Commissioners v. Prinz, 32 Ky. Law Rep., 359, 105 S. W., 948.

(l) Garbage. Condict's Adm'r v. Jersey City, 46 N. J. Law, 157; Kuehn v. Milwaukee, 92 Wis., 263; 65 N. W., 1030.

(m) City Hall. Snider v. St. Paul, 51 Minn., 466, 53 S. W., 763; Wilcox v. Rochester, 82 N. E., 1119; Kelly v. Boston, 186 Mass. 165, 71 N. E., 299; Eastman v. Town of Meredith, 36 N. H., 284; Worden v. Town of New Bedford, 131 Mass., 23.

OPINION OF THE COURT BY JUDGE SETTLE—Affirming.

On August 30, 1906, Simon J. Schwalk lost his life while going to some part of the city hall in Louisville upon an elevator used in the building. The city hall is owned by the appellee, city of Louisville, and practically the whole of the city's business is conducted within its walls.

The appellant, Columbia Finance & Trust Company, was appointed and duly qualified as administrator of Schwalk's estate, and on March 27, 1907, instituted this action in the court below to recover of the appellee city damages for his death; it being, in substance, alleged in the petition as finally amended that the death of its intestate was caused by the negligence of appellee, its agents, and servants in failing to maintain the elevator in a reasonably safe condition for use, and in permitting it to be operated by an inexperienced and incompetent negro boy. After the petition had been twice amended, the circuit court sustained a demurrer to it, and, appellant refusing to plead further, judgment was rendered dismissing the action. Appellant's dissatisfaction with that ruling and judgment resulted in this appeal.

The judgment of the circuit court is bottomed upon the theory that the duty of the city of Louisville to provide and maintain a city hall for the use of its officers and agents and as a place for transacting its business affairs is a public and governmental duty and obligation for the negligence of its agents and servants, in the performance of which the city is not liable in an action for damages. This court is fully committed to the doctrine thus announced. As said in Taylor v. Owensboro, 98 Ky. 271, 32 S. W. 948, 17 Ky. Law Rep. 856, 56 Am. St. Rep. 361: "Municipal governments are auxiliaries of the state government. They are created principally to aid in securing a proper government of the people within the boundaries of such municipalities, and to make more effectual the maintenance of public order." Louisville Bridge Co. v. City of Louisville, 81 Ky. 189; 5 R. 16; City of Louisville v. Commonwealth, 1 Duv. 295, 85 Am. Dec. 624.

The Constitution of the state gives full recognition
to municipal corporations, and that they are to be
treated as parts of the governmental machinery and
necessary auxiliaries in carrying out the ends of government. Under section 170 of the Constitution,
which declares that "public property used for public
purposes" shall be exempt from taxation, it has been
held by this court that waterworks, a park, public
wharf, and even bonds owned by a city and applied
exclusively to governmental or public uses cannot be
subjected to taxation. City of Louisville v. Commonwealth, 1 Duv. 295, 85 Am. Dec. 624; City of Owensboro v. Commonwealth, 105 Ky. 344, 49 S. W. 320. 20
Ky. Law Rep. 1281, 44 L. R. A. 202; Board of Councilmen City of Frankfort v. Commonwealth, 94 S. W.
648, 29 Ky. Law Rep. 699; Commonwealth v. City of
Covington, 128 Ky. 36, 107 S. W. 231, 32 Ky. Law Rep.
837, 14 L. R. A. (N. S.) 1214. Under the rule stated
by the foregoing authorities, appellee's city hall is
exempt from taxation. As the maintenance of a city
hall for the use of the court, officers, and employes of
a municipality, as well as for the transaction of its
business, is but the exercise of a purely governmental
function, it would seem to follow that the city cannot
be held liable for acts of negligence on the part of its
officers or agents engaged in its work or business
therein.

The general rule on this subject is well stated in
Burdick's law of Torts as follows: "Nonliability of
City—There is a substantial agreement that it is not
liable for the torts of its fire or police departments,
nor for those of its boards of health or education; nor
for those of any other officers, agents, or servants in
the discharge of functions which primarily belong to

the state, but the performance of which it has delegated to the municipality. Neglect of officers in
guarding prisoners, or in caring for jurymen, or in
keeping courthouses, townhouses, jails, or other public buildings in repair, will not subject the corporation
to legal liability. Nor will the negligence of an employe of a charity hospital render the city which maintains it, liable to damages." The doctrine thus stated
by Burdick has been applied by this court to relieve
cities and towns of responsibility for the torts or negligence of their agents in the following cases: Twyman's Adm'r v. City of Frankfort, 117 Ky. 518, 78 S.
W. 446, 25 Ky. Law Rep. 1620, 64 L. R. A. 572; Pollock's Adm'r v. City of Louisville, 13 Bush, 221, 26
Am. Rep. 260; Jolly's Adm'r v. Hawesville, 89 Ky.
279, 12 S. W. 313, 11 Ky. Law Rep. 477; Prather v.
Lexington, 13 B. Mon. 559, 56 Am. Dec. 585; Having v.
Covington, 78 S. W. 431, 25 Ky. Law Rep. 1617; Ernst
v. Covington, 116 Ky. 850, 76 S. W. 1089, 25 Ky. Law
Rep. 1027, 63 L. R. A. 652, 105 Am. St. Rep. 241;
Clark v. Nicholasville, 87 S. W. 300, 27 Ky. Law Rep.
974; Jones v. City of Corbin, 98 S. W. 1002, 30 Ky.
Law Rep. 374; Board Park Com'rs v. Prinz, 127 Ky.
460, 105 S. W. 948, 32 Ky. Law Rep. 359. And also
held in the cases further cited to exempt state and city
eleemosynary institutions from such liability. Leavell v. Western Ky. Asylum, 122 Ky. 213, 91 S. W.
671, 28 Ky. Law Rep. 1129, 4 L. R. A. (N. S.) 269;
Williamson v. Industrial School of Reform, 95 Ky.
251, 24 S. W. 1065, 15 Ky. Law Rep. 629, 23 L. R. A.
200, 44 Am. St. Rep. 243.

In respect to such nonliability for defects in its public buildings, such as a city hall, prison, school-house,
or other structure used for public or governmental

purposes, or the negligence of its employes in their care, cities seem to be placed by the law on the same footing with the state and the counties thereof as to buildings owned and used by them in aid of government; and in the recent case of Simon v. Gregory, 120 Ky. 116, 85 S. W. 751, 27 Ky. Law Rep. 509, it was held by this court that neither Jefferson county, the county judge, members of its fiscal court, jailer, nor other of its county officers could be made liable in damages for injuries received by one through the fall of an elevator in the Jefferson county courthouse. According to the great weight of authority, cities and towns are not liable for negligence in the performance of a public, governmental duty imposed upon them for public benefit, and from which they in their corporate or proprietary capacity derive no pecuniary profit. However, the universally recognized liability of such municipalities for negligence is not keeping their streets in repair affords an exception to the general rule, which, as said in Snider v. City of St. Paul, 51 Minn. 466, 53 N. W. 763, 18 L. R. A. 151 (a case almost identical in point of fact with this): "We think the courts would do better to rest either upon special consideration of public policy or upon the doctrine of stare decisis than to attempt to find some strictly legal principle to justify the distinction. * * *"

It is, however, insisted for appellant that a municipality is charged with the performance of duties of a private and corporate character as well as those of a political or governmental nature, and that, as to the former, the municipality stands upon the same footing with a private corporation and may be held to the same responsibility with a private corporation for injuries resulting from its negligence. This is undoubtedly true, but unfortunately for this contention in maintaining a city hall appellee does not act in its capacity as a private corporation, but, as we have attempted to show, in the performance of a purely governmental function, because of which no liability resulted to it from the death of appellant's intestate. If it could be demonstrated by allegation and proof that the building in which the intestate met his death is maintained by appellee merely as an investment for profit, expected to be realized by its sale or in the way of rents from private persons occupying it as tenants, or it were devoted to any other use for which appellee charged and received remuneration, manifestly appellant's contention that, with respect to its liability for the death of the intestate, appellee should be regarded as on the footing of a private corporation, would be sound.

But appellee has not put the building in question to such a use as any of those mentioned, but, on the contrary, erected, and has always used it, as and for a city hall, within and from which to manage and conduct the affairs and business of the municipality. It is, in brief, a building wholly devoted to public and governmental uses. This being true, we deem it our duty to adhere to the doctrine announced by past deliverances of this court, that a municipal corporation is not amenable to actions for negligence in the performance of public duties incident to the exercise of its governmental functions; that persons employed in the performance of such duties by the municipal corporation act as public officers, charged with a public service, and, being mere agencies or instruments by which such public duties are performed, that the doctrine of respondeat superior does not apply to such employments. To hold otherwise and impose upon the municipality responsibility for the negligence of such employes would indirectly fasten upon it a liability from which it is by law or consideration of public policy exempt.

We will not enter upon a discussion of the authorities from the courts of other states relied on in argument by counsel in support of their respective contentions, as we should be and are controlled in the conclusions we have reached by this court's several previous adjudications of the questions herein involved. Being of opinion that the law exonerates appellee from responsibility for the death of appellant's intestate, the judgment is affirmed.

NUNN, C. J., dissenting.

CASE 71.—PROSECUTION BY COMMONWEALTH OF BEACH HARGIS FOR MURDER.—December 1, 1909.

Hargis v. Commonwealth.

Appeal from Estill Circuit Court.

J. P. ADAMS, Circuit Judge.

Defendant convicted and appeals.—Affirmed.

1. Judges—Prejudice—Time for Objection.—An objection to the trial judge on the ground of prejudice raises a question of jurisdiction, and, t> b? avai'able must be made before plea'- ing to an indictment, or moving for bail, or for a continuance, unless the basis of the objection be after discovered facts.

2. Judges—Disqualification—Prejudice.—The statement by the commonwealth's attorney that he had "camped on the trail of" defendant's father, and now proposed to "camp on de- fendant's trail, and put him where he belonged," does not show such prejudice as to disqualify him to act as judge, he being subsequently appointed to that office, in the trial of defendant for murder.

Hargis v. Commonwealth.

3. Judges—Disqualification—Statements.—Where a statement by
a judge in reference to a case is capable of two constructions,
that which is consistent with good faith should be preferred.

4. Judges—Disqualification—Burden of Proof.—The burden of
proof is on defendant in a criminal prosecution who alleges
that the judge will not give him a fair trial.

5 Criminal Law—Evidence—Judicial Notice.—The court takes
judici l notice that it would not be unnatural for the commonwealth's attorney to state, on hearing that a homicide of an
unusual character had been committed, that he would prosecute the case with all his power.

6. Homicide—Trial—Instructions—Self-Defense.—It was proper
to instruct that defendant had no right to kill deceased, unless he believed, and had reasonable grounds to believe, that
he was "then and there"in danger of death or great bodily
harm, and it appeared' to defendant in the exercise of "reasonable judgment" that there was no other safe way to avert
the danger.

7. Homicide—Trial—Instructions—Self-Defense.—It is proper for
an instruction on self-defense to allow the previous acts
of deceased to be considered only in determining whether defendant was in danger at the time of the homicide.

8. Criminal Law—Trial—Refusing Instructions.—Where the subject of self-defense is fully covered by the court's instruction,
it is not error to refuse defendant's request on the same
subject.

9. Criminal Law—Appeal—Harmless Error—Instructions.—The
refusal of a proper instruction is not available on appeal,
where it was less favorable to defendant than the one given
by the court on the same subject

10. Criminal Law—Trial—Instructions.—An instruction that the
law presumes defendant innocent until his guilt is proved beyond a reasonable doubt, and if on the whole case, or on
any material fact necessary to establish his guilt, there is a
reasonable doubt of his guilt, they should find him not guilty,
could not have been misleading.

11. Criminal Law—Change of Venue—Discretion of Court.—Under Cr. Code Prac. Sec. 281, the change of venue in a criminal
prosecution is within the discretion of the court.

12. Criminal   Law—Appeals—Review—Discretion   of   Court—
Change of Venue.—As no exception can be taken to an order
for a change of venue (Cr. Code Prac. Sec. 281), such order
is not subject to review.

13. Homicide—Defenses.—It is no defense to a prosecution for
the murder of defendant's father that deceased taught him to

carry a weapon, encouraged him to drink whisky, and to associate with disreputable men.

14. Homicide—Evidence — Self-Defense—Previous Difficulties.—
Where defendant was allowed to show previous assaults on him by deceased, he cannot complain that the details of such assaults were excluded.

15. Homicide — Evidence — Self-Defense — Uncommunicated Threats.—Though the threats by deceased, made two hours before the homicide, were not communicated to defendant, evidence thereof is admissible to show the state of deceased's mind at the time of the homicide.

16. Homicide—Appeal—Harmless Error.—Under Cr. Code Prac. Sec. 240, directing the reversal of a conviction for error prejudicial to the substantial rights of defendant, a conviction of murder will not be reversed for the exclusion of evidence of previous uncommunicated threats by deceased, where such evidence would only be cumulative of uncontradicted testimony fully showing the state of deceased's mind toward defendant.

17. Contempt—Misconduct of Attorney.—Filing an affidavit by defendant in a criminal prosecution alleging prejudice of the judge, and asking the appointment of a special judge, does not constitute contempt of court by the attorney.

18. Criminal Law—Appeals—Harmless Error—Misconduct of Court.—The error of fining defendant's attorney for contempt in presenting an affidavit of prejudice of the judge is harmless, where the trial took place a year afterward in another county on a change of venue.

W. O. BRADLEY attorney for appellant.

W. A YOUNG, D. B. REDWINE, J. J. C. BACH, SAM H. KASH and THOS. L. COPE of counsel.

POINTS AND AUTHORITIES.

1. It was error for the court to refuse to retire from the bench. Givens v. Crawshaw, (55 S. W., 905) 21 Ky. Law Rep., 1619; Massie v. Commonwealth, 93 Ky., 588; Powers v. Commonwealth, 114 Ky., 237; Ky. Journal Pub. Co. v. Gaines (116 S. W., 268) 33 Ky. Law Rep. 402.

2. It was error for the court to grant a change of venue in the case or to preside in any way after the affidavit was filed.

3. It was the duty of the Court to have given all the law of the case. Williams v. Commonwealth, 80 Ky., 312; Cook v. Commonwealth, 10 Ky. Law Rep., 222; L. & N. R. R. Co. v. Common-

wealth, 13 Ky. Law Rep., 925; Trimble v. Commonwealth, 78 Ky. 176; Heilman v. Commonwealth, 84 Ky. 457; Buckles v. Commonwealth, 113 Ky. 799.

4. The court erred in failing to define the words "malice aforethought" and "feloniously." Section 673 b., 2 Vol. Bish. Crim. Law; Ludwig v. Commonwealth, 22 Ky. Law Rep., 1108; Whatton's Homicide, 3rd Ed., page 3; State v. Sims, 71 Mo., 538; Bobb v. State, 12 Tx. App., 491; Richardson v. State, 28 Tx. App., 216; Harrell v. State, 41 Tx. Crim. Rep., 507 (55 S. W., 824); Ewing v. Commonwealth, 111 S. W., 355.

5. On requiring defendant to exercise a reasonable judgment the court erred. He was entitled to act upon the belief based upon reasonable grounds, taking into consideration all the surroundings. Haney v. Commonwealth, 5 Ky. Law Rep. 203; Coffman v. Commonwealth, 10 Bush, 495; Radford v Commonwealth, 9 Ky. Law Rep., 280; Bledsoe v. Commonwealth, 9 Ky Law Rep., 1002; Estep v. Commonwealth, 86 Ky., 39 Adkins v. Commonwealth, 32 S. W., 243; Oakley v. Commonwealth, 10 Ky. Law Rep., 885.

6. The court, in limiting the right of the defendant to shoot, by saying that he could not act up to had some other safe way in which to avert the danger, erred. Coffman v. Commonwealth, 10 Bush, 495; Radford v. Commonwealth, 9 Ky. Law Rep., 380; Kinglesmith v. Commonwealth, 7 Ky. Law Rep., 744.

7. The court erred in the 5th instruction by submitting to the jury what were the material facts necessary to establish guilt.

8. The defendant was entitled to the instruction that he had a right to act if he believed, and had reasonable grounds to believe that he was in immediate danger which reasonably appeared to him, whether or not the danger in fact existed. Rapp v. Commonwealth, 14 B. Mon., 622; Meridith v. Commonwealth, 18 B. Mon., 49; Haney v. Commonwealth, 5 Ky. Law Rep., 205; Holloway v. Commonwealth, 11 Bush, 344; Mundy v. Commonwealth, 81 Ky., 233; Ayers v. Commonwealth, 108 S. W., 320; Adkins v. Commonwealth, 82 S. W., 242; Radford v. Commonwealth, 9 Ky. Law Rep., 380; Bledsoe v. Commonwealth, 9 Ky. Law Rep., 1002; Estep v. Commonwealth, 86 Ky., 39; Amos v. Commonwealth, 16 Ky. Law Rep., 158.

9. It was error in the court to refuse to allow the defendant his mother, and grandmother to prove that defendant at the time of the several assaults by his father, did and said nothing to bring them on and did not resist them, and that his father had taught him to carry weapons and associate with disreputable men and encouraged him to drink whisky.

10. The court erred in refusing to allow the witness, Isom, to state that two hours before the killing, the deceased said he

would kill defendant before night and that he was done with him forever.

11. The court erred in failing to caution the jury that the testimony as to the moral character of the defendant, was incompetent, except in so far as it might or might not affect his credibility and in refusing appellant the right to prove that his moral character was attributed generally to the conduct of his father.

12. The court erred in excluding the testimony of Mrs. Day at page 168 Record, as to the assault by deceased on appellant.

Petition for re-hearing by W. O. BRADLEY and D. B. REDWINE for appellant.   ·

POINTS AND AUTHORITIES.

1. Section 968 of the Kentucky Statutes does not fix any time when a petition swearing a judge from the bench is to be filed further than, of course, it should be before the trial.

2. The word "trial" refers to a decision on the issues in a case. Bovier's Law Dictionary. Title, "Trial."

3. Under the Statute, defendant could not swear the judge from the bench on the trial of a motion for bail, and having withdrawn his motion for a change of venue before same was passed upon, he cannot be prejudiced thereby. Givens v. Crawshaw, 21 Ky. Law Rep., 1619; the cases of Kentucky Central R. R. Co. v. Kenney, 82 Ky., 154; Bales v. Ferrell, 20 Ky. Law Rep., 1564, referred to by the Court, do not sustain the rule declared by the court.

4. From the time of the decision in Turner v. Commonwealth, 2nd Met., 619, rendered February 20, 1859, up to the decision of German Insurance Co. v. Landrum, 88 Ky., 433, rendered in 1889, a period of thirty years, affidavits drawn in the language of the Statute were universally recognized as proper and no question was made as to a waiver by reason of preliminary motions and the changing of that rule amounts to a changing of the Statute itself.

5. The majority opinion in this case is diametrically opposed to the published opinion of this court in Powers v. Commonwealth, 114 Ky., 241.

6. If the facts stated in the affidavit are such as to prevent an official of personal integrity from presiding, their truth must be assumed. Powers v. Commonwealth, 114 Ky., 241. Or even if the facts in the affidavits do not import intentional unfairness, but if true might create an impression upon the affiant that the judge would be unable to give a fair trial, the judge should retire from the case. Givens v. Crawshaw, 21 Ky. Law Rep., 1619.

7. The majority opinion in this case and in the Powers case cannot both fail to stand. One or the other is the law.

8. The judgment should be reversed, even though a fair trial has been given, if the affidavit is sufficient. Kentucky Publishing Co. v. Gaines, 110 S. W., 268 (33 Ky. Law Rep., 402.

9. The witness Isom, who was not allowed to testify, was not corroborated by three witnesses, but only one aside from defendant. It was error to refuse the testimony of Mrs. Day, showing a threat to kill the defendant. This Court cannot speculate on the effect of testimony. Coppage v. Commonwealth, 3 Bush, 532; Kenned v. Commonwealth, 14 Bush, 361.

10. Although preliminary motions were made, they can constitute no waiver if not passed on by the Court. Givens v. Crawshaw, supra.

JAMES BREATHITT, Attorney General, T. B. BLAKEY, Assistant Attorney General, for Commonwealth.

The Commonwealth in its brief in this case makes the following points and cites the following authorities:

1. The motion and affidavit requiring judge to vacate the bench insufficient in this case. Ky. Journal Pub. Co. v. Gaines, 33 Ky. Law Rep., 404; German Insurance Co. v. Landram, 88 Ky., 433; Turner v. Commonwealth, 2 Met., 625; Ky. Stat., Sec. 968; Massie v. Commonwealth, 93 Ky., 590; Givens v. Crawshaw, 21 K. L. R., 1618; Powers v. Commonwealth, 24 Ky. Law Rep., 1007; Wathen, Mueller & Co. v. Commonwealth, 116 S. W., 236; Schmidt v. Mitchell, 101 Ky., 592; Smith v. Commonwealth, 108 Ky., 53; Hargis v. Marsum, 31 Ky. Law Rep., 795; Sparks v. Colson, 22 Ky. Law Rep., 1369; Vance v. Fields, 11 Ky. Law Rep., 388.

2. There was no error in granting the change of venue on petition of the commonwealth. Commonwealth ex rel., Atty. Gen., &c., v. Cowans, 125 Ky., 821, and cases cited.

3. The venire was properly summoned from Madison county. Section 194 Criminal Code; Brafford v. Commonwealth, 13 Ky. Law Rep., ——; Roberts v. Commonwealth, 94 Ky., 504; Mosely v. Commonwealth, 27 Ky. Law Rep., 214.

4. Exceptions to testimony by Commonwealth properly sustained. White v. Commonwealth, 31 Ky. Law Rep., 271.

5. It was not error to permit an employed attorney to read the indictment and state the case. Sections 219 and 220 Criminal Code; Roberts v. Commonwealth, 94 Ky., 499.

6. The instructions in this case fairly present the law. Ludwig v. Commonwealth, 22 Ky. Law Rep., 1108; Ewing v. Commonwealth, 111 S. W., 355; Robertson's Ky., Criminal Law & Procedure, 221; Rush v. Commonwealth, 78 Ky., 268; Jolly v. Common-

wealth, 22 Ky. Law Rep., 1622; Stout v. Commonwealth, 123 Ky.,
184, and cases cited; Brooks v. Commonwealth, 16 Ky. Law Rep..
265; Williams v. Commonwealth, 25 Ky. Law Rep., 1504; Stephens
v. Commonwealth, 20 Ky. Law Rep., 545; Pennington v. Commonwealth, 24 Ky. Law Rep., 321; Austin v. Commonwealth, 19 Ky.
Law Rep., 477; Sparks v. Commonwealth, 3 Bush, 117.

OPINION OF THE COURT BY JUDGE HOBSON—Affirming.

Beach Hargis shot and killed his father, James
Hargis. He was indicted for murder, and on a trial
before a jury was found guilty as charged; his punishment being fixed at confinement in the penitentiary
for life. The court entered judgment on the verdict,
and he appeals.

The first question arising on the appeal is in regard
to the refusal of the regular circuit judge to vacate
the bench. The affidavit filed by the defendant in
support of his motion that the regular judge should
retire from the bench, and that a special judge should
be appointed, is as follows: "The defendant and
affiant, Beach Hargis, states that the judge of this
court, Hon. James P. Adams, will not afford him a
fair and impartial trial, and will not impartially decide an application for a change of venue in this case,
and that said judge is and has been a bitter partisan
Republican and has an unkind and prejudicial feeling
against the defendant and all the family of the Hargises. He says: That for a number of years preceding this time there existed in this county a deadly enmity and feud between the Hargis family and its
friends, he and his father being among the number,
and others of the opposing political party, and those
whose tendencies and sympathy was with them, he
and his father and the Hargis family being Democrats, and those opposing them being Republicans, or
persons who sympathized with them. That many in-

dictments were found against his father and others and many trials had, and that at the time of his father's death that enmity and unfriendliness existed. That the Hargises were charged with being responsible for the death of various persons, and a number of said indictments were found against them, charging them with conspiracy in the murder of a number of persons who had been killed.

He says: That the Hargises, especially his father and himself, to the best of his ability, were active Democrats and active workers for that party at the polls. That during the time aforesaid the said Judge Adams was a candidate for commonwealth's attorney, and he and his father actively worked against him. That said Adams being defeated in his race, on the face of the returns, instituted a contest which was very bitter, and in which his father and others were charged with partisanship and illegal conduct. That after this the judicial district was changed by legislative act, and said Adams, having won his contest, became the commonwealth's attorney in the district as it is at present constituted, and prosecuted the Hargises, his father among others, with great activity and bitterness. That whilst said Adams was acting as commonwealth's attorney, Judge Riddell, the circuit judge of this district died. Whereupon the said Adams was appointed judge by the acting Governor in this district. He states that at the time he killed his father said Adams was commonwealth's attorney in this district, and he has discovered, for the first time since the adjournment of the last term of this court, expressed himself with great bitterness against this defendant, saying that he had 'camped upon his father's trail,' and now he proposed to 'camp upon

this defendant's trail and put him where he belonged.'
He says that after his trial for bail said Adams said
that he would never allow any man bail who had killed
his father. For the foregoing reasons, he asks that
the said Adams retire from the trial of the case, and
another judge be selected or appointed as the case
may be, under the statutes.''
    The indictment was returned on February 18, 1908.
At that term the defendant demurred to the indictment. His demurrer was overruled, and he excepted.
The trial was set for the thirteenth day of the term.
On that day he filed affidavits for a continuance, and
later he filed his petition and motion for a change of
venue in the action. Before the proof was heard on
the motion for a change of venue, he withdrew the
motion. The case was continued for the term, and at
the special term in August he filed the affidavit above
quoted to remove the regular circuit judge from the
bench. In the meantime he had made a motion for
bail, and this had been heard and overruled by the
circuit judge.
    The rule is that an objection to the trial judge
raises in effect a question of jurisdiction, and the objection, to be available, must be made before an appearance to the merits of the action or the submission
of preliminary motions by either party preparatory to
a trial. Kentucky Central R. R. Co. v. Kenney, 82
Ky. 154, 6 R. 17; German Insurance Co. v. Landram,
88 Ky. 433, 11 S. W. 367, 592, 10 Ky. Law Rep. 1039;
Vance v. Field, 89 Ky. 178, 12 S. W. 190, 11 Ky. Law
Rep. 388; Russell v. Russell, 12 S. W. 709, 11 Ky. Law
Rep. 547; Bales v. Ferrell, 20 Ky. Law Rep. 1564, 49
S. W. 759. There is nothing in any of the later cases
in conflict with the rule laid down in these cases. It
is held, however, in all the cases, that matters which

have been since discovered may be set up by affidavit. Vance v. Field, 89 Ky. 178, 12 S. W. 190, 11 Ky. Law Rep. 388. The whole of the affidavit above quoted, except the last paragraph, refers to matters which the defendant knew at the preceding term when he enter ed his general demurrer to the indictment, when he filed his application for a change of venue, and when he made a motion for bail. If, in a criminal case, the defendant were allowed thus to experiment with the circuit judge, and at a succeeding term to swear him from the bench because his experiments had not turned out as he would like them, the door would be open for a practice well calculated to bring the administration of criminal law into disrepute. The rule is a sound one which requires the defendant to make his objection promptly to the circuit judge, and which precludes him from making an objection where he elects to proceed with the case before him without objection. The only part of the affidavit therefore which it is necessary for us to consider is the last paragraph.

The statement attributed to the circuit judge, was made when he was commonwealth's attorney in the district, and when he was not circuit judge, and had no reason to anticipate that he would be. He was speaking as commonwealth's attorney. When he declared that "he had camped upon his father's trail and now proposed to camp upon the defendant's trail and put him where he belonged," he was simply expressing what he would do as commonwealth's attorney. The law made it his duty as commonwealth's attorney to prosecute all infractions of law occurring in his district. It made it his duty to camp upon the trail of all those who were charged with committing felonies, and to put them where they belonged. The words do not necessarily import any personal hostility to the defendant. On the other hand, taking this whole paragraph together, it would simply indicate that the officer had in mind the performance of the duties which the law imposed upon him.

The office of circuit judge is one of great dignity and responsibility. Perhaps the peace and good order of the district more largely depends upon him than any other one person. The people of the district should not be deprived of the services of the regular judge for trivial causes, or on account of declarations made by him which do not necessarily show such a state of mind as would make him unfit to hold the court for the occasion. If what he says is capable of two constructions, then that which is consistent with his good faith should be preferred. The burden is on the defendant to show facts manifesting that the circuit judge will not grant him a fair trial, and he does not do this when he attributes to the circuit judge a statement which may as naturally be construed innocent as otherwise. It does not appear from the affidavit that, while he was commonwealth's attorney, the circuit judge had taken any part in the prosecution. No facts are stated in regard to this.

The only thing alleged is the declaration as commonwealth's attorney as to what he would do. The court must take judicial knowledge that the commonwealth's attorney travels around the circuit with the judge, and that, when he would hear at some point on the circuit that a homicide had been committed, it would not be unnatural that he should say where the facts were, as in this case, unusual, that he would prosecute the case with all his power. We do not

think that a declaration by a commonwealth's attorney, when informed that a crime had been committed,
that he would prosecute the case as best he could,
should disqualify him from thereafter acting as circuit judge, nothing more appearing, for this is nothing more than he should be expected to do; and to say
that his declaration that he intended to do what he
would naturally be expected to do, it was his duty to
do and what disqualifies him from acting as circuit judge, would be in effect to say that the commonwealth's attorney, if afterwards appointed circuit
judge, could not properly preside on the trial of any
crime which was charged to have been committed in
his district while he was commonwealth's attorney.

The proof for the commonwealth on the trial
showed in brief these facts: On the night before the
homicide, Beach Hargis had gone to his father's store
and asked one of the clerks to let him have a pistol.
The clerk declined to give him a pistol out of the
stock, but told him that his father's pistol was there
in the drawer of his desk, and he could take that. The
defendant got the pistol, but said nothing to his
father, although he was then in the store. The next
morning between 9 and 10 o'clock, the defendant was
sitting in a barber shop. His face was swollen. He
told the barber his father had hit him in the mouth
and hurt him there. A man who looked like his father then passed by. He raised up in the chair, threw
his hand back, and said, "I thought that was the old
man." About an hour later he drank a bottle of
Brown's Bitters, and said to a bystander, "Did you
hear about the old man mashing my mouth?" and
added that it was hard to take. Some two hours
later, he appeared at a drug store kept by his brother-
in-law, Dr. Hogg. There he drew out his pistol, and

was waving it about, pointing it in the direction of a bystander and his brother-in-law. From this drug store, after a few minutes, he went to his father's store. It was a double store-room. His father was in one room, and he entered the other and took a seat in a chair not far from the front door.

While he was sitting there in the chair, a man in the other room asked his father where he was. His father pointed him out tó the man, and said: ''There he sits. I have done all I can for him, and I cannot go about him or have anything to do with him.'' A few minutes later his father said to another man who was in the room: ''I don't knôw what to do with Beach. He has got to be a perfect vagabond, and he is destroying my business, and if Dr. Hogg lets him stay there he will ruin his business.'' After saying this to the man, the father walked in the direction of where the defendant was sitting. There were a number of persons in the store. As his father approached, the defendant got out of his chair and walked around behind a spool case that was sitting on the end of the counter. No words were spoken. The first sound that anybody heard was the report of a pistol. His father was then about three feet from him. A struggle ensued between them, during which the pistol was shot four times more; all five of the shots taking effect in the father. Persons in the store ran up, and when they got to them the father had the son down and had the pistol, which he handed to one of them, saying, ''He has shot me all to pieces.'' The father died in a few minutes.

The proof for the son was, in substance, that the father came up to him, struck him in the face, and began choking him. When he felt his eyes bulging out, he drew his pistol and shot him, and, his father continuing to choke him, he fired the other four shots in the struggle; the last two being fired from the floor. The proof for the defendant also showed that the father was drinking. Taking all the evidence, we think it is reasonably clear that the father was un- armed, and that he was shot by the son while he was approaching him, and before he had touched him. Two witnesses who were on the outside of the store were looking through the window, and their testi- mony, as well as the testimony of the persons in the store, confirms this conclusion. We think it also rea- sonably clear from the evidence that the son was maudlin drunk, and but for this the unfortunate homicide would not have occurred. He showed that he was under the impression that his father had left the store, and that he went there to meet an uncle, but expecting no difficulty. He also showed: That about a week before his father had beat him unmercifully with a ramrod, that previous to this he had whipped him with a rope, and on the last occasion had struck him in the mouth with his fist, and had got upon him on the floor and churned his head against the floor; that he had taken his pistol from him, and had threat- ened to shoot him with it, but had been prevented from doing this by the interference of a bystander; and that he had then declared that he would kill him. There was also evidence that the son had said that the old man had beaten him up; but he would never get the chance to do it again; also that he had de- clared, when his father had taken a pistol away from him when drunk, that every time he got drunk and was having a good time they had to do something to him, and that he aimed to kill his father and certain other persons whom he named.

The court gave the jury instructions aptly submitting to them the law of murder and manslaughter. The instruction on self-defense is in these words: ''Although the jury may believe from the evidence beyond a reasonable doubt that the defendant, Beach Hargis, shot and killed James Hargis with a pistol loaded with powder and leaden ball as defined by the first or second instruction, still if they further believe from the evidence that at the time he did said shooting and killing, if he did do it, he believed, and had reasonable ground to believe, that he was then and there in immediate danger of death or great bodily harm then about to be inflicted on him, or which reasonably appeared to the defendant about to be inflicted on him, by the said James Hargis, and there appeared to the defendant in the exercise of a reasonable judgment no other safe way to avert the danger or to the defendant apparent danger, if any, but to shoot and kill said James Hargis, then, in that event, they will find the defendant not guilty on the ground of self-defense or apparent necessity.''

We see no objection to the instruction. The court properly used the words ''then and there.'' The defendant had no right to kill his father unless he was then and there in danger. What had taken place before was only to be considered by the jury in determining whether he was then in danger. What his father had previously done would throw light on this question; but it was not competent for any other purpose, for the defendant had no right to kill his father if he was not at the time in danger. A man may not take life unless it was necessary, or apparently necessary, for him to do so. The court did not err in using the words ''a reasonable judgment.'' The defendant cannot be excused for killing another if he acted upon grounds not reasonably sufficient to warrant a man in so doing. There is nothing in the instruction about retreat. The defendant is not excused for killing another unless in case of necessity, and this is all that the instruction requires. The instruction given contained the whole law, of the case on self-defense, and the court did not err in refusing to give the instruction which the defendant asked. The defendant was in no wise prejudiced by the failure of the court to define the words "malice afore-thought" and "feloniously." If these words had been defined according to the approved definitions, the instructions as a whole would have been less favorable to the defendant than they were as given by the court. The fifth instruction could not possibly have mis-led the jury. The court had told the jury what facts were necessary to constitute the defendant's guilt, and when he told them, in instruction 5, that the law presumed him innocent until his guilt was proved beyond a reasonable doubt, and if upon the whole case, or upon any material fact necessary to establish his guilt, they had a reasonable doubt of his having been proved guilty, they should find him not guilty, the jury could not have misunderstood the instruction.

We find no error of the court in sending the case to Estill county on the changing of the venue. The circuit court has a wide discretion in matters of this sort, and this court will not interfere where the discretion has not been abused. The trial was had in the county of Estill, and a large part of the jury was brought from Madison county. The case had been tried once before, and the circuit judge finds as a fact that he could not obtain a jury in Estill county after having made a fair effort in good faith to obtain a qualified jury free from bias, by reason, among other things, of the wide circulation given the facts of the case. Matters of this sort are by section 281 of the Criminal Code of Practice committed to the discretion of the circuit judge, and, as by that section no exception can be taken to his ruling, it is not subject to review here. Howard v. Commonwealth, 118 Ky. 1, 80 S. W. 211, 81 S. W. 704, 25 Ky. Law Rep. 2213, 26 Ky. Law Rep. 363.

The defendant offered to prove by his grandmother and others that his father had taught him to carry a weapon, encouraged him to drink whisky, and had caused him to associate with disreputable men, thus rearing him in a manner calculated to bring about the result which followed. The court properly excluded this evidence. It is no defense for the defendant when he kills another that his father reared him badly, and it is immaterial that the person killed was his father. The enforcement of the laws of the commonwealth which the defendant violated are in no manner affected by the way he was reared. The court allowed proof to be made of the previous assaults by the father upon the son. The defendant complains that the court did not allow him to prove the particulars of these assaults as fully as he should have done. The court, however, seems to have followed substantially the rule laid down by this court in White v. Commonwealth, 125 Ky. 699, 102 S. W. 298, 1199, 31 Ky. Law Rep. 271, 720. In that case the court said: "We do not mean to say that it would have been proper for the court to have allowed evidence as to all the details of the cutting and wounding of appellant by Layne, or of the assault made upon him by the latter with a club; but the fact that both assaults occurred, the general character of the injuries received by appellant at the hands of Layne, and the further fact that the latter was the attacking party, should have gone to the jury in evidence.'' The evidence which the court admitted got before the jury fairly and fully the assaults made by the father on the son in the previous difficulties, and showed clearly that the father had treated the son in a most inexcusable manner.

The defendant complains that he was not allowed to prove by the witness James Isom that about two hours before the killing he met James Hargis, and he then said to him that he would kill the defendant before night, and that he was done with him forever. The witness had not communicated this threat to Beach Hargis; but, although it had not been communicated to the defendant, it was competent to show the frame of mind of James Hargis at the time. Miller v. Commonwealth, 89 Ky. 653, 10 S. W. 137, 10 Ky. Law Rep. 672; Young v. Commonwealth, 29 S. W. 334, 17 Ky. Law Rep. 18. The evidence should have been admitted. This was error. We find no other substantial error in the admission of evidence in the record. So the question arises: Should a judgment be reversed and a new trial granted for this error? The defendant showed by several witnesses, who were entirely uncontradicted or impeached, that his father a week before had pointed a pistol at him and threatened to kill him, and the conduct of the father at that time was clearly shown. If the evidence of Isom had been admitted, it would only have served to corroborate these three uncontradicted witnesses, and the proof as to the conduct of the father on those occasions was such that we are satisfied the testimony of Isom would really have added nothing to an understanding of the case by the jury. The fact that the deceased may have made a threat beforehand is simply evidence to show the condition of his mind at the time of the homicide. In addition to the witnesses who testified as to the previous declarations of the father and his previous acts, there were two witnesses to the declarations made by him just before he walked to where the defendant was. The fact is, the defendant had his father's pistol. The father was unarmed. The shooting was done before a word was spoken, and when the father was at least three feet from the defendant. The storeroom had a number of people in it, and it is hard to believe that the defendant, if he had been sober, could have thought that he was then and there in danger of death or great bodily harm at the hands of the father.

Section 340 of the Criminal Code of Practice originally read as follows: "A judgment of conviction shall be reversed for any error of law appearing on the record." Under this provision many criminal cases were reversed by this court, and so, the better to promote the administration of justice, the Legislature added to the section these words: "When upon consideration of the whole case the court is satisfied that the substantial rights of the defendant have been prejudiced thereby." The plain purpose of the amendment was to provide that a judgment of conviction should not be reversed unless upon consideration of the whole case the court was satisfied that the substantial rights of the defendant had been prejudiced by the error complained of. This had been the rule for a long time under the Civil Code, and the purpose of the amendment was to make the rule in criminal cases practically the same as in civil cases. Under the former provision, the court was required to reverse when it found an error in the record. It was

not allowed to speculate as to what was the effect of
the error. The amendment was aimed to change this
rule and to provide that no case shall be reversed
where the defendant has had substantially a fair trial
of the merits of his case. We have in a number of
cases so construed the amendment. Rutherford v.
Commonwealth, 78 Ky. 639, 1 R. 410; Whiteneck v.
Commonwealth, 55 S. W. 916, 56 S. W. 3, 21 Ky. Law
Rep. 1625; Bailey v. Commonwealth, 58 S. W. 425, 22
Ky. Law Rep. 512; Ward v. Commonwealth, 91 S. W.
700, 29 Ky. Law Rep. 62; Stacy v. Commonwealth, 97
S. W. 39, 29 Ky. Law Rep. 1242.

In Collett v. Commonwealth, 121 S. W. 426, where,
as here, there had been an error in the admission of
evidence, this court, affirming the judgment, said:
"The jurisdiction of this court in criminal cases is
wholly statutory. We have only such jurisdiction as
the law confers. One of the limitations upon our
jurisdiction is that a judgment of conviction shall not
be reversed for an error of law appearing in the
record, unless, upon a consideration of the whole case,
the court is satisfied that the substantial rights of the
defendant have been prejudiced thereby." In this
case, as in that, the defendant relied in substance
solely on the plea of self-defense. The right of self-
defense was clearly presented to the jury by the instruction which the court gave. The admission of
this uncommunicated threat would not have served in
any wise to show that the defendant believed that he
was in danger at the hands of his father at the time
he shot him, for it was unknown to him. It could
only have illustrated his father's state of mind and
served to show the purpose for which he approached
him; but, in view of the great mass of evidence heard

on the trial as to what had occurred before and what had occurred then, it is manifest that this evidence, if admitted, would have been only cumulative, and could have had no controlling effect upon the trial. On the whole case, we are satisfied from the record that the defendant has had substantially a fair trial on the merits of his case. To reverse the judgment for this error would be to overlook the amendment of the Code, and to follow the old rule which the amendment was designed to abolish.

When the defendant filed his affidavit asking that the circuit judge vacate the bench, the court fined the attorneys for contempt of court in filing the affidavit. This was error. The defendant was on trial, and he had a right to determine whether he was willing to try the case before the regular circuit judge or not. He had a right to require his attorneys to file the affidavit. If the affidavit was false, the proper way to punish it was by an indictment for perjury. An affidavit that the regular circuit judge will not afford the defendant a fair trial would, but for the statute, be necessarily a contempt of court, and, if the attorneys may be fined for filing such an affidavit in one case, they may be fined in all cases, and the statute allowing the affidavit to be filed amounts to nothing. We therefore think that it cannot be a contempt of court under the statute to exercise the statutory right; but the defendant was not prejudiced by this on the trial, for the reason that it all took place in Breathitt county before the venue was changed, and it could have had no effect on the trial before a jury in Estill county a year afterwards.

Judgement affirmed.

BARKER, J. (dissenting). I am unable to concur in the opinion of the majority of the court in·this case. I think the affidavit filed by the defendant, that he could not obtain a fair and impartial trial before the presiding judge, was more·than sufficient, and the judge should have vacated the bench and allowed a special judge to be appointed to try the case. The opinion sets forth the affidavit of the defendant in full, and, without recopying it here, I deem it sufficient to refer to it in the opinion.

The affidavit shows that, at the time the homicide for which the defendant was being tried was committed, the presiding judge, Hon. James P. Adams, was commonwealth's attorney in the district where it took place. As soon as the killing occurred, the duty of the commonwealth's attorney with reference to the prosecution began. It was his duty as soon as the homicide was committed to take charge of the case in so far as that was possible or practicable, and to do everything that was necessary, if he thought a crime had been committed, to prosecute the criminal. After the defendant had killed his father, the affidavit shows —and it must be taken as true—that the then commonwealth's attorney said of the defendant "I have camped upon his father's trail and now I propose to camp upon the defendant's trail and put him where he belongs."

The commonwealth's attorney, in his mind, began the prosecution of the defendant when he made this speech. It was a declaration upon his part that he then took charge of the prosecution and intended to see that the defendant was put where he belonged. Before the indictment, however, the regular judge of that district died and the commonwealth's attorney, James P. Adams was appointed judge in his stead.

So that the result of what happened was that the attorney against the defendant and for the commonwealth was placed upon the bench to try the defendant whom he had theretofore been prosecuting. It was not necessary, in order to begin the prosecution, that anything should actually be done. The bias of the prosecuting attorney against the defendant was a mental bias, and it seems to me highly improper that one who had such bias should be allowed to sit in judgment upon the trial of the case which involved the life or liberty of the defendant whom the judge had theretofore prosecuted. It will not be disputed, of course, that the defendant was entitled to a fair and impartial trial, and, in order that he might have this, it was necessary that he should have an unbaised judge to preside upon the trial of the case. The defendant was entitled to have a judge preside upon the trial of his case who had not expressed an opinion that he was guilty of the charge against him. If the judge who presided upon the trial in this case said what is charged in the affidavit there can be no doubt that he had made up his mind as prosecuting attorney that Beach Hargis was guilty of murder, and that he intended to follow him up until he was convicted; and if we analyze the language used and give to it the meaning which those who use it ordinarily intend, there can be no doubt of the soundness of this conclusion. "I have camped upon his father's trail, and will camp upon his."

The expression comes from the frontier. To camp upon one's trail is to follow him up day by day and when nightfall comes the pursuer camps upon the trail of the pursued, so that he can resume his pursuit when morning comes. The Indian camps upon the trail of the white man he is following to kill or despoil; the hunter camps upon the trail of the game whose life he covets; and the revengeful man camps upon the trail of the enemy he desires to punish. The expression has a sinister sound, and augurs ill for the object of it. It means unremitting pursuit until the purpose of the pursuit is accomplished, and this is what the prosecuting attorney meant when he used the language charged against him. He intended to prosecute Beach Hargis until he was convicted, for that is what is meant by putting him where he belonged. The prosecuting attorney meant that Beach Hargis was guilty of murder, and that he intended to put him either upon the gallows or within the walls of the penitentiary. I do not believe that there can be two opinions as to the meaning of the language used, and its use showed a mental status which disqualified the speaker from occupying the position of a judge in the very case of which he was speaking. The statute (section 968, Ky. St. [Russell's St. sec. 2824]) requires the presiding judge to retire and give place to a special judge "if either party shall file with the clerk of the court his affidavit that the judge will not afford him a fair and impartial trial, or will not impartially decide an application for a change of venue." This court, in construing this statute, has uniformly required the affidavit to state the facts which show why the judge will not afford the party filing the affidavit a fair and impartial trial. This I think was done in this case by the affidavit under consideration.

I do not mean to reflect in any way upon the character or general fairness of the learned judge whose conduct is under discussion. On the contrary, it gives me great pleasure to say of him that I believe him to be an upright, honest, and learned magistrate, whose

record as a judge entitles him to the confidence of all.
I do not believe he was conscious of being biased
against the defendant; but, on the contrary, he was of
opinion that, when he left the position of prosecuting
attorney and took a seat upon the bench as judge, he
could afford the defendant a fair and impartial trial.
The rights of the defendant, however, do not turn
upon the private belief of the judge as to his own fairness; the right to another judge turns under the statute upon the question whether the facts stated show
that the judge cannot properly preside. I cannot believe that any man who has been advocate in a litigation can afterwards properly preside as judge in that
litigation. The commonwealth's attorney is the advocate employed by the state in a given territory to
prosecute crime, and he is paid a salary for so doing.
As soon as homicide is committed in his district, as
said before, it is necessary and proper that he should
at once take charge of it and do all that the interests
of the commonwealth demand with reference to it.
This makes him literally an' attorney in the case and
gives to his mind such a bent or direction with reference to it as seems to me renders it improper that he
should afterwards be judge of the matter. It is altogether irrelevant whether or not the judge was conscious of being biased; the bias of mind of which we
are not conscious is more dangerous than that of
which we are conscious. If we have cause to suspect
that our mind is prejudiced against one with whom
we have to deal, we may battle against it and overcome it and perhaps do him justice; but, if we are
unconscious of the bias we have, then our prejudices
robe themselves in the garments of truth, and we mistake them for truth, and are unable to resist their
influence.

Upon the trial of the case the defendant offered to prove by James Isom that about two hours before the killing the witness met James Hargis, who said to him that he would kill his son, Beach, before night, and that he was done with him forever. This evidence was excluded, presumably upon the ground that this threat had not been communicated to the defendant, Beach Hargis; but it is admitted in the opinion that it was competent for the purpose of showing the frame of mind of James Hargis at the time of the killing. The opinion then holds that, while it was error on the part of the trial court to exclude this evidence, it was not prejudicial to the substantial rights of the defendant. It seems to me that this conclusion is erroneous. I cannot agree that it is the province of the court to weigh this proposed evidence and say that it was not prejudicial to the defendant to exclude it.

On the contrary, it seems to me, if true, to be most important to the interest of the defendant. The defendant showed by his mother and his grandmother that his father on several occasions prior to the killing had beaten him in a cruel manner, from the effect of which he had been confined to his bed for several days after the occasion, and he offered to show by these ladies that the father threatened to kill his son while he was beating him, and would have killed him but for the fact that he was prevented from so doing. The court excluded the testimony that the father had threatened to kill his son, and that he would have killed him but for the interference of outside parties; and of this ruling the defendant also complains. I think this evidence was competent. The father was beating his son, presumably, to reform him, and the average juror would be of the opinion that, although the son was of age, yet he should not resist the exercise of parental authority when administered for his own good. Now, when the father approached Beach in the store, upon the fatal occasion when the killing took place, and began to chastise him as he testifies, it was very important for him to know whether the father was simply intending to chastise him, or whether he intended to make an assault upon his life; and, if upon other occasions when he had begun to chastise the boy he had to be restrained by outside parties from murdering him, then Beach had a right to think that his life was in danger on the occasion of the killing when the father commenced to beat him. A boy would not be justified in killing his father simply because the parent was proceeding to administer rational corporal punishment for the good of the son; but if the son knows that the father is a savage, vindictive man, utterly without pity or remorse, and liable, under the influence of passion, to imitate the crime of Ivan the Terrible by killing his own child, then the son had a right to treat him, not as a parent correcting errors, but as a savage foe making a murderous assault.

The jury could not understand the peril in which Beach Hargis stood without knowing all that had gone before. If the defendant was to be justified at all, he was to find his justification in the savage cruelty of the conduct of his father towards him in the past, and he had a right to have the jury view the killing for which he was tried with this evidence before them in order that they might truly estimate the danger within whose pale he stood at the time of the homicide. James Hargis is shown in this record to have been a savage, cruel man; that he had a high vindictive temper, and allowed neither fear nor remorse nor pity to come between him and the objects of his passionate resentment. The frame of mind of the father shown by the excluded evidence warranted the boy in shooting in defense of his life, when, perhaps, he would not have been justified if the father had been in a different frame of mind. I think the jury should have had this evidence and weighed it along with the other testimony, and I am of opinion that it was highly prejudicial to the interest of the accused to exclude it. James Hargis was a man of violence and blood. He had established in the county of Breathitt a reign of terror, under the influence of which the law was paralyzed and its ministers overrun. He is pictured as a man of gigantic frame, savage temper, and indomitable courage. He had surrounded himself with armed mercenaries, whose minds he inflamed with drink, and who seemed willing to do his bidding even to the point of assassinating his enemies without fear of the consequence of their crimes and without remorse or pity for the result. He had not only broken down the law and terrorized its officers, but he had made the temple of justice itself the rendezvous for assassins who, sheltering behind its walls, reddened its portals with the blood of its votaries. He literally ingrafted upon the civilization of the twentieth century the savagery of the fifth, and introduced into a community of law and order the merciless ferocity of the middle ages.

I am of opinion that the character of this man should have been fully presented to the jury, and especially as the case had been transferred by a change of venue to a county where, perhaps, he was not so well known as in Breathitt. To shoot one's father seems almost an inexcusable crime, and is so considered by the average man. If it is to be justified at all, it must be justified by showing a very extraordinary occasion. Beach Hargis knew his father, knew his savage and ferocious temper, knew his pitiless heart, and his gigantic strength; and, so knowing, he had a right to presume that his life was in danger, when, if his father had been of a different temperament, he would not have been justified in such a conclusion.

I do not believe that this defendant has had a fair and impartial trial. I believe that the judge who presided in the case was disqualified for the reasons above given, and that the error pointed out in regard to the refusal to admit the testimony of Isom, Mrs. Hargis and her mother was so prejudicial to to the defendant's interest as to warrant a reversal of the case.

For these reasons, I am constrained to dissent from the opinion of a majority of the court.

NUNN, C. J. I concur in the dissenting opinion for two reasons only: First, the circuit court judge should have vacated the bench upon the filing of the affidavit; and the other is for the rejection of Isom's testimony. Isom's testimony not only showed the state of mind of Judge Hargis at the time of the conflict, but it would have tended to corroborate the defendant's theory that his father made the first assault. The affidavit filed to cause the circuit court judge to vacate the bench contained only two mat-ters worthy of notice, one of which is mentioned in the dissenting opinion, and the other is a statement to the effect that the judge was personally prejudicial and hostile to defendant, either of which should have caused him to vacate the bench.

I concur in all that is said in the dissenting opinion on the two questions referred to, but disapprove of the remainder.

CASE 72.—ACTION BY C. M. LANGDON AGAINST HARRY EL-
LISON AND OTHERS.—December 7, 1909.

Ellison, &c. v. Langdon

Appeal from Pulaski Circuit Court.

M. L. JARVIS, Circuit Judge.

Judgment for plaintiff, defendant appeals.—Af-'
firmed.

Sheriffs and Constables—Bonds—Collection of Taxes—Penalties.—
Where a deputy sheriff executed bonds to the sheriff authorized by the statute, requiring him to pay over to plaintiff all
sums legally collected by him as taxes, etc., the sureties were
liable for his failure to pay over to the sheriff the 6 per cent.
penalty imposed by Ky. St. 1903, Sec. 4143, on delinquents
which the deputy collected, whether such penalty belonged
to the county and state or to the taxpayers, because the
sheriff, with his owns means and borrowed money, paid to
the county and state all the taxes for which he was bound
before they became delinquent.

DENTON & WALLACE attorneys for appellants.

It is clear in the case that the appellee did not pay off the
taxes on December first, to accomodate the County, State or
people, but was actuated solely by the prospect of gain on the
transaction.

We therefore conclude:

1. That appellee by his own acts prevented the happening of
the only contingency upon which the tax-payer was due either
the State or County, any sum whatever as interest or penalties,
that therefore there was no penalty or interest to be or that
could be legally collected from the taxpayer.

2. Conceding that Ellison wrongfully collected any penalties from the people, this does not entitle the appellee to the same or any part of the money, so wrongfully collected, and he will not be heard to ask for a sum of money to which neither he nor his deputy have any right.

AUTHORITIES CITED.

·Ky. Statutes, Section 1885, Section 4143; Adams v. Saunders. 46 Southern Reporter, 960; Commonwealth, etc., v. Pate, etc., 85 S. W., 1096; Fidelity & Deposit Co., of Maryland, v. Logan County, 119 Ky. Reports, 428; Hill v. Fleming, etc., 107 S. W., 764

WESLEY & BROWN attorneys for appellee.

The penalties, for which this action was instituted, are part of the "taxes on the lists of the above mentioned precincts." They have not been paid; therefore the terms of the bond have ٫been broken and appellee is entitled to recover thereon.

AUTHORITIES CITED.

Kentucky Statutes, Section 4143; Commonwealth, &c., v. Pate, &c., 85 S. W., 1096; Fidelity & Deposit Co., of Maryland, v Logan County; 119 Kentucky Reports, 428.

OPINION OF THE COURT BY CHIEF JUSTICE NUNN— Affirming.

Appellee was sheriff of Pulaski county, Ky., for four years, including the years 1900 and 1901. Appellant Harvey Ellison was his deputy, and the other appellants were Ellison's sureties on his bond for the two years mentioned. The stipulations in the bonds for each of the two years named were the same. We copy from one of the bonds that part which has reference to the question at issue, to-wit: "We further agree and bind ourselves that we will hold the said Langdon harmless as to the collection of taxes placed in the said Ellison's hands for collection. The said Ellison having agreed to take the books and collect the taxes for the following precincts: Glades, Dalla, and Burdine—and said Harvey Ellison, by taking said books, became responsible for all taxes therein to said sheriff, and we are hereby bound to said sheriff that said Ellison shall fully and truly pay to said C. M. Langdon, in the amounts and at the time required by the statutes of the state of Kentucky, all taxes on the lists of above-mentioned precincts, including state, revenue, county levy, road tax, and any and all other taxes or revenues coming into his hands as such deputy sheriff for collection by virtue of his said office; it being distinctly understood that, by the acceptance of the books and tax list for said precincts, said Ellison became responsible to said Langdon for the whole thereof, except such as is released in pursuance of law, and entirely relieved said Langdon of the collection of said taxes or any part thereof." Appellee instituted suit upon these bonds, and recovered a judgment for $276, from which this appeal is prosecuted.

Appellants admitted owing $23 to appellee, and they tendered this amount with their answer, claiming that no greater amount should be recovered of them. They contend that the balance of the judgment consists of the "6 per centum additional on the tax" due and unpaid by the taxpayers after the first day of December in each year, as provided in section 4143, Kentucky Statutes of 1903, which statute went into effect in 1894. They did not deny that the deputy had collected that per centum from the taxpayers, but alleged that appellee was not entitled to it, for the reason that the taxpayers were entitled to have it returned to them, or it was due the county and state. It was shown, without contradiction, that the sheriff, with his own means and with money he borrowed for that purpose, paid the county and state all the, taxes for which he was bound before the 1st of December in each of the years, and obtained a quietus from both the county and state. By section 4143, supra, it is provided: "Any person or persons, failing to pay their taxes by the 1st day of December in the year following the assessment for such taxes, shall pay 6 per centum additional on the tax so due and unpaid. * * * The Auditor, in his settlement with the sheriff, shall charge him with the several penalties accruing under the provisions of this act."

This court, in the case of Commonwealth v. Pate, 85 S. W. 1096, 27 Ky. Law Rep. 623, said: "By section 4143, Ky. Stat., any person failing to pay his taxes by the 1st day of December after it is due, shall pay a penalty of 6 per cent. on the amount unpaid, and it is the duty of the sheriff to collect the penalty, as well as the principal, and must pay it over to the proper authority before the 1st day of the succeeding January, or himself pay a penalty of 6 per cent. on the amount wrongfully withheld."

Appellee contends that he is entitled to this per cent. collected by appellant from delinquent taxpayers in the three precincts mentioned to reimburse him for the interest on the money he advanced to the county and state for them and to save himself the penalties provided in the section of the statute referred to. This question, however, is not before us, and we do not decide it. If the county and state, or the taxpayers, are entitled to this fund, they have a right to look to the sheriff and his sureties for it. The bonds were executed to the sheriff, as authorized by the statute, and they required appellant Ellison to account for and pay over to appellee all sums legally collected by him. The statute fixes 6 per cent. as a penalty against delinquents, and requires them to pay that amount as a penalty for their delinquency; but it is not provided or intimated in the statute that the taxpayers should be relieved from it if the sheriff advanced the taxes for them before he became delinquent and a like penalty assessed against him.

It is our opinion that the judgment of the lower court is correct, and it is therefore affirmed.

CASE 73.—ACTION BY THE ADMINISTRATOR OF I. ꝋ. LEWIS DECEASED AGAINST THE BOWLING GREEN GAS LIGHT CO. FOR THE WRONGFUL DEATH OF SAID DECEDENT.—March 17, 1909.

Lewis' Adm'r v. Bowling Green Gas Light Co.

Appeal from Warren Circuit Court.

JOHN M. GALLOWAY, Circuit Judge.

Judgment for defendant, plaintiff appeals.—Reversed.

1. Evidence—Res Gestae.—In an action for death of decedent through contact with an electric wire which had fallen from the poles. what decedent said on taking hold of the wire as to his purpose in grasping it was admissible as part of the res gestae.

2. Electricity—Injuries Incident to Production—Companies and Persons Liable.—A company supplying electricity cannot escape liability for negligence in the manner of distribution by turning it onto private wires, or on the wires of another concern, which are not safely arranged to receive and transmit the current.

3. Electricity—Injuries Incident to Production—Care Required. —A company distributing electricity through public streets is held to the highest degree of care to keep its lines in a safe condition.

4. Electricity—Injuries from Broken Wires—Failure to Inspect
—Negligence—Questions for Jury.—In an action for death
of·decedent, through contact with a sagging and defectively
insulated electric wire, whether defendant, who used the
wire for transmitting electricity, and who knew that the line
had not been inspected or repaired for two years, and that
the insulation was much worn off, was negligent in failing to
inspect and discover the break for more than 12 hours in the
daytime, was for the jury.

5. Negligence—Contributory Negligence—Questions of Law and
Fact.—While ordinarily, when there is no conflict in the evidence, it is a question of law whether the admitted facts constitute contributory negligence, yet, if it be a question whether plaintiff's act at the time was that of an ordinarily prudent
person under the same circumstances, the question is for the
jury.

6. Electricity—Injuries from Broken Wires—Contributory Negligence—Question for Jury.—In an action for death of decedent through grasping a broken electric wire which had fallen
from the poles, whether decedent was guilty of contributory
negligence, held, under the evidence, a jury question.

WRIGHT & McELROY and JOHN B. GRIDER for appellant.

POINTS AND AUTHORITIES.

1. Where defendant placed a deadly current of electricity upon
an unsafe line, it is responsible for injuries occurring by reason
of the defective condition of the line, whether defendant owned
the line or not. Thomas' Adm'r v. Maysville Gas. Co., 21 Ky. Law
Rep. 1609.

2. Where defendant uses the dangerous agency of electricity
for its private gain and transmits it by means of wires, it is
bound at its peril to use the highest degree of care to protect the
public and to keep its wires perfectly insulated at places where the
public have the right to be for business or pleasure, and shall use
the highest degree of care by constant inspection to see that the
lines are kept safe. McLaughlin v. Louisville Electric Co., 18
Ky. Law Rep., 639; Overall v. Louisville Electric Co., 20 Ky. Law
Rep., 759; Mangans' Adm'r v. Louisville Electric Co., 9 S. W.,
703; City Owensboro v. Knox, 76 S. W., 191; Sweitzer's Adm'r v.
Citizen's Gen. Electric Co., 21 Ky. Law Rep., 608.

3. Defendant was guilty of gross negligence, not only by failing to inspect line and see that it was safe, but by failing to test
it, from 5 o'clock Sunday morning until 6 o'clock that evening.
Brown v. Consolidated Light, Power & Ice Co., 109 S. W., 1032.

4. The test of contributory negligence is not always found in the failure to exercise the best judgment or to use the wisest precaution, * * * * but it is to consider whether a prudent person in the same situation and having the knowledge possessed by the one in question, would have done the alleged negligent act. Thompson's Commentaries on Law of Negligence, Vol. 1, Sections 171-173.

5. In order that an act shall be deemed one of contributory negligence per se, it must have been done contrary to a statutory duty, or it must appear so opposed to the dictates of common prudence that the Court can say without hesitation or doubt that no careful person would have committed it. L. & N. R. Co. v. Walton, 13 Ky. Lew Rep., 460; Ashland Coal & Iron Co. v. Wallace, 19 Ky., Law Rep., 853.

6. The lower court erred in taking the case from the jury, and should have permitted the jury to say, under all the circumstances whether I . O. Lewis was guilty of such contributory negligence as would prevent a recovery.

SIMS, DUBOSE & RHODES for appellee.

AUTHORITIES.

1. The Appellee was not required to exercise the highest degree of care at the time and under the circumstances where and when the accident occurred. McLaughlin v. Light Company, 18 Ky. Law Rep., 693.

2. It was contributory negligence for the Appellant's testator to take hold of a live wire in the manner and under the circumstances shown in this case. Mayfield Water & Light Co. v. Webb's Administrator, 111 S. W., 202; I. C. R. R. Co. v. Wilson, 23d Ky. Law Reporter, p. 684.

OPINION OF THE COURT BY JUDGE O'REAR—Reversing.

The Bowling Green Gaslight Company furnished the electric power for a private electric light line extending beyond the city limits of Bowling Green, to supply some suburban residents with lights for their dwellings. One of the wires got down and parted in two places. It hung from the poles and partly on a fence or tree, so that it was sagging some six or eight feet above the ground and alongside of the highway in front of I. O. Lewis' residence. The insulation was worn off the wire in many places. It had not been inspected by the gaslight company since it had been put up—for about two years. The voltage used on this wire was about 1,200 or 1,300 watts. One kilowatt is ordinarily fatal to life where a human body forms part of the circuit. Mr. Lewis was about 70 years old, hale, and in possession of his mental faculties. Walking along the public highway in front of his premises, and seeing this loose wire sagging to within a short distance from the ground, he stepped over and took hold of it, probably to pull it down so as it would be out of the way, when he was shocked and killed by the current of electricity in it. What his purpose was in taking hold of the wire we do not know, because the trial judge would not allow the witness to state what Lewis said as he took hold of the wire. What he then said was as clearly competent as what he did, and was, in fact, part of his act. The accompanying statement of an act is a verbal act, and, as it illustrates the physical act, is treated as part of the res gestæ.

This suit was by the personal representatives of Lewis to recover for his death, on the ground that the gas company was negligent in not looking after the insulation and safety of the wire, and in turning into it such a dangerous voltage of electricity without knowing that the wire was in safe condition along the highway where people might be expected to come in contact with it. The trial court gave the jury a peremptory instruction to find for the defendant at the close of the evidence in the case. The correctness of that ruling is the question presented here for review.

It may be assumed that the trial judge did not base his ruling upon the fact that the gas company did not own the line, as it has been authoritatively declared that the distributor of such a deadly agency as electricity cannot escape liability for negligence in the manner of distribution by turning it onto private wires, or on the wires of another concern, which are not safely arranged to receive and transmit the current. Thomas' Admr. v. Maysville Gas Co., 108 Ky. 224, 56 S. W. 153, 53 L. R. A. 147.

The evidence was that the wire in question was broken at one or two places, and was hanging down as stated, and that on the night previous to the death of Mr. Lewis a witness saw sparks and flames emitted from the wire at a point where on the next morning it was discovered to be in two. The wire was without insulation in many places; it had rotted or broken off, and had not been repaired. That condition had existed for some months. The wires (two of them constituting a circuit) were strung on opposite sides of the posts along the highway, attached to the posts by glass brackets, and were thus placed 8 to 12 inches apart. They were so close as that, when they or one of them became loose, they were in danger of swinging together and touching, creating a short circuit. This would melt the wires, letting them fall to the ground. Appellee had not inspected this line for defects since it was built some two years before, and had not caused it to be repaired. Under these facts we think the case was one for the jury, both as to the company's negligence, and the decedent's contributory negligence. The company could not escape its responsibility as the dispenser through the public streets and roads of such a stealthy, deadly force as an electric current of such

high voltage upon insecure lines of wire, where the
public might reasonably be expected. No more could
it dispense with the duty of inspecting the wires, from
time to time to see that they were securely fastened
and properly insulated, although the lines were not
owned by it. When it used the lines, it was its duty
to see to their proper and safe condition. This duty
was not discharged by the exercise of ordinary care,
but required the highest degree of care to keep them
safe. If the wire broke because of the storm of
Sunday morning (the injury occurred late Sunday
afternoon), and if appellee did not know it was
broken, and could not in the exercise of that degree
of care exacted of it by the law have discovered it,
then it would not be negligent in failing to discover it; but, having knowledge of the manner in which
the wires were strung, the length of time they had
been exposed and in use, and that the insulation was
off much of the wire, whether then it was negligent
in failing to inspect and discover the break, from
whatever cause it may have occurred, for more than
12 hours in the daytime, is a question for the jury.

As to the plea of contributory negligence: Ordinarily, when the facts are admitted, and where there
is no conflict in the evidence, it is a question of law
whether they constitute contributory negligence; but
it is not always so. Although the facts may be admitted, still if it be a question whether the act of the
plaintiff at the time was such as an ordinarily prudent person would have done under the same circumstances, the jury ought to be permitted to say
whether, under the circumstances, it was or was not
negligence, but for which the defendant's negligence
would have been harmless. If the act relied on is
admitted and is clearly negligent, or is clearly not

negligent, the court as a matter of law should by instructions to the jury dispose of the matter; but, although the proof is all one way as to the act, the act itself may be of such doubtful character as to render it an issue of fact, as much so as if the act itself were not of a doubtful character, but the evidence tending to establish or to disprove it was. If the decedent knew that was a live wire, and knew the danger of touching it as he did, the act would be undoubtedly negligence on his part which would defeat a recovery for his injury. If he did not know, and had not reason to believe, it was a live wire, but, on the contrary, had reason to believe the electric current was not turned onto it, his was not such an act as an ordinarily prudent person might have done under the same circumstances. At least, it was not necessarily so. His purpose might have been to place the wire so that when the current was turned on it would be out of the way to do damage.

It is claimed that the insulation is not a protection to human life when the voltage is so high as was that in use in this instance, but there was evidence to the contrary of that contention. We think the whole matter should have gone to the jury under the usual instructions in such cases as to the care exacted of the gas company and of the decedent, and as to what would constitute negligence in each.

Judgment reversed and remanded for a new trial.

CASE 74.—ACTION BY C. J. LITTLE' AGAINST THE CONTI-
NENTAL REALTY CO. AND OTHERS TO RECOVER
FOR SLANDER TO TITLE OF LAND.—March 17,
1909.

Continental Realty Co., &c. v. Little

Appeal from Perry Circuit Court.

L. D. LEWIS, Circuit Judge.

From an order overruling a demurrer to plaintiff's
petition, defendants appeal.—Reversed.

1. Libel and Slander—Slander of Title—Construction of Petition.
    —A petition, averring that plaintiff "is the owner and in
    actual possession of one-half of 522 oak trees," standing on
    a tract of land described, and which further states that plain-
    tiff "has a deed to the said property," and that defendants
    are alleging that a certain company is the owner of the tract
    of land described in the petition, and by reason of such alle-
    gations are greatly injuring plaintiff's title to the "said prop-
    erty" will not be construed as alleging title to the land but
    only to the trees, and that defendants were seeking to slan-
    der plaintiff's interest in the trees.
2   Libel and Slander—Slander of Title to Property.—What Con-
    stitutes.—The owner of a one-half interest in trees on land is
    afforded no action for slander of title bv false statements that
    a certain company owns the land.
3. Corporations—Liability for Acts of Officials—Slander of Title
    to Property.—A corporation is not liable in an action for slan-
    der of title because of declarations made by the president
    and secretary of the company, where it is not shown that
    such declarations were made by them in their official capacity,
    and by direction of the corporation, or in the apparent scope
    of their authority as its officers.
4. Pleading—Conclusions—Slander of Title to Property.—A peti-
    tion, in an action for slander of title to land, which sets out
    certain allegations made by defendants, but which does not
    state that they were false or maliciously made, and does not
    charge that the market value of plaintiff's property was there-

by impaired or lessened, or that he was prevented from selling or using it, but which merely alleges that he was injured and his title slandered by the alleged statements, is insufficient; the allegations as to injury and slander of title being mere conclusions unsupported by statements of fact.

5.   Libel and Slander—Slander of Title to Property—Actions— Petition.—A petition, in an action for slander of title, to property because of alleged declarations of defendants, must set out the words constituting the slander and the special damage resulting therefrom.

6   Libel and Slander—Slander of Title to Property—Petition.—A Petition, in an action for slander of title to land, must allege that plaintiff holds the legal title to the land and is in possession of it, in order to recover as against a defendant setting up a claim thereto.

MARTIN T. KELLY attorney for appellant.

We insist that defendants demurrer to the petition should have been sustained:

1.   Because the petition does not state a course of action against any of the defendants. Perkins v. Maysville. Dist. Camp Meeting Association, 10 Ky. Law Rep., 781, 10 S. W., 659; Ogders on Libel & Slander, Am. Ed. 368; Ky. Statutes, Sec. 11; Campbell v. Disney, 93 Ky., 41.

2.   Because there is no equity in the petition and a court of law is the proper place to settle and adjust the matters in dispute.   Parker, &c., v. Shannon, 121 Ill., 452, 13 N. E., 155; Spelling on Injunction, Secs. 343 and 369; Lex. City Nat. Bank v. Guynn, 69 Ky., (6 Bush) 486; Barker v. Warren, 6 Ky. Law Rep., 86; Hillman v. Hurley, 82 Ky., 626; Moses v. Christian, 46 Ky., (7 B. Monroe) 422; Pomeroy's Equity Jurisprudence, Sec. 1358; Spelling on Injunction, Sec. 344; Burket v. Griffith, 13 L. R. A., 707; Reges v. Middletown, 29 L. R. A., 66 to 69; Flint v. Hutchinson Smoke Burner Co., 16 L. R. A., 243; Boston Diatel Co. v. Florence Mfg. Co., 114 Mass., 69, 19 Am. Rep. 31.

3.   The petition is defective in that it does not allege that the plaintiff is the owner of the land or that he has any title thereto.

GOURLEY, REDWINE & GOURLEY for appellee.

AUTHORITIES CITED.

17 Encyclopedia of Pleading & Practice, 279, 330: Barker v. Warren, 6 Ky. Law Rep., 86; Williams v. Ayrault, 31 Barb. N. Y., 264.

OPINION OF THE COURT BY CHIEF JUSTICE SETTLE—
.Reversing.

This is an appeal from a judgment of the Perry
circuit court overruling a demurrer filed by each of
the appellants to appellee's petition. It therefore
presents for our consideration but one question,
namely, whether or not the petition states a cause of
action.

The action was brought in equity by the appellee, C.
J. Little, against the appellants, Continental Realty
Company, F. L. Whittaker, and Martin Kelley; it being alleged in the petition that the Continental Realty
Company is a corporation, that F. L. Whittaker is
its president, and Martin Kelly, its secretary. It
is not clear from the language of the petition whether
the action is one to quiet title or to recover for slander
of title. The petition begins with the averment that
appellee "is the owner and in the actual possession of
one-half of 522 oak trees," standing upon a tract of
land on the waters of Troublesome creek in Perry
county; the land being described by metes and bounds,
courses and distances. The petition contains the further averment that appellee "has a deed to the said
property." As it does not allege that appellee owns
or has either actual or constructive possession of the
land upon which the oak trees stand, but does in express terms allege his title to and actual possession of
one-half of 522 oak trees standing on the land, we
must infer that the deed received by appellee for "the
said property" merely conveyed him one-half of the
trees, and that by the words "the said property" is
meant one-half of the trees, and nothing more.

The petition does not disclose the name of the owner of the other half of the 522 oak trees, or of the

land; nor does it contain any explanation of the failure to give the name of such owner, or any reason
for not making him a party to the action. As it is
not alleged that appellee's half of the 522 oak trees
have been marked or set apart to him, it is apparent
that his interest in the trees is a'n undivided half
thereof. Hence it would seem necessary that the
owner of the other undivided half of the trees should
be made a party to the action. The fact that this
was not done may, it is true, amount to a mere defect
of parties, which could be corrected by the filing of a
special demurrer to the petition; but it is here mentioned as one of the evidences of the vague and intangible nature of appellee's claim to the relief sought
in the petition. It is also, in substance, alleged in the
petition that the appellants Whittaker and Kelley are
giving it out in speeches that the appellant Continental Realty Company is the owner of the tract of land
described in the petition, and by reason of such
speeches are greatly injuring appellee's title to the
"said property." As the only property the petition
alleges appellee has title to is an undivided half of 522
oak trees, and it nowhere alleges that he has title to
the land upon which the trees are standing, we must
conclude that the words "said property" refer, as in
previous connection, to appellee's undivided half of
the oak trees, and for the same reason must also conclude that in further alleging in the petition that appellants have no title to "said property," and that, in
claiming appellee has not title thereto, they were
seeking to injure him and to slander and becloud his
title to "said property," was again meant appellee's
undivided half of the trees.

In view of the fact that the petition does not set up
title in appellee to the land on which the trees stood,

we are unable to comprehend how he could have been or can in the future be injured, or his title to one-half the oak trees injured or beclouded by the alleged declarations of Whittaker and Kelley that the Continental Realty Company owns the land. Its ownership of the land is not inconsistent with appellee's ownership or possession of one-half of 522 white oak trees standing thereon, if, as alleged in the petition, the latter's ownership of the trees is evidenced by a deed or other written instrument. If, as alleged in the petition Whittaker and Kelley declared appellee had no title to the half of the 522 oak trees claimed by him, and that the title thereto was in the Continental Realty Company, that fact would not impose any liability upon the corporation, even in an action for slander of title, unless such declaration was made by them in their official capacity as president and secretary, respectively, and by direction of the corporation, or in the apparent scope of their authority as its officers; none of which facts will be found to have been alleged in the petition. Perkins v. Maysville District Camp Meeting Association, 10 S. W. 659, 10 Ky. Law Rep. 781; Odgers on Libel and Slander (Am. Ed.) .368.

It is not charged in the petition that the statements of Whittaker and Kelly complained of were false, or that they were maliciously made; nor is it charged that the market value of appellee's half of the 522 oak trees was thereby impaired or lessened, or that he was thereby prevented from selling the timber or interfered with in its use. The averment that he was injured and his title slandered by the alleged statements was a mere conclusion, unsupported by any statement of fact showing such injury or any damage. If the action could be treated as one for slander of title resulting from the alleged declarations of Whittaker and Kelley, there could be no recovery, for the petition does not set out the words constituting the slander of title, and no special damage is alleged, both of which are essential in such a case. Burkett v. Griffith, 90 Cal. 532, 27 Pac. 527, 13 L. R. A. 707, 25 Am. St. Rep. 151. It is not averred that Whittaker or Kelley set up any claim to the land or timber in or for themselves, but that they 'did so for and on behalf of the Continental Realty Company, which, as we have already said, was unaccompanied by other necessary allegations showing that they were authorized to make such claim in behalf of the corporation. If the language of the petition could be construed to mean that it asserts title in appellee to the land, it obviously fails to allege his possession of the land, and to maintain an action quia timet the plaintiff must allege that he holds both the legal title and possession of the land, in order to recover as against a defendant setting up claim thereto.

The petition being fatally defective, the circuit court erred in overruling appellant's demurrers.

Wherefore the judgment is reversed, and cause remanded, with direction to sustain each of the demurrers and for further proceedings consistent with the opinion, including leave to appellee, should it be asked, to amend his petition.

CASE 75.—ACTION BY HARVEY McDONALD'S ADMINISTRA-
TOR AGAINST THE WALLSEND COAL & COKE
CO. FOR CAUSING THE DEATH OF PLAINTIFF'S
INTESTATE.—March 17, 1909.

McDonald's Adm'r v. Wallsend Coal & Coke Co.

Appeal from Bell Circuit Court.

M. J. Moss, Circuit Judge.

From a judgment of non-suit, plaintiff appeals.—
Reversed.

1. Master and Servant—Injuries to Servant—Contributory Negligence.—Coal mine employes entitled to use the tracks of an
   electric railway into the mine when leaving the mine at
   the close of the day's work, may assume that the employer
   will not run cars into the mine while they are going out,
   and an employe is not chargeable with contributory negligence for failing to anticipate that cars will be run into the
   mine.

2. Master and Servant—Injuries to Servant—Contributory Negligence.—An employe placed suddenly in a position of peril
   by the negligence of the employer is not bound to exercise a
   correct judgment, and is not chargeable with contributory negligence because he failed to take the safer of the two ways
   open to him.

3. Master and Servant—Injuries to Servant—Contributory Negligence.—Coal mine employes, leaving the mine at the close
   of the day's work, used an electric railroad track, which
   was the only way provided for them. The employer ran cars
   into the mine while the men were coming out at an excessive speed without any headlight or gong. An employe on
   the cars, suddenly coming on the men, sought to escape,
   leaving the track at the side where he was walking, but the
   entry was too narrow to enable him to clear the track, and
   he was killed. The passage was dark, being only lighted
   by the miner's torches. Held, that the employe was not as
   a matter of law guilty of contributory negligence.

McDonald's Admr. v. Wallsend Coal & Coke Co.

4. Judges—Disqualification—Bias.—The bias of a judge does not legally disqualify him from trying a case, unless it causes him to act corruptly or with such oppression as to be equivalent to corruption, and the cause for the removal of a judge must be such that, if he assumes to act in spite of it, it involves his personal integrity, or makes it improper that a man of integrity should preside in that matter, and the mere fact that a judge is unfriendly to personal injury suits does not disqualify him from trying a personal injury action.

5. Judges—Disqualification—Affidavit—Sufficiency.—An affidavit to remove the regular judge on the ground of bias filed by plaintiff in action for injuries while a coal mine employe, which stated that the judge was a stockholder and officer in a coal mine, that it was thought that he was inimical to the interests of the miners, that he was on friendly social terms with mine operators and that it was the common talk among lawyers and citizens that his friendliness to mineowners and unfriendliness toward damage suits created a bias in his mind, which made it difficult for an employé to get a fair trial of his case, did not state facts showing affirmatively a personal bias toward the litigant or his case essential to remove a judge on the ground of bias.

6. Judges—Bias—Affidavit—Time to File.—An affidavit to remove the regular judge because of his disqualification by bias must be presented promptly on the discovery of the facts.

B. B. GOLDEN attorney for appellant.

W. T. DAVIS of counsel.

The facts, contained in this record, disclose that the appellee owned and operated at the time of the injury complained of a mining plant known as a Drift Mine in which there were numerous entries and cross entries in which it had in use electrical motors with which to haul its coal from the mine. There were some hundred or more miners on this occasion employed in these mines. The deceased, Harvey McDonald, a man of good education, fifty years of age, after having finished his day's work in his room in these mines, together with twelve or fifteen others, was coming out of the mine. They were in the main cntry and the only avenue which all of the miners had to travel in order to get out of the mines, and into them, and were within about six or eight hundred feet of the drift mouth when sudden.

McDonald's Admr. v. Wallsend Coal & Coke Co.

ly and almost without a moment's warning this motor with more than twenty empty cars attached to it, without sounding the gond·and without the headlight burning and coming at an unusual and dangerous rate of speed ran among these men, all of whom sprang to the sides of the entry for safety. The deceased in his haste and excitement happened to get off the track and to the rib side at a point where the track was so near the rib side that portions of the motor and cars came violently in contact with him, knocking him down and dragging him about eighteen feet against a post that was so near the track that the cars had been scraping against it theretofore so often that they had cut a grove in it and his leg was broken and he was injured on his head, back, and body, and internally, so that he died within two or three days after the injury.

WM. LAW and O. V. RILEY for appellee.

CONCLUSION FROM THE TESTIMONY.

The testmony showed the following clear conclusions:

1. That the injured man and the others with him at the time of the accident were traveling along the motor-way during the work-time of the motor-crew, and thus unnecessarily and imprudently exposed themselves to danger.

2. That the injured man did not exercise that vigilence for his own safety that a prudent person would have done under the circumstances nor as other persons along with him did.

3. That the motorman did not fail to do anything that he could or should have done to have averted the injury after seeing the deceased in peril.

QUESTIONS OF LAW.

If these conclusions from the testimony are well founded, there are but two questions of law for the Court to consider so far as the merits of the action are concerned, which are as follows:

1. Was it negligence in appellee for the trip to have been made without the electric-light on the motor, when the crew each had a driver's lamp burning in his cap, and the trip was being made in regular time, and when the noises from the operations of the motor are more timely and effective warnings than the head-light if burning, or gong had it been used, could have been?

2. If this be held in the affirmative, then the question of deceased exercising due care for his own safety, the time, place and the manner of the accident being considered. alone remain.

OPINION OF THE COURT BY JUDGE O'REAR—Reversing.

Harvey McDonald, a miner in the service of appellee, was injured by being run against by an electric motor and train of cars in appellee's mine in Bell county. There was a custom, as well as an agreement between the mineowner and the miners, that the latter were to "shoot" their coal twice a day—at 11:15 a. m. and 4:15 p. m. One hundred to 150 coal miners worked in the mine. When they had cut under the face of the coal far enough to place a charge of powder in a drilled hole at the top and fire it off, the coal would be knocked down. The smoke and gas generated by the discharge made it impossible for the miners to stay in the rooms and passages for awhile after the shots were fired; so it was arranged that all should shoot about the same time, which was near enough to quitting time, whether for the noon rest or in the evening, that the mines would clear of smoke and gas before the men went back to work. From the time of shooting 15 minutes were allowed the miners in which to get out of the mine. On the day appellant's intestate was injured the miners began shooting about 4:15, the intestate among the others. As they set off the charges, they withdrew and started out the main entry to leave the mine, which was the only way out. Electric motors were used to take in the empty coal cars, and to draw out the loaded cars. These motor cars had a speed of about 12 miles an hour. The main entry was about five feet high. The entry varied in width, but at places was less than six feet. The entry was not straight. An overhead wire to the side of the entry transmitted the current of electricity, which was fed to the motor by a trolley from the side of the motor car. At 4:15 p. m. the motor car was on the outside of the mine. The motorman then notified the mine boss that the headlight on this car was out of fix, and was not of use. The gong on the car was also out of repair, and could not be sounded. The mine boss promised to have the car repaired by morning, but directed the motorman to take in another lot of empty cars. The motorman demurred on account of having no headlight, and because it was then shooting time, and the miners would be coming out. The mine boss looked at his watch and told the motorman that, if he would hurry up, he could make it in time. The motor car, coupled to about 20 empty coal cars, then started in the mine, running at its highest speed. When in the mine about 1,200 or 1,500 feet, and directly after it had passed around a curve, the train ran into a squad of miners who were walking along the track coming out of the mine after their day's work. There was no warning of the approach of the train except the humming noise made by the trolley, and the noise of the cars on the rails. The noise, of course, indicated that a motor was running on that track, but whether coming in or going out it would not very well indicate. As the trolley passed the retaining brackets electric flashes would appear at those points. But, as the cars were around the bend, these flashes would not show further than the bend. The intestate was in this squad of miners. Their walking and talking made some noise, and the frequent discharges of the blasts in the rooms, which were then being set off, further confused the sounds. This was the situation when the train dashed into the midst of this company of miners. They jumped to the side of the track for safety. But decedent McDonald failed to reach a place of safety.

At the point where he jumped off the track the entry was too narrow to admit his person in the clear at the side of the cars. As they passed, they struck him, caught him, and rolled him along the side of the mine, bruising and mangling him so that he died within three days. This suit is by his administrator to recover for the negligent destruction of the life of the intestate. At the close of the plaintiff's evidence, which disclosed the foregoing facts, the court gave the jury a peremptory instruction to find for the defendant. It is supposed this instruction was based upon the fact that the intestate was himself guilty of contributory negligence, but for which he would not have been hurt. The contributory negligence in this case is thought to have consisted of two factors: One, the decedent was either inattentive and failed to listen for the cars, or, hearing them, failed to exercise due care for his own safety; the other is that on the opposite side of the entry where he was struck there was room enough for him to have stood in safety while the cars passed.

We cannot doubt it was negligence, we might say criminal negligence, in running that train of cars at that time and under the circumstances at such high speed without headlight or gong to announce its approach. It was such an utter disregard of the lives of the men who were known to be coming out that entry, and who had to walk along the track, the entry being too narrow in many places to admit of their walking by the side of the track, or to get into a place of safety by its side, as makes the master liable for any injury inflicted upon them by reason of that act. Nor was it certain that the decedent was guilty of contributory negligence. He had a right to use the track to walk upon in coming out the mine. No other way was provided him. He had the right to assume that the master would not run the motor car into the mine while the miners were coming out—particularly not at the speed run in this instance—and without a head-light or gong on the motor car. He was not required to give attention to or to anticipate what reasonably he had not cause to suspect. Besides, he had not control of the other miners' movements—their walking, talking, and laughing as they went along the passage way, nor the shooting that was going on in the rooms along the route. All these matters tended to confuse sounds, which were equally well known to the master and those operating the motor car, and decedent had the right to assume that with knowledge of such conditions the master would regulate the running of the trains so as to make the situation as safe for the miners as the conditions admitted of. When, contrary to such reasonable presumptions, the master ran the train of cars recklessly in the entry so as to suddenly imperil the decedent, he was not bound in such emergency to exercise correct judgment, or to select the safer of the two ways presented to his mind in that moment. He had the right to act upon impulse, as he was deprived by the master's negligence of a reasonable opportunity to exercise judgment. The impulse would be to take the nearest apparent means of safety. That was to leave the track at the side where he was walking, which he did. He probably had not time to cross the track. He took the chance of being able to find a safe place on his side. The passage was dark, narrow, and low. The only light was the feeble rays shed by the miner's cap torches. In choosing the means that he did the decedent acted as any ordinary person might have done under the circumstances. Whether he was guilty of contributory negligence at all on the evidence now in the record was barely presented so as to let the question go to the jury. But it was not such, in any event, as to make his conduct as a matter of law a bar to his right of recovery for the injuries which his master's negligence had inflicted. The motion for the peremptory instruction ought to have been overruled.

This action was begun in 1905. The docket of the Bell circuit court is said to be large. The issue was made up in this case some two years ago, and one trial was begun, but was discontinued for the plaintiff, owing to illness in his lawyer's family. When the case was called the last time for trial, plaintiff filed an affidavit to remove the regular judge of the court because of his disqualification by bias. The facts disclosed, so far as they are facts, instead of rumors and suspicious, had existed since before the beginning of this case, and were known to the plaintiff and to his counsel from the beginning. No effort was made when this suit was filed, or at the first term of the court thereafter, to remove the judge because of his alleged bias. On the contrary, the parties submitted their case to his rulings. The judge is charged with being unfriendly to personal injury suits, and as himself being connected with a coal mining corporation. The judge is not charged with corruption, nor with being personally hostile to the litigant, nor as entertaining a particular antipathy toward the plaintiff or his suit. It is said he does not look with favor upon litigation growing out of personal injuries. It is likely some judges have just the opposite feeling concerning such suits. But we do not see that that fact necessarily disqualifies the judge from presiding at the trial of such cases in his court. Judges, like other men, have their notions of right and wrong, which may not agree with the law of the matter. Their alleged bias may, so far as they are concerned, be a matter of conscience. Unless it causes them to act corruptly, or with such oppression as to be equivalent to corruption, we do not see how it can legally disqualify the judge as an official. A juror may not look with favor upon personal injury suits, or say that he may, and in his previous service his predilections have in some manner affected, or colorably affected, his verdicts. Would that subject him to challenge for cause in all cases of that nature? We doubt it. A judge will not be removed for the same causes always that a juror may be peremptorily challenged for. The cause to remove a judge must be one which, if he assumes to act in spite of it, involves his personal integrity, or which makes it improper that a man of integrity should preside in that matter. German Ins. Co. v. Landrum, 88 Ky. 433, 11 S. W. 367, 592. It is not always corrupt. So far as the man's own conscience is concerned, it may be innocent. But it must be such a cause as that an impartial mind would conclude that a person so situated would not probably, and could not, give a fair trial in the case. The substance of the complaint in this case is that the judge was a stockholder and officer in a coal mining company; that it was thought he was "inimical" to the interests of the miners; that he is on friendly, social terms with mine operators; that it was common talk among certain lawyers and citizens that his friendliness to the mine-owners and unfriendliness toward damage suits created a bias in his mind, which made it difficult for the workman to get a fair trial of his case. The latter is stated as a deduction from the predicate, much of which is "rumor of the county," and talk of certain lawyers who had been disappointed in court. This affidavit in this case involves more the question of character than of particular bias in the judge. The latter only is a matter reviewable by this court. Character is for the people in their elections or for the Senate sitting as a court of impeachment. The lack of character is such as disqualifies the man altogether. If an appellate court could say in such instance that the judge must vacate the bench upon complaint of any litigant who attacked his general character as a man, we must sit necessarily as a court of impeachment, which we cannot do. And it would result, if we did, that that judge could try only such cases as the litigants and lawyers in his court would suffer him to try. No; we cannot review these sweeping general charges. We have not the jurisdiction to do so. The trial judge's position is a hard one to fill. It is hard to please a losing litigant. Some lawyers when they lose are not convinced by the judge's judgment—perhaps ought not to be. But, if these conditions are allowed to constitute a basis for impeaching the judge without trial, the circuit judiciary are indeed in a most unenviable condition; for, when attacked by an affidavit, the judge must sit dumb as to the truthfulness of the grounds charged. He cannot deny them, though he may know them to be false. He cannot call witnesses to refute them. He cannot even cross-examine his accuser. He must confine himself to deciding, by the standard erected by the law, whether the affidavit is sufficient to require him to vacate the bench in that case. It must be a delicate and embarrassing situation. Nevertheless he alone must first pass judicially upon the matter. Hence it is that the

634 KENTUCKY REPORTS. [Vol. 135.

McDonald's Admr. v. Wallsend Coal & Coke Co.

statute has been construed that the affidavit must state facts. German Ins. Co. v. Landrum, supra; Sparks v. Colson, 109 Ky. 711, 60 S. W. 540; Schmidt v. Mitchell, 101 Ky. 570, 41 S. W. 929, 72 Am. St. Rep. 427; Hargis v. Marcum, 103 S. W. 346, 31 Ky. Law Rep. 795; Ky. Journal Co. v. Gaines, 110 S. W. 268, 33 Ky. Law Rep. 402. They must show affirmatively a personal bias toward the litigant or his case (Massie v. Commonwealth, 93 Ky. 588, 20 S. W. 704), and must be presented promptly upon their discovery (German Ins. Co. v. Landrum, supra; Ky. C. R. R. Co. v. Kenny, 82 Ky. 154; Vance v. Field, 89 Ky. 178, 12 S. W. 190; Russell v. Russell, 12 S. W. 709, 11 Ky. Law Rep. 547; Bales v. Fennell, 49 S. W. 759, 20 Ky. Law Rep. 1564). The affidavit in this case did not fill those requirements. That seems to be admitted in the argument, but we are asked to go further in this case. We find no warrant to do so.

For the error in granting the nonsuit the judgment is reversed, and cause remanded for a new trial under proceedings consistent herewith.

CASE 76.—PROSECUTION AGAINST ROBERT BROWN AND
OTHERS FOR ROBBERY.—March 18, 1909.

Brown, &c. v. Commonwealth

Appeal from Bell Circuit Court.

M. J. Moss, Circuit Judge.

Defendant convicted and appeals.—Affirmed.

1. Indictment and Information—Formal Requisites—Signature
   of Public Prosecutor.—Since the Code does not·require the
   commonwealth's attorney to sign an indictment, the signing
   or printing by mistake of the name of a person to it as commonwealth's attorney who is not such officer does not invalidate it.
2. Robbery—What Constitutes—Force—Putting in Fear.—To
   constitute robbery, the person robbed must be deprived of
   property by force, or by putting him in fear.
3. Robbery—Sufficiency of Evidence.—Evidence tnat one of
   defendants asked prosecutor for a dime with which to buy
   beer, and that, on the latter's drawing some money from
   his pocket, the other defendant suddenly and forcibly
   wrenched the money from prosecutor's hand, and fled with
   it, authorized a conviction for robbery, and an instruction
   on larceny was properly refused.

J. G. ROLLINS counsel for appellants.

W. B. HAYS of counsel.

The judgment herein should be reversed, because:
   1. The evidence does not show that anything of value was
taken from the man, Roberts, said to have been robbed.
   2. Because the court failed to give the jury the whole law of
the case by instructing them on the law of grand and petrt
larceny.
   3. The court erred in its first instruction to the jury in this;
if either Charley Woods or Pearl Wiggins aided Robert Brown,

the court instructs the jury to find both guilty, although the other may not have so aided him.

JAMES BREATHITT attorney general by TOM B. McGREGOR assistant attorney general.

Section 262, Criminal Code, provides: "Upon an indictment for an offense consisting of different degrees, the defendant may be found guilty of any degree not higher than that charged in the indictment, and may be found guilty of any offense included in that charged in the indictment."

Section 263 of the Code provides in part: "The offenses named in each of the subdivisons of this section shall be deemed degrees of the same offense in the meaning of the last section. The third sub-division of that section is: "All offenses of larceny."

Roberson's Criminal Law, Section 295, reads· "Robbery being a higher grade of crime than larceny, the former includes the latter, and if, under an indictment for robbery, the aggravating matter essential to constitute the crime be not proven, the defendant may be convicted of grand, or of simple, larceny."

Commonwealth v. Prewitt, 82 Ky., 240; Sullivan v. Commonwealth, 9 Ky. Law Reep., 420; Bibb v. Commonwealth, 33 Ky. Law Rep., 726; Jones v. Commonwealth, 115 Ky., 592; Dawson v. Commonwealth, 74 S. W., 701; Snyder v. Commonwealth, 21 Ky. Law Rep., 1538.

OPINION OF THE COURT BY CHIEF JUSTICE SETTLE— Affirming.

The appellants, Robert Brown, Charlie Woods, and Pearl Wiggins were indicted, tried, and convicted of the crime of robbery, the punishment of each being fixed at confinement in the penitentiary two years. Appellants ask a reversal of the judgment of conviction.

Numerous errors are assigned, but only two of them are relied on for the reversal asked. The first complaint is that the court erred in overruling appellant's demurrer to the indictment. At the close of the indictment appears the name of G. A. Denham, as commonwealth's attorney of the Twenty-Sixth judicial district, when it should have contained the name of J. B. Snyder, present commonwealth's attorney, of the judicial district. Denham was the predecessor in office of Snyder, and it is admitted that the indictment against appellants was written upon a partly printed form, which was one of a lot that had been procured by Denham while commonwealth's attorney, and that in preparing the indictment Snyder forgot to erase the name of Denham and write his own in lieu thereof as commonwealth's attorney. The error did not affect the validity of the indictment. In the case of Sims v. Commonwealth, 13 S. W., 1079, 12 Ky. Law Rep. 215, it is said: ''The Code does not require the commonwealth's attorney to sign the indictment. It makes no difference whether the person signing the indictment was a county or commonwealth's attorney. The law did not require either to sign it.''

If, as thus held, neither the county nor the commonwealth's attorney is required by the Code to sign the indictment, it necessarily follows that the signing or printing by mistake of the name of a person to it as commonwealth's attorney who is not such officer would not invalidate it. The mistake could have no other effect that would the absence from the indictment of the name of the commonwealth's attorney or county attorney. It is further insisted for appellants that the trial court erred in failing to instruct the jury as to the law in respect to larceny, and that the evidence upon which they were convicted, if it showed them guilty of any crime, more directly tended to prove them guilty of larceny than robbery; and, $6 being the amount of which the owner was deprived by them, they should have been convicted of petit larceny if convicted at all; whereas the instructions that were given only contained the law as to robbery, and compelled the jury to find appellants guilty of that crime, or to acquit them. It remains to be seen whether the evidence supports this contention. That introduced by the commonwealth conduced to prove that William Roberts and another man named Johnson were in the city of Middlesboro on the night of the robbery, having gone there from the state of Virginia. Together they walked along one of the streets of the city until they reached a point in front of the Shady Grove saloon and near a restaurant, where they met two negro men and a negro woman. The negro woman was Pearl Wiggins, and one of the negro men the appellant Charles Woods. The other man was a one-eyed negro, but there was contrariety of evidence as to whether he was the appellant, Robert Brown, or another one-eyed negro known as "Bram." Upon meeting the three negroes something was said by Johnson to them, and the appellant Charles Woods then started away with Johnson, ostensibly for the purpose of conducting him to a barber's shop, leaving Roberts with the other negroes. At that juncture Pearl Wiggins asked Roberts for a dime to buy a bucket of beer. Evidently intending to comply with her request, Roberts drew some money from his pocket, and after he did so the one-eyed negro man with Pearl Wiggins suddenly, and with force and violence, snatched or wrenched the money from Roberts' hand. and with equal suddenness swiftly fled and escaped with it. The amount thus taken was $6. The arrest of the three appellants speedily followed. Mrs. Gerrish, a witness for the commonwealth, was standing in the door of the restaurant, in plain view of the parties, when the robbery occurred, and claimed to have seen the entire transaction. She testified that the negro man, who snatched the money from Roberts' hand and ran away with it was a one-eyed man, and identified the appellant Brown as the guilty person. Two other witnesses testified that he was in a negro restaurant on an alley in the rear of the Shady Grove saloon immediately before the robbery, and one of them said that he was then trying to borrow a bucket to get some beer for Pearl Wiggins. The evidence fails to show that he was seen at the place of the robbery after its occurrence. The appellants, Brown and Pearl Wiggins, admitted all the facts as to the robbery, except they claimed that it was the one-eyed negro Bram, and not Brown, who siezed and fled with Roberts' money. They also proved by two or more witnesses that Bram resembles Brown; that he, too, was seen near the scene of the robbery shortly before it was committed, and that immediately thereafter he left Middlesboro, and has not since returned.

While the evidence was conflicting as to the identity of Brown and as to Woods' connection with the crime, we are unable to say that it furnished no basis for the verdict of the jury. It was for the jury to say whether Brown or Bram was the money-snatcher, and whether Woods and Pearl Wiggins were aiders and abettors in the commission of the crime. We are not at a loss to understand how the jury constructed from the evidence as a whole the theory that each of the appellants contributed to the crime charged; the part assigned Woods being to get Johnson separated from Roberts that he might not assist the latter to resist the robbers, the act of Pearl Wiggins in asking of Roberts the dime to buy beer being a subterfuge to get him to pull the money from his pocket that Brown might be afforded the opportunity to forcibly take it from him, and Brown's part of the enterprise to possess himself by force of the money after Roberts drew it from his pocket. The evidence clearly shows that force was required and used to deprive Roberts of his money, and to constitute robbery the person robbed must be deprived of his property by force, or by putting him in fear. In Davis v. Commonwealth, 54 S. W. 959, 21 Ky. Law Rep., 1295, it was held the fact that the defendant snatched money from the hand of another was evidence of actual violence, which entitled the prosecution to an instruction to the jury to convict if the money was taken against the owner's will, by actual force. And in Jones v. Commonwealth, 112 Ky., 689, 66 S. W., 633, 57 L. R. A., 432, 99 Am. St. Rep., 330, it was also held that, where defendant snatched a pocketbook from the hand of another so quickly that he had no chance to actively resist, there was such a taking by violence as authorized a conviction under an indictment for robbery.

The trial court did not err in failing to give an instruction under which the jury might have found appellants guilty of larceny. There was indeed no proof of larceny; it was wholly and altogether to the effect that Roberts' money was taken from him by force and with such violence and suddenness as gave him no opportunity to resist the robbers. The crime was therefore robbery, and the instruction authorizing the jury to find appellants guilty of robbery, together with the one as to the reasonable doubt, gave to the jury all the law of the case.

Wherefore the judgment is affirmed.

CASE 77.—ACTION BETWEEN WILLIAM CORNWALL, Jr.,
AND ANOTHER, AND SALLY W. C. HILL AND
ANOTHER FOR THE CONSTRUCTION OF A WILL.
March 19, 1909.

Cornwall, &c v. Hill, &c.

Appeal from Jefferson Circuit Court (Chancery
Branch, First Division).

SHACKELFORD MILLER, Judge.

From the judgment William Cornwall, Jr., and
another appeal.—Reversed.

1. Wills—Construction—Time of Taking Effect.—Ky. St.1909, Sec.
   4839 (Russell's St. Sec. 3962), provides that "a will shall be construed.* * * to speak and take effect as if executed immediately before the death of testator, unless a contrary intention appears." Held, that where it appears that a will
   was made in contemplation of a settlement with creditors,
   and a conveyance for carrying out that plan was made in
   about a month after its execution, the will should be read as
   speaking from the date of conveyance rather than that of its
   execution.

2. Wills—Construction—Equality of Beneficiaries.—The construction of the will, which produces equality is preferred to
   one that produces inequality, and it will not be presumed
   that testator intended to prefer one of his children to the
   others, unless this appears from a fair reading of the will.

3. Wills—Construction—Division of Property.—A will construed
   with reference to the condition of testator's property and the
   contemplated compromise and settlement with creditors, and
   held, that testator intended to divide his estate equally between his three children, and that the daughter was not entitled to a one-third interest in a certain factory before a
   division of the estate.

D. W. FARLEIGH AND ALFRED SELLIGMAN counsel for appellants.

vol. 135—41

The following rules of law with reference to the construction of wills may be aidful:

1. The presumption that the testator intended to make an equal distribution of his estate among his children and the construction which will produce equality· is to be preferred over·one which will produce inequality.

2. Extrinsic facts may be considered by the Court in construing a will, to "enable the Court to place itself in his situation, to see things as he saw them, and to apply his language as he understood and intended it. Page on Wills, Section 817.

3. The general intent of the will must be given effect. In the case at bar there is a general equal devise of all the estate, real and personal. This general intent must be given effect.

AUTHORITIES CITED.

Hill, etc.; v. Cornwoll & Bros. Assn., 95 Ky., page 512; Page on Wills, Section 817; Page on Wills, Section 463.

BODLEY & BASKIN for appellees.

CLASSIFICATION OF QUESTIONS DISCUSSED AND AUTHORITIES CITED.

1. Where a testator devises all his property to three children and by a later clause makes a special devise to one of them, the special devise must be paid and the residue divided under the general clause.

2. Effect must be given to all clauses of a will, and they must be reconciled if possible. Moss v. Cross, 17 B. Mon., 735; 29 Am. & Eng. Ency.. 350 and 363; Hunt v. Johnson, 10 B. Mon., 342; Jacob v. Jacob, 4th Bush, 110; Howard v. Howard, 4th Bush, 495; Adie v. Cornwell, 3 T. B. M., 279; Delph v. Delph, 2nd Bush, 171; Proctor v. Duncan, 1st Duvall, 318; Hickman v Holliday, 6 T. B. M., 582.

3. If all clauses can not be reconciled, the last clause making a special devise must prevail. (Same authorities.)

4. A later clause is not repugnant to a· former clause unless it entirely destroys it. It if does destroy it, the later clause stands. Sweet v. Chase, 2nd N. Y., 73.

5. The title to property specially devised passes as of the death of testator's death, and the income from that property vests immediately in the devisee. 49 Century Digest, column 2709, and citations.

6. Where a special devise is used for payment of general debts, whether interest is thereby stopped or not, the devisee is entitled to interest with annual or biennial rests. In this case

only simple interest was allowed. Page v. Holeman, 82 Ky., 576; Montjoy v. Lashbrook, 2 B. M., 261; Celsaons v. Caldwell, 7 B. M., 171; Grigsby v. Wilkinson, 9th Bush, 91.

OPINION OF THE COURT BY JUDGE HOBSON—Reversing.

William Cornwall, Sr., died testate, a resident of Jefferson county in March, 1895, leaving three children surviving him, two sons and a daughter. His will was duly admitted to probate, and this controversy has arisen between his children as to its construction, the two sons insisting that the estate is left to the three children equally, and the daughter that one-third of the property known as the "factory of Cornwall & Bro." goes to her in addition to one-third of the estate. The will, after a clause appointing the two sons as executors without bond, as far as material, reads as follows:

"I give all my real and personal property I may die possessed of to my executors, or executor, in trust for the purposes named in this, my last will, and my rents or incomes of my estate, after paying taxes, insurance and repairs shall be equally divided among my children, viz: My sons, William and Aaron W. Cornwall, and my daughter, Sally W. Hill. Any interest I may have in the manufacture of soap and candles at the time of my death may be continued by my executors or executor with my sons as partners or at the election of my sons be continued as stock in a manufacturing corporation, or invessted in the stock of a corporation that may be formed for manufacturing soap and candles; or my sons may take my interest at its value as shown by the books at the time of my death and pay for the same in one- two and three years time, without security, paying interest at the

rate of six per cent. per annum. The value of my
interest shall be ascertained by taking stock at the
usual time which is any of the summer months when
candle market is usually stopped. Or the stock may
be taken if my sons so elect to do so, as near the time
of my death as may be deemed to involve the least
loss of time and business. And the election herein-
above may be exercised by my sons after taking the
account of stock. My daughter's share of any money
coming to her under this will, or her share of any real
estate shall be held by my executors, or executor, in
trust for her separate use, free from the control of
any husband she may have, and she may will it to
any child or children she may have who may survive
her.

"The income from rents or dividends, if any that
may accrue for my daughter, shall be paid to her only
on her receipt, free from any debt or claim of any husband she may have. She shall not anticipate the income by drawing orders or by creating debts or pledg-
ing it for any purpose, and if she should the amount so
anticipated or pledged shall be forfeited and distributed to my other children then living, or to their descendants then living. And in the event of any husband
she may have surviving her, said husband shall have
no estate of curtesy in said property of my daughter
nor any interest therein by virtue of his married relation. In the event that the portion of the factory
known as the factory of Cornwall & Bro. now belonging to my daughter, should again become my property, I devise said portion to my daughter and her
heirs forever as her separate estate, free from the
control of her husband, R. E. Hill, or any husband
she may have and it shall not be subject to any right
of curtesy or any other right in or to him by virtue

of his marriage to my daughter or by virtue of any other circumstance or condition whatever. I direct that no debt or claim which I may now have or here after have against my children or either or any of them shall be made against them or either or any of them; but that all and every one of said claims or debts against my children or any of them shall be considered as paid and cancelled to the full extent as if there never had been any claim against them or either of them. And I expressly direct that no claim or debt that I now have against my children or either of them or any of them shall ever be considered as an advancement to them or either of them; and that under no circumstances shall any debt or claim I may now have or may hereafter have against any of my children or either of them be subject to the rule or principle of advancement.''

To understand the will it will be necessary to read it in the light of the facts surrounding the testator at the time. William Cornwall and John Cornwall, doing business under the name of Cornwall & Bro., operated a candle and soap factory in Louisville for many years before the death of John Cornwall, which occurred in the year 1867. After his death the property was sold and was bought by William Cornwall, Jr., who conveyed two-thirds of it to his father, retaining one-third himself. They continued to run the manufacturing business in the name of Cornwall & Bro. In 1874, when Aaron Cornwall became of age, William Cornwall, Sr., conveyed to him a one-third interest in the factory property; the two sons and the father operating it from that time on in the old name of Cornwall & Bro. In 1875, the daughter having become of age, the father conveyed to the two sons the remaining third of the property which he then owned in trust for her use, reserving in himself the power of revocation; the firm paying her as rent $1,000 a year. Thus things ran along until 1891, when the firm, having become insolvent, made an assignment for the benefit of their creditors; their debts amounting to about $350,000. The assignee proceeded with the settlement of the trust and paid several dividends to the creditors. In the year 1894 the Cornwalls undertook to make a compromise with their creditors, and finally did make a settlement on the basis of $60,000. To raise the $60,000 it was arranged that William Cornwall would revoke the deed to the daughter, and the two sons would convey to him their interest in the factory property, and he would then convey this property, together with some other land he had in Texas and a warehouse property owned by him and his sons, to the Louisville Trust Company, the Louisville Trust Company to furnish him $60,000, and to ˙sell the land when a sale could be made, so far as necessary, and to convey back to William Cornwall, Sr., so much of the property as was left after the payment of the debt. The arrangement was carried out, the deeds were made, and the creditors were settled with. The will is dated November 24, 1894. The agreement between the parties as to the conveyance of the property to the Louisville Trust Company was made on December 4, 1894. The deeds were executed on January 2, 1895. William Cornwall, Sr., died the following March. After his death in the year 1900 the Louisville Trust Company sold the factory property and the warehouse property for $30,000. Its debts then amounted to something over $23,000, and it turned over the surplus to the executors of William Cornwall, Sr. It is conceded that the factory property in this sale brought $14,000. Mrs. Hill insists

that one-third of this, with interest, should be paid
to her. Whether she is entitled to it or not depends
upon the question whether the event took place that
the third of the factory property belonging to Mrs.
Hill again became the property of William Cornwall,
Sr. It is evident from the will as a whole that the
testator, at the time the will was made, contemplated
reopening the factory and running it as before. What
he had in his mind was that after the creditors were
paid, and he got his affairs straightened out, he wished his daughter not to lose by the revocation of the
deed of trust in her favor. While the will was made
on November 24th, and the written agreement for the
conveyance of the property on December 4th, and the
deeds were not made until nearly a month afterwards,
still it is perfectly manifest from the will that the will
was written in contemplation that the composition
with the creditors should be carried out, and it should
read as speaking rather from that time than from the
date of its execution, pursuant to section 4839, Ky. St.
(Russell's St. Sec. 3962): "A will shall be construed
with reference to the real and personal estate com
prised in it, to speak and take effect as if it had been
executed immediately before the death of the testator
unless a contrary intention shall appear by the will,"
In the contract of December 4th, it is provided that
the conveyance to the trust company shall be upon
trust that it shall collect all choses in action assigned to it, and sell so much of the land as may be necessary, and that, as soon as its debt was paid, all the
residue of the property should be "the individual
property of William Cornwall, Sr.," and should be
conveyed by the trust company to him. When the
testator speaks in the will of the event of the factory
property again becoming "my property," he evident-

ly had in mind the event of the trust company recon-
veying the property to him after the payment of his
debt, as specified in this written contract. By the
deed which he made to the trust company, it was provided that the deed was made "to the end that the title
to said entire property known as the factory property shall be vested in fee simple in said Louisville
Trust Company." At the time of his death the title
to the property was in the Louisville Trust Company.
What he contemplated was that, if he and his sons
got the factory property back, he wished his daughter
to be placed where she was before he revoked the
deed of trust for her benefit; but he died without getting the property back. At his death the title to the
land was in the Louisville Trust Company, and all that
he had was an obligation on the part of the Louisville Trust Company to convey back to him the remainder of the property left after the payment of the
debt to the trust company. The title to the factory
property was not in him when he made his will, and although the two sons conveyed to him their interest in
it, this interest was charged with the debts of the firm
which had to be settled, and their conveyance to him
was only made that he might convey the entire property to the trust company, so all these deeds should be
read together; their evident purpose being merely
to pass the title through him to the trust company.
and not to vest any title in him, until the $60,000 was
paid.

Taking the will as a whole, it leaves no doubt that
the testator was equally devoted to all three of his
children. He had not in mind giving one a preference over the others. His sole purpose, as exhibited
by the whole instrument, was to treat them all alike
and with exact justice. He did not intend that a

sum equal to one-third of the proceeds of the factory property should be paid to his daughter out of his estate before the two sons received anything from the estate. The careful wording of the will to the effect that no advancements are to be charged, when read in connection with the words directing an equal division among the three children, forbids such a conclusion. The construction of a will which produces equality is preferred to one that produces inequality, and it will not be presumed that the testator intended to prefer one of his children to others, unless this appears from a fair reading of the will. The whole will here shows a purpose on the part of the testator to put all his children on equality without regard to what had theretofore been received by each of them. To adopt the construction of the will urged by the daughter would be in effect to make the value of her one-third of the factory property a first charge upon his whole estate left after the payment of the debts, in the event the testator revoked the trust deed to her. That is not the event he had in mind. He had in mind the event of getting back his property and going on again with the business of Cornwall & Bro., as shown by the preceeding words of the will. The revocation of the trust to the daughter was only a step to vest the property in the trust company. The event he had in mind was the property revesting in him. It would then be his to devise. If at the date of the will he had revoked the deed of trust to his daughter and had stopped there, he would have had no interest in the factory property to devise to her, for his creditors would then have subjected the property to their claims. He had at that time no interest in the manufacture of soap and candles to devise, for he had assigned everything for the payment of his debts. All this part of the will must therefore be regarded as prospective and as made in contemplation of the composition with his creditors which he had in hand, and in view of a subsequent carrying on of his business after his debts were settled; but he died the following March, before his plans were carried out, and before the portion of the factory property then owned by his daughter became his property within the meaning of the will. We are therefore of opinion that the three children will take the estate equally under the will.

Judgment reversed and cause remanded for a judg-ment as above indicated.

CASE 78.—SUIT BETWEEN NANNIE COOK AND CLARENCE HART AND OTHERS FOR THE CONSTRUCTION OF THE WILL OF JOHN JOHNSON. SR., DE-CEASED.—March 19, 1909.

Cook v. Hart, &c.

Appeal from Nelson Circuit Court.

SAMUEL E. JONES AND WM. E. RUSSELL, Successive Judges.

From the judgment Nannie Cook appeals.—Re-versed.

1. Wills—Construction—Intention of Testator.—In construing a will, the court must determine the intention of the testator from a consideration of the entire will, and the intention, when ascertained, will be cārried into effect, though the technical meaning of words is disregarded, and though words must be supplied.

2. Wills—Estates Devised—"Heirs."—Testator devised real es-tate to the children of a deceased daughter, to a son, and to his daughter C. gave his daughter N. a specified sum, gave $10,000 in bonds to the son in trust for his daughter B. to pay to her the income for life and at her death the principal

to be divided among his "heirs" in accordance to the number of children which each might then have, division to be per stirpes, and gave the residue to his son and two daughters, C. and N., and the children of the deceased daughter, Held, that the word "heirs" meant testator's children, and that the trust fund on the death of B. must be divided among the stocks, giving to each stock in proportion to the number of children of that stock; each of the three children of the testator being a stock, and the children of the deceased daughter being another stock.

L. A. FAUREST for appellant.

QUESTION DISCUSSED AND AUTHORITIES CITED.

Under the sixth clause of the will of John Johnson, the fund therein disposed of should be divided according to the number of children that each child of the testator (other than Bettie Johnson) had living at the death of said Bettie Johnson. 21 Cyc., 419, 426; Edmonds v. Edmonds, 31 Ky. Law Rep., 396; Tucker v. Tucker, 78 Ky., 503; Mitchell v. Simpson, 88 Ky., 125; Hughes v. Clark, 16 Ky. Law Rep., 41: Gordon's Adm'r v. C., N. O. & T .P. R. R. Co., 89 Ky. 50.

JOHN A. FULTON for appellee.

A. W. HALSTEAD of counsel

CONSTRUCTION OF CLAUSE OF WILL AS FOLLOWS, VIZ:

"I devise to my son John, in trust for my daughter, Bettie, ten (10) one thousand dollar Logan County bonds, the net income to be paid her every six months as long as she lives and at her death the principal is to divided among my heirs in accordance to the number of children which they may have, said devision to be per stirpes."

The legatee for life of this fund is now dead and the question is now on the distributing of this fund among the "heirs" of the testator.

The word "heirs" embraces the grand children of testator living at the making of the will and whose parent (child of testator) was dead at said time, as well as children of testator, and entitles such of them as have children living at death of legatee for life to share in this fund on same terms with the children of testator, i. e., "in accordance to the number of children which each may then have."

2. A clear gift is not defeated or cut down by later expressions
less clear and certain. Wells, &c., v. Newton, &c., 4 Bush, 158;
Cromie's Heirs v. Louisville Orphan's Home Society, 3 Bush, 365;
Black's Legal Dictionary; Jarman on Wills, 5th Ed. Vol. 2, page
61; Jarman on Wills, 5th Ed., Vol. 1, page480; Schouler on Wills,
2nd Ed., Secs. 54, 474; Rood on Wills, Secs. 449, 494.

OPINION OF THE COURT BY CHIEF JUSTICE SETTLE—
Reversing.

This appeal involves a construction of the will of
John Johnson, Sr., who died in Nelson county in May,
1891. The will is in words and figures as follows:

"I, John Johnson, Sr., of the county of Nelson and
State of Kentucky, do make and publish this my last
will and testament hereby revoking any former will
which I may have heretofore made:

"(1)   I desire my just debts and funeral expenses
paid.

"(2)   I devise to the children of my dead daughter,
Mary Hart, to be equally divided among them, their
farm above Bardstown on which their father now resides; and in the distribution of my estate I value
said farm at twelve thousand dollars. I make no
charge whatever against them for rent or for use of
said farm, nor for taxes which I have paid on it. In
fact I want this valuation of the farm to cover all advancements to them and their mother. I also give
them three thousand dollars.

"(3)   I devise to my son John, all of my real estate
south of the Beechfork and in the settlement of my estate I value said land at fifteen thousand dollars, and
this valuation is to cover any and all advancements
made to him, whether in the way of use of the place,
taxes thereon, or otherwise.

"(4)   I devise to my daughter, Cassie, my home
place, containing about 600 or 700 acres to be hers as

long as she lives, and at her death to go to her children. I also give all the homestead and kitchen furniture, provisions, live stock, farming implements, gears, buggy and harness. Also all the meat, corn, hay and oats on hand at my death, and $5,000.00 in money. All of which I value at $15,000.

"(5) I devise to my daughter, Nannie Cook, $15,000.

"(6) I devise to my son, John, in trust for my daughter Bettie, ten (10) $10,000.00 Logan county bonds, the net income to be paid her every six months, as long as she lives, and at her death the principal to be divided among my heirs in accordance to the number of children which each may then have; said division to be 'per stirpes.' I also give to my daughter, Bettie, the right to occupy a room in the house which I hereby devise to Cassie as long as she (Bettie) may live or remain unmarried.

"(7) I give to Octavia Barnes $400.00, provided she stays with and helps Cassie with her housework for four years after my death.

"(8) The real estate which I devise to my son, John, is to be his only during his life and at his death to go to his children.

"(9) I also give my son, John, the stock in the Louisville & Nashville Railroad Company.

"(10) I hereby constitute and appoint my son, John, the executor of this will and ask the court to allow him to qualify without giving security. As executor he is to have no commissions in any part of my estate, except upon that part used in paying my debts and funeral expenses and costs of administration, and that disposed of under the twelfth clause of this will. I appoint my friend, Ben Johnson, as the legal adviser of my executor.

"(11)   In case any of my devisees should institute legal proceedings to break or annul this will then such as do shall have no part of my estate.

"(12)   All of the remainder of my estate I want equally divided among John Johnson, Nannie Cook and Cassie Barnes, and the children of Mary Hart. The Hart children to have one-fourth, and John, Cassie and Nannie, each to have one-fourth.   Bettie is to have no more of my estate than the income from the Logan county bonds and a comfortable room in my house as hereinbefore set out.''

At the time of his death the testator owned real and personal estate amounting in value to $120,000. Four of his children were then living, viz., John Johnson, Jr., Nannie Cook, Cassie Barnes, and Bettie Johnson, the last an unmarried daughter. Another daughter, Mary Hart, died before the testator, leaving surviving her three children, Clarence Hart, Al. J. Hart, and John Hart, all adults. It will be observed that the will of the testator, with the exception of $10,000 in Logan county bonds bequeathed by the sixth clause to his daughter Bettie Johnson, devised all the residue of his estate to his three other children and the sons of his deceased daughter, Mary Hart, one-fourth to each of the children, and one-fourth to the three sons of Mrs. Hart jointly. It will further be observed that the $10,000 in Logan county bonds disposed of by the sixth clause of the will were bequeathed by that clause to John Johnson, Jr., in trust for Bettie Johnson; the net income thereof to be paid the cestui que trust every six months "as long as she lives and at her death the principal to be divided among my heirs in accordance to the number of children which each may then have; said division to be per stirpes.''

Bettie Johnson died April 27, 1908, and shortly
thereafter the appellant, Nannie Cook, filed in an action which had previously been brought in the Nelson
circuit court by the executor to settle the testator's
estate and was still on the docket, a supplemental answer and cross-peition setting up the death of Bettie
Johnson and averring that at the time of her death
she (Nannie Cook) had 12 children, her sister, Cassie
Barnes 5 children, and her brother, John Johnson, Jr.,
4 children, all of whom were living, and that the 3
sons of her deceased sister, Mary Hart, were still living, making altogether 24 grandchildren of the testator. The pleading in question contained a prayer for
the distribution of the $10,000, the income of which
Bettie Johnson had received down to the time of her
death, in the proportion of 12-24 to the appellant Nannie Cook, 5-24 to Cassie Barnes, 4-24 to John Johnson, and 1-24 each of the three sons of Mary Hart, deceased. At the succeeding term of the court, Clarence Hart and A. J. Hart filed a joint answer to the
cross-petition of the appellant, Cook, in which they
claimed to be "heirs" of the testator in the meaning
of the sixth clause of the latter's will, and alleged
that at the time of Bettie Johnson's death Clarence
Hart had 10 children, A. J. Hart 2 children, and their
brother, John Hart, had no children. The answer,
while admitting that Mrs. Cook had 12 children, Mrs.
Barnes 5, and John Johnson 4, denied the right of the
parents to demand a distribution of the fund in question on the basis proposed in the cross-petition, and
averred that at the time of the death of Bettie Johnson there were living 33 children of the "heirs" of
the testator, and that the fund left by Bettie
Johnson should be distributed as follows: 12-33
to Mrs. Cook; 5-33 to Mrs. Barnes; 4-33 to John John-

son; 10-33 to Clarence Hart; 2-33 to A. J. Hart; and to John Hart nothing. The special judge by whom the case was tried in the court below construed the will according to the contention of the appellees Clarence and A. J. Hart, and entered judgment distributing the fund in controversy as asked by them. Nannie Cook, being dissatisfied with the judgment prosecutes this appeal.

The language of the sixth clause of the will very clearly shows it was the intention of the testator that the remainder in the trust fund, the income of which his daughter Bettie had enjoyed until her death, should be distributed to certain persons in proportion to the number of children each might have at the time of Bettie's death. The difficulty is as to the identity of the beneficiaries. It is urged in behalf of appellees that the word "heirs" is a technical term meaning the persons to whom the estate would go in case of intestacy, which it is claimed would include them with the children of the testator, and therefore entitle them to take, as to this fund, under the sixth clause of the will as do the testator's own children; that is, in proportion to the number of children each has. While the word "heirs" is generally given the meaning attributed to it by appellees in this case, it its sometimes used in the sense of children. In construing a will the matter of first importance is to arrive at the intention of the testator, and, when ascertained, the intention must be carried into effect, even though the technical meaning of the words must be disregarded in order to do so. In deed, as held by this court in Edmonds' Ex'r v. Edmonds' Devisees, 102 S. W., 311, 31 Ky. Law Rep., 396, courts will sometimes supply words to carry into effect the manifest purpose of the testator.

The whole context must be considered, and the intent arrived at from a consideration of the entire will, and not from the technical meaning of a single word found in the will. The rule stated is expressed in 21 Cyc. 426, as follows: " 'Heirs' is generally construed as meaning children, where the context so requires, where it is necessary that the term should be so construed in order to carry out the clear intent of the instrument." It will also be found that this rule has often been recognized by this court. Tucker v. Tucker, 78 Ky., 503; Mitchell v. Simpson, 88 Ky., 125, 10 S. W., 372; Hughes v. Clark, 26 S. W., 187, 16 Ky. Law Rep., 41. To construe the word "heirs," in the will under consideration as meaning the testator's children, would seem to carry out the intention of the testator as manifested by all other parts of his will. In disposing of the bulk and residue of his estate, he provided for the three children of his deceased daughter, Mrs. Hart, just as he would have provided for the mother had she been living. So her three children were, together, given the bulk of the estate, what each of the testator's living children, except Bettie, received. Nowhere in the will did the testator indicate that these grandchildren or any of them, should have any greater rights than their mother would have had if alive, or than the other children were given.

Does the testator, in disposing of the $10,000 fund by the sixth clause of the will, direct such a distribution of it as manifested any change of his purpose with respect to the sons of Mrs. Hart, as clearly manifested in all other parts of the will? We think not. It is true the sixth clause introduced a new method of distribution as to the $10,000 fund, viz, that it should be distributed to his children, according to the num-

ber of children each might have; but its language indicates no change of the testator's intention, as expressed in all other parts of the will, that the three
sons of Mrs. Hart should together take of that fund
what their mother, as the parent of the three children,
would have been entitled to receive of the fund had
she been living. The testator knew when the will was
executed that his daughter, Mary Hart, was then
dead, so, for the purpose of showing that he did not
intend the number of children her children might have
should be considered in distributing the fund mentioned in the sixth clause, he therein directed that the
division should be "per stirpes." In other words,
it was intended by the testator that the fund remaining at the death of his daughter Bettie should be divided among the stocks, giving to each stock in proportion to the number of children there were of that
stock. Thus Nannie Cook was one stock, and had
12 children; Cassie Barnes was another stock, and had
5 children; John Johnson was another stock, and had
3 children. If such was not the basis of distribution
in the mind of the testator the words "said division
to be per stirpes" would be utterly meaningless. This
construction would carry out the manifest purpose
of the testator to give the children of Mary Hart what
the mother would have taken if living; but the construction contended for by appellees and adopted by
the circuit court would not only render nugatory the
words "said division to be per stirpes," but would
give two of the testator's grandchildren an advantage
over their brother who has no children, and allow
them more of the estate than their mother could have
taken under the will had she lived. We do not believe
the language of the will authorizes the conclusion that
the testator thus intended to unduly favor one stock;

but that his intention, as shown by the entire will, was to so dispose of his property that all of his children and the children of his deceased child should participate in his bounty in the following proportion: 12-24 to Nannie Cook; 5-24 to Cassie Barnes; 4-24 to John Johnson; 3-24 to the Harts—that is, 1-24 to each of the Harts.

Wherefore the judgment is reversed, and cause remanded, with direction to the circuit court to set aside the judgment appealed from and enter in lieu thereof another conforming to this opinion.

CASE 79.—ACTION BY THE MONTICELLO CONSTRUCTION COMPANY AGAINST E. O. STONE, LEO. F. SANDERS, A. MILLER AND OTHERS AND JOE MARSH TO RECOVER CERTAIN SUBSCRIPTIONS TO A PROJECTED RAILROAD FROM TATEVILLE TO MONTICELLO.—March 19, 1909.

Stone &c. v. Monticello Construction Co.

Appeal from Wayne Circuit Court.

Wm. H. Holt, Special Judge.

Judgment for plaintiffs, defendants appeal.—Reversed.

1. Corporations—Capital Stock—Subscription to Stock—Actions on Subscriptions.—Where persons agreed to subscribe for stock in a railroad construction company to be organized the subscriptions to be binding only upon the bona fide subscription of a certain amount and the execution of an agreement by a committee of subscriptions with a railroad company for construction of a railroad, an action could be maintained in the name of the corporation on the subscription agreement; the conditions having been complied with.

2. Jury—Qualifications—Relationship to Stockholders in Corporation Suing for Subscription.—A juror would not be disqualified to serve, in an action by a corporation to recover on a

subscription for stock, merely because he was related to a stockholder in the corporation other than a party to the action and who had no real interest in the action.

3. Jury—Peremptory Challenge—Examination of Jurors.—A party in a civil action having the right to strike off three jurors without cause, he may ask questions which may enable him to know who the jurors are and their relationship, that he may exercise his right intelligently, though the answers to them would not disqualify the jurors.

4   Corporations—Conditional Subscription to Stock—Other Subscriptions—Subscriptions in Good Faith.—In an action by a corporation on subscriptions to stock, which were to be binding if a certain amount were subscribed in good faith, a subscription, made by a person whose apparent ability was not such as a person of ordinary prudence would have deemed reasonably sufficient to meet the assessments on the stock as they might be expected to be made, was not made in good faith though it was not made for the purpose of fraud and the directors did not know of such fraudulent intention.

5. Corporations—Conditional Subscriptions to Stock—Subscription by Corporation—Good Faith.—A subscription by a corporation is not invalid, within the meaning of such condition as not made in good faith, because made in violation of the subscriber's articles of incorporation; the subscriber having waived that defense and paid the subscription.

STONE & WALLACE, McQUOWN & BECKHAM and HARRISON & HARRISON for appellants.

O. H. WADDLE & SON attorneys for appellee.

CRESS & CRESS of counsel.

AUTHORITIES CITED.

1. As to the validity of subscription papers for the organization of Corporations. Twin Creek & Coalmansville Turnpike Road Co. v. Lancaster. 79 Ky., 552; Bullock v. Falmouth. etc., Turnpike Co., 85 Ky., 184; Cadiz Railroad Co. v. Roach, 24 Ky. Law Rep., 1761; Curry v. Ky. Western R. R. Co., 25 Ky. Law Rep., 1372.

2. As to the construction of the phrase "in good faith" in contracts. Seymour v. Cleveland, 68 N. W., 171; Wright v. Mattison, 59 United States, 50; Crouch v. First Nat'l Bank, 40 N. E., 974; Docter v. Furch, 65 N. W., 253.

3. The burden of proving a precedent negative condition in contracts. 16 Cyc., 1928; Malone v. Ruffino, 79 Am. St. Rep., 127; Great. Western R. R. Co. v. Bason, 30 Ill., 347.

4. As to the competency of jurors. Kemper v. City of Louisville, 14 Bush, 87; Ky. Wagon Co. v. City of Louisville, 97 Ky., 548; Searsburg Turnpike Co. v. Cutler, 6 Vt., 315; Lewis v. Hilsborough, etc., 23 S. W. 338.

OPINION OF THE COURT BY JUDGE HOBSON—Reversing.

Some years ago a corporation known as the "Cumberland River & Nashville Railway Company," was organized for the purpose of building a railroad from Corbin, Ky., through Wayne county, into Tennessee. It made a contract for the building of the road from Tateville to Monticello, and this contract was sublet by the original contractors to Plunkett, Edwards & Clark. Some work was done upon the road between Tateville and Monticello, and then it developed that the railroad company was without means. The people about Monticello were very anxious to secure a railroad and they began to organize a construction company which was to finance the building of the road from Tateville to Monticello. With this view the following written contract was signed by a number of persons interested in the building of the railroad: Whereas it is proposed to organize a corporation with a capital stock of $100,000.00 divided into shares of $100.00 each under the name of the Monticello Railroad Construction Company, with its chief office at Monticello, Kentucky; said corporation to be organized for the purpose of constructing and building railroads and especially for the purpose of constructing and building the Cumberland River & Nashville Railroad, and taking over to itself all contracts now existing for building the said railroad from the Cincin-

nati Southern Railway near Tateville, Kentucky, to
Monticello, Kentucky, and for such other work of construction as may be contracted for: ''Now we, the
undersigned, agree to take the number of shares set
opposite our names and to pay for same at the rate
of $100.00 each in installments as called for by the
directors hereafter to be elected. It is further
agreed that this subscription shall not be binding until
there shall have been $80,000 of the capital stock of
the said company subscribed for in good faith. It is
further agreed that this subscription shall not be binding until an agreement and contract is entered into by
a committee of the subscribers hereto, and the Cumberland River & Nashville Railroad Company, for the
construction of said railroad from Tateville to Monticello, Kentucky, nor until satisfactory arrangements
shall have been made with the present contractors
now at work and holding contracts for work upon said
line. Done at Monticello, Kentucky, this October 1,
1907.'' In October, 1907, when the necessary subscription was said to have been made, the Monticello
Construction Company was organized. After the organization of the company, satisfactory arrangements
were made with the contractors holding contracts for
work upon the line, and a contract was entered into
by a committee of the subscribers and the Cumberland
River & Nashville Railroad Company for the construction of the railroad from Tateville to Monticello.
Certain subscribers refused to pay their subscription
when called for, and this suit was brought against
them by the Monticello Construction Company to recover the amount they had subscribed. The defendants pleaded that $80,000 had not been in good faith
subscribed, and relied on this fact to defeat the action
on the subscription paper. On a trial of the action,

there was a judgment in favor of the plaintiff, and the defendants appeal.

It is insisted for the defendants that the contract is simply an agreement to subscribe for stock when the corporation should be organized and the conditions set out in the agreement complied with, and that under the ruling of this court in Mt. Sterling Coalroad Company v. Little, 14 Bush, 429, no action can be maintained upon the contract in the name of the corporation; but the latter cases fully maintain the right of action, holding that the rule was correctly stated in the case referred to, but by inadvertence was incorrectly applied. Twin Creek, etc., Turnpike Co. v. Lancaster, 79 Ky., 552; Bullock v. Falmouth, etc., Turnpike Co., 85 Ky., 184, 3 S. W., 129; Cadiz R. R. Co. v. Roach, 114 Ky., 934, 72 S. W., 280; Curry v. Ky., etc., R. R. Co., 78 S. W., 435, 25 Ky. Law Rep., 1372.

On the trial of the case, the defendants desired to interrogate the jurors as to whether any of them were related by blood or marriage to any of the other stockholders in the construction company. The court refused to allow the question answered and of this the defendants complain. The other stockholders in the construction company were not parties to the action. They had no interest in the action except such as the mere fact that they were stockholders in the corporation gave them. The rule is that a juror or judge is not always disqualified in a suit by a corporation merely because he is related to some of the stockholders in the corporation. The stockholders themselves would not be qualified to be jurors, but it would be carrying the rule further than it has been carried to say that in a case like this all their relatives were also disqualified. It was held in New York Life in surance Company v. Johnson, 72 S. W., 762, 24 Ky. Law Rep.,· 1867, that a policy holder in a mutual life insurance company was not disqualified as a witness, under section 606 of the Civil Code of Practice, on the ground that his interest was so infinitesimal as not to amount to a real interest. We see no reason why this should not apply here, for it clearly appears from the record that the other subscribers to the contract have no real interest in the controversy. Their object was simply to get a railroad, and the proof shows their stock is worth nothing. The authorities holding that a kinsman of a stockholder in a corporation is incompetent as a juror rest upon the ground that the stockholder is beneficially interested in the result of the litigation. 24 Cyc., 274; 17 Am. & Eng. Encyc. 1126. Here the stockholders have no real interest in the litigation. On another trial the court will allow counsel for defendants to ask the panel the questions indicated, as they will thus be enabled to exercise their right of peremptory challenge more intelligently. Questions may be asked the panel, though the answer to them would not disqualify the juror, where the facts sought might be ground for the party striking off the juror. As he has the right to strike off three without cause, he may ask questions which may enable him to know who the jurors are and their relationships.

At the conclusion of the evidence, the court properly instructed the jury that they should find for the plaintiff unless they believed from the evidence that $80,000 had not been subscribed to the capital stock of the company in good faith, and that in this event they should find for the defendant. To define what was a subscription in good faith, he then gave the jury the following instruction: "If the jury believe from the evidence that the stock subscribed to the plaintiff company was subscribed with the intent and expectation to pay for it, and that the party would be able to do so, and without any purpose or intention to engage or assist in the commission of a fraud, then any such subscriptions were made in good faith; but, if any subscription was made without intending and without ability to pay, and for the purpose of committing or assisting in the commission of a fraud upon the co-subscribers and upon the plaintiff, the Monticello Con- struction Company, and its board of directors knew of such intention or inability to pay and such purpose or intention to assist in committing a fraud, then any such subscriptions would not have been made in good faith.'' In 1 Morawetz on Corporations, Sec. 141, the rule on the subject is thus stated: ''It is necessary also that the required amount of capital be subscribed by persons apparently able to pay the assessments which may be made upon their shares. Fictitious sub- scriptions or subscriptions made by persons unable to contribute their proportion of the capital, do not sat- isfy the requirement that the whole capital of a cor- poration shall be subscribed before its members can be assessed; but, if the required number of subscrip- tions has been obtained in good faith from persons ap- parently able to perform their duties as shareholders, it is no defense to an action against a shareholder that some of the subscribers have proved to be insolvent '' See, also, Penobscot, etc., R. R. Co. v. White, 41 Me., 512, 66 Am. Dec. 257; Lewey's Island R. R. Co. v. Bolton, 48 Me., 451, 77 Am. Dec. 239, 10 Cyc., 400, 20 Am. & Eng. Encyc., 937. The purpose in getting up the Monticello Construction Company was to get up the money necessary to build the railroad. A sub- scription which was not made by a person apparently able to pay it would not be a subscription in good faith within the meaning of the contract, although it was not made for the purpose of committing a fraud, and the defendants were not required to show that the board of directors knew of any such fraudulent inten- tion. In lieu of the instruction given, the court should have told the jury that a subscription in good faith was one made by a person apparently able to pay the assessments which might reasonably be expected to be made upon the stock, although the subscriber prov- ed to be insolvent, but that a subscription was not in good faith if made by a person whose apparent abil- ity was not such as a person of ordinary prudence would have deemed reasonably sufficient to meet the assessments on the stock as they might be expected to be made. While the proof was conflicting there was some evidence tending to sustain the defense. The instruction given by the court did not fairly present the case to the jury and was prejudicial to the substantial rights of the defendants under the evidence.

The proof, on another trial, as to the ability of the subscribers in contest to pay, will be limited to the facts known to the witnesses. Hearsay and in- formation from others will be omitted, except it may be shown what information the directors had as to the ability of the subscribers in contest, as this will il- lustrate whether they exercised ordinary care in ac- cepting the subscriptions as made by persons of ap- parent ability to pay. The court will allow proof of all statements made in the presence of any of the di- rectors by any of the subscribers tending to show a want of apparent ability to pay on their part.

The subscriptions made by corporations which have been paid are not invalid because not warranted by their articles of incorporation. When the corporation has waived this defense and paid its subscription, it cannot be said not to have been made in good faith.

Judgment reversed, and cause remanded for a new trial and further proceedings consistent herewith.

CASE 80.—ACTION BY MONTICELLO CONSTRUCTION CO. AGAINST McCONNAGHY TO ENFORCE CERTAIN SUBSCRIPTIONS TO A PROJECTED RAILROAD FROM TATESVILLE TO MONTICELLO, KY.—March 19, 1909.

McConnaghy v. Monticello Construction Co.

Appeal from Wayne Circuit Court.

. WILLIAM H. HOLT, Special Judge.

Judgment for plaintiff, defendant appeals.—Affirmed.

Corporations (Sec. 81.)—Subscription to Stock—Liability of Subscriber—Acquiescing in Binding Force of Subscription.—The subscribers to the stock of a corporation to be formed, on the condition that the subscription should not be binding unless a specified sum should be subscribed in good faith, met, passed on the question of the amount of bona fide subscriptions, and proceeded to organize the corporation, electing, as treasurer and director, defendant, who was a subscriber and present at the meeting, and who acquiesced in the action taken. He acted as director for over a month, making no objection that the necessary amount of stock had not been subscribed for in good faith. Held, that his conduct was such as to necessarily induce his associates to believe that he consented to the subscriptions as satisfying the condition, and he could not contend, in an action against him by the corporation to recover his subscription, that it was not binding because the condition as to the amount of bona fide subscriptions had not been fulfilled.

STONE & WALLACE, HARRISON & HARRISON and Mc-
QUOWN & BECKHAM for appellant.

CRESS & CRESS and O. H. WADDLE for appellee. .

OPINION OF THE COURT BY JUDGE HOBSON—Affirming.

This case is in all respects similar to the case of E. O. Stone and Others v. Monticello Construction Company (this day decided) 117 S. W., 369, except that one question is made here which did not arise in those cases. McConnaghy subscribed for 20 shares of stock. When the persons who were getting up the subscriptions had obtained subscriptions amounting to $80,000, they called a meeting of the subscribers. McConnaghy was present at that meeting and presided. At that meeting the question was discussed whether the necessary subscriptions had been raised. The paper was footed up, and thereupon the meeting concluded to organize the company. About three-fourths of the subscribers were present, and they signed the articles of incorporation, McConnaghy among the rest. Thereupon a board of directors was elected, which included McConnaghy. He accepted the position of director and attended several meetings of the board A committee was appointed to make the necessary arrangements with the railroad company and with the contractors. McConnaghy participated in these matters. The committee reported, their report was accepted, and the contracts were closed; McConnaghy being present when the contracts were discussed. He remained a director for something over a month, and then resigned; but at no time during the month did he make any objection that any of the subscriptions had not been made in good faith or were insufficient.

It was distinctly understood at the meeting at which the company was organized that they were organizing because they had secured bona fide subscriptions amounting to $80,000.

We do not decide that McConnaghy would be estopped by acquiescing in the organization of the company that night, if he did not in fact know as much about the subscribers then as he learned afterwards; but he was a managing agent of the corporation. He knew that the subscribers were proceeding upon the idea that the necessary subscriptions had been obtained. His acquiescence in the organizing of the company, and his subsequent action as a director in proceeding with the business of the company, was a consent on his part that the necessary subscribers had been obtained. In any view of the case, it was incumbent on him, when he knew the company was organized and was going on with its business upon the idea that the necessary subscribers had been obtained, promptly to look into the matter and to make known his objections before his associates proceeded further in a matter, where he knew they were assuming that he was consenting to the acceptance of the subscriptions as made in good faith. The company was preparing to assume considerable liabilities, and, while he does show by his own testimony that he objected to the contracts being made, he does not show that he at any time objected on the ground that the necessary subscribers had not been obtained in good faith. His conduct was such as would necessarily induce his associates to understand that he consented to the subscription as satisfying the terms of the written contract. He was in a position where he was bound to speak and act promptly, and where silence necessarily misled his associates, and therefore was equivalent to consent. The managing agent of a corporation, in a matter of this sort stands on a different footing from one of the subscribers who takes no active part in its affairs. His proceeding with the business of the corporation as he did was necessarily a consent on his part to treat the subscriptions as valid, and this consent he cannot withdraw to the prejudice of his co-subscribers. In the case of Stone v. Monticello Construction Company, above referred to, we decided that a subscription was not made in good faith if the directors in the exercise of ordinary prudence should not have accepted it. Whether the necessary subscriptions had been obtained was the first question the directors were to decide. If the necessary subscription had not been raised, there was nothing to do as the company had no means outside of the subscription. It was incumbent on McConnaghy, as one of the directors, to decide whether the necessary subscription had been raised before anything was done by the company. They elected him treasurer, and he accepted the office. His conduct was an acceptance of the subscription for the company, and, after he so accepted it for the company, he cannot be permitted to say for himself against it that the subscription was not sufficient. Under the evidence, the court, for the reasons given, should have instructed the jury peremptorily to find for the plaintiff, and the defendant was therefore not prejudiced by the instruction which the court gave.

Judgment affirmed.

CASE 81.—ACTION BY BENTLEY SMITH'S ADMINISTRATOK
AGAINST THE NATIONAL COAL & IRON COM-
PANY FOR CAUSING THE DEATH OF PLAIN-
TIFF'S INTESTATE.—March 23, 1909.

Smith's Adm'r v. National Coal & Iron Co.

Appeal from Bell Circuit Court.

M. J. Moss, Circuit Judge.

From a directed judgment for defendant, plaintiff
appeals.—Reversed.

1. Master and Servant—Injuries to Servant—Sufficiency of Evi-
    dence—Employment.—In an action for the death of a boy
    while working in a coal mine, evidence held to show that he
    was employed by defendant's foreman.
2. Master and Servant—Unlawful Employmant of Infant—Mas-
    ter's Liability.—Under St. 1909, Sec. 331a (Russell's St.
    Secs. 3237-3251a(5)), making it unlawful to employ any child
    less than 14 years old in a mine, read in connection with St.
    1909, Sec. 466 (Russell's St. Sec. 3), permitting one injured
    by the violation of a statute to recover from the offender
    any damage sustained by reason of the violation, an infant
    employed in a mine in violation of the statute, can recover
    damages sustained in consequence of its violation, and wheth-
    er the injury occurred when the boy was at his place in the
    mine, or going or coming to work, was immaterial.
3. Death—Action for Death—Right of Action.—An action to re-
    cover for death by wrongful act can only be maintained under
    St. 1909, Sec. 6 (Russell's St. Sec. 11), enacted pursuant to
    Const. Sec. 241, giving a right of action for death by wrong-
    ful act; no such right of action existing at common law.
4. Death—Action—Defenses—Contributory Negligence—Neglect
    of Statutory Duty.—Contributory negligence is a defense to
    an action brought pursuant to St. 1909, Sec. 6 (Russell's St. Sec
    11),giving a right of action for death by wrongful act, for
    the death of an infant while employed in a coal mine in
    violation of St. Sec. 1909, Sec. 331a (Russell's St. Secs. 3237-
    3251a (5)), prohibiting the employment of infants under 14
    years old in a mine.

Smith's Adm'r. v. National Coal & Iron Co.

5. Negligence—Contributory Negligence—Infants.—An infant is
    only required to exercise such care as may reasonably be ex-
    pected from one of his age under like circumstances; the law
    recognizing his lack of mature discretion.
6. Master and Servant—Infants—Contributory Negligence—Jury
    Question.—In an action for the death of a boy killed while
    working in a coal mine by falling between the cars while rid-
    ing out from work, whether he used ordinary care in pass-
    ing over the cars under the circumstances held for the jury.

R. S. ROSE for appellant.

Ky. Stat., Carroll Edition, 1903, 331a; Ky. Stat., 466; 45 N. Y.,
630; 60 S. W., 180; Big Hill Coal Co. v. Abney's Adm'r, 101 S. W.,
394; 30 L. R. A., p. 82, John Queene, by &c., v. Dayton Coal &
Iron Co.; Iron & Wire Co. v. Green, 108 Tenn., 161; Bailly on
Personal Injuries, Sec. 1291; Wm. Rollin, by &c., v. R. J. Reynolds
Tobacco Co., 141 N. C., 300 also 110 Ill., 648; American Car
Foundry Co., v. Amentrout, 214 Ill., 509; Alsoi 116 Ill., 121; Morris v. Stanfill, 81 Ill., 264; Mickey v. Stender, 164 Ind., 189;
Brower v. Lock, 31 Ind., 353; Wolf v. Norman & Co., 128 Iowa,
261; Sterling v. Union Carbile Co., 142 Mich., 284: Margaret Lena-
han v. Paterson Coal Mining Co., 12 L. R. A., N. S., 461; Marino
v. Lehmaris, 173 N. Y., 530, also 61 L. R. A., 811 also 48 L. R. A.
68; Chicago Coulterville Coal Co., v. Fidelity Coal Co.. 130 Fed.
p. 957; Durant v. Lexington Coal Mining Co., 97 Missouri, 62, also
142 Mich., 677; Godfrey v. Baetyville Coal Co., 41 S. W., 10, secs
26, 30, 31, and 32, Ky.; City of Hendorson v. Clayton, 57 S. W., p.
1; Monteith v. Kokimo Wood Enameling Co., 58 L. R. A., p.
Thompson on Negligence, Sec. 10; White on Personal Injuries
in Mines, Sec., 16; Andriacus Adm'r v. Pineville Coal Co., 90 S.
W., 235; Sutton's Adm'r v. Wood, 85 S. W., p. 201; Hollingsworth
v. Pineville Coal Co., 74 S. W., 205; Mosley's Adm'r v. Black Dia-
mond Coal & Coke Mining Co., 109 S. W., 306.

BARKER & WOODS AND D. B. LOGAN for appellee.

OPINION OF THE COURT BY JUDGE HOBSON—Reversing.

Bentley Smith lost his life in the mine of the National Coal & Iron Company, and this action was
brought to recover for his death under section 6, Ky.
St. (Russell's St. Sec. 11), on the ground that his

death resulted from an injury inflicted by the negligence or wrongful act of the company, in this, that he was under 14 years of age and had been employed by the company in violation of the statute, which then read as follows: "That it shall be unlawful for a proprietor, foreman, owner or other person to employ any child less than fourteen years of age in any workshop, factory, or mine, in this state; that unless said proprietor, foreman or owner shall know the age of the child, it shall be his or their duty to require the parent or guardian to furnish a sworn statement of its age, and any swearing falsely to such by the parent or guardian shall be perjury and punishable as such." Section 331a, Ky. St. (Russell's St. Sections 3237-3251a 5). This statute is to be read in connection with section 466, Ky. St. (Russell's St. Sec. 3): "A person injured by the violation of any statute may recover from the offender such damage as he may sustain by reason of the violation, although a penalty or forfeiture for such violation be thereby imposed."

The plaintiff showed on the trial these facts: Bentley Smith was the son of Elliot Smith, who was a miner regularly employed in the mine. He took his son on one occasion to the mine and asked the foreman if he would let the boy work with him. The foreman asked him how old he was. He answered that he was not 14. The foreman then said that he was too young to work in the mine, and the boy was sent home. Shortly after this, about the 1st of May, Elliot Smith was injured in the mine so he could not work. His little boy then said to him: "I want to work in the mine. You are mashed up, and our house rent is to pay, and we have got to live." The father told him not to go in the mine, but notwithstanding

this he did go to work in the mine, getting out coal on
his father's number. When he went in the foreman
said to the boy, "Son, you have to work now, do you,
since your father got hurt?" The boy said, "Yes,
sir," and he went on in the mine. The foreman
came around where the boy was at work, showed him
how to shovel, and told him how to run under the
coal. The coal which the boy got out was weighed
by the man who weighed the coal for the other miners,
and was credited to his father, amounting to $10.58.
The company kept the money for the rent of the
house in which the family lived. On the 18th of May
about noon, when a shot was to be fired, the boy
started out of the mine, and, as was customary with
the miners, rode out on the loaded cars of coal. There
were six or seven cars in the train. The boy got up
on the rear car. A friend of his was on the car next
to the front. There were quite a number of men on
the cars. The boy was walking over the cars toward
the front, when he fell between the third and fourth
car and was run over and killed. On this proof the
circuit court instructed the jury peremptorily to find
for the defendant apparently on the idea that the
death of the child was due to his own act in walking
over the cars. It is insisted that the court properly
so instructed the jury, as he was not then serving the
master, and his injury was due to his own want of
care.

The boy was serving the master in the mine. He
had been getting out coal all the morning. It was
necessary that he should leave the mine at noon when
the shots were fired. In leaving the mine he was in
the regular course of his duty, and it was customary
for all the miners to ride out on the cars or to ride
in on them. The statute which forbids the employ-

Smith's Adm'r. v. National Coal & Iron Co.

ment of children in mines is for their protection. It was a violation of the statute for the child to be employed in the mine. The evidence was plainly sufficient to show that he was employed; and, as he was injured in the mine while going from his place of work to the shaft, it cannot be said that he was not injured in the course of his employment in the mine. The statute made it unlawful for him to be employed in the mine, and whether he was injured while at his work in the mine, or in going to his work or coming from his work, is immaterial. It has been held by this court in several cases that, where a statute prohibits a thing for the benefit of a person, he may maintain an action to recover damages sustained by reason of the violation of the statute. City of Henderson v. Clayton, 57 S. W. 1, 22 Ky. Law Rep. 283, 53 L. R. A. 145; Hutchison v. L. & N. R. R. Co., 108 Ky. 619, 57 S. W. 251; City of Henderson v. O'Haloran, 114 Ky. 188, 70 S. W. 662, 59 L. R. A. 718, 102 Am. St. Rep. 279; Sutton v. Wood, 120 Ky. 23, 85 S. W. 201. We see no reason why this principle should not be applied to infants who are injured when employed in violation of the statute, for manifestly the purpose of the statute is to protect infants from the dangers attending the forbidden employments, which by reason of their youth they would not fully appreciate. While there is some conflict in the authorities, the weight of authority seems in favor of the rule that the breach of the statute is actionable negligence whenever it is shown that the injuries were sustained in consequence of the employment. Queen v. Dayton Coal Co., 95 Tenn. 458, 32 S. W. 460, 30 L. R. 82, 49 Am. St. Rep. 935; Rolin v. Reynolds Tobacco Co., 141 N. C. 300, 53 S. E. 891, 7 L. R. A. (N. S.) 335; American Car Co. v. Armentraut, 214 Ill. 509, 73 N. E. 766;

Nickey v. Steuder, 164 Ind. 189, 73 N. E. 117; Iron &
Wire Co. v. Green, 108 Tenn. 164, 65 S. W. 399; Sterling v. Union Carbide Co., 142 Mich. 284, 105 N. W.
755; Woolf v. Nauman Co., 128 Iowa, 261, 103 N. W.
785; 1 Thompson on Negligence, Sec. 10; 2 Labatt on
Master & Servant, 2177.

This is an action to recover for the death of the
intestate.   No cause of action existed at common law
to recover for death, and an action to recover for the
death of a person can only be maintained in this
state by virtue of section 6, Ky. St., enacted pursuant to section 241 of the Constitution.   It is well settled that contributory negligence may be pleaded as a
defense to an action brought under this section.
Passamaneck v. Louisville, etc., R. R. Co., 98 Ky. 195,
32 S. W. 620; Clark v. L. & N. R. R. Co., 101 Ky. 34,
39 S. W. 840.   As the action can only be maintained
under the statute referred to, and as contributory
negligence may be pleaded as a defense to an action
under the statute, it necessarily follows that contributory ngligence may be relied on by the defendant in
bar of the plaintiff's action.   A child under 14 years
of age is only required to exercise such care as may
be reasonably expected of a child of his age under
like circumstances.   The law takes into consideration
that children lack the discretion of grown persons,
and that a child under 14 years of age may reasonably
be expected to do things which an older person would
not do.   Whether the intestate used ordinary care in
passing over the cars as he did is a question for the
jury.   Ornamental Iron, etc., Co. v. Green, 108 Tenn.
161, 65 S. W. 39.   Of course, as we have not the proof
of the defendant before us, we now only pass upon
the case as presented by the proof for the plaintiff.
On the proof for the plaintiff the court should have

refused to give a peremptory instruction to the jury to find for the defendant.

Judgment reversed, and cause remanded for a new trial, and further proceedings consistent herewith.

BARKER, J., not sitting.

CASE 82.—ACTION BY J. McADOO AND OTHERS AGAINST L. W. GRAHAM AND OTHERS.—Dec. 10, 1909.

Graham, &c. v. McAdoo, &c.

Appeal from Fulton Circuit Court.

R. J. BUGG, Circuit Judge.

From the judgment defendants appeal.—Affirmed.

1. Corporations—Operation—Control by Court.—The courts will not interfere with the management of a corporation, because it is not being successfully operated. unless there is actual fraud, or such a wasting of the corporate property as practically amounts to fraud.

2. Corporations—Mismanagement—Fraud—Sufficiency of Evidence.—Evidence held sufficient to show such mismanagement of a corporation as authorized the appointment of a receiver and the sale of the property.

LEE HESTER and EDW. THOMAS for appellant.

H. H. BARR, T. N. SMITH and W. J. WEBB for appellees.

OPINION OF THE COURT BY JUDGE BARKER—Affirming.

The Fulton Electric Light & Power Company was organized in the year 1899, under the general corporation laws of the state of Kentucky, with an authorized capital stock of $30,000, divided into shares of the par value of $100 each, and was authorized under the terms of its charter to manufacture and sell electric light, heat, and power, and to deal in coal and ice. It is located in the city of Fulton, Ky., where it has since its organization been engaged in the business which it was chartered to do. It is a valuable property, and constitutes the subject-matter of this litigation. In 1906 L. W. Graham was elected the president and general manager, his brother-in-law, William Robinson, was elected vice president, and his sister-in-law, E. C. Robinson, the wife of William Robinson, was appointed secretary. The board of directors consisted of L. W. Graham, L. C. Graham, his wife, William Robinson, his brother-in-law, J. H. McClure, and C. E. Rice. As soon as L. W. Graham was elected president, there developed a powerful opposition to him from all of the stockholders outside of his family; and it may be said that from that time until the appointment of a receiver by the circuit court the history of the corporation has been exceedingly violent and stormy. Without going into this phase of the case with minuteness, it may be said that the two factions among the stockholders have been at daggers' points all of the time, and frequently a general and free fight was imminent, although, happily, this extremity was not actually reached. That faction of the stockholders which constitutes the appellees here own in the aggregate 150 shares of the capital stock of the corporation, while L. W. Graham, his wife, his brother-in-law, and sister-in-law together own 150 shares; it thus appearing that the shares of the capital stock are equally divided between the warring factions. After L. W. Graham had operated the plant for a year, this action was instituted by the appellees for the purpose of having a receiver appointed to take charge of the property, and for a dissolution of the corporation and a sale of the plant as a whole. The basis of this claim on the part of the appellees was alleged to be the fraudulent acts of Graham in the management of the corporation, his wrongful appropriation of its money to his own use, his reckless wastefulness and unbusinesslike methods in the management of the plant, and his fraudulent refusal to allow the appellees to participate in or have any influence in the management of the corporation, or even to examine its books or know what was being done with their property interests. Graham and his associates denied all these allegations, and the issues between the parties were made up along these lines. Pending the litigation the circuit judge appointed R. N. Chowning receiver, who took charge of the corporate property and operated the plant under the orders and direction of the court. After the introduction of a great deal of evidence on both sides, the case was submitted for final judgment, and the circuit judge rendered a judgment continuing the receiver and ordering a sale of the property as a whole. From this judgment, this appeal has been prosecuted.

The condition of affairs between the two factions, who are appellants and appellees here, is an anomalous one. Each owns an equal number of shares of the capital stock, and yet, by reason of the fact that L. W. Graham is president and authorized to cast the deciding vote where there is a tie, he is enabled to entirely monopolize the management of the corporation and to exclude the appellees from any participation therein. Prior to his election as president, the board of directors consisted of seven stockholders; but after his election he proceeded to have the number reduced to five, and this enabled him, out of the bosom of his own family, to put in a sufficient num-

ber of directors to entirely control the management
of the corporation. This could not have been done
if the number had remained at seven, as before his
election. But by reducing the number to five, and
electing himself and his wife and brother-in-law into
the board, he secured absolute control of the corporation, by having a majority of the directors in his interest. In his testimony he explains this change in
the number of directors by saying that prior to his
election the appellees, who then had control of the
corporation, had fixed the number of directors at
seven, in violation of the charter, and that he had
the number reduced in order to comply with the charter. In this statement he is inaccurate, as a reference
to the charter will show. That instrument provides
on this subject that the number of directors shall not
be less than five; but there is nothing in it which prohibits the number from being greater than five. This
manifest error as to the facts concerning the reduction of the number of directors accentuates the charge
that it was made to enable Graham to more readily
control the affairs of the corporation by directors
selected from the bosom of his own family. The evidence shows that as soon as he was elected president
he had his salary increased, as were also the salaries
of the minor officers. It also shows that L. W. Graham conducted the affairs of the corporation in an
exceedingly slovenly and unbusinesslike manner, if it
does not authorize the conclusion that his actions and
conduct amounted to fraud. It appears, also, that
under the prior management the corporation had been
prosperous and earned dividends, which were paid to
the stockholders; but since his election and during
his management it has not made money, but has be-

come indebted to the extent of several thousand dollars.

One of the items relied upon by the appellees to establish the fraud of L. W. Graham was that his books showed that he gave two checks for payment of two car loads of coal from the Crabtree Coal Company, although it appeared that he only purchased one car load from that company, and he was able to make no satisfactory statement with regard to who got the money represented by the second check. This was a comparatively small matter, and, standing by itself, might be allowed to go unchallenged; but when we find, as appears from the testimony of Miss Tate, the bookkeeper of his own selection, that he constantly collected bills due the corporation and appropriated the money to his own use, and would make settlements not oftener than once or twice a month, and then she simply took his word for the amount he owed the corporation, and entered the items in accordance with his dictation, we are forced to conclude that his conduct was recklessly unbusinesslike, if not fraudulent. It also appears that three or four pages of the daybook were torn out, thus making it impossible for anyone to know what items were concealed by the destruction of the leaves upon which they had been entered.

The appellees further point out, and this was admitted by Miss Tate, that at Graham's dictation she had entered an item of $473 on the labor account, and some time afterward, by his direction, she erased this item and entered an item of $5 in its place. This Graham explained by saying that the $473 was in large part for lawyer's fees he had to pay for litigation which had been imposed upon him by appellees, and he thought at first this should be charged to the corporation, and he had therefore charged it to the labor account, but afterwards concluded that he ought to consult the board of directors about the item, and he therefore required the bookkeeper to erase the first entry and replace it with the small item before mentioned. As to this, we are forced now to take his word, as there is no other explanation of it in the record. It also appears that several pages of the impression or letter book were torn out, and no rational explanation was given of this.

Appellees point out that L. W. Graham and his wife originally owned 75 shares each of the corporate stock, and they charge that, in order to make his brother-in-law and sister-in-law eligible as officers of the corporation, he and his wife transferred to them each 5 shares of the stock, and for the purchase money took the notes of the vendees, with the stock as collateral security; and there is testimony in the record tending to sustain the charge that this was done so as to make it possible that the family could control the affairs of the corporation. Now, under this situation of affairs, what is the duty of the court with reference to the final disposition of the corporate property? It is conceded at the outset that the courts are without jurisdiction to take from a majority of the stockholders the management of a corporation simply because they are not successfully operating it; that is, that they are not operating it so as to make money. The general rule is, as stated by counsel for appellants, that the courts will not interfere with the management of a majority, unless there is actual fraud, or such a wasting of the corporate property as practically amounts to fraud. Therefore it is not necessary to review any of the authorities cited by counsel for appellants on this subject. The case discussed in the brief is not the question we have here. This is not a management of the corporate property by a majority of the stockholders. On the contrary, the appellees own precisely as much stock as do appellants, and yet they have not been permitted to have any voice or influence in the management of the corporation, or the fixing of the salaries of officers, or in deciding who the officers should be. There seems to us to be substantial grounds for the charge that L. W. Graham so cunningly arranged matters as to enable him, although he and his faction owned but half of the stock, to obtain the absolute control and management of the corporate property, very much to its detriment and to the injury of the appellees. If he had allowed the number of directors to remain at seven, then he would, perhaps, have been forced by circumstances to select a majority of these officers from stockholders other than his own family; but, having reduced the number to five, as said before, he could, out of the bosom of his own family, readily select a majority of the directors, and thus absolutely control the whole situation by voting for himself and for his own measures.

We think this record shows that the corporation, prior to the time Graham obtained control, had been managed with economy and success, and that since he has had control it has been managed in a very unbusinesslike and wasteful manner, and that a continuation of his management will inevitably result disastrously to the corporate property; that it is to the interest of all the stockholders that the corporation should be dissolved and the property sold, in order that it may be purchased by one faction or the other, and thus restore a harmony in the management which it is evident never can be obtained while the situation remains as it now is.   To leave these warring stock-holders as they were prior to the time of the appoint-ment of the receiver by the circuit court would be but to insure the wrecking of the property. We are of opinion that there was sufficient evidence of mis-management, if not actual fraud, to authorize the in-terposition of the chancellor in the appointment of a receiver, and for his judgment in ordering the prop-erty sold.   When the case returns to the circuit court, the chancellor will doubtless order the sale on such terms as to time as will enable either party to pur-chase it if they desire, and this will insure such an active competition between the factions, and perhaps others, for the property, as will insure that there will be no sacrifice of it at the sale.

We are strengthened in the opinion we have reached by the fact that we are concurring in the con-clusion of facts arrived at by the learned circuit judge. He was on the ground. He, perhaps, knew all the parties, their position in society, their credi-bility as witnesses, and his opinion should not be lightly set aside, but, on the contrary, should be up-held and maintained,unless the appellate court is firm-ly of the opinion that his conclusion is contrary to the weight of the evidence, which is not true in the case before us, as we have expressed above.

In conclusion, believing, as we do, that it is for the substantial interest of all parties concerned that the judgment of the circuit court should be affirmed, it is so ordered.

CASE 83.—ACTION BY J. D. GROVER AGAINST THE BLUE
GRASS TRACTION COMPANY.—December 7, 1909.

Blue Grass Traction Co. v. Grover

Appeal from Franklin Circuit Court.

R. L. STOUT, Circuit Judge.

Judgment for plaintiff, defendant appeals.—Reversed.

1. Highways—Defects—Liability.—A county is not liable for
    injuries to a traveler on a defective county highway; the
    county being an arm of the state government exercising
    a part of the powers of the state, created by the Legislature
    for that purpose.

2. Bridges—Defects—Liability.—A contract between a county,
    railroad company, and a traction company, which provided
    for a change in the location of a county highway crossing
    the railroad track at grade, and which required the railroad
    and traction companies to construct an overhead bridge at
    their own expense, and which bound the traction company
    to keep the bridge in repair, contemplated that the county
    should be free from the burden of maintaining the bridge,
    and the traction company only assumed to do for the county
    what it otherwise would have been compelled to do, and was
    not liable for injuries to a traveler caused by a defect in
    the bridge.

3. Highway—Defects—Liability.—Though the county authorities
    or its representatives may be indicted for maintaining a pub-
    lic nuisance, occasioned by maintaining a defective highway,
    or bridge forming a part thereof, yet there is no liability for
    damages to persons injured thereby.

ALLEN DUNCAN, STOLL BUSH and BRADLEY for appellant.

B. M. LEE and JAMES BRADLEY for appellee.

OPINION OF THE COURT BY JUDGE HOBSON—Reversing.

Previous to the building of the Blue Grass Traction line between Georgetown and Lexington, the turnpike between those places crossed the railroad track of the Cincinnati Southern Railroad at grade. When the traction company was about to build its line, it was agreed between it, the railroad company, and the Fayette fiscal court to deflect the turnpike a little to one side and cross the railroad where it ran through a cut; the traction company agreeing to put up and maintain a bridge at this point free of cost to Fayette county, and Fayette county agreeing to maintain the turnpike from the points where it left the old line on each side to the bridge. The arrangement was carried out, the bridge was built; but the successor of the traction company failed to keep it in order, and by reason of its being out of order a valuable race mare belonging to J. D. Grover, while crossing over the bridge, had her foot to slip through the floor, and was injured about the knee in such a manner as, it is claimed, unfitted her for racing purposes. He brought this suit against the present traction company for the injury to his mare, and recovered a judgment for $5,000. The traction company appeals.

There was little controversy in the evidence as to the value of the mare; and, while the proof was conflicting as to the extent of her injuries, we cannot, under the proof, disturb the verdict on account of the amount of the damages found. The only material question in the case which it is necessary for us to consider is whether the traction company is liable to Grover for the injury to his mare. The turnpike was a county highway. It is well settled that the county is not responsible to a traveler on the highway who is injured by a defect in it. Moberley v. Carter County, 5 Ky. Law Rep. 694; Shephard v.

Pulaski Co., 18 S. W. 15, 13 Ky. Law Rep. 672. The bridge was a part of the county highway, and, unless the traction company became liable by reason of its contract with the fiscal court, or by some other fact shown in the case, then it is not liable to Grover for an injury to his mare while traveling on the public highway by reason of a defect in it. The contract referred to so far as material is as follows: "This contract made and entered into this the 31st day of March, 1902, by and between the Fayette fiscal court of Fayette county, Kentucky, as party of the first part and the Cincinnati, New Orleans & Texas Pacific Railway Company and the Georgetown & Lexington Traction Company, as parties of the second part, witnesseth: That for and in consideration of the mutual covenants, promises and agreements herein contained, it is hereby agreed: (1) That the party of the first part will consent and permit and does hereby consent and permit that the parties of the second part may remove the roadbed of the Georgetown and Lexington turnpike from where same is now located and place the said roadbed and the pike thereon upon the fills to be constructed by the parties of the second part, according to the plans and profiles which have heretofore been prepared and which have been and are now approved by the parties hereto; a copy of said plans and specifications is hereto attached and made a part hereof. * * *   (2) That the parties of the second part hereby agree to construct the pike upon the fills and remove the pike as it is now located as well as to construct the proposed overhead bridge at their own proper cost and expense, and the Georgetown & Lexington Traction Company, its successors and assigns, agree to maintain said bridge at their own cost and expense, but this is not to be construed as an agreement on the part of the parties of the second part to maintain or keep in repair or renew the metal on said pike so placed by them on said fill. It is agreed that all of said work shall be done under the supervision of the superintendent of Fayette county and according to the plans and profiles and specifications which have heretofore been prepared and approved by the parties hereto. * * * The old turnpike shall remain open to the public until the new road is completed and accepted by the fiscal court. The bridge is to be built and forever maintained by the Georgetown & Lexington Traction Company, and its successors and assigns, free of cost to Fayette county. The bridge shall not be less than (24) twenty-four feet wide in the clear and so constructed that the whole of the floor shall be level and suitable for public travel. It shall be forever maintained by the Georgetown & Lexington Traction Company, or whatever company that may own and operate the Georgetown & Lexington Electric Railway free of cost to Fayette county.''

It has been held that neither the county judge nor the justices composing the county court nor the road overseer, whose duty it is to keep the road in order, are liable in an action for damages to a traveler injured on the highway by reason of a defect in it. Wheatly v. Mercer, 9 Bush, 704; Hite v. Whitley Co. Court, 91 Ky. 168, 15 S. W. 57, 12 Ky. Law Rep. 764, 11 L. R. A. 122. It was also held in Coleman v. Baker, 111 Ky. 131, 63 S. W. 484, 23 Ky. Law Rep. 513, that a supervisor of roads is not responsible to a person injured by reason of the breaking down of a bridge on the county highway. In Moss v. Rowlett, 112 Ky. 121, 65 S. W. 153, 358, 23 Ky. Law Rep. 1411, the same rule was applied to a contractor who had undertaken to keep the road in order in a county where the roads were maintained by taxation. The reason underlying these opinions is that the county is an arm of the state government exercising a part of the powers of the state, and created by the Legislature for that purpose. To hold that the county is not responsible for a defect in the highway, but that the contractor who agrees with the county to discharge the duty which the law places upon the county, is responsible to a traveler injured by a defect in the highway, would be to overlook the reason upon which the rule rests; for if such ability existed the county would be unable to make contracts for the keeping in repair of its highways on as reasonable terms as it can where it must only pay a reasonable price for the necessary work; because, if the contractor assumes the greater liability, he must necessarily take this into consideration in fixing the price for which he may do the work. We cannot see that there is any substantial distinction between this case and that of a contractor who agrees to keep the road in order as in Moss v. Rowlett. The traction company only undertook by the contract to keep the county bridge in repair, and thus relieve Fayette county of an expense which would otherwise fall upon it. What was in the minds of the contracting parties is not difficult to see. The fiscal court and the railroad company wished to get rid of the grade crossing with the dangers attendant upon it; but the fiscal court did not wish to assume the additional burden of maintaining the bridge. The traction company wished to avoid the danger attendant upon operating its cars over the grade crossing, and so the agreement was reached by which the railroad company bore a part of the expense of making the change in the turnpike, and the traction company assumed the entire burden of maintaining the bridge. No duty was imposed by the contract on the railroad company as to building or maintaining the bridge, and it will be observed that in the second clause of the contract the traction company agrees to maintain the bridge at its own cost and expense, and in the last clause of the contract it is twice stipulated that the bridge is to be built and forever maintained by the traction company "free of cost to Fayette county." In other words, it is clear from the contract that what the parties had in mind was that Fayette county should be free forever from the burden of maintaining the bridge. It is simply a contract by which the traction company assumes to do for Fayette county what it would otherwise be required to do; and by this contract it assumes no greater liability than Fayette county was under. In maintaining the bridge it simply acts for Fayette county, and it is under no greater responsibility than it would be if, instead of contracting to keep the bridge in repair, it had contracted to keep that part of the pike in repair which led from the old pike to the bridge; for the bridge was an essential part of the pike, and a contract to maintain the bridge imposed no greater liability than a contract to maintain any other part of the pike. The fact that the bridge was over the track of the railroad company in no way affects its liability. The railroad company was not required to build the bridge. It did not build it, and, if Fayette county had built this bridge over the railroad track, the railroad company would have been in no wise responsible to Grover, if Fayette county had allowed it to get out of repair. The fact that the county made a contract with another to do this work for it in no way affected the liability of the railroad company.

It is earnestly insisted that the defective bridge in the county highway was a public nuisance and that any one injured by a public nuisance may recover; but the bridge in question was no more a public nuisance than the bridge in the case of Moss v. Rowlett, or the defects in the other cases referred to, and this case cannot be distinguished from them on this ground. Any such defect in a county highway is a public nuisance, and, if a liability may be imposed on this ground here, it may be in all such cases. The county authorities or its representatives may be indicted for maintaining a public nuisance; but for reasons of public policy a liability for damages to persons injured thereby has not been imposed. Appellee relies upon the cases in which water companies have been held liable to the property owner for the loss of his property by fire due to their failure to maintain a sufficient water supply pursuant to their contracts made with the city. Graves Co. Water Co. v. Ligon, 112 Ky. 775, 66 S. W. 725, 23 Ky. Law Rep. 2149, and cases cited. But these cases rest upon the ground that the city in making the contract with the water company for water for fire protection contracted on behalf of its inhabitants and for their benefit. The city was under no obligation to furnish its inhabitants with a supply of water, and in furnishing a water supply the water company acted for itself, and not in the discharge of any obligation of the city to its inhabitants. Here the obligation to maintain the county highway rests primarily upon the county, and the traction company, when it undertook to maintain the bridge free of cost to Fayette county, simply undertook to do what Fayette county otherwise would have been under obligation to do. As Fayette county, if it had maintained the bridge, would have been under no obligation to pay appellee for the injury to his horse, such damages cannot be said to be reasonably within the contemplation of the parties when it was contracted that the traction company would maintain the bridge free of cost to Fayette county. The case would be the same, if, by reason of the defect in the bridge, the rider had been thrown from the horse and killed. To hold the traction company liable for such damages on a contract to maintain the bridge free of cost to Fayette county would be to extend the obligation of the contract beyond the fair and natural meaning of its terms. We therefore conclude that the appellant is not liable for the injuries sued for.

Judgment reversed, and cause remanded for further proceedings consistent herewith.

CASE 84.—PROSECUTION AGAINST ABE ALLISON FOR VIO-
LATION OF LOCAL .OPTION LAW.—December 2,
1909.

Allison v. Commonwealth

Appeal from Hardin Circuit Court.

WEED S. CHELF, Circuit Judge.

Defendant convicted and appeals.—Reversed.

1. Indictment and Information—Joinder of Offenses.—Under the
    common-law rule providing that an indictment may contain
    several counts charging violations of the same grade and
    punishment, an indictment merely charging in separate
    counts a sale, within 12 months, of liquor in violation of the
    local option law, without stating the facts with such particu-
    larity as distinguishes one violation from any of the others,
    charges but one offense.
2. Indictment and Information—Joinder of Offenses.—Under
    Civ. Code Prac. Sec. 126, providing that an indictment, ex-
    cept in the cases mentioned in section 127, must charge but
    one offense, an indictment not charging an offense within
    section 127 can charge only one offense, and an indictment
    charging more than one offense is void for duplicity, and
    all offenses not included in section 127 must be stated in
    separate indictments; and this rule applies to misdemeanors,
    which may be prosecuted by penal actions.
3. Penalties—Actions.—Where the procedure is by penal ac-
    tion as many violations of the law of the same grade and
    punishment may, under the Code, be set out as the common-
    wealth desires.

H. L. JAMES for appellant. .

JAS. BREATHITT, Attorney General, TOM B. McGREGOR,
Assistant Attorney General, and CHAS. H. MORRIS for commonwealth.

OPINION OF THE COURT BY JUDGE LASSING—Reversing.

The only question involved in this case is the suffi-ciency of the indictment. Appellant was indicted in the Hardin circuit court for the illegal sale of liquor in Hardin county, where the local option law was in force. The indictment contains six separate counts. A demurrer was interposed by the defendant, and overruled, whereupon a motion was made that the commonwealth be required to elect upon which one of the six counts the defendant should be tried. This motion was likewise overruled. The case was heard by a jury, and under instructions given by the court the jury found the defendant guilty on two counts, and not guilty on four. It failed to specify in its verdict upon which of the counts it found the defend-ant guilty and upon which not guilty. Upon this ver-dict judgment was rendered for $120, the amount fixed by the jury for two violations of the local option law. There is no bill of evidence in the case; no mo-tion or grounds for a new trial having been filed. So the sole question is: Does the indictment support the verdict and judgment predicated thereon?

It is insisted, for the appellant, that the indictment was in direct violation of section 126 of the Code, which is as follows: "An indictment, except in the cases mentioned in the next section, must charge but one offense, but, if it may have been committed in different modes and by different means, the indict-ment may allege the modes and means in the alterna-tive"—that under this Code provision but one offense might properly be charged in an indictment, and that the attempt on the part of the commonwealth to charge six separate and distinct offenses in the same indictment rendered the indictment bad, and the com-monwealth should have been required to elect which of the six counts it would stand upon. For the commonwealth it is urged that the indictment is good, and that, under the case of South v. Commonwealth, 79 Ky. 493, any number of counts may be put in one indictment, provided in each count the circumstances of each violation are stated with particularity.

At the outset we may state that, even if it should be conceded that an indictment might charge in separate counts several violations of the law of the same grade, still the indictment in the present case would be bad, for the reason that the facts and circumstances surrounding each violation attempted to be set out and alleged in the indictment are not stated with such particularity as to enable one to distinguish one alleged violation from any of the other five set out in the indictment; for they each simply charge a sale within 12 months next preceding the finding of the indictment, and, of course, proof on any one would necessarily cover the proof on all, and it would be impossible to tell, when proof was offered, to which count it was intended to be applied. We are of opinion that, even under the common-law rule here contended for by the commonwealth, and which authorized an indictment to be drawn containing several counts charging violations of the law where the offenses were of the same grade and punishment, the indictment as presented charges but one offense, and the trial court should have so told the jury; but the indictment in this particular could easily be cured, and, if cured, would it then be good? If the dictum in South v. Commonwealth is to be followed, it would; but, as far as we have discovered, the rule announced in South v. Commonwealth has not been followed— indeed, the principle therein apparently laid down seems to have been an inadvertence on the part of the court, which for the time being overlooked the fact

that the Code was intended to abrogate the common-
law rule, and that, while formerly more than one offense might be charged in an indictment, where each
was set out with particularity in a separate paragraph, now this is no longer admissible, and an indictment that charges more than one violation of the
law is void for duplicity.

In Ellis v. Commonwealth, 78 Ky. 130, this court
held that, where the indictment charged more than
one offense, a demurrer should be sustained. And in
Commonwealth v. Powell, 71 Ky. 7, the court held
that, if the indictment sufficiently alleged two or more
distinct and separate offenses, it would be defective
for duplicity and consequent uncertainty as to the
precise charge on which conviction would be sought.
The only exception to the rule denying the right of
the commonwealth to charge more than one offense
in the indictment is in that class of cases where it is
frequently quite difficult to distinguish one offense
from another, and under section 127 of the Civil Code
of Practice certain of these offenses last referred to
may be charged in one indictment, to wit, larceny and
knowingly receiving stolen property, larceny and obtaining money or property on false pretenses, larceny
and embezzlement, robbery and burglary, robbery
and assault with intent to rob, and passing or attempting to pass counterfeit money or United States
currency or bank notes, knowing them to be such, and
having in possession counterfeit money or United
States currency or bank notes, knowing them to be
such, with the intention of circulating the same. These
latter offenses are the only ones which, under our
present Code provision, may be united in one indictment. All other offenses, whether of the same grade
or not, must, under section 126 of the Civil Code of

Practice, be stated in separate indictments. Nor does the fact that misdemeanors may be prosecuted by penal actions militate against this rule, for the reason that procedure by penal action is regulated by Code provision just as indictments are, and hence, where the procedure is by penal action, as many violations of the law of the same grade and punishment may be set out as the state desires to include in one action, because distinctly authorized by the Code.

We are of opinion that the court erred in not sustaining the demurrer to the indictment as presented, or at least to five counts therein, and he should have limited the commonwealth in the instructions to a recovery for one violation.

For his failure to do so, the judgment is reversed, and cause remanded, with instructions to sustain the demurrer, with leave to resubmit.

CASE 85.—ACTION BY ARRENA CRUTCHER AGAINST THE
SOUTH COVINGTON & CINCINNATI STREET RAIL-
WAY COMPANY FOR DAMAGES FOR PERSONAL
INJURIES.—December 9, 1909.

South Covington & Cincinnati Street Ry. Co. v. Crutcher

Appeal from Campbell Circuit Court.

J. W. YUNGBLUT, Circuit Judge.

Judgment for plaintiff, defendant appeals.—Reversed.

1. Carriers—Injuries to Passengers—Contributory Negligence—
Action—Emergency.—Plaintiff, a woman 69 years of age, was
injured while riding on defendant's street car by a collision
between the car and an ice wagon approaching each other
at right angles at a crossing. Plaintiff saw the wagon and
the danger of collision, just before it occurred, when she got
up and stepped to the other side of the car as she saw other
passengers doing; and, when the collision occurred, she was
thrown forward onto the back of a seat, and the tongue of
the wagon, entering the car, dragged down over her back
and hip. Held, that plaintiff's act in moving from her position was done in an emergency not of her creation, and
the fact that she made an unwise choice of means to escape
did not constitute contributory negligence.

2. Street Railroads—Injuries to Passengers.—Street Car Collision—Duty of Motorman.—A street car motorman in approaching a crossing, while bound to keep a lookout for persons or vehicles crossing or about to cross the track, is not
required to stop and look up and down the street he is
crossing; his primary duty being to look ahead and observe
persons or vehicles approaching the track within the ordinary range of his vision while so looking, being entitled to presume that the driver of a vehicle approaching the track will
have his team under control.

3. Carriers—Injuries to Passengers—Streets—Collision with Ice
    Wagon—Negligence.—Where an ice wagon which collided
    with a street car at a crossing was not within the motor-
    man's ordinary range of vision as he was looking ahead when
    he started to cross the track, but was approaching the
    crossing at a high rate of speed, and when the motorman saw
    that a collision was imminent, and stopped the car in the
    middle of the street, the wagon was only 10 or 12 feet distant,
    and to have kept the car in motion would have increased the
    force of the collision, the motorman was not negligent in
    failing to observe the wagon earlier or in stopping the car.

L. J. CRAWFORD for appellant.

A. M. CALDWELL for appellee.

OPINION OF THE COURT BY WM. ROGERS CLAY, COM-
MISSIONER—Reversing.

Appellee, Arrena Crutcher, instituted this action
against the South Covington & Cincinnati Street
Railway Company to recover damages for personal
injuries. The jury returned a verdict in her favor
for $200. From the judgment based thereon this
appeal is prosecuted.

The accident occurred at the intersection of Pearl
and Pike streets, in Cincinnati, Ohio, on May 20,
1908. Pearl street runs east and west, and Pike
street begins on the north side of Pearl and runs a
short distance up a rather steep hill. As the street
car reached the middle of Pike street, it came in contact with an ice wagon coming down that street. The
tongue of the wagon passed through one of the windows of the car and injured appellee. Her account
of the accident is as follows: "I got on board of
the car there, and went over, and, when we came to
Pearl and Pike, there this accident occurred. An
ice wagon came down the street. They were going,
of course, I suppose at a pretty good rate of speed.

I couldn't exactly state the speed at the time that the car was traveling; but I saw the wagon coming, and I thought in all probability there was danger. So I waited a few minutes. I seen the other passengers get up, step to the opposite side of the car. I thought, well, there will be an accident. I will rise up and step into the aisle. And I was sitting with my right side against the window. When I raised partially up, just as I raised the crash came, and the tongue of the wagon came through the window and caught me, when I was only about halfway raised, over my right shoulder, and, of course, as they fell down, it throwed me forward on to the back of the seat in front of me, and the tongue dragged down over my back and right hip. Of course, it stunned me a little bit. And that was the way that accident occurred.'' Appellee further testified that she saw the wagon coming as she looked up Pike street, for she could see up that street a short distance before she reached the corner. She also testified as follows: ''Well, the reason I thought so (that there would be an accident) was because the ice wagon was very near and coming very rapidly down the street. I didn't see as well as I could understand it how an accident could be avoided. I don't know, I thought that perhaps the car would pass swiftly enough over Pike street to escape a collision. Of course, I didn't have an idea whether it would hit the window or not; but I thought, well, I will get up and step to the other side of the car, as I saw the other passengers going that way over.'

Thomas Lewis, another witness for appellee, testified substantially as follows: ''The grade on Pike street is very steep. When the car reached Pike street, the motorman did not do anything, but kept

on coming pretty fast. If he had looked before
crossing, there was nothing in the way to prevent him
from seeing the wagon. When the wagon was within
10 feet of the car, the motorman rang his bell, and
stopped the car. The car was stopped in the middle
of the street. When it stopped, the wagon ran into
it.'' This witness also made the following statement:
''The reason I am satisfied he stopped it, because, if
he hadn't stopped the car, I think there would have
been more of an accident than what there was, I am
satisfied the motorman stopped the car, but he stopped it with a sudden stop. all at once. If he had kept
on, he would have avoided the accident.''

Thomas Donahue, appellant's motorman, gave the
following acount of the accident: ''Well, about the
time before the accident, going west on Pearl street
there was a big express wagon. Whether it came
from the depot I don't know, but it was in the front
of me, and, of course, he would not get out of the
track, and he turned to go up Pike street. Well, of
course, I was going slow at the time. I could not
go fast because I was following him up. When he
turned the corner of Pike street, of course, I gave her
about half speed, and I happened to hear something.
I could not see anything because this big black covered wagon was in the shade of the ice wagon. When
I got just by there, I could see her coming, and, then
this ice wagon was tearing down the street, it stunned
me for a minute. I did not know which way to go or
what to do or anything else because I knew that I
would get hit. He would get me anyhow, so I
didn't know what to do. So I tried to make for the
opposite side of the street, and I says, no, I cannot
make it, he will get me anyhow. So I just waited;
stood there thinking that he would slow his horses

around, and go the other way; but he did not wheel the wagon because I was a little over halfway of the street, and I just had to stand there and take it.   If he had slewed around the other way down Pearl street, he would have just taken the whole end of the car out, because the wagon would be turned around, slewed around, and taken the whole front end of the car off.   So I tried to avoid it the best way I could, so I stopped.   I think, if I had been going at the time when the accident occurred, it would have took and done more damage that what it did.''   This witness further testified that the driver of the wagon tried to go east.   After the wagon which was in front of the car turned up Pike street, witness saw the ice wagon.   He then put on half speed, and started across the street at the rate of five or six miles an hour.   Just as he put on half speed the ice wagon was right on top of him.   He then had no time to get out of the way.   The wagon was coming like the fire department.

John Swis, the conductor, testified that he did not notice the ice wagon until it was within 10 feet of the car.   So far as he knew, there was no wagon in front of the car.   The ice wagon was coming down the street very rapidly.

Edward Riggs, a passenger on the car, testified as follows: ''Well, as we came to the corner there, why, there seemed to be a wagon in front of the car.   I remember the motorman ringing his gong.   Right after that wagon had turned out, why, an ice wagon came down Pike, and the pole and the horse's head came in the side of the car, broke the side out, and scattered glass.   I ducked my head down to get out of the way of the glass.   The motorman seemed to be doing the best he could for to stop his car immediately.   If he

hadn't, we would all have been caught on that side
of the car.   The pole would have taken out the whole
side of the car there.''

Harry Evans, a passenger on the car, testified that
when he saw the ice wagon it was 10 or 12 feet from
the car; that the wagon was coming very rapidly.
The motorman rang the gong several times and stopped the car.   The ice wagon was going even faster
than the fire department does sometimes.

John Adam Skinner, a passenger on the car, testified that just as they got to Pike street he saw the
ice wagon dashing down that street, and before he
knew it the tongue had crushed through the car.   He
thought the driver endeavored to turn his team to
the east.

Two grounds are urged for reversal: First, the failure of the court to award appellant a peremptory instruction; second, contributory negligence on the part
of appellee.   We shall discuss the second contention
first.

The evidence shows that appellee was 69 years of
age.   It is insisted that she was guilty of contributory
negligence in getting up and going to the other side
of the car.   When her whole evidence is read, it is
manifest that there was but a short period of time
intervening between the time she saw the wagon and
the time it came in contact with the car.   Thus an
emergency was presented.   She was not placed in a
perilous position by any act of hers.   She had a right
to make a choice as to the means to be used to avoid
the peril.   The making of an unwise choice under
such circumstances does not constitute contributory
negligence.   Louisville & Nashville R. R. Co. v. Molloy's Adm'x, 107 S. W. 217, 32 Ky. Law Rep. 745.
The only question in the case is whether or not a

peremptory instruction should have gone in favor of
the appellant. While one witness expressed the
opinion that had the motorman proceeded across the
street he would have avoided the accident, this witness does not state facts which tend to support this
conclusion. When the car reached the middle of the
street, the ice wagon was within 10 or 12 feet of it,
and the circumstances all indicate that, had the car
gone on, the ice wagon, instead of striking the car
about the third window from the front, would have
struck it near the center of the car, or towards the
rear; and the impact would of necessity have been
much greater, because both the wagon and the car
would have been in motion. Thus it will be seen that
there are no facts tending to show that the act of
the motorman in stopping the car constituted negligence. It is mere speculation to say that had he
gone on across the street he would have avoided the
accident. All the circumstances tend to rebut this
presumption. It is manifest that the only negligence
on the part of the motorman, if there was any, consisted in his failing to observe the approach of the
wagon, or in attempting to cross the street in the face
of the danger likely to arise from coming in contact
with the ice wagon. As a street car approaches a
street crossing, it is the duty of the motorman to
keep a lookout for persons or vehicles crossing or
about to cross the track. In discharging this duty
he is not required to stop and look up and down the
street he is crossing. His primary duty is to look
ahead, and to observe persons or vehicles approaching the track within the ordinary range of his vision
while so looking. He has the right to presume that
the driver of a vehicle approaching the track will have
his horse or horses under control. Were he required

to look up or down the street to avoid coming in contact with a runaway horse attached to a vehicle, a most uncommon occurrence, he might strike a vehicle or a person crossing the track, a very common occurrence, and thus injure such person or one of his passengers by his failure to keep a proper lookout. There is nothing in the evidence to show that the motorman saw the ice wagon until it was within 10 or 12 feet of the car. Nor is there any evidence tending to show that it was within the ordinary range of his vision as he looked ahead and started across the street. When the car stopped in the middle of the street, the wagon was then 10 or 12 feet distant. It was coming like the fire department; that is, at a very rapid rate. That being the case, the wagon must have been a considerable distance up the street when the motorman started the car across. It was not negligence, therefore, on his part to fail to observe the wagon when he could not see it and at the same time keep a proper lookout ahead.

For the reasons given, we conclude that the trial court erred in refusing to instruct the jury to find for appellant.

Judgment reversed and cause remanded for a new trial consistent with this opinion.

CASE 86.—ACTION BY T. M. GILMORE & CO. AGAINST W. B.
SAMUELS & CO. TO RECOVER BROKERAGE FEES.
December 8, 1909.

Gilmore & Co. v. Samuels & Co.

Appeal from Nelson Circuit Court.

SAMUEL E. JONES, Circuit Judge.

Judgment for defendant, plaintiff appeals.—Reversed.

1. Brokers—Agreement for Compensation—Consideration.—The
   undertaking by a broker to effect a sale of property is a consideration sufficient to support the contract for the payment
   of commissions thereof.
2. Corporations—Authority of Officers—Sale of Manufactured
   Product.—A corporation president expressly authorized by the
   board of directors "to sign the corporate name to all papers
   pertaining to the business of" the corporation has authority
   to contract with a broker for the sale of the manufactured
   product on hand, and to be manufactured during a period of
   five years.
3. Contracts—Construction—Entire or Severable Contracts.—In
   determining whether a contract is to be treated as an entirety
   or as severable, the intention of the parties must control, and
   this intention is to be determined by the terms of the contract itself.
4. Contracts—Construction—Entire or Severable Contract.—A
   contract between plaintiff, a broker, and defendant, a distill-
   ing company, authorized plaintiff to sell for a specified commission defendant's manufactured product on hand and to be
   manufactured during a period of 5 years, and provided that
   the purchaser of the product should have an option to purchase the distillery at the end of five years, or, if the contract be extended for an additional five years, as therein provided, the purchaser should have an option to purchase the
   distillery at the end of the second five years, plaintiff to receive a specified commission for selling the distillery in
   addition to that for selling the product. Held, that the con-

tract was severable, and defendant's officer who made it having authority to sell the product, that portion of the contract is enforcable, even if that relating to the sale of the distillery was invalid for want of authority to make it.

5. Contracts—Validity—Mental Capacity.—To render a contract invalid for mental incapacity of a party thereto, it is not enough to show that such party was at times, by the use of drugs, by disease, or other cause, lacking in mentality, but the evidence of defective mind must relate to the immediate time of making the contract.

6. Corporations—Contracts—Validity—Mental Capacity of Officer —Evidence.—Evidence held to show that a corporate officer in making a corporate contract had sufficient mental capacity to do so, and fully understood the transaction.

7. Corporations—Contracts—Validity.—A corporate contract cannot be set aside for mental incapacity of the president who executed it, where another corporate officer who had the active management and control of the concern's affairs assisted in, and advised the making of the contract.

JOHN S. KELLEY, JOHN A. FULTON AND R. C. CHERRY, for appellant.

NAT W. HALSTEAD, D. A. McCANDLESS AND E. E. McKAY for appellee.

OPINION OF THE COURT BY JUDGE LASSING—Reversing.

This litigation grows out of an attempt on the part of T. M. Gilmore & Co. to recover of W. B. Samuels & Co. brokerage fees for the sale of 3,266 barrels of whisky at 50 cents per barrel. The plaintiff, T. M. Gilmore & Co., is a corporation engaged in the whisky brokerage business in the city of Louisville. The defendant, W. B. Samuels & Co., is a corporation owning and operating a distillery in Nelson county, Ky. On the 29th day of November, 1906, T. M. Gilmore & Co. procured from W.B. Samuels & Co. the following writing: "Samuels, Ky., Nov. 29, 1906. This writing witnesseth that W. B. Samuels & Co., incorporated, of Nelson Co., state of Kentucky, have this day employed and do hereby employ, constitute and authorize T. M. Gilmore & Co., incorporated, of Louisville, Ky., to make a contract for and on its behalf for the sale of its distillery property at Samuels Depot, in Nelson county, Kentucky, and twelve hundred and sixty-six barrels of whisky in its bonded warehouses of the manufacture of fall 1905 and spring 1906 and the future product of said distillery on the following terms and conditions, namely: .

The said twelve hundred and sixty-six barrels of whisky at the price of thirty cents per proof gallon, original gauge; the purchaser to take and pay for same not less than two hundred barrels each and every two months from the date of sale, and the cost of carriage additional after the date of sale to be added to the price. To sell two thousand barrels to be manufactured during each and every distillery season from this date, with an option to the purchaser to take and require to be made for him one thousand barrels additional each season if he required or any proportion thereof, for a period of five years from this date and the purchaser to have the privilege of renewing this contract and extending same for an additional period of five years, provided he gives notice of his intention to renew the contract on or before the first day of July next preceding the date of expiration of the first five-year period. The price of said whisky to be hereafter manufactured to be twenty-five (25c) cents per proof gallon based on corn at 45 cents per bushel in Louisville as shown by bills for same, or in the event that the price of corn should advance the price of the whisky to be increased ¼ of a cent per gallon for each cent advanced per bushel in corn above 45 cents and if corn declines the price of the whisky to be reduced ¼ of a cent per gallon for each cent decline in the price of corn below 45 cents. The whisky manufactured hereafter to contain 30 per cent. of small grain and to be sound and merchantable.

If, during any season the price of corn should exceed 75 cents, then no whisky is to be made except at option of purchaser, but the full amount shall be produced during the life of this contract in such amount each season as the distiller can produce, but rot exceeding 3,000 barrels per season except at distillers' option. Cooperage to be first class 8 or 10 hoop barrels, and the distiller to deliver the whisky as required f. o. b. cars at Samuels, Ky. Outs to be guaranteed not to exceed one gallon over and above the government allowance on each barrel separately. Storage to begin first of each month following month cf inspection and to be at the rate of 5 cents per barrel per month. Goods to be paid for on the 10th of each month succeeding the month of manufacture or delivery of warehouse receipts. Buyers to have cption of having a portion of each crop made in such name or names as he may designate other than W. B. Samuels & Co., and buyer is to have the brand of W. B. Samuels placed on any or all of the whisky made under this contract, at his option.

Said W. B. Samuels & Co. is to establish and maintain a bottling room suitable for bottling in bond, suitable to meet the requirements of purchaser in bottling the whiskies of said distillery, and said bottling house must be established without delay so as to take care of any orders buyer may give for the bottling of any whiskies now in the W. B. Samuels & Co. warehouses which buyer may purchase on the market. Purchaser is to furnish, for bottling in bond, at Samuels, Ky., all cases, bottles, corks, labels, etc., without cost to W. B. Samuels & Co., and W. B. Samuels & Co. is to furnish labor in bottling said goods and charge for same as follows: Half pints 60 cents per case. Pints 40 cents per case. Fives 25 cents per case. Fours 25 cents per case. Also to sell the distillery plant and lands containing about 14 acres more or less at Samuels Depot, in Nelson county, Ky., being all the lands owned by said W. B. Samuels & Co., together with the distillery warehouses and all other improvements, buildings, fixtures, and machinery thereon, also all brands, good will etc,, for a consideration of $25,000.00, excluding, however, accrued storage up to time of transfer of said property, and personal property consisting of barrels, barrel material, grain, coal, etc.

The purchaser of the whisky under any contract which may be made by said T. M. Gilmore & Co., to have the option to purchase said distillery at the end of the said first five-year period, or, if contract is extended for an additional five years, then the purchaser to have the option to purchase said distillery plant and premises, at said price at end of second five-year period. Said W. B. Samuels & Co. agrees to make a deed of general warranty to the purchaser except as to the lien in favor of the United States government. Said W. B. Samuels & Co. agree to pay in the event of this sale to T. M. Gilmore & Co. a commission of fifty (50) cents per barrel on each and every barrel of whisky taken by purchaser under this contract, said commission to be paid as goods are delivered and paid for, and in the event that the purchaser in the exercise of his option takes the distillery, it is to pay a commission to T. M. Gilmore & Co. of (5) five per cent., when deed is made and notes are given or cash paid. In case distillery is destroyed

W. B. Samuels & Co. is not to be required to fulfill
this contract, but in the event it should rebuild the
distillery then it shall perform the contract for the
remaining portion of the term. Said W. B. Samuels
& Co. further agrees that in the event of the making
of a contract by T. M. Gilmore & Co. as hereinbefore
authorized to keep and perform said contract with the
successors or assigns of person with whom same may
be made. This option limited to five days from date
of this paper. W. B. Samuels & Co., by M. A. Samuels, Prest.''

Acting on the authority given under this contract,
T. M. Gilmore & Co., within the time limited, closed a
deal with R. H. Edelen & Co., by the terms of which
they purchased all the whisky and the output of the
distillery with a right to buy the distillery property
as set out in the authority or contract under which
Gilmore & Co. was acting. W. B. Samuels & Co. was
notified that this sale had been consummated, and it
at once, through its president, wrote a letter to R. H.
Edelen & Co., in which it refused to ratify the sale
made by Gilmore & Co. on the ground that the authority for making same had not been properly executed
by the W. B. Samuels Company, and that the writing
signed by its president had not been approved by the
board of directors. R. H. Edelen & Co. thereupon
brought suit in the Nelson circuit court to compel the
specific performance of the contract. A demurrer
was filed to this petition, and, being sustained, plaintiff declined to plead further, and its suit was dismissed. Upon appeal here the judgment of the circuit court was affirmed, on the ground that the court
would not compel the specific performance of a contract of that nature. Thereafter T. M. Gilmore &
Co. filed a suit in the Nelson circuit court, wherein it

sought to recover its brokerage fees for the sale of
1,266 barrels of whisky, which were on hand at the
time the sale was entered into, and the 2,000 barrels
which had been manufactured by said company between the date of the execution of the contract and
the filing of this suit.

W. B. Samuels & Co. answered, and, in addition to
traversing the allegations of the petition, interposed
the following defenses: (1) That the writing sued on
was not the act and deed of W. B. Samuels & Co., and
that the company was not bound by the unauthorized
act of its president; (2) that at the time of the execution of this writing M. A. Samuels was not competent
to contract; (3) that she was over-reached and deceived in its execution by T. M. Gilmore; and (4) that
it was without consideration.   In its reply, the affirmative matter in each of these several defenses set up
in the answer was traversed, and plaintiff also set
up the business relations theretofore existing between
it and defendant, its previous employment to sell this
same property, the organization of defendant and its
mode of conducting business, and the circumstances
under which the contract sued on was made and entered into.   This affirmative matter in the reply was
traversed of record, and on the issues thus made the
case proceeded to trial.   At the conclusion of all the
testimony, the court peremptorily instructed the jury
to find for the defendant, which was done, and the
plaintiff's petition was dismissed.   From that ruling
and judgment this appeal is prosecuted.

The record discloses the following state of facts,
about which there is practically no dispute: The defendant company was organized many years ago for
the manufacture and sale of whisky, and W. B. Samuels, for whom it was named and who organized the

company, was its principal stockholder, chief officer, and general manager. At his death the stock which he owned in this corporation passed under his will to his widow, M. A. Samuels, and his son, H. M. Samuels. It appears that he owned 275 shares of stock. M. A. Samuels, his wife, received thereof 247 shares, and H. M. Samuels, his son, 28 shares. The only other stockholders in the company at that time were D. P. Simons, who owned three shares, and Adams, Taylor & Co., of Boston, Mass., who owned two shares. It appears that both Simons and Adams, Taylor & Company were merely nominal stockholders; Simons being made a stockholder for the purpose of perfecting the organization, and Adams, Taylor & Co. for trade purposes, in order to advertise the output of the distillery as being their own manufacture. M. A. Samuels, H. M. Samuels, and D. P. Simons were the board of directors of the corporation. M. A. Samuels was its president, D. P. Simons vice president, and H. M. Samuels its secretary and treasurer, and, as such, he had the active management and control of the corporation, and looked after the conduct of its business.

After the death of W. B. Samuels, a meeting of the stockholders was held on the 25th of August, 1902, at which time the stock owned by him was formally transferred to his wife and son, and three shares were issued to D. P. Simons for the purpose of perfecting the organization. It appears that the certificate for these three shares of stock was signed in blank by D. P. Simons and delivered to H. M. Samuels, and was thereafter kept by him in the company's safe, so that at most he was but a nominal owner of the stock. On that same day the following order was placed upon the minute book of the company:

"On motion it is ordered that M. A. Samuels, president, and H. M. Samuels, secretary and treasurer of the incorporators above, are authorized to sign the corporate name to all papers pertaining to the business of said corporation." The business of the corporation was carried on by M. A. Samuels and H. M. Samuels. They managed, conducted, and controlled its affairs without any further meeting of the board of directors, so far as the minute book shows, until February 11, 1907, when a meeting was called for the purpose of employing counsel to defend the suit brought by plaintiff. M. A. Samuels, who executed the contract relied upon, was at the date of its execution about 65 years of age. She was in poor health, and had been for some time, was much of the time confined to her bed, and was a victim of the drug habit. She did not read the contract, but it was read over to her by T. M. Gilmore. This contract was first discussed with her son, H. M. Samuels, and he was present at the time it was read to his mother, and its various provisions discussed, and he saw her execute it.

It is further made to appear that in the summer of 1906, and some months before the execution of the contract sued on, the defendant had employed the plaintiff to sell the product of this distillery and an interest in the distillery property, and that, under said employment, plaintiff undertook to sell the property, and did find a prospective purchaser, who, for some reason, declined to close the contract, although at that time it appears both M. A. Samuels and H. M. Samuels were desirous of having it carried out. When this sale had fallen through, T. M. Gilmore, of T. M. Gilmore & Co., testifies that it was understood between him and the defendant that he would seek to find another purchaser, and that, in furtherance of this general understanding, he continued to try and make sale of this property, or to find a purchaser for it, and did sell a part of the whisky on hand, and later, after discovering that it was possible to make a deal with R. H. Edelen & Co. that he believed would be acceptable to the defendant company, he procured the execution of the contract sued on. This contract was obtained under the following circumstances: John S. Kelley, a member of the firm of R. H. Edelen & Co., at the instance of T. M. Gilmore, met H. M. Samuels and T. M. Gilmore at the distillery plant, at the date upon which the contract was executed, and together discussed the proposed sale of the output and distillery plant, and their agreement and understanding was reduced to writing and later submitted to M. A. Samuels, the president of the company, who executed same as above set out. It appears that the price agreed upon as commission for the sale of the whisky on hand, and the annual output was the usual and customary brokerage fee for conducting such sales.

When reduced to their last analyses, the defenses interposed by the defendant are two: First, that the contract sued on is an entirety and not severable, and that, as neither the president nor the president and secretary and treasurer had authority to sell and dispose of the distillery property, the contract into which they entered with plaintiff, by which they authorized its sale, together with the sale of the whisky on hand and the annual output of the distillery for five years, is void; and, second, that at the date of its execution the mind of M. A. Samuels, the president of the company, was so weakened and enfeebled by the continued and protracted use of morphine that she did

not know and understand what she was doing, and
that for this reason the company is not liable or
bound upon the contract. The other defenses interposed are wholly without merit, for there is nothing
in the record to justify the charge that a fraud was
practiced upon the president, M. A. Samuels, in the
execution of the contract, and the undertaking on the
part of a broker to effect a sale of property has so
frequently been held to be a consideration sufficient
to support the contract, as evidenced by the following authorities: Cook v. Fryer, 3 Ky. Law Rep. 612;
Jacob v. Buchanan & Bros., 11 Ky. Law Rep. 861;
Simrall v. Arthur, 13 Ky. Law Rep. 682; Tamplet &
Washburn v. Saffell, 15 Ky. Law Rep. 94—that the
defense of want of consideration cannot be seriously
considered.

We will first dispose of the question as to whether
or not this is a severable contract, and, for the purposes of this case, we will proceed upon the theory
(without so deciding) that the president of a company, even though advised and counseled by the secretary and treasurer, who is also a member of its
board of directors, has no authority to sell and dispose of the real estate owned by the corporation in
the absence of express authority from the board of
directors so to do, when the business of the corporation is not that of buying and selling real estate.
Here the president of the company undertook,
through the plaintiff, to sell the whisky on hand, together with such whisky as should be manufactured
during the next five years, and the distillery property
itself. The business of this corporation was the manufacture and sale of whisky. It can hardly be seriously questioned, in the absence of any express authority from the board so to do, that the president or

the secretary and treasurer, having the active management of the company, had the right to sell whisky
on hand, and such as it should from time to time manufacture, as this was the business in which the corporation was engaged. But, when we find that the
board of directors had expressly authorized the president and the secretary and treasurer to do such acts
as were necessary to the proper and successful conduct of the company's business, we must conclude that
in the execution of the contract sued on, in so far as
it authorized and directed a sale of the whisky on
hand, and such as should be manufactured during the
time specified in the contract, the president was acting clearly within the express authority given by the
board of directors.

We have, then, a contract, a part of which is authorized by the board of directors, and which, therefore, the president had a right to execute, and a part
of which, as stated, for the purpose of this case only,
she had no right to execute. Are these so connected
and interwoven as that they must be treated as a
whole, or may this contract be separated into its com-
ponent parts and such as were authorized carried into
effect? It is not always an easy matter to determine
just what contracts are severable, and what are not.
The text-writers and authorities agree that in determining whether a contract shall be treated as severable or as an entirety the intention of the parties will
control, and this intention must be determined by a
fair construction of the terms and provisions of the
contract itself. In 3 Page on Contracts, Sec. 1484,
we find the rule thus stated: "In determining whether
a contract is entire or severable, the intention of the
parties is paramount, and, if this intention is clearly
expressed, no question can arise as to which class of

contract it is. This intention is, however, often not clearly expressed, as the parties have generally no clear idea whether the contract is entire or severable, and no definite idea of the legal consequences which would follow from its being in either class. The intention of the parties must therefore be deduced from the language used by the application of the ordinary rules of construction. The rules of construction are applied differently, however, in the different classes of cases in which the question whether the contract is entire or severable may arise. If this question arises in connection with the illegality of one covenant, the general principle applies that the courts will uphold a contract, if, by fair construction, it is possible to do so, rather than overthrow it. Accordingly the test chiefly relied upon in such cases is whether the parties have apportioned the consideration on the one side to the different covenants on the other, one of which covenants is illegal. If the consideration is apportioned so that for each covenant there is a corresponding consideration, the contract is severable, and the illegality of one covenant does not make the rest unenforceable. If, on the other hand, the consideration is not apportioned, and the same consideration supports a legal and illegal covenant, the contract is entire, and is already unenforceable.''

On the question of apportionment of the consideration, we find in the same authority, under section 1486, the following: "In determining questions of performance, the fact that several covenants are each supported by a distinct consideration, which consideration is thus separately apportioned, is often enough to show that the covenants are severable.'' In 2 Parsons on Contracts (9th Ed.) p. 517, we find the rule stated in this manner: "The question whether a contract is entire or separable is often of great importance. Any contract may consist of many parts; and these may be considered as parts of one whole, or as so many distinct contracts entered into at one time, and expressed in the same instrument, but not thereby made one contract. No precise rule can be given by which this question in a given case may be settled. Like most other questions of construction, it depends upon the intention of the parties, and this must be discovered in each case by considering the language employed and the subject-matter of the contract. If the part to be performed by one party consists of several distinct and separate items, and the price to be paid by the other is apportioned to each item to be performed, or is left to be implied by law, such a contract will generally be held to be severable. And the same rule holds where the price to be paid is clearly and distinctly apportioned to different parts of what is to be performed, although the latter is in its nature single and entire.''

In Story on Contracts (5th Ed.) p. 28, the author thus states the rule: ''The weight of opinion and the more reasonable rule would seem to be that where there is a purchase of different articles, at different prices, at the same time, the contract would be several as to each article, unless the taking of the whole was rendered essential either by the nature of the subject-matter, or by the act of the parties.'' Our court has in many instances, viz., Craddock v. Aldridge, 5 Ky. 15; Allen v. Sanders, 46 Ky. 593; Berryman v. Hewit, 29 Ky. 462; C. & O. R. R. Co. v Shelbyville, B. & O. R. Co., 117 Ky. 95, 77 S. W. 690, 25 Ky. Law Rep. 1265, been called upon to construe contracts where the issue was made to turn on the question as to whether they were severable or not, and it has uni-

formly been held that, where the plain language of
the contract did not force a contrary construction, the
contract has been held severable in order that the
intention of the parties might be carried out as far
as possible.

In the case of Craddock v. Aldridge, supra, Aldridge contracted with Craddock to build a house for
a certain sum of money, to be completed at a certain
time. One-fourth of this money was to be paid
when the work was begun, one-fourth when the roof
was finished, and the remainder when the house was
completed. It was held that this was a severable
contract. Again, in Allen v. Sanders, supra, where
the plaintiff agreed to build a house for the defendant by a specified time, and defendant agreed to pay
$50 in cash and the balance when the work was com-
pleted, it was held that there was a severable contract, and the covenant calling for the payment of
$50 in cash could be enforced. See, also, Leonard v.
Dyer, 26 Conn. 172, 68 Am. Dec. 382; Patton v. Gil-
mer, 42 Ala. 548, 94 Am. Dec. 665; Mechanics' Nat.
Bank v. Frazer, 86 Ill. 133, 29 Am. Rep. 20; Scott v.
Kittanning Coal Co., 89 Pa. 231; Pierson v. Crooks,
115 N. Y. 539, 22 N. E. 349, 12 Am. St. Rep. 831;
Coleman v. Insurance Co., 49 Ohio St. 310, 31 N. E.
279, 16 L. R. A. 174, 34 Am. St. Rep. 565.

Applying these general principles to the contract
under consideration, we find that it is expressly
agreed that the plaintiff shall receive from the defendant 50 cents per barrel for each barrel of whisky
which it sold for the defendant, and that, in the
event the purchaser of the whisky exercises the option
given to purchase the real estate, then the plaintiff
shall receive for his compensation for effecting this
sale 5 per cent. of the gross sum realized from the

sale of the real estate. His compensation for the sale of the whisky is in no wise made to depend on the sale of the real estate. Suppose, for instance, that the contract had been closed by the defendant, and that it had accepted the terms of the sale to Edelen & Co., and Edelen & Co. had received the whisky which the defendant had on hand when the contract was made, and had annually thereafter received the whisky as it was manufactured, and then at the end of five ·years had declined to exercise its right and close the option to purchase the real estate, could the defendant be heard to say that it would not pay to the plaintiff the commissions called for in the contract for the sale of the whisky? We think not. Then, as the sale of the whisky was in no wise made dependent upon the sale of the real estate, it seems very clear that the parties, when entering into this contract, did not intend that the plaintiff's compensation for the sale of the whisky would be made in any wise to depend upon his ultimate sale of the real esate. In fact, from the plain language of the contract, it is apparent that they each understood that the commissions for the sale of the whisky were due and payable when the terms of the sale thereof were complied with, to wit, the whisky delivered and paid for; whereas, it could not be determined whether the plaintiff would under this contract be entitled to any commission on the sale of the real estate until the expiration of five years from the date of the contract and Edelen & Co. had made it known whether or not they would exercise their option and take the property.

Thus, by the provisions of the writing sued on, the plaintiff was authorized to sell the whisky which the defendant company at that time owned and should

vol. 135—46

manufacture during the next five years at the prices agreed upon in the contract, and, if he succeeded in doing so, he should be paid 50 cents per barrel for his services. There can be no doubt whatever that the parties themselves clearly understood that the sale of the whisky under this contract was not dependent upon the sale of the real estate, and that the purchaser of the whisky under this contract was in no wise compelled or required to purchase the real estate in order to enable him to close the contract for the purchase of the whisky. We think the contract is a severable contract, and that portion thereof which the plaintiff company was authorized to make should be carried out and complied with by defendant, unless it be found that defendant should be excused from its performance because at the time the contract was executed its president was not competent to know and understand its terms, and was not capable of making a contract for which the defendant company should be held answerable.

This raises a novel question. The defense of want of capacity has frequently been interposed by individuals in seeking to escape liability upon contracts into which they have entered, but we are cited to no case where a corporation has sought to be excused from performing its contract upon the sole ground that its representative who made the contract for it did not have sufficient mental capacity to know and understand the character and effect of the transaction. This lack of precedent is due, perhaps, to the fact that a corporation enjoys many advantages which the individual does not. It is an artificial being whose affairs are in general not affected by the sickness, mental derangement, or death of one of its officers. The law requires that its business shall be under the management and control of certain officials, and, in the event of the disability of any one of these to act, provision is made that others in line of succession shall discharge the duties of those thus incapacitated. The duties which are usually discharged by the president in case of disability properly fall upon the vice president, and, if he should likewise be under some disability, then upon the secretary, treasurer, or other officer as the law designates, for in contemplation of law the incapacity, death, or removal from office of one official does not break the continuity in the chain of the conduct of the company's business. Still the company in every transaction must act through some one, and, if it shall be made to appear that the officer or agent representing it was at the time of the transaction complained of so lacking in mentality that he could not enter into a contract for himself, we can see no good reason why it should be held that the company for which he attempts to act should not be excused upon the same ground.

But, in order that it may avail itself of this right, it must be clearly established that the said contracting agent did not, at the time the contract was entered into, have sufficient capacity to know and understand what he was doing, and that this fact was not known to other officers or agents of the company, or, if known to them, they did not know that such officer was attempting to act for or represent the company. It is not enough to show that such contracting agent was, by the use of drugs, disease, or from other cause, at times lacking in mentality, but the evidence of the defective mind must relate immediately to the time when the transaction complained of was being entered into.

In this case the defendant has utterly failed to establish either of the points necessary to enable it to escape liability under its contract; for, while it is shown that Mrs. Samuels had for many years been addicted to the use of morphine, and was in poor health at the time of the execution of this contract, and her physician testifies that her mentality had by reason thereof been very much weakened, she has by her own testimony given in this case shown that upon the day of the transaction complained of she knew and understood what she was doing. Her deposition was not given until many months after the date of the contract, and yet she remembers perfectly well the whole transaction, and how she was called to the telephone by her son and notified that he wanted to bring the plaintiff's representative out to see her, to which arrangement she finally consented. She details the order in which they came into the house, what was said and done by each, what her physical condition was on that day, with what she was suffering, and how many doses of morphine she had taken and how much at a dose. She shows plainly in her deposition that she then understood that she was giving an option upon the whisky on hand, the plant and its output, which was satisfactory to her son, and she says, and it is shown in the record, that she relied upon his judgment in a large measure, if not exclusively, in the conduct of their business. In the light of this testimony on her part, in spite of the opinion of her physician and others who have testified that she did not, we are constrained to believe that she did know and understand what she was doing at the time she signed the contract in question.

But even if the evidence led us to entertain a contrary view, and to hold that she did not at that time have mental capacity to contract, still defendant must fail in its contention for the further reason that in its execution the secretary and treasurer of the company, who was also a director and had the active management and control of its affairs, participated. In fact, he assisted in the draft of the contract and discussed its terms and provisions, and not until they were acceptable to him was his mother, the president, conferred with in regard thereto. Here, then, we have a contract entered into between plaintiff and defendant in which the defendant is represented not only by the president, whose capacity to contract is questioned, but by another officer of the company, her son, H. M. Samuels, who had equal authority to represent it and whose mental ability is in no wise impaired. He and his mother owned practically all of the stock of this corporation. In its welfare and success he was most vitally interested. If he had not wanted the contract executed, or the company had not been satisfied with its terms and provisions, instead of going to his mother and requesting her to enter into it for the company, he should have objected to her signing it; and, if he regarded her as mentally incompetent to transact business, he should have so stated to the plaintiff.

The fact that he did not object to plaintiff seeing his mother and discussing the matter with her and contracting with her relative thereto is another evidence that he did not regard his mother as incompetent to transact business, and that neither they nor their attorney so regarded her is further evidenced by the fact that when, a few days after the contract had been entered into, the company through its president notified Edelen & Co. that they would not carry out the contract, the ground upon which they sought to escape liability was not want of capacity upon the part of its president, who made the contract, but because she had not first obtained authority so to do from the board of directors.

The contract being a severable one, and there being no merit in the contention of appellee that in the execution of the contract it was not properly represented, the record discloses no defense whatever to plaintiff's suit, and, this being made to appear, a peremptory instruction should have been given the jury to find in favor of plaintiff, under the terms of the contract, 50 cents per barrel for each barrel of whisky on hand at the date of its execution and such as was manufactured during the succeeding year.

The judgment of the lower court is therefore reversed, and the case remanded for further proceedings consistent herewith.

CASE 87.—ACTION BY FRANK CORBIN AGAINST JENNIE M.
SMITH.—December 3, 1909.

Smith v. Corbin

Appeal from Fayette Circuit Court.

WATTS PARKER, Circuit Judge.

Judgment for plaintiff, defendant appeals.—Affirmed.

1. Evidence—Parol Evidence—Rights of Parties.—The rights of parties to a contract are to be determined by the contract as written, where ne'ther fraud nor mistake in its preparation or terms is alleged.

2. Vendor and Purchaser—Contracts—Construction.—The purchaser of a lot agreed to pay a certain price therefor, and deposited certificates of membership in an investment company as collateral security; the vendor also retained a lien for the purchase price. The purchaser was to keep up the payments on the certificates, and had the right to pay the purchase money with maturing coupons on the certificates. The certificates were to be returned to the purchaser when the purchase price had been paid. The investment company failed, and the vendor sued to enforce his lien. Held, that as the contract provided that the purchaser should pay the dues to the investment company, and that only the maturities should be accepted as payments on the purchase price, the purchaser's assignee was not entitled to a credit upon the purchase price for dues paid on the certificates.

3. Vendor and Purchaser—Contracts—Fraud.—Fact that the vendor knew of the financial unsoundness of the investment company as well as its hazardous and illegal methods of business, and represented to the purchaser that the coupons would mature at regular intervals during each year until the purchase money would be paid, and thereby induced the purchaser to continue payment to the investment company until it went into the hands of a receiver, but for which representations she would not have done so, were not fraudulent

representations which would vitiate the contract of sale, it
not being alleged that the vendor was an officer or agent or
even a stockholder in the company, or that such knowledge
came to him through any connection he had with its affairs,
nor that the representations were made when or before the
purchaser or her assignee became investors in the investment
company, nor as an inducement to them to invest therein nor
that the vendor knew of the assignment by the purchaser of
her interest and rights under the contract until it was made
nor that the assignee was induced by the representations to
accept the assignment; it further appearing that the purchaser acquired the certificates four months before the contract of purchase was made.

4. Vendor and Purchaser—Contract—Fraud—Representations.—
The vendor's representation that the coupons would mature regularly if the purchaser continued the payment of
dues on the certificates was, at most, a mere expression of
opinion.

5. Vendor and Purchaser—Contract—Validity.—The certificates
being held by the vendor merely as collateral, there being an
unqualified undertaking by the purchaser to pay the consideration for the lot, the fact that the investment company's
business was an unlawful lottery would not affect the validity
of the contract of sale of the lot.

6. Appeal and Error—Presumptions—Validity of Contract.—The
answer not alleging facts from which it could be said that
the investment company's business was conducted as a lottery, it would be presumed on appeal, after a verdict for plaintiff, that the contract for purchase of the lot was not made
illegal by the manner in which the investment company conducted its business.

7. Contracts—Validity—Enforcement of Valid Parts of Contract
Partly Illegal.—Where there are contained in the same instrument distinct engagements by which a party binds himself
to do certain acts, some of which are legal and some illegal,
the performance of those which are legal may be enforced,
though the performance of those which are illegal may not.

J. ALEXANDER CHILES for appellant.

FORMAN & FORMAN and DON FORMAN for appellee.

OPINION OF THE COURT BY JUDGE SETTLE—Affirming.

This is an appeal from a judgment of the Fayette
circuit court enforcing a vendor's lien asserted by

appellee against certain collateral and a lot on Chestnut street in the city of Lexington owned by appellant, and directing a sale of the property in satisfaction of the lien debt and costs of the action.

It appears from the record that appellant's sister, Maggie Smith, in June, 1897, obtained by purchase certain certificates of membership or stock, with coupons attached, in the Southern Mutual Investment Company, of Lexington, and that, desiring to utilize this stock in the purchase of a house and lot from appellee, she in October, 1897, entered with him into a written executory contract whereby he sold and agreed to convey her by proper deed, upon the full payment by her to him of $1,300 with interest from date, a house and lot situated on Chestnut street, Lexington, known on the plat of the city as lot 219. In the contract a lien was retained on the lot to secure the payment of the purchase money. The contract recited that the second party, Maggie Smith, had taken out in the Southern Mutual Investment Company six certificates of membership with coupons attached; and the contract provided: "The said certificates shall be and they are hereby assigned to the first party (appellee) to be held by him as collateral to secure the payment of said purchase price, and the said first party alone is authorized to collect and receipt for all the maturing coupons on the said certificates or renewals thereof, until the said purchase price with interest is fully paid to him."

The contract also provided: "That the said second party (Maggie Smith) will each and every month, beginning on the 15th day of October 1897, pay to the Southern Mutual Investment Company according to its rules, the dues of the said certificates or renewals ––that is to say, $2.00 per month on each of said certificates or renewals thereof;   *   *   *   but when all of said purchase price and interest is paid, as agreed upon, said first party (appellee) shall turn over and deliver said certificates to said second party, and they shall be free from all claims of the first party.'' The contract contained the further provision that: ''If at any time the second party should be three months in default on any of the said payments to the Southern Mutual Investment Company, then all of the unpaid purchase money above agreed upon with interest thereon up to that date shall be due and payable, and the said first party shall have the right to carry the said certificates in the said Southern Mutual Investment Company and to own the same absolutely as his property, and the second party shall have no interest therein nor claim thereon whatever.''

Yet another provision of the contract required Maggie Smith to keep the house on the lot she purchased insured for appellee's benefit as long as any of the purchase money remained unpaid. It will be observed that the purchaser had the right to pay the purchase money upon the lot with maturing coupons, and that she was to continue the certificates of membership in the investment company, and to meet all dues that might accrue thereon until the purchase money was fully paid. Pursuant to the contract, she took possession of the lot, procured insurance on the house, paid the dues, and continued the certificates for several years and until she sold, and in writing assigned and conveyed them, together with her interest in the lot and all her rights under the contract to her sister, the appellant Jennie M. Smith, who took the place of Maggie, and in the writing between them assumed all the undertakings and liability of Maggie imposed by the contract of the latter with appellee.

Jennie M. Smith, after thus taking the place of Maggie in the contract with appellee, continued as Maggie had done the insurance upon the property, the certificates of membership in the Southern Mutual Investment Company, and also to pay the dues thereon, until the company became insolvent and its property and business went into the hands of a receiver under an order of the Fayette circuit court. When this event occurred, appellant quit paying dues upon the certificates of membership of which she was the owner, and as none of the coupons maturing after the appointment of the receiver were paid by the company to appellee, and no part of what remained of the purchase money due on the lot was thereafter paid him by appellant, he, as allowed by the contract, brought suit against appellant for the balance of purchase money, and to enforce his lien upon the lot and certificates of stock he held as collateral to satisfy the amount due.

It appears that appellee down to the time of the appointment of the receiver had been paid by appellant and her sister Maggie, through the investment company, from maturing coupons, divers sums amounting in the aggregate to $316.80. In the mean-time the house situated on the lot appellee sold had been destroyed by fire and the insurance thereon, amounting to $665.00, was also received by appellee, and for that as well as the $316.80 appellant was entitled to credit upon the amount sued for. By the judgment rendered in the lower court appellee recovered $1,300, with 6 per cent. interest from October, 1897, and costs of the action, credited by the various sums making up the $316.80 as of the dates they were paid, respectively, and by the insurance of $665 as of the date it was received by appellee. Appellant,

however, complains of the judgment and the action
of the circuit court in rejecting the defenses interposed to a recovery by her answer, and it is now our
duty to determine whether there is any merit in her
complaint.

The answer as finally amended set up, in substance,
the following matters of defense: (1) That, in addition to the credits and insurance admitted by appellee,
appellant and her sister paid to the investment company in dues upon the certificates of stock deposited .
with appellee as collateral $954.21, for which it was
alleged she was also entitled to credit. (2) That she
was ignorant of the antecedents and character of the
Southern Mutual Investment Company and of its
system and methods of business, but that appellee
was informed thereof and of the financial unsoundness of the company, as well as its hazardous and
illegal methods of conducting its business; yet that
with such knowledge he, by fraudulently representing
to her that the coupons would mature at regular intervals during each year until the purchase money
due him upon the lot would be paid, induced her to
continue the payment to the company of dues until
its assets and business went into the hands of the receiver; but for which representations she would not
have done so. (3) That the manner in which the
Southern Mutual Investment Company conducted its
business made it in effect a lottery, the operation of
which was contrary to law, and that, as the executory
contract under which she purchased the lot of appellee obligated her to pay him therefor through the
investment company and its methods were illegal, the
contract became tainted with such illegality and entitled her to its rescission and an accounting by which
appellee should be charged with, and appellant allow-

ed to recover, all the moneys he had received from her and her assignor upon the lot. The circuit court by sustaining a motion to strike out certain parts of the answer and sustaining a demurrer to what remained, held that the matters set out above did not constitute a defense, and in that conclusion, after mature reflection, we concur.

As to the claim for additional credits from the payment of dues, it is sufficient to say that the rights of the parties are to be determined by the contract as written, and, as neither fraud nor mistake in its preparation or terms is alleged, we must accept its meaning as expressed. It specifically provides that appellee only had the right to, and should be paid, the maturities. Moreover, he agreed to accept as payment upon the purchase price only the maturities, and these appellant and her assignor agreed he should receive, to be applied, first, in liquidation of the interest on the purchase money, and, secondly, as credits upon the principal. By the terms of the contract, appellant and her assignor had to pay the dues to the investment company, but, as to what application should be made of them after they were paid, that instrument is silent. But appellant would have been compelled to pay the dues so long as she continued the certificates of membership in the investment company even if not indebted to appellee, or after completing the payment of what they owed him. It is not claimed that appellee failed to credit appellant or her assignor by any payment received from the investment company, or that he was negligent in failing to collect or demand of the company the money upon any matured coupon to which he was entitled. We conclude, therefore, that no credit should have been allowed in the judgment for the dues.

We are also convinced that the plea of fraud is not good. While it was charged that appellee knew of the financial unsoundness of the investment company and of its hazardous and alleged illegal business methods, it is not alleged that he was an officer or agent or even a stockholder in the company, or that such knowledge came to him through any connection he had with its business or affairs. Besides, it was not averred that the alleged fraudulent representations were made when or before appellant or her assignor became investors in the investment company, or as an inducement to them to invest therein. On the contrary, as before stated, it appears that appellant's assignor acquired the certificates of membership of the company in June, 1897, and that her purchase of the lot of appellee was on the following October, four months later. She did not, therefore, invest with the company at the instance of appellee, and he probably did not know of the investment until he sold her the lot.

It does not appear from the averment of the answer that appellee knew of the assignment to appellant of her sister's interest and rights under her contract with him until after it was made, nor was it alleged that she was induced by the alleged fraudulent representations of appellee to accept the assignment or assume in her sister's stead the obligations it imposed. But, after all, an analysis of the answer and several amendments will show that the alleged fraudulent representations of which appellant complains were simply that appellee assured her the coupons would mature regularly, if she continued the payment of dues thereon. This, at most, was but an expression of opinion on his part; and judging the investment company at the time, in the light of her past experience with it, she had the same means of knowing as did appellee, with what regularity the coupons carried by her in the company would mature.

The facts averred in the answer as amended do not show particular knowledge of the condition of the affairs of the investment company on the part of appellee, or that he had any peculiar means of knowing it; nor did he sustain any such relation of trust or confidence to appellant or her assignor, or to the investment company, as would make what he said support an action for fraud or deceit, although what he said with reference to the maturity of the coupons may have been exaggerated or untrue. So we think it should be considered that in entering into the contract made by them the parties were upon an equal footing, and that they had equal opportunity of investigating and knowing the subject-matter of the contract in all its details.

We are further of opinion that appellant cannot avoid the contract or ask its rescission on account of the manner in which the Southern Mutual Investment Company conducted its business. However illegal its business methods, it is not alleged in the answer or amendments that appellee had any connection therewith either as an officer, agent, or privy of the· investment company. Nor is it alleged that he in any manner furnished or advanced money, property, or other thing of value to the appellant or her assignor with which to aid the lottery, if it were a lottery, or that he was in any way to participate in the winnings or profits, if any, which might accrue to the appellant or her assignor from their investment in the company. The contract shows that appellee was only to receive from appellant and her assignor the $1,300, with interest from October 10, 1897, the agreed price of the lot; and, in the event more maturities arose than was necessary for the payment of this fixed sum, with interest, the excess was, under the contract, to be absolutely the property of appellant. The certificates were held by him simply as collateral, and whenever there was paid to him the consideration for the lot, with interest, the certificates were to be returned by him to the appellant. It is patent from the contract that there was an unqualified promise and undertaking on the part of appellant and her assignor to pay the consideration for the lot, whether such payment should be accomplished through the maturity of coupons or otherwise. Its payment by means of the maturities was simply a method adopted for the convenience of appellant and her assignor, presumably, by their choice.

The facts alleged in the answer as amended do not afford such information as to the business methods of the Southern Mutual Investment Company as will enable us to say that its business was conducted after the manner of a lottery, and, in the absence of such information, we must presume that the contract between appellant and appellee was in no way made illegal by the manner in which the investment company conducted its business. Martin v. Richardson, 94 Ky. 183, 21 S. W. 1039, 14 Ky. Law Rep. 847, 19 L. R. A. 692, 42 Am. St. Rep. 353; Bibb, etc., v. Miller, etc., 11 Bush, 306. But if it were true that the investment company's manner of doing business constituted it a lottery, the fact that appellee was to be paid by means of its maturing coupons cannot invalidate the contract with reference to the sale of the lot; it being the duty of appellant to pay the balance of purchase money due thereon in some other way, if the insolvency of the investment company prevented her from doing so by means of the maturing coupons. So, in any event, the contract between appellant and appellee should be upheld in so far as it was not contrary to law. In other words, it is a well-known rule of law that where there are contained in the same instrument distinct engagements or covenants by which a party binds himself to do certain acts, some of which are legal and some illegal, the performance of those which are legal may be enforced, although the performance of those which are illegal may not. Brown's Adm'r v. Lankford's Adm'r, 3 Bibb, 497; Beach on Contracts, Sec. 1426; Parsons on Contracts (6th Ed.) p. 517.

It should be borne in mind that the contract in question was not one between appellant, or her assignor, and the investment company; nor is the investment company a party to this action, or in any way seeking to benefit from the contract. The action is simply one on the part of appellee to recover the balance of purchase money due on the lot and to enforce the lien retained therefor. The failure of the investment company, through insolvency, did not relieve appellant of the obligation imposed by the contract to pay the balance of purchase money. It merely destroyed the means by which she had expected to pay it, left it in part unpaid, and compelled her to resort to some other means of raising the money. So in no way can it be said that the failure of the investment company to continue the payment of maturing coupons prevented appellee from compelling by suit payment of the balance of purchase money due him upon the lot. It is clear, therefore, that appellant's plea that the investment company was a lottery did not constitute a valid defense to the action.

The record disclosing no error in the judgment, the same is affirmed.

CASE 88.—ACTION BY JOHN RAYMONDS' ADMINISTRATOR AGAINST THE LOUISVILLE RAILWAY CO.—December 14, 1909.

Louisville Ry. Co. v. Raymond's Adm'r

Appeal from Jefferson Circuit Court (Common Pleas Branch, Third Division).

MATT O'DOHERTY, Judge.

Judgment for plaintiff, defendant appeals.—Reversed.

1. Death—Action for Death—Statutory Cause of Action—New Cause of Action.—At common law, though an action to recover for pain and suffering of a person injured might be revived by his personal representative, still, where death resulted immediately, no action could be maintained therefor. Const. Sec. 241, provides that, when the death of a person shall result from an injury inflicted by a wrongful act, damages may be recovered therefor, the action until otherwise provided by law to be prosecuted by the personal representative of decedent. Ky. St. sec. 6 (Russell's St. sec. 11). passed in pursuance thereof, provides how the remedy shall go and to whom belonged. Held, that the Constitution and statute did not create a new cause of action distinct from that which accrued to decedent.

2. Election of Remedies—Rule at Common Law—Single Remedy for Wrong.—It is a rule of the common law to allow only one remedy for one wrong, though several different remedies may be provided.

3. Election of Remedies—By Administrator—Effect Upon Beneficiaries.—If an administrator should elect to sue upon the common-law right of action for injuries to his decedent, and it should be made to appear to the court on the settlement of his accounts that the death of decedent was due to the

injury the court would not permit his election to defeat the statute, and would treat the fund in his hand so recovered as belonging to those who would be its beneficiaries if he had sued under the statute.

4. Evidence—Secondary Evidence—Absence of Predicate—Physician's Death Certificate.—The statute does hot make a physicians death certificate evidence in judicial proceedings, and, where it was not shown that the physician had died, the certificate was inadmissible; his testimony being the best evidence.

FAIRLEIGH, STRAUS & FAIRLEIGH and HOWARD B. LEE for appellant.

POPHAM & WEBSTER and MORTON K. YONTS for appellee.

OPINION OF THE COURT BY JUDGE HOBSON—Reversing.

John Raymond was struck by a street car of the Louisville Railway Company on October 16, 1906. On November 24, 1906, he made a compromise with it by which he accepted $20 in full settlement of all claims which he had against it as a result of the accident. He died on May 19, 1907, and on May 1, 1908, this action was brought against the railway company by his personal representative to recover damages for the loss of his life; it being alleged that his death was the result of the injury he received, and that this was by reason of the negligence of the railway company. The company pleaded in bar of the action, among other things, the written settlement which it had made with the decedent. The circuit court sustained the plaintiff's demurrer to this paragraph of the answer, and, the case having been tried, there was a verdict and judgment in favor of the plaintiff for $3,500. The railway company appeals.

The first question arising upon the appeal is as to the propriety of the action of the court in sustaining the demurrer to that part of the answer pleading the settlement made with the deceased. In Eden v. Lexington, etc., R. R. Co., 14 B. Mon. 204, it was held by this court that, though an action to recover for pain and suffering of a person injured might be revived by his personal representative, still, where death resulted immediately, no action could be maintained for the loss of the life of a human being. To remedy this ruling, which was made in the year 1853, at the next session of the Legislature in the year 1854 (Act 1853-54, p. 175, c. 964), an act was passed which provided that, if the life of any person not in the employment of a railroad company should be lost by reason of its negligence, the personal representative might maintain an action and recover damages "in the same manner that the person himself might have done for any injury where death did not ensue."

By another section of the same act it was provided that, if the life of any person was lost by the willful neglect of another, then his personal representative should have the right to sue and recover damages for the loss of his life. See 2 Stanton's Rev. St. p. 510. Under this statute, the employes of a railway company were placed upon a different footing from other persons, and only railway companies were made liable to an action for death unless there was willful negligence. The statutes thus stood until the revision of 1873 (Gen. St. 1873, c. 57, Sec. 3), when the Legislature modified the section as to willful neglect by providing that "the widow, heir or personal representative of the deceased" might bring an action. Gen. St. 1888, c. 57, pp. 774, 777, Sec. 3. Under this amendment, it was held by the court that, where the decedent left no widow or children, there could be no recovery for his death under the willful neglect section. Henderson v. K. C. R. R. Co., 86 Ky. 389, 5

S. W. 875, 9 Ky. Law Rep. 625. So it was that rail-road companies were not liable for the death of their employes unless there was willful neglect, and the deceased left widow or children. Other corporations or persons were not liable at all except in case of willful neglect, and only then when the deceased left widow or children. Thus matters stood when the constitutional convention met in 1891.

To put all persons and corporations on the same footing, and to allow a recovery in all cases whether the deceased left widow or children or not, they adopted the following: "Whenever the death of a person shall result from an injury inflicted by negligence or wrongful act, then, in every such case, damages may be recovered for such death, from the corporations and persons so causing the same. Until otherwise provided by law, the action to recover such damages shall in all cases be prosecuted by the personal representative of the deceased person. The General Assembly may provide how the recovery shall go and to whom belong; and until such provision is made the same shall form part of the personal estate of the deceased person." Const. Sec. 241. At the first meeting of the General Assembly after the adoption of the Constitution the following provision was made by statute: "Whenever the death of a person shall result from an injury inflicted by negligence or wrongful act, then in every such case, damages may be recovered for such death from the person or persons, company or companies, corporation or corporations, their agents or servants, causing the same, and when the act is willful or the negligence is gross, punitive damages may be recovered, and the action to recover such damages shall be prosecuted by the personal representative of the deceased.

The amount recovered, less funeral expenses and the cost of administration, and such costs about the recovery, including attorney's fees, as are not included in the recovery from the defendant, shall be for the benefit of and go to the kindred of the deceased in the following order, viz.: (1) .If the deceased leaves a widow or husband, and no children or their descendants, then the whole to such widow or husband. (2) If the deceased leaves either a widow and children or a husband and children, then one-half to such widow or husband and the other one-half to the children of the deceased. (3) If the deceased leaves a child or children, but no widow or husband, the whole to such child or children. If the deceased leaves no widow, husband or child, then such recovery shall pass to the mother and father of deceased, one moiety each, if both be living; if the mother be dead and the father be living, the whole thereof shall pass to the father; and if the father be dead and the mother be living, the whole thereof shall go to the mother; and if both father and mother be dead, then the whole of the recovery shall become a part of the personal estate of the deceased; and after the payment of his debts, the remainder, if any, shall pass to his kindred more remote than those above named, as is directed by the general law on descent and distribution." Ky. St. Sec. 6 (Russell's St. Sec. 11).

The decision of this court in the case of Eden v.· Lexington, etc., R. R. Co., followed a like decision in the courts of England. To meet that decision the English Parliament passed what is known as "Lord Campbell's act" in 1846, which was more or less followed in our act of 1854, and by like acts in other states both before and since. The purpose of Lord Campbell's act and the various acts in this country following it was to do away with the common-law principle that a civil action could not be maintained to recover damages for the death of a human being. It was steadily maintained by this court under the acts in force previous to the adoption of the present Constitution that, if a person was injured and did not die immediately, an action might be maintained after his death by his personal representative upon the cause of action which accrued to him at the time of his injury, and in point of fact many actions were maintained by personal representatives in this way where there could be no recovery for damages because the decedent left no widow or children, or where for other reasons a recovery could not be had under the statute for his death. But, while it was steadily maintained that the personal representative might sue upon the common-law cause of action which had accrued to the decedent if he survived the injury for a time, it was steadily maintained that he could not sue upon this cause of action, and at the same time sue under the statute to recover for the death of his · decedent.

Both before the adoption of the Constitution and since, it has been held that in such a case the personal representative must elect whether he will sue upon the common-law cause of action which accrued to the decedent or upon the cause of action accruing to him under the statute. See Hansford v. Payne, 11 Bush, 285; Conner v. Paul, 12 Bush, 144; Donahue v. Drexler, 82 Ky. 157, 56 Am. Rep. 886; Hackett v. Louisville, etc., R. R. Co., 95 Ky. 236, 24 S. W. 871, 15 Ky. Law Rep. 612; L. & N. R. R. Co. v. McElwain, 98 Ky. 700, 34 S. W. 236, 18 Ky. Law Rep. 379, 34 L. R. A. 788, 56 Am. St. Rep. 385; O. & N. R. R. Co. v. Barclay, 102 Ky. 16, 43 S. W. 177, 19 Ky. Law Rep. 997. In

Lewis v. Taylor Coal Company, 112 Ky. 851, 66 S. W. 1045, 23 Ky. Law Rep. 2218, 57 L. R. A. 447, the court, reviewing its previous decisions on the subject, said: "At common law the right of action for the injury to the person abated on the death of the party injured. Under Ky. St. Sec. 10 (section 2), the cause of action for personal injury, causing physical and mental suffering, does not abate on the death of the injured person, except actions for assault, slander, and criminal conversation, and so much of the action for criminal conversation as is intended to recover for personal injury. These questions are reviewed by this court in Railroad Company v. McElwain, 98 Ky. 700, 34 S. W. 236, 18 Ky. Law Rep. 379, 34 L. R. A. 788, 56 Am. St. Rep. 385. So, under the principles of the common law, if appellee had, through its agent, inflicted the injury which resulted in physical pain and mental suffering and death, neither cause of action would have survived.

This court has held that the cause of action for damages resulting in death cannot be joined with the cause of action for physical pain and mental suffering; that a recovery for one bars an action for the other." In the subsequent case of L. & N. R. R. Co. v. Simrall, 104 S. W. 1199, 32 Ky. Law Rep. 240, the court, responding to the petition for rehearing, said: "Nothing in the opinion was intended as an intimation that there could be two actions maintained for a single wrong—one to recover for pain, suffering, etc., and another for the death of the person injured where he afterwards died. It has been often held that two such actions cannot be maintained for one wrong—the personal injury." It was pointed out by this court in Conner v. Paul, and in Donahue v. Drexler, that the statute allowing a recovery in the case of death was only intended to enlarge the remedy and to allow a recovery when, under the facts, the decedent might have recovered if he had not died. It was accordingly held under that statute, and has been held under the present statute, that contributory negligence on the part of the decedent bars a recovery. Passamaneck v. Louisville R. R. Co., 98 Ky. 195, 32 S. W. 620, 17 Ky. Law Rep. 763; Clarke v. L. & N. R. R. Co., 101 Ky. 34, 39 S. W. 840, 18 Ky. Law Rep. 1082, 36 L. R. A. 123; Toner v. South Covington, etc., R. R. Co., 109 Ky. 41, 58 S. W. 439, 22 Ky. Law Rep. 564. There can be no substantial distinction between acts done by the decedent at the time of the injury or after the injury as affecting the right of his personal representative to recover where such acts on his part would bar him from recovering.

The rule that a personal representative cannot sue upon both causes of action is based upon the ground that the defendant committed a single wrong, the negligence or wrongful act which caused the injury, and that, while the law gives two remedies for the wrong, it was not contemplated that two recoveries should be had for one wrong. The plain purpose of the act of 1854 was simply to do away with the common-law holding that no recovery could be had when death resulted immediately. The cause of action by that act was vested in the personal representative, and it was manifestly intended only to give him a remedy in cases where before there had been no remedy. The debates of the Constitutional Convention show that their purpose was to remove the inequalities which existed under the statutes then in force. They put actions for death from negligence or wrongful act on the same plane, and they manifestly did not intend to interfere in any way with the common-law right

of action which accrued to the person injured where
he survived the injury, and died subsequently. They
used no words showing an intention, however, to allow
two actions to be maintained by the personal representative for one wrong, and we think it manifest
that, if there had been no further legislation, it would
hardly be maintained that under the Constitution two
actions might be maintained by the personal representative, one to recover for pain and suffering, etc.,
and the other for the death of the decedent.

But manifestly the statute was only intended to
carry into effect the provisions of the Constitution;
and, while it provides how a recovery shall go in an
action to recover for death from negligence or wrongful act, this manifestly was not to create a right of
action in the beneficiaries, but only to protect the recovery for their benefit from the claim of others.
When the Legislature passed this statute, this court
had several times held that the personal representative could not sue upon both causes of action, and if
the Legislature had contemplated changing that rule,
and allowing two actions to be maintained for one injury, it must be presumed it would have clearly so
declared; for it has long been a rule of the common
law to allow only one recovery for one wrong, although several different remedies may be provided.
If notwithstanding his settlement the representative
of the decedent may recover in this action, he might
equally recover if the decedent had brought a suit
and recovered a large sum for his injury before his
death. The amount of the settlement is not material
except as the amount paid may throw light on the
good faith of the settlement, and that question is not
now here, as the court sustained a demurrer to the
plea.

The precise question we have before us was before the English court in Reed v. Great Eastern R. R. Co., 3 Q. B. 555. The court among other things said: "The intention of the statute is, not to make the wrongdoer pay damages twice for the same wrongful act, but to enable the representatives of the person injured to recover in a case where the maxim 'Actio personalis moritur cum persona' would have applied. It only points to a case where the party injured has not recovered compensation against the wrongdoer. It is true that section 2 provides a different mode of assessing the damages, but that does not give a fresh cause of action." A like conclusion was reached by the Supreme Court of South Carolina in Price v. Railroad Co., 33 S. C. 556, 12 S. E. 413, 26 Am. St. Rep. 700. The precise question before us was also before the Supreme Court of Vermont under statutes very similar to ours in Legg v. Britton, 64 Vt. 652, 24 Atl. 1016; and it was there held that a recovery on the cause of action which accrued to the decedent was a bar to an action to recover for his death. To the same effect, see Hecht v. O. M. R. R. Co., 132 Ind. 507, 32 N. E. 302; Dibble v. N. Y., etc., R. R. Co., 25 Barb. (N. Y.) 183; Lubrano v. Atlantic Mills, 19 R. I. 129, 32 Atl. 205, 34 L. R. A. 797; Littlewood v. N. Y., 89 N. Y. 24, 42 Am. Rep. 271; Hill v. Penn. R. R. Co., 178 Pa. 223, 35 Atl. 997, 35 L. R. A. 196, 56 Am. St. Rep. 754; So, Bell Tel. Co. v. Cassin, 111 Ga. 575, 36 S. E. 881, 50 L. R. A. 694; Hughes v. Auburn, 161 N. Y. 96, 55 N. E. 389, 46 L. R. A. 636. See, also, note to L. & N. R. R. Co. v. McElwain, 34 L. R. A. 788. The authorities on the subject are consistent and uniform. 13 Cyc. 325; Cooley on Torts, 263; Shearman & Redfield on Negligence, Sec. 140.

In 6 Thompson on Negligence, Sec. 7028, the rule is thus stated: "The right of action in the personal representatives it has been held depends, not only upon the character of the act from which death ensued, but also upon the condition of the decedent's claim at the time of his death. If the claim was in such a shape that he could not then have enforced it had death not ensued, the statute gives the executors no right of action, and creates no liability whatever on the part of the person inflicting the injury. Therefore, where in an action by the personal representative of a person to recover damages for his death, caused by the wrongful act of the defendants, it was shown that the defendants settled with the deceased in his lifetime, and paid him the amount of his claim on account of the injury, it was held that this would bar the plaintiff's action. Such a release is invalid if secured by unfair means.'

We have not been referred to any contrary authorities outside of this state. The cases in this state which are relied on as contrary to the rule prevailing elsewhere do not sustain that conclusion. The case of Donahue v. Drexler, which is sometimes cited as an authority to the contrary, was based on an entirely different statute. Merrill v. Puckett, 93 S. W. 912, 29 Ky. Law Rep. 595. In Meyer v. Zoll, 119 Ky. 480, 84 S. W. 543, it was held that a settlement by a parent for an injury to his child would not bar an action by the personal representative of the child. But in that case two actions lay for the injury to the child, one by the parent and one by the child. The action by the parent had been settled; but there had been no action brought by the child, and no settlement made of the right of action existing in his favor. In Sturges v. Sturges, 126 Ky. 80, 102 S. W. 884, 31 Ky. Law Rep.

537, 12 L. R. A. (N. S.) 1014, it was held that the fund arising from a recovery for the death of the decedent under the statute must pass as directed by the statute, and could not be controlled by his will. The power to make a will is regulated by the statute, and, the statute having also regulated how this fund should pass, he could not make a will which would prevent the application of the statute. There was nothing in either of these cases to bring before the court the question here presented, and neither of them was intended to conflict with the previous cases.

We therefore conclude that the circuit court erred in sustaining the demurrer to this paragraph of the answer. Ordinarily, unless the decedent is insolvent, the beneficiaries of the recovery will be the same whether the administrator sues upon the common-law right of action which accrued to the decedent or upon the statutory right of action to recover for his death, and so no confusion will arise by his election to sue upon the former rather than upon the latter. But, if he should elect to sue upon the common-law right of action, and it should be made to appear to the court on the settlement of his accounts that the death of the decedent was due to the injury, the court would not permit his election to defeat the statute, and would treat the fund in his hands so recovered as belonging to those who would be its beneficiaries if he had sued under the statutes. The defendant offered in evidence a copy of the death certificate made by the attending physician, Dr. Yandall Roberts, showing the cause of the death of the decedent. It showed that he died of tuberculosis.

The court properly refused to allow the certificate to be read in evidence; it not appearing that Dr. Roberts is dead. If he were dead, a different question would be presented. While the statute requires the physician to give the death certificate, there is nothing in the statute making the certificate evidence in judicial proceedings, and it stands entirely on a different plane from the return of an officer made pursuant to law under his official oath. The law requires the best evidence, and the best evidence is the testimony of Dr. Roberts, if living. There was sufficient evidence to take the case to the jury, and we cannot disturb the verdict of the jury on the ground that it is palpably against the evidence.

On another trial of the case the court will give to the jury instruction No. 4, approved by this court in Goldstein v. Louisville R. R. Co., 115 S. W. 195, with the modification there suggested.

Judgment reversed and cause remanded for further proceedings consistent herewith.

Nunn, C. J., dissenting.

CASE 89.—ACTION BY CARTER HELTON AND ANOTHER
AGAINST A. J. ASHER.—December 7, 1909.

Helton, &c. v. Asher

Appeal from Bell Circuit Court.

M. J. Moss, Circuit Judge.

Judgment for defendant, plaintiffs appeal.—Re-versed.

1. Covenants — Covenants Against Incumbrances — Breach —
    Measure of Damages.—The measure of damages for breach
    of covenant against incumbrances by the existence of an ease-
    ment on the land is the diminution in the value of the premis-
    es thereby, and, where it has been extinguished, the measure
    of damages is the injury sustained between the date of the
    deed and the extinguishment, together with the expenses of
    such extinguishment.

2. Evidence—Admissibility—Damages—Opinions.—In an action
    for breach of a covenant against incumbrances by the exist-
    ence of an éasement on the land, witnesses testifying to the
    damages must state the difference in value of the premises
    with and without the easement, and should not be permitted
    to state that the property is damaged in a certain sum.

3   Covenants—Warranty—Breach—Damages.—Where the pur-
    chaser has lost the entire property conveyed, the vendor is
    liable on his warranty, in addition to the cost for the con-
    sideration paid him with interest, but, where only part of the
    property conveyed has been lost. he is liable. in addition to
    the cost only for such proportionate part of the consideration
    paid him as the part lost bears to the whole property.

4   Covenants—Warranty—Breach—Damages.—A purchaser, who
    resisted an action by a third person to establish a tramroad
    through the land, resulting in a decree establishing the same
    at a point where it damaged the land much less than it
    would be damaged by the location demanded by the third per-
    son, can recover, on the vendor's covenant against incum-
    brances, the legal cost of the action including a reasonable
    attorney's fee, though the vendor told the purchaser not to
    contest the action.

5. Covenants—Knowledge of Defects.—That either or both of
    the parties knew at the time of the conveyance that the gran-
    tor had no title in part or in whole does not affect the right
    to recover for breach of a covenant and knowledge by the
    purchaser of the existence of an incumbrance on the land
    does not prevent him from recovering damages. where he pro-
    tects himself by proper convenants in the deed.
6. Evidence—Parol Evidence—Varying Covenants in Deeds.—
    Parol evidence is not admissible to vary a covenant in a
    deed, but it is admissible to show fraud or mutual mistake, or
    explain a patent ambiguity.
7. Covenants—Breach.—The rule that a covenant against incum-
    brances does not embrace an entry by the state in exercise
    of the right of eminent domain, and that a purchaser must
    be held to know of the existence of a public highway on the
    land at the date of the purchase and to have made his bar-
    gain with the knowledge of the inconvenience resulting from
    it. does not apply to a private passway over the land, and
    that the purchaser knew thereof when he purchased does not
    prevent him from recovering damages, where he protects
    himself by covenant against incumbrances.

A. G. PATTERSON and N. R. PATTERSON for appellants.

N. J. WELLER for appellee.

OPINION OF THE COURT BY JUDGE HOBSON—Reversing.

On February 2, 1902, A. J. Asher conveyed by deed
of general warranty to Carlo Helton a tract of eight
acres of land lying in Bell county.   On April 26, 1906,
Carlo Helton conveyed the land by deed of general
warranty to Carter and Farmer Helton, who built
upon it a storehouse, residence, and other buildings.
Previous to the sale to Carlo Helton, Asher had
granted to Taylor and Crate a right of way over the
eight acres for a tramroad to get out logs to market.
After the purchase of the land by Carter and Farmer
Helton, and after they had settled upon it, Taylor and
Crate proposed to run the tramroad across it.   This
they resisted.   Thereupon Taylor and Crate brought

a suit against them, and obtained in the circuit court an injunction restraining them from interfering with the construction of the tramroad over the route proposed by them. The Heltons notified Asher of the suit when it was brought, and, when the injunction was obtained, they brought the case before a judge of this court on a motion to dissolve the injunction. On the hearing of that motion, it was determined that the tramroad should not be built on the route selected by Taylor and Crate, but on another route at a part of the premises, where it would be less injurious to them.

On the return of the case to the circuit court, a final judgment was entered as indicated by the judge of this court. Thereupon the Heltons brought this suit against Asher on the covenant of warranty to recover damages for the taking of the easement over the land by Taylor and Crate, and for their cost in the injunction suit. Asher filed an answer to the petition, in which he denied the plaintiff's allegations as to the damages sustained, and pleaded in another paragraph that, when he sold the land to Carter Helton, he informed him of the easement which had been granted to Taylor and Crate, and Carter Helton agreed to take the land subject to the easement. He also alleged that Carter and Farmer Helton when they purchased from Carlo Helton had like notice. The court sustained a demurrer to this paragraph of the answer. The case coming on for trial before a jury, Asher testified that, when the suit was brought by Taylor and Crate, the Heltons came to him about it, and he told them that there was no use in defending the suit, that Taylor and Crate were bound to win it, and that they should just let the judgment go, that they answered that they were going to fight the suit

vol. 135—48

to the bitter end, as they had a good man behind them. At the conclusion of the evidence, the court allowed Asher to file an amended answer to conform to this proof, in which he pleaded these facts in bar of any recovery of the cost incurred in the former action.

The court then gave the jury these instructions:

"No. 1. The jury will find for the plaintiffs the difference, if any, as shown by the evidence, between the market value of the eight acres of ground mentioned in the evidence before the time of the laying of the tramroad thereon by Taylor and Crate and the market value of said land after the laying of said tramroad, not to exceed the sum of $300.

"No. 2. If the jury believe from the evidence that the plaintiffs or either of them expended money in resisting the claim and right of Taylor and Crate to lay said tramroad over said land and using same asserted by said Taylor and Crate in the Bell circuit court and elsewhere in the courts, and further believe from the evidence that it was necessary on the part of the plaintiffs to expend said money for said purpose, and further believe from the evidence that the amount so expended by said plaintiffs in resisting the claim of said Taylor and Crate was reasonable, then the jury will find for the plaintiffs the reasonable amount so expended by them not to exceed the sum of $300, unless the jury further believe from the evidence that the defendant Asher, before said sum of money was expended by plaintiffs, if any, requested said plaintiffs or either of them not to expend said money in the defense of said claim, and offered to pay the plaintiffs or either of them the damage they would sustain by the laying of the said tramroad over the said land and using same in which event they will find for the defendant on this account."

The jury found a verdict for the defendant, and, the court having entered a judgment dismissing the plaintiffs' petition, they appeal.

The first instruction is not strictly accurate. The rule on the subject is thus stated in 11 Cyc. 1166: "The diminution in the value of the premises resulting from the existence of an easement thereon is as a rule the measure of damages in an action for the breach of the covenant against incumbrances. Where the easement has been extinguished, the measure of damages is the injury sustained between the date of the deed and the removal of the incumbrance, together with the expenses incident to such removal." The witnesses testifying as to the amount of damages should be required to state what the difference in value of the premises is with and without the easement as established by the court considering the time for which it exists, and they should not be allowed to state generally that the property is damaged in a certain sum by reason of the easement. It is manifest from the proof that the easement as established does depreciate the value of the property at least to some extent. The verdict for the defendant as to this is palpably against the evidence. Where the vendee has lost the entire property conveyed, the vendor is liable on his warranty in addition to the cost for the consideration paid him with interest, but, where only part of the property conveyed has been lost, he is liable in addition to the cost only for such proportionate part of the consideration paid him as the part lost bears to the entire property. Cox v. Strode, 2 Bibb, 275, 5 Am. Dec. 603; Hunt v. Orwig, 17 B. Mon. 85, 66 Am. Dec. 144; Robertson v. Lemon, 2 Bush, 304. On another trial the court will so modify instructions as to express this.

The second instruction should not have been given. If the Heltons had not defended the suit, the tramroad would have been constructed across the property in such a way as to seriously damage them. By resisting the action they secured its establishment at a point where it damages the premises very much less. The damages which they may recover on account of the taking of the land for the tramroad must be measured by the location as it was in fact made by the court, and this was the result of their defending the suit, and bringing the matter before a judge of this court for decision. Asher gets the benefit of their exertions in the decreased damages which he must pay on account of the injury to the property; and the fact that they succeeded in materially modifying the injunction and in defeating the location claimed by Taylor and Crate is conclusive that their resistance was both reasonable and necessary. On the facts shown, the court under the evidence should have told the jury to find for the plaintiffs their legal cost incurred in that action as taxed by the clerk, including a reasonable attorney's fee to their attorney. The fact that Asher told them not to defend the suit and to let the tramroad go through, in no way affects their right to recover against him their cost in the action. They had a right to protect themselves as well as they could from Taylor and Crate, and then to look to Asher for redress on his warranty. We do not mean to say that they could make a capricious defense at his expense, but they had the right to use all reasonable means for their protection, and the result of the case shows that what they did was reasonable. If Asher had wished to stop the litigation and protect himself, he should have tendered to the Heltons the amount of damages he was willing to pay. They could then have known with some intelligence what course to pursue.

The court did not err in sustaining the demurrer to so much of Asher's answer as pleaded that Carlo Helton bought the land with notice of the easement theretofore granted to Taylor and Crate. The writing is the best evidence of the contract between the parties in the absence of fraud or mistake. The rule is thus stated in 11 Cyc. 1066: "The fact that either or both of the parties knew at the time of conveyance that the grantor had no title in a part or in the whole of the land does not affect the right of recovery for a breach of covenant. Knowledge on the part of the purchaser of the existence of an incumbrance on the land will not prevent him from recovering damages on account of it, where he protects himself by proper covenants in his deed. In some jurisdictions, however, it is held that where the incumbrance does not affect the title, but only the physical condition of the property, as in the case of an open notorious easement, of which it is the servient tenement, the purchaser must be presumed to have seen it, and to have fixed his price with reference to the actual condition of the land at the time, and that such incumbrance is no breach of the covenant; and the same is true of easements and servitudes imposed by law."

Again, on page 1155, it is said: "Parol or extrinsic evidence is not admissible to contradict, vary, or materially affect a covenant, although it may be received to show fraud or mutual mistake in the original execution of the instrument, or to explain a patent ambiguity." In Bird v. Bank of Williamstown, 13 S. W. 430, 11 Ky. Law Rep. 868, the railroad ran across the land at the time of the purchase, and the company

had possession of its right of way.   In Butt v. Riffe,
78 Ky. 354, the county highway ran over the land at
the time of the purchase and the public had possession
of it.   These cases fall within the exception referred
to in the authorities quoted.   In Butt v. Riffe the
court said: "Such covenants have never been held to
embrace an entry by the state in the exercise of the
light to eminent domain.   It is no eviction for which
the grantor can be made liable when the land is taken
for public use; and the purchaser, when a public highway is on the land at the date of his purchase, must
be held to know of its existence, and to have made
his bargain with a knowledge of the inconvenience
resulting from it."   But it was further there held
that as to a private passway the rule was different.
Sanders v. Rowe, 48 S. W. 1083, 20 Ky. Law Rep.
1082, rests upon the ground of fraud or mistake.

    Judgment reversed, and cause remanded for a new
trial.

CASE 90.—ACTION BY A. A. VAN BUREN AGAINST THE
WEISSINGER TOBACCO COMPANY TO RESCIND
CONTRACT.—December 17, 1909.

Weissinger Tobacco Co. v. Van Buren

Appeal from Jefferson Circuit Court (Chancery
Branch, Second Division).

SAMUEL B. KIRBY, Judge.

Judgment for plaintiff, defendant appeals.—Affirmed.

1. Corporations—Officers—Authority of President.—Where the
president of a corporation was, under the by-laws, the chief
executive officer and head of the company, with general control of its business, and with knowledge of the other directors,
was engaged in placing treasury stock, he was authorized to
represent the corporation in such matters, and any fraudulent
representation he made while trying to place the stock were
within the scope of his employment and bound the corporation.

2. Corporations—Stockholders' Action — Issue. — In an action
against a corporation to rescind subscription to stock for
fraudulent representations, where the only defenses made
were a general denial and an offer to issue the shares of
stock subscribed for, and the other stockholders were not
parties, the corporation could not raise the defense that plaintiff could not have his subscription canceled and recover from
the corporation the full amount paid by him, because the other
stockholders who also subscribed and paid for stock were
misled in the same way.

3. Corporations—Capital Stock—Subscriptions Induced by Fraud
—Remedy of Subscriber.—Where plaintiff was induced to subscribe to corporate stock on the fraudulent representation
of the president, with full authority to act, that $70,000
had been paid for the plant which the corporation had purchased and was to operate, while in fact only $50,000 had
been paid for it, and the stock was never issued to the sub-

scriber, he could have the contract of subscription rescinded and recover the subscription price paid therefor.

BULLITT & BULLITT for appellant.

WEHLE & WEHLE, A. S. BRANDEIS and LOUIS B. WEHLE for appellee.

OPINION OF THE COURT BY WM. ROGERS CLAY, COMMISSIONER—Affirming.

Charging that he was induced to purchase 20 shares of the capital stock of the Weissinger Tobacco Company by the fraudulent representations of its authorized agent, appellee, A. A. Van Buren, instituted this action against appellant, Weissinger Tobacco Company, to rescind the contract of subscription and to recover the sum of $2,000 which he paid for said stock, together with interest thereon from the date of payment. The court below gave judgment in favor of appellee, and the Weissinger Tobacco Company appeals.

In 1895 the Green River Tobacco Company owned a plant at Maysville, Ky., which it desired to sell. Henry Y. Weissinger, who had been connected with that company, persuaded several New York men to put in $50,000 for the purpose of buying the plant, with the understanding that he (Weissinger) would furnish $20,000 so as to raise the sum of $70,000, which sum he represented to be the purchase price of the plant. The Weissinger Tobacco Company was then formed. For the purpose of organizing this company, the New York capitalists subscribed for 500 shares, Henry Y. Weissinger for 194 shares, and William Marshall Bullitt and L. H. McHenry for 3 shares each. The subscription by Bullitt and McHenry were made in order to permit them to qualify as directors; they being selected for the purpose of representing the interests of the eastern subscribers. Thus it will be seen that 700 shares of stock were subscribed for in all. The Green River Tobacco Company, by deed dated July 1, 1905, conveyed the Maysville plant to the Weissinger Tobacco Company. The consideration expressed in the deed was $70,000 cash, and the receipt of that sum was acknowledged.

On July 11, 1905, the first meeting of the board of directors was held. Henry Y. Weissinger was elected president, and William Marshall Bullitt secretary-treasurer. The acquisition of the Green River plant was ratified. Weissinger then began to solicit subscriptions for the 300 shares of stock which remained in the treasury of the company. Appellee, A. A. Van Buren, was a former resident of Louisville, but for several years had been residing part of the time in Boston and the remainder of the time in Florida. He became acquainted with Weissinger while living in Kentucky. On August 10, 1905, he received a letter from Weissinger soliciting a subscription for some of the treasury stock of the Weissinger Tobacco Company. In this letter Weissinger used the following language: "You will observe this property was reported on by two auditors, and there is no question as to its value. We have paid $70,000.00 for the Green River Tobacco Company, and have organized the Weissinger Tobacco Company." Accompanying this letter was a prospectus purporting to furnish information with reference to the organization of the new company, and giving the amount of its capital stock, the value of its assets, etc. This prospectus contains the following statement: "Capital stock to be $100,000.00 at the par value of $100.00 per share. $70,000.00 has been subscribed by eastern capitalists, and the property of the Green River Tobacco Company has been purchased with the $70,000.00, leaving a balance of $30,000.00 unsold, which will represent the cash working capital.'' On the second page of the prospectus, under the heading, ''Distribution of Capital,'' there is this line: ''Cash paid for the plant, $70,000.00.''

From the foregoing it will be seen that Weissinger represented to appellee that stock worth $70,000 had been subscribed for, and that $70,000 had been paid in cash by the Weissinger Tobacco Company for the plant of the Green River Tobacco Company. As a matter of fact, only $50,000 was paid for the plant, and the record does not disclose that any further sum was ever paid. It does appear, however, that Weissinger represented to Bullitt that he (Weissinger) was to pay $20,000 additional to the Green River Tobacco Company. It was afterwards ascertained by the members of the directory that Weissinger was only expecting to pay $12,500 for the plant, and in return for that was proposing to get $20,000 in stock of the Weissinger Tobacco Company. In other words, he was to get a commission of $7,500, and the real purchase price of the property was $62,500, instead of $70,000. As a matter of fact, none of the $20,000 was ever paid. Therefore, when Weissinger represented to appellee that $70,000 had been paid for the plant, $50,000 was all that had been actually paid, and was all that was ever paid. On the faith of the letter and prospectus sent to him, appellee agreed to and did subscribe for $2,000 worth of stock. He thereupon mailed to Weissinger a check for that amount, payable to the order of Henry Y. Weissinger, president. Accompanying the check was a statement to the effect that he was sending the check to cover his subscription for 20 shares of treasury stock in the

Weissinger Tobacco Company. Appellee subsequently wrote several letters and sent some telegrams demanding his stock certificate. Receiving no satisfactory answer, he then communicated with his attorney, who promptly took steps to have the contract of subscription rescinded.

The twelfth by-law of appellant company provides that the president shall be the chief executive officer and head of the company, and shall have the general control and management of its business and affairs, subject, however, to the right of the directors to delegate any specific power to any other officer or officers of the company. Weissinger was not only a director, but president, of the company. He not only had the authority given in the above by-law, but he was engaged, with the knowledge and consent of the other directors, in placing the treasury stock. It is due to the other directors, Bullitt and McHenry, to say that they had no knowledge of the fraudulent representations made by Weissinger, and when they ascertained that Weissinger was not only deceiving them, but others, they immediately took steps to remove him from the position he occupied. However, as Weissinger was president of the company, and had general control and management of its business and affairs, and as he, with knowledge of the other directors, was engaged in placing the treasury stock, he was authorized to represent the corporation in the matters thus intrusted to him, and any fraudulent representations he made to appellee while trying to place the stock in question were necessarily made within the scope of his employment and bound the corporation which he represented. P. C. & St. L. R. R. Co. v. Woolley, 12 Bush, 451; Toll Bridge Co. v. Betsworth, 30 Conn.

380; Clark & Marshall on Corporations, Sections 717, 721; Cook on Corporations, Sec. 726.

While it does not appear that the Weissinger Tobacco Company received the benefit of the $2,000 paid for the stock subscribed for by appellee, yet the money was paid to the president of the corporation, who was authorized to manage its business and to sell its stock. It follows that the money paid by appellee was a payment direct to the corporation. Martin & Co. v. Logan, 99 S. W. 648, 30 Ky. Law Rep. 799. According to the doctrine now firmly established, there are several remedies open to a subscriber induced to subscribe by fraud. Among such remedies is the right to have set aside the subscription contract and recover the payments made on such subscription. Cook on Corporations, Sec. 152; Prewitt, Trustee, v. Trimble, 92 Ky. 176, 17 S. W. 356, 36 Am. St. Rep. 586. But it is insisted by counsel for appellant that the sole question involved on this appeal is whether or not one stockholder, having been induced to enter into an improvident subscription for stock, is entitled to have his contract of subscription canceled and to recover from the corporation the full amount paid by him, regardless of the other stockholders who also subscribed and paid for stock and were misled in the same way as appellee.

This question, however, was not raised in the record. The other stockholders are not parties to the action. No such defense was made by them, or for them by the Weissinger Tobacco Company. The only defenses made were a general denial and an offer to issue the 20 shares of stock. If the corporation had desired to depend upon the ground set forth in the brief of counsel for appellant, it should have done so by a pleading showing that all the stockholders were deceived, and were therefore in the same predicament. While it may be true that the eastern stockholders were also deceived by Weissinger, yet, so far as the record before us shows, they may have known that only $50,000 was, as a matter of fact, to be paid for the plant. None of those stockholders testified in this case. What would have been the rights of all the stockholders had the corporation, for them, or the stockholders, themselves, made the defense in this action that they were all deceived in the same manner as appellee, and therefore stood upon a plane of perfect equality with appellee, we deem it unnecessary to decide. No such question is presented in the record. The only question before us is the right of appellee, who was induced by the fraudulent representations of appellant's authorized agent to purchase the stock in question, and to whom, as a matter of fact, the stock was never issued, to have the contract of subscription rescinded and to recover the subscription price. Upon the facts before us, there can be no doubt of appellee's right to recover.

For the reasons given, the judgment is affirmed.

CASE 91.—ACTION BY C. BOTHWELL AGAINST H. F. CORUM.
—December 9, 1909.

Bothwell v. Corum

Appeal from Knox Circuit Court.

H. C. FAULKNER, Circuit Judge.

Judgment for plaintiff, defendant appeals.—Reversed.

1. Bills and Notes.—Drafts—"Negotiable Instrument."—An instrument in writing, signed by the drawer and containing an unconditional order to pay a certain sum in money at a fixed future date to the order of a specified person, and addressed to a drawee, named therein, was a "negotiable instrument."

2. Bills and Notes—Indorsement—"Notice" of Equity.—To constitute notice of an infirmity in a negotiable bill indorsed before maturity, the indorsee must have actual knowledge of the infirmity or defect, or knowledge of such facts that his action in taking the instrument amounts to bad faith, as provided by Ky. St. Sec. 3720b, subsec. 56 (Russell's St. Sec. 1925).

3. Bills and Notes—Drafts—Transfer—Bona Fide Purchaser.—Where there was nothing on the face of certain drafts transferred to plaintiff before maturity to indicate knowledge of any infirmity in the instruments or the title of the indorser, indicating bad faith of the indorsee in taking them, and the indorsements were regular, the drafts being transferred to the indorsee before maturity in consideration of his payment of 90 per cent. of their face, he was a holder in due course, and was not subject to any defense available as between the drawer and the payee, as provided in Ky. St. Sec. 3720b, subsec. 57 (Russell's St. Sec. 1926).

4. Bills and Notes—Action by Indorsee—Pleading.—Where an indorsee for value before maturity denied any knowledge or notice of the fraud relied on by defendant to defeat the action, it was not material that the indorsee's denial that the instruments were obtained by fraud was insufficient.

JAMES M. GILBERT for appellant.

B. B. GOLDEN for appellee.

OPINION OF THE COURT BY WM. ROGERS CLAY, COM-
MISSIONER—Reversing.

On February 24, 1906, the American Jobbing Association, by its manager, S. G. Dunley, drew six drafts
on appellee, H. F. Corum, of Artemus, Ky., each for
the sum of $52.58 and payable to the order of the
American Jobbing Association, in four, six, eight,
ten, twelve, and fourteen months after date. Each
of these drafts was accepted by Corum. Thereafter,
and before the maturity of the drafts, the American
Jobbing Association sold them to appellant, C. Bothwell. Each draft was indorsed by the American
Jobbing Association and delivered to appellant. Appellant paid 90 cents on the dollar for each draft.
Upon the maturity of the first three drafts, appellant
instituted this action against appellee to recover
thereon. During the pendency of the action, the
other three drafts matured and were set up in an
amended petition. Appellee defended on the ground
that the drafts were procured by fraud, and that appellant purchased same with notice thereof. The
jury returned a verdict in favor of appellee. From
the judgment based thereon, this appeal is prosecuted.

Appellant contends that the trial court erred in
refusing to award him a peremptory instruction.

The evidence, in brief, is as follows: Appellee, H. F.
Corum, testified that some time in February, 1906, a
salesman by the name of T. M. Morris came to his
store for the purpose of inducing him to purchase a
lot of jewelry. The salesman told appellee that he
could pay for the jewelry along every two or three
months, and at the end of twelve months they would
send a man and take up the jewelry left on hand—
that is, the balance of the unsold goods—and give

him credit for it. The firm then shipped the jewelry, and a few days thereafter the drafts came. At first, appellee refused to sign the drafts, but a man by the name of Dooley came and persuaded him to sign them. Dooley made the same representations to him as the other salesman; that is, that appellee could pay for the jewelry as long as he sold it, and at the end of 12 months they would send a man to take it up, and, if appellee owed them anything at the end of that time, he was to pay them what he owed, and they would give him credit for the balance. He then signed the drafts with that understanding. Had it not been for that understanding, he would not have signed them.

After that, appellee sold some of the jewelry, and found that it did not give satisfaction. The jewelry was not as represented by the agent. He thereupon wrote the American Jobbing Association that he desired to return the jewelry and pay them for that which he had sold. He received no answer to his letter. Upon cross-examination appellee testified as follows: "Q. You don't undertake to say when this paper was transferred to Bothwell, the plaintiff in this action? A. No, sir. Q. You don't undertake to tell the jury what amount Bothwell paid for this paper, do you? A. I don't know what he paid for it. Q. You don't undertake to tell the jury anything about Bothwell knowing anything about the transaction between you and this company, do you? A. No, sir; I don't. Q. So, then, you can't say to the jury that the transaction between him and this American Jobbing Association wasn't a genuine transaction? A. No, sir." Appellee further testified that he accepted the instruments sued on, that he was then 21 years of age, and had a fairly good common-school education.

Appellant testified that he was 31 years of age. He resided in Iowa City, Iowa, and was engaged in the loan and brokerage business, and was engaged in that business during February, 1906. The American Jobbing Association was a partnership. It was owned by W. F. Main. Appellant was in no wise interested in the American Jobbing Association, nor was he related, directly or indirectly, to any of its officers or employes. He paid 90 per cent. net for the drafts in question. They were indorsed by the American Jobbing Association and delivered to him, and he paid for them before maturity. The drafts were complete and regular on their face. None of them had been dishonored at the time he purchased them, and he had no notice of any defect in their title. The drafts were indorsed and transferred to him in good faith and for a valuable consideration and before maturity. At the time he had no notice of any defect in the title of the person negotiating the drafts, and no notice of any infirmity in the instruments. The drafts were purchased on May 29, 1906, and were indorsed and delivered to him on that day.

On the back of each draft are the following indorsements:

"4196.

"Bank—Nat. Bk. of John A. Black,
  "Address Barbourville, Ky.

"May 29, 1906
  "Pay to the order of C. Bothwell.
  "American Jobbing Association,
  "By C. H. Dayton, Mgr.

"Pay to the order of
  "Johnson County Sav. Bank,
  "Iowa City, Iowa, C. Bothwell.

"Pay any bank or banker, or order.
"Johnson County Savings Bank,
"Iowa City, Iowa,
"Geo. L. Folk, Cashier.
"Says return."

It is evident that each of the drafts in question fulfilled the requirements of a negotiable instrument; each is in writing and signed by the drawer; each contains an unconditional order to pav a sum certain in money; each is payable at a fixed future time; each is payable to the order of a specified person; each instrument is addressed to a drawee, and he is named in the instrument with reasonable certainty. Not only is each draft a negotiable instrument, but each was actually negotiated by the indorsement of the holder, the American Jobbing Association, and the negotiation was completed by delivery.

The question, then, arises: Was appellant a holder in due course? It is apparent from the record that each draft is complete and regular upon it face. Appellant became the holder of each draft before it was due and without notice that it had previously been dishonored. He took them in good faith and for value. He swears that at the time they were negotiated to him he had no notice of any infirmity in the instruments or defect in the title of the person negotiating them. While appellee testifies to facts going to show fraud on the part of the agent of the American Jobbing Association, he testifies to no facts going to show that appellant had notice of the fraud. To constitute notice of an infirmity in an instrument or defect in the title of the person negotiating the same, the person to whom it is negotiated must have actual knowledge of the infirmity or defect, or knowledge of such facts that his action in taking the instrument amounts to bad faith. Ky. St. Sec. 3720b, subsec. 56. The proof in this case fails to come up to either one of these requirements of the statute. There is nothing in the case to show that appellant had actual knowledge of the infirmity or defect, or knowledge of such facts that his action in taking the instruments amounted to bad faith. On the contrary, his evidence, which is unimpeached by that of any other witness or by any circumstances in the case, tends to show that he acquired the drafts before maturity, for value, and without notice of any infirmity therein or defect in the title of the American Jobbing Association, which indorsed, delivered, and sold the drafts to him.

Nor is there anything upon the drafts themselves tending to show knowledge of such facts on the part of appellant as would constitute bad faith on his part in ,taking them. The indorsements are simply the usual indorsements to be found upon any draft which may be sold, indorsed, and delivered, and then deposited at a bank for collection. It is apparent, therefore, that appellant was a holder in due course. That being the case, he took the drafts free from any defect of title of prior parties, and free from defenses available to prior parties among themselves. Ky. St. Sec. 3720b, subsec. 57. We therefore conclude that the trial court erred in refusing to instruct the jury peremptorily to find for appellant.

Nor is there any merit in the contention of appellee that he is entitled to judgment on the face of the pleadings. While appellant's denial that each of the instruments was obtained by fraud was insufficient, yet he did deny the only matter materially affecting his right to recover; that is, any knowledge or notice of the fraud relied on.

Judgment reversed and cause remanded for a new trial consistent with this opinion.

CASE 92.—SUIT FOR INJUNCTION BY THE STATE NATIONAL
BANK AGAINST D. P. RICHARDSON, CITY TAX
COLLECTOR, OF FRANKFORT.—December 14, 1909.

Richardson Tax Collector v. State National Bank

Appeal from Franklin Circuit Court.

R. L. STOUT, Circuit Judge.

From a judgment granting the injunction, defendant appeals.—Reversed.

1. Taxation—Local Assessments—Bank Stock.—Prior to 1906,
    the tax assessment of national banks for local purposes was
    made by the state board, and the tax collected on their
    certificate of the amount of the assessment. Act March 15,
    1906 (Laws 1906, p. 136, c. 22, art. 4, subd. 2), providing for
    taxing shares of banks and trust companies, took local taxes
    out of the jurisdiction of the state board, and required the
    assessment for local taxes to be made by the local "assessing
    officer." The Court of Appeals in November, 1907, held that
    the state board was required to make an assessment for the
    year 1906, for state purposes under the act of March 15, 1906,
    even though an assessment had been made under the prior
    law. Held, that the local "assessing officer" was required to
    make a similar assessment for local purposes; it being mani-
    fest that the Legislature did not intend when changing the
    officer who was to make the local assessment to require an
    assessment for state purposes for 1906, and to omit from as-
    sessment for local purposes shares of bank stock for that
    year.

2. Taxation—Local Assessment of Bank Stock—Duties of As-
    sessing Officer.—Though the local assessor could not assess
    shares of stock in a national bank previous to the time Act
    March 15, 1906, took effect for previous to that time he had
    no such authority and though he was required by previous
    statutes to return his book, and the assessment was complet-
    ed before the act took effect, the Legislature which had impos-
    ed upon him these duties could impose others upon him, and
    did so by providing for a local assessment of the shares of
    bank stock for local purposes.

3. Taxation—Retrospective Assessment of Property.—The state may provide for the retrospective assessment of property for taxation.

4. Taxation—Local Assessment of Bank Stock—Ordinances— Construction of Statute.—Ky. St. Sec. 3403 (Russell's St. Sec. 1467), provides that where any property has not heretofore been assessed for taxation, or has been improperly assessed, or where notice of the time and place of the meeting of the board of supervisors of tax has not heretofore been properly or regularly given, cities of the third class can pass an ordinance directing the assessment of such property, etc., and that its object is to insure the collection of any unpaid taxes, and that the provisions shall not extend back for more than five years. Act March 15, 1906, provided for the taxing of shares of banks and trust companies at the same rate as for other personalty, which was to be assessed by a local assessing officer. Held, that, where the local assessing officer had not made an assessment of the shares of stock of a bank for 1906, the council had authority under section 3403 to provide for its assessment, as that section applied to all cases "where property has not been assessed for taxation"; the word "heretofore" being required to be read as referring to the time of the passing of the ordinance, and the five years allowed being counted, not from the time of the passage of the act, but from the time the assessment is made.

WM. CROMWELL for appellant.

HELM & HELM for appellee.

OPINION OF THE COURT BY JUDGE HOBSON—Reversing.

The State National Bank brought this suit to enjoin the city of Frankfort from assessing its shares of stock for taxation for city purposes for the year 1906 under Acts 1906, p. 134, c. 22; it being alleged in the petition that a special board of supervisors had been appointed under an ordinance of the city council, and were about to assess the property. The city filed an answer, in which it was alleged that no assessments of the shares had been made for city purposes for the year 1906, and that no tax had been paid thereon, admitting that it was the intention of the board to assess the shares of stock without deducting therefrom the value of the United States bonds held by the bank. The plaintiff demurred to the answer, the court sustained the demurrer, and, the city failing to plead further, a judgment was entered granting an injunction as prayed in the petition. The city appeals.

Section 3403, Ky. St. (Russell's St. Sec. 1467), which is part of the act governing cities of the third class to which Frankfort belongs, among other things provides as follows: "Where any property has not heretofore been assessed for taxation or where same has been irregularly or improperly assessed, or where notice of the time and place of the meeting of the board of supervisors of tax has not heretofore been properly or regularly given, said city is authorized to pass an ordinance directing the assessment of such property and making correction in any assessment irregularly or improperly made, and giving notice of the place and time of the meeting of any board of tax supervisors, so that any taxpayer may appear before same. The object of this section is to insure the collection of any unpaid taxes, and for that purpose any of the said cities may, if it deems it necessary, appoint a special board of tax supervisors, whose duty it shall be to assess for taxation any omitted property or to correct any improper or irregular assessments, or to hear any complaints as to the assessment or value of any property upon which the taxes have not been paid. When any property is assessed or any assessment corrected, or where any taxpayer has the opportunity of being heard for previous years, the tax rate and levies and liens for such years shall apply and the provisions of this section shall not extend back for more than five years." The ordinance passed by the council was enacted pursuant to this section. The proceedings by the city were regular. The first question in the case is: Was the defendant liable to the tax? For it is admitted that the property has not been assessed and the tax has not been paid.

The act of 1904, providing for the taxation of the shares of national banks, required them to make certain reports on the 1st day of March, and to pay the taxes on the 1st day of July. The provision of the act as to the assessment of the shares is as follows: "The Auditor, Treasurer, and Secretary of State are hereby constituted a board of assessment for the purpose of fixing the value of shares of all national banks in this state. It shall be the duty of the Auditor, immediately after the board of assessment has fixed the value of the shares of national banks to furnish each bank with a statement of the value fixed on its shares and the amount of tax due thereon, and the bank shall have thirty days from the time of receiving the notice to go before the board, and ask for a change in the valuation, and the board, after hearing such evidence as may be submitted, may change the valuation and assessment as it may deem proper, and the action of the board shall be final. Each bank shall be entitled to have deducted from the total valuation placed on its shares by said board, the assessed value of its real estate in this state. It shall be the duty of the national banks to list with the county assessor of each county its real estate, and pay the taxes thereon to the sheriff. The Auditor shall at the expiration of thirty days after final action by said board, certify to the county clerks of said counties where national banks are located, the value of the shares of the bank, less the assessed value of its real estate, and such

certificates shall be by each county clerk filed in his
office and be by him certified to the proper collecting
officer of the county, city, town or taxing district, for
collection, and each county, city, town or taxing district shall be entitled to collect taxes on such valuation, except in such cities and towns as otherwise provided." Acts 1904, p. 146, c. 66. This act only applied to national banks. It did not apply to state
banks. Under the act, the assessment was made for
city taxes in Frankfort, not by a local assessor, but
by the state board, and the tax was collected by the
city on the assessment as certified by that board.

Under this act it was held in Marion Nat. Bank v.
Burton, 121 Ky. 876, 90 S. W. 944, 28 Ky. Law Rep.
864, 10 L. R. A. (N. S.) 947, that national banks were
entitled to a deduction of their United States bonds
for the reason that the state banks which were assessed under a different statute were entitled to the
deduction, and that, under the act of Congress, the
national banks must be placed on the same footing
as the state banks. This ruling applied to all taxes,
both state and local. That opinion was delivered on
January 31, 1906. The Legislature was then in session, and, to remedy this evil, it enacted the act of
1906, which placed state banks and trust companies
on the same footing as national banks, and required
their shares of stock and the shares of stock in national banks all to be assessed in precisely the same
manner. There had, in fact, been no discrimination
under the previous act, but it was the possibility of a
discrimination that required the court to hold that
under the act of 1904 national banks were entitled to
a deduction of their United States bonds. The act
of 1906, after providing that the state board should
assess shares of stock of all banks and trust com-

panies, contained this provision as to the assessment for local taxation: "Every state bank and trust company incorporated under the laws of this commonwealth, and every national bank doing business therein and located in any county, city, town or taxing district in this commonwealth shall make to the assessing cfficer of the county, city, town, or taxing district a report similar to that required by this sub-division to be made to the state board of valuation and assessment for assessment for state purposes.

The assessing officer of the county, city, town, or taxing district wherein any trust company, state and national bank is situate, shall assess the shares of such trust company, state and national bank for taxation for county, city, town and taxing district purposes in the manner prescribed in this subdivision for assessing the same by the state board of valuation and assessment for taxation for state purposes, and such officer shall make out and return the assessment to the proper authorities of the county, city, town or taxing district, at the same time and manner as prescribed by law for the return of the assessment of personal property therein. In assessing the shares of banks for county purposes the assessor shall make the return upon a separate blank and shall not be included in the recapitulation sheet made by the county clerk and furnished to the Auditor, but shall be returned to the county board of supervisors. The equalization, collection, penalties and all laws relating thereto, now provided by law for other personal property in the county, city, town or taxing district, shall apply in like manner to the collection of the taxes herein provided for; any county, city, town or taxing district, not now having the right to collect such taxes by suit, is hereby authorized and empowered so to do." See Acts 1906, p. 136, c. 22.

The act also contained these provisions: "All laws
or parts of laws in conflict or inconsistent with this
act, providing for other methods of taxation of
shares of national banks, or the taxation of trust companies and state banks, incorporated under the laws
of this commonwealth, and the collection of taxes
thereon, are hereby repealed. All national banks,
trust companies and state banks shall file with the
Auditor their reports herein provided for on or before the 15th day of April, 1906, and annually thereafter on or before March the first. Said reports shall
be made up to and including the first day of the preceding September."

The act contained no emergency clause. It was
approved March 15, 1906, and so took effect 90 days
after the adjournment of the Legislature. The last
clause of the act is in these words: "If any section
in this bill shall be held to be unconstitutional, that
fact shall not affect any other section of the act, it
being the intention of the General Assembly in enacting this bill to enact each section separately, and if
any proviso or exception contained in any section of
this bill shall be declared unconstitutional, that fact
shall not affect the remaining portion of said section;
it being the intention of the Legislature to enact each
section of said bill and each proviso and exception
thereto separately." In Hager v. Citizens' National
Bank, 127 Ky. 192, 105 S. W. 403, 914, 32 Ky. Law
Rep. 95, the act was held valid by this court and applicable to state taxes for the year 1906; that is to
say, it was held that the state taxes for the year 1906
should be assessed and collected under this act, and
that the national banks as to their state taxes were
not entitled to a deduction for that year of the value
of the United States bonds held by them, but the

question as to their right to the deduction as to local taxes was not there before the court, and was not passed on. That question is presented on this appeal.

In point of fact the state board of valuation had not allowed to any state bank a deduction on acouṇt of United States bonds held by it previous to the act of 1906. The state banks were in fact discriminated against under the decision in Marion National Bank v. Burton; for the national banks when given the deduction of their United States bonds as ḟollowed under that decision were placed in a more favorable position than the state banks enjoyed, and they were thus given an immunity from taxation which the Legislature had not intended to allow. The result was that the Legislature undertook to remedy the evil by the act of 1906, and to this end the provisions of that act as to the returns for the year 1906 were inserted. The court in Hager v. Citizens' National Bank held that, if the state board had made an assessment before the act of 1906 took effect, it would have been its duty to make another assessment after that act took effect. The court said: "If it had not been intended that the taxes for 1906 were to be assessed under the act, there was no need for a special repealing clause in this subdivision; and the sixth clause must otherwise be rejected as meaningless. It is true that the act did not take effect until June 11th, but the Legislature plainly intended that the assessment should be made under it, and it was done. Even if an assessment for 1906 had been made before the Legislature met, it should have directed another assessment to be made and the taxes to be paid under it. And so, if the board had made an assessment under the act of 1904, it would have been its duty after June 11, 1906, to have made an assessment under the act of 1906, and the taxes should have been paid under that assessment.''

There was the same necessity for this legislation as to local taxes as there was to state taxes. The Legislature endeavored to correct an imperfection in the existing law, and the correction would have been imperfect if it had not applied to the year 1906; for there was the same necessity for a remedy as to the taxes for the year 1906 as there was for the taxes of the subsequent years. . Under the previous act, the assessment for local purposes was made by the state board, and the taxes were collected on their certificate of the amount of the assessment. The act of 1906 took local taxes out of their jurisdiction and required the assessment for local taxes to be made by the local "assessing officer." If, as has been held, the state board was required to make an assessment for the year 1906 for state purposes, it must follow that the local "assessing officer" was also required to make a similar assessment for local purposes; for the Legislature manifestly did not intend when it simply changed the officer who was to make the assessment to require the assessment to be made for state purposes for 1906, and to omit from assessment for local purposes the shares of stock for that year. The two assessments are provided for in the same act, in the same connection, and manifestly for the same purpose, the local assessment for local purposes being merely substituted for an assessment by the state board as under the former law. The local assessor could not have assessed the shares of stock in a national bank previous to the time the act of 1906 took effect; for, until that act took effect, he had no authority to make an assessment of such shares of stock for any purpose. It is true that by the previous statutes he was to return his book, and the assessment was completed long before the act of 1906 took effect; but this was all by statute, and the Legislature which had imposed upon him these duties could impose upon him other duties, and this it manifestly intended to do by that part of the act of 1906 which provides for a local assessment of the shares of stock for local purposes.

It is true that the taxes are levied under the statute as of date January 1st; but, while this is true, the assessment may be made after January 1st, the value of the property to be fixed as of the date when the assessment should have been made. The state may provide for the retrospective assessment of property. In this case no assessment of the property had been made for 1906, and none could be made; for, as held by this court, it was the duty of the state board to proceed under the act of 1906, and under that act they had no jurisdiction to make an assessment for local purposes. When it is settled, as held in Hager v. Citizens' National Bank, that, if the state board had made an assessment for state purposes before the act of 1906 took effect, it would have been its duty, after that act took effect to make an assessment as provided thereby, it must follow, that, if the state board had made an assessment for local purposes before the act of 1906 took effect, it would have been the duty of the local "assessing officer" after that act took effect in like manner to make an assessment pursuant to it; for the act of the state board as to the assessment for the state and for local purposes stands on the same plane, and the Legislature had the same power to require a new assessment in one case as in the other. The act of 1906 shows clearly that the state board was not to make local assessments under it, and as no other officer but it could assess these shares before it took effect, when this jurisdiction was taken from it, and transferred to the local "assessing officer," the manifest meaning was that he was to make the assessment which under the former law the board was to make. The mere change of officers was not intended to exempt the banks from taxation.

We also conclude that, when the local "assessing officer" had not made an assessment of the shares of stock of the State National Bank, the council was authorized by section 3403, Ky. St., above quoted, to provide for its assessment; for it was property subject to assessment, and which had not been assessed for taxation. The operation of this section is not confined to property which has been omitted from assessment by the assessor; but it applies in all cases "where any property has not heretofore been assessed for taxation." When we read the whole section, it is evident that the word "heretofore" is to be read as referring to the time of the passing of the ordinance. The act creates the board of supervisors of tax, and this section provides for the correction of their work; its object is "to insure the collection of any unpaid taxes;" and the five years allowed by the last clause are to be counted, not from the passage of the act, but from the time the assessment is made. Aside from section 3403, the powers granted the common council of third-class cities are fully as broad as those granted towns of the fifth class. Compare Ky. St. sections 3265, 3289, subsecs. 1, 12, 3281, 3637, and 3644 (sections 1282, 1306, 1298, 1643, 1650, and 1682). In Muir v. Bardstown, 120 Ky. 739, 87 S. W. 1096, 27 Ky. Law Rep. 1150, we sustained an ordinance under the latter sections providing for the assessment of property that had escaped taxation.

Judgment reversed, and cause remanded for further proceedings consistent herewith.

BARKER, J., dissenting.

Dissenting opinion by Judge Barker.

I am unable to concur in the opinion of the court. If my only reasons for dissenting were those given in the dissenting opinion of Hager v. Citizens' National Bank, 127 Ky. 192, 105 S. W. 403, I should not feel impelled now to dissent, but there are other and vital reasons why I cannot concur in the opinion, which I will state as briefly as I can. The opinion holds that the decision in that case is conclusive, or, at least, that there is no substantial difference between the two cases; and this idea runs through the whole opinion. The two cases are essentially different.

1. In that case the assessment involved was the assessment for the current year. In this case the assessment sought to be made in 1908, for the taxes of 1906, is necessarily a retrospective assessment, governed by different principles, as I shall presently show.

2. In that case the court held that, there was no particular time named within which the assessment should be made, it might be made at any time during the current fiscal year. In this case, as the only assessment for local purposes required by the act must be made "at the same time and manner as prescribed by law for the return of the assessment of personal property therein," and as it is conceded in the opinion of the court that the time for the assessment of the tax of 1906 for the purposes of cities of the third class (to which Frankfort belongs) had expired "long before the act of 1906 took effect," the two cases

differ materially in that respect, and it is an important difference.

3. In that case, as the time for the assessment for the current year had not expired, the court thought that the act of 1906 could be made to apply as a remedial statute, without giving it a retroactive operation. In this, as the time has expired, it is necessary to give the act of 1906 a retroactive effect, and the court does so in the opinion, in which I think the court errs vitally, and I shall presently review the authorities on that question, particularly the decisions of the Supreme Court, since that is the court of final resort on the question of the right to deduct United States bonds, as well as the question whether the tax rests upon assets or upon shares of stock.

The difference between the cases of an assessment for the current year and a retrospective assessment is that in the former it is the duty of the officers who by the law are charged primarily with the duty of assessing to assess during the current year, and if the law under which their power to assess for the year should be repealed during the current year, and another substituted, which is remedial in nature, then there is much force in the argument that the authority entitled to receive the tax should not be allowed to suffer by the failure to assess before the repeal, and that now, there being no law in force under which there could be an assessment, except the substituted or remedial statute, the assessment should be made under the latter. This I understand to have been the position of the court in the Hager Case. But, on the other hand, it is well settled by the decisions of this court that a retrospective assessment must be made under the law as it existed as of the time to which the assessment related, which in this instance is January 10, 1906, when the act of 1904 was in force. Again, a retrospective assessment has as its necessary basis the failure to assess by the officers primarily charged with the duty; and since the purpose of the law is to supply or correct that failure, it would seem to follow that the person authorized to perform the omitted duty should be governed by the law which would have governed the actions of the officers primarily charged with the duty if they had not cmitted to perform it; and that is the result of the previous decision. If that principle should be applied to this case, the resultant effect would necessarily be an affirmance of the judgement, because it is demonstrable, as well as admitted in the opinion, that "the exclusive right to assess was in the board of valuation and assessment until the act of 1906 became effective July 11, 1906." The act of 1906 took the power of assessing for local purposes from the board, and put it in the hands of the local assessors. Therefore the failure of the state board, which possessed the exclusive power to assess for local purposes from March 1, 1906, until July 11, 1906, when the act of 1906 became effective, must necessarily have been under the act of 1904, and therefore, the substituted duty should be performed under the same act; and it is conceded that, if the act of 1906 does not apply, there was the right, in the appellee, under the prior decisions of this court, to have had deducted from the aggregate value of the shares the value of the United States bonds held by it, which, if allowed, would necessarily have resulted in an affirmance of the judgment, because it is conceded of record that the total book value of the shares at the date the assessment should have been made, as well as when it

vol. 135—50

was attempted to make it, was $190,870; that of that amount $15,000 was represented in tangible property, upon which the taxes for all purposes had been paid, leaving a balance of book value of shares at $175,870, whereas, the face value of the United States bonds held by the appellee from January, 1906, continuously to the present time, is $187,600. There is nothing in this record which justified the court in saying: "In point of fact the state board of valuation and assessment had not allowed to any state bank a deduction on account of United States bonds held by it previous to the act of 1906." The record has absolutely nothing in it on that subject.

The statement that "the state banks were discriminated against under the decision in Marion National Bank v. Burton" is certainly opposed to the decision of that case, which proceeded upon the opposite theory; and the statement "that national banks were thus given an immunity from taxation which the Legislature had not intended to allow" is equally opposed to the Burton Case, because it became the duty of the court in that case, in construing the statute, to declare the intention of the Legislature, and it declared that the Legislature did intend that the deduction should be made. The court further says in the opinion: "The court in Hager v. Citizens' National Bank held that, if the state board had made an assessment before the act of 1906, it would have been its duty to make another assessment after the act took effect"— and then proceeding, as I think and shall presently show, from the erroneous premises, the court further says: "When it is settled, as held in Hager v. Citizens' National Bank, that if the state board had made an assessment for state purposes before the act of 1906 took effect, it would have been its duty, after that act took effect, to make an assessment as provided thereby, it must follow that, if the state board had made an assessment for local purposes before the act of 1906 took effect, it would have been the duty of the local assessing officers, after the act took effect, in like manner to make an assessment pursuant to it.'' This last statement, based on the first, which in its turn is based, as I think, on an erroneous conception of the effect of the decision in the Hager Case, is very radical and in distinct opposition to at least five other cases, decided by this court, three of which have been reported, and another (decided last June) has been marked for publication. Two of these opinions were rendered by Judge O'Rear, two by Judge Hobson, and one by Judge Lassing.

I think the first statement quoted as to the effect of the decision in the Hager Case must have come from a somewhat hasty reading of the opinion in that case, which was rendered by Judge Carroll. What was really said in the Hager Case was this: ''Even if the assessment for 1906 had been made before the Legislature met, it could have directed another assessment to be made, and the tax to be paid under it. And so if the board had made an assessment under the act of 1904, it would have been its duty after June 11, 1906, to make an assessment under the act of 1906, and the tax should have been paid under that assessment.'' This, I take it, must mean that it would have been the duty of the board, if the Legislature had so directed, to have made another assessment, and the constitutional right of the Legislature to have so ordered may, for the purpose of the argument, be conceded. If it was intended in the opinion to say that the board of its own power, without the special legislative authority referred to, could have made an-

other assessment after a final assessment, already
made and completed, by the lapse of 30 days, without
any complaint of the taxpayer, then the court has
overruled at least five well-considered cases, without
dignifying them by the slightest mention.

The first of these is that of Coulter v. Louisville
Bridge Company, 114 Ky. 47, 70 S. W. 29, 24 Ky.
Law Rep. 809. In that case, upon the report of the
bridge company, duly filed, the board of valuation
and assessment, after considering the matter, wrote
on the jacket in which the assessment papers are preserved the words "No franchise." After the members of that board went out of office and different
men were elected to fill the place, the board as reor-
ganized, proceeded to consider de novo the question of
the assessment upon that report, and reached the
conclusion that the company ought to be assessed for
a franchise, and valued the franchise at $662,998,
and demanded a tax thereon, which, with penalty,
amounted to $4,167.89. Thereupon the bridge com-
pany filed in the Franklin circuit court its suit in
equity, and enjoined the assessment before it became
final, and this court, having considered the question,
determined that, while there was no assessment made
by the old board, it had determined that there was
nothing upon which to base a franchise assessment,
and had therefore written the words "No franchise,"
and that that was conclusive both of the state and
bridge company. In illustration of that conclusion,
the court used the following language: "If the board
of 1898 had fixed a valuation of $100,000 on appellee's
franchise, acting under the same circumstances as
shown in this case, and appellee had paid the tax,
could appellant and his associates, constituting the
present board, have ignored that action, and revalued

and reassessed the franchise? If they could, then there is no end to this thing. Nor would there be to any assessment or listing of any property for taxation by any assessing board or assessor. We are of the opinion, and hold, that when the proper assessing officers, within the time and substantially the manner prescribed by the statute, have acted in considering and fixing the valuation upon property liable to assessment for taxation, and no relief has been obtained within the time allowed by statute for correcting their action, if erroneous, that action is final. The judgment and action of the assessor based upon the legal evidence then obtainable and at hand, and as fixed by statute, when recorded in the proper tax lists, in the very nature of things should be conclusive upon the state, as well as against the taxpayer. Such being the judgment below, it is affirmed.'' That opinion was delivered by Judge O'Rear.

In the case of C., N. O. & T. P. R. R. Co. v. Commonwealth, 115 Ky. 281, 72 S. W. 1119 (opinion by Judge O'Rear), in which the same question arose, it was said: ''Under the authority of Coulter, Auditor, v. Louisville Bridge Company, we hold that the action of the board was conclusive, and after the expiration of the time for hearing complaints for reduction is binding alike upon the state and the railroad company.''

In Commonwealth v. American Tobacco Co., 96 S. W. 466, 29 Ky. Law Rep. 746 (opinion by Judge Hobson), the Bridge Company Case was again approved; and in the case of Commonwealth v. Ledman, 127 Ky. 621, 106 S. W. 247, 32 Ky. Law Rep. 247 (opinion by Judge Lassing), where the same question was presented, it was said: ''From the report as filed by the company and such other information as it may

possess it (referring to the board) assesses the property at a fair valuation, and when once so assessed
the action of the board is final and conclusive, and
no further action can be taken leading to a further
assessment or revaluation of the property.''

In the case of Commonwealth v. Southern Pacific,
120 S. W. 311 (decided last June), marked to be officially reported—opinion by Judge Hobson—the same
question was again presented, and Judge Hobson
quoted from the Bridge Company Cases the language which is quoted above.

But the opinion of the court in this case goes further, much further, than it is said the opinion in the
Hager Case went, because it must be admitted, and I
think is substantially admitted in the opinion, that the
board of valuation and assessment must have omitted to make an assessment before the local officers,
acting in a supplementary way, in other words, performing the substituted duty, could have proceeded
at all. And yet it is said that even though the board
had made the assessment for local purposes, before
the act of 1906 became operative, as it was its clear
duty to do—in other words, had not failed or omitted
to do its duty in respect to the local assessment—still
it would have been the duty of the officers charged
with the performance of the substitute duty to have
ignored the assessment and performed their supposed substitute duty, without the existence of the
jurisdictional fact necessary as a basis for the right
to proceed, and in so doing should ignore the assessment duly and properly made, and should assume
there had been a failure of duty on the part of those
officers charged primarily with the duty.

If this can be done, then, in the language of the
court, ''Where is this thing to end?'' If the con-

clusion of the court is right, then the same thing would be true, even if the taxpayer had paid the taxes due on the assessment. Such a conclusion would be entirely unprecedented and appalling to the profession and to the state. That conclusion of the court is worked out on the theory that the law of 1906 is retroactive in its operation to such an extent as to make it amount to a legislative command on the local officers to ignore assessments for the year 1906 and to proceed with the assessment without what has universally been conceded to be the necessary basis for such proceeding. I think it must be admitted that the legislative language be so plain as to exclude all doubt before such a construction could be placed upon it. There should be no possible escape from it.

The most critical examination of the statute fails to disclose a single sentence pointing to the conclusion that the Legislature intended the act to apply to local taxes for the year 1906. But the whole language and spirit of the act is to the contrary—that it was intended to act only prospectively. The Legislature is presumed to have known (and a large majority of the members did know) that even before the act was passed, and certainly long before the act became operative, all of the local assessments had been made for the tax of 1906, and that perhaps 95 per cent. of the tax due thereon had been paid.

Under these circumstances there is not the slightest reason for supposing that the Legislature intended anything but a prospective operation. The only section in the act that bears to the slightest extent upon the assessment of local taxes is section 4 of the original act (section 4092c, Carroll's St. 1909, Russell's St. Sec. 6078), and copied in full in the opinion, and certainly there is no language in that section in-

dicating anything but a prospective operation. That
section provides that the assessment for local pur-
·poses shall be made "at the same time and manner
as prescribed by law for the return of the assessment
of personal property therein." An examination of
the statutes upon that question shows that the county
assessment must be completed by January 1st. Ky.
St. sections 4046-4059 (sections 5937-5951). The assessment in cities of the first class must be completed, and taxes are due thereon, by January 3d.
Section 2997 (945). In none of the other cities is the
assessment delayed longer than May 1st. In cities of
the third class the assessment must be completed by
March 10th. Under such conditions it seems to me
to be absolutely plain that, when the Legislature declared the assessment for local purposes under the act
of 1906 should be "at the same time" that other assessments for local purposes were made, it could not
have contemplated any other assessment before the
next one after the adoption of the act. This proposition seems to me to be so plain that no argument
can make it plainer.

The court quotes, as though it should be given a
preponderating influence, section 4092 of the Kentucky Statutes, giving the banks until after April
15th to file their reports before the Auditor; but that
section of the act became wholly inoperative when
the Legislature determined it would not add an emergency clause, but would let the act become operative
under the Constitution, 90 days after the adjournment. In the next place, the section has absolutely
nothing to do with local assessments, but only state
taxes, as the reports for local purposes must be made
to the local officers at an entirely different time, and
only the reports which are to serve as a basis for

state taxes are returned to the Auditor. The court says: "The state may provide for the retrospective assessment of property." That is, of course, conceded; but the question is, Has it done so? Having seen that the language, and the spirit, too, in my judgment, really point unerringly to a strictly prospective construction, I shall now briefly consider what the result of the authorities is.

In Endlich on Interpretation of Statutes, Sec. 271, it is said: "Indeed, the rule to be derived from a comparison of a vast number of judicial utterances on this subject seems to be that, even in the absence of constitutional obstacles to retroaction, a construction giving to a statute a prospective operation is always to be preferred, unless a purpose to give it a retrospective force is expressed by clear and positive command, or to be inferred by necessary, unequivocal, and unavoidable implication from the words of the statute taken by themselves, and in connection with the subject-matter and the occasion of the enactment admitting of no reasonable doubt, by precluding all questions as to such intention."

This court, in the case of Watts v. Commonwealth, 78 Ky. 331, said: "It is a sound rule of construction that a statute shall have a prospective operation only, unless its terms show clearly a legislative intention that it operate retrospectively." And in Lawrence v. City of Louisville, 96 Ky. 598, 29 S. W. 451, 27 L. R. A. 560, 49 Am. St. Rep. 309, it is said: "In some cases retrospective legislation may be upheld. However, the words of a statute ought not to have a retrospective operation unless they are so clear, strong, and impressive that no other meaning can be annexed to them, or unless the intention of the Legislature cannot be otherwise satisfied." See, also, the case of Ohio Valley Telephone Co. v. City of Louisville, 123 Ky. 193, 94 S. W. 17, 29 Ky. Law Rep. 631, which in some of its aspects is strikingly like this case. In that case we said: "The fiscal year of the city of Louisville, then as now, began on the 1st day of September and ended on the 31st day of August in each year. All property was assessed for municipal purposes as of the 1st of September of each year, and the lien of the city for taxes of a given year began on that day; so that when the act of November 11, 1892, authorizing the assessment of corporate franchises for state and municipal taxation, became a law, more than two months of the fiscal year for which the tax bill herein sued on issued had already expired, and, unless the rule against retrospective taxation is to be ignored, there is no legal foundation for it."

The Supreme Court, in the case of United States v. American Sugar Co., 202 U. S. 577, 26 Sup. Ct. 719, 50 L. Ed. 1149 said: "We are to remember there is a presumption against retrospective operation, and we have said that words in a statute ought not to have such operation 'unless they are so clear, strong, and imperative that no other meaning can be annexed to them,' or 'unless the intention of the Legislature cannot be otherwise satisfied.' " In United States v. Burr, 159 U. S. 78, 15 Sup. Ct. 1002, 40 L. Ed. 82, there was under consideration of the United States court a statute which took effect August 28, 1894, but the first section of which provided as follows: "That on and after the 1st day of August, 1894, unless otherwise specially provided for in this act, there shall be levied, collected and paid upon articles imported from foreign countries or withdrawn from consumption and mentioned in the schedules herein contained, the rates of duty which are by the schedules and paragraphs respectively prescribed, viz." It was held that, notwithstanding this language, the act did not apply to transactions completed when the act became a law; that is, to goods which were imported between August 1st and August 28th.

Without burdening this opinion unnecessarily with authorities, it is sufficient to say that both in this court and in the Supreme Court the principle is thoroughly established that a retrospective construction will not be given to a statute unless, in the language of this court in the Watts Case, supra, its terms "show clearly a legislative intention that it operate retrospectively," and in the Lawrence Case, supra, these terms "must be so clear, strong, and impressive that no other meaning can be annexed to them," and as stated by the Supreme Court in the Sugar Company Case, "these terms must be so strong, clear, and impressive that no other meaning can be annexed to them." With the authorities of these two courts being so emphatic upon this proposition, I do not see how it can be legally possible to conclude that the Legislature intended the act of 1906 to be given a retrospective operation, so as to include the tax for 1906, assessable in this instance as of March 10th.

For these reasons, I am constrained to dissent from the opinion of the majority of the court.

CASE 93.—ACTION BY J. E. GAITSKILL AND OTHERS AGAINST THE BURLEY TOBACCO SOCIETY.—December 17, 1909.

Burley Tobacco Society v. Gaitskill

Appeal from Clark Circuit Court.

J. M. BENTON, Circuit Judge.

From a decree appointing a receiver for defendant, it appeals.—Reversed.

Account—Time for Bringing Action—Conditions—Precedent.— Where a corporation, for the purpose of selling tobacco grown by its members, markets the crops of two years and disburses to its members 99 per cent. of the sum realized, and there are certain features of the business unsettled, and some claims of the corporation and certain suits against it pending in court, and the expense necessary to defend the suits and other items of expense have not been ascertained, a complaint by members for an accounting, is premature.

PENDLETON, BUSH & BUSH, T. L. EDELEN, J. H. HAZEL-RIGG and JOHN R. ALLEN for appellant.

JOUETT & JOUETT and APPLEGATE & CLARK for appellees.

OPINION OF THE COURT BY JUDGE O'REAR—Reversing.

A receiver was appointed by the judge of the Clark circuit court for certain money, books, and other property of the appellant society, at the suit of appellees, four members of the society, who complained that it had failed to distribute as it should all the proceeds of sales of the 1906 and 1907 pools of tobacco. Appellant is a corporation organized in January, 1907, without capital stock, for the purpose of promoting the interests of the growers of burley to- bacco in certain counties of Kentucky, Ohio, and In- diana, and to sell the tobacco of its members. The crops of 1906 and 1907, pooled with it, it sold during the fall of 1908 and summer of 1909. The sum real- ized was nearly $20,000,000, 99 per cent. of which has been disbursed to the members of those pools. Cer- tain features of· the business are yet unsettled, some claims on the part of the society, amounting to some $130,000, and which are pending in court, have not been adjudged, and certain suits against the society and some of its members for damages arising, it is alleged, out of the course of the business, have not yet been disposed of. Those suits involve about $900,000. The expense necessary to defend them has not yet been ascertained. Other items of expense connected with the pools of 1906 and 1907 have not been ascertained or settled. In this state of affairs, complaint by members for an accounting in court is premature. The appointment of the receiver was un- authorized by the state of the record, or by the situa- tion disclosed by it. No·other questions are consid- ered or determined.

Judgment reversed, and cause remanded for pro- ceedings consistent herewith.

CASE 94.—ACTION BY THOMAS BROWN BY NEXT FRIEND
AGAINST THE CHESAPEAKE & OHIO RAILWAY
COMPANY AND OTHERS.—December 7. 1909.

Brown v. C. & O. Railway Co.

Appeal from Pike Circuit Court.

A. J. KIRK, Circuit Judge.

Judgment for defendant, plaintiff appeals.—Reversed.

1   Negligence—Child Playing About Railroad Turntable—Petition in Action for Injury.—In an action for injury to a child
    playing about a railroad turntable   the petition alleged:
    that it was very attractive to children as a merry-go-round;
    that they had been attracted to it and used is as such for a
    considerable time previous to the injury, with full knowledge
    of defendant's agents and servants in control thereof; and
    they often went on it with full knowledge of defendant; that
    it was not securely fastened, a minute description of the fast-
    ening being given; that children of seven or eight years old
    could easily remove the fastening, and had done so with full
    knowledge of defendant's servants in charge thereof; and that
    defendant negligently failed to provide a secure fastening.
    which could have been done with but little expense and
    trouble, though children were constantly using it as a play-
    thing with full knowledge of defendant, who also knew that
    it was very dangerous for them to do so. Held not objection-
    able as not alleging that it was particularly and unusually
    attractive to children and was easily accessible and a source
    of danger to them.

2. Courts—Turntable Doctrine as Sound Law—Decisions of
    Courts of Other States.—The "turntable doctrine," by which
    railroad companies are held liable for injuries to children
    playing about turntables left unguarded or not securely fas-
    tened, will not be departed from by the Supreme Court of
    this state as unsound, though the courts of several states have
    seemingly repudiated it.

3. Negligence—Turntable Doctrine—Statement of Rule of Law.—
. If a railroad company can with slight expense and little inconvenience keep its turntables guarded or locked so as to prevent trespassing children from using them, they should be
compelled to do so, and, if they fail to perform this duty, they
should be made liable in damages for any injury occasioned
to children of tender years in playing with them.
4. Negligence—Injury to Child Playing About Turntables—Proximate cause—Acts of Third Persons.—The acts of third persons
in putting in motion an unlocked turntable, whereby a child
was injured, is not the proximate cause of the injury, and
does not relieve the railroad from liability for its negligence
in failing to make it secure.

ROSCOE VANOVER and R. C. BURNS for appellant.

WORTHINGTON, COCHRAN & BROWNING and J. M. YORK
for appellee.

OPINION OF THE COURT BE CHIEF JUSTICE NUNN—
Reversing.

This appeal is from a judgment of the Pike circuit
court sustaining a general demurrer to and dismissing the petition and amended petition as to appellee
The action was instituted by appellant against appellee and two persons by the name of Saad, to recover
damages occasioned by the loss of a foot by appellant on appellee's turntable in the town of Pikeville,
Ky. The action is undisposed of as to the Saads.
The only question to be determined upon this appeal is whether or not the petition stated a cause
of action against appellee.

The injury occurred on the 11th day of April,
1909, on a turntable which was constructed by appellee in the town of Pikeville, about 65 feet from a
public highway. The Saads negligently removed
the fastening and set the turntable in motion, which
attracted appellant, a boy of 12 years of age, and
he entered upon, and while playing thereon one of

his feet was crushed to such an extent that it was rendered useless. The petition as amended, which relates to the negligence charged against appellee, is as follows :"The plaintiff, Thomas Brown, • • says: That at the time of the injuries complained of plaintiff resided with his father, John Brown, a distance of about 300 yards from defendant company's turntable at which he was injured. That said turntable is, and was at the time of plaintiff's injury, complained of, situated a distance of 65 feet from the public highway or public road running through the lower end of the city of Pikeville, and running from Pikeville down Big Sandy river. That defendant company's main line of road and right of way intervene between the said public road and said turntable. That, immediately prior to the time plaintiff received the injury complained of, defendant company had said turntable fastened by a draw bolt placed between the rails on the switch line leading to said turntable, said draw bolt being placed where the said switch intersects with said turntable, said draw bolt being a bar of iron weighing 55 pounds, 4 feet 10 inches long, 3 inches broad, 1 inch thick, and with flanges at each end of said draw bolt, so that flange together with the width of the bar made it 10 inches wide at each end of said draw bolt, and same was placed at the point where the switch intersects with the turntable so that one side of the flange at each end of the draw bolt would be against the rails on the switch line and the other side of the flange at each end of said draw bolt would be against the rails on the said turntable, and in this way said turntable was held in its place and could not be removed or moved until said draw bolt was removed which was done by slipping said draw bolt either

way, so that the entire flange at 'each end of said
draw bolt would be entirely on the rails of the switch
line, or if slipped the other way so that the flange
would be entirely on the rails of the turntable, and
if said draw bolt was slided on the said rails either
way so that the turntable would revolve without
lifting the draw bolt from its place, and that it was
necessary to only slide it until it passed the point of
intersection as above set out. That at the time of
the plaintiff's injury it was negligently removed by
the defendant, Jasper Saad, and the defendants Jasper Saad and Sam Saad were negligently revolving
said turntable and using it as a merry-go-round
when plaintiff was attracted to it and by it, and was
playing on same without any knowledge of the danger attending same at the time he received the injuries complained of. That said draw bolt was an
insecure fastening, and said draw bolt could easily
be removed and slipped to either side by a child
seven or eight years old, so that said turntable would
revolve, and small children had previous to the time
of the injuries complained of been in the habit of removing said draw bolt and using said turntable as a
merry-go-round, and said turntable was very attractive to children to use same as a merry-go-round, and
was very dangerous to so use same. That the agents,
servants, and employes of the defendant company in
charge of said turntable knew that it could easily be
unfastened and set in motion by children, and that
it could easily be unfastened by small children, and
knew that it was attended by great danger to do so,
and knew that small children had been in the habit
of unfastening and using same as a merry-go-round
previous to the time of the injuries complained of.
vol. 135—51

That said turntable was situated in a part of the city
of Pikeville that was much frequented by small children, as well as by other children, and this fact was
also known to the agents, servants, and employes of
defendant company in charge of said turntable at
and previous to the time of the injuries complained
of.   That a lock and key could easily have been
placed on said turntable, and the same kept locked
when not in use by the defendant company, and no
harm could have then come to any one. And that it
was perfectly practicable to have done so without interfering with the reasonable use of said turntable by
defendant company and with very slight trouble to
defendant company.''

Appellee's counsel present the following reasons
in support of the judgment of the lower court: First,
the "turntable doctrine" is not a sound principle of
law and should not be adopted by this court. Second,
the petition does not state a cause of action under
that doctrine, even if it be sound.   Third, whether
sound or unsound, it has no application to the case
at bar for the reason that appellee had securely fastened the turntable, and had, in any event, performed
its lawful duty in this respect. Fourth, that the proximate cause of appellant's injury was the negligent
conduct of appellee's co-defendants, Sam and Jasper Saad, and that there is no negligence shown upon the appellee's part, which can be said to have
been the direct or proximate cause of the injury to
appellant.   The second and third propositions require but little notice.

Appellee claims that it is not alleged in the peti
tion that the turntable was particularly and unsu-
ally attractive to children, and that it was easily accessible to children and a source of danger to them.

It is alleged that it was very attractive to children as a merry-go-round, and that they had been attracted to it and used it as such for a considerable time previous to the injury, and with the full knowledge of appellee's agents and servants in control thereof. It was not only alleged that it was accessible to children, but that they often went upon it with the full knowledge of appellee. It was alleged in the petition that the turntable was not securely fastened, and a minute description of the fastening is given, and it is alleged: That children seven or eight years old could easily remove the fastening, and had done so with the full knowledge of appellee's agents in charge of the turntable; that appellee had negligently failed to provide a secure fastening, which could have been done with but little expense and trouble, although children were constantly using it as a plaything with the full knowledge of appellee, who also knew that it was very dangerous for them to do so.

The first proposition of appellee's counsel is that the "turntable doctrine," which has been so often adhered to by this court, the courts of the majority of the states of the Union, and the Supreme Court of the United States, is unsound and should be departed from by this court. After a careful consideration of the question and authorities, we decline to depart from the doctrine, although the courts of several states have seemingly repudiated it. However, the opinions mostly are by divided courts and based on dicta. The first case referred to as repudiating the doctrine is the case of Frost v. Eastern Railroad, 64 N. H. 220, 9 Atl. 790, 10 Am. St. Rep. 396.

The turntable in that case "was fastened by a toggle, which prevented its being set in motion, unless the toggle was drawn by a lever, to which was attached a switch padlock, which, being locked, prevented the lever from being used, unless the staple was drawn.

At the time of the accident, the turntable was fastened by the toggle; but it was a controverted point whether the padlock was then locked. When secured by the toggle, and not locked with the padlock, the turntable could not be set in motion by boys of the age and strength of the plaintiff.'' On this issue the court decided the case in favor of the railroad, and stepped aside to show its disapproval of the turntable doctrine as declared in the case of Sioux City R. R. Co. v. Stout, 17 Wall. 657, 21 L. Ed. 745.

Another case which is relied on very strongly by appellee's counsel as showing the unsoundness of the doctrine is Walsh v. Fitchburg R. R. Co., 145 N. Y. 301, 39 N. E. 1068, 27 L. R. A. 724, 45 Am. St. .Rep. 615. In that case the facts, as they appear in the opinion, show that the turntable was surrounded by an embankment from three to nine feet high, and was not easily accessible except by the company's track which led to it. The child injured, with two or three others, went to the turntable and was playing with it; but there is not a statement or intimation in the opinion that children had previously made use of this turntable as a plaything, or, if they had, there was no allegation that the company's agents in charge of it had any information of that fact. Therefore the facts of that case easily distinguish it from the one before us.

In commenting on the turntable doctrine and the decisions holding that a /recovery cannot be had in ''turntable'' cases, Thompson, in his Commentaries on the Law of Negligence (volume 1, page 952) says:

"Some of the courts, chiefly in those portions of our country which are dominated by railroad and other corporate influences, have balanced the lives and limbs of children of tender years against the slight inconvenience on the part of the railway company of keeping its turntables locked, and have decided that such a company is not liable in damages for the death or injury of a child, received while playing with an unguarded and unfastened turntable, although situated in a populous district where children play in great numbers. Some of these cases put the doctrine on the cold and draconic ground that children, although of tender years, are responsible for the consequences of their trespasses the same as adults, and that the mere fact that one trespassing upon the grounds of a railroad company is such a child does not raise any duty on the part of the company towards the trespasser."

In the same work (volume 2, page 528) after commenting upon the great danger to children in allowing turntables to be left insecurely fastened, and stating that railroad companies should, when they can with slight expense and inconvenience, keep their turntables locked or guarded so that children could not use them, and that if they fail to do so they should be required to respond in damages, continues as follows:

"This, on the one hand, allows the railway company the reasonable use of its property, while at the same time it refuses to release it from these obligations of social duty which rest upon all men in a state of civilized society. Decisions of authoritative courts contravening this doctrine no doubt exist; but the author does not hesitate to characterize them, as he has always done whenever he has had occasion to

comment upon them, as being cruel, wicked, and blots
upon the jurisprudence of civilized communities."

Appellee's counsel and some of the authorities referred to as repudiating the turntable doctrine announce the correct general rule of law to be: The
owner or occupier of real property is under no obligation to make it safe for the benefit of trespassers,
intruders, mere volunteers, or bare licenses, and contend that the rule is applicable alike to adults and
infants; that there cannot, in reason, be any distinction between them. The only exceptions they make
to this general proposition are: First, when the owner of property expressly or impliedly invites persons
upon his premises, he assumes the duty of exercising
reasonable care to prevent their injury from dangerous obstructions thereon or defects therein; second,
he cannot use his premises in such a way that
the use so made of them inflicts injury upon the persons or property lawful in the use of or upon adjoining premises; third, the owner of ground abutting on
a public highway cannot suffer pitfalls, or other nuisances dangerous to public travel, to remain so near
the margin of such highway that persons in the lawful use of same are liable to receive injuries therefrom.

The fourth and only other exception, we quote:
"As an exception to the first rule, it may be stated
that if the owner intentionally or wantonly places
upon his premises a dangerous instrumentality or
obstruction for the express purpose of inflicting injury, then he is liable if an injury results, for no one
can lawfully use even his own property for the purpose of inflicting a wanton or intentional injury."
If this is correct law, then the owner of property
would have to commit a felony before he would be

liable in damages for injuries inflicted, for it would certainly be a crime for an owner of property to place upon it a dangerous instrumentality for the express purpose of inflicting injury or death upon another, if his attention was acomplished; This is not, and should not be, the law. If this principle were announced as the law in every state in this Union, in this age when there is such a clamor and frenzy to accumulate dollars, it would be destructive to humanity, and especially to infants and other unaccountable beings. The correct rule of law is, and should be, that if a railroad company can with slight expense and little inconvenience keep its turntables guarded or locked so as to prevent trespassing children from using them, they should be compelled to do so, and, if they fail to perform this duty, they should be made liable in damages for any injury occasioned to children of tender years in playing with them. Suppose a farmer owned a pasture through which he knew children passed daily in going to and returning from school, and that he should turn a vicious animal into this field, and take no steps or precautionary measures to prevent it from injuring some one or more of the children, although he knew that it was likely to do so, under the rule contended for by counsel for appellee and the opinions referred to, the owner would not be responsible in damages, unless he intended to accomplish the result which followed. This is not the law of this state, and, in our opinion, should not be of any jurisdiction.

The turntable doctrine has been considered and approved by this court in several cases. The case of Branson's Adm'r v. Labrot, 81 Ky. 638, 50 Am. Rep. 193, was where Labrot and others owned or had control of an uninclosed lot of ground on which they

stacked some lumber. It was alleged in the petition in that case: That they stacked the lumber
in a negligent and unsafe manner; that the children
in the vicinity of the lot had frequented it for years
for the purpose of play, which fact was well known
to Labrot and others, when they piled their lumber
thereon; that the children continued to resort to
the lot for the same purpose after the lumber was
placed there with the knowledge of Labrot and others;
that the lumber, which was defectively stacked, fell
and crushed the life out of Bransom's infant son.
The lower court in that case, as did the court in the
case at bar, sustained a demurrer to the petition and
amended petition.

This court, however, reversed the action of the lower court, and said: "As a general rule, the owner of
land may retain to himself the sole and exclusive
use and occupation of it; but, as property in lands
depends upon municipal law for its recognition and
protection, the individual use and enjoyment of it
are subject to conditions and restraints imposed for
the public good, and from a reasonable and humane
regard for the welfare and rights of others. * * *
It is held that a party is guilty of negligence in
leaving anything in a place where he knows it to be
extremely probable that some other person will un-
justifiably set it in motion, to the injury of a third
person." Counsel in that case contended for the following rule, to wit: "The owner of private grounds
is under no obligation to keep them in a safe condition for the benefit of trespassers, idlers, bare licensees, or others who may come upon them, not by
invitation, expressed or implied, but for pleasure or
to gratify their curiosity, however innocent or laud-
able their purpose may be." In commenting on this,

the court said: "If this rule is to be interpreted so as to relieve the owner of private grounds from all, or even reasonable, care for the safety of those who without invitation, may come upon them, it is not a reasonable and humane rule, for the owner has no right to wantonly injure even an actual trespasser." The court also quoted with approval, in that case, from the case of Souix City Railroad Company v. Stout, 17 Wall. 657, 21 L. Ed. 745, the leading case establishing the turntable doctrine, as follows: "In the case of Railroad Company v. Stout, 17 Wall. 657, 21 L. Ed. 745, it was held that the care and caution required of a child is, acording to its maturity and capacity, only to be determined in each case by the circumstances of that case, and that a railroad company might be held liable, on the ground of negligence for a personal injury to a child of tender years in a town or city, caused by a turntable, built by the company on its uninclosed land, left unguarded and unlocked, in a situation which rendered it likely to cause injury to children." To the same effect are the cases of Keffe v. Milwaukee R. R. Co., 21 Minn. 207, 18 Am. Rep. 393; Koons v. St. Louis R. R. Co., 65 Mo., 592, and Whirley v. Whitman, 1 Head (Tenn.) 610.

The case of Kentucky Central R. R. Co. v. Gastineau's Adm'r, 83 Ky. 119, approved the principle announced in the Stout and Labot Cases. In that case the boy was between 14 and 15 years, and the court said: "We are aware that it has been held in some cases, as, for instance, in Flower v. Railroad Co. (69 Pa. 210, 8 Am. Rep. 251), supra, that, if the deceased is a trespasser, his being of tender years makes no difference, because the company is under no duty to him which requires his protection; but, in our opinion, age should be considered upon a question of contributory neglect, and one should exercise reasonable care to anticipate and prevent an injury to a child of such tender years as to have little or no discretion, although he may be technically a trespasser. His condition excuses his concurrent negligence. Humane considerations require such a rule." See, also, the cases of L. N. R. R. Co. v. Popp, 96 Ky. 99, 27 S. W. 992, 16 Ky. Law Rep. 369; Swartwood v. L. & N. R. R. Co., 33 Ky. Law Rep., 785, 111 S. W. 305, 19 L. R. A. (N. S.) 1112; City of Owensboro v. York, 117 Ky. 294, 77 S. W., 1130, 25 Ky. Law Rep. 1397, 1439; Board of Councilmen v. Allen, 82 S. W., 292, 26 Ky. Law Rep., 581; Merschel v. L. & N. R. R. Co., 121 Ky., 620, 85 S. W. 710, 27 Ky. Law Rep., 465; I. C. R. R. Co. v. Wilson, 63 S. W., 608, 23 Ky. Law Rep., 684.

The remaining question necessary to be determined is whether appellee is relieved from liability, if negligent in failing to make secure its turntable, by the acts of its codefendants, Sam and Jasper Saad, who put the turntable in motion. The authorities seem to be one way on this question. In the case of Gulf Colorado & Santa Fe Railway Co. v. McWhirter, 77 Tex., 356, 14 S. W., 26, 19 Am. St. Rep., 755, this question was also involved, and the court said: "If it be conceded that the person who put the turntable in motion was sui juris, this would not relieve the appellant from liability, though another party might also be liable. If an accident occurs from two causes, both due to negligence of different persons, but together the efficient cause, then all the persons whose acts contribute to the accident are liable for an injury resulting, and the negligence of one furnishes no excuse for the negligence of the other." And after cit-

ing many cases from other jurisdictions, cites the following text-books to support the proposition, to wit:
"Cooley on Torts, 823; Bishop on Noncontract Law,
518; Shearman & Redfield on Negligence, 35; Thompson on Negligence, 1088; Wharton on Negligence,
144.".

The case of Snyder v. Arnold, 122 Ky. 557, 92
S. W., 289, 28 Ky. Law Rep., 1250, was where appellees negligently stacked a lot of lumber near to and
partly on a sidewalk, and allowed it to remain there
in its dangerous position for some time. Appellant,
a boy of about nine years of age, was passing along
on the walk and stopped by the side of the lumber,
and at that moment a wagon loaded with rock was
moved by, and the hub struck the lumber pile and
caused it to fall upon the boy and injure him. Appellees in that case claimed that they were not
responsible, even if they were negligent in letting
the lumber remain at that place, for the reason
that the driver of the wagon, a third person who was
in no way connected with them, caused the lumber to
fall which resulted in the boy's injury. In considering the question the court said: "It will thus be seen
that the sole question in the case is: What was the
proximate cause of the injury? And this is one of
the most difficult and important questions presented
in the trial of negligence cases; it being an established principle of law that there can be no recovery
for an act of negligence unless it was the proximate
cause of the injury complained of.

If the conduct of appellees in piling the lumber at
the place, in the manner it was piled, and in permitting it to remain in that position, was not the proximate cause of the injury to appellant, he cannot
recover. If the injury is traceable to the negligent

and careless manner in which the lumber was piled, although the immediate cause of the accident was running the wagon against the lumber, the appellant may recover. In our opinion the controlling and determining question in this case is : Were appellees guilty of negligence in piling the lumber and permitting it to remain in the position it was in when struck by the wagon? If there was no negligence on their part in this particular, then appellee cannot recover, because the injury to him was due to the driver of the wagon. On the other hand, if they were guilty of negligence in the respect mentioned, the negligence, or carelessness of the driver of the wagon will not excuse them, as the mere fact that another person concurs or co-operates in producing an injury, or contributes thereto in any degree, whether large or small, is of no importance.'' See, also, the cases of Bransom's Adm'r v. Labrot, supra, and Edington v. Railroad Co., 116 Iowa, 410, 90 N. W., 95, 57 L. R. A., 561.

For these reasons the judgment of the lower court is reversed and remanded for further proceedings consistent herewith.

CASE 95.—ACTION BY J. D. PORTER AND OTHERS AGAINST
MATTIE PORTER.—December 17, 1909.

Porter v. Porter, &c.

Appeal from Butler Circuit Court.

JOHN M. GALLOWAY, Circuit Judge.

Judgment for plaintiffs, defendant appeals.—Reversed.

1. Deeds—Description of Property—Certainty.—A deed to a
tract of land "lying in Butler county, Ky., and described as
follows: Our entire interest in the S. A. T. Porter farm except
½ acre more or less on the north east corner of said farm
where J. D. Porter now lives," is not void for insufficiency of
description, there being evidence that S. A. T. Porter had
an interest in only one tract in that county and that
she had lived on that tract for many years after her husband's death, that the tract was known as the "S. A. T. Porter
land," and that J. D. Porter had purchased one-half acre of
that tract.

2. Executors and Administrators—Distribution of Estate—Sale
of Property—Relief.—Two brothers interested in equal parts
with other brothers and sisters in their father's estate deeded
their interest in the property to a third brother, and, after
the death of the third brother, induced his widow to return
the deeds to them; the deeds not having been recorded, the
consideration for one of them not having been paid, and the
consideration for the other being returned to the widow. Held,
that, in an action by another brother and sister for the sale
of the land and division of the proceeds, the two brothers
who deeded their interest should not have been relieved from
their contract of sale, the deeds by them being sufficient, but
that the court should have decreed that the consideration for
such deeds should be paid them out of the amount of the
proceeds which descended to the deceased brother who had
purchased their interest.

3. Executors and Administrators—Distribution of Estate—Actions—Pleading.—In an action brought by one of the devisees for the sale of the land of the testator and division of the proceeds, the widow of one of the devisees who claimed the greater part of the property, and who had been in possession of the land for a number of years after the court decided that she and her children were not entitled to have their interests set apart and a homestead allowed them out of the same, because the real estate had been converted into personalty by the provisions of the will, filed an amended pleading, in which she alleged that she was the widow of one of the devisees named, alleged that he left surviving him five infant children who had resided with her, that her husband had left no property or provisions for her and the children, except two horses, one cow, one wagon, and some household goods not worth exceeding $200, and a part interest in a legacy, and asked that $730 be set aside out of the legacy to supply the deficiency in the property on hand at the death of her husband. Held, that a demurrer to the item of $730 was properly sustained, as it was impossible to determine the amount she was entitled to; the value of the household goods not being alleged.

4. Conversion — Reconversion. — Testator directed in his will that, after all of his children had an equal outfit at the death of his wife, his land be sold and equally divided between all of his children. In another clause he gave his executor power, provided certain things happened, to sell the land and divide the proceeds between the children equally. Held that in the absence of an election by the devisees to treat the land as realty, the will converted it into personalty, and a reconversion of the devisees can only be affected by the joinder of all the devisees in such election, and such election is not shown by deeds conveying the interests of the devisees in the land or the proceeds thereof.

GARDNER & HOLMES for appellant.

GORE & BUNCH for appellees

OPINION OF THE COURT BY CHIEF JUSTICE NUNN—
Reversing.

In the month of March, 1874, the will of J. D. Porter was duly probated in the Butler county court, and recorded in the clerk's office. He owned at his

death 400 or 500 acres of land which he had purchased from different persons, but all formed one
body. He also owned some personal property. The
will, beginning with the third clause, is as follows:

"3rd. I will after all my debts are paid that the
remainder of my estate belong to my beloved wife
and her children.

"4th. I will that my wife and children remain on
the place until they marry or become of age.

"5th. I will that all of the children who are not of
age be made equal in property with those who have
married or may marry, that is I want them to have
the same outfit.

"6th. I will that should my wife Sally die and
there should not be a sufficient amount of perishable
property on the place to make the youngest children
equal in an outfit that they be made equal out of
the proceeds of the land; an outfit is understood to
mean horse, saddle and bridle, bed and clothing, cow
and calf.

"7th. I will that after all my children have had
an equal outfit at the death of my wife Sally that my
land be sold & divided equally between all my children.

"8th. I will that my wife Sally shall abide at my
old residence or on a place that shall be purchased
by my executor out of the proceeds of the old residence. should she live to become disabled from age
or affliction that she shall be provided for out of my
estate.

"9th. I will that my son William A. Porter be
my executor and that he in the event of certain things
that may come up in the division of the land on which
I now reside that may render the place ill convenient
and unprofitable that he shall have power to sell and

make a deed to the old residence and invest the money in land again which shall be the general property of all the children at the death of Sally my wife. Should my son William A. outlive my wife Sally he shall have power to sell my land and make a deed and divide the proceeds equally between my children that may be left after paying all expenses without security.''

The widow of J. D. Porter died in the early part of the year 1908. She remained a widow and resided on the land as requested by the will. J. D. Porter, the testator, had 11 children, some of whom died prior to his death and left children surviving them. The testator's estate, under the will, was to be divided into 11 equal parts. Sam Porter, a son, resided on the place with his mother and cared for her until his death in 1905, and his widow and children resided with and supported the old lady from that time until her death. Sam Porter, while residing on the farm with his mother, purchased the interests of several of his brothers and sisters, nieces, and nephews in the land or its proceeds, amounting in all to 23-33 of the whole. A part of the consideration for these interests, or, at least, some of them, was that Sam was to live with and support his mother during her lifetime, which, in our opinion, he complied with until his death, from which time his widow and children substantially carried out his contract in this respect.

This action was instituted in the month of October, 1908, by John D. Porter, a brother, and sister against the other heirs and interested parties for a sale of the land and a division of the proceeds among them. The main purpose of the suit, as stated in the petition was ''to test the question whether the devisees owned an interest in the real estate or

in the proceeds thereof.'' The infant children of
Sam Porter, deceased, and his second wife answered
the children by guardian ad litem, and claimed that
they owned 23-33 of the land, and asked that their
interests be set apart in a body, and that the widow
and infant children be allowed a homestead therein.
They also alleged that two of the appellees, J. B.
and J. E. Porter, had sold and conveyed to their
father, Sam Porter, their interests in the property;
that the consideration named in the conveyances
from J. E. Porter was $40 cash in hand, and that
Sam would take care of his mother the remainder of
her life; that the consideration named in the deed
from J. B. Porter to Sam was $60 which appears by
the deed to have been cash in hand, but, in fact,
was not, and Sam still owed it with its interest at his
death. It is further alleged that after the death of
Sam the deeds just referred to having never been
recorded, J. B. and J. E. Porter went to Sam's
widow and wrongfully induced and persuaded her to
surrender the deeds to them. J. E. Porter returned
the $40 which he had been paid by Sam to his widow,
and J. B. Porter surrendered the papers he had
showing that Sam owed him the $60. They alleged
that this was a wrong perpetrated against their interests, and asked that J. B. and J. E. Porter be
compelled to return these deeds to them; that they be
recorded and that they be adjudged the owners of
these two interests. The lower court sustained a demurrer to these pleadings upon the ground that by
the terms of the will of J. D. Porter his real estate
was converted into pensonalty, and that it must be
sold and the proceeds divided among those in interest,
and consequently the widow and children were not en-

titled to a homestead in the land. The court also adjudged that the deeds from J. B. and J. E. Porter were void for want of description, and conveyed no title or interest to Sam Porter in the property. The widow and children objected and excepted to this judgment.

The action of the court in declaring the deeds executed by J. E. and J. B. Porter void for want of description is the first question that arises on this appeal, and we will dispose of it now. As the descriptions in the deeds are in substance and effect the same we will copy but one, to wit: "Do bargain, sell and convey unto the said party of the second part, a certain tract or parcel of land lying in Butler county, Ky., and described as follows: Our entire interest in the S. A. T. Porter farm except 1-2 acre more or less on the north east corner of said farm where J. D. Porter now lives." In our opinion this description was sufficient. The testimony shows that S. A. T. Porter had no claim to or interest in any other land in that county; that she had resided on that farm for many years after her husband's death. The description given disposed of their interests in the S. A. T. Porter land in Butler county. The land referred to was known as the S. A. T. Porter land. The statement to the effect that it was the same land out of which one-half acre had been previously sold to J. D. Porter upon which he resided made certain the land described, as it was shown in the record that J. D. Porter had purchased one-half acre off of one end of the Porter survey upon which he erected a dwelling and resided for many years. The case of Hyden v. Perkins, 119 Ky., 188, 83 S. W., 128, 26 Ky. Law Rep., 1099, and the authorities therein ·cited, settle the question. The court should not have relieved J. E. and J. B. Porter from their contract of sale of the property; but J. E. Porter should have the $40 and its interest returned to him by Mrs. Sam Porter to whom he paid it when he got his deed from her, and J. B. Porter should be allowed the purchase money due him for his interest to-wit, $60, with its interest, which should be paid him out of the proceeds of the sale of Sam Porter's 23-33. When the court determined that Sam's widow and children were not entitled to have their interests set apart and a homestead allowed them out of same, because the real estate had been converted into personalty by the provisions of the will of J. D. Porter, the widow filed an amended pleading, in which she alleged that she was the widow of Sam Porter, gave the date of his death, and further alleged that he left surviving him five infant children who had at all times resided with the petitioner; that Sam left no property or provisions for her and the infant children, except two horses, one cow, one wagon, and some household goods not worth exceeding $200, and 23-33 interest in a legacy of J. D. Porter. She asked that $737 be set aside to her out of this legacy to supply the deficiency in the property on hand at Sam's death. She also alleged that she as Sam's widow was entitled to one-half of the surplus of the personalty, including the legacy, after the payment of Sam's debts. The court sustained a demurrer to this pleading and dismissed it, and this presents the only question that remains to be considered.

We are of the opinion that the court did not err in sustaining the demurrer as to the item of $737 claimed by reason of the deficiency in the articles of personal property, which is authorized to be set apart to widows and infant children by the statute.

The pleading is very defective. It was impossible for the court to determine any certain amount that she was entitled to. She stated that she received "two horses, one cow, one wagon, and some household goods not worth exceeding $200." She did not state what the household goods were. She only gave it as her opinion that they were not worth exceeding $200. The two horses and wagon were all that she was entitled to under this head, but she was entitled to another cow and calf or $20 in lieu of them. The household goods might have covered every article in that line allowed by the statute. It is our opinion, however, that the court erred with reference to her claim of interest in the proceeds of the sale of 23-33 of the land. By the will of J. D. Porter the real estate he owned was converted into personalty and the devisees took it as such. By the third and fourth clauses of the will he devised the farm to his wife and children until they married or became of age. The widow never married, but all the children became of age before her death. By the seventh clause of his will he provided as follows: "I will that after all of my children have had an equal outfit at the death of my wife, Sally, that my land be sold and divided equally between all my children."

In the ninth clause he gave his executor power, provided certain things happened, to sell the land and divide the proceeds among his children equally. After the death of their mother, the life tenant, the children instituted this action to have the land sold, and the proceeds divided as directed by the will.

The doctrine that land directed to be converted into money by a testator is to be regarded as a money legacy is well established, and has been long recognized by the courts of this state, subject, it is true, to an election by the devisees whether to treat it as realty or personalty; but, in the absence of an election to regard it as realty, the law stamps it as a money bequest. See Jarman on Wills, 756; Arnold's Exors. v. Arnold's Heirs, 11 B. Mon. 89; Williams on Executions, 767; Bowling's Heirs .v. Dobyn's Admr., 5 Dana, 434; Field's Heirs v. Hallowell & Co., 12 B. Mon. 517; and Hocker, et al. v. Gentry, et al., 3 Metc. 473, and the authorities there cited.

The cases of Rawling's Exor., &c. v. Landes, &c., and Holeman, &c. v. Landes, &c., 2 Bush, 158, are conclusive of the question at issue. It appears in those cases that Jacob Holeman devised to his wife for life 200 acres of land, and directed that at her death the land be sold by his executor and the proceeds divided among his children and two grandchildren. Subsequent to Holeman's death his daughter, Mary, a devisee, married one Benjamin Rawlings, and died childless in the year 1845, and her husband survived her only about a year, when he died, leaving surviving him as his only child and residuary devisee appellant, John W. Rawlings, by a former marriage. Mary's brothers and sisters sought to recover the interest in the proceeds devised to her in this 200 acres of land. John W. Rawlings, a child of Benjamin by a former marriage, claimed it for the reason, as he claims, the will of Holeman had converted the land into personalty, and it was therefore given to Mary as a money legacy and upon her death her personal property passed, under the statutes, to her husband, and, when he died, it passed to Rawlings, his only son. The court upheld Rawlings in his contention, and gave him the interest in the proceeds of the sale of the 200 acres of land which had been devised to Mary Rawlings. In discussing the character of interest Mary took under this bequest, the court said: "Was this an interest in realty or personalty? The doctrine that land directed to be converted into money by a testator is to be regarded as a money legacy and is now equally well established, and has long been recognized by the courts of this state in the cases before cited, as well as by numerous of the other American states and in England, subject, it is true, to an election by the devisees whether to treat it as realty or personalty; but, in the absence of an election to regard it as realty, the law stamps it as a money bequest." In view of the authorities, there is no escape from the conclusion that under the will of J. D. Porter his real estate was converted into personalty in so far as it affected his devisees, and they took money legacies rather than an interest in the realty. If Benjamine Rawlings, in the case just quoted from, took the interest of his wife after her death in the 200 acres of land devised to her by her father, Jacob Holeman, then appellant in the case at bar, Mrs. Sam Porter, took the interest provided for by statute in the interest or money legacy devised to her husband, Sam Porter, by his father in the will under consideration. It was provided in the statute as it existed in 1905, the date of Sam's death, that the wife should have one-half of the deceased husband's personal estate. Therefore appellant, Mrs. Sam Porter, is entitled to one-half of 23-33 of the proceeds of the sale of the real estate after the payment of Sam's liabilities and the expenses of the sale; but out of her portion she must refund to J. E. Porter the amount she received from him when she returned to him the deed or writing hereinbefore referred to.

Appellee's counsel admit the correctness of the rule above stated, but claim that there has been a reconversion by the devisees; that they elected to take the land, instead of the proceeds thereof. It is true that it is a well established rule that the devisees may elect to do so, but the facts do not support the contention of appellee's counsel in this case. The authorities seem to consider it necessary, in order to create a reconversion of property, for all the devisees to join in the election, which was not done in this case. On the contrary, this action was brought to carry out the intention of the testator by selling the land and dividing the proceeds as directed by the will. It is true Sam received many deeds or writings from his brothers and sisters which had the effect to convey or transfer to him their interests in the land or the proceeds thereof, but this fact does not show an election to change the devise from one of personalty to one of realty. Some of the heirs did not convey their interest to any one, but held it under the will until their mother's death.

For these reasons, the judgment of the lower court is reversed and remanded for further proceedings consistent herewith.

CASE 96.—ACTION BY M. N. JONES AGAINST THE LOUIS-
VILLE TOBACCO WAREHOUSE COMPANY.—September 24, 1909.

Jones v. Louisville Tobacco Warehouse Co.

Appeal from Franklin Circuit Court.

R. L. STOUT, Circuit Judge.

Judgment for defendant, plaintiff appeals.—Reversed.

1. Fraudulent   Conveyances — Transfers   Between   Husband and wife—Validity as to Third Persons—Registration.—
   Under Ky. St. Sec. 2128 (Russell's St. Sec. 4631), providing
   that a transfer of personal property between husband and
   wife shall not be valid as to third persons, unless in writing
   and recorded, a surrender of tobacco by husband to wife, not
   reduced to writing or recorded, was invalid as to his other
   creditors.

2. Fraudulent Conveyances—Rent Lien—Effect of Invalid Transfer of Property to Landlord.—A surrender of tobacco by husband to wife being invalid, as to other creditors under Ky. St.
   Sec. 2128 (Russell's St. Sec. 4631), because not reduced to
   writing and recorded, left unchanged her superior landlord's
   rent lien, under section 2317 (Russell's St. Sec. 4574), on the
   tobacco raised on the land leased by him of her.

3 Landlord   and   Tenant — Rent   Lien — Enforcement —
   Loss of Right.—Under Ky. St. Sec 2317 (Russell's St. Sec.
   4574), giving the landlord a superior lien for a year's rent on
   produce of the leased farm, but for no rent that has been
   due for more than 120 days, and providing that if the produce
   be removed openly from the leased premises, without fraudulent intent, and not be returned, the landlord shall have his
   lien on it for 15 days from its removal, and may enforce it
   against the property wherever found, where after the end of
   the year for which a farm was rented, at which time the rent
   became due, the tenant, being indebted for the rent, surrendered tobacco raised 'on the farm to the landlord, which sur-

render was invalid as against the tenant's other creditors because the landlord was his wife, and she then shipped the tobacco to defendant to sell as her agent, and it .sold it, applied
the proceeds on the tenant's debt to it, and refused to pay the
landlord, all this within 15 days after the removal of the
tobacco from the premises and 120 days after the termination
of the lease—the landlord's right of action against defendant
to enforce its lien against the proceeds accruing when it refused to pay her the same was not lost by failure to bring
the action within 120 days after the rent became due.

4. Fraudulent   Conveyances — Partial   Individuality. — A
    lease by the wife of the lessee and another not being re-
    corded, its provision that the landlord shall have a lien on
    the crop for the rent is invalid as to creditors so far as con-
    cerns the lien given the wife.

5. Subrogation—Nature and Theory of Right.—Subrogation is
    only allowed where there is some equitable reason for it.

6. Subrogation—Voluntary Payment.—One who pays a debt for
    another voluntarily is not ordinarily subrogated to the
    rights of the creditor.

7. Pleading—Subrogation—Conclusions.—The allegation of the
    petition that plaintiff, one of two landlords, who paid to the
    other landlord her part of the rent was subrogated to the
    rights of the other, is a mere legal conclusion· it being neces-
    sary to state the facts showing a right of subrogation.

B. G. WILLIAMS and J. MORGAN CHINN for appellant.

BROWN & NUCHOLS for appellee.

OPINION OF THE COURT BY JUDGE HOBSON—Reversing.

Appellant, Maggie N. Jones, brought this suit
against the Louisville Tobacco Warehouse Company
to recover the proceeds of certain tobacco which she
alleged she had shipped to it in March, 1900, and it
had sold as her agent.   The warehouse company
claimed the right to hold the money as the property of
John W. Jones, the husband of Maggie N. Jones, on
account of a debt which he owed to it contracted about
the year 1896.   The circuit court sustained a de-

murrer to the plaintiff's reply to the defendant's answer, and, she declining to plead further, dismissed
her petition. From this judgment she appeals.

The facts admitted by the demurrer are these:
Maggie N. Jones and her mother, Minerva Noel, owned a farm in Franklin county, and on March 1, 1905,
they entered into the following written contract by·
which they rented the farm to J. W. Jones: "For and
in consideration of the sum of nine hundred dollars
($900.00) to be paid on or before the first day of
March, 1906, we, Mrs. Minerva Noel and Maggie N.
Jones of the first part have this day rented to J. W.
Jones of the 2nd part of our farm known as the S. M.
Noel farm for the term of one year. Parties of the
first part reserve for their own use the tenement
house at front gate, the two tenement houses at the
mouth of branch, the pump house and right of way to
said tenement house and pump house right of way
over and for repairing of pipe line by the distillery
company and also the slop privilege at the new cattle
sheds. First parties also reserve a lien on all crops
grown on said farm until moneys for rent are paid.
First parties reserve all right for seeding purposes
in the fall of the year. First parties are not to repair any fencing on said farm. Possession of farm
to be given 1st of March, 1905, given up March 1st,
1906. , Second party is allowed to work lands on
farm any way he wants to, or to sublet any lands that
he wants to, or to plow any lands, and is to do all the
repairing on barns, fencing, etc., at second parties
own expense. Minerva Noel, Maggie N. Jones, J. W.
Jones." On March 1, 1906, Jones owed $550 of the
rent, and Maggie N. Jones then paid to Mrs. Noel
her part of the rent, and thus became entitled to all
the rent as between her and her husband. He had

sublet the farm the year before to a number of tenants who had raised a crop of tobacco on it, under
contracts by which they were to have one-half of the
tobacco and he one-half. J. W. Jones then surrendered to Maggie N. Jones his half of the tobacco which
was then on the place, and she took possession of it
and shipped it to the warehouse company. The net
proceeds of half of the tobacco when sold by the
warehouse company amounted to $214.54. The rent
contract above quoted was not recorded. The arrangement by which J. W. Jones surrendered to his
wife his one-half of the tobacco was verbal, and not
reduced to writing or recorded. Section 2128, Ky.
Stat. (Russell's St. § 4631), which gives the wife the
right to make contracts as a single woman, contains
this proviso: "A gift, transfer or assignment of personal property between husband and wife shall not
be valid as to third persons, unless the same be in
writing, and acknowledged and recorded as chattel
mortgages are required by law to be acknowledged
and recorded; but the recording of any such writing
shall not make valid any such gift, transfer or assignment which is fraudulent or voidable as to creditors or purchasers." It is insisted for the warehouse company that, as the transfers between the
husband and wife were not recorded, they were void,
and the title to the tobacco still remained in the husband. Section 2317, Ky. Stat. (Russell's St. § 4574)
is as follows: "A landlord shall have a superior lien
on the produce of the farm or premises rented, on the
fixtures, on the household furniture, and other personal property of the tenant, or undertenant, owned
by him, after possession is taken under the lease·
but such lien shall not be for more than one year's
rent due or to become due, nor for any rent which

has been due for more than one hundred and twenty days. And if any such property be removed openly from the leased premises, and without fraudulent intent, and not returned, the landlord shall have a superior lien on the property so removed for fifteen days from the date of its removal, and may enforce his lien against the property wherever found.'' It is conceded that under this section the wife had a lien on the tobacco for her rent; but it is insisted that this lien was lost because it was not asserted within 120 days after the rent fell due or within 15 days after the removal of the tobacco from the premises.

In Eberhardt v. Wahl, 124 Ky. 223, 98 S. W. 994, 30 Ky. Law Rep. 412, Mrs. Eberhardt and her husband, Jacob, executed two notes to a bank for $250 for money borrowed by him. To secure the first note he pledged 10 shares of stock which he owned and to secure the second note she pledged 10 shares of stock which she owned. She paid to the bank $250 of her own money, intending to pay the note which was secured by the pledge of her own stock. But the bank applied it to the payment of the first note which was secured by the pledge of her husband's stock. She applied to the bank to correct the mistake, and was told by the bank officers that all that was necessary was that her husband should deliver to her the 10 shares of stock which had been released to secure her in the $250 which she had paid, and protect her against liability on the second note. This was accordingly done, but the agreement was not recorded. In this condition of things another creditor attached the husband's 10 shares of stock. It was held by this court that the arrangement between the husband and wife was void, and that the wife acquired no lien on the husband's 10 shares of stock by reason of the transfer of the stock to her by him. But it was also held that the bank had a lien on the 10 shares of stock, and that the wife, having paid the note to the bank which was secured by the stock, was entitled to be subrogated to the lien of the bank under the circumstances, independently of any transaction between her and her husband. See, also, Stroud v. Ross, 118 Ky. 630, 82 S. W. 254, 26 Ky. Law Rep. 521. In Marquess v. Ladd, 100 S. W. 305, 30 Ky. Law Rep. 1142, the tenant, while the tobacco was on the leased premises, turned over his interest in the crop to the landlord under an agreement that he should retain possession of it and place it upon the market with the Dark Tobacco Protective Association, where it was to remain until sold, and that out of the proceeds of it when sold the landlord was to pay himself what the tenant owed him and pay the remainder to the tenant. Under this arrangement the landlord took possession of the tobacco, and in stituted no proceedings to enforce his lien. More than 120 days after the expiration of the lease suit was brought to enforce a mortgage given by the tenant before the tobacco was turned over to the landlord; and it was insisted that the landlord had lost his lien by failing to institute proceedings to enforce it. Rejecting this claim the court said: "When the agreement between the landlord and the tenant was made in November, 1904, the landlord had a superior lien upon the tenant's interest in the tobacco to secure the payment of the money and property advanced to him, and the crop was on the leased premises. This lien he had the right under the statute to enforce at any time within 120 days after the expiration of the tenancy. The purpose of the statute was to secure the landlord for advances made to his tenant by giving him a lien upon the crop. If, after the crop has been planted and at any time during the period for which the lien of the landlord exists, the tenant for any reason concludes to deliver his interest in the crop to the landlord as security for advances made, we cannot percieve any reason why the lien in this way may not be perserved. An agreement of this kind does not extend the lien of the landlord beyond the statutory period, as the legal effect of it is the same as if the landlord had instituted legal proceedings to enforce the collection of his lien, and had acquired possession of the crop under process of the court. Creditors of the tenant cannot be prejudiced by an agreement of this character because the landlord holds the tenant's interest as a pledgee, and must acount for whatever surplus remains after discharging his debt.''

Under the statute, a gift, transfer, or assignment of personal property between husband and wife is invalid as to third persons unless in writing, acknowledged and recorded as chattel mortgages are required to be acknowledged and recorded. The surrender of the tobacco by Jones to his wife was a transfer of personal property, and, not being reduced to writing or recorded, was invalid. After that arrangement was made, the parties stood where they were before it was made. It took from the wife no right she then had and it added nothing to her rights. Before that surrender was made, she had a lien on the tobacco for her rent under the statute, and this superior lien she continued to have after the arrangement was made. The rent was not due until March 1, 1906. The tobacco was sold during that month. When the tobacco was sold, her demand against the warehouse company accrued, and, it then refusing to pay her the

money, her right to the money was in no wise affected by the fact that she did not bring her suit against
the warehouse company until December 10, 1906. The
tobacco having been sold and the proceeds being in
the hands of the warehouse company, her right of
action against it accrued when it refused to pay the
money over to her, and, this all having occurred within 120 days after the rent became due, her delay in
suing after the liability accrued did not prejudice
the warehouse company. There is nothing in the
case to show that the tobacco had been removed from
the premises more than 15 days before it was received or sold by the warehouse company and the proceeds applied by it upon its debt against J. W. Jones.
No opinion is indicated as to what would be the effect
of such removal in a case like this. The circumstances indicate that only a short time elapsed after the removal of the property from the premises before its
receipt and sale by the warehouse company.

The written lease provided that the owner
of the land should have a lien on the crop
for the rent, but, as this was not recorded, the
special contract was invalid so far as it stipulated
for a lien on the crop in favor of the wife. It was
valid, however, as to Mrs. Noel. She had a lien by
virtue of the contract on the crop of tobacco as
against the warehouse company whose debt was
created in the year 1896. It is alleged in the petition
that Mrs. Jones when she paid Mrs. Noel her part of
the rent became subrogated to her rights. But no
facts are alleged showing a right of subrogation. One
who pays a debt for another voluntarily is not ordinarily subrogated to the rights of the creditor. Subrogation is only allowed where there is some equitable reason for it. The allegation that the plaintiff

was subrogated to the rights of Mrs. Noel is only a
conclusion of the pleader. The facts must be stated
showing a right of subrogation, if the plaintiff bases
her right of recovery upon the lien given Mrs. Noel
in the lease; but the plaintiff is entitled to a lien under the statute for the rent due her.

We therefore conclude that the court erred in sustaining the defendant's demurrer to the plaintiff's
reply. On the return of the case the parties will be
allowed to amend their pleadings if they desire to
do so.

Judgment reversed, and cause remanded for further proceedings consistent herewith.

Extended Opinion and Response to Petition for
Rehearing.

O'REAR, J. It appears that Mrs. Jones shipped
the tobacco to appellee as her factor. Section 4768,
Ky. St. (Russell's St. § 2530); J. S. Phelps & Co. v.
Barkley, 40 S. W. 384. Appellee, as factor, could not
deny the title of its principal. When it accepted her
consignment of tobacco as her property, it became
estopped thereafter to deny to appellant's prejudice
that the title to the tobacco was hers.

Appellee argues that the lien is given by statute
upon the property—not its proceeds. But the statute
deals alone with the status, independent of a contract
enlarging or restricting it. It is still competent for
the parties to contract with respect to property of the
tenant or leased premises. While, as between husband and wife, such contracts must be in writing to
affect "third persons," by the expression it is meant
that others may deal with the former owner on the
faith of his ostensible ownership, unaffected by se-

cret transfers. The provision as to recordation of the contract is to give a notice of the changed title. Obviously, if the party dealing with it knows equally well from other sources that the title is in the wife, but he buys from the husband, knowing that the wife is ignorant of the transaction, he is not the kind of "third person" intended to be protected by the statute. The statute aims at promoting honesty, not trickery, and is meant to enlarge, not to restrict, married women's property and contractual rights. It ought to be given a liberal construction to effectuate the legislative purpose.

The transaction between the husband and wife was not meretricious. The transaction itself was valid. The only thing lacking was the publicity necessary to protect "third persons" who might deal with it. The possession of the wife was of itself notice that she had some sort of claim upon the property. If her possession was obtained in fact by reason of the transfer of the tobacco in satisfaction of her lien, it preserved her lien, independent of the statute, as against all the husband's creditors who had notice of the facts; and her possession was of itself notice of the facts. The relation of landlord and tenant between the husband and wife gave her, under the statute, a lien, regardless of the contract between them, which is attacked by the appellee because not recorded. She never relinquished that lien. Her consignment of the tobacco to appellee for sale was in line to preserve her dominant equity; and, when appellee accepted the consignment on her account, it undertook as her agent to sell the tobacco on her account alone, and to remit to her the proceeds of the sale, less its commissions and expense in the matter. The

15 days given by the statute has no place in this case.
Nor has the 120-day provision. They were merged
in her consummated equity, when she took charge of
the tobacco to sell it on account of her liens in liquidation of the rent due her.

Petition overruled.

CASE 97.—ON APPLICATION FOR REHEARING.—December 17,
1909.

Smith's Adm'r v. North Jellico Coal Co.

Motion for rehearing overruled.

For former opinion see 114 S. W. 785, 131 Ky. 196.

OPINION OF THE COURT BY JUDGE HOBSON—Overruling.

When this case was pending before us on appeal,
the transcript was read by five of the seven judges,
and the case most thoroughly discussed on several
occasions in consultation before the opinion was rendered, after which a majority of the court reached
the conclusion that the judgment awarding a peremptory instruction to the jury to find for the defendant
should be affirmed.

On the petition for a rehearing the transcript has
been re-read by two of the judges, and all of the material parts of the evidence read in consultation to
the whole court, and we have again thoroughly discussed and considered the question involved; we
still think the original opinion contains a correct

exposition of the law governing the case, under all the facts as shown in the transcript.

The. petition for rehearing is therefore overruled.

DISSENTING OPINION BY JUDGE NUNN.

The facts as stated in the opinion delivered do not agree with my construction of them. Therefore it is necessary for me to state my reasons for dissent. ing. A misunderstanding by the court of the facts as they appear in the record is the only way that I can account for the result.

In considering this case, it should be kept in mind that the court was not asked to reverse a judgment based upon a verdict of a properly instructed jury, but its duty, and only duty, was to carefully examine the record, and ascertain, first, whether appellant stated in his pleadings a cause of action; if so, then to determine whether he introduced any or a scintilla of testimony sustaining his alleged cause of action. If it was found that he had complied with these requirements, he was entitled to have his case submitted to the jury. All the decisions of this court on the question sustain the proposition. If appellant introduced any testimony supporting his alleged cause of action, it is then the duty of this court to reverse the action of the lower court in giving the peremptory instruction. It was a violation of the lower court's lawful duty to usurp the functions of the jury in weighing the evidence and deciding the case as it thought the evidence warranted. The Constitution of the state guarantees to persons the right of trial by jury, and, when a court takes this right from a person, it usurps its power. It is not contended that appellant failed to state a cause of action in his pleadings. Therefore the only question to be con-

sidered is: Was there any or a scintilla of evidence
introduced sustaining appellant's cause of action?
Upon this matter I will not content myself with the
bare assertion that there was; but will quote from
the testimony of each and every witness introduced,
showing that there was not only a "scintilla," but
much testimony sustaining his cause of action.

There were ten witnesses introduced, only seven of
whom gave testimony upon the question involved.
The other three were the widow, the administrator,
and the physician who attended him by whom the
extent of Smith's injuries and the cause of his death
were shown. It is conceded that the law required
appellee to furnish Smith a reasonably safe place in
which to perform his work, and to use reasonable
care to keep it reasonably safe for that purpose.
This is a general rule of law that cannot be successfully controverted. The term "reasonably safe
place" must be construed in connection with the work
to be performed. There cannot be found in a coal
mine, powder house, or similar places a safe place
to labor. The meaning of the phrase is that the mas-
.ter must use due care, considering the place where
the work is to be done, in making the place reasonably safe and in keeping it so. If the character of
the work is unusually dangerous, there then arises
the necessity of more care on the part of the master
to provide and keep a reasonably safe place for the
protection of the employe, and more care is also required on the part of the employe to save himself
from injury.

The following quotation from the case of Pfisterer
v. Peter & Co., 117 Ky. 501, 78 S. W. 450, 25 Ky.
Law Rep. 1605, emphasizes this principle, to-wit:

"A master employing a servant impliedly engages
with him that the place in which he is to work and

the tools or machinery with which he is to work or by which he is to be surrounded shall be reasonably safe. It is the master who is to provide the place and the tools and the machinery, and, when he employs one to enter into his service, he impliedly says to him that there is no other danger in the place, the tools, and the machinery than such as is obvious and necessary. Of course, some places of work and some kinds of machinery are more dangerous than others, but that is something which inheres in the thing itself, which is a matter of necessity, and cannot be obviated. But within such limits the master who provides the place, the tools, and the machinery owes a positive duty to his employe in respect thereto. That positive duty does not go to the extent of a guaranty of safety, but does require that reasonable precautions be taken to secure safety, and it matters not to the employe by whom that safety is secured, or the reasonable precautions therefor taken. He has a right to look to the master for the discharge of that duty; and if the master, instead of discharging it himself, sees fit to have it attended to by others, that does not change the measure of obligation to the employe, or the latter's right to insist that reasonable precaution shall be taken to secure safety in these respects.' ''

I will now proceed to show from the record that appellee did not furnish Smith a reasonably safe place to work, or use any care whatever to put and keep it in a reasonably safe condition. James Woodward, the helper of Smith at the time he received his injuries, in speaking of the place where Smith was killed, testified as follows: "Q. Now, tell the jury if there was a hill seam there, and, if there was, where it ran with reference to the entry? A. Yes; there

was one. Q. Describe that seam the best you can as
if you were describing a crack in a room? The
width or depth and how it ran with reference to the
entry and neck of the room? A. It ran across the
entry and across into the corner of the room neck.
Q. Which side of the room neck? A. Left-hand side.
Q. Tell the jury what kind of a top that was at this
room neck and along that entry at that place. A.
Most of it was bad top. Q. What do you mean by
'bad top'—rotten top? A. Yes, sir. Q. Do you know
whose duty it was to look after that? A. I suppose
the bank boss was supposed to look after it. Q. To
what extent was that bad top around in that neighborhood? A. Most of it around there was bad.''

George Owens, with reference to the same subject,
testified as follows: ''Q. Describe the condition at the
top of that mine where the room neck was turned off
where Smith was hurt? A. I don't know whether
the room was cut the last time I was in there before
he was hurt. There was loose slate hanging in places.·
It is called a bad entry.''

Henry Davidson testified as follows: ''Q. Tell the
jury if you know what was the condition of that top.
A. It was a pretty bad top. Q. What is a bad top?
A. Loose, bad top. Q. Is there such a thing as a rotten top? A. Yes, sir. Q. Tell the jury whether or
not this was rotten? A. Yes, it was rotten. Q. Did
you notice any hill seam there? A. Yes. Q. Explain
to the jury. If they weakened the top, how they do
it? A. It runs in on the rib and weakens one side
of it. Q. State whether or not the slate is more liable
to fall where there is a hill seam than where there is
none? A. Yes, sir. Q. What ought to be done to
make it safe in case of a hill seam? A. It ought to
be timbered to make it safe.''

We find that there was ample proof that appellee failed to furnish Smith a reasonably safe place to work; but it is said or intimated in the opinion that it was the duty of Smith to call for props and place them so as to protect himself. This is not the fact. It was not his duty to clean up this room or entry, and make them safe by the use of props or by other means. The witness Woodward, in speaking of the duties of Smith, testified as follows: "Q. The only thing he (Smith) was connected with was simply running that machine? A. Yes. Q. The company had other men to look after props and other work? A. Yes."

Witness Owens said: "Q. In cutting that entry, Smith had nothing to do about fixing the roof? A. No, Sir; it wasn't his duty to fix the roof."

Witness Davidson testified as follows: "Q. What duties are incumbent on the man who runs the machine? A. Cut coal for the loaders. Q. In what way do they ascertain where to cut? Who directs them to the place where they shall cut? A. The man that loads the coal. Q. What are the duties of the machine man with reference to looking after the safety of the roof where he works? A. He ain't got any I don't suppose. Q. Who does that? A. The loaders. Q. State whether or not it is the duty of the machine man, when he goes to cut this coal, after he understands a place is ready—is it his duty to look after the roof or safety of a place where he cuts? A. They hardly ever do. He takes the loader's word for whatever he tells him."

Thomas Profit gave the following testimony: "Q. State what you do as a loader? A. I clean the place up ready for the machine man to cut. Q. Does the machine man get any part of your wages? A. No,

sir. Q. Do you have any connection with his wages
in your work? Does he pay you anything or dó you
pay him anything out of your wages? A. No, sir.
Q. Does the machine man have anything to do with
what you do? A. No, sir. Q. What does the machine man do? A. He cuts coal. Q. Operates the
machines? A. Yes, sir. Q. Is that all he does? A.
Yes, sir.'

John Profit also said: "Q. Are you acquainted
with the duties of the machine man? A. Yes, sir.
Q. What does he do? A. He just cuts the coal. Q.
After he cuts the coal, does he have anything further
to do with it? A. No, sir. Q. After he cuts the place,
what does he do with his machine? A. Loads it up
and goes to another place, where it is cleaned up. Q.
How does he know where to go and when the place
is ready? A. The loaders generally tell him. Q. How
do they report to him? A. When they get a place
cleaned up, they tell him it is ready. Q. When you
tell him it is ready, what does he understand that to
mean? (Defendant objects. Objection sustained.)"

It was the duty of the loaders to clean up the room
and pull down the loose slate, and prop the entry for
the protection of the machine man and his helper.
The witness Aaron Jones testified that he and one
Mullens were employed by appellee as 'loaders, and
continued as follows: "Q. Where was he (Smith)
when you saw him last before the slate fell on him?
A. Unloading his machine to cut that. Q. Who had
charge of that place where the slate fell on him?
A. Me and Richard Mullens. Q. Your duties were
to load coal. A. Yes, sir. Q. What other duties did
you have? A. Pull down all loose slate. Q. Who did
you pull the slate down for, and what for? A. For
the machine man, to keep it from falling down in his

way. Q. What do you mean when you say you are
ready for him to go to work? A. I've done my duty.
Q. What does he understand? A. That I have done
my duty. Q. Does he understand that you have tested it and made it safe? A. Of course, he does. Q.
It is the duty of the loader to notify the machine man
when he is ready? A. Yes, sir.''

The witness Owens testified as follows: ''Q. What
was the duty of the loader as to preparing the place
for the machine man to work? A. It was his place
to see that the place was all right for the machine
man, and pull down loose slate, and see that the
props were all right. Q. State whether or not the
machine man had anything to do about looking after
the roof of the mine where he worked or whether
that was his duty? A. I don't suppose it was his
duty. Q. To whom was he to look for conditions? A.
He was to go to the loader if the place was not in
shape. He looked to the loader to see that his place
was all right.''

The witness Thomas Profit also testified: ''Q. How
long have you followed the occupation as a loader?
A. About seven or eight years. Q. Tell all the duties
of a loader? A. To see that the room is cleaned up.
Pull down the loose slate and fix it up for the machine man to cut. Q. Why does he pull the slate
down? A. To keep the machine man from getting
hurt. Q. Who is it that looks after the safety of the
place where the machine man works? (Defendant
objects; objections sustained.) Q. Did the company
have anybody to inspect these places and make them
safe for these men? A. Yes. Q. Who was that? A.
Gin hands.''

See the quotation from his testimony copied above.
The witness John Profit said: ''Q. What particular

employment did you have in the mines and do you
have now? A. Loading coal. Q. How long have you
been engaged in that occupation? A. Eight or nine
years. Q. Tell the jury what is the duty of a coal
loader and what he does. A. His duty is to clean up,
I suppose, and pull down the slate. Q. What does he
load? A. Coal. Q. What else do you do, if anything?
A. That's all—load coal and set timber. Q. Do you
do anything else? A. Yes, sir; pull slate."

I have shown that there is testimony in the record
that the place where Smith was put to work was very
unsafe. Indeed, this is conceded in the opinion by
the court. I have also shown that it was not Smith's
duty to make or keep it in a safe condition. This
duty devolved upon the loaders or "bank boss," Martin. I will now proceed to show that the bank boss,
Martin, marked the place, which was, in effect, an
order to Smith to cut this room neck, where he was
killed; that Martin knew of the hill seam, which
crossed the roof of the entry at an angle of about 45
degrees and entered the place that Smith was directed to cut; that he told a witness that he was going to prop it, and that he also knew of the rotten
condition of the roof, and so did the loaders, for
some time before Smith was killed. And there is
not the slightest testimony appearing in the record
that they or any of them informed Smith of these conditions, nor is there any testimony showing that
Smith knew of these facts, except from the statements of some of the witnesses to the effect that they
supposed he knew as the defects were patent to them.
The witness Aaron Jones, one of the loaders, after
stating that Smith had made one cut in that room the
evening before to a depth of four and a half or five
feet, continued as follows: "Q. Had you seen the

bank boss, David Martin, after that first cut, had been taken out? A. No, sir. Q. When had you seen him? A. That morning before I finished taking it out. Q. Whereabouts? A. Right at that place. Q. What was said between you and him at that time? A. Nothing more than he said he was going to set timber. Q. Where? A. On the entry. Q. On the entry of this room that had been drawn off at this time? A. Beyond the entry where the hill seam went across. Q. How did this hill seam run with reference to this room neck? A. I think it run kinder anglin into the neck. Q. Martin was there on that morning before you had moved all the coal? A. Yes, sir. Q. Did you call his attention to the hill seam? A. No, sir; it was plain for everybody to see. Q. He said that he was going to have timber put there? A. Yes, sir. Q. Did he say for what purpose? A. Across that hill seam in the entry. Q. What did he say about it being needed? A. Just said he was going to put it there. Q. Did he say why? A. No, sir; because I knowed what he was going to put it there for. Q. What was the reason he was going to put that timber there? A. To keep slate from falling. Q. Did he know who had been cutting in that place? A. Yes, sir. Q. How do you know? A. He saw Smith waiting for another place to cut before he came down there. Q. How do you know? A. He said he did. Q. How did you know that Mr. Martin knew that Mr. Smith was working on that entry? A. Every bank boss knows exactly where his machine men are at work. Q. Did he understand that Smith would be back there to work when you got that coal moved that morning? A. Yes, sir." That the loaders knew of this defect, see the quotations from other testimony.

The statement in the opinion that "Smith had cut in some eight or ten feet and the coal had been taken out" is a mistake; and there is not the slightest testimony in the record supporting it. All the witnesses who spoke upon the subject stated that there had been only one cut made in the room with the machine, and that it would only cut 4½ or 5 feet, and the coal had been taken out of that preparatory for Smith to make another cut. When he was making the second cut, sitting on his board about nine feet in length, facing the coal in the room and managing his machine, he received his injuries, which shows that he was inevitably sitting near the edge of the entry. The testimony shows that the piece of slate that fell was six or more inches thick, six or seven feet long, and four or five feet wide; that it first gave way in the edge of the entry at the hill seam, and ran to a feather-edge in the room. The witness Davidson, after describing the board and the machine that Smith was using and the depth of the first cut, stated that it required two cuts with the machine to undermine the coal in the room which was ten or more feet wide, and continued as follows: "Q. Now, after he has made these cuts and there is a hill seam across the entry running to that neck, is there any trouble about the bank boss timbering that to make it safe? A. No, sir. Q. Is that the usual and proper way to make it safe to timber it? (Defendants object. Objections sustained.) Q. If the hill seam ran clear across would it not tend to strengthen it? A. Yes; it would have saved the entry. Q. It would have prevented the slate from starting to break in the entry and running on down in the neck? A. Yes."

The court concludes its opinion by saying in effect that it appeared from the evidence that it was the duty of Smith to call for props when he needed them, and, having failed to do so, he could not recover. It is true the testimony shows that, when any employe in the progress of his work discovered any dangerous place, it was his duty to make it known, and have it made safe or do it himself. This is a self-evident proposition, but in this case there was no evidence whatever ,that Smith discovered these defects, or had any information with reference thereto. At least two of the witnesses of the seven testified that they had no knowledge of these defects prior to the falling of the slate, but it is shown that the bank boss, Martin, at least, knew of this hill seam, and regarded it as being dangerous, and said that he. was going to have it propped. At the time he made this statement, he knew he had marked out this dangerous place for Smith to cut a room, and knew that Smith was then waiting for the room to be prepared for him to make another cut; but, notwithstanding this knowledge on his part, he not only suffered and permitted, but in effect ordered Smith to continue to work before it was propped, and without giving him warning of the danger. But, suppose the proof does show that Smith saw the hill seam, it is not decisive of the fact that he knew the danger and risk incident thereto and that he was assuming in working thereunder. The proof only shows that he had been working in the mine as a machine man for about twelve or eighteen months. There is not a scintilla of evidence that he had ever been engaged to remove slate or to prop rooms or entries to make them safe. In view of these facts, the following quotation from Ashland Coal & Iron Railway Co. v. Wallace, 101 Ky. 640, 42 S. W. 747 (19

Ky. Law Rep. 849), is in point, to-wit: "Defects in
the roof of a mine which might/ be perfectly apparent to the eye of a competent inspector might have no
significence to a laborer or an employe who had had
no experience in this special employment; and it
would be unreasonable to charge him with contributory negligence simply because he sees defects, unless
a reasonably intelligent and prudent man, would under like circumstances, have known or apprehended
the risks which those defects indicated. The dangers.
and not the defects alone, must be so obvious that a
1easonably prudent man would have avoided them in
order to charge the servant with contributory negligence." Appellee's position in this case, which is in
effect sustained by the opinion of the court, is that
every laborer in its mine must look out for himself;
that he must stop his work, investigate the conditions
of his surroundings, and, if he finds dangerous places,
he must make them safe. To do this would require
a loss of time to each hand of 30 or more minutes a
day; and would of necessity require that every man
upon entering a mine be an experienced miner. However, this is not true, unless there be a special contract to that effect. It would change all rules of law
with reference to the subject, and would involve the
coal companies in such a loss that they could not survive any length of time. In addition to this, employes should not be required to bear this loss of
time, unless there is a special contract to do so. As
this action was brought under the provisions of the
Constitution and statutes, it was not required of appellant to allege and prove that Smith did not know
of the defects in the roof and the dangers incident
thereto; but it devolved upon appellee to allege and

prove that he did know, not only of the defects, but also of the dangers likely to result therefrom.

In the case of Lexington & Carter County Mining Co. v. Stephens' Adm'r, 104 Ky. 508, 47 S. W. 323 (20 Ky. Law Rep., 696), the court, after discussing the principle applicable to an action brought for personal injuries when death did not ensue, said: "But it must also be remembered that a recovery in such cases is authorized by the common law, and that at common law no recovery can be had for injuries resulting in the immediate death of the person injured. The right to recover in case of death is authorized by the constitution and statutes enacted by the Legislature, which give an absolute right to recover where death ensues from the negligence or wrongful act of the defendant, and it will be observed that the statute makes no reference to the knowledge or contributory negligence of the decedent; and, while it may be true that the administrator or heir would not be allowed to recover in a case where the decedent had knowledge of the danger or risk he was about to incur, yet such negligence is a matter of defense, and, to be made available, must be pleaded and proved by the defendant. Any other construction of the law would, in effect, make it a dead letter, for the reason that, the injured party being dead, it would be impossible to prove that he was not aware of the danger, or that he could not with reasonable diligence have ascertained the danger." I have shown from the record that appellee's mine, in which Smith was employed to labor was defective and dangerous; that he lost his life by reason thereof; that it was the duty of appellant to make the place where Smith was injured reasonably safe, and to use ordinary care to keep it so; that it was not the duty of Smith to do this; but this duty was assigned to the bank boss and the loaders, and they utterly failed to perform their duty in this respect.

The only question left is as to the contributory negligence of Smith. There is no proof that he was negligent, except a few of the witnesses assume that he knew of the defects in the roof, because, in their opinion, the defects were patent. There was not the slightest intimation that Smith had any experience or knowledge in examining the roof of mines for the purpose of ascertaining defects and securing them with props. He was an experienced machine man. The question of the contributory negligence of Smith barring a recovery should unquestionably have been submitted to the jury and the court erred in refusing to do this. The case of Ashland Coal & Iron Railway Co. v. Wallace, supra, was one where the facts were very similar to the case at bar. It appears that in that case the person injured was an experienced miner, and was at the time of his injuries laying track in an entry of the mine. In that case the court said: "In actions like this questions of negligence are for the jury to determine. The ordinary care which parties are required to use in the discharge of their respective duties varies so much with the situation of the parties and the circumstances of each particular case that the policy of law to relegate these questions to juries has long been settled. The application of these rules of law to this case clearly authorizes its submission to the jury. The testimony does not present a record where all reasonable men must draw the inference either that the plaintiff was guilty of, cr that the defendant was free from, negligence. The testimony is conflicting. It is probable that, if the mine owner in this case had sent an experienced, suitable and competent person after the removal of the coal by Harris on Saturday evening to inspect the roof of this entry at that place, the defects would have been discovered and remedied; and, as to the contributory negligence of decedent which is complained of, in view of the fact that he was primarily employed as a tracklayer by the day—at $1 a day—and it not being his special duty to see after the safety of the roof of the entry, we think he had a right to presume that the defendant had inspected and knew the roof from which this coal had been so recently removed to be reasonably safe. This work was performed in dark passages in the earth, with no light to guide decedent except the flickering rays of the small lamp in his hat, which rendered it specially difficult for him to have noted other than obvious defects.'' See, also, the cases of Crabtree Coal Mining Co. v. Sample's Adm'r, 72 S. W. 24, 24 Ky. Law Rep., 1703, and McFarland's Adm'r v. Harbison & Walker Co., Southern Department, 82 S. W. 430, 26 Ky. Law Rep., 746.

In view of the facts stated and the authorities cited, I am compelled to dissent from the opinion of the court delivered in this case.

CASE 98.—ACTION BY WILLIAM ROBINSON AGAINST THE
CHESAPEAKE & OHIO RAILROAD CO—December
17, 1909.

Chesapeake & Ohio R. R. Co. v. Robinson

Appeal from Floyd Circuit Court.

A. J. KIRK, Circuit Judge.

Judgment for plaintiff, defendant appeals.—Reversed.

1. Carriers—Injury to Passenger—Contributory Negligence—
   Question for Jury.—It is not negligence per se for a passenger
   to alight from a moving train.
2. Carriers—Injury to Passenger—Contributory Negligence—
   —Question for Jury.—In an action for injuries to a passenger while alighting from a moving train at his station, evidence held to require the submission to the jury of the issue whether he exercised reasonable care in alighting, though the station was not announced.
3. Carriers—Carriage of Passengers—Announcement of Station. While a carrier must, as required by Ky. St. Sec. 784 (Russell's St. Sec. 5333), announce the station, it need not insure that a passenger hear it, provided the announcement is made in such a manner that the persons in the car having ordinary hearing and paying ordinary attention will hear it.
4. Carriers—Injury to Passenger—Stopping Train at Station.—
   A carrier must stop its train at the stations a reasonable time for passengers to alight.
5. Carriers—Carriage of Passengers—Lighting Depot Platforms.—A carrier must have its depot platforms lighted so as to be reasonably safe for persons to board and alight from trains, but, where the trainmen are on the platform with their lanterns to furnish passengers light during the time the train stops, the carrier is not liable because they do not remain on the platform after the train starts.
6. Carriers—Injury to Passenger——Setting Down Passengers—Allowing Time to Alight.—Where a carrier failed to announce a station as required by Ky. St. Sec. 784 (Russell's St. Sec. 5333), or failed to light its depot platform so as to afford a passenger a reasonably safe place to alight, and the passenger by reason of the failure to announce the station

was delayed in alighting from the train; so that, when he undertook to alight, the train started suddenly when he was stepping from it, and he was injured, the carrier was liable; but, where the carrier called the station and stopped the train a reasonable time for passengers to alight, and the passenger failed to alight during that time and until after the train started it was not liable.

7. Carriers Injury to Passenger—Care Required of Passenger.—Though a carrier is negligent in failing to announce the station or to have its depot platform lighted, a passenger must exercise such care as a person of ordinary prudence would under similar circumstances usually exercise, and where he fails to do so and is injured, he cannot recover.

WALTER S. HARKINS, WORTHINGTON, COCHRAN & BROWNING, F. D. WALLACE and JOSEPH D. HARKINS for appellant.

MAY & MAY for appellee.

OPINION OF THE COURT BY JUDGE HOBSON—Reversing.

William Robinson was a passenger on a train of the Chesapeake & Ohio Railroad Company from Catlettsburg to Prestonsburg. In getting off the train at Prestonsburg, he fell upon the platform as the train was pulling out, and· his foot was caught under the wheel and crushed. He brought this action to recover for his injury, and a judgment having been rendered in his favor upon a verdict of the jury, assessing the damages at $1,500, the railway company appeals.

The train reached Prestonsburg about 8 p. m. It was a dark rainy evening. The testimony of Robinson is to the effect that no notice was given of the arrival of the train at the station, and that, while the train was standing there, he learned that it was at Prestonsburg, and immediately got up and went out to get off; that, as he was getting off, the train gave a jerk which caused him to fall and his foot was caught and injured. He also testified that there was no light on the platform, that it was dark, and there was only a light in the station window. The testimony for the railroad company was, in effect, that the station was properly called out; that there were some 20 odd passengers for that station who got off when the train stopped; that the train stood there from 5 to 7 minutes; and, after the passengers had all gotten off, the conductor went to the baggage car to look after the unloading of some baggage, and, when it was off, ordered the train forward; that after the train had started, Robinson and his companion, Sizemore, came out on the platform without the knowledge of the conductor or any of the trainmen. As to what then occurred one of the witnesses for the railroad company whose testimony was supported by other witnesses for the defense testified as follows: "While standing on the rear end of my coach, I observed two men coming forward from the coach behind, and, on approaching the front end of their coach, one argued that it was the town of Prestonsburg, and the other claimed it wasn't, and at the same time the one that claimed it was Prestonsburg said: 'I am going to get off.' Q. Then what happened? A. By that time the train had started to move very slowly, and one of the men went down the steps and jumped off backwards. He fell and rolled on the platform of the station. I leaned forward, and saw some one pull him away from the train. Q. What did the other man do? A. He started down the steps immediately after the first man had jumped, and also jumped off backward. He rolled along the platform of the station, and his legs extended over the track." The first man who jumped off was Sizemore, and he escaped without injury. Robinson was the second man who jumped off after Sizemore. The defendant's testimony also showed that Robinson had two gallon jugs of whisky, also a quart of whisky, and that he had taken four drinks as he came along on the train. He and Sizemore were more or less under the influence of whisky. On this evidence the court gave the jury the following instructions:

"(1)   If the jury believe and find from the evidence that the plaintiff, William Robinson, was a passenger aboard the defendant's train, and had paid for a first-class fare from Catlettsburg, Ky., to Prestonsburg, Ky., and that the defendant, Chesapeake & Ohio Railroad Company, by its agents, servants and employes in charge of the train, at the time of the injury complained of, failed to call Prestonsburg station in the car in which plaintiff was riding within a reasonable time before its arrival at Prestonsburg station, from which calling plaintiff was notified it was to stop, and if the jury further believe and find from the evidence that the defendant, Chesapeake & Ohio Railroad Company, failed and neglected to light its station grounds and platform in such a manner as to afford plaintiff reasonably safe means of alighting from the train, and departing therefrom, and that the plaintiff by reason of such failure or neglect to so call said station or light its station and platform, the plaintiff was delayed in getting off the train, and while attempting to get off the car started, thereby causing plaintiff to jump off the car, and in so doing was caught and injured as complained of, then you will find for the plaintiff such damages as you may believe from the evidence he had sustained, if any, not exceeding the sum claimed in the petition, $1,900.

"(2)   The court instructs the jury that if they should believe and find from the evidence that the plaintiff in attempting to alight from the train did so while the same was moving, and that in consequence thereof he was thrown down and injured, the law is for the defendant, and the jury will find for it."

It is manifest that the verdict of the jury is not warranted by the evidence under the instructions of the court; for the evidence leaves no doubt that the train was in motion before Sizemore jumped off, and Robinson's own testimony shows that he was jerked by the motion of the train, while he was yet standing on the platform of the car. It is earnestly insisted for the defendant that the court should have instructed the jury peremptorily to find for it. This would be correct under the evidence if the rule obtained in this state that it is per se negligenc in a passenger to step from a moving train, but this court has steadily refused to adopt this rule, holding that it is a question for the jury whether the passenger in getting off as he did exercised ordinary care: for in many cases when a train is apparently moving very slowly it may reasonably appear to a prudent person safe to step from it. In view of our previous decisions and the evidence that the station was not announced, we have reached the conclusion that under the scintilla rule this case should go to the jury cn the question whether Robinson, if the station was not announced, exercised reasonable care in getting off as he did. It is true that Sizemore had fallen, but it may be he did not know this when he stepped cff, or he may have thought that Sizemore's fall was due to some other cause than danger in getting off. L. & N. R. R. Co. v. Eakins, 103 Ky. 472, 45 S. W. 529, 46 S. W. 496, 47 S. W. 872; I. C. R. R. Co. v. Whittaker, 57 S. W. 465, 22 Ky. Law Rep. 395; I. C. R. R. Co. v. Glover, 71 S. W. 630; L. & N. R. R. Co. v. Arnold, 102 S. W. 322, 31 Ky. Law Rep. 414. The instructions of the court are erroneous, in that they required no sort of care on the part of the plaintiff.

Although the defendant was negligent, the plaintiff could not negligently jump off the train, and hold it responsible for his injury. The defendant was required to call the station in the car in which the plaintiff was riding; but it was not required to insure that the plaintiff heard the call. These words should have been omitted from the first instruction: "From which calling plaintiff was notified it was to stop." The plaintiff's injury was not due to a lack of light about the station grounds, and only the failure to light the platform should have been set out in the instruction. It was the duty of the railway company to announce the station and to stop the train a reasonable time for passengers to get off. It was also its duty to have its platform lighted so as to be reasonably safe for persons to get on and off the train while the train was at the station; but, when the trainmen were on the platform with their lanterns to furnish the passengers light to get off during the time the train stopped for this purpose, the company is not liable because they did not remain on the platform with their lanterns after the train started. The statute requires the station to be called in the car twice. Ky. St. Sec. 784 (Russell's St. Sec. 5333). There was no controversy as to Robinson's being a passenger on the train or as to his having paid his fare, or as to the fact that the train had stopped at the station from five to seven minutes before Robinson got off. In lieu of instruction 1, the court should have told the jury that if they believed from the evidence that the defendant's agents in charge of the train in question failed to announce twice Prestonsburg station in the car in which plaintiff was riding within a reasonable time before its arrival at that station, or that the defendant failed to light its platform in such a manner as to afford the passengers

a reasonably safe means of alighting from the train
while the train stopped for that purpose, and that
the plaintiff, by reason of such failure to announce
the station, was delayed in geting off the train, and,
when he undertook to get off, the train started suddenly as he was steppng from it, and he received the
injury sued for by reason of the failure to announce
the station or to have the platform lighted while the
train stood at the platform for the purpose of receiving or letting off passengers, the jury should find for
him the damages he thereby sustained unless they
find as set out in No. 3. By another instruction the
court, in lieu of instruction 2, should have told the
jury that if the defendant called the station twice in
the car in which plaintiff was riding as set out in No.
1, and stopped the train at Prestonsburg a reasonable time for passengers to alight therefrom, and the
plaintiff failed to get off during this time and until
after the train had started, he could not recover. By
a third instruction the court should have told the
jury that, although the defendant was negligent as
set out in No. 1, still it was incumbent on the plaintiff
to exercise such care for his own safety as a sober
person of ordinary prudence, situated as he was.
would usually exercise, under like circumstances, and
that if he failed to do so, and but for this would not
have been injured, the jury should find for the defendant. By a fourth instruction the court should have
told the jury that the announcing of the station
should be made in such a manner that the persons in
the car having ordinary hearing and paying ordinary
attention would hear it. These instructions with one
defining the measure of damages cover the law of
the case.

Judgment reversed and cause remanded for a new
trial.

INDEX.

BANKRUPTCY—Continued—   Page.

debt, plaintiffs could pursue him in the state courts and
obtain a personal judgment against him, though he had
been adjudged bankrupt, upon which, after the federal
court had exercised its jurisdiction, the writ of fieri facias
might issue; but, pending the proceedings in bankruptcy,
the state court should stay its execution until the bankruptcy case is finally adjudicated. Idem................ 164

4. Bankruptcy—Construction of Statutes.—Act of 1856 (Ky.
St. Secs. 1910—1917), providing that a mortgage by a
debtor in contemplation of insolvency and to prefer certain creditors shall operate as an assignment of all his
property for the benefit of all creditors, except as provided, such transfers to be under the control of equity,
etc., is not a bankrupt or insolvency statute. Idem...... 164

5. Bankruptcy—Preferential Mortgages by Insolvent.—Ky.
St. Sec. 1910, makes a mortgage by a debtor in contemplation of insolvency and with design to prefer creditors
an assignment of all the debtor's property for benefit
of all creditors, except as provided. Section 1911 (section
2105) gives equity control of perferential mortgages made
by a debtor in contemplation of insolvency upon petition
of an interested person within six months after the transfer is lodged for record or the property is delivered.
Bankr. Act July 1, 1898, c. 541, Sec. 3a (2), 30 Stat. 546
(U. S. Comp. St. 1901, p. 3422), makes the transfer while
insolvent of any portion of his property by a debtor to his
creditor with intent to prefer the creditor an act of bankruptcy, and provides that a petition may be filed against
an insolvent who has committed an act of bankruptcy
within four months after commission of the act. Sec.
60b makes a preference given four months before filing
a petition voidable by the trustee. Held, that the federal
statute does not invalidate either a perferential mortgage
by an insolvent debtor or his voluntary deed of assignment, and if such mortgage is not attacked within the
time which will give the bankrupt court jurisdiction, or if
the assignor is not proceeded against by his creditors or
does not file petition to be adjudged a bankrupt within
the four months allowed by the federal statute, the instruments may be enforced and the parties thereto
granted appropriate relief by the state court when· invoked within six months, and, where the state court has
been invoked and has taken jurisdiction and possession of
the property, it may proceed to a final adjudication,

Carriers.

Carriers.

Carriers.

                  Carriers.

Carriers.

Carriers.

Contracts.

Contracts—Corporations.

Corporations.

Corporations.

Criminal Law.

Criminal Law.

Criminal Law.

Criminal Law,—Death.

vol. 135—56

Deeds.

DEEDS—Continued—   Page.

who claimed the greater part of the property, and who
had been in possession of the land for a number of years
after the court decided that she and her children were
not entitled to have their interests set apart and a homestead allowed them out of the same, because the real
estate had been converted into personalty by the provisions of the will, filed an amended pleading, in which
she alleged that she was the widow of one of the devisees
named, alleged that he left surviving him five infant
children who had resided with her, that her husband had
left no property or provisions for her and the children,
except two horses, one cow, one wagon, and some household goods not worth exceeding $200, and a part interest
in a legacy, and asked that $730 be set aside out of the
legacy to supply the deficiency in the property on hand at
the death of the husband. Held, that a demurrer to the
item of $730 was properly sustained as it was impossible to
determine the amount she was entitled to; the value of
the household goods not being alleged. Idem............ 814

5.   Conversion—Reconversion.—Testator directed in his will
      that, after all of his children had an equal outfit at the
      death of his wife, his land be sold and equally divided be-
      tween all of his children. In another clause he gave his
      executor power, provided certain things happened, to sell
      the land and divide the proceeds between the children
      equally. Held, that in the absence of an election by the
      devisees to treat the land as realty, the will converted it in-
      to personalty, and a reconversion of the devisees can only
      be affected by the joinder of all the devisees in such elec-
      tion and such election is not shown by deeds conveying
      the interest of the devisees in the land· or the proceeds
      thereof.   Idem.. 814

DESCENT AND DISTRIBUTION—

1.   Descent and Distribution—Conveyances by ·Heirs—Debts
      of Intestate—Bona Fide Purchaser for Valuable Con-
      sideration.—Under Ky. St. 1909, Sec. 2078, providing that
      any estate aliened by the heir or devisee before suit
      was brought shall not be liable to the creditors of dece-
      dent in the hands of a bona fide purchaser for a valuable
      consideration unless action is instituted within six months,
      a "bona fide purchaser for a valuable consideration" is
      one who in good faith buys the land and pays therefor.
      Buchanan v. Boyd's Exor., &c...................... 94

Divorce and Alimony.

EXECUTORS AND ADMINISTRATORS—Continued.   Page.
   at a subsequent term to set aside such appointment and
   appoint the one entitled to it. Phillips v. Hundley. &c.... 269
2. Pleading—Affidavits—Pleadings Executed in Another
    State—Sufficiency.—A pleading or affidavit to be used in
    Kentucky must be made and verified as required by the
    laws thereof, though executed in another state. Crane &
    Breed M'f'g Co. v. Stagg's Adm'r...................... 428
3. Executors and Administrators—Actions Against—Verifi-
    cation of Claims.—Ky. St. Sec. 3870, provides that all
    demands against the estate of a decedent shall be
    verified by the claimant's written affidavit. Civ. Code
    Prac. Sec. 544, defines an affidavit as a written declara-
    tion under oath made without notice to the adverse
    party. Sec. 550, subsec. 1, provides that any affidavit by
    law may, unless otherwise expressed, be made by his agent
    or attorney if he be absent from the county. Section 117
    provides that an affidavit of a private corporation must be
    verified by its chief officer or agent, etc., or if it have
    no such officer or agent in the county in which the action
    is brought, that it may be verified by its attorney. Sec-
    tion 549, subsec. 2, provides, that an affidavit may be
    made out of the state before any officer or person who
    may be authorized pursuant to section 564 to take deposi-
    tions and section 564 authorizes the taking of deposi-
    tions out of the state before a notary public, etc. Held,
    that the affidavit of a nonresident corporation claimant
    against the estate of a decedent may be made before a
    notary at its chief office or principal place of busi-
    ness in the state of its residence by its chief officer, or
    in his absence from the county of its principal place of
    business by its treasurer or other authorized agent,
    the affidavit in the latter case to show the official title of
    the chief officer, his absence from the county, and the
    authority of the treasurer or other agent to make the
    necessary affidavit, and such an affidavit which does not
    purport to have been made by the corporation's chief
    officer, or state that he was absent from the county, or
    that the corporation's treasurer, in the absence of its
    chief officer from the county, was authorized to make the
    affidavit is insufficient. Idem...................... 128
4. Executors and Administrators—Actions Against—Affida-
    vit of Claim—Sufficiency.—Under Ky. St. Sec. 3871, pro-
    viding that, if any part of the demand of a claimant
    against a decedent's estate has been paid, the affidavit of

claim shall state the payment and, when it was made,
to the best of affiant's knowledge and belief, an affidavit
of claim upon an account which embraces sales of merchandise from claimant to decedent covering a period of
four years, aggregating $1,463.71, upon which decedent
had made during that period numerous payments, all
credited on the account, amounting to $1,062.91, leaving a
balance due of $400.80, which affidavit treated the balance,
not as a balance, but as representing decedent's entire
indebtedness from start to finish, was insufficient. Idem.. 429

5. Executors and Administrators—Actions Against—Affidavit
of Claim—Sufficiency.—Under Ky. St. Sec. 3870, which requires that, when a person other than the claimant
against a decedent's estate makes affidavit to the claim,
he shall state in his affidavit that he believes the claim to
be just, and shall give the reason why he so believes, an affidavit by an employe of a claimant on an account against
an estate giving as the only reason for his belief as to the
correctness of the account, that he had examined plaintiff's books, and found that the account against decedent
appeared on the books as on the copy of the account to
which his affidavit was attached, is insufficient. Idem 429

6. Executors and Administrators—Suit to Compel Settlement
by Administrator—Necessity for Verified Affidavits of
Claims—Where a creditor sued in equity to compel the settlement of an estate by an administrator, under Civ. Code
Prac. Sec. 428, and the payment of debts, including plaintiff's claims, making the administrator, decedent's heirs,
and such of the creditors as were known to plaintiff,
defendants, and the petition charged that the administrator was delayed settlement, stating the amount of the estate's indebtedness, the value of its property, that the personal property was not sufficient to pay the debts, alleged
the necessity for a sale of realty for such purpose, asked
a reference of the case to a master commissioner for
taking proof as to creditor's claims, and reporting assets
and liabilities of the estate, and closed with a prayer for
personal judgment for plaintiff's debt, with interest, and
for a settlement of the estate, etc., it was unnecessary
that payment of plaintiff's claim should have been demanded of the administrator before the institution of the action, and it was error to dismiss the suit because of
a failure of plaintiff to present such affidavit, the object
of the statute requiring the claimant, before bringing
an action on his claim to make demand of payment, being

Vol. 135]   INDEX.   899

Land.

Libel and Slander.

Master and Servant.

Master and Servant.

Master and Servant—Measure of Damages.

Municipal Corporations.

MUNICIPAL CORPORATIONS—Continued   Page.

persons traveling thereon extends to cases where the obstruction or unsafe condition of the street is brought
about by persons other than the agents of the city; but
the party seeking to recover for failure to perform such
duty must show that the city had knowledge of the defect, or might have had knowledge thereof by the use
of reasonable care. City Mayfield v. Hughley........... 532

9. Municipal   Corporations—Character—Taxation—Liability
for Defective Sidewalks.—It is no defense to an action
against a city of the fourth class for personal injuries
from falling on a defective sidewalk that the territory
where the accident occurred had been annexed too late
to be subject to taxation that year, and that the taxes
for subsequent years were sufficient to improve streets
or sidewalks, since the charter of such cities gives them
the right to build sidewalks and assess the cost against
the abutting property, so that it was unnecessary for
the city to levy any general tax for such purpose. Idem. 532

10. Municipal Corporation—Defects in Sidewalks—Notice.—
Where it was shown that an excavation which lowered
a sidewalk and allowed an obstruction to protrude, over
which the plaintiff fell, was made about three months
prior to the accident, the city was chargeable with notice
of the obstruction. Idem.............................. 532

11. Municipal   Corporations—Classification—Validity.—The
laws providing for the organization and powers of the
various classes into which cities may be divided under
the Constitution, requiring the legislature to assign the
various cities to the classes in which they belong, are
general laws, where they are made applicable alike to
all cities falling within the designated class, and the laws
governing cities of the first class are general laws,
though they are applicable in fact to only one city. Specht
v. City Louisville 548

12. Municipal Corporations—Police and Fire Commissioners
—Holding Over.—Ky. St. 1909, sec. 3137, part of the
charter of cities of the second class, provides that four
persons shall be appointed as police and fire commissioners for a term of one, two, three, and four years, respectively and thereafter yearly, as their terms of office
expire, respectively, there shall be one appointed for a
term of four years. Held, that such a commissioner
does not hold over after expiration of his term till his
successor is appointed and qualified, there being no pro-

MUNICIPAL CORPORATIONS—Continued   Page.

PAWNBROKERS—Continued—   Page.
   pawnbroker's license did not authorize the pawnbroker
   to sell pistols at retail without taking out a license for
   the sale of pistols. Stevens, &c. v. City of Louisville.... 24

PENALTIES—See Indictment and Information.

PERPETUITIES—
1. Perpetuities—Construction of Deed.—A deed conveying
    land to a turnpike company for a tollhouse, and providing
    that when the house should cease to be used for such
    purpose the land and building should revert to certain
    persons named, did not create a perpetuity, in violation
    of Ky. Stat., 1909, sec. 2360, since the grantee might at
    any time with the sale of its turnpike convey the use of
    tollhouse and ground to its vendee, and under section
    2359, the reversioners might at pleasure sell their re-
    versionary interest. Patterson, &c. v. Patterson, &c.... 339
2. Deeds—Construction—Condition Subsequent—Covenant—
    Conditions subsequent are not favored, and, if it is
    doubtful whether a clause in a deed be a condition or a
    covenant, courts will incline to the latter construction.
    Idem 339
3. Perpetuities—Conveyances for Highway.—The statute
    against perpetuities (Ky. St. 1909, sec. 2360) does not ap-
    ply to a conveyance of land for a public highway, or
    for its use in connection with the operation of a turn-
    pike, which is a public highway. Idem................. 339
4   Perpetuities—Reversions—Construction.—Where a deed
    conveyed land to a turnpike company for use for a toll-
    house, a provision that on cessation of such use the land
    should revert to certain named persons, instead of her-
    self, was valid. Idem................................. 339
5. Pleading—Demurrer—Effect.—On demurrer to the peti-
    tion the facts therein alleged must be accepted as true.
    Idem 339

PERSONAL INJURIES—See Carriers, 6, 7, 16, 17.

PLEADING—See Bills and Notes, 1, 7; Executors and Administrators, 2.
1. Pleading—Answer—Admissions—Failure to Deny.—Aver-
    ments of a petition are confessed by failure to deny them.
2. Bankruptcy—Discharge—Claims Barred.—Creditors who
    had actual notice of the adjudication of their debtor in
    bankruptcy, and of the steps taken in the proceedings,

Pleading.

PLEADING—Continued—   Page.

dant in buying and selling tobacco, and plaintiffs knew,
when defendants filed a petition in bankruptcy that the
venture would result in loss leaving defendants indebted
to plaintiffs, though the exact amount was not then known
and could not be known until the rest of the tobacco was
sold. Held, that plaintiffs had an "unliquidated claim"
against defendants within section 63, subd. "b" which
was provable when plaintiffs filed their petition, and
was barred by failure to present it, and the provisions of
the bankrupt act, permitting nonbankrupt partners to
administer the assets, did not relieve them from reporting
to the court the amount received in the settlement of
the partnership affairs; its purpose not being to defeat the
rights of creditors of bankrupt partners. Idem............ 141

6. Bankruptcy—Construction of Act—Provable Debts.—The
provision of Bankr. Act July 1, 1898, c. 541, 30 Stat. 544
(U. S. Compt. St. 1901, p. 3418), relating to provable debts,
should be construed to make all debts fairly within its
meaning provable debts, in order to effectuate the purpose
of the act in relieving insolvents, and any doubt whether
a debt is provable or whether it is an unliquidated demand
which may be made provable, should be resolved in favor
of its provability. Idem............................ 141

PLEDGES—

1. Pledges—Delivery and Possession—Written Instruments—
Bonds—Validity.—A bank issued to depositors certificates
terms "mortgage certificates of deposit," which recited
the deposit, and that the certificate was secured by an
equal amount of bonds or lien notes. When such certificates were issued, the bank would indorse on one of its
mortgage bonds or lien notes the fact that it was pledged
as security for certificates issued, and the bond or note so
indorsed was placed in a box retained by it with others
similarly indorsed, and a similar indorsement was made
on the register opposite the entry of such bond or note,
and, when such indorsed bonds or notes were paid, another bond or note belonging to the bank was indorsed
and placed in the box with the others. The indorsements
were not dated and ordinarily not signed by the bank
officers. Ky. Stat. Sec. 1908, makes every charge upon
personality, unless actual possession in good faith accompanies it, void as to any creditor prior to the recording of
the charge. Held, that a pledge of personality could only be

Railroads.

Railroads.

SCHOOLS AND SCHOOL DISTRICTS—Continued—   Page.
    under section 4458, providing that, in a common school dis-
    trict election to levy a district tax for common schools,
    any resident widow or spinster, who is a taxpayer, or who
    has children within school ages, may vote, such persons
    may vote upon the question of tax for a graded school
    in a proposed graded common school district. Act March
    24, 1908 (Acts 1908, p. 133, c. 56), establishes in some
    particulars a radical departure from the pre-existing sys-
    tem, but without any design to render the system as a
    whole inharmonious, and provides that graded common
    school districts operating under special charter or es-
    tablished by popular vote in school districts operating in
    municipal districts established under special charter, and
    supplementing the state school fund by a local tax of
    a certain amount, shall retain their present boundaries and
    be exempt from the provisions of the act. Held, that the
    effect of the prohibition of the act of 1908 was to re-enact
    section 4464-4500a as part thereof, and the graded com-
    mon school districts operating under special charter or es-
    tablished by popular vote remained unaffected by the
    later law in their boundaries, government, and regula-
    tion; but the later act, providing that all resident males
    over 21 years of age shall have the right to vote at elec-
    tions, women are no longer entitled to vote in graded and
    common school elections. Idem............................ 488
4. Schools and School Districts—Levy of Tax—School Elec-
    tion—Manner of Voting.—Ky. Stat. 1909, Sec. 4467, relat-
    ing to the voting upon the question of establishing
    a graded common school and a tax to maintain it,
    provides that on the day set apart for the election
    the officers shall open a poll and propound to each voter
    the question, "Are you against or for the graded common
    school tax?" and his vote shall be recorded for or against
    the same as he may direct, which has been held to
    require a viva voce vote on the subject of taxation.
    Act March 24, 1908 (Acts 1908, p. 133, c. 56), which in
    effect re-enacted the former act as a part of the latter act,
    makes no provision as to how the votes shall be taken,
    whether by ballot or otherwise, though in an election for
    trustees, voting by special ballot and the manner of
    preparing and furnishing the ballots are all provided for.
    Held, that the intent was that the vote on the question
    of the tax should be viva voce. Idem 489

Schools and School Districts.

Taxation.

Taxation.

Taxation.

TAXATION—Continued— Page.

properly assessed, or where notice of the time and place
of, the meeting of the board of supervisors of tax has not
heretofore been properly or regularly given, cities of the
third class can pass an ordinance directing the assessment of such property, etc., and that its object is to insure the collection of any unpaid taxes, and that the provisions shall not extend back for more than five years.
Act March 15, 1906, provided for the taxing of shares of
banks and trust companies at the same rate as for
other personalty, which was to be assessed by a local
assessing officer. Held, that where the local assessing
officer had not made an assessment of the shares of stock
of a bank for 1906, the council had authority under
section 3403 to provide for its assessment, as that
section applied to all cases "where property has not
been assessed for taxation;" the word "heretofore" being
required to be read as referring to the time of the passing
of the ordinance, and the five years allowed being counted, not from the time of the passage of the act, but
from the time the assessment is made. Idem.......... 773

TELEGRAPH AND TELEPHONES—

Telegraphs and Telephones—Regulation—Charges—"Business Service."—The words "business service" in a telephone company's franchise fixing the maximum rate for
such service mean the ordinary service between business
men and other citizens within the radius specified, and do
not include service rendered to a telegraph company under a joint traffic arrangement which does not increase
the cost of the service rendered by the latter company.
East Tenn Telp. Co. v. City Harrodsburg.............. 216

TRIAL—

1 Appeal and Error—Consolidation of Actions—Discretion
of Trial Court—Review.—The action of the court in directing that an original cause of action and a cause of
action presented by cross-petition shall be heard together
by the same jury will not be disturbed unless it appears
that, in the exercise of a sound discretion, the court
should have ordered separate trials before separate
juries. Doyle v. Offutt & Blackburn.................... 296

2. Jury—Competency of Jurors—Prior Service—Similar
Cause—In actions by buyers of seed wheat based on the
seller's warranty that the wheat was good, and the fact

Wills.

Wills.

Wills.

Wills.

vol. 135—60

Wills.